T0265714

Practical Guide to
Personal Financial Awareness

What Every High School Graduate Should Know About Money

James A. Lorenz, CFEI®
Edited by Todd A. Richardson, CPA

From high school to retirement, a comprehensive,
easy-to-understand guide for managing your money
that promotes a mindful approach to personal finance

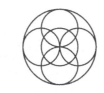

Heuristics Press
Published in U.S.A.

Heuristics Press LLC / James A. Lorenz
630 Black Hawk Dr.
Marysville, OH. 43040

Library of Congress Control Number Information (LCCN)
Name: Lorenz, James, 1951-, author.
Title: Practical Guide to Personal Financial Awareness / James A. Lorenz.
Description: Marysville, OH: Heuristics Press LLC / James A. Lorenz (2024)
Includes bibliographical references and index.

LCCN: 2022919453 (print) https://www.loc.gov/
Subjects 1 LCSH: Economics Education - United States.

ISBN: 979-8-21809-261-0 (pbk : alk. Paper)
ISBN: 979-8-35093-207-2 (eBook)

BISAC: BUS050000 - Business and Economics / Personal Finance / General

Ordering Information: Please visit the publisher's website at:
https://heuristicspress.com/

Printed in the United States of America   10 9 8 7 6 5 4 3 2 1

Book Highlights and Features

This book is a down-to-earth guide for managing your finances that provides a mindful and holistic approach to personal money matters. It is also a personal story documenting one man's journey to financial awareness and the trials and tribulations along the way. Having successfully navigated the rough and often murky waters of personal finance, Lorenz provides many real-world examples combined with life lessons learned. This book is an overview of personal finance concepts that can help the average person deal more effectively with money situations in their lives, whether it's buying a car or home, investing for retirement, paying for college, or improving their credit score. The book is packed with relevant and interesting anecdotes describing financial situations that many have been or will go through. These are interspersed with important financial concepts and useful tips, delivered in an easy-to-read conversational style.

This is a financial literacy book that covers a wide range of personal finance subjects and can help the average person gain control of their finances. It is both entertaining and educational and is an interesting blend of money education and mindful awareness. Topics include income, expenses, cash flow, assets, net worth, credit scores and credit reports, budgets, home, and vehicle buying, as well as college/student loans, investing, taxes, insurance, retirement, and financial scams. Chapters include Web research exercises to find and use online financial tools, as well as guided examples to determine your personal financial indicators (PFIs). With over thirty hands-on exercises, the book can be considered an "encyclopedic personal finance workbook." Readers can use the Personal Financial Spreadsheet (PFS), which is available for download from the publisher's Website, and customize it to their needs. A print version of the PFS is also included in the book. Each chapter contains the following components:

1) **Chapter Overview** - Brief description of the main chapter content and highlights
2) **Chapter PFS and PFI Integration** - PFS (Personal Financial Spreadsheet) and PFI (Personal Financial Indicator) ties to chapter content
3) **Chapter Exercise List** - Exercises that pertain to the chapter
4) **Chapter Notable Quotes** - Integrated quotes that supplement the chapter content
5) **Chapter Main Content** - Explanation of concepts and illustrative tables and figures
6) **Chapter Tips and Summaries** - Key points and terms of the chapter
7) **Chapter Exercises** - Hands-on exercises and Web research to reinforce concepts

Contents

Dedication

This book is dedicated to my wife Mary and our daughters Jessica and Natasha,
for their love and encouragement, as well as their patient support and editing assistance.

Acknowledgements

I would like to thank the following individuals for their influence and inspiration.

- Financial teachers and radio talk show hosts Clark Howard and Dave Ramsey
- Spiritual teachers Deepak Chopra and Eckhart Tolle

I would also like to thank the members of my professional advisor group. They have not only provided valuable services to Mary and me over the years, but they have been instrumental in the development and validation of content for this book.

- Todd Richardson, CPA - Tax advisor and book financial editor
- Trent Schuler, CFP - Financial advisor
- Julie Spain, Attorney - Business legal advisor
- Dustin Hughes, Attorney - Estate legal advisor
- Andrew Conley, PLCS - Insurance advisor (Auto/Home/Business)
- Jim Hogan, MSFS - Health care and Medicare Planning

Preface

I have been collecting notes, quotes, and anecdotes for years. When I retired, I decided to consolidate them in this book. In the financial arena, I am self-taught (College of Hard Knocks). The most notable exception is my Certified Financial Education Instructor (CFEI®) credential, which was conferred by the National Financial Educators Council (NFEC) upon my taking a rigorous course and passing the final exam. The quotes below refer to the fact that, over the years, it seems that I have had to make my own financial mistakes in order to learn the lessons, rather learn from the mistakes of others.

Quote P-1: "Experience holds a dear school, but some will learn in no other." - Ben Franklin

Quote P-2: "A smart person learns from their mistakes. A smarter person learns from the mistakes of others, but the smartest person learns from the mistakes and success others." - Anonymous

I decided to write the book because I felt that someone other than I should learn from my mistakes, especially our two daughters. Also, there just seems to be a lot of confusion and misinformation regarding personal finance. My hope is that the information presented here will help others navigate the turbulent waters of the financial world and help them make good decisions while avoiding some of the mistakes I made.

Introduction

The title of this book is **Practical Guide to Personal Financial Awareness**. It's kind of a long title, but each word contributes something to the meaning. The book is a blend of nuts-and-bolts basic money management along with some more mindful prosperity concepts. Merriam-Webster defines the words in the title as follows:

- **Practical:** Capable of being put to use or account: useful
- **Guide:** Something that provides a person with guiding information
- **Personal:** Of, relating to, or affecting a particular person: private, individual
- **Financial:** Relating to finance or financiers (and money)
- **Awareness:** The quality or state of being aware: knowledge and understanding that something is happening or exists

The subtitle is **What Every High-School Graduate Should Know About Money.** The audience is anyone who can read at a high-school level and who wants to learn more about how to make, spend, save, invest, and manage money. Since the information is presented logically, and financial terms are defined in layman's language along the way, most people should be able to get through it fairly easily. Also, you don't have to be a math whiz to get a lot out of this book. If you can add, subtract, multiply, and divide using a calculator, you can manage your financial affairs. People of all types can benefit from this book, although not everyone will be able to take advantage of all the options discussed therein due to various factors, including their attitude toward money, personal financial situation, and family environment. The book content is appropriate for high school all the way through a person's retirement years. They have one common denominator: they all share a desire to know more about how to manage their money and not be taken advantage of, both important factors in most people's lives. We are not teaching or promoting entrepreneurship here, although it is covered to some extent within the book. Rather, we are talking about the application of basic common sense and having an awareness of the world of personal finance. This includes key financial concepts, methods, and terminology that can help make your life less stressful and hopefully, more enjoyable. This is a hands-on book that makes use of a comprehensive and customizable Personal Financial Spreadsheet (PFS) to help you understand your finances.

Many good financial books are available that go into detail on a wide range of money topics. This book takes a high-level common-sense approach that provides some general suggestions and guidelines for managing your finances and avoiding pitfalls. However, it also provides some specific information about tried-and-true methods to help you manage your finances. Most of the concepts and principles presented are not overly complicated and are applicable to most people, whether they have a lot of money or not. They also apply whether interest rates, inflation, the stock market, unemployment, or other economic factors are up or down. This book is being written during the infamous Covid-19 pandemic, against the backdrop of a war and the worst inflation the world has seen in forty years, among other global issues. Nevertheless, the financial principles and concepts are basically the same, and once you have established a sound financial strategy, it is important to stay the course and not be swayed by world events. I am standing on the shoulders of many intelligent people whose works have preceded and inspired me. Over my teaching career I have been told that I do a good job of breaking down and explaining complex subjects, such as computers and networking technologies. Hopefully with this book I have done the same for personal money matters.

Quote I-1: "When you talk, you are repeating what you already know. But if you listen, you may learn something new." - The Dalai Lama

This book is relatively concise, given the range of topics covered, and focuses on awareness of the most common day-to-day money issues and the mistakes people make with regard to the same. I purposely do not get bogged down with the nitty-gritty nuances of every financial concept, term, and investment vehicle. The focus in this book is on the most important concepts and strategies, as well as financial problem-solving tools, which are available to the average person. I encourage you to further research topics that are of interest to you or particularly applicable to your financial circumstances. The book is also somewhat like a financial encyclopedia, with the chapters broken down into topic areas that are affected by money.

Your financial situation and monetary needs will vary based on your age, employment status, lifestyle, and many other factors. This book is not meant to be all things to all people. It is a money book written by a nonmoney person to help other nonmoney people navigate the shark-infested waters of the financial world. It is a compilation of some useful money management tools, concepts, practices, and principles. The information in this book is presented in a way that will help you make better financial choices while saving money and avoiding being taken advantage of. Many of the concepts are basic, and you may already be employing them. The knowledge, tips, and practices described here can be valuable to anyone that makes and spends money, irrespective of whether they have a lot of it or not. In fact, if these basic principles and concepts are adhered to, you may find you have more money and financial security than when you started reading it. You may also sound like you are financially literate in conversations when the subject of money comes up!

For many people, financial terminology is like a foreign language. Each chapter in this book introduces various relevant terms used in the world of finance. They are presented and explained in layman's language to help simplify concepts. So, when you hear acronyms and terms like "APR," "fiduciary," and "net worth," you will have at least a basic idea of what they mean.

Options for Reading the Book:
I recommend reading all twenty of the book chapters in sequence. However, if you do not read all the chapters, be sure to at least read the bulleted ones listed below. The information presented in these five chapters could have a direct impact on the financial awareness level of most people.

- Chapter 1: Financial Literacy Perspectives (also an intro to mindful awareness)
- Chapter 8: Credit Scores and Credit Reports
- Chapter 9: Credit and Credit Cards
- Chapter 13: Investing Basics
- Chapter 20: Attitude of Gratitude and Prosperity

Also, you can choose to read chapters based on content and your needs and interests. Each chapter can stand on its own so you can scan the table of contents and pick and choose those chapters that are of most interest to you or relevant to your current financial situation. If you are thinking of buying or selling a home, read Chapter 11: Buying or Renting a Home. If you are in the market for a used car, read Chapter 12: Buying or Leasing a Vehicle. If someone in your family is college bound, read Chapter 17: Education. Jobs, and Student Loans. If you are math-averse, you can just scan the text of each chapter, rather than focus on the formulas and spreadsheets presented. You can still get a lot of out of this book, and you can always come back to the formulas if desired.

The Personal Financial Spreadsheet (PFS)
This spreadsheet is the real heart of this book, and I use it as a central document to help me manage our finances. It is a basic Microsoft Excel (.xlsx) spreadsheet that is kind of old school and has evolved over a period of ten or more years. Portions of it are included in this book where they are referenced. All seven pages (or sheets) of the PFS Excel spreadsheet, with formulas and sample data, are included in Appendix A. Chapter 2 is dedicated to the Personal Financial Spreadsheet (PFS), describing its structure, contents, and how to best use it.

The Personal Financial Indicators (PFIs)
In addition to the PFS, the Personal Financial Indicators or PFIs are another important component of the book. The PFIs are simple money formulas that can be used to evaluate a person's financial condition. Although we cover fifteen of them in the book, we have prioritized them and created our "Top Ten" list, which are the ones we focus on. Many of these PFIs are used by banks and other lenders as a benchmark to decide whether to loan you money, how much, and at what interest rate, whether for a house, car, or personal loan. Being aware of these indicators and monitoring them is crucial to your financial health.

Most of the PFIs are ratios that are represented as a percentage (%), such as Debt-to-Income (DTI) and Debt-to-Credit (DTC). The other PFIs are dollar amounts ($), such as Personal Cash Flow (PCF) and Personal Net Worth (PNW). For consistency and brevity, I have tried to come up with a good three-letter acronym (TLA) for each of the fifteen indicators. The financial industry is full of three-letter acronyms to begin with (e.g., APR and ROI), so I apologize for adding to the number of TLAs, but using the acronym was the best way I found to reference the concept without have to expand it to three words every time it was used. The PFIs are referenced throughout the book, and using TLAs was the most efficient way to keep the book from getting any bigger than it already was. All fifteen of the PFIs with description, chapter where used, and formula to calculate them are included in Appendix B: Personal Financial Indicators (PFIs).

Chapter 1
Financial Literacy Perspectives

Chapter Overview:

This chapter introduces the concept of financial literacy and provides an overview of the main subject areas addressed by the field of personal finance education. It emphasizes how the lack thereof can impact your life and promotes the offering of personal finance courses in high school. Examples of financial literacy initiatives at the state and national levels are identified. The chapter provides a backdrop based on some of my own personal financial experiences. It describes the use of the "Offsite Meeting" for families becoming more financially aware. The "Personal Financial Spreadsheet (PFS)" is described, along with its use as a guide when reviewing your current finances and financial goals. The chapter also describes some of the more common personal finance problems that can result from being finically illiterate. It introduces mindful awareness and its importance in financial affairs as well as other life areas. The chapter is divided into three parts:

- **Part 1: Financial Literacy Overview**
- **Part 2: Financial Literacy Problems**
- **Part 3: Financial Literacy Solutions**

A short quiz is provided to help you determine your current knowledge of personal finance concepts. Refer to **Exercise 1-1** below and take the financial knowledge quiz to get started and see how you fare.

Chapter PFS Integration:

This chapter introduces the "Personal Financial Spreadsheet" (PFS), which is the foundation of the book and can be used as a centralized reference repository for your financial information. Chapter 2 provides an overview and describes the function and structure of the PFS and sheets that it includes. Appendix A contains screenshots of the seven sheets (tabs) of the PFS with sample data entered.

Chapter Exercise:
- **Exercise 1-1: General Financial Knowledge Quiz**

There are many financial tests available on the Internet that can help you gauge your current financial awareness level. Before you start reading this book, take the basic sixteen-question test from the American Association of Retired People (AARP). It provides a good selection of personal finance questions that can help you evaluate your current level of financial knowledge. The topics and content of the quiz are relevant and current. If you get them all correct, you have a good foundation to build on. Take the quiz again after reading this book and compare your before and after scores.

Note: As you take the quiz, read the explanation of the answer to gain additional knowledge irrespective of whether you get the correct answer to a question. The answers to these quiz questions, and much more, are found within the pages of this book. The link to the AARP "Test Your Money Smarts" financial literacy test is provided here. You may need to turn off your ad blocker to view the quiz. If you have difficulty accessing the quiz, do a search for "financial knowledge quiz" and you will find several from reputable sources.

https://www.aarp.org/money/budgeting-saving/info-01-2014/test-your-money-smarts.html

Chapter Notable Quotes:

Quote 1-1: "Awareness is the greatest agent for change." - Eckhart Tolle

Quote 1-2: "Life is hard. It's even harder if you are ignorant." - John Wayne

Quote 1-3: "Give a person a fish, feed them for a day. Teach them to fish, feed them for a lifetime." - Lao Tzu

Quote 1-4: "Learn from the past, plan for the future and live in the present." - Anonymous

Quote 1-5: "It is a great and powerful feeling to pay off your credit cards on your way to being debt free." - Anonymous

Quote 1-6: "Life is 10% what happens to you and 90% how you react to it." - John Maxwell

Part 1: Financial Literacy Overview

What is Financial Literacy?
There are many variations for the definition of "Financial Literacy." Wikipedia provides a concise and accurate financial literacy definition as follows:

"The possession of the set of skills and knowledge that allows an individual to make informed and effective decisions with all of their financial resources."

Over the last twenty years or so, we have seen a heightened awareness with regard to financial literacy or more appropriately financial "illiteracy." Many initiatives have been developed surrounding this important topic. The following are contributing factors to the problem:

- **Lack of basic personal finance education**
- **Increased complexity of personal finance**
- **More savings and investment options available**
- **Increasing number of financial scams**

It's no wonder the average person gets confused and has difficulty when it comes to making financial decisions. Fortunately, we have also seen an increased willingness and ability by various organizations to teach financial literacy content to deal with this serious problem. Comprehensive and well-funded efforts toward imparting financial literacy have sprouted from private companies and professional organizations in addition to the government-driven efforts—at both the national as well as state level—aiming at the same. This section just highlights a few of the initiatives and efforts that are currently underway and their approach to addressing financial literacy.

Financial Literacy Initiatives

The following organizations have launched financial literacy initiatives, developed standards and model curricula, and implemented local and nationwide financial literacy programs. The organization, the initiative, and the Website are listed here for more information on what each organization is doing. This is a sampling of organizations and their financial education offerings. Regarding state initiatives, nearly every state in the U.S. has initiated and/or implemented standards and programs to provide guidance to school districts and instructors.

American Institute of Certified Public Accountants (AICPA)

360 Degrees of Financial Literacy. Visit the AICPA Website at: https://www.aicpa-cima.com/home/ or the 360 Program Website: https://www.360financialliteracy.org/

Ohio Department of Education (ODE):

Learning Standards for Financial Literacy for grades K-12.
https://education.ohio.gov/Topics/Learning-in-Ohio/Financial-Literacy/Financial-Literacy-in-High-School

Note: Many other states have or are developing similar programs and requirements.

U.S. Department of the Treasury - Financial Literacy and Education Commission (FLEC)

National financial education Website (MyMoney.gov) and a national strategy on financial education. https://www.mymoney.gov

Council for Economic Education (CEE) and Jump$tart

National Standards for Personal Financial Education
https://www.councilforeconed.org/new-national-standards-for-personal-financial-education

National Financial Educators Council (NFEC)

Certified financial education instructor training, standards and course materials.
https://www.financialeducatorscouncil.org

Financial Literacy Subject Areas

The word "literacy" simply means the ability to read and write a language. By any measure the world of finance has its own, often cryptic, language and a high percentage of the U.S. population is financially illiterate. The average citizen has never taken a personal finance course in any educational setting. This results in considerable pain and suffering, much of which is avoidable with some basic personal finance education. The lack of education and the fact that each person has preconceived ideas and attitudes toward money can make financial education especially challenging.

Based on subject areas identified in the financial literacy education initiatives listed previously, the following is a distillation of the common subject areas for an audience aged eighteen and older. Financial literacy education offerings will cover some or all of these topics to one degree or another, but the student should come away with at least a basic understanding and awareness of each of the fourteen key areas, listed below. Armed with this knowledge, they can formulate a plan and take action to improve their financial situation. The topics may be sliced and diced differently depending on the presenter, but these are the core financial literacy subject areas you will learn about by reading this book.

1. **Income**
2. **Expenses**
3. **Budgeting**
4. **Financial Accounts**
5. **Saving**
6. **Buying, Borrowing, and Debt**
7. **Credit and Loans**
8. **Credit Profile Scores and Reports**
9. **Basic Investing**
10. **Insurance and Risk**
11. **Retirement Planning**
12. **Estate Planning**
13. **Economic and government influences**
14. **Personal finance planning**

Practical Guide to Personal Financial Awareness - Chapter Titles and Content

Refer to this book's table of contents or the chapter listing below to see how the financial literacy topics listed above are addressed. In addition to the core topics, other financially related topics—such as auto buying, home buying, taxes, paying for college, and financial scams—are included. Although this book has a chapter on insurance, the subject is also covered in chapters where it relates directly to the topics being presented, such as auto, home, and life insurance.

By the time you finish this book, you should be aware of the key personal finance areas and be financially literate. You should be familiar with the terminology for each area and conversant when it comes to personal financial subjects. You should have acquired some basic skills and techniques by which you can evaluate and manage your finances effectively with some degree of confidence.

Quote 1-1: "Awareness is the greatest agent for change." - Eckhart Tolle

Developing awareness of personal financial deficiencies is a key aspect of financial literacy education. This simply means addressing areas you were previously unaware of and identifying problem areas that need improvement. You cannot change that which you are not aware of. Financial literacy education increases awareness.

Part 2: Financial Literacy Problems

Problems and Mistakes Due to Financial Illiteracy

There are other types of literacy in addition to financial. For example, some people might be considered "computer literate" (knowledgeable of computers). It seems that each discipline has its own language, and the world of finance is no exception. There is no area of literacy that affects so many aspects of a person's life as that of financial literacy.

People come in all colors, shapes, and sizes and so do their financial situations and problems. Most people make financial mistakes throughout their lifetimes, many of which can be attributed to lack of financial knowledge or illiteracy. Note that problems can also be created, and mistakes made due to inaccurate financial knowledge. This can be a result of misinterpretation or taking financial advice from family members and unqualified advisors. Remember, it's not so much what you don't know that creates problems, it's "what you know that just ain't so." Educators these days are faced with many challenges, but one of the biggest is the sheer volume of "knowledge" available and how to help students become critical thinkers and overcome the fallacies, conventional wisdom, and misinformation they may encounter.

Most personal finance problems can be grouped into one of four major areas: Income/Expenses, Assets/Liabilities, Credit/Debt, and Insurance/Risk. These are areas of financial difficulty for most people and where financial corrective measures are most often applied. These four financial areas are presented sequentially in this book.

Quote 1-2: "Life is hard. It's even harder if you are ignorant." - John Wayne

The Penalties and Price of Ignorance - My Story
In the quote above, the word "ignorant" simply means "lacking knowledge." That term certainly applied to me in my early years, especially with regard to my finances. By the time I was thirty years old, I was divorced, broke, and in debt up to my eyeballs. I had had a car repossessed, had declared bankruptcy, and had dropped out of college. I eventually went back to college and got my Bachelor of Science degree in Computer Information Systems. However, with such a dismal financial track record, my credit rating was understandably very poor. Not a very promising financial start for adulthood. Some of the lessons shared in this book are ones that I learned in my thirties and many others, in my fifties or later. After making many mistakes in my earlier life, I have become somewhat successful financially, primarily through a fairly conservative lifestyle and adopting appropriate investment strategies with help from a qualified financial advisor. But a person should not have to wait until late in life to learn the basic lessons of personal finance.

It is becoming evident that teaching these subjects at the K-12 level and especially requiring personal finance education prior to graduating high school, makes for a more rounded education. It is an essential part of preparing young people for their entry into the real-world job market and high-school graduates for personal financial success. A high-school degree should prepare the graduate for at least a basic functional role in society, of which financial literacy is a big part. We are not talking about teaching people to be entrepreneurs or how to get rich. We are talking about the basics of how to manage and invest your money and avoid getting ripped off. Educators and parents are increasingly working together to help students be financially successful in life. Individuals who develop some basic financial literacy skills early on can lead more productive and satisfying lives. The focus of this book is on developing confidence and competence when it comes to dealing with money matters.

For the average person, much of their financial knowledge is acquired by making mistakes and, hopefully, learning from them. In my opinion, every high-school student should take a basic money management or financial literacy course before they graduate, and school districts across the country are moving in that direction. Since not all high-school graduates go on to college, large segments of our population may be left to flounder in the world of personal finance if they don't receive the requisite financial knowledge before leaving high school. Unfortunately, these people will likely have to learn the hard way (like I did) and make mistakes with their finances that could have been avoided.

Teaching Young People About Money

We have just started to teach our five-year-old granddaughter how to recognize and count money, starting with the basic coins and the one-dollar bill. We mix them up and, if she can identify them and put them in the right order based on value (penny, nickel, dime, quarter), she gets to put the coins in her piggy bank. Most recently she has begun to understand the actual value based on how many "cents" each coin is worth and is able to add up a group of coins and give you the total. Next, we are going to pretend she's going to the store, and she has a certain number of coins that she can use to buy things. She will have to determine what she can buy based on the value of the coins she has. She loves playing the game, and it gives us something fun and educational to do. She gets to keep the coins for one round of the games when she comes over. When the piggy bank gets full, she gets to dump the coins out, count them, and buy something for herself for real. There is a lot of motivation to learn the coins and develop a habit of saving. It also teaches the concept of delayed gratification.

Figure 1-1: The Piggy Bank

Back in My Day

When I was young, parents did not share or discuss financial information with their children, even as they reached their late teens. Credit cards were just beginning to proliferate, but many people operated on a cash-only basis. Now you cannot book an airline flight or rent a car without a credit card. When I was growing up, your credit score was known by your creditors but unknown to you! Even today, most parents do not take advantage of teachable money moments. Most just take care of their own finances, and the children have little understanding of what is being done for them, even if they go off to college.

Quote 1-3: Give a person a fish, feed them for a day. Teach them to fish, feed them for a lifetime." - Lao Tzu

Most financially successful people have been taught to fish (through example or assistance) or they were able to learn it on their own through trial and error. The first credit card I had was a Sears card, and I did not take it seriously. I made many mistakes (missed payments, went over my limit, etc.), and they cancelled my card. My first (practice) marriage was to a financially irresponsible woman (I was equally so), and we managed to screw up our credit royally. We bought a more expensive car than we could afford, and it was repossessed because we could not make the payments. Soon we separated and then got divorced. I declared bankruptcy way back in 1987, which provided a serious wakeup call for me, especially since I still had to pay the bankruptcy attorney and some debts that could not be discharged. I was determined that my children would not make the same mistakes as I did, or at least I would do my best to make sure they knew some basic financial concepts to help them get started on the right track.

Money, Marriage, and the Fruits of Ignorance

Issues regarding money are a common source of life problems. There are many issues that people deal with, but four of the main ones are these:

- **Lack of information and incorrect information**
- **Living outside of your means** (spending more than you make)
- **Inability (or unwillingness) to manage your money**
- **Lack of communication** (partner, spouse, creditors)

Money problems resulting from the above can cause relationships to degrade and marriages to fail. It is estimated that money problems contribute to the breakup of over 50 percent of failed marriages. A study conducted by Ramsey Solutions found that the number one issue couples fight about is money. According to the study, money fights are the second leading cause of divorce, behind infidelity. The study is a bit dated, but I doubt that it has changed much in the last five years. I believe that money-related problems are the number one cause of relationship breakups, either directly or indirectly. Poor money management can contribute to a miserable and stressful life in general, as well as depression and anxiety, which can contribute to a dismal outlook with little hope for the future. In a relationship, the partner's views and behavior regarding money are easily as important as those on politics, religion, and child rearing. It's healthy to be able to discuss these topics and see eye-to-eye or at least understand the others viewpoint. It is critically important, for the success of the relationship, to come to an agreement on how to conduct your financial affairs. Money is not the root of all evil, but abusing it and lack of understanding regarding it can have devastating effects on your life. All this points to the pressing need for more and better personal financial education, a challenge that fortunately is being addressed by many sectors of our society.

My parents never discussed money or finances in my presence. We did not have much, if any, family discussion of finances, debt, etc. This was not because we were in bad shape financially but because those were subjects that were deemed ones young people did not need to know about. My parents probably felt uncomfortable or inadequate discussing the subject or simply did not want to take the time. Even into my teens, all I knew about our finances was how much our house cost, and I had some idea of how much money my dad made. I also knew he had some passive income in the form of rental properties. My mother did not work outside the home and was totally dependent on my father for money. She wanted a divorce but had no income by which she could support herself. So, she went back to college at age forty-five and received her master's degree in library science. After that she divorced my father, moved to another state, and started a new life and career as a librarian. Lack of financial knowledge and the "I want it all now" mentality contribute significantly to money problems. My mother was able to take the time necessary to re-educate herself while raising a Family of four and then went out on her own after saving up enough to rent an apartment and manage her own finances.

Who Pays the Bills?
Who in your family is primarily responsible for finances? If the answer is you, then ask yourself if your partner or another trusted person could take over if something happened to you. Typically, there is not much communication between partners or other family members when it comes to finances. It is not uncommon for a family member to pass away and not even leave a will. Would your spouse know what joint accounts you have and how to get to them online? Do they know who the primary account holder is for credit cards and other financial accounts? Good luck trying to get information about a credit card if you are not the primary card holder, even if you are an authorized user. The Personal Financial Spreadsheet (PFS) included with and referenced throughout this book can be a valuable tool to record and monitor your financial accounts.

Note: The PFS is introduced in Part 3 of this chapter and Chapter 2 is largely dedicated to the PFS, its structure, and how to use it.

Surprisingly, couples frequently get married and don't know what each other's goals, financial status, or thoughts are regarding important things such as finances, retirement, home ownership, careers, and insurance. Few couples know or even care about their spouse's creditworthiness, let alone their political or religious views. It is not uncommon for one spouse to have good credit and the other to have poor credit and, when they marry, their financial histories co-mingle. Does your partner know your combined credit scores? If they don't, it can result in a painful revelation when they try to get financing for a car or home. When I got married (the second and final time), I paid the bills and pretty much managed the finances (while my wife made most of the money). We made it a point to share the important aspects of our finances and wrote down our financial goals as a couple.

Part 3: Financial Literacy Solutions

Opportunities for Financial Awareness - Teachable Moments

Growing up with me as their father meant many teachable moments for our daughters, regarding financial concepts as well as other subjects. For example, I would ask them to calculate the tip when we went to a restaurant. When we were on road trips, I would I tell them how many gallons the gas tank in the car held and how many miles per gallon the car got. I would then tell them that the tank was half full and ask them to figure out how far we could go before we ran out of gas. I would also ask them that, if gas cost a certain price per gallon, how much it would cost us to fill up if we stopped at a gas station. They got bored quickly with these exercises, but they got the idea. Of course, most newer cars now display on the dashboard the number of miles you can cover on the gas you have left (range). With hybrid vehicles this is not so much of an issue but with electric vehicles it is important. Our daughters have used what we taught them to enter adulthood and are both successful financially. They have thanked us multiple times for taking the time to help educate them on money matters along the way.

Another teachable moment was when I had our daughters read the Clark Howard book: *Clark Smart Kids* when they were teenagers and summarize the five main points they'd gleaned from the book. I actually paid them to read it to give them a real financial incentive! It was not as much fun as hanging out with their friends, but they did seem to get something out of it. When our oldest daughter got her first job, we asked her to put away 10 percent of her pay into a starter mutual investment fund -which grew to a decent sum over time. Although she complained about saving money for retirement at such a young age (and, of course, her friends made fun of her for it), she came to realize she did not really miss the money. In the process she was investing and beginning to understand the money concept of "pay yourself first," which means you set aside a percentage of your paycheck for yourself before you buy anything else.

When our girls turned eighteen, we took some time to explain what a credit card was, how it worked, the importance of interest rates and paying your balance in full. Around the time they turned 18, both girls had received their first credit card, with some help from us, of course. We also opened a bank checking account for each of them. I went into the bank with them to meet with a real live banker. This exposure helped them become familiar with banking and less intimidated by banks and bankers. When our daughters graduated from college, they each had a four-year credit history and their credit ratings were in the 700-750 range, which is not bad for someone in their early twenties. Chapter 8: Credit Scores and Credit Reports explains these critical financial awareness topics in detail.

Recently, I picked up our granddaughter from school and needed to stop at the bank, so I took the opportunity to bring her into the bank with me and introduced her to my bankers. They struck up a conversation with her and she came to realize that the bank is more than just bricks and mortar, although I did point out the gigantic safe that houses people's safe deposit boxes. She watched the teller count money out for me, and the tellers talked to her about what she was expecting for Christmas.

Better Late than Never

One of our daughters took a course in personal finance in her senior year at college, and it covered a wide range of financial topics. At least she got exposed to personal finance before she joined the workforce. The following is an excerpt from an email our daughter sent us regarding the personal finance course.

"I just had a tidbit of interesting information to share with you. I just completed Part 1 of my personal financial plan, which I must do for my finance class. I had to compare credit cards and banks based on APR, cash back, late fees, and annual fees and provide a spreadsheet to compare credit cards."

This kind of knowledge is very valuable and can go a long way in helping someone to be more confident and competent in dealing with money and credit. It's too bad she had to wait until her senior year in college to be exposed to it. Better late than never, I suppose!

The Financial Offsite Meeting

My wife and I take a day off once a year and stay in a hotel (especially important for those of you who have children) for what we call our "Financial Offsite Meeting." The "Offsite meeting" is a corporate concept whereby a group of employees such as department managers or the members of a particular department go offsite to another location to have meetings. They do this so they can focus their attention on important issues and not be disturbed by the daily office distractions. For my wife and me, it means we can get out of the house for a couple of days and break up the routine. We share our thoughts on future plans and take stock of our financial status, as well as discuss short- and long-term goals. We write out an agenda for use in our "offsite" so we can clarify the purpose and expected outcome of the session. We usually go out to dinner, to treat ourselves, after we have worked our way through the agenda.

The Personal Financial Spreadsheet (PFS)

Another practice that my wife and I employ at our offsite meetings is using the Personal Financial Spreadsheet (PFS) as a guide to review our financial status. During this process we go over our PFS, and we make sure that both of us understand the accounts that are listed, what they are for, and how they can be accessed. We record about 90 percent of our financial information in the spreadsheet and keep it updated so it has become our central "go to" document for all things financial. For this reason, the PFS should not be accessed or updated on a non-secure Internet connection. Listed below are examples of the financial data in our spreadsheet and subjects we discuss at our offsite meetings that are part of our personal financial plan.

- Assets
- Our current income (gross)
- Our current monthly expenses
- Our current budget and any adjustments
- Credit card balances and limits
- Bank accounts balances
- Current Savings and Investments accounts
- Retirement accounts balances
- Insurance policies
- Completed and upcoming home related plans or projects
- Auto-related plans
- Planned purchases, projects and vacations

The Personal Financial Spreadsheet (PFS) and How to Get One
By reading this book, you will have the necessary information to build your own PFS. However, you can download the spreadsheet template from the publisher's Website and use it to record your financial data. Refer to **Exercise 2-2: Download the Personal Financial Spreadsheet (PFS) Template,** in Chapter 2. The structured data-gathering exercises in the book provide instructions on what data you will need to collect to complete each of the seven sheets that make up the PFS. Appendix A contains screenshots of all PFS sheets in sequence, with sample data entered. The PFS is not complicated, and if you are familiar with Excel, you can build the PFS just by looking at the screenshots in Appendix A. You will also develop a personal financial plan as part of **Exercise 19-1 (Fin-Plan Section 1): Gather Personal Financial Planning Data**. As you progress through the chapters in this book you will find that even just starting to take care of your money matters helps build confidence and can improve other areas of your life.

The PFS, which is the core of this book, uses some very simple math and formulas. You don't have to be a math whiz to manage money effectively; simply being motivated and conscientious is enough. My wife and I go over the spreadsheet periodically (usually at our annual offsite financial planning meeting) so we can verify the accuracy and content and understand the implications of our financial data. It is important that both partners are familiar with their personal finances in case something happens to one of them. The PFS can help ensure that both partners have up-to-date information in a centralized location that is readily accessible. In addition to updating our spreadsheet regularly and in preparation for our offsite meetings, I also copy the spreadsheet and update it to create a new one each year. I update assets, liabilities, income, expenses, and credit card information, etc. Chapter 2 describes the PFS, and other chapters in this book frequently refer to various sections in the spreadsheet. The complete seven-page spreadsheet, with formulas, is in Appendix A. The personal financial spreadsheet contains the following sheets (or tabs). (See Table 1-1.)

Table 1-1: Personal Financial Spreadsheet (PFS) - Sheet Title and Tab Names

Seq.	PFS Chapter: Sheet Title	Tab Name
1	PFS 3-1: Income, Expenses, and Cash Flow	Income-Exp
2	PFS 5-1: Assets, Liabilities, and Net Worth	Assets-Liab
3	PFS 9-1: Credit and Credit Cards	Cred-Cards
4	PFS 11-1: Home Info and Maintenance	Home-Info
5	PFS 12-1: Auto Info and Maintenance	Auto-Info
6	PFS 16-1: Insurance Policy Info	Insure-Pols
7	PFS 19-1: Financial Planning and Projects	Fin-Plan

Mindfulness (Mindful Awareness) - Definition, Application, and Benefits

I have included a small section on the topics of mindfulness and awareness because many of us go through much of our lives mindlessly and unaware (myself included). It's like we are on autopilot and somewhat unconscious as we go about our business. We can sit there at the table and eat a meal while hardly tasting the food as we shovel it in, let alone thanking the plants and animals that gave their lives for our nutrition. The study and adoption of the Eastern wisdom tradition of mindfulness can provide a different perspective. It can help us to focus on the present moment, learn from our mistakes, and overcome obstacles to become more successful with our finances and life in general. The mental and physical health benefits of these spiritual traditions or life philosophies are well documented. They are increasingly being adopted and are merging with modern medicine, along with meditation, Yoga, and Tai Chi. These traditions have been around for thousands of years and are becoming more mainstream in Western culture. If you do a search for "mindfulness" or "mindful awareness" you may be surprised by the number of hits you get and the variety of organizations represented.

Mindfulness includes awareness and acceptance. Awareness allows us to focus our attention on the present moment. Acceptance allows us to impartially observe a situation and accept it for what it is rather than try to change it or resist it. Being aware and acceptant allows us to focus on solutions rather than our anger and fighting the situation. Awareness can shed light on and help correct nonproductive behavior. You cannot correct what you are not aware of. Mindful Awareness helps you focus on the now, the only place you can have any effect. The past does not exist except in our memories and the future can only be imagined, as it has not yet happened. So, neither the past nor the future exists, even though we spend much of our lives thinking about them rather than living in and paying attention to the present. It does not do any good to dwell on past financial mistakes or worry about the future. You can't change the past, but you can learn from it, and you can change the future by living fully in the present and doing your best. The future is what we make it. If you take care of the present, the future will take care of itself. Here's a mindful quote from the Gratitude Affirmations in Chapter 20: Attitude of Gratitude and Prosperity.

Quote 1-4: "Learn from the past, plan for the future, and live in the present." - Anonymous

The present moment is the only real opportunity we have to make changes that can affect the course of our lives. When you become aware of a problem and acknowledge it exists, that is the first step in correcting it. Improving your financial situation is not a short-term endeavor that ends with taking a course on personal finance or reading a book. That is the beginning of your quest for financial enlightenment. This book is just a starting point for your path toward financial literacy. I have been following this path for over ten years and have studied personal finance much of that time. Once you start, it becomes a gratifying lifelong pursuit to develop proficiency and control with regard to your finances. You can derive a great deal of satisfaction and peace of mind knowing that your finances are under control. For many people, it all starts with awareness. Being in the present moment and aware of your opportunities is key, along with a willingness to take action. But this does not happen overnight. I know a couple that made a conscious commitment to get rid of their credit card debt and it took them two years of dedicated conscious awareness to get there. Here's a quote that describes how they felt when they achieved their goal.

Quote 1-5: "It is a great and powerful feeling to pay off your credit cards on your way to being debt free." - Anonymous

Here's one more quote that helps tie together the importance of mindful awareness in financial affairs as well as other life areas. This is what's meant by acceptance; the willingness to take responsibility for a situation; and work to correct it rather than worry, blame and complain.

Quote 1-6): "Life is 10% what happens to you and 90% how you react to it." - John Maxwell

I am not a guru, but I do try to meditate daily and be thankful for what I have. I'm not religious, although I was raised in a Christian environment, but I am becoming more spiritual. Just as one would set aside time for physical exercise, I try to allocate time each day to exercise the mind and spirit. Time spent on mental and spiritual development is considered by many to be equally important as physical exercise. Dr. Stephen Covey, the author of the book *The 7 Habits of Highly Effective People*, refers to this as "Sharpening the Saw," which is the 7th habit in his book. According to Covey, "Sharpen the Saw" means preserving and enhancing the greatest asset you have—you. It means having a balanced program for self-renewal in the four areas of your life: physical, social/emotional, mental, and spiritual." What does all this have to do with personal finance you might ask. It is about awareness and balance. If you can maintain a healthy balance between the physical, mental, emotional, and spiritual aspects of your life, managing your finances will be a lot easier.

I try to be aware in the present moment as often as I can and consciously use all five senses when possible. More information on mindfulness and gratitude can be found in Chapter 20: Attitude of Gratitude and Prosperity. Not everyone will be successful in reaching all their financial goals, but through desire, dedication, and diligence—along with some guidance and education—you can achieve a great deal of success, financially and otherwise. However, it is easy to start thinking about the past and waste the opportunities of the present. We can learn from the past but not dwell on it. Negative thinking and focusing on previous financial failures, your current financial problems, or dismal future financial outcomes can undermine anyone's efforts to get ahead. In pursuit of financial awareness, be aware enough to not neglect other areas and people in your life. Here are a couple of examples of how awareness can help financially in your life: (1) You are aware enough to offer assistance to someone and then are able to take advantage of an opportunity that may turn into a new job, and (2) You are aware of potential financial scams, so you do not get duped and lose money.

A major benefit to being mindful or mindfully aware is being conscious enough to stop for a moment and take a couple of deep breaths, to appreciate the beauty and abundance that surrounds you and is present at any given moment. Just stop occasionally, and observe, notice, and appreciate. A good practice to help you focus on the present rather than the past or the future, is to slow down and focus on the five senses: sight, hearing, touch, smell and taste. In all aspects of your life, use this simple acronym memory jogger to help you remember the **Four "M.A.T.H Bee's." Just do the Math!**

- Be Mindful
- Be Aware
- Be Thankful
- Be Here Now

Chapter 2
The Personal Financial Spreadsheet (PFS)

Chapter Overview:
This chapter introduces methods by which you can evaluate your current financial status and identifies some steps you can take to help ensure that you are moving in the right direction regarding money matters. The scenarios described herein address the impact of one's financial lifestyle on one's whole life. The chapter is divided into two parts. Part 1 focuses on personal financial awareness and how to develop it, and Part 2 focuses on the Personal Financial Spreadsheet (PFS), its structure, how it evolved, and how to best make use of it.

Note: Screenshots of the actual "Assets, Liabilities, and Net Worth" sheet, with sample data entered, are provided in **Part 2** of this chapter to explain the components of a typical PFS sheet. See **Figure 2-1** in **Part 2** of this chapter (two instances). Refer to **Appendix A** for screenshots of all seven PFS sheets in sequence.

- **Part 1: Personal Financial Awareness Challenges**
- **Part 2: The Personal Financial Spreadsheet (PFS)**

Chapter PFS Integration:
The PFS is the foundation of this book and can provide a centralized location for the money-related aspects of your life. Using the available template, you will enter your data to create a PFS for yourself to help manage your finances. This chapter describes the PFS contents, how to enter data, how to manage it, how to keep it secure, and how to use it as a financial reference tool. Appendix A contains screenshots of the seven tabs (sheets) of the PFS with sample data.

Chapter Exercises:
- **Exercise 2-1: Compare Password Management Apps**
- **Exercise 2-2: Download the Personal Financial Spreadsheet (PFS) Template**

Chapter Notable Quotes:
Quote 2-1: "I find the great thing in this world is not so much where we stand, as in what direction we are moving." - Oliver Wendell Holmes

Quote 2-2: "If you can't measure it, you can't improve it." - Peter Drucker

Quote 2-3: "Each morning we are born again. What we do today is what matters most." - The Buddha

Part 1: Personal Financial Awareness Challenges

How are you doing financially? Do you feel like you are moving in the right direction regarding money? Where do you stand now, and where are you going? The first quote above by Oliver Wendell Holmes can be applied to any aspect of our lives including mind, body, spirit, and relationships. However, it is especially relevant to developing financial awareness. It reminds us to look at where we are currently regarding money, and ask ourselves if we are improving or making progress. Fortunately, where we are currently is not as important as whether we are moving in the right direction. The right direction generally means an improvement in some area of our lives, and for the purposes of this book, it means less debt, more prosperity, and more abundance in general. It is important to be honest about your current situation and focus not on past mistakes but on how you can improve and educate yourself, so as to not repeat those mistakes!

Keep in mind that if you are staying in one place with some aspect of your life, and not improving, you are most likely losing ground as time marches on. This does not mean you have to burn yourself out competing in the rat race to be successful, but I like this related saying: "If you're not making any mistakes, it's because you're not doing anything." You will make mistakes; everyone does. Take account of them, learn from them, and move forward. Have you ever heard the saying "The harder I work, the luckier I get"? Hard work, perseverance, and dedication can compensate for a lot of shortcomings and help you to move toward your goals. Don't expect to solve all your problems at once. Remember, it's slow and steady that wins the race, especially in pursuit of financial stability and well-being. Some days are better than others. Sometimes you're the windshield, sometimes you're the bug.

The Top Twelve Financial Action Items
As with other aspects of our lives, if we do not like where we stand financially, we can choose to change direction, though this may not happen overnight. Financial changes can be made gradually, and if we have clear, achievable goals and are making progress, that's what counts. It takes time and some effort to undo years of bad financial habits and decisions, but if you are committed and have the right attitude, you CAN do it! Millions of people have, regardless of their background or circumstances. The following Top Twelve Financial Action Items, listed in Table 2-1, are examples of specific actions that you can take or start working on to improve your financial situation and develop personal financial awareness. The list is not intended to be exhaustive, but these are my Top Twelve, more or less in order of importance or priority. However, Action Item number twelve (review your insurance policies for coverage vs. cost) should probably be closer to the top of the list. The rest of this book builds on the Top Twelve list.

Preview of What's to Come!
I have included these here because they are twelve of the most important things you can do to significantly improve your financial situation, according to many financial advisors. Other advisors may disagree, but these are my Top Twelve. There are certainly other things you can do, but this should be considered the "A" List, in my opinion. You may be familiar with some or all of these, but there is no expectation that you should understand or be able to accomplish them at this point. So, you only need to start thinking about them to increase awareness and ask yourself what they mean to you. Some might ask why list these here so early in the book, but I subscribe to the philosophy espoused by Dr. Stephen Covey in his book *The 7*

Habits of Highly Effective People. Habit 2 is "Begin with the end in Mind." So, Table 2-1 is basically a list of personal financial goals that can be achieved by reading this book and taking appropriate action. The action items in the table can be thought of as milestones that you can check off as you progress toward financial awareness. Perhaps you have already achieved some of these and are working on others. As you are progressing through the book or when you finish, come back to this chapter and look at the table to see how many of these items you have achieved or feel confident about. The "Top Twelve" financial action items (AIs) are part of goal setting for your personal financial plan, in Exercise 19-1.

Note: Assuming Action Item #1 to be: "Read this book."! Action Item #2 should probably be: "Seek the assistance of a professional financial advisor" to help you build your financial plan and facilitate your financial journey. Since you are reading this book you have already started on the top 12 financial action items!

Table 2-1: The Top Twelve Financial Action Items (A/Is)

A/I#	Description	Notes
1	Read this book	You have already started on the Top Twelve list
2	Build your Personal Financial Spreadsheet (PFS) by recording your financial data.	The PFS is included with this book and can be downloaded from the publisher's Website. Refer to Exercise 2-2 for instructions.
3	Make payments to creditors on time.	Most import credit rating factor
4	Create and monitor a basic monthly budget.	Where does your money go?
5	Decrease discretionary spending.	Easiest expense to control
6	Reduce your monthly fixed expenses where possible.	Long term results benefit
7	Reduce high-interest credit card debt.	Biggest problem for many people
8	Add to an emergency fund savings account.	Crucial to weathering a financial storm
9	Add to an investment account, such as a 401K or IRA.	Crucial for retirement lifestyle
10	Check your credit score and credit report regularly.	Critical creditworthiness indicators
11	Review credit card and bank statements carefully.	Interest, fees, unauthorized charges. Promotes financial awareness
12	Review your insurance policies for coverage vs. cost.	The right type of insurance and adequate coverage can protect you and your investments.

Making Financial Changes - The Challenge

The key to personal financial awareness is to gain enough knowledge and skill so that you can be consciously aware of the options you have in most financial situations and work steadily toward achieving your goals. Your financial situation and available options will likely be different from the next person's. The Top Twelve Financial Action Items list assumes you have a job with regular income and a positive cash flow (more income than outgo), and for many of us that is not the case. It will be easier for some people to accomplish the goals on the list than others but anyone with desire, dedication, and diligence can make significant financial progress if they stick to it. Set small, achievable goals initially and reward yourself along the way.

The "divide and conquer" method seems to work well, so you might just target one or two of the Top Twelve each month. Start with a goal of paying your bills on time. Once you start, any progress you make will help you to keep going in the right direction. Maybe you don't pay all your bills on time. Pay the most critical ones or the ones with the highest interest rate or the ones with lowest balance, and from month to month, try to improve. If you are having trouble, call the creditor's accounting department and talk to them directly and explain your situation.

Note: Many credit card statements include contact information with 1-800 numbers that you can call for free credit counseling. You can also contact the National Foundation for Credit Counseling (NFCC) at: https://www.nfcc.org for information on debt management plans. The NFCC provides many free services, including counseling on credit and debt, bankruptcy, student loans and more.

Lots of people are having financial difficulties these days. A phone call to the creditor goes a long way, and you may be surprised at how creative and cooperative they can be. As you tackle the goals on the list, put a check mark next to the ones where you feel you are making progress. You can also number them in the order you think you can accomplish them. Another approach is to put an A, B, or C priority next to each of them based on the order in which you want to attack them.

In addition to the Top Twelve Financial Action Items listed in Table 2-1, refer to Table 2-2—which shows the names of the seven sheets of the PFS—to help you get an idea of what this spreadsheet can do for you, and jot down some notes or questions you may have.

Table 2-2: Personal Financial Spreadsheet (PFS) Sheet Titles and Notes

Seq. #	Sheet Title / Name	Notes / Questions
1	**Income, Expenses, and Cash Flow**	
2	**Assets, Liabilities, and Net Worth**	
3	**Credit and Credit Cards**	

4	**Home Info and Maintenance**	
5	**Auto Info and Maintenance**	
6	**Insurance Policy Info**	
7	**Financial Planning and Projects**	

Moving in the right direction financially does not mean you do not suffer setbacks or unexpected expenses or that you do not indulge yourself occasionally, but, on average, you are improving. Read the following scenarios to clarify what is meant by moving in the right direction financially.

Personal Financial Scenario #1:
You decide to buy a new couch and take on debt of $3,000 by acquiring a credit card from the store where you bought the couch. The monthly minimum payment is around thirty dollars, and the annual interest rate is 25 percent. If you pay the minimum payment each month, it will take a long time (years) to pay off the couch and you will end up paying a lot of interest. Your old couch was in good shape and could have been cleaned, but you wanted a new couch. This purchase and the taking on of more high-interest debt might be considered a move in the "wrong direction" for some people's financial situation, especially if they already have a lot of other credit card debt. Instead of buying the couch, you could have decided to pay off one of your high-interest credit cards over six months and improve your financial situation. This might also have improved your credit score, thus moving you in the "right direction" financially. You may still be in debt (most people are), but if you're making progress, decreasing your outgo and/or increasing your income, you're probably moving in the right direction.

Don't get me wrong; sometimes you may spend money on or go into debt for things that you want but may not need. This may not move you in the "right" financial direction, but you simply must have them, and they improve your quality of life, so you choose to indulge yourself. All of us have done this at one time or another. As a personal example, I would not give up my big screen TV and sports channels or my smartphone regardless of how much debt I may have!

Personal Financial Scenario #2:
Let's say "Person A" does not make a lot of money. They have little spending money (discretionary income) and not much saved, but they are working hard. They have a good attitude and are taking courses at the local community college. They are working on increasing their knowledge and investing in themselves. They do not overspend and are paying off their credit cards. They are cooking at home instead of going out to dinner. They drive an older, relatively dependable car and have no car payment. They are renting an apartment and saving for a down payment on a house. Although they might not have much now and may not appear to be as successful as some other people, you could say they are improving their financial

situation and generally moving in the right direction, although perhaps at a somewhat slower rate than they would like.

Contrast Person A's situation with "Person B," who takes home a sizable paycheck. Person B has two expensive, late model cars that are leased, and they live in a large expensive home in a nice neighborhood. They have large amounts of credit card debt, which is growing, since they go out to eat a lot. They are paying minimum payments on their credit cards. They do not have much in savings for an emergency. They have two big car lease payments and a big house payment. Who is better off, Person A or Person B? Who is moving in the right direction financially? The person driving the nice car may appear to be more financially successful, but Person A, who is working hard and living within their means, may sleep better at night. Some would argue that Person B may be better off because they have a big paycheck coming in and could pay down their debt more quickly if they wanted to, but that contention assumes they will not continue to charge their credit cards to the limit. It also assumes they will continue to be employed. Since they have little in savings for an emergency fund, if Person B loses their job, it could result in the loss of one of their cars and possibly their house.

Admittedly the above two examples are overly simplistic and do not paint a complete picture of the finances for Persons A and B. However, they illustrate the point that where you are is not as important as the direction you are going in and demonstrates that looks can be deceiving. Many people do not take responsibility for their spending habits and do not plan or budget when it comes to spending money. Many of us have been financially irresponsible (including myself) at one time or another, but if we are moving in the right direction, that's what counts!

Measuring Your Progress

Quote 2-2: "If you can't measure it, you can't improve it." - Peter Drucker

The second quote for this chapter is from Peter Drucker, considered by many to be the father of modern business management. This is a key tenet of Quality Control, which can be applied to almost any aspect of business or one's personal life, for that matter. From a financial standpoint, if you are not aware enough of a potential problem area to monitor it, you won't know if it's getting better or worse. That is, of course unless you've received a notice in the mail informing you of the "problem." This is one of the main reasons that people get into trouble financially. In most cases they are simply not monitoring how much they are spending and its potential impact on their financial situation. It could be that they are not "financially aware" or maybe they assume that if there is a problem, they, or someone else, will just deal with it later. You cannot change or correct what you are not aware of. This is true whether you have a lot of money or very little. The interesting thing about the Drucker quote is that, just by measuring or monitoring a process, the situation frequently improves. This is due mainly to the fact that someone is watching or paying attention and is known as the "Hawthorne effect." This is great for people trying to improve their financial situation because just by monitoring an aspect of their finances, with heightened awareness, they can frequently improve it.

Most people do not keep track of (measure or monitor) what they are spending or their upcoming financial obligations, and consequently it is easy to overspend. They just whip out the credit card when they want to buy something. For example, when they're dining out with a group of friends and the bill comes, they might say "I've got it." Perhaps they feel it impresses other people. What does not impress people is when their server comes back and tells them that the credit card charge has been declined.

Most Americans that have a credit card carry a balance of thousands of dollars and most are paying minimum monthly payments. No wonder people have credit problems and get into trouble financially. Most people are not aware of how much they have already charged on a particular credit card and don't know how close they are to their credit limit. Few people even know what their credit limit is for a given credit card, let alone the interest rate. I know because I was one of these people until I got a notice from the credit card company telling me that I had exceeded my credit limit. In order to keep the credit card, I had to make a large payment soon. I also paid a hefty fee for going over my credit limit. In addition, they increased my interest rate to the maximum for future purchases (to nearly 30 percent!). I was not monitoring or measuring my spending. I was out of control and unaware. I was clearly moving in the wrong direction financially!

Quote 2-3: "Each morning we are born again. What we do today is what matters most." - The Buddha

Part 2: The Personal Financial Spreadsheet (PFS)

Note: Part 2 of this chapter is the introduction and explanation of the PFS. Figure 2-1a below is a screenshot of the entire Assets, Liabilities, and Net Worth sheet (Tab Assets-Liab) with all three sections shown. This sheet is used as an example and is included here at the beginning of Part 2 as a preview. There are many references to this sheet in Part 2. The same screenshot Figure 2-1b is included near the end of Part 2 of this chapter for convenience.

Figure 2-1a: PFS Sheet - Assets, Liabilities, and Net Worth – All Sheet Tabs Shown

	A	B	C	D	E	F	G
1	**ASSETS, LIABILITIES and NET WORTH**		Book Build: Ch. 5			Updated: MM-DD-YYYY	
2							
3	**<<< Sect 1: Assets >>>**						
4	Owner	< Liquid Assets (Name / Type) >	Institution	Notes	Curr. Value	Monthly Contrib.	Beneficiary / Formula
5	Joint	Bank Checking Acct 1	Bank	Cash	1,000	0	Joint
6	Joint	Bank Checking Acct 2	Bank	Cash	5,000	0	Joint
7	Joint	Emergency Fund (EF) - Online Savings Acct	Savings-Co	EF Goal = $27,000	13,700	300	Emergency Fund Acct - Joint
8	Joint	Savings Acct. - Short-Term (Ass./Inc.)	Anytown Bank	Savings	15,000	200	Joint
9	Joint	Money Market Acct (MMA)	Anytown Bank	Savings	5,000	200	Joint
10	Joint	5-Yr Certificate of Deposit (CD)	Anytown Bank	Savings	10,000	200	Joint
11	Ted	Pension (Ass./Inc./Ret.)	Pension Co.	Retire: Defined benefit	60,000	0	Amy
12	Ted	401K (Ass./Inc./Ret.)	Mgmt Co.	Retire: Stock Funds	75,000	0	Amy
13	Amy	403B Retirement Plan (Ass./Ret.)	Mgmt Co.	Retire: Stock Funds	35,000	500	Ted
14	Ted	IRA Invest (Stocks/Bonds) (Interest/Dividends)	Invest-Co.	Retire: Stock Funds	45,000	300	Amy
15		Other liquid asset			0	0	
16		Other liquid asset			0	0	
17		Other liquid asset			0	0	
18				Total Liquid Assets:	264,700		=SUM(E5:E17)
19							
20		< Non-Liquid Assets (Name / Type) >					
21	Joint	Home Value (Appraised)	Mortgage Co.	Appraised value	250,000	Ref. Sect 2: Liabilities for Mortgage balance	
22	Joint	Auto values (total) (Car and truck)	Cars Paid for	Estimated values (10k+20k)	30,000		
23	Joint	Jewelry & Other	Other Assets	Appraised values	10,000		
24		Other Non-liquid asset			0		
25		Other Non-liquid asset			0		
26				Total All Major Assets:	$554,700		=SUM(E5:E25)-E18
27							
28				Total Moly Save/Invest Contrib:		1,700	=SUM(F5:F25)
29							
30				Saving-to-Income (STI %):		19.1%	=F29/'Income-Exp'!C21
31							
32			EF Goal is $27,000	Emerg Fund-to-Exp: (EFE %):		50.7%	=E7/('Income-Exp'!C76*6)
33							
34				Liquid Assets-to-Exp:	No. Months:	59	=E18/('Income-Exp'!C76)
35							
36	**<<< Sect 2: Liabilities >>>**						
37							
38	Owner	Liability Name / Type	Institution	Notes	Amount		
39	Joint	Home Mortgage Balance	Mortgage Co.	Secured debt	170,000		
40	Joint	Auto Loans (balance owed)	Various	Secured debt	0		
41	Joint	Credit Card Debt (See Cred-Cards Tab)	Various	Unsecured debt	5,000		
42	Joint	Home Equity Line of Credit (HELOC)			5,000		
43	Amy	Credit Card - XYZ Visa			1800		
44	Ted	Credit Card - QRS M/C			600		
45		Other Liability			0		
46		Other Liability			0		
47				Total Major Liabilities:	$182,400		=SUM(E39:E46)
48							
49	**<<< Sect 3: Net Worth >>>**			Total Personal Net Worth (PNW$):	$372,300		=E26-E47
50	(Net Worth = Total Major Assets - Total Major Liabilities)			(Includes Home Equity)			
51							

< > ••• Income-Exp **Assets-Liab** Cred-Cards Home-Info Auto-Info Insure-Pols Fin-Plan Incom

The Evolution of the Spreadsheet

Over time, my financial affairs became more complicated and difficult to keep track of. So, I started to record the key pieces of our financially related information using what we called the **Personal Financial Spreadsheet** or **PFS**. There are probably similar spreadsheets out there, but the PFS is what my wife and I came up with after years of managing our finances. It is a planning tool that tracks the common financial information that a typical family would need. It is tailored to the financial needs of our family. A generic version of it is included with this book, that is not overly complex, and can be modified as necessary to fit your situation. The basic form is presented in this chapter with some suggestions as to how you could modify it, along with suggestions on how to manage it. The entire set of seven sheets (also called a workbook), is included in this book as Appendix A, along with the necessary built-in formulas. It is also downloadable from the publisher's Website as instructed in Exercise 2-2.

The PFS uses some very simple math and a few basic formulas. You may recall the memory jogger device "My Dear Aunt Sally" (MDAS) from a math class you might have taken in junior high or high school. The abbreviation MDAS stands for Multiplication, Division, Addition, and Subtraction and is the order or sequence in which you perform basic math operations. The sequence can be altered using parentheses and exponentiation (powers). So, if you can handle good old Aunt Sally, you can probably handle this spreadsheet. You don't have to be a math whiz to manage your money; simply being motivated and willing to learn is enough. This is a very important point since a lot of people are apprehensive when it comes to math, spreadsheets, and computers in general. You will be provided with everything you need to create your own PFS (if you choose) and manage it effectively. Lots of realistic sample entries are provided throughout the book to make it easier to enter your own data and information.

The Benefits of Using the Spreadsheet

Managing your finances requires some time and diligence, but not really a whole lot, considering the benefits. Like many things, once you take the time to set it up, it's fairly easy to maintain. Just the process of doing this is eye-opening and educational. The payoff or return on your time invested, as with reading this book, is very high and worth every minute. The PFS is a good way to record where you are financially and monitor or keep track of which direction you are going in. It also provides a central location in which to record key pieces of your financial life. It reduces the need to leaf through files and piles of papers; however it does require you to update the spreadsheet periodically (preferably monthly) based on the piles of papers you are collecting. It is still important to keep the hard copy statements of your accounts (usually for three to six months of history). The spreadsheet can save you a lot of time trying to find information kept in stacks or folders in a filing cabinet. It also provides a snapshot of what accounts you have and where you stand financially with each of your accounts. My wife and I use this spreadsheet to prepare for our annual meeting with our financial advisor. It may be a kind of old-school way to manage our finances, but I like the fact that it provides full visibility to our financial information without hiding the data and formulas behind a user interface.

The PFS Structure

The PFS is a simple spreadsheet developed using Microsoft Excel software. It has been refined based on experience and advice, and it has evolved over the years to become the primary financial management tool for our family. It is the foundation of this book. The spreadsheet contains the essential components of personal finance and helps me to sleep better at night. This spreadsheet can provide a centralized place to record your financial information and will help you get a handle on your finances. Using it, you can establish a baseline or starting point from which you can gauge your progress. The PFS is a useful tool that can help you budget and track many types of common financially related information. These include assets, liabilities, expenses, insurance, credit cards and more.

Note: There are multiple spreadsheet programs that are compatible with Windows and Apple OS. Tablet and Smartphone versions that run on iOS and Android are also available. As the PFS has evolved in its various forms over the years, it has been field tested in the real world. The latest iteration of the PFS contains seven tabs, or sheets, which encompass most financially related aspects of our lives.

The titles and names of the seven PFS sheets are listed in Table 2-3, which shows the sheet title as it appears in Cell A1 (e.g., "Income, Expenses, and Cash Flow") at the top of each sheet. Table 2-3 also shows the tab name, which is the abbreviated sheet title name and is the actual name of the sheet (e.g., "Income-Exp"). The Sequence Number (Seq. No.) is the order they appear in the PFS workbook. Refer to Figure 2-1 (a or b) for a screenshot of PFS sheet 2, Assets, Liabilities, and Net Worth. The screenshot also shows all seven tabs across the bottom of the screen. The tab (or sheet) names are listed in Table 2-3 and can be seen in Figure 2-1.

Table 2-3: PFS Sequence, Sheet Titles, and Tab Names

Seq. No.	Sheet Title (Cell A1 of each sheet)	Tab Name (Actual Sheet Name)
1	Income, Expenses, and Cash Flow	Income-Exp
2	Assets, Liabilities, and Net Worth	Assets-Liab
3	Credit and Credit Cards	Cred-Cards
4	Home Info and Maintenance	Home-Info
5	Auto Info and Maintenance	Auto-Info
6	Insurance Policy Info	Insure-Pols
7	Financial Planning and Projects	Fin-Plan

The main value of the spreadsheet is that it encourages you to document or record most of your financial information in a single centralized location that is password protected and encrypted. They say that what you write down you have a reasonable chance of remembering, and just the process of writing it down or recording it increases awareness. There's an old Chinese proverb that goes thus: "That which I hear I forget. That which I see I remember. That which I do I understand." This is the approach we take in this book. We introduce the topic and kind of talk about it, and then we do an exercise that requires some research and documentation, and make choices and decisions based on this. Then, in the PFS exercises we enter actual spreadsheet data, which is hands-on.

Not everyone will be able to take full advantage of each of the sheets, but they contain information that is common and familiar to most people. Refer to Figure 2-1: PFS Sheet - Assets, Liabilities, and Net Worth and Table 2-3 as you read on.

Personal Financial Spreadsheet (PFS) Sheet and Personal Financial Indicator (PFI) Calculations
The seven PFS sheet tabs are listed below along with their main purpose and PFS/PFI interaction. Most chapters have references to either PFS sheets or PFI calculations or both. The PFS sheets contain your financial data and the PFIs do the calculations. Each of the seven PFS sheets has one or more PFIs or other calculations imbedded in it.

Sheet 1: (Tab name Income-Exp) Is for recording your income and expenses, from which the PFS will calculate your Debt-to-Income (DTI) ratio, and Personal Cash Flow (PCF). This is a critical area for all of us. This is where budgeting takes place.

Sheet 2: (Tab name Assets-Liab) A screenshot of the Assets, Liabilities, and Net Worth sheet is shown here as a prime example of a PFS sheet (See Figure 2-1). It is relatively simple but has all the elements of the more complex PFS sheets. This sheet helps you determine what you own (assets) and what you owe (liabilities). By documenting assets and liabilities with the required inputs, this PFS sheet will calculate your Emergency Fund to-Expenses (EFE) ratio, Savings-to-Income (STI) ratio, and your Personal Net Worth (PNW). Along with income and expenses, this is a good place to start when analyzing your financial situation. It's important to know where you stand with your assets and liabilities to create a baseline.

Sheet 3: (Tab name Cred-Cards) is for recording credit card information and helps you get a handle on what cards you have, what their credit limits are, how much you owe and how much you are budgeting to pay per month. Once you enter your credit card information with the amount owed and credit limit for each card, the PFS will calculate your current credit utilization or Debt-to-Credit (DTC) ratio.

Sheet 4: (Tab name Home-Info) provides a place to collect all your home-related, primarily financial information (whether you are renting or buying). By entering your monthly housing expenses and Gross Income, the PFS will calculate your Housing-to-Income (HTI) ratio.

Sheet 5: (Tab name Auto-Info) does the same thing for automobiles irrespective of whether you have one car or three cars. Most people have some form of transportation that can be tracked, and the maintenance monitored here. Once you enter your monthly transportation expenses and Gross Income, the PFS will calculate your Transportation-to-Income (TTI) ratio.

Sheet 6: (Tab name Insure-Pols) is dedicated to insurance policies and documents the policies you have and with which companies, policy numbers, premiums, etc.

Sheet 7: (Tab name Fin-Plan) Section 1 helps you create a comprehensive personal financial plan that you will develop with the help of your professional advisors, primarily your Certified Financial Planner (CFP) or another financial advisor. Section 2 helps track major planned projects and purchases.

Note: Screenshots of all seven sheets of the PFS, with sample information entered, are included in Appendix A of this book. You can build the entire PFS just by looking at the screenshots in Appendix A. Refer to Option B below.

Download PFS Template and Enter Your Data

You download a copy of the Excel-compatible PFS, with all seven sheets, from the publisher's Website. Refer to **Exercise 2-2: Download the Personal Financial Spreadsheet (PFS) Template** at the end of this chapter. This allows you to obtain a current copy of the PFS template for reference and use with the other chapters in the book. You will be instructed to enter your data into the PFS template as necessary as you progress through the book. The downloaded PFS template is read-only but you can change this when you open the file so you can edit it. To open the spreadsheet, you will need Microsoft Excel or compatible spreadsheet software. You can use the template along with the screenshot figures provided in each chapter and Appendix A. Each PFS sheet has a corresponding "Book Build: Ch. X" indicated at the top of the sheet. You enter your financial data based on the relevant chapter exercises and data tables you filled out with each chapter. The downloaded PFS sheets contain pre-formatted headings, cells, and formulas, with blank data rows and other entry fields, where you can enter your own data. Sample entries are provided in the first seven sheets and blank data entry fields are provide in the last seven (-F) sheets (forms). Non-data entry fields and formulas in the PFS template are protected. Whether you build the PFS from scratch or download it, you enter your own data for each of the seven sheets from the data tables you filled out in conjunction with the exercises and screenshot figures provided in each chapter.

Note: After downloading the pre-formatted PFS template file, make a backup copy and save it before making changes to the original. After you are finished adding your data you can convert this file to be read-only.

The Baseline PFS

Once you have a baseline version of the spreadsheet created, you can copy the spreadsheet at the start of each year and rename it to whatever you want (e.g. JAL-PFS-Fin-2024.xlsx). This allows you to keep backup and historical versions, and you can then update the latest copied version with information for the current year. This spreadsheet can be created from scratch to meet your needs using the screen shot information provided in Appendix A.

Note: If you are new to Excel, or spreadsheets in general, there are many books and tutorials that can help you get up to speed quickly. The PFS is easy to work with and does not use any advanced functions or formulas.

The PFS and Spreadsheet Columns and Rows (Refer to Figure 2-1)

Like all spreadsheets, the PFS is made up of vertical lettered columns (A, B, C) and horizontal numbered rows (1, 2, 3), the intersection of which identifies a cell. In Figure 2-1, the label "Section 1: Assets" is in Cell A3 and the "Liquid Assets" column label is entered in Cell B4. The sample asset data entry rows start in Cell B5 and end in Cell B18. An extra blank row starting in Cell A19 is provided to make it easier to insert more rows if you need them. If you need to add more liquid assets, just type over the "other" entries that are already there rather than add rows.

Note: If you add or remove rows between Cell A8 and A18, the formula in Cell E20 for Total Liquid Assets will automatically adjust to cover the range of rows you need.

Spreadsheet Navigation Tips

Spreadsheets can be large, and it is helpful to know how to quickly move around. The cell that your cursor is currently in is always displayed in the formula bar. By pressing the Control key plus the Home key (**Ctrl + Home**) you can move to cell A1 (like Home base) in the top left corner of the spreadsheet. By pressing Control plus the End key (**Ctrl + End**) you can move to the bottom right of the spreadsheet. Pressing the Control key and the letter G key (**Ctrl + G**) prompts you for a cell to Go to. Just enter the cell reference (e.g., E20) and press the Return key (New Line or Enter) to go to that cell. There are many more spreadsheet shortcuts. These are just a few of the more useful ones. As with many things, the 80/20 rule applies, whereby you can do 80 percent of the tasks you need to do using 20 percent of the tools available.

Using the Assets, Liabilities, and Net Worth PFS Sheet as an Example

Whether you build your spreadsheet from scratch or download the pre-built template, you can replace the sample information in the cells and delete or insert new rows for your information. It is not recommended to add or remove columns, as that can change formulas and the function of the sheet. Figure 2-1 shows the second PFS sheet with a sheet title of "Assets, Liabilities, and Net Worth" (Tab name Assets-Liab) and some sample data entered. The figure shows the entire screen or PFS sheet with all three sections: Assets, Liabilities, and Net Worth. Other sheets may be smaller or larger, so you may see only a portion of the screen in a screenshot.

Important Note: The screenshots of some of the PFS sheets may be somewhat difficult to read (see Figure 2-1) due to the small type and amount of data on the sheet. They are provided in the book for reference when discussing the actual spreadsheet and various elements of it. It is assumed that you will have a copy of the real PFS spreadsheet (downloaded in Exercise 2-2) available and will be reviewing it along with the book using Excel or another spreadsheet program. If you do not have a copy of the actual spreadsheet available, you can refer to Appendix A, which has all seven sheets of the PFS broken into smaller pieces. If you have a digital copy of the book (eBook) you can expand and contract the spreadsheet screenshots to zoom in on things that may be difficult to read. Also, you have a complete print version of the entire spreadsheet in Appendix A of the book.

The asset accounts and dollar amounts shown in Figure 2-1 are fictitious, as are Ted and Amy, but are realistic examples and represent some of the possible assets you could have. In Figure 2-1, note the sheet title name "Assets, Liabilities, and Net Worth" in the upper left corner. The sheet title for all seven of the core PFS sheets starts in Cell A1, and is highlighted in yellow on the actual PFS. Section titles, such as Assets and Liabilities, are also listed in Column A under the sheet title and are bolded and highlighted in orange on the actual PFS. The Totals and Subtotals sections of all PFS sheets, such as Total Liquid Assets in Figure 2-1, are bolded and highlighted in green on the actual PFS. Table 2-4 shows how the "Total Liquid Assets" formula is entered and displayed in the spreadsheet, as an example. Review the bulleted items below in conjunction with Figure 2-1 and Table 2-4.

Figure 2-1b: PFS Sheet - Assets, Liabilities, and Net Worth – All Sheet Tabs Shown

	A	B	C	D	E	F	G
1	ASSETS, LIABILITIES and NET WORTH		Book Build: Ch. 5			Updated: MM-DD-YYYY	
2							
3	<<< Sect 1: Assets >>>						
4	Owner	< Liquid Assets (Name / Type) >	Institution	Notes	Curr. Value	Monthly Contrib.	Beneficiary / Formula
5	Joint	Bank Checking Acct 1	Bank	Cash	1,000	0	Joint
6	Joint	Bank Checking Acct 2	Bank	Cash	5,000	0	Joint
7	Joint	Emergency Fund (EF) - Online Savings Acct	Savings-Co	EF Goal = $27,000	13,700	300	Emergency Fund Acct. - Joint
8	Joint	Savings Acct. - Short-Term (Ass./Inc.)	Anytown Bank	Savings	15,000	200	Joint
9	Joint	Money Market Acct (MMA)	Anytown Bank	Savings	5,000	200	Joint
10	Joint	5-Yr Certificate of Deposit (CD)	Anytown Bank	Savings	10,000	200	Joint
11	Ted	Pension (Ass./Inc./Ret.)	Pension Co.	Retire: Defined benefit	60,000	0	Amy
12	Ted	401K (Ass./Inc./Ret.)	Mgmt Co.	Retire: Stock Funds	75,000	0	Amy
13	Amy	403B Retirement Plan (Ass./Ret.)	Mgmt Co.	Retire: Stock Funds	35,000	500	Ted
14	Ted	IRA Invest (Stocks/Bonds) (Interest/Dividends)	Invest-Co.	Retire: Stock Funds	45,000	300	Amy
15		Other liquid asset			0	0	
16		Other liquid asset			0	0	
17		Other liquid asset			0	0	
18				Total Liquid Assets:	264,700		=SUM(E5:E17)
19							
20		< Non-Liquid Assets (Name / Type) >					
21	Joint	Home Value (Appraised)	Mortgage Co.	Appraised value	250,000	Ref. Sect 2: Liabilities for Mortgage balance	
22	Joint	Auto values (total) (Car and truck)	Cars Paid for	Estimated values (10k+20k)	30,000		
23	Joint	Jewelry & Other	Other Assets	Appraised values	10,000		
24		Other Non-liquid asset			0		
25		Other Non-liquid asset			0		
26				Total All Major Assets:	$554,700		=SUM(E5:E25)-E18
27							
28				Total Mo'ly Save/Invest Contrib:		1,700	=SUM(F5:F25)
29							
30				Saving-to-Income (STI %):		19.1%	=F29/'Income-Exp'!C21
31							
32			EF Goal is $27,000	Emerg Fund-to-Exp: (EFE %):		50.7%	=E7/('Income-Exp'!C76*6)
33							
34				Liquid Assets-to-Exp:	No. Months:	59	=E18/('Income-Exp'!C76)
35							
36	<<< Sect 2: Liabilities >>>						
37							
38	Owner	Liability Name / Type	Institution	Notes	Amount		
39	Joint	Home Mortgage Balance	Mortgage Co.	Secured debt	170,000		
40	Joint	Auto Loans (balance owed)	Various	Secured debt	0		
41	Joint	Credit Card Debt (See Cred-Cards Tab)	Various	Unsecured debt	5,000		
42	Joint	Home Equity Line of Credit (HELOC)			5,000		
43	Amy	Credit Card - XYZ Visa			1800		
44	Ted	Credit Card - QRS M/C			600		
45		Other Liability			0		
46		Other Liability			0		
47				Total Major Liabilities:	$182,400		=SUM(E39:E46)
48							
49	<<< Sect 3: Net Worth >>>			Total Personal Net Worth (PNW$):	$372,300		=E26-E47
50	(Net Worth = Total Major Assets - Total Major Liabilities)			(Includes Home Equity)			
51							

< > ··· Income-Exp | **Assets-Liab** | Cred-Cards | Home-Info | Auto-Info | Insure-Pols | Fin-Plan | Incom

Table 2-4: PFS Sheet Assets-Liab - Total Liquid Assets Formula - Example

PFS Sheet Element	Cell Location	Contents/Value
Cell Descriptor/Label	D18	"Total Liquid Assets"
Formula (actual)	E18	=SUM(E5:E17)
Formula (value)	E18	$264,700
Formula (text)	G18	=SUM(E5:E17)

- The text descriptor "Total Liquid Assets:" is in Cell D18.
- The actual formula for Total Liquid Assets is entered in Cell E18 and displays in the formula bar at top of screen (not shown).
- The value that results from the formula is displayed in Cell E18.
- That same formula is also entered and shows in Cell G18 as text, for reference.
- The text formula shown in Cell G18 doesn't do anything but show you what the real formula in Cell E18 should look like.
- The same is done for all the other formulas on all the seven main sheets in the PFS spreadsheet (See Appendix A to review all seven sheets).
- If you select the cell that actually contains the real formula (Cell E18), the calculated value appears in the cell itself, and the formula appears in the Formula Bar (not shown) in the upper left area of the screen. Use this as a double check measure to ensure that you have entered the formulas correctly if you build your own sheet or if you make changes. This assumes the sheet is not protected.

Note: The Assets-Liab tab at the bottom of the screen is the active tab and is highlighted. The tab names of the other six sheets appear across the bottom of the PFS. Selecting one of these tabs will take you to that sheet.

Note: Each of the seven main core PFS sheets contains an "Updated" field entry in the upper right corner. As you work with the PFS, if you make changes to the static entry field names or your data, be sure to update the date using the format shown: mm-dd-yyyy.

Personal Financial Spreadsheet Sheet - Purpose and Contents Overview
The PFS is designed to provide a framework with a big-picture view of your finances with detailed data just a click away on one of the seven tabs. It may not be as refined as some of the database-driven tools available, but it gives you financial awareness that comes from having about 90 percent of your financial data in one place with transparency and visibility. You can drill down quickly by selecting one of the seven sheet tabs (financial categories). Table 2-5 shows the PFS Sheet Tab Name with a description of the main sections in the sheet along with content information and the primary chapter where the sheet is covered. This table is provided as an overview along with Table 2-6 and previous tables to give you a good idea of the actual data in each of the PFS sheets prior to working with them.

Table 2-5: PFS Sheet Descriptions and Contents

Sheet #: Tab Name (Build Chapter) PFS#	Description / Contents
Sheet 1: Income-Exp (Build Ch 3) PFS 3-1	**Sheet Title/Name: PFS 3-1: Income, Expenses, and Cash Flow** Contains 3 sections: Income Sources, Expenses (fixed and discretionary) and Cash Flow. Section 1, Sources, lists the income sources with name/type, institution, and monthly amount. Section 2, Expenses (outgo) is divided into two categories: fixed and discretionary. Each expense includes the name/type, institution, the monthly payment amount, and method of payment. Section 3 shows the monthly Cash Flow (positive or negative) which is calculated by subtracting total monthly expenses (fixed and discretionary) from monthly income.
Sheet 2: Assets-Liab (Build Ch 5) PFS 5-1	**Sheet Title/Name: PFS 5-1: Assets, Liabilities, and Net Worth** Contains 3 sections: Assets, Liabilities, and Net Worth. Section 1, Assets (what you own), lists the asset person, name or type, institution where it is kept, notes, and asset value, as well as the beneficiary. Section 2 lists liabilities (what you owe), and includes person, name or type, and amount of liability. Section 3 shows Net Worth, which is calculated by subtracting total liabilities from total assets.
Sheet 3: Cred-Cards (Build Ch 9) PFS 9-1	**Sheet Title/Name: PFS 9-1: Credit and Credit Cards** Central record for credit card related information. Contains one main section which lists the card issuer/sponsor/brand, primary card holder and authorized users, the last four digits of the credit card number, the credit limit, the current balance (update monthly), the annual percentage rate (APR), and Rewards notes regarding things like cash back and foreign transaction fees. Lastly, the credit limit is totaled for each card and the credit card balance (unsecured debt) is totaled. **Note**: It is also a good idea to include a note if there are any monthly charges that are automatically charged/paid with each card or if the card is the default for use with online transactions. This is especially important if a card is stolen or lost and is replaced with a new card with a different number.
Sheet 4: Home-Info (Build Ch 11) PFS 11-1	**Sheet Title/Name: PFS 11-1: Home Info and Maintenance** Central record for home related information. Contains two main sections, the first is home info such as mortgage, sales price, as well section 2 with maintenance and home improvement projects. Section 1 information includes #brms/baths, square footage, lot size, owner, address, parcel #, assessed value, property taxes, mortgager, mortgage payment, loan #, current mortgage balance, last sale price, homeowner Ins., home warranty Ins., HOA dues, renters ins., and property tax.

Sheet 5: **Auto-Info** **(Build Ch 12)** **PFS 12-1**	**Sheet Title/Name: PFS 12-1: Auto Info and Maintenance** Central record for auto purchase/lease, as well as key dates and mileage for various maintenance items. Contains two main sections. Section 1 lists the vehicle model year, manufacturer, and model. Year purchased, and mileage are recorded as well as the last time important items were serviced or replaced such as tires, oil changes and wipers. Section 2, the Maintenance Record, contains information on the company performing the service, the date, mileage, and a brief description of the work done to the vehicle. A column is also provided to record the cost. The description does not need to be detailed but it's nice to be able to go back to the spreadsheet and see that, for example, for one of your cars, you had Company X replace the water pump, alternator and serpentine belt on a specific date at a specific mileage, and that they warrantied the work (parts and labor) for one year.
Sheet 6: **Insure-Pols** **(Build Ch 16)** **PFS 16-1**	**Sheet Title/Name: PFS 16-1: Insurance Policy Info** Central record for insurance related policy coverage and premium information. Contains one main section which lists who the insurance policy is for and type, insurance carrier, phone no., policy no., amount of coverage, monthly premium, payment method and notes. The Monthly Insurance cost is totaled.,
Sheet 7: **Fin-Plan** **(Build Ch 19)** **PFS 19-1**	**Sheet Title/Name: PFS 19-1: Financial Planning and Projects** This sheet provides a template you can use to create a personal financial plan that you will develop with the help of your professional advisors, primarily your CFP. This tab is included with the seven main tabs to provide a place to record and budget for planned future major purchases and projects. It consists of two main sections. Section 1 is Personal Financial Planning Goals. Section 2 (optional) is for Major Purchases and Projects, such as home improvement, purchasing a new car, or other big-ticket plans, like a vacation.

Note: The PFS is an extensive topic, portions of which are covered in most of the book chapters, as shown in Table 2-6.

Table 2-6: Chapter and Related PFS Sheets

Book Chapter Number and Name	Main PFS Tab	Notes
1: Financial Literacy Perspectives		
2: The Personal Financial Spreadsheet (PFS)	Assets-Liab	
3: Income, Expenses, and Cash Flow	Income-Exp	
4: Budgets and Frugal Living	Fin-Plan	
5: Assets, Liabilities, and Net Worth	Assets-Liab	
6: Banks and Checking Accounts	Assets-Liab	
7: Savings and Banking Services	Assets-Liab	
8: Credit Scores and Credit Reports	Cred-Cards	
9: Credit and Credit Cards	Cred-Cards	
10: Buying, Borrowing, and Debt	Fin-Plan	
11: Buying or Renting a Home	Home-Info	
12. Buying or Leasing a Vehicle	Auto-Info	
13: Investing Basics	Assets-Liab	
14: Retirement Requirements	Fin-Plan	
15: Income Tax Basics	Income-Exp	
16: Insurance and Risk Management	Insure-Pols	
17: Education. Jobs, and Student Loans	Assets-Liab	
18: Scams and Rip-Offs	N/A	
19: Personal Financial Planning	Fin-Plan	
20: Attitude of Gratitude and Prosperity	N/A	
Appendix A: PFS sheets and data	All	Screenshots of all sheets

The "College" and Other Optional Tabs

The seven main sheets are a starting point, and you can add (or delete) as you need them. The spreadsheet can be modified to suit your financial situation by adding tabs for such things as planned "Vacations" and a "To Do" or "Action Items" sheet for keeping track of important financial tasks you want to accomplish within a certain timeframe (e.g., weekly, monthly, or yearly). You may also want to add a sheet for "Medical" or "Med-Drug" to record and track related information.

Another good example of an optional tab is the addition of a sheet for college. When our daughters began attending college, I added another tab to track sources of funds and expenses. We used it to keep track of the financial status of each of the girls separately but kept all the information on one sheet for both girls. This sheet was very important, over a five-year period, as we were keeping track of tuition, books, room, and board. In addition, we kept track of the money the girls contributed to their college education, which included student loans and income from their part time jobs as well as our 529 plans and related spending. I have not included this tab in the book due to its complexity, but it is an example of how you can customize and use the spreadsheet to manage most any money-related project. However, Chapter 17: Education, Jobs, and Student Loans contains college-related financial information, such as 529 plans and other ways to help pay for college.

Backing Up the PFS to Your Smartphone

In addition to local, cloud, external USB, flash drive, and other backup methods, you can also send a copy of your PFS as an email attachment to your smartphone (iPhone or Android) and browse it, although the type is pretty small. This also effectively creates a backup of the PFS. I edit my PFS on my laptop and send it, using my laptop email address, to my iPhone email address when I finish updating data or modifying the spreadsheet. I always have a current version for reference. When you tap the email attachment, it downloads it, so it can be viewed using the built-in iOS email viewer. You can copy and paste from the viewer. You can also use the built-in Excel-compatible spreadsheet iOS app called Numbers to search and even edit the PFS. Apple iOS also includes a Word-compatible Word-processing app called Pages. In addition, you can download an iOS app version of Excel and Word. You can also store the PFS in the cloud using Microsoft Office/365 for iOS and access it from your laptop or iPhone. Figure 2-2 shows how to set the password for an Excel spreadsheet.

Note: If you encrypt your PFS and require a password, you may have issues with it being automatically backed up to the cloud using OneDrive and AutoSave because of the encryption.

Figure 2-2: Spreadsheet Password Security

Spreadsheet Security

When I first started using the spreadsheet, for each account (checking, savings, 401K, etc.). I kept the institution names, account numbers, Web URLs, login user IDs, and passwords within the spreadsheet itself. I realized that this was not very secure, as anyone who could access the spreadsheet could access my accounts! Now I encrypt the spreadsheet with a password of its own, and I keep only the last four digits of my account numbers in the spreadsheet, and I keep the full account numbers and login information in a separate place. The spreadsheet resides on my laptop and the logins/passwords reside in a password management application (app) on my smartphone. Refer to **Exercise 2-2: Download the Personal Financial Spreadsheet (PFS) Template** for how to protect the PFS workbook by creating a password and prompting the user for the password if they try to open it. (See Figure 2-2)

Password Management Apps

Password apps provide a way to secure all your passwords and other sensitive information such as Website logins, credit cards, identity cards, private notes, and other information. Most of them have strong bank-level encryption for logins and passwords and account numbers. Be sure to use a secure network when working with the spreadsheet and be sure to back up your data to a USB/flash drive or the Cloud on a regular basis. Do not update or transfer the PFS on a network that is not secure.

Do a search for "best free password apps" and you will see several of them available. There are some very good ones that are either free or very low cost, and some are free to download and try. Read the reviews for the various password management apps and decide which one best meets your needs. Some popular password managers that are highly rated, include (alphabetically) Bitwarden, Dashlane, LastPass, and Norton.

Keep security-related spreadsheet information in a password app on a smartphone. Examples of the types of information that can be stored offline in a smartphone include the institution name, actual account numbers, phone numbers and the Web URL, as well as login IDs, passwords, and answers to security questions for online accounts.

Refer to **Exercise 2-1: Compare Password Management Apps**, at the end of this chapter to assist you in selecting a password app. Also refer to Table 2-7 below and make a copy of it for use with Exercise 2-1.

Table 2-7: Password Management Apps Comparison (Form)

App Name	Cost	Notes

The Personal Financial Spreadsheet (PFS) in Action

So why should put your financial information into the spreadsheet (PFS)? The main reason is to gather the bulk of your financial information into a centralized and easily accessible location. It will take some time to enter your information, but during this process you will learn a lot about spreadsheets, and more importantly, become more familiar with your finances. Remember, the spreadsheet does not only contain data related to your assets, income, expenses, bank accounts and investments, but also home projects, auto maintenance, your insurance policies, and much more. Email a copy of your finished spreadsheet to your smartphone account and save it in a folder called "Finances." You can use it as a mini database to look up data whenever you need to, since you will usually have your phone with you. If you need to lookup recalls on your vehicle using the VIN, you've got it in the PFS on your smartphone.

I keep a copy of my PFS on my iPhone. It comes through very clean, although very tiny, but it's readable and you can enlarge it easily. You can also rotate the phone to look at the spreadsheet horizontally in landscape mode. You can tap on each of the seven tabs to access the data on each sheet using the built-in Excel compatible App called Numbers. So, the other day I was sitting in my car and the "Maintenance Required" light came on. I wondered when I had last had maintenance done on this car. I opened the PFS workbook on my iPhone and was able to go to the Auto-Info tab and see exactly what maintenance had been performed on my cars, by whom, and when. Of course, this assumes that I had updated the data on the spreadsheet periodically as things changed so that the information I was looking at was current and accurate.

Spreadsheet Record Keeping
Hardcopy records may be kept in a fire-proof safe at home or a safe deposit box at a bank. In addition, this is a place to keep a video or hardcopy record of all your possessions. You can use a smartphone to record videos that can be used when making an insurance claim. What if a tornado hits? Make a list of important documents and keep them handy and stored in a place where you can get them quickly when/if you must leave in a hurry.

Also create an inventory list of the documents that you put in your safe deposit box so that you have a record of what is in it. We have made a handwritten list of what is in our bank safe deposit box, taken a photo of it on our smartphones, kept a copy at home, and put a copy in the safe deposit box. The list includes our social security cards, passports, copies of our drivers' licenses, and our vehicle titles as well as our birth certificates, marriage license, wills, and powers of attorney.

Refer to Exercise 2-2 below to obtain a current copy of the PFS template for reference and use with the other chapters in the book. To open the spreadsheet, you will need Microsoft Excel or compatible spreadsheet software.

Chapter 2 Exercises

Exercise 2-1: Compare Password Management Apps
In this optional exercise, you will research password management apps. To assist you in selecting an app, you can make a copy of Table 2-6. Do a Web search for "best password apps" or search for them individually and compare the features to determine which ones best serve your needs. If you already have a password management app and are happy with it, you can skip this exercise.

Exercise 2-2: Download the Personal Financial Spreadsheet (PFS) Template
In this exercise, you will download a **read-only** copy of the pre-formatted Personal Financial Spreadsheet (PFS) template Excel file for reference when using this book. You can print the first seven sheets of the workbook if desired (eight including the Cover sheet).

- You can edit the file by clicking the "Edit Anyway" button after you open the file.

- The first seven sheets are examples and are protected. The second seven sheets are the template for entry of your financial data.
- The downloadable PFS has a Cover Page (unnumbered) where you can enter your personal information if desired.
- The first seven sheets (tabs) of the PFS template workbook are prepopulated with sample data and are the same as those found in Appendix A of the book. (e.g., Cred-Cards)
- The last seven sheets are data entry "Form" sheets with "-F" appended to the tab name (e.g., Cred-Cards-F).
- Use the first seven sheets for reference only and enter your data into the last seven "Form" sheets of the workbook (and/or make copies of the book screenshots).
- To enter data for one of the seven sheets you should make a copy of the form in the book or print the blank form from the downloaded workbook template file. Next gather your data and enter it into the paper form manually. This allows you to take notes as you go. Transfer your data to the actual PFS sheet later.
- This workbook has fifteen sheets total counting the "Cover" sheet.

As part of this exercise, you will protect your PFS workbook by applying a password to the entire workbook (spreadsheet) to prevent anyone from seeing your financial information. You will go to the publisher's Website for additional instructions on downloading the PFS workbook template file.

Note: Workbook/sheet static entries (headings and other non-data cells) are protected as are formulas, which are color-filled. You can click on any non-data cell but you will not be able to see the contents (in the case of formulas) or edit (change) the contents of the cell.

Download the PFS template file:
1. Go to the publisher's Website at: https://heuristicspress.com/ and select "Books" from the Home page menu.
2. Download the PFS Excel spreadsheet template file from the Website and save a copy locally (e.g., Desktop). Name it PFS-ZZZ.xlsx where ZZZ is your initials.
3. Protect the PFS workbook using a password. To do this, open the workbook by selecting the file and pressing **Enter** (or Return key).
4. From the **File** menu select **File/Info/Protect Workbook/Encrypt with Password**. Enter the desired password, click OK, and save the file. Be sure to write the password down and keep it in a safe place, such as your password management app. The next time you try to open the workbook, you will be prompted for the password. (This applies to Excel 2016 and compatible apps.)

Chapter 3
Income, Expenses, and Cash Flow

Chapter Overview:

This chapter covers financial topics related to the first sheet of the Personal Financial Spreadsheet (PFS), with a tab label of "Income-Exp" and sheet title "Income, Expenses, and Cash Flow." This sheet contains approximately 50 percent of the information for the seven pages of the PFS. The Income-Exp sheet provides a foundation for the budgeting process since all your income and expenses are recorded there. This chapter is divided into five parts with Parts 1–3 corresponding to the three main sections of the Income-Exp sheet. Part 4 explains the Debt-to-Income (DTI) and Personal Cash Flow (PCF) ratios and formulas. Part 5 provides an explanation of Personal Financial Indicators (PFIs), which are introduced in this chapter and used throughout the book.

- **Part 1: Income Sources**
- **Part 2: Expenses - Outgo**
- **Part 3: Housing Expenses and Housing-to-Income Ratio**
- **Part 4: Debt-to-Income Ratio and Personal Cash Flow**
- **Part 5: Personal Financial Indicators and Performance Ratios**

Chapter PFS and PFI Integration:

This chapter explains the purpose and components of the PFS Income-Exp sheet, which provides a way to record your income sources as well as recurring expenses to determine your approximate monthly Personal Cash Flow (PCF). The key Personal Financial Indicators or PFIs related to income and expenses, such as Debt-to-Income (DTI) and Housing-to-Income (HTI) ratios, are built-in and calculated by the Income-Exp sheet. Each part of this chapter describes a section and explains the related terminology, while providing details and instructions for entries.

Note: Refer to Appendix A, which includes all seven sheets of the Personal Financial Spreadsheet (PFS) with sample data entered.

PFS Income-Exp Sheet - Owner's Background - Meet Amy and Ted

The sample financial data shown in the PFS screenshots throughout this book belongs to a fictitious couple named Ted and Amy. Ted retired at age sixty-seven and has Social Security income and a couple of other retirement sources that he is drawing on. These include a 401k and a pension, both from former employers. He is taking retirement distributions from his 401K and is receiving monthly payouts from his pension. He also has a part-time job at a hardware store and a small furniture repair business on the side. Amy is sixty-two and working full-time with a salary and benefits as an instructor with the local college. She teaches economics and personal finance. She plans to retire in about five years and is contributing to her employer-matched 403B plan. Ted is on Medicare and Amy has health and life insurance through her employer.

Note: Ted's and Amy's age or life stage may not be the same as yours, but they have several income sources and expenses that you will probably be able to relate to, if not now, then at some time in your life. You may know about them now or will learn about them as you progress through the book. For example, Amy contributes to a 401K with an employer match at work and is nearing retirement. A young person in their twenties and working a full-time job might ask when they should start contributing to a 401K. If one is available with their current employer, then the answer is "now." The sooner the better! If you can, start putting away 10 percent of your gross pay while you're in your twenties and continue to do that until you retire. You will likely be a millionaire by then and will thank yourself when you reach retirement age or sooner. If a 401K plan is not available through work, you can start an Individual Retirement Account (IRA) for yourself. Starting to save and invest early is the single most important factor in building a sizable nest egg for retirement. Refer to Chapter 13: Investing Basics, and Chapter 14: Retirement Requirements.

Chapter Exercise:
- **Exercise 3-1: List PFS Income and Expenses**

Chapter Notable Quote:
Quote 3-1: "Cash flow is what's left after subtracting what you have to pay from what you have to pay it with." - Anonymous

PFS Income-Exp Sheet Overview
The Income-Exp sheet is the largest and most complex of all the PFS sheets and consists of three main sections which are named thus:
- **Section 1: Household Income**
- **Section 2: Expenses**
- **Section 3: Cash Flow**

The Household Income main section provides for entry of all forms of household income from multiple sources. The second section, Expenses, is divided into three subsections, each of which is subtotaled.
- **Housing Required Monthly Expenses** (e.g., Home mortgage payment)
- **Other Required Monthly Expenses** (e.g., Auto loan payment)
- **Discretionary Monthly Expenses** (e.g., Dining out expense)

The third section, Cash Flow, uses the totals from the Household Income and Expenses sections to calculate your Personal Cash Flow. See Figures 3-1, 3-2, 3-3, and 3-4 for screenshots of sections of the Income-Exp sheet as well as Tables 3-1, 3-2, 3-3, and 3-4 for sample data entries and instructions.

Figure 3-1: Household Income Section of Income-Exp Sheet (sample entries)

	A	B	C	D	E
1	**INCOME, EXPENSES and CASH FLOW**	Book Build: Ch. 3			Updated: MM-DD-YYYY
2					
3	**<<< Sect 1: Household Income >>>**				
4	**< Income Source (Who/Type/Asset/Income/Retmt.) >**	**Institution**	**Monthly Gross**	**Monthly Net**	**Notes / Formulas**
5	Ted - Social Security (Inc.)	US Govt	1,500	1,300	DD Chkg: X9999
6	Ted - Pension (Inc./Ret.)	Pension Co.	750	600	DD Chkg: X9999
7	Ted - 401K (Ass./Inc./Ret.)	Mgmt Co.	1,000	800	DD Chkg: X9999
8	Ted - Part time job at Hardware store (Inc.)	Anytown Hardware	800	600	Regular income (1040 wages)
9	Ted - Small furniture repair business (Ass./Inc.)	Ted's Furniture Repair	500	500	
10	Ted - Rental Property (Ass./Inc.)	Anytown Mortgage Co.	750	600	Rental income less maint exp.
11	Amy - Full-time Instructor Salary (Inc.)	Anytown College	3,000	2,600	
12	Amy - 403B Contribution (Ass./Ret.)	Mgmt Co.	0	0	For retirement
13	Joint - Money Market Acct (MMA) (Ass./Inc./Ret)	Anytown Bank	100	70	
14	Joint - Savings Acct. - Emergency Fund (Ass./Inc) - Interest	Anytown Bank	100	70	
15	Joint - Savings Acct. - Short-Term (Ass./Inc.) - Interest	Anytown Bank	100	70	
16	Joint - Savings 5-Yr.CD - Long-Term (Ass./Inc.) - Interest	Anytown Bank	100	60	
17	Joint - Invest IRA Acct Income (Stocks/Bond Interest and Dividends)	Invest-Co.	200	150	
18					
19					
20					
21	**Total Monthly (GROSS) Income:**		**$8,900**		=SUM(C5:C20)
22	**Total Monthly (NET) Income:**			**$7,420**	=SUM(D5:D20)
23					
24	**<<< Sect 2: Expenses >>>**				
25					

Income-Exp   Assets-Liab   Cred-Cards   Home-Info   Auto-Info   Insure-Pols   Fin-Plan   Income-Exp-F   Assets-Liab-F   Cred-Cards-F   ··· + ⋮ ◀

Part 1: Income Sources

Household Income Section Overview

Refer to Figure 3-1: Household Income Section of Income-Exp Sheet (sample entries).

This section allows for multiple household income entries and includes Gross Income (GI) and Net Income (NI) entries for each income source identified. As the income sources are entered, they are totaled as gross or net monthly income, or both, depending on what you enter. Most of the Personal Financial Indicator (PFI) ratios, such as Debt-to-Income (DTI), use Gross Income. However, Net Income is used with the Personal Cash Flow (PCF) calculation and is also very important.

Income Types - Active vs. Passive

There are basically two main categories or types of income: Active income, often referred to as "ordinary" or "earned" income; and Passive income, sometimes referred to as "unearned" income. Active income can be a salary, hourly wages, or tips and commissions that an employee might receive (W2 income). It can also result from working a regular part- or full-time job or income earned through self-employed contract work (1099 income). With Active income, you are employed by an employer where you trade X number of hours for Z number of dollars. Passive or unearned income, as the name implies, is income derived from assets and sources that can generate income in the background with minimal management or involvement required from the asset owner. Passive income can include silent partner interest in a small business; rental properties; and investments such as stock dividends, bond yields, and savings interest. Income from retirement accounts such as a 401k or IRA may also be considered passive. Check with your tax advisor. Active income is usually taxed as "ordinary" income, whereas Passive income may be taxed as ordinary income or as capital gains.

Note: Personal income (gross and net) can include both active and passive forms of income. The terms Personal Gross Income (PGI) and Personal Net Income (PNI) are used to distinguish them from a business which also has gross and net income.

Personal Gross Income (Monthly)

This is pre-tax income (before taxes and deductions) and any pre-tax and nontaxable income that you want to include in the ratio calculation. Alimony and other forms of income can be included in this category if desired. For a regular wage earner, PGI is what their employer pays them weekly, bi-weekly, or monthly, before taxes and any deductions. The PFS Income-Exp sheet uses monthly income entries to calculate Gross and Net income for a family. Where more than one person in a household may have earned income or a person may hold multiple jobs, the various income sources can be combined for use in Personal Financial Indicator (PFI) calculations and are referred to as "household income." Many financial health indicators make use of Gross Income—which remains a fairly consistent comparison amount, since it is not affected by taxes and deductions—which can vary considerably depending on the individual or family. The Personal Gross Income (PGI) Personal Financial Indicator PFI 3-1 is shown here, which is calculated in the Income-Exp sheet shown in Figure 3-1.

PFI 3-1: Personal Gross Income (PGI) - Formula/Calculation
(Personal Financial Indicator #PFI-1)

Total Gross Income, All Sources Individual or Household (before taxes) = PGI ($)

Total Monthly Gross Income, All Sources = PGI ($) = $8,900

(PFS Income-Exp sheet example)

Personal Net Income (PNI)

Net Income is what the employee receives after taxes and deductions have been taken out and can vary significantly from one wage earner to the next, even if their Gross Income is the same. For the purposes of this book, the Personal Net Income (PNI) indicator is calculated by summing up the Net Income entries you provide as input to the PFS Income-Exp sheet. The spreadsheet does not record tax entries. The Personal Net Income (PNI) Personal Financial Indicator PFI 3-2 is shown here, which is calculated in the Income-Exp sheet shown in Figure 3-1.

PFI 3-2: Personal Net Income (PNI) - Formula/Calculation
Personal Financial Indicator (#PFI-2)

Gross Income (-minus-) Taxes (Federal and State) = PNI ($)

Total Monthly Net Income Sources = PNI ($) = $7,420

(PFS Income-Exp example - sheet does not record tax entries)

The common Personal Financial indicators (PFIs) referenced in this and other chapters use gross monthly income in their calculations. These include Debt-to-Income (DTI), Savings-to-Income (STI), Housing-to-Income (HTI) ratios, and several others.

Note: The Personal Cash Flow (PCF) calculation in the Income-Exp sheet uses Net Income, which is calculated based on the Net Income entries you provide from your income sources. Commonly referred to as "Take-home Pay," Net Income is gross pay minus deductions (refer to your pay stub and/or W2). Deductions will vary depending on the employer and the employee but usually fall into one of three categories: Taxes, Insurance, or Savings. It is beyond the scope of this book to address the variables involved in payroll deductions. Common automatic payroll deductions include the following:

- **Federal Taxes** (include Social Security and Medicare)
- **State and City Taxes** (depending on the state and city)
- **Insurance** (Health, Life, Disability)
- **After-tax Savings Transfers** (CDs, Short-term savings, etc.)
- **Pre-tax Retirement Contributions** (401K, 403B, IRA, or Pension)

Note: If you are having an automatic payroll deduction taken out of your pay to put into a savings account, this will show up as a deduction and result in lower net pay. You can add the monthly amount you're contributing back to your Cash Flow as a Net Income source, so that it is accounted for and reflected as a positive in your overall cash flow dollar amount.

Income and Benefits
A regular W2 employee may be paid an hourly rate plus overtime or may be paid based on an annual salary. Either way, it normally comes down to a weekly pay period. Base pay can be supplemented by the employer with commissions and bonuses (active income) and stock options (passive income). In addition, included with the employee's regular income is typically a package of benefits and other incentives to create the total benefits package. So, a particular job may pay a salary of $50,000 per year, but with the benefits, the total value added by the compensation package could be worth an additional $10,000. If the job offers bonuses and/or commissions, the value added could be considerably higher. The benefits package varies considerably from one employer to the next but can include the following:

- **Retirement Plan** (401K – with potential match)
- **Paid Time Off** (PTO)
- **Health Insurance** (Individual/family)
- **Life Insurance**
- **Tuition Reimbursement**

When comparing jobs, be sure to quantify the benefits for each one so that you compare apples to apples. For example, if two jobs pay the same base salary of $50,000 per year but one has a 401K with a 5 percent employer match available and the other has a 401K with no match, the job with the 401K match will potentially be much better for the employee, financially, over the long haul. As another example, a friend of ours recently accepted a position that allows her to work from home two out of five days a week. With two young children, working from home may be considered a major benefit, which needs to be quantified when comparing jobs.

Note: Some benefits may be taxed as ordinary income, as they are essentially a form of compensation.

Common Income Sources
Table 3-1 lists examples of common income sources along with a brief definition. These are the types of income that the average person could have, depending on their life stage. Your actual income sources will vary depending on your age, employment status, and financial situation. For a family, the combination of these income sources is referred to as household income. Most of the information in this book and the Personal Financial Spreadsheet (PFS) assumes you are working (employed) or have some form of regular income. Figure 3-1 shows the income portion of the Income-Exp sheet with Ted and Amy's income source data entered. Your PFS sheet should list all your household income sources so the totals can be calculated for Gross and Net Income as shown in Figure 3-1. In Exercise 3-1, at the end of this chapter, when entering data into Table 3-5 and the Income-Exp sheet, focus on Gross Income, but try to obtain both Gross and Net amounts for each income source you enter to give a more complete picture of your income, even if you must estimate. Without complete income and expense data entries, you will not be able to get an accurate value for Personal Cash Flow (PCF). Keep in mind that your Net Income entered in the Income-Exp sheet is used to calculate PCF. Refer to Chapter 15: Income Tax Basics, for additional information on income sources.

Non-monthly Income Sources
All income and expense entries in the Income-Exp sheet are monthly amounts in order to compare apples to apples. When entering Gross or Net Income into the Income-Exp sheet, be sure to adjust the amount if you are not paid monthly. For example, if you get paid every two weeks, you should multiply your gross or net pay times two before entering it in the spreadsheet. If you are paid based on an annual salary, divide it by twelve before entering it in the spreadsheet. See Figure 3-1 for a screenshot of Section 1: Household Income.

Note: Personal financial awareness regarding income means awareness of opportunity.

Table 3-1: Income Section - Example Sources of Income

Income Type/Name	Description	Notes
Ordinary income (net)	Ordinary income from employer (net amount after taxes and deductions taken out)	Used with Personal Cash Flow (PCF) and Potential Saving Ratio (PSR)
Ordinary income (gross)	Ordinary income from employer (with no taxes or deductions taken out)	Used with Debt-to-Income (DTI) ratio and other calculations.
Self-employment	Consulting, contract work, small business salary	
401K and 403B accounts	401K (private) and 403B (public) - Tax deferred retirement income.	Investment accounts for retirement. Defined contribution plan.
Stocks	Investment in a company, ex: Cisco, Apple	Can pay monthly dividends.
Bonds	Purchase of interest-bearing notes that lend money to a company, organization, or municipality (ex: city or state).	Can pay monthly yields.
Social Security	Monthly payments from government, based on contributions and past income history.	Usually taxable income
Pension plan	Monthly payments from an employer (public or private) based on contributions from past income.	Investment accounts for retirement. Defined benefit plan.
Alimony/Child support	Monthly payments from ex-spouse	Optional entry in PFS
Royalties	Payment from sales of publications (books, music, videos, etc.)	Usually taxable income
Savings Income	Interest on deposits	Usually taxable income
Rental Income	Income from rental of assets such as home, apartment, Vrbo/Airbnb, Storage shed, etc.	Usually taxable income

Part 2: Expenses - Outgo

Note: Refer to Income-Exp sheet, Section 2: Expenses. Also refer to Figure 3-2: Housing Required Monthly Expenses Section of Income-Exp Sheet.

Section 2: Expenses Overview
This portion of the sheet allows you to record the amounts you pay out (outgo) on a monthly basis. It then subtotals your expenses by "Total Housing Required Monthly Expenses," "Total Other Required Monthly

Expenses," as well as "Total Discretionary Monthly Expenses." The "Total Monthly Expenses (outgo) - ALL TYPES" is compared to "Total Monthly Gross Income" and used to calculate your Debt-to-Income (DTI) ratio or percentage, a key financial indicator that is looked at by any potential creditor. In addition to totaling housing-related fixed monthly expenses, this section of the spreadsheet also calculates the Housing-to-Income (HTI) ratio or percentage. HTI is the percentage of your gross income you spend per month on housing-related expenses.

The Expenses section of the PFS Income-Exp sheet is shown in Figure 3-2. See Table 3-2, which lists the major expense categories, as well as Tables 3-3 and 3-4, which provide examples of the various expense categories. Expenses are amounts paid out, usually monthly, for various purchased items or services. They are usually paid from the income sources available, assuming income exceeds outgo. Expenses can be fixed or variable.

Fixed Expenses

These are expenses that remain consistent from month to month, although they can vary somewhat. Examples include a car payment, a rent payment, or an insurance premium. Expenses can be grouped by category such as home, auto, medical, or other—depending on your circumstances—and can be summarized as a subtotal for each group. The main thing with fixed expenses is that the payment is the same or changes very little from month to month. The PFS can subtotal the fixed expense amount for subgroups, like housing, and then calculate a total for all fixed expenses. Fixed expenses are ideal candidates for AutoPay.

Variable Expenses

These are expenses that can change from month to month, such as utilities, gas, or a credit card payment. With a credit card, you can choose to pay more than the minimum (good), pay off your balance (better), or pay only the minimum (not good, but sometimes necessary).

Mandatory (required) vs. Discretionary (optional) Expenses

Another way to characterize expenses is "mandatory" (required) or "discretionary" (optional). An example of a mandatory fixed expense is your car or home loan payment (mortgage). If you do not make the required minimum payment on time, it can damage your credit score or even result in repossession. On the other hand, you can choose to pay more than the minimum car or home payment, which will pay off the loan more quickly and save interest. Mandatory/discretionary and fixed/variable expense categories and examples are shown in Tables 3-2, 3-3, and 3-4.

Table 3-2: Categories and Examples of Expenses

Category	Example	Notes
Mandatory Fixed	Car payment	Payment is required and is the same until loan is paid off (Most expense entries).
Mandatory Variable	Credit card payment	Payment varies but minimum payment required.
Discretionary Fixed	Groceries	More or less consistent dollar amount but you can choose not to purchase certain items or purchase other items due to cost or health considerations.
Discretionary Variable	Dining out	Based on choice and lifestyle.

Examples of fixed and variable mandatory (required) monthly expenses for a typical U.S. homeowner are shown in Table 3-3. Examples of monthly discretionary expenses are shown in Table 3-4.

Table 3-3: Monthly Mandatory (Required) - Fixed/Variable Expense Examples

Mandatory (Required) Expense Description	Payee	Payment	Fixed / Variable	Notes
Mortgage (*PITI)	XYZ Bank	1300	F	
Water / Sewer	City municipality	50	V	
Trash / Recycle	County municipality	20	F	
Electric / Gas	Power Co.	180	V	Average
Medical / Prescriptions	Pharmacy	200	V	
Security/Smoke	Security Co.	50	F	
Cell Phone	Provider	280	V	
Internet	ISP	60	V	
Cable/Satellite TV	Cable/Sat Co.	50	V	
Home Maintenance	Various	100	V	

*PITI – Principal, Interest, Taxes (property) and Insurance (homeowners). Used with Housing to Income (HTI) calculation (introduced in this chapter and Chapter 11). Note that homeowner's insurance is not listed as an example here as it is typically included in the mortgage payment along with property taxes.

Note: For Mandatory (required) variable expenses, like utilities, you can add up the amount for the January through December monthly bills and divide it by twelve to get an average. Or, you can add the high and low months amount and divide by two, and then record the average in the table.

Table 3-4: Monthly Discretionary Expense Examples

Discretionary Expense Description	Amount	Notes
Groceries	500	
Dining out	200	
Gas	200	
Auto maintenance	100	
House cleaning	115	
Lawn mow / landscape	80	
Vacations	300	
Misc. personal care (haircuts, etc.)	250	
Misc. other (e.g., Daycare cost)	800	

Part 3: Housing Expenses and Housing-to-Income Ratio

Housing Required Monthly Expenses

Figure 3-2 shows the Housing Required Monthly Expenses section of the Income-Exp sheet. This is the largest category of fixed expenses for most people, since it includes the home mortgage or rent amount. It lists the main housing expenses and then subtotals them as shown in Cell C41. Note: the actual contents of Cell C41 is the formula to sum up housing expenses, and if you select Cell C4,1 it will show the calculated value in the Cell C41 and show the actual formula in the Formula Bar at the top left corner of the screen (See Figure 3-2). This formula is also entered as text in Cell E41 for reference. The formula shown in Cell E41 is nonfunctional and is there for display only.

Note: The term "housing" is used when referring to home-related expenses, including rent expenses, and is a broader term. The term "home" is generally used when referring to an individual home-related expense or line item.

Figure 3-2: Housing Required Monthly Expenses Section of Income-Exp Sheet

	A	B	C	D	E
24	<<< Sect 2: Expenses >>>				
25					
26	< Housing Required Monthly Expenses >	Institution	Monthly Payment	Payment Method	Notes
27	Housing Expense Name / Type				
28	(Required Housing Expenses)				
29					
30	Home - Mortgage PITI (or Rent)	Anytown Mortgage	1,800	O/L Bill Pay	Bank X9999 (Escrow Tax/Ins)
31	Home - Homowners Assoc, Dues (HOA fees)	Subdivision HOA	100	O/L Bill Pay	O/L: www.xyzprop.com - Qtrly
32	Home - Water/Sewer/Trash/Recycle	Anycounty Services (Avg)	175	O/L Bill Pay	CC x9999 (one bill)
33	Home - Electricity/Gas	Anytown Electric/Gas (Avg)	250	Auto-Pay	CC x9999 (one bill)
34					
35	(Optional Housing Expenses Included)				
36	Home - Security/Smoke alarm	XYZ Security	50	Auto-Pay	Auto Pay CCx9999
37	Home - TV Cable	Anytown TV	85	Auto-Pay	Auto Pay CCx9999
38	Home - High Speed Internet	Anyprovider Internet	50	Liquid Assets-Exp (LAE)	No. of Months
39	Home - Pest Control	Anytown Pestsbegone	40		Billed Qtrly CCx9999
40	Other			Auto-Pay	
41	Total Housing Required Monthly Expenses		$2,550		=SUM(C30:C40)
42					
43	Housing-To-Income Ratio (HTI %)		28.7%		=(C41/C21)
44	= (Required Housing Expenses / Gross Income)				(HTI Ratio < 30% is OK)

Housing-to-Income (HTI) Ratio

Figure 3-2 shows a screenshot of the PFS Housing subsection of the Expenses section of the Income-Exp sheet with sample entries. This portion of the Expenses section is separated because of the large amount of monthly expenses it represents for most people, and it is the major component of the Housing-to-Income (HTI) ratio financial indicator. In addition to totaling home-related fixed monthly expenses, this section of the spreadsheet also calculates the HTI percentage, shown in Figure 3-2 at the bottom of the screen. HTI is determined by taking the monthly expenses that make-up your mortgage payment (PITI = Principal + Interest + Property Taxes + Homeowner's Insurance), plus any homeowner's association dues, and then divides that total by your Monthly Gross Income (See Part 1). Most lenders like to see an HTI ratio of less than 30 percent (less is better). This means you spend less than 30 percent of your gross income on housing-related expenses. Refer to Chapter 11: Buying or Renting a Home for additional information on the Housing-to-Income (HTI) PFI as well as the Income-to-Home (ITH) projection PFI.

Other Required Monthly Expenses (Includes Loans and Credit Line Payments)

Figure 3-3 shows the Other Required Monthly Expenses subsection of the Expenses section of the Income-Exp sheet. This is the second-largest category of expenses for most people since it includes various types of insurance as well as student loans, personal loans, and auto loans. Revolving credit lines, such as credit cards, are also included in this section of the spreadsheet, along with potentially a Home Equity Line of Credit (HELOC) or second mortgage. It can grow to be very large dollar-wise, eclipsing the house expense category for some people. This subsection of the sheet separates the monthly expenses (payments) that have a balance (like a car loan or credit card) from those that don't (like an insurance premium). It provides a total for all "Other" expenses as well as a total for the balance owed on those monthly expenses that carry a balance. The formula in Cell C73 sums up all monthly fixed expenses (most of which are mandatory) other than the housing-related expenses. The formula in Cell D74 totals the balances for all loans and credit lines. Note: the actual contents of Cell C73 is the formula to sum up "Other Required Expenses." If you select this cell, the calculated value will display in the cell, but the actual formula displays in the Formula

Bar at the top left corner of the screen. This formula is also entered as text in Cell E73 for reference. The formula in E73 is nonfunctional and is there for display only.

Credit Cards and Credit Line Entries

Although the monthly payment on the revolving lines of credit (mainly credit cards) is not a fixed amount, they frequently carry a balance from one month to the next, and a payment of at least the minimum is required. Also, it is a good idea to set a fixed payment on credit cards that is more than the minimum to help pay them off more quickly and simplify budgeting.

Revolving credit entries in the Loans and Credit Line Required Payments section can and do change frequently. When adding credit card entries to the PFS Income-Exp sheet, only include credit cards that have a significant balance (like maybe over $500) so you can track them as part of your expenses and budget. If you pay off your credit cards when you receive the statement, do NOT include them in the Income-Exp sheet. However, be sure to add them to the PFS Cred-Cards sheet, which keeps track of all your credit cards, whether you carry a balance or not. The balances are also entered in the Cred-Cards sheet. The Cred-Cards sheet is covered in Chapter 9 - Credit and Credit Cards.

Non-Monthly Billed Expenses

If any of your expenses are billed other than monthly, you must convert them to monthly before recording them in Tables 3-6 and 3-7 or entering them in the Income-Exp sheet for Exercise 3-1. For example, if your homeowner's association (HOA) dues are paid quarterly (every three months), you must divide the quarterly payment amount by three to convert to a monthly amount. If an insurance premium is billed/ paid annually, you must divide the amount paid by twelve to arrive at the monthly amount. Just be sure to divide by the appropriate number to convert to monthly expenses so that the spreadsheet formulas will produce accurate results.

Exercise 3-1 at the end of the chapter has you gather all your income and expense data using copies of Tables 3-5, 3-6, and 3-7. Or you can enter the data directly into the Income-Exp sheet. After all the data for the Household Income section is entered (See Figure 3-1) you will need to provide the Expenses section entries for Housing Required Monthly Expenses (See Figure 3-2), Other Required Monthly Expenses (See Figure 3-3), and Discretionary Monthly Expenses (See Figure 3-4). Once the income and expense data are provided, the spreadsheet will calculate three important Personal Financial Indicators (PFIs):

- **Housing-to-Income (HTI) Ratio (%)** - (Income-Exp sheet Section 1)
- **Debt-to-Income (DTI) Ratio (%)** - (Income-Exp sheet Section 2)
- **Personal Cash Flow (PCF) ($)** - (Income-Exp sheet Section 3)

Figure 3-3: Other Required Monthly Expenses Section of Income-Exp Sheet (sample)

	A	B	C	D	E
	< Other Required Monthly Expenses >	Provider Name / Desc	Monthly Payment	Loan Balance	Payment Method
47	Insurance - Ted Medicare Part B - Medical	Social Sec / Medicare	160	0	Auto deduct from SS Chk Dep
48	Insurance - Ted Medicare Part D - Drug Coverage	Large-Med-Co.	70	0	Auto-Pay EFT Chk Acct X9999
49	Insurance - Ted Medicare supplemental	XYZ-MediCo Supplem Plan	120	0	Auto-Pay EFT Chk Acct X9999
50	Insurance - Ted Vision & Dental	ABC-Medical	40	0	Auto-Pay EFT Chk Acct X9999
51	Insurance - Ted Long Term Care (LTC)	AnyInsCo LTC	200	0	Auto-Pay EFT Chk Acct X9999
52					
53	Insurance - Amy Health (Thru employer, incl. Life, Vis., and Dent)	Anytown College	230	0	Auto deduct from paycheck
54	Insurance - Amy LTC Long Term Care (LTC)	AnyInsCo LTC	210	0	Auto-Pay EFT Chk Acct X9999
55					
56	Home Property Tax	County Auditor (Yrly/12=$200)	0	0	(Incl w/ Mort Pmt - $9,999/YR)
57	Insurance - Home Owners	BigInsCo (Yrly Prem/12 = $50)	0	0	(Incl w/ Mort Pmt - $9,999/YR)
58	Insurance - Umbrella	BigInsCo (Yrly Prem/12 = $20)	20	0	Auto Yrly CC#9999 ($9,999/Yr)
59	Insurance - Auto (Car ABC and XYZ)	BigInsCo (Yrly Prem/12)	100	0	Auto Yrly CC#9999 ($9,999/Yr)
60					
61	(Loan and Credit Line Required Payments)	(Include Loans, Credit Cards, and Credit Lines if Carry Monthly Balance)			
62	Auto Loan - Ted - ABC Car	ABC Car Finance Co.	0	0	Paid Off!
63	Personal Loan - Ted	Personal Loan Bank	0	0	Paid Off!
64	Student Loan - Amy	Student Loan Bank	0	0	Paid Off!
65	Other Loan				
66					
67	Home Loan (Mortgage balance)	Anytown Mortgage Co.	0	170,000	(Pmt in Housing Section)
68	Home Equity Line of Credit (HELOC)	Anytown Bank	300	5,000	Open credit line $30,000
69	Credit Card - Amy - XYZ M/C	XYZ Credit Card	400	1,800	
70	Credit Card - Ted - QRS M/C	QRS Credit Card	100	600	
71	Other CC1				
72					
73	Total Other Required Monthly Expenses		$1,950		=SUM(C47:C72)
74	Total Loan and Credit Line Balances			$177,400	=SUM(D62:D72)

Refer to **Exercise 3-1: List PFS Income and Expenses** at the end of this chapter, which will help you identify your income and expenses to enter them into your PFS Income, Expenses, and Cash Flow sheet.

Part 4: Debt-to-Income Ratio and Personal Cash Flow

(Refer to Income-Exp Sheet, Section 2 – Debt-to-Income)

(Refer to Income-Exp Sheet, Section 3 – Cash Flow)

(Refer to Figure 3-4: DTI and Cash Flow Sections of Income-Exp sheet)

Debt-to-Income (DTI) Ratio (%)

By entering your income sources and monthly expenses, the Income-Exp sheet can calculate your Debt-to-Income (DTI) ratio and Personal Cash Flow (PCF) (See Figure 3-4). Your DTI ratio is a key factor that lenders consider when deciding whether to loan you money for a car or home. It is one of the most important Personal Financial Indicators (PFIs). Your DTI (also referred to as "debt load") is basically your total fixed mandatory (required) monthly debt payments divided by your monthly gross income. The DTI section of the Income-Exp sheet totals all your fixed monthly mandatory expenses and then divides the total by your total Gross Income to determine your DTI ratio.

PFI 3-3: Debt-to-Income (DTI) Ratio - Formula/Calculation
Personal Financial Indicator (#PFI-3)

Required Monthly Expenses (/divided by/) Monthly Gross Income = DTI (%)

$4,500 / $8,900 = .505 (*100) = 50.6%

(PFS Income-Exp sheet example)

Opinions vary, but most financial people would probably agree that your DTI ratio (or percentage) should be less than 40 percent. This means you spend less than four of every ten dollars you make on mandatory or required expenses (excluding discretionary expenses). Some lenders require a DTI ratio of 38 percent or less. These expenses can be fixed or variable. Examples include your mortgage or rent payment, car loan, and student loan or credit card payment, and are made up of your entries into Housing Required Monthly Expenses and Other Required Monthly Expenses subsections of the Income-Exp sheet. Refer to Figure 3-4 for the calculated results and formulas used. Additional information on DTI is covered in Chapter 11: Buying or Renting a Home.

Figure 3-4: DTI Ratio, Discretionary Expenses, and Cash Flow Sections - Income-Exp Sheet

	A	B	C	D	E
76	Total Required Monthly Expenses (Used w/ DTI & EF)		$4,500		=C41+C73
77					
78	Debt-to-Income Ratio (DTI %)		50.6%		=(C76/C21)
79	= (Required Monthly Expenses / Gross Income)				(DTI Ratio < 40% is OK)
80					
81					
82	< Discretionary Monthly Expenses >				
83	Groceries	Various	400		
84	Dining out	Various	200		Need to track; incl fast food
85	Gas	Various	300		Varies, work miles, cost of gas
86	Auto maint	Various	100		All cars avg
87	Personal care (hair, massage, gym, etc)	Various	250		
88	House clean	Various	90		
89	Lawn mow / landscape / snow remov.	Various	50		
90	Vacations	Various	300		Try to keep under $3600/yr
91	Misc - other		300		Check CCs for avg / mo.
92					
93					
94	Total Discretionary Monthly Expenses		$1,990		=SUM(C83:C93)
95					
96	Total Monthly Expenses (outgo) - ALL TYPES		$6,490		=C76+C94
97					
98	<<< Sect 3: Cash Flow >>>				
99					
100	Monthly Personal Cash Flow (PCF) ($)	(Positive or Negative)	$930		=D22-C96
101	(Total Mo. Net Income minus (-) Total Mo. Expenses)				
102					
103	Potential Savings Ratio (PSR) (%)	% of PCF for Savings	12.5%		=(D22-C96)/D22
104	(or PCF-to-Net Income (NI) ratio)				
105	(Total Moly NI minus (-) Total Moly Exp) / Moly NI)				
106					
107	PCF ($$) x PSR (%) = Moly Dollars Avail. for Savings	$$ of PCF for Savings	$117		=C100xC103

Discretionary Monthly Expenses

Figure 3-4 also shows the Discretionary Monthly Expenses subsection of the Income-Exp sheet right after the DTI ratio section. Discretionary expenses are optional by definition and vary greatly from one person to the next. They are not included with the DTI ratio calculation because it only includes monthly expenses that are required. However, discretionary expenses are included with required expenses for the Personal Cash Flow calculation in Section 3: Cash Flow. This is because you want to include ALL of your expenses or money spent on a regular basis (required or not). Also, you want to compare it to your NET Income, which is after taxes have been taken out. Refer to Personal Net Income (PNI) in Part 1. So, you basically want to maximize your stated expenses and minimize your stated income to achieve a more realistic cash flow dollar amount to work with. Refer to Appendix B for a complete listing of all personal financial health indicators, such as PCF and DTI ratio, and other ratios and indicators used in this book.

Personal Cash Flow (PCF) Overview

Quote 3-1: "Cash flow is what's left after subtracting what you have to pay from what you have to pay it with."
– Anonymous

Cash flow, for the purposes of this book, is defined as the amount of money you have coming in (income from whatever sources) monthly as compared to your expense obligations or "outgo" on a monthly basis. The difference between the two is "Personal Cash Flow" or PCF. Personal Cash Flow is one of the most important personal financial indicators and is the amount of money you have left over after paying all your bills. From a business or investor's perspective, cash flow may refer to an investment's ability to produce income. For example, you might purchase a Duplex rental property whereby you have a positive cash flow if both units are rented to tenants consistently. If one of your tenants skips town, you might have a negative cash flow for your investment.

Importance of Cash Flow

If your income is greater than your outgo, you will have more disposable income and may be able to go out to dinner more often or put more into savings and investments. Cash flow involves active budgeting so that outgo does not exceed income. It's also called "living within your means." Cash flow is actually more important on a daily basis than net worth, as it determines your lifestyle to a great extent. Every year, businesses fail due to over-investment in capital equipment, among other things, and then not having enough cash flow to pay the monthly bills or payroll and keep the doors open. Personal Cash Flow (PCF) is extremely important to your financial well-being and quality of life. You could have a huge nest egg saved or a trust fund set up in your name, thereby making your net worth look very good, but if you can't tap into it or there are penalties and fees involved, it may not have a positive impact on cash flow. Various personal financial management and budgeting tools (smart phone and other apps) are available to help you budget and manage your finances to keep your cash flow on the positive side. These are discussed in Chapter 4: Budgets and Frugal Living.

Cash Flow and Debt-to-Income indicators are commonly used when assessing the financial health of a business or potential investment, and they are equally valuable when assessing personal financial health. Personal Cash Flow (PCF) is calculated by taking your monthly total net income minus (-) monthly total expenses. The result can be positive or negative, but hopefully, yours is positive. If it's not, you may have some work to do. Your PCF is a key personal financial health indicator that can help you get a handle on your finances. It is the basis for your Potential Saving Ratio (PSR), which is calculated by taking a percent of your PCF if your cash flow is positive. Once you know your PCF, it should remain fairly consistent from month to month unless you make significant changes to income or expenses or both. Having a positive cash flow is the main factor that allows you to set money aside toward savings and investment or paying down your debts. It's not uncommon, but if you have a negative cash flow, you are fighting a losing battle because you have more cash flowing out than flowing in. Note that in Table 3-1, there are various types of income-producing sources listed, but for most, you need to have a positive cash flow, or uninvested money from some source, to take advantage of them.

PFI 3-4: Personal Cash Flow (PCF) Formula/Calculation
Personal Financial Indicator (#PFI-4)

Total Monthly NET Income (-minus-) Total (ALL) Regular Monthly Expenses = PCF ($)

$7,420 - $6,490 = $930

(PFS Income-Exp sheet example)

Your Personal Cash Flow and Personal Net Worth Statements
You can create your own Personal Cash Flow (PCF) statement for a given time period by simply monitoring and recording your cash flow on a monthly basis. If you update the Income-Exp sheet of the PFS monthly, you can compare your Income, Expenses, and Cash Flow from one month to the next. You can then graph the trend over time to see if you are moving in the right direction. A Personal Net Worth (PNW) statement (See Chapter 5) is usually paired with the PCF statement as two of the primary documents of your financial plan. You can create your own spreadsheet or print the two PFS sheets Income-Exp and Assets-Liab at the first of each month. The Personal Net Worth statement (also called a balance sheet) adds up your Assets and subtracts total Liabilities to calculate your Personal Net Worth (PNW). Your PCF statement and PNW statement work together to provide the foundation for your finances. An increase in income or decrease in expenses will increase cash flow and vice versa. For example, let's say your cash flow is positive and you decide to pay off your car loan, which was costing you $500 per month, and the balance you owed was $2,500. Your PCF will increase by the amount of your car payment. However, if you pay off your car loan with money from your savings account (an asset), your PNW will decrease by the loan balance payoff of $2,500, but that could be offset by the interest saved on the auto loan and the fact that you now have more equity in your car, since it's paid off. By paying off the car with savings, you will lose the interest that

could have been earned with the savings account. But the interest saved on the auto loan would probably be more than the yield paid by the savings account.

Note: Personal Financial Awareness is developed by monitoring key personal financial health indicators over time. Awareness opens the door to action.

Ways to Improve Cash Flow

Cash flow is what you have flowing in (income) minus what you have flowing out (outgo) or expenses. Positive cash flow means you have discretionary income, which can allow you to save and invest more and potentially live a more abundant and prosperous lifestyle. Other than a windfall, there are primarily two ways to improve cash flow: (1) increase income (active or passive), or (2) decrease outgo (expenses).

Increasing Income

Buying and holding quality investments is a viable way to increase one's net worth but some people just don't have the money to do so. One must have excess cash or liquid assets to be able to take advantage of a lot of the financial opportunities that may present themselves. Many of us are living paycheck to paycheck and simply do not have extra cash lying around to put into an IRA or buy stocks or bonds, and the only way we'll get to a position where we have that flexibility is to deal with our present situation, which means we must either increase our income or decrease our expenses in order to achieve positive cash flow. There are three main ways to increase your income if you do not have a positive cash flow:

- **Option 1** - Take on more active income generation (increase hours, change jobs, work a second job, ask for a raise)
- **Option 2** - Explore passive liquid income options (rent out a room or sell assets—stocks, collectibles, or something else)
- **Option 3** - Invest in yourself (start a small business, build your resume, take courses to increase your salary, sell stuff on the Internet)

Decrease Expenses

The other way to increase your positive cash flow is to decrease your expenses. Use the "Four Rs" method (Review, Reduce, Remove, and Revise) to help identify areas where you can reduce costs. All these ideas can be applied to the budgeting process as described in Chapter 4: Budgeting and Frugal Living. For each of your monthly expenses try to apply at least one of the Four R's and set a target of a 10 percent reduction in your overall monthly expenses.

- **Review** - All bills and account statements (check for errors and invalid charges)
- **Reduce** - Discretionary spending (decrease spending for non-essential items like dining out)
- **Remove** - Non-essential expense items (eliminate services not used or used infrequently)
- **Revise** - Agreements and contracts (negotiate new terms: lower interest rates, increased credit limits, longer terms, increased principal paid on loans to pay off early)

To help with the Four Rs process, you will want to first look at all your expenses, divide them into Optional and Essential, and total the dollar amount for each group. The Optional group total is the first place to look to reduce expenses and increase your positive cash flow. Next, apply the Four R's as described above. This is similar to how we approach the "Green" conservation initiatives using the Three Rs (Reduce, Reuse, and Recycle). Get the family involved and see what kinds of ideas they come up with to help reduce outgo.

Play the Expense Reduction Game

You could take the expenses in the order that they appear in the **PFS Income-Exp** sheet and assign one to each family member. Then you could play a money game wherein each family member (depending on age, etc.) could present their "Expense Reduction Plan" for the expense assigned and present/discuss it with the group. You might be surprised at what they come up with. A major plus is that it increases the financial awareness of the person presenting and the family as a whole. And who knows, someone might come up with a great idea!

Personal Cash Flow (PCF), Potential Saving Ratio (PSR), and Budgets

Your PCF is an important financial health indicator that can help you get a handle on your finances. It is the basis for your Potential Saving Ratio (PSR), which is calculated by taking a percentage of your PCF. After entering all your Net income sources and all your monthly expenses you should be able to get a reasonably accurate estimate of your monthly PCF, which is essentially the cash or dollar amount you have left over after you subtract your total monthly expenses, from your monthly net income. This in turn dictates your Potential Saving Ratio (PSR), also known as Cash-Flow-to-Net Income ratio. Assuming that your cash flow is positive, you can determine what percentage of your PCF you wish to put away toward savings. Refer to the Income-Exp sheet in Figure 3-4, which shows a positive PCF of $950 and a PSR of 12.5 percent. This means that you have about 12.5 percent of your monthly cash flow (PCF) available as discretionary income to pay down your debt or use for savings and other investments.

Three Savings Buckets

There are three savings buckets that you can set up, in order of priority: Emergency fund, Short-term savings, and Long-term savings. By determining your PCF and PSR, you can develop a budget that will help you achieve your saving goals, which is one of the main reasons to set up a budget. Admittedly, the PSR dollar amount in the spreadsheet is only $117/month (12.5 percent of $930). That's not much to work with but, if you put a hundred dollars of that into a savings account at 4 percent interest compounded monthly, at the end of a year (twelve months) you would have $1,222 in your account. That does not account for inflation, but it makes a point. And you would still have over $800 per month from your PCF available for other discretionary spending. Without a budget, many people would just spend whatever is available until they're out of cash and then wait for the next paycheck. Most financial advisors recommend putting away 10 percent of your Gross pay toward savings. Again, be careful that you don't set savings goals that are too aggressive, such that you reduce monthly PCF too much and get into a bind. That said, savings is one of the most liquid assets, and you could correct the cash flow issue very rapidly by tapping into your savings. The important thing is to set realistic savings goals, budget accordingly, and be consistent from month to month.

<u>PFI 3-5: Potential Saving Ratio (PSR) Formula/Calculation</u>

Personal Financial Indicator (#PFI-5)

Personal Cash Flow (/divided by/) Monthly Net Income = PSR (%)

$930 / $7,420 = .125 (x 100) = 12.5 %

(Multiply PCF ($930) * PSR (12.5%) = $117/mo. toward savings)

(PFS Income-Exp sheet example)

The PFS Income-Exp sheet is an excellent source of information for building a budget. All of your income sources and expenses should have already been entered upon completion of chapter **Exercise 3-1: List PFS Income and Expenses** and entered your data into
PFS sheet Income, Expenses, and Cash Flow.

Cash Flow Factors to Consider with Credit Cards

Many things factor into cash flow, but the bottom line is that if you have enough monthly income to cover your monthly expenses, you should have a positive cash flow. Be careful, however, as this can be misleading. You could be paying the minimum on your credit cards and appear to have a healthy positive cash flow, but you could also be paying 25 percent interest (which is a LOT of interest) on the outstanding balance. Although technically you have a positive cash flow, it will take you a LONG time to pay off the credit card debt you have accumulated. On the other hand, if you pay your credit card balance off each month, you will have a lower positive cash flow but one that more realistically represents your ability to pay your debts. Paying the minimum on your credit cards is like trying to put out a raging fire with a watering can!

Aggressive Debt Payoff Effect on Cash Flow

With regard to cash flow, there is such a thing as being "house poor" or "car poor," meaning that your house payment or car payment is so large you can barely afford it, and you can't afford to do much else. Some people can also be overly aggressive when paying off credit card debt. While their motives may be good, paying the debt off too quickly can result in cash flow issues and potential problems with regard to just paying regular bills from month to month. Even in this day and age, there are many people who feel the need to pay off their mortgage so that they can say they "own" their home. They frequently pay more than the basic mortgage payment each month to bring down the principal or loan balance. If this does not create a cash flow problem, then more power to them.

Part 5: Personal Financial Indicators and Performance Ratios

Financial advisors and stock market analysts use many tools to determine which companies to invest in and make buying decisions based on various performance ratios. A few of the more common ones are

Debt-to-Equity (DTE) ratio, Earnings Per Share (EPS), Price-to-Earnings (PE or PTE) ratio, and Return On Investment (ROI). These types of indicators and other metrics are routinely applied to companies of all types and sizes to gauge their financial health. Using ratios can help determine investment potential and provide a common way to compare one company to another.

Assessing Personal Financial Health

Corporations have cash flow, and individuals have cash flow. Corporations have net worth, and individuals have net worth. The same types of ratios or indicators that are used to gauge a corporation's financial health can be applied to an individual to measure how they are doing financially. How do you know if you are moving in the right direction financially? There are many ways to measure your progress toward your financial goals. These can include monitoring of savings accounts, investment accounts, acquired assets, cash flow, your credit score, current debt load, net worth, automation of bank accounts, and much more. There are about fifteen or so Personal Financial Indicators (PFIs) that you could look at to evaluate a person's financial condition. Fortunately, most financial health assessments can be accomplished using just a subset of them. We prioritized these and came up with our "Top Ten," which are covered in this book and listed below in order of appearance. Many of these are used by lenders to decide whether to loan you money, how much, and at what interest rate. The impact of these indicators on your ability to borrow money—whether for a house, car, or personal loan—cannot be overstated. Being aware of these indicators and monitoring them to keep your finances on track is crucial to your financial health.

Most of the PFIs are ratios that are represented as a percentage (%), whereas some of them are dollar amounts ($). The four main "Dollar Amount" PFIs, which you have already worked with, are Personal Net Income (PNI), Emergency Fund Goal (EFG), Personal Cash Flow (PCF), and Personal Net Worth (PNW). They are listed here, along with our top six "Ratio" PFIs, for a total of ten key indicators. Four of these—Housing-to-Income (HTI), Debt-to-Income (DTI), Personal Cash Flow (PCF), and Potential Saving Ratio (PSR)—are covered in this chapter. They are calculated in the PFS Income-Exp sheet based on your input. The other six Ratio (%) Indicators are covered in subsequent chapters. These "Top 10" Indicators or PFIs form a good basis for analyzing personal financial health and are listed in Table 3-1, with a description of their purpose and how they are calculated. There are several common three-letter acronyms (TLAs) used in the financial world to describe Personal Financial Indicators (PFIs), such as DTI for Debt-to-Income and DTC for Debt-to-Credit. I have tried to come up with a logical and unique TLA for each of the other PFIs (fifteen in total) that are discussed in this book, to keep things consistent and make them easier to remember.

Your Financial Dashboard

You can think of the PCF and PNW "Dollar Amount" indicators along with the six "Ratio" indicators as gauges on your financial dashboard (See Figure 3-5).

- Personal Cash Flow (PCF) is like your Speedometer (How fast you are going)
- Personal Net Worth (PNW) is like your Gas Gauge (How much gas is in your tank).

The Ratio (%) PFIs represent the other gauges, such as Engine Temperature, Oil Pressure, Oil Temperature, Charging Voltage, and Transmission Temperature, all of which are critical to the operation of your vehicle. These all have a "normal" reading or range, and if the gauge is reading significantly above or below the normal range, it could indicate a serious problem. If you don't keep track of the indicator gauges in your car, you may have a mechanical malfunction. If you don't keep track of the financial indicators in your life, you may have a financial malfunction!

Figure 3-5: Personal Financial Indicators - The Gauges of Your Financial Dashboard

Table 3-5: The Top Ten Personal Financial Indicators (PFIs)

Ratio Based (%) PFIs: Acronym/Name	Formula/Calculation	Chapt
1. DTI - Debt-to-Income (%)	Monthly Reqd. Exp/ Gross Income	Ch. 3
2. STI - Savings-to-Income (%)	Monthly Savings/Gross Income	Ch. 7
3. HTI - Housing-to-Income (%)	Monthly Housing/Gross Income	Ch. 3
4. TTI - Transport-to-Income (%)	Monthly Transportation/Gross Income	Ch. 12
5. DTC - Debt-to-Credit (%)	Credit Used/Credit Limit	Ch. 9
6. EFE - Emerg. Fund-to-Expenses (%)	EF Balance/(Monthly Reqd. Exp. x 6)	Ch. 5
Dollar Amt. ($) PFIs: Acronym/Name	**Formula/Calculation**	**Chapt**
7. PNI - Personal Net Income ($)	Gross Income (minus) - Taxes = PNI ($)	Ch. 3
8. EFG - Emergency Fund Goal ($)	Monthly Reqd. Expense (times) * 6 = EFG($)	Ch. 4
9. PCF - Personal Cash Flow ($)	Monthly Net Income (minus) - Expenses	Ch. 3
10. PNW - Personal Net Worth ($)	Assets (minus) - Liabilities	Ch. 4

Note: DTC, STI, HTI and TTI as well as other key PFIs are covered in subsequent chapters where they apply. The slash symbol (/) in a formula means "divided by".

Personal Financial Awareness

PFI Ratios and Percentages

A percentage is a special type of ratio that is usually expressed as a single number (from 0-100) followed by the percent sign (e.g., 50%). A percentage can also be expressed as a fraction with some number divided by (over) 100 (e.g., 50/100), or as a two-digit decimal (usually) that is less than or equal to 1.00. (e.g., .50).

- **Fractional Percentage:** **50/100**
- **Decimal Percentage:** **.50**
- **Display Percentage:** **50%**

All the Personal Financial Indicator (PFI) "Ratios" used in this book and in the Personal Financial Spreadsheet (PFS) are percentages and are indicated using the percent sign (%). For example, one of the most used and important PFI ratios is the Debt-to-Income or DTI ratio, and prospective borrowers (home or auto) need to have a DTI ratio of less than 40 percent. This means their fixed monthly expenses (mortgage, car loans, etc.), do not exceed 40 percent of their gross income per month. For example, let's say Amy's monthly fixed expenses (debts) are $2,000 and her gross monthly pay (income) is $5,000. To calculate her DTI ratio, we divide her debt by her income, which comes to .40. To convert the decimal .40 to a percentage we multiply it by 100. So, Amy spends about 40 percent of her income to pay her debts each month. The DTI ratio or percentage will always be less than 1.00 unless Amy's monthly expenses exceed her income, in which case she is living beyond her means and needs to talk with a financial counselor.

Amy's DTI ratio: $2,000 / $5,000 = .40 * 100 = 40%

Note: All "ratio" PFIs in this book and in the PFS, give a decimal result and must be multiplied times 100 to get the actual percentage. If you have a formula that produces a decimal result (e.g., .50) in your PFS, you can change the display format of the cell to Percentage (e.g., 50%).

PFI Ratios - Comparing Apples to Apples

The nice thing about ratios is that they allow you to compare apples to apples. It doesn't make any difference how much money one person makes as compared to another because you are comparing ratios or percentages. The main goal with ratios is to stay within an acceptable percentage range for a given PFI or indicator. You can be making a lot of money, but if you are also spending a lot of money, your DTI ratio could be more than 40 percent and you might be considered a bad credit risk if you go to buy a car or a house. On the other hand, someone who makes a lot less but has a DTI ratio of 30 percent or lower, might be considered a better credit risk, because they are living within their means. If your DTI is significantly over 40 percent.you could be living beyond your means. Two people with very different financial situations can have the same ratios regarding debt, credit, homeownership, and other personal financial indicators.

Chapter 3 Exercise

Exercise 3-1: List PFS Income and Expenses

This is a three-part exercise. In Part A, you will list your income sources and dollar amounts. In Part B, you will list your expenses. In Part C, these will be entered into PFS sheet Income-Exp. The PFS was downloaded in Chapter 2 Exercise 2-2. Even if you do not plan to enter your information into the spreadsheet at this time, go ahead and enter your data in the table forms provided. You can do the calculations manually if you want to.

Note: Before starting this exercise, make copies of Table Forms 3-5, 3-6 and 3-7. You may also want to print off a couple of your latest checking and savings account statements, and use the income deposits and expense transaction entries for the tables and PFS sheet Income-Exp.

Part A: List your Income Sources (monthly gross and net)

Take a few minutes to think about and list your major monthly income sources and the approximate amounts per month in Table 3-6 or a copy of it. Refer to this chapter for examples of income sources and enter those that pertain to your financial situation. Make copies of Tables 3-6, 3-7, and 3-8 or, if you are using the workbook concept, write in the sources and amounts in the tables provided. Figure 3-1 shows examples of PFS Income Sources. Be sure to include active earned income sources (W2 wages and 1099 for household members). You may also include passive income sources (alimony, investment dividends and rental income). The Income sources listed here can be transferred to the PFS sheet Income, Expenses, and Cash Flow (Income-Exp Tab name) downloaded in Exercise 2-2.

Note: When entering income data into Table 3-6 and the Income-Exp sheet, focus on Gross Income but try to obtain both gross and net amounts for each income source you enter. This will give a more complete picture of your income, even if you must estimate. Without complete income and expense data entries, you will not be able to get an accurate dollar amount for your Personal Cash Flow. If you do not have the corresponding Gross or Net Income amount, just enter Zero (0) as a place holder for now. Refer to Table 3-1 for examples of income sources.

Table 3-6: Monthly Gross/Net Income Sources Listing (Form)

Income Source Who / Type	Institution	Monthly Gross	Monthly Net	Notes

Part B: List your Expenses (monthly actual)

List your major mandatory (required) expenses related to home and auto and their approximate amounts in Table Form 3-7. Refer to Figures 3-2 and 3-3 for additional examples. Other expenses such as insurance premiums and regular monthly credit card payments as well as medical payments can also be entered here. Some typical mandatory expenses are provided in Table Forms 3-7 and 3-8. Enter amounts for those that pertain to your financial situation. For utility entries such as gas, electric, and water, try to come up with a monthly average. For example, you can add the June and January electric or gas bills and divide the result by two to come up with an approximate monthly average for the year. Do not include discretionary expenses.

Note: If any of your expenses are billed other than monthly, you must convert them to monthly before entering them into the table or spreadsheet. For example, if your homeowner's association (HOA) dues are paid quarterly, you must divide the quarterly payment amount by three to convert to a monthly amount. If an insurance premium is billed/paid annually, you must divide the amount paid by twelve to arrive at the monthly amount. Just be sure to divide by the appropriate number to convert to monthly expenses so that the spreadsheet formulas will produce accurate results.

Table 3-7: Monthly Mandatory Expense Listing (Form)

Mandatory Expense Description	Payee	Payment	Fixed / Variable	Notes
Mortgage (PITI)				
Water				
Sewer				
Trash				
Electric				
Gas				
Security/Smoke				
Phone				
Internet				
TV				
Home Maintenance (avg)				
Auto 1 Payment				
Auto 2 Payment				
Life insurance Premium				
Auto Insurance Premium				
Health Insurance Premium				

Enter discretionary expenses in Table 3-8. Refer to Figure 3-4 for additional examples. Estimate the approximate amounts for those expenses that apply to you. The expenses listed in these tables can be transferred to the actual PFS sheet - Income, Expenses, and Cash Flow (Income-Exp Tab).

Table 3-8: Monthly Discretionary Expense Listing (Form)

Description	Amount	Notes
Groceries		
Dining out		
Gas		
Auto maintenance		
House cleaning		
Lawn mow / landscape		
Vacations		
Misc. personal care (haircuts, etc.)		
Misc. other (e.g., Daycare cost)		

Part C: Enter Data for PFS Sheet - Income, Expenses, and Cash Flow (Income-Exp Tab)

Using the PFS template downloaded with Exercise 2-2, enter your income sources and expenses as well as the amounts, into the blank data entry areas provided in the PFS sheet Income-Exp. To assist you, refer to the forms you filled out in Part A and Part B as well as chapter figures and Appendix A, which show sample entries.

Chapter 4
Budgets and Frugal Living

Chapter Overview:
This chapter covers the budgeting process as it relates to your income and outgo or Personal Cash Flow (PCF) and provides a review of the Potential Saving Ratio (PSR) indicator. It explains how to apply the 50/30/20 Budgeting Rule and introduces the Savings-to-Income (STI) ratio indicator as well as the Emergency Fund (EF). It describes personal budgeting and financial apps and their features. Specific frugality tips are provided on how to spend less and save money with respect to your home and auto, as well as some general tips for living frugally. Exercises are provided to help you research financial budgeting apps and create a monthly budget.

Chapter PFS and PFI Integration:
The chapter does not cover a specific Personal Financial Spreadsheet (PFS) sheet but does review the Income-Exp sheet, which addresses PCF and PSR indicators from Chapter 3, as input to the budgeting process. The chapter introduces the Savings-to-Income (STI) ratio indicator and Emergency Fund (EF) as well as the 50/30/20 Budgeting Rule. In addition, the chapter makes use of a preformatted Microsoft Excel budget template that is packaged with the Excel application. The template allows you to create a Personal Monthly Budget. Most of the information needed to create the budget can be obtained from the PFS Income-Exp sheet data entered previously in Exercise 3-1: List PFS Income and Expenses and Tables 3-1 through 3-7 in Chapter 3. The Microsoft Excel budget template is NOT part of the PFS, which is included with this book. The Excel budget template should not be commingled with the PFS.

Chapter Exercises:
• **Exercise 4-1: Create Personal Monthly Budget from Excel Template**
In this exercise, you will use a preformatted Microsoft Excel template to create a Personal Monthly Budget. This template displays as an option when you start the Excel application (newer versions) without first selecting a file to open. You can scroll through the templates available. Figure 4-1 shows the initial Excel screen from which you can begin to build the budget spreadsheet. There are two parts to the exercise: Part A, to locate pertinent budget data, and Part B, to create the budget.

• **Exercise 4-2: Compare Budgeting and Financial Apps**
This exercise will help you identify and compare the budgeting and financial apps that are of interest to you. You will do some research and select the one that best fits your needs.

Chapter Notable Quotes:
Quote 4-1: "A budget is telling your money where to go instead of wondering where it went" - John Maxwell
Quote 4-2: "If you don't have any money, don't spend it." - Mother

What Is a Budget?

A budget is essentially a plan for how you want to manage your income, expenses, cash flow, and savings. It is a systematic way of determining how you want to spend your money to accomplish your financial goals for a specific time period. It is a form of cash flow management with a focus on savings and spending. Budgeting involves decisions pertaining to where you need or want to spend your money and what future expenses you want to save for. Using a budget, you can compare projected expenses to actual expenses and determine which of your expenditures are wants and which are needs. You can also develop your budget around your lifestyle. By monitoring your budget monthly, you can track your spending over time and determine where adjustments need to be made. A budget is basically a financial tool that can be used to determine estimated and actual spending in various categories in order to accomplish your financial goals. A budget can be written on a piece of paper, entered in a spreadsheet, or kept in one of the many budgeting apps that are available.

Budget Benefits

The main benefit of a budget is that it requires you to pay closer attention to your finances and helps you actively plan how you want to spend your money. That which you do not monitor, you cannot control. The budgeting process helps you monitor your income and outgo and control your spending habits. For example, if you just got paid and have $1,000 in your checking account, you might think you could go shopping for some new clothes. However, if you have a stack of bills, your rent is due, and your car's gas tank is empty, you don't have as much money as you think because most of it is already spoken for! Having a budget can help you monitor and control your spending to avoid living beyond your means. Setting up a budget and deciding how much you want to spend in each category is not difficult, but sticking to the budget can be. By creating a budget, you can plan ahead to make sure you have enough money for necessities while saving for other short- and long-term purchases and expenses.

Without a budget, you may decide to buy a high-end TV to get ready for football season. If you have a budget, and one of your goals is to save for a new kitchen countertop, you can decide against buying the new TV at this time in order to save for other, higher-priority items. (On second thought, to heck with the budget, buy the TV! You have to keep your priorities straight!) Another benefit of having a budget is that it encourages delayed gratification. And by delaying or holding off on certain purchases, you give yourself more time to do research and compare products, so you can frequently get a better deal. All kidding aside, waiting to buy the TV is probably a good idea, since it will probably go on sale toward the end of the year anyway, when the new models come out.

Having a budget will increase your awareness of your finances, and you will be able to, perhaps slowly, improve your financial situation. Set small milestones at first and, when you achieve them, treat yourself as a reward. Even small achievements should be celebrated to help you develop a positive money mindset. Slow progress is better than no progress!

The Budgeting Process

To create a budget, you need to know your monthly income and outgo, both of which were determined in Chapter 3. You should also have already identified those expenses that are mandatory (required) and those that are discretionary (optional). Budgeting and saving are closely related, as you will frequently limit spending in specific categories (e.g., dining out) while saving for other categories (e.g., vacation). The first step in creating a realistic budget is to record your Net Income, calculated in Chapter 3 using the PFS Income-Exp sheet. Next, review your spending history, based on the required and optional expenses identified in Chapter 3. Keep in mind that budgets are dynamic, and yours will need to be adjusted over time as your financial situation and goals change.

The 50/30/20 Budget Rule

Many financial advisors recommend using the 50/30/20 Budget Rule as a general guide to categorize and prioritize spending. The "50/30/20" refers to the percentage allocated to the three main categories of expenditures. The rule can be implemented as an overlay using the PFS Income-Exp sheet in conjunction with Exercise 4-1. You can print off the Net Income and Expense portions of the Income-Exp sheet and next to each, expenditure, mark it as "E," "D," or "S." Total the amount spent for the monthly expenses in each of the three major categories and then compare that to your net income to see how close you are to the recommended percentages. If you have automatic payroll deductions taken out of your paycheck toward savings or 401K for retirement, be sure to give yourself credit, as those deductions represent contributions to the "S" category, and they reduce take home pay. The general recommendation for the 50/30/20 rule is to spend a percentage of your Net (after-tax) Income as indicated below.

- **50 percent = Essential Spending** (Mortgage, Rent, Utilities, Transportation, Insurance, Food)
- **30 percent = Discretionary Spending** (Dining Out, Entertainment, Personal Care, Vacations)
- **20 percent = Savings** (Emergency Fund, Short Term savings, Investment/Retirement, Debt Paydown)

To come up with target dollars for each category, take your Net Income and multiply it times each of the three percentages (50 percent, 30 percent, and 20 percent). If your Net Income is $2,000 per month, you would multiply it times 50 percent (.50) to calculate the Essential spending category target amount or goal of $1,000 (not to exceed).

50/30/20 Budget Rule:	**= Net Income = $2,000 / Month**
Essential spending allocation	**= Net Income × .50 = $1,000**
Discretionary spending allocation	**= Net Income × .30 = $600**
Savings/debt paydown allocation	**= Net Income × .20 = $400**

So, if you tallied up all your Discretionary category expenses (marked with "D") and it equals $800/month, you are $200 over budget for that category, according to the 50/30/20 rule. The overage is probably at the expense of the Savings category, and you would need to look at each Discretionary expense to see where you can cut back.

Personal Cash Flow (PCF), Potential Saving Ratio (PSR), and Budgeting
Your Personal Cash Flow (PCF) is a key personal financial health indicator that can help you get a handle on your finances. It is the basis for your Potential Saving Ratio (PSR), which is calculated by taking the percentage of your PCF that you wish to allocate to savings. Refer to PFS Income-Exp sheet Section 3: Cash Flow.

As a brief review, recall that your income sources and monthly expenses were entered into the Income-Exp sheet in Chapter 3 to determine your monthly Personal Cash Flow (PCF). This is the dollar amount you have left over after you subtract your total monthly expenses from your monthly net income. If you have a positive cash flow, you are living within your means. If your cash flow is negative for several months in a row, you may be living beyond your means. PCF determines your Potential Saving Ratio (PSR) or Cash-Flow-to-Net Income ratio (See Figure 3-4). Assuming that your cash flow is positive, you can decide what percentage of your PSR to put away toward savings. If your PSR is 20 percent of your PCF, this is considered discretionary income and means that 20 percent of your cash flow (PCF) can be used toward savings and other investments or to pay down high-interest debt. So, if your monthly PCF is $1,000 and PSR is 20 percent, you have $200 per month to put into savings. In the Income-Exp sheet (Figure 3-4) the following numbers and calculations are used:

- **Personal Cash Flow (PCF** is Monthly Net Income – Total Expenses) = $930
- **Potential Saving Ratio (PSR** is PCF / Monthly Net Income x 100) = 12.5%
- **Discretionary Monthly Income** toward savings (PCF$ x PSR%) = $117

Note: Multiply your PCF ($930) times your PSR (12.5 percent) to get your discretionary income ($117) that can potentially be used toward savings and investments and to pay down debt.

The Savings-to-Income (STI) Ratio Indicator
Another key Personal Financial Indicator (PFI) that can help you decide how much to set aside (budget) toward savings and investments is the Savings-to-Income (STI) indicator, one of the "Top Five PFI Ratios" listed in Chapter 3.

The STI is easier to calculate as compared to the PCF/PSR and is focused more on savings and investments as compared to debt payoff. Where the PSR helps determine your "potential" savings ratio, as the name implies, the STI ratio can tell you what your current monthly savings/investment amount is compared to your Gross Income and help you decide how you might change it. Using the STI ratio, you can determine whether you are within the recommended range (10-20 percent), based on current monthly contributions being put into savings or investments. STI is determined by taking total monthly savings/investment contributions (excluding money you are putting into your Emergency Fund or EF) and dividing by monthly Gross Income. If you wish to include money budgeted for debt paydown you can increase the range to 10-30 percent.

PFI 4-1: Saving-to-Income (STI) Ratio - Formula/Calculation
Personal Financial Indicator (#PFI-6)

Saving/Invest Monthly Contributions (/divided by/) Monthly Gross Income = STI (%)

$1,700 / $8,900 = .19 (*100) = 19.0%

(PFS Income-Exp and Assets-Liab sheet example)

The total of your entries for contributions toward savings and investment assets in the PFS Assets-Liab sheet is linked to Total Gross Income in the PFS Income-Exp sheet in order to calculate STI. STI is based primarily on entries to the Assets-Liab sheet and should include regular monthly contributions to the following types of accounts:

- Savings accounts (excluding emergency fund)
- Certificates of Deposit (CDs)
- Money Market Accounts (MMAs)
- Pension - defined benefit retirement plans
- IRA, 401K, and 403B defined contribution retirement plans

The STI percentage should generally be between 10-20 percent of your monthly Gross Income from the Income-Exp sheet, with 10 percent being the minimum and 20 percent being more aggressive. If your STI percentage is less than 10 percent, consider adding to your savings and or investing contributions if you can. If it is greater than 20 percent, consider allocating a percentage toward paying down high interest such as that on credit cards.

Your Emergency Fund: Priority 1

When it comes to budgeting, one of the first steps you can take toward financial stability is to set up an Emergency Fund (EF). Also referred to as a "Rainy-Day Fund," this is money set aside from your paycheck and usually deposited in a savings account. It's a place to keep money that is not to be touched unless you are confronted with a genuine emergency. You should only access your EF money when faced with a significant financial setback, such as a major auto repair or the loss of a job. Establishing and building an emergency fund should be one of your first financial goals. Notice that the contributions to your emergency fund are usually excluded from the savings/investments pool for indicators like STI. Savings in general and your EF are top priorities when it comes to budgeting and building your financial foundation. The message is that you don't get to count it as a saving unless it is over and above the EF contribution level. If you already have an EF, and it is built up to the recommended level, then more power to you!

The Emergency Fund Goal (EFG) for a person in their working years should be six times their required monthly expenses, so they could make ends meet on a strict budget for about six months if they lost their job. And for a retired person, it is recommended that they should have twelve times their required monthly expenses as their EFG. So, if you're a working person and your required monthly expenses total $4,500, then your emergency fund target should be $4,500 x 6 or $27,000. If you are retired, the target should be $54,000. Required monthly expenses should include things like your mortgage or rent, car payment, utilities, and food. The EFG formula is shown below. Additional information on the Emergency Fund and EFG is covered in subsequent chapters.

PFI 4-2: Emergency Fund Goal (EFG) - Formula/Calculation
Personal Financial Indicator (#PFI-7)

Monthly Required Expenses (*times*) 6 (or 12) = EFG ($)

$4,500 x 6 = $27,000

(PFS Income-Exp and Assets-Liab sheet example)

Note: Additional information on the STI and EFE ratios is presented in Chapter 7: Savings and Banking Services and Chapter 14: Retirement Requirements.

Pay Yourself First
One of the keys to successful saving and investing is to "pay yourself first." This simply means putting away some money from each paycheck before you have a chance to spend it. The key is to put away a set amount that you can spare on a regular basis (preferably monthly). For savings and investments, you can put your plan on autopilot by setting up automatic payroll deduction or debits to your checking account. This happens in the background, and most people don't miss the money. When they check their account balance, they are often pleasantly surprised. Also, be sure to count those deductions toward your savings goals by adding them back to your net pay amount. By determining your PCF and PSR, you can develop a budget that will help you put away 10–20 percent of your gross pay toward savings and investing. The important thing is to set realistic savings and lifestyle goals and budget accordingly.

Recording Expenses
Budgeting spreadsheets and apps have the ability to record expenses quickly and easily in real time. One of the most important things you can do that contributes to successful budgeting is to keep a record of the following for a specific period (e.g., a month) each time you spend money.

Refer to **Exercise 4-2: Compare Budgeting and Financial Apps**. Note that some budgeting apps can record how much you spend and on what, depending on which accounts you add for monitoring.

- When did you spend it? (Date)
- What did you spend it on? (Movie)
- How much did you spend? (Twenty dollars)
- What category is it in? (Entertainment)

If you can do this, then you should be able to keep to a budget. The bottom line literally is that, if a person wants to find out where their money is really going and keep to a budget, they need to be diligent about keeping records of how much they spend and on what. As with many things, the hardest part is getting started. Just commit to try it for a week or a month and see how it goes. You might be amazed, and some minor spending adjustments could lead to major savings. If you record each expenditure in a note on your smart phone, you can always go back and organize or categorize it. Or you can enter it into one of the many budgeting and financial apps you can find when doing **Exercise 4-2: Compare Budgeting and Financial Apps**. Many of these apps monitor your credit and debit card usage and will record and categorize the expenditure for you.

Personal Monthly Budget Expense Categories
A budget spreadsheet or app can have many or just a few categories into which you break down your expenses, depending on how much detail you want to track. Most budget software comes with preset categories that would be appropriate for most people, but these can usually be customized to the user's needs. To prepare for creating a monthly budget in Exercise 4-1, classify the expenses you identified in the PFS Income-Exp sheet (Exercise 3-1) by referring to those categories identified below. Focus on the nonessential lifestyle items.

Exercise 4-1 will help you build a personal monthly budget spreadsheet based on a Microsoft-provided Excel template. Refer to Figures 4-1 and 4-2. The budget template is prepopulated with example budget dollar amounts in various expense categories and formulas that will perform calculations when you make changes or overwrite existing entries. In addition to your income, the expense categories of the Personal Monthly Budget in Exercise 4-1 include the following (in no particular order):

- **Housing**
- **Transportation**
- **Loan payments**
- **Savings deposits**
- **Investments**
- **Loans**
- **Taxes**
- **Insurance**
- **Food**
- **Personal care**
- **Pets**
- **Gifts and Donations**
- **Entertainment**

You don't have to budget for and track everything in all categories. Just focus on the top five repeat offenders that have the most impact on your cash flow. Most of these will be variable discretionary expenditures that fall into categories such as entertainment, personal care, and food (and drink), etc. You need to monitor and minimize all expenses, but you don't have much control over mandatory (required) fixed expenses such as housing and taxes. Review the categories listed above and refer to Chapter 3 for a review of the types of expenses in the Income-Exp sheet.

Refer to **Exercise 4-1: Create Personal Monthly Budget from Excel Template** at the end of this chapter, which will help you record monthly budgeting information into categories. The data you enter in this budget template will come from what you entered previously into **Exercise 3-1: List PFS Income and Expenses** from Chapter 3. You will use a preformatted Microsoft Excel template that is packaged with the Excel application. The template allows you to create a Personal Monthly Budget using a prepopulated and preformatted spreadsheet to enter your planned and actual budgeting data and categories. Most of the information needed to create the budget can be obtained from Exercise 3-1 and Tables 3-1 through 3-7 (in Chapter 3). You can make copies of the relevant screenshots and tables to use as a reference while entering your budget template data.

Figure 4-1: Personal Monthly Budget Template <u>Selection</u> Screen (Exercise 4-1)

Figure 4-2: Personal Monthly Budget Template <u>Startup</u> Screen (Exercise 4-1)

Personal monthly budget

Provided by: Microsoft Corporation

Make your financial health a priority with this Excel monthly budget template. It tracks your monthly expenditures by income and expenses, including housing loans, transportation costs, and more. This accessible personal monthly budget template by Excel is easy to use—just fill in a few cells and the rest is calculated automatically. You can even compare projected costs with actual costs to hone your budgeting skills over time.

Download size: 55 KB

Budgeting Tools Overview

Some banks offer apps that help you plan and keep to a budget if you have a checking and/or savings account with them. With a budgeting app, you can determine how much you are spending each month in various categories and where you need to cut back to achieve your savings goals. There are several good budgeting calculators that you can download and use to create a **budget** plan. Some of the apps provided by major banks allow their customers to do regular banking tasks as well as budget planning and tracking with their mobile app. You can also use the tried-and-true spreadsheet method to set up and monitor your budget. Mobile Banking apps are discussed in Chapter 6: Banks and Checking Accounts, and Automatic Savings apps are covered in Chapter 7: Savings and Banking Services. Nearly everyone has a smart phone these days, and there are many budgeting apps to choose from, including apps available for both iPhone and Android as well as other platforms. In conjunction with online bill payment, these apps can be very helpful in managing your finances. Check with your bank to see if they have a spend/save/budget app available or can recommend one. You can also use PC- or Mac-based software along with a corresponding mobile app to create and manage a budget while tracking your expenses. If you are not achieving your goals, you can make changes to your budget and modify your spending habits.

Budgeting and Financial Management Apps

The smartest, easiest, and possibly the cheapest way to create and manage a budget is by using what is called a "budgeting financial app". Some of the more popular ones include these (listed alphabetically): Empower, EveryDollar, Goodbudget, Mint, and YNAB (You Need A Budget). Search the Web for "best budget app". There are many low-cost and no-cost options available, and each has strengths and weaknesses. Many provide free and for-cost financial services. The preceding apps are listed in alphabetical order, and their mention here is not intended as an endorsement of any of these apps. Most of the personal financial apps available tend to focus on either budgeting or investing. Table 4-1 lists several criteria that can be used to compare apps of this type. Most of the apps have multiple functions, such as savings, investing, budgeting, cash flow analysis, and net worth. Most also have graphing capabilities with varying levels of sophistication (bar, pie, point/plot, etc.) to monitor trends over time.

Centralizing Accounts with Financial Apps
Some budgeting/financial apps allow you to centralize access to various types of accounts such as checking, savings, loans, and credit cards. Some can also provide help with investments and retirement planning. To consolidate all your accounts within an app, you must give them permission to access your accounts. The Personal Financial Spreadsheet (PFS) included with this book essentially centralizes most of your financial account data, as well as home and auto information, in one place and you can view it all very quickly. The advantage is you have privacy and only you have visibility into the spreadsheet. The disadvantage is that you need to keep the balances updated (monthly). With some of the financial apps, once you set them up, they can import transactions, and update themselves automatically. This is because they have access to your actual financial accounts. However, if you have not given full access to all your accounts, you may be seeing a partial picture when they show you things such as net worth and cash flow.

Note: Third-party online money management services that consolidate your accounts can be concerning and may display advertising. The top-rated personal financial management apps have millions of users and excellent security measures in place. Exercise caution when using these apps.

Many of the budgeting tools or apps provide online user guides, demos, and tutorials to help you get started. Take some time to read current reviews and get familiar with some of the more popular apps. You can download one or two of the free ones or ones with a free trial and play around with them. In addition to the built-in guides and demos, there are YouTube video tutorials available for many of the apps that cover the main steps to get started. There is a wealth of information available on budgeting apps and related tools, as well as cost and features. Table 4-1 provides a way to compare personal budgeting and financial management mobile apps, based on features and capabilities, with sample entries provided. There are a number of good apps to choose from. You can search for and read reviews on many of them. Some of these apps are more basic while others are more robust. They are accessible from a tablet, desktop, or mobile device.

Refer to **Exercise 4-2: Compare Budgeting and Financial Apps** at the end of this chapter, which will help you identify and compare those budgeting and financial apps that are of interest to you. You will research some of the apps that are available and choose one that best fits your needs. Table 4-2 is provided as a blank form of Table 4-1 for you to copy and use in your research to compare apps.

Table 4-1: Budgeting and Financial Apps Comparison

Software developer	App ABC Company	App XYZ Company	
Cost	Free	Free trial, $10/mo.	
Budget planner	Yes	Yes	
Money/Expense tracker	Yes	Yes	
Envelop system	No	Yes	
Investing capability	Yes	Some	
Retirement planning	Some	No	
Goal setting	No	No	
Cash Flow analysis	Yes	Yes	
Net Worth tracker	No	Yes	
Free credit score and monitor	Yes	No	
Checking account	No	Yes	
Comprehensive financial	Yes	Yes	
Centralized accounts	Yes	Yes	
User workshops/demos/guides	Yes	No	
Zero base budgeting	No	Yes	

Make Use of Available Budgeting Tools

The use of various personal financial apps can help improve your financial health and enable you to manage your finances more effectively. Three of the key tools discussed are listed here. Others will be introduced in subsequent chapters.

- **Use a Banking App (online or mobile) -** You can use automatic bill pay (AutoPay), but you have to carefully manage your bank account to ensure funds are available when payments are scheduled.
- **Use an Automatic Savings App -** Establish a savings account and contribute to your emergency fund.
- **Use a Budgeting/Financial App -** Set up a budget, centralize access to your financial accounts, track investments, and get a handle on your expenses and outgo.

Decrease Expenses

As a brief review from Chapter 3, you can give yourself more flexibility in budgeting and increase your positive cash flow by decreasing your expenses. Use the "Four Rs" method (Review, Reduce, Remove, and Revise) to help identify areas where you can decrease costs. All these cost reduction ideas can be applied to the budgeting process. For each of your monthly expenses, try to apply at least one of the Four Rs and set a target of a 10percent reduction in actual expenditure vs estimated. expenses.

- **Review -** All bills and account statements (check for errors and invalid charges)
- **Reduce -** Discretionary spending (decrease spending for non-essential items like dining out)
- **Remove -** Non-essential expense items (eliminate services not used or used infrequently)

- **Revise** - Agreements and contracts (negotiate new terms: lower interest rates, increased credit limits, longer terms, increased principal paid on loans to pay off early)

Frugal Living Tips – Home, Car, and Other

Note: Personal Financial Awareness regarding expenses means awareness of frugality and ways to function more economically without sacrificing quality of life. (Merriam-Webster: *economical* - careful in the management of money or resources. By being *frugal*, the family is able to stretch its monthly budget.)

Some people think those who claim to be frugal are just cheap, and in some cases, this may be true. However, frugal people can be very generous, especially if it's for a good cause. They spend their money wisely and distinguish between wants and needs while trying not to buy things they can do without. When buying things they need, they often buy less expensive versions that will do the job. Some people take this as a personal "frugality challenge," and do a lot of research to find the best functionality for the least cost. They will often opt to fix things that are broken rather than buy new ones. On the other hand, they may buy a better quality and more expensive product that will last longer and have better resale value.

Frugal living and budgets go hand in hand, as budgets allow you to decide where you want to spend your money and keep track of how much you spend. Whether you are saving for a car or vacation or just trying to get a handle on your credit card debt, a frugal lifestyle can help you get there. By adjusting some of your spending habits and keeping to a budget, you can be more frugal and still have money for things you really want or need. Do a Web search for "frugal living budget," and you will find many sources of information. Some general frugality tips and suggestions are listed here, along with some more specific ones related to your home and auto.

General Frugality Tips

Many of the suggestions presented here in the general, home, and car tips sections are common sense, and frugal types are already doing them. By following some of these tips, you can improve your quality of life and save quite a bit of money which can be used for other things.

- Some businesses, utilities, and health care providers offer a discount for prompt payment. They frequently charge a penalty fee for late payment, so try to make your payments on time to both obtain the discount and save paying the penalty fee.
- Try not to accumulate too much stuff. It requires time and maintenance. The more stuff you have, the more you have to keep track of and worry about.
- Consider the minimalist approach, which is a major social trend. It will help you understand the life-enhancing benefits of living with less.
- Consider yourself a caretaker of your stuff while you are alive. You don't really own anything anyway. Someone else will own your stuff when you are gone.
- Clip coupons and take advantage of online coupon services such as Groupon.

- Use one of the coupon browser tools that automatically search for and apply coupons when you shop online.
- Buy store brands, as long as they are comparable to name brands.
- Take advantage of "Buy One Get One free" or "BOGO" offers if the product is one you will use often enough to justify getting two of it.
- Shop at "dollar" stores when possible. But watch yourself, as the dollars can add up.
- Go "Green" by adopting the three conservation Rs: Reduce, Reuse, and Recycle.
- Drink filtered tap water instead of bottled water. Fill discarded plastic bottles with filtered tap water, which can be better tasting, cleaner, and better for the environment than bottled water.
- If you go to a movie, go to an afternoon matinee, which is usually cheaper.
- If you go out to eat, go at lunch time, when you can frequently get the same meals for less.
- When paying bills, call and ask if you can pay over the phone with a credit card. You can often do this with no fee being levied, and you may get rewards points or cash back. In some cases, you have the option of using an automated system or talking to a representative. There is usually no charge if using the automated system, but you may be charged if you talk to a live person.
- Try to pay your credit card bills in full, if you possibly can without creating cash flow problems, or at least pay more than the minimum amount due to avoid interest charges.
- Pay your bills with online bill pay unless you are paying with a credit card to get cash back. You save the cost of an envelope, and a stamp, and the time spent addressing the envelope. You also save the cost of a check and the time writing the check. In addition, you have a digital record of your payment.
- Use AutoPay, when possible, to pay mandatory (required) fixed monthly payments. You may get a discount and will avoid missed payments.

Home Frugality Tips
- Bundle homeowner's and auto insurance to save money and possibly include umbrella insurance (and renter's insurance if appropriate). Choose a reputable, financially stable insurance company that can provide auto, home and umbrella insurance at a reasonable cost. Check that their AM Best carrier rating is A or better (See Chapter 16). If you currently have multiple providers, see if you can combine or bundle policies with a single insurer. Shop around and you may be able to save money and simplify your life.
- Set high deductibles on your auto and home insurance policies, and save or invest what you save on your monthly premiums in case you need it to cover the deductible in case you have a claim.
- Consider renting instead of buying a home if you are not planning on living there for at least three years. The cost of home ownership is considerably more than the monthly mortgage payment and, if you sell, you will typically pay realtor fees of about 6 percent of the sale price.
- Assuming you buy a home for $100,000 and make no improvements to increase its value, and, assuming no appreciation, when you sell it, you will only get $94,000 or less after deducting sales commissions and closing costs.
- If you buy, try to buy the least expensive home, which fits your needs, in the nicest neighborhood.

- Remember, the three most important things when buying a home are these: (1) location, (2) location, and (3) location.
- When buying a home, buy with resale in mind, but be sure your own needs and wants are satisfied first.
- Try not to buy too much home with high mortgage payments and become "house poor."
- It is better to have a thirty-year mortgage and pay it off faster than to have a fifteen-year loan with a higher payment and risk getting into a cash flow bind financially.
- Exercise caution if buying a timeshare. Resale may be an issue, and they usually have high maintenance fees.
- For insurance purposes, take a narrated video and photos of each room in your house and what is in it.
- Contact your utility companies (e.g., electric, gas, and water) and ask what you can do to reduce costs.
- Total your utility costs for the year and divide by twelve to get a monthly average and pay a more consistent payment to help with budgeting. Most utility companies will help you do this.
- Consider "living small" instead of "living large." Tiny houses (less than 500 sq. ft.) are very popular and represent a major architectural trend.
- Make small improvements to your house while you live there. Do not spend a lot on improvements and then expect to get this investment back when you sell.
- Regular updates and improvements can keep your home fresh and marketable if you should need to sell it.
- Kitchen and bath improvements provide the best returns.
- Many homeowners paint a house twice, once when they buy it (move in) and once when they sell it (move out).
- Avoid home warranties if you are a homeowner. They are good for a buyer if the seller provides one to help sell the house.
- Insulation and quality windows are a good investment and help reduce heating/cooling costs.
- Eliminate your land line phone to save money. Most people have cell phone service anyway.
- Watch for cramming fees (false charges) on your phone bill.
- When buying home appliances, basic models will get the job done. You don't need a super digital designer fridge. Consumer Reports magazine rates the cheaper models better in some cases.
- Burglar Alarm (smoke & fire) - Look for monitoring services with low monthly fees and no contract.
- Beware of home improvement scams. Always check references, and make sure they are licensed and bonded. Do not pay up front. They might take the money and run. Also do not sign anything at the first meeting!
- Beware of roofing scams in particular. Recently, after a windstorm, a guy came to my door and told me it looked like there might be some damage to the roof. He said he would get up there and check it out and let me know what he found, and that his company worked closely with the insurance companies and may be able to get my roof replaced, (which was only 8 years old). I called a local

roofing company that I had previously done business with, and the owner stopped by and checked out the roof and said there was no problem. I also called my neighbor across the street. He took a shot of it with his smartphone and sent it to me, saying it didn't look like there was damage that he could see. We then posted a warning to our neighborhood about this scam company.

- Don't file a claim against your homeowner's insurance unless it's for something major. The insurance provider may increase your premiums or worse, cancel your policy. Keep a high deductible (like $5,000) to help lower your premiums.
- When renting a home or an apartment, buy renter's insurance. It's not expensive and, if you need it, you will be glad you have it.

Auto Frugality Tips

- When buying a car, the monthly payment is only the start of the involved cost. The actual cost of ownership includes insurance, gas, and maintenance (oil changes, tires, brakes, etc.). So, the $300/month car payment could turn into a $500/month outgo easily, when factoring in other expenses. A good rule of thumb is to take the estimated monthly payment for an auto and double it to come up with a realistic amount that it will actually end up costing on a monthly basis.
- Avoid car leases unless you have a good reason not to (like owning a business).
- For a car purchase, do not go for a low monthly payment and a longer term. Finance it for the fewest number of months that will fit your budget. You will pay a lot less interest.
- Don't finance for more than five years (sixty months). If you can afford the payment, forty-eight months is best. If you can't afford the forty-eight -month payment, consider scaling back and buying an older used car that has a good repair record.
- Use the Auto 20-4-10 Rule for purchasing a vehicle (20 percent down, four-year max loan term, transportation budget not to exceed 10 percent of your gross income. See the first bullet point above).
- Don't buy a new car. Buy one that is three to five years old, with low mileage. It may still have some of the factory warranty left. If you do buy a new car, buy at the end of the year.
- Buy a dependable car with a good repair record. Check with Consumer Reports magazine.
- Keep the cars you buy for a long time and take good care of them. If you take care of your car, it will take care of you. My truck is ten years old and looks new.
- Use a spreadsheet to track the maintenance and repair of your cars. Refer to the Auto-Info sheet of the PFS. Record all repairs and replaced maintenance items, like tires, wipers, and batteries.
- Check your battery, tires, and brakes on a regular basis.
- Keep your tire pressure at the factory-recommended settings. It will increase gas mileage, improve the ride, and the tires will last longer.
- Keep your gas tank at least a quarter full so you don't run out and have to walk.
- If the number of miles you drive is fairly consistent on a monthly basis, consider selecting a day of the month and filling up to help with budgeting.

- When buying a new car, forgo the extended warranty. You will have double coverage for a while. If you choose to buy it for a new car (or newer used car), ask if there is a manufacturer-backed extended warranty available.
- When buying a car, negotiate the best deal without a trade, then bring the trade into it. Be willing to walk away and consider selling your trade-in as a private party.
- Use an online car purchasing service, like the one "Consumer Reports" provides, to get a good deal and minimize the high-pressure sales pitch.
- The single most important maintenance item to keep a car running is an oil and filter change.
- Consider changing the car's oil and filter every five thousand miles if it uses regular oil. You could save a lot of money and oil and reduce pollution. Many newer cars running synthetic oils can be changed every ten thousand miles, depending on driving conditions. Follow the owner's manual recommendations.
- Shop at retail stores that offer gas savings. You can save as much as ten to thirty cents per gallon. I use a credit card for gas that pays four percent cash back.
- Buy auto insurance with a high deductible for a lower premium and shop around. I've seen premiums from $250/month to $500/month for the same coverage. Be sure to save the deductible amount in your rainy-day emergency fund! Check that the insurance carrier you plan to switch to is AM Best rated as "A," or better for financial strength and credit rating (See Chapter 16).
- Find a good, dependable (not cheap) mechanic. By doing so, you can save a lot of money over time. Ask your friends and others for a recommendation. Check online for ratings and feedback.
- Beware of auto service scams where they charge for work but may not have actually done it. They prey on women in particular.
- Beware of some used car dealers. They may be able to get you financed but at a very high interest rate.
- When buying a used car be sure to check its history with Carfax or a similar service, to determine its repair history and if it has been in an accident.
- Take the car to a trusted mechanic and have it checked out.
- When buying a new or used car check "Consumer Reports" and user-feedback Websites.
- When renting a car, your current auto insurance provider may cover you when driving the rental. Verify this with your carrier for U.S. and foreign rentals.
- Buy "certified pre-owned" if possible. You usually get a good car with an extended manufacturer's warranty. Many manufacturers offer certifications on late model used cars. A certified pre-owned auto warranty is the next best thing to a new car warranty.

Refer to the Auto Buying Leasing Tips section at the end of Chapter 12: Buying or Leasing a Vehicle, for more money-saving tips on autos.

Chapter 4 Exercises

Exercise 4-1: Create Personal Monthly Budget from Excel Template

In this exercise you will use a preformatted Microsoft Excel template to create a personal monthly budget. You will need access to a licensed version of Microsoft Excel or Microsoft Office to make use of this template and others that are available, although you can create your own with a compatible spreadsheet program. This template displays as an option whenever you start the Excel application (newer versions) without first selecting a file to open. Figure 4-1 shows the initial Excel screen from which you can select the Personal Monthly Budget template to begin to build the budget spreadsheet. Figure 4-2 shows the Personal Monthly Budget startup screen from which you can click the "Create" button to begin working with the template. There are two parts to this exercise: Part A to locate pertinent budget data and Part B to create the budget.

Note: This Microsoft provided Excel spreadsheet template is NOT part of the Personal Financial Spreadsheet (PFS) and the two should not be commingled.

Part A: Locate Budget Data to be Entered. Identify monthly income and expenses from the PFS Income-Exp sheet and record them on a sheet of paper or copy the relevant sections of the Income-Exp sheet. You may also want to copy Chapter 3 Tables 3-1 through 3-7 for reference when entering your income and expense data into the Excel Personal Monthly Budget template.

Part B: Create Personal Monthly Budget from Template

1. Explore the budget spreadsheet template to become familiar with it before starting to create the spreadsheet and entering data. The template contains a lot of explanatory text.
2. Open the Excel app without specifying a file to get to the initial screen like Figure 4-1.
3. Select the Personal Monthly Budget template.
4. Review the information on the primary template screen, which should look like Figure 4-2, and then click on the "Create" button.
5. The spreadsheet will load and display. It has two tabs, "Start" and "Personal Monthly Budget," with the "Start" tab being selected by default. Read the information "About this Template" on the "Start" tab and be sure to read the notes on how to manage instructional text in Column A and other information on the main sheet template itself, tab Personal Monthly Budget.
6. Click the Personal Monthly Budget tab to access the main spreadsheet.
7. Use the data from the PFS Income-Exp sheet, that you entered previously in Chapter 3 Exercise 3-1, and record your information in the Personal Monthly Budget spreadsheet template as appropriate.
8. Input your budget data as necessary to build your Personal Monthly Budget.
9. When you are finished adding data, save the file. The default Excel file name for the file is Personal monthly budget1. When you go to save the file, you can change the name to PMB-XXX-1, where XXX is your initials, or whatever you choose. If you want to try different things, you can create two or three versions (-1, -2 and -3) and experiment.

Note: If you get confused or make mistakes, you can just exit the Excel application without saving the template file, and then start again.

Exercise 4-2: Compare Budgeting and Financial Apps

To assist you in researching budgeting and financial apps, Table 4-1 compares features of various apps and shows examples of what to look for in terms of desirability. Table 4-2 is a form to enter your findings. Select two or more apps to see which ones have the best features. Use Table 4-1 as an example and make a copy of Table 4-2. List the apps across the top and the features to be compared down the left side. You can use the features provided or add your own. Do a Web search for "personal budgeting apps" or for "budgeting and financial apps."

Table 4-2: Budgeting and Financial Apps Comparison (Form)

Comparison Feature	App 1 Name	App 2 Name	Notes
Software developer			
Cost			
Budget planner			
Money/Expense tracker			
Envelop system			
Investing capability			
Retirement planning			
Goal setting			
Cash flow analysis			
Net Worth tracker			
Free credit score and monitor			
Checking account			
Comprehensive financial			
Centralized accounts			
User workshops/demos/guides			

Chapter 5
Assets, Liabilities, and Net Worth

Chapter Overview:
This chapter explains what assets and liabilities are and how they interact to determine your Personal Net Worth (PNW). The chapter also covers the second sheet of the Personal Financial Spreadsheet (PFS) with a tab label of "Assets-Liab." The chapter then explains liquidity and basic taxation terms relative to assets, as well as the role your home plays in the equation. The difference between tangible and intangible assets is explained. An exercise is provided to help you record your assets and liabilities in the PFS Assets, Liabilities, and Net Worth sheet. Examples of assets, liabilities, and Personal Net Worth (PNW) are provided.

Chapter PFS and PFI Integration:
The chapter focuses on the Assets, Liabilities, and Net Worth PFS sheet, which provides a centralized location to record your assets (equity items) as well as liabilities (debts). The sheet then calculates your approximate net worth from the input provided. By combining the net worth from multiple people in a family, you can determine the net worth of the household. The chapter focuses primarily on the PFI 5-1 Personal Net Worth (PNW) financial indicator, but also references the Personal Cash Flow (PCF) and Emergency Fund (EF) indicators from previous chapters. Two new asset-related indicators, PFI 5-2 Emergency Fund-to-Expenses (EFE) and PFI 5-3 Liquid Assets-to-Expenses (LAE), are introduced. These are both part of the Assets-Liab sheet and are linked to the Income-Exp sheet via the Required Monthly Expenses total. They are two critical indicators that could make the difference in getting through tough financial times.

Chapter Exercise:
  • **Exercise 5-1: List PFS Assets and Liabilities**

Chapter Notable Quote:
Quote 5-1: "Your net worth to the world is what's left after subtracting your bad habits from your good ones"
- Benjamin Franklin

Personal Net Worth (PNW) and Personal Cash Flow (PCF)
The Personal Net Worth (PNW) statement (also called a balance sheet) adds up your assets and subtracts total liabilities to calculate your net worth. Your Personal Cash Flow (PCF) statement (See Chapter 3) and Personal Net Worth (PNW) work together to provide the foundation for your finances. Basically, assets are what you own and liabilities are what you owe, and you want to have more assets than liabilities. An item can be both an asset and a liability. For example, if you have a car you are making payments on (a loan), you have a debt obligation that is a liability. If it's worth more than you owe, then you have some equity, which is an asset. If you pay off the car loan and then sell the car, you've just converted your car asset to a cash asset (minus the loan payoff amount). However, if you decide not to sell the car, your "asset" will usually be worth less as time goes on, as it will continue to depreciate. But if it runs great and it's paid for,

who cares? You have basic transportation and that's all some people want or need. Depending on its value and condition, you might even be able to reduce your insurance coverage and premium and improve your cash flow.

What You OWN (Assets) -minus- What You OWE (Liabilities) = Net Worth

The PFS Assets-Liab Sheet
The asset entries occupy the top and middle sections of the Assets-Liab sheet (See Figure 5-1 or the actual PFS sheet tab Assets-Liab). Examples of asset entries include checking accounts, savings accounts, investments, stocks and bonds, precious metals, etc., that belong to you and that have monetary value. In Figure 5-1, the Assets section is divided into Liquid Assets and Non-Liquid Assets, as described below.

Liquid and Non-liquid Assets Section 1 – Row Reservations
The top four data rows (R5-R8) of the Liquid Assets section are reserved for specific highly liquid accounts, such as checking and savings. The first two rows, R5 and R6, are reserved for your checking accounts. Row 7 is reserved for your Emergency Fund (EF) savings account, with the target EF Goal entry. Row 8 is reserved for a second savings account, if needed. If you have a Money Market Account (MMA) or Certificate of Deposit (CD), you can use Rows 9 and 10 by just typing over the current sample MMA and CD entries. There are several unused "Other" rows in the Liquid Assets and the Non-Liquid Assets sections if you need to add more entries of your own.

Liabilities Section 2
The liability entries in the lower section of the Assets-Liab sheet (See Figure 5-2) are amounts you owe for various debts, typically mortgages and installment loans, such as personal or auto loans. The difference between Assets and Liabilities is your Net Worth. Refer to the tables and figures that follow for further explanation and sample entries for the Assets, Liabilities, and Net Worth sections of the Assets-Liab sheet and its structure.

Asset Categories and Classifications
Assets can be categorized in various ways, such as Asset Class, Tangibility, Liquidity, and Tax Status. Asset classes are groups of similar types of investments that are subject to the same regulations. Financial advisors often use asset class to diversify portfolios across multiple types of investment assets. They are generally grouped into one of three main assets classes or categories:

- **Equities** (Stocks and other ownership investments)
- **Fixed Income** (Bonds and Securities)
- **Cash Equivalents** (Cash, Savings, CDs, MMAs)

A fourth category is sometimes listed called "Alternative Investments," which can include real estate, commodities, and other "ownership" types of investments. However, most of the alternative investments are variations on equities.

Note: Additional information on investment types, asset classes, and diversification can be found in Chapter 13: Investing Basics.

Tangible vs. Intangible Assets

Tangible assets are those assets that physically exist, such as office equipment, buildings, and property. You can touch and see them. Intangible assets are nonphysical things that have a monetary value. Examples include intellectual property like a copyright for a book or a patent for an invention. That said, a savings account is considered a tangible asset, even though it cannot be seen or touched. It does exist and has some physical characteristics. The majority of assets are tangible.

Assets and Liquidity

Assets are money accounts and nonmoney salable items of value that can be converted to spendable cash. They can be classified based on varying degrees of "liquidity." Liquidity refers to your ability to exchange an "asset" for cash. For example, a checking or savings account is said to have "high liquidity." These types of accounts are the most liquid since you can write a check, transfer funds to someone, go to the auto teller, or walk into your bank and withdraw cash with little time delay. These are money accounts that you can tap into at any time. Assets such as retirement accounts can be classified as "Qualified" or "Nonqualified." Qualified accounts such as 401K and 403B plans and pensions are tax deferred and may be classified, depending on the type, as "Low-to-Medium Liquidity" assets. This is because there are delays, and you usually must pay taxes and penalties if you take money out early. Assets such as traditional savings and other nonqualified accounts are considered high liquidity, as there are no penalties to take money out. Most retirement accounts like the 401K and 403B are usually considered low liquidity but are included in the "Liquid" category in the Assets-Liab sheet where Assets are divided into "Liquid" and "Nonliquid." This is because you could tap into them early, in an emergency, even though you would pay penalties and taxes. In addition, if you were at or near retirement age, you could begin taking distributions without penalties, although you would pay taxes. Also, all liquid and semi-liquid assets including your emergency fund (EF) come into play when calculating the PFI 5-3 Liquid Assets-to-Expenses (LAE) ratio.

Note: Your checking account (or cash in your wallet) is the most liquid asset and rates a "ten" on the liquidity scale (where ten is the most liquid), whereas your home is probably your least liquid asset and rates a "one". Every other asset is somewhere in between. Your home asset liquidity rating of "one" does not have to do with its value or how much equity you have in it; it just means that it would be difficult to extract the value or equity from it quickly.

Keep in mind that, even though an asset may be fairly liquid, there may be fees to pay and/or penalties if the asset is liquidated or cashed in early, as is the case with Certificates of Deposit (CDs) and Money Market

Accounts (MMAs). Items such as valuable antiques, collector cars, and stamp collections and jewelry can be included as assets; however, it may be difficult to establish their value and doing so may require a licensed appraiser. Also, something is worth what someone will pay for it, not necessarily what you or an appraiser thinks it is worth. In general, something is considered an asset if it has intrinsic value, if you can borrow against (leverage) it, and/or if you can turn it into cash.

Figure 5-1: PFS Assets Section of Assets-Liab Sheet (sample entries)

	A	B	C	D	E	F	G
1	**ASSETS, LIABILITIES and NET WORTH**		Book Build: Ch. 5			Updated: MM-DD-YYYY	
2							
3	**<<< Sect 1: Assets >>>**						
4	Owner	< Liquid Assets (Name / Type) >	Institution	Notes	Curr. Value	Monthly Contrib.	Beneficiary / Formula
5	Joint	Bank Checking Acct 1	Bank	Cash	1,000	0	Joint
6	Joint	Bank Checking Acct 2	Bank	Cash	5,000	0	Joint
7	Joint	Emergency Fund (EF) - Online Savings Acct	Savings-Co	EF Goal = $27,000	13,700	300	Emergency Fund Acct. - Joint
8	Joint	Savings Acct. - Short-Term (Ass./Inc.)	Anytown Bank	Savings	15,000	200	Joint
9	Joint	Money Market Acct (MMA)	Anytown Bank	Savings	5,000	200	Joint
10	Joint	5-Yr Certificate of Deposit (CD)	Anytown Bank	Savings	10,000	200	Joint
11	Ted	Pension (Ass./Inc./Ret.)	Pension Co.	Retire: Defined benefit	60,000	0	Amy
12	Ted	401K (Ass./Inc./Ret.)	Mgmt Co.	Retire: Stock Funds	75,000	0	Amy
13	Amy	403B Retirement Plan (Ass./Ret.)	Mgmt Co.	Retire: Stock Funds	35,000	500	Ted
14	Ted	IRA Invest (Stocks/Bonds) (Interest/Dividends)	Invest-Co.	Retire: Stock Funds	45,000	300	Amy
15		Other liquid asset			0	0	
16		Other liquid asset			0	0	
17		Other liquid asset			0	0	
18				Total Liquid Assets:	264,700		=SUM(E5:E17)
19							
20		< Non-Liquid Assets (Name / Type) >					
21	Joint	Home Value (Appraised)	Mortgage Co.	Appraised value	250,000	Ref. Sect 2: Liabilities for Mortgage balance	
22	Joint	Auto values (total) (Car and truck)	Cars Paid for	Estimated values (10k+20k)	30,000		
23	Joint	Jewelry & Other	Other Assets	Appraised values	10,000		
24		Other Non-liquid asset			0		
25		Other Non-liquid asset			0		
26				Total All Major Assets:	$554,700		=SUM(E5:E26)-E18
27							
28				Total Moly Save/Invest Contrib:		1,700	=SUM(F5:F26)
29							
30				Saving-to-Income (STI %):		19.1%	=F29/'Income-Exp'!C21
31							
32			EF Goal is $27,000	Emerg Fund-to-Exp: (EFE %):		50.7%	=E7/('Income-Exp'!C76*6)
33							
34				Liquid Assets-to-Exp:	No. Months:	59	=E18/('Income-Exp'!C76)

`< >` Income-Exp | **Assets-Liab** | Cred-Cards | Home-Info | Auto-Info | Insure-Pols | Fin-Plan | Income-Exp-F | Assets-Liab-F | Cred-Cards-F ···

The Asset Beneficiary

In the Assets section of the Assets-Liab sheet, you can enter the name of the asset recipient or beneficiary in the last column. This is the person who will take ownership of an asset should the current owner pass away. For a married couple, the beneficiary is usually the other partner. A beneficiary is typically specified for assets such as CDs, MMAs and 401Ks. Having a beneficiary identified for assets can be a factor regarding contested wills, estate inheritance and probate proceedings.

Your Home as an Asset

A house might be considered an asset depending on how much equity (sales value minus amount owed) you have, although financial experts might disagree. Some would argue that unless it generates income, it is a liability, since you pay money into it (for mortgage and maintenance). However, if you rent out a portion of the house, it can produce an income stream and would then clearly be considered an asset. Even if you don't rent it out but still consider it an asset, it usually takes a while (typically a few months or more) to get the equity (value) or cash out of a house. If you are a homeowner, your house is typically your least liquid asset. Some financial people would not include your home equity in the net worth equation. They might argue that you would need to sell your home to obtain equity from it. And even if you sold your home, you would still need some place to live. You also need to factor in closing costs, which can be substantial. As the seller, you will typically pay a sales commission of about 6 percent of the selling price.

On the other hand, you can borrow against the equity of your home with a Home Equity Line of Credit (HELOC) or home equity loan, the interest on which may be tax deductible. In addition, you might be able to sell your home in a good market and make quite a bit on the sale. Gains up to $250,000 are tax exempt for an individual if the home has been their primary residence for two of the last five years. You could sell your home and take the proceeds and move to a less expensive region. You could also downsize and move into an apartment or downsize to a smaller, cheaper home (tiny home trend). So, if you consider your home an asset and choose to include home equity in your net worth equation, you just need to acknowledge that your net worth will go up or down depending on whether you include the home equity or not. Note that home equity is included as an asset in Table 5-1.

Your Home as an Investment
While your home may be considered an asset, some financial planners do not recommend viewing it as an investment, especially one that counts toward your retirement. For most people, their home is a place to live with associated expenses, and the value could go up or down depending on market conditions, interest rates, and other factors. That said, in today's seller's market (which could be different tomorrow), you can make a decent return on investment (ROI) if you are willing to move every couple of years and/or adjust your lifestyle.

Table 5-1 lists examples of common assets along with a brief description of each. These are the types of assets that the average person might have and that would be added to the "Assets-Liab" sheet of the PFS. Your list of assets will most likely be different. In the table, assets are monetary possessions that can vary in liquidity (H, M, L), as shown below.

- **High (H)** = Very liquid - easy to extract cash quickly
- **Moderate (M)** = Liquid - but may take several days or weeks to extract cash
- **Low (L)** = Relatively difficult to extract the cash quickly

Asset Gains and Tax Status
Table 5-1 also classifies various assets based on Tax Status or how the gains (profits) are typically treated: Taxable (T), Tax Deferred (D), or Tax Free (F). With taxable accounts, you pay taxes on interest or gains as they are earned. Examples include savings and individual stocks. Taxable asset accounts are not tax deferred. Tax-deferred accounts are referred to as "qualified accounts," and you generally don't pay tax on the money put into these accounts or the gains until you withdraw from them, usually at retirement. Different types of investments are covered in later chapters. If you need help deciding which types of investments to make with respect to taxes, you should contact a financial professional, such as a CPA or CFP, to discuss what is best for you and your financial situation. Investments and are covered in Chapter 13: Investing Basics, and taxes are covered in Chapter 15: Income Tax Basics.

Table 5-1: Examples of Asset Types and Classifications

Asset Name / Type	Description / Notes	Liquidity (H/M/L)	Tax stat (T/D/F)
Cash on hand	Could be in your wallet or under your mattress	H	N/A
Checking account	Bricks and mortar bank or online	H	T
Savings account	Bricks and mortar bank or online	H	T
Stocks	Equities - Individual shares or mutual funds	M	T
Bonds	Loans to U.S. government and other organizations, that bear interest	M	T
Traditional IRA (Individual Retirement Account)	Before tax investment account. Usually invested in stock market but can be most any form of investment. Contributions and gains are tax deferred. You don't pay income tax until cash is withdrawn.	M	D
Roth IRA	After-tax investment account. Usually invested in stock market but can be most any form of investment. Never pay tax on gains (tax free).	M	F
401K Plan	Contributions and gains are tax deferred. Retirement savings account for employees of private companies and self-employed individuals. Usually made up of stocks.	M	D
403B Plan	Tax deferred retirement savings account for public employees. (Police, teachers, etc.) and non-profit organizations. Usually made up of stocks.	M	D
Certificates of Deposit (CDs)	Purchased timed money accounts	M	T
Annuity (Fixed/Variable)	Usually, tax deferred retirement investment offered by many insurance Companies.	M	D
Money market account (MMA)	Long term savings account. Higher interest yield but higher minimum balance required.	M	T
529 Plan (college)	College savings account. Usually invested in stock market. Gains are not taxed if used for college expenses.	M	F
Precious metals	Purchased gold/silver. Can be in an IRA or direct purchase.	M	T or D
Jewelry	Appraised value	L	T or F
Coin collection	Rare coins that can appreciate in value.	L	T
Stamp collection	Rare stamps that can appreciate in value.	L	T

Home (equity)	Value of residence minus mortgage balance.	L	F
Business interests	Partnerships, etc.	L	D
Rental property	Income producing asset.	L	D
1969 Camaro SS 396	Antique American muscle car that can appreciate in value.	M	T

Sample entries for the Assets-Liab PFS sheet are shown in Figures 5-1 and 5-2 as well as Tables 5-2 and 5-3. Tables 5-4 and 5-5 provide space for entering your own assets and liabilities. Prior to starting on **Exercise 5-1: List PFS Assets and Liabilities**, you can make copies of Tables 5-4 and 5-5 and record your name and the current date on them. Or you can just use a separate sheet of paper to record your assets and liabilities for entry into the Assets-Liab sheet in Exercise 5-1. Note that asset values and dollar amounts for liabilities can be approximate (rounded to the nearest ten or hundred dollars) as they are likely to change from month to month. These are only sample entries and are not recommendations for asset allocation.

Note: The Home Value asset entry is the appraised value of the home and does not consider the mortgage (loan balance). The mortgage balance is recorded in the Liabilities section of the spreadsheet and is subtracted from the assets to calculate net worth.

Liabilities and Secured Debt

Liabilities are major financial obligations for which you are responsible and that can be paid for out of your assets over some period of time. Typically, assets are the things you own that have value, and liabilities are the loans and debt that you owe. Liabilities are usually large chunks of indebtedness that represent major purchases. They can be classified as "secured" or "unsecured." Secured liabilities, such as a home or car, are secured by the major purchase that has value as collateral. Secured liabilities can be repossessed by the creditor that loaned the money to purchase the item. Unsecured liabilities are those that are generally not associated with a major purchased item. A car for which you have taken a $20,000 auto loan is considered a secured liability and could be repossessed. The balance on a credit card, although it can be substantial, is not secured and is made up of many smaller purchases. As an example, let's say you charged the purchase of a $1,500 big screen TV on one of your credit cards. You have also previously charged about $500 for other smaller purchases, including dinner at restaurants. Your total balance on the credit card is now approximately $2,000, for which you are liable. The bulk of the liability is the TV, but the credit card balance is considered unsecured debt. The company you purchased the TV from will probably not attempt to repossess your TV. If you really want something and it becomes an unsecured liability, be sure to do some research and get the best one for the money.

Note: When adding up your liabilities, keep in mind they typically consist of major financial obligations like mortgages, rent, installment loans, and high-balance revolving credit accounts. They typically do not include expenses such as utilities, transportation, or entertainment.

DTI debts and loans are the major liabilities that increase your Debt-to-Income ratio, which was covered in Chapter 3. DTI is the percentage of your monthly gross income that you are using to pay off major debt and should not exceed 40 percent. Examples of major liabilities that are factored into your Debt-to-Income (DTI) ratio include these:

- **Auto loan**
- **Home mortgage**
- **Student loan**
- **Personal loan**
- **Credit card debt**

Personal Net Worth (PNW)

Do you know what your net worth is? Most people do not have any idea. A person's net worth is essentially the value of their total major assets minus their total major liabilities at a given point in time. In this book we refer to it as your "Personal Net Worth" or PNW. PNW is one of the key Personal Financial Indicators (PFIs). Your net worth can change daily. It is like a snapshot of your current financial status or how much value your assets have as compared to how much you owe. A Net Worth Statement is also referred to as a "balance sheet" and can give you some idea of where you stand overall (plus or minus). An example of an asset is a savings account. An example of a liability is a loan against a car. Many people have a savings account, and many have a car loan.

Note: While net worth is a very important indicator in determining your overall financial health, it is cash flow that determines your lifestyle. If an asset—such as stocks or property—increases in value, it can increase your net worth, and by the same token, if it decreases in value, it can decrease your net worth. If the asset generates income, it can also affect your net cash flow.

Assets are not the same as income, and liabilities are not the same as expenses (outgo). Your monthly income and expenses, although closely related, are separate from assets and liabilities. Assets and liabilities are totals of how much you own and how much you owe, and together, they determine your net worth. Income and expenses are how much you take in and how much you spend on a monthly basis, and together, they determine your cash flow. These topics were covered in Chapter 3 - Income, Expenses, and Cash Flow.

Calculating Personal Net Worth (PNW)

PNW is calculated as shown below in PFI 5-1. The result can be positive or negative, and hopefully it's positive. The calculation is simple. The hard part is determining the value of your nonmonetary assets and how much equity you have. Adding up your liabilities (debts) can be eye-opening. Note that Total Major Assets, in the example, includes home equity (appraised value minus mortgage balance). Total Major Liabilities includes the mortgage balance as well as major installment loan purchases and credit card debt but does not include monthly expenses or money spent on house and auto maintenance. Refer to Figure 5-2 for the formulas and cells in the spreadsheet that match the cells referenced here for PFI 5-1:

Total Major Assets (Cell E26) - Total Major Liabilities (Cell E47) = Total PNW (Cell E49)

PFI 5-1: Personal Net Worth (PNW) Formula/Calculation
Personal Financial Indicator (#PFI-8)

Total Major Assets (Equity) (-minus-) Total Major Liabilities (Debt) = PNW ($)

$554,700 - $182,400 = $372,300

(PFS Assets-Liab sheet example)

Figure 5-2: PFS Liabilities and Net Worth Sections of Assets-Liab Sheet (sample entries)

	A	B	C	D	E	F	G
36	<<< Sect 2: Liabilities >>>						
37							
38	Owner	Liability Name / Type	Institution	Notes	Amount		
39	Joint	Home Mortgage Balance	Mortgage Co.	Secured debt	170,000		
40	Joint	Auto Loans (balance owed)	Various	Secured debt	0		
41	Joint	Credit Card Debt (See Cred-Cards Tab)	Various	Unsecured debt	5,000		
42	Joint	Home Equity Line of Credit (HELOC)			5,000		
43	Amy	Credit Card - XYZ Visa			1800		
44	Ted	Credit Card - QRS M/C			600		
45		Other Liability			0		
46		Other Liability			0		
47				Total Major Liabilities:	$182,400		=SUM(E39:E46)
48							
49	<<< Sect 3: Net Worth >>>			Total Personal Net Worth (PNW$):	$372,300		=E26-E47
50	(Net Worth = Total Major Assets - Total Major Liabilities)			(Includes Home Equity)			

Income-Exp Assets-Liab Cred-Cards Home-Info Auto-Info Insure-Pols Fin-Plan Income-Exp-F Assets-Liab-F Cred-Cards-F

Simple Net Worth Example

The following net worth example in Table 5-2 assumes you have $200,000 in total assets and $130,000 in liabilities. Remember that net worth is a snapshot of assets and liabilities and can change daily. The numbers shown here are examples, and a real net worth case would have more entries depending on the individual or household finances.

Table 5-2: Simple Net Worth Example

Entry	Amount	Notes
Assets:		
Savings account	$20,000	
Stock portfolio	$30,000	(Current value)
Home est. sale value	$150,000	(Appraised value)
Total Assets:	**$200,000**	
Liabilities:		
Home mortgage balance	$100,000	

Car loan balance	$20,000	
Credit card debt	$10,000	
Total Liabilities:	**-$130,000**	
Net Worth:	**$70k**	($200,000 assets minus $130,000 liabilities)

Your net worth can and does change often, as mentioned previously. Your stock portfolio could be worth $50,000 today, but the stock market could go down tomorrow, and your portfolio may be worth only $45,000. Your net worth would decrease and be $5,000 less than it was. If the value of your stocks went up to $60k, your net worth would increase by $10,000. If you have a teenager living with you, your net worth can decrease very rapidly!

Using Assets to Pay Off Debt
Your Personal Cash Flow (PCF) (See Chapter 3) and Personal Net Worth (PNW) work together to provide the foundation for your finances. An increase in income or decrease in expenses will increase cash flow and vice versa. For example, let's say your cash flow is positive and you have a car loan, which is costing you $500 per month, and the balance you owe (payoff amount) is $2,500. You decide to use your savings (an asset) to pay off your car loan (a liability). This will have the effect of increasing your monthly Personal Cash Flow (PCF) by the amount of your car payment. However, your Personal Net Worth (PNW) will decrease by the loan balance payoff of $2,500 but could be offset by the interest saved on the car loan and the fact that you now have more equity in your car.

Note: In general, it is a good idea to pay down high-interest debt (like credit cards) sooner rather than later if you have the cash flow to do it. Using savings, which may pay 2 percent interest, to pay off a credit card at 19 percent interest is just plain smart money management, as long as you don't tap into your emergency fund.

Emergency Fund Goal (EFG) and Emergency Fund-to-Expenses (EFE%)
Your Emergency Fund (EF) is one of the most important building blocks for your financial house. And your Emergency Fund-to-Expenses (EFE) ratio is an important Personal Financial Indicator (PFI). Recall from Chapter 4 that the Emergency Fund Goal (EFG $) dollar amount should be six times the required monthly expenses for a working person. This is the amount you would have in your EF if it was fully funded. Having enough money saved in your EF and other liquid assets to get you through hard times is good for your mental as well as your financial health. You can start small, but the important thing is to establish an EF savings account and add to it on a regular basis.

Determine your EFE ratio (%) by totaling your monthly required expenses from the Income-Exp sheet and multiplying that by six, which is your target EF amount or goal (EFG). Then divide your current EF savings balance by the target amount to get a percentage that indicates how close you are to reaching your goal. Below are the results using the sample data numbers from the example in Chapter 4. Let's say you are working full-time and have been steadily adding to your EF for the last four years and currently have $13,700 saved in your EF. Your required monthly expenses (from the Income-Exp sheet sample entries) are $4,500, and your target EF goal is $27,000 (4,500 x 6). Dividing your EF balance of 13,700 by 27,000 equals .507 or appx 51 percent. So, you are halfway there and moving in the right direction! The PFI 5-2 EFE formula is shown here with calculations from the PFS.

PFI 5-2: Emergency Fund-to-Expenses (EFE)
Personal Financial Indicator (#PFI-9)

Current EF Balance (/divided by/) (Monthly Required Expenses * 6) = EFE (%)

$13,700 / (4,500 * 6) = .507 (*100) = 50.7%

$13,700 / (27,000) = .507 (*100) = 50.7%

(PFS Income-Exp and Assets-Liab sheet example)

Liquid Assets and Your Emergency Fund - So You Think You'd Survive?
Another important indicator that relates to expenses, and your ability to cover them with your assets in the event of an emergency, is the Liquid Assets-to-Expenses projection (LAE). The EFE is based solely on the amount you have in your EF to see how close you are to funding it to the recommended levels (6 x required monthly expenses). So, if your EF was fully funded based on your monthly required expenses of $4,500 and you lost your job, you could hang in there for about six months. The LAE indicator is similar but includes not only your EF but all your other liquid assets (total value snapshot) and divides your total liquid assets ($264,700 in the Assets-Liab sheet) by your required monthly expenses ($4,500 in the Income-Exp sheet). The LAE indicator is measured in months, rather than as a percentage (like Debt-to-Income – DTI ratio) or in dollars (like Personal Cash Flow - PCF). The LAE can help to determine how many months you could go without an income based on the total value of your liquid assets and required monthly expenses. Examples of liquid assets that should be included in the LAE calculation are listed below. Checking account balances and alimony may be included if desired.

- **Checking accounts (optional)**
- **Emergency Fund (EF)**
- **Non-EF Savings accounts**
- **Certificates of Deposit (CDs)**
- **Money Market Accounts (MMAs)**
- **Pensions (defined benefit retirement plans)**
- **IRAs, 401Ks, and 403Bs (defined contribution retirement plans)**

Assets such as 401K and 403B retirement plans will be discussed further in Chapter 13: Investment Basics and Chapter 14: Retirement requirements. These retirement plans are, admittedly not very liquid, and carry some stiff penalties if you tap into the funds before retirement. Also, early withdrawals are taxed as ordinary income. However, in an emergency, you can use that money to make ends meet. You just need to factor in the penalties and taxes if you should choose to do so. For example, if you take $1,000 out of an IRA before retirement, and your effective tax bracket is 25 percent, you must hand over $250 to the IRS, plus the 10 percent penalty amount! The PFI 5-3 LAE formula is shown here with calculations and sample data from the PFS. Using the sample data in the PFS Assets-Liab sheet, you could hang in there for about fifty-nine months or about five years with no income, before you completely exhaust your semi-liquid assets. This does not factor in what the market might do over that time frame or what social welfare programs might be available.

PFI 5-3: Liquid Assets-to-Expenses Projection (LAE)
Personal Financial Indicator (#PFI-10)

(Total Liquid Assets) (/divided by/) (Monthly Required Expenses) = LAE (#Mo.)

$264,700 / 4,500 = 59 Months (Appx.)

(PFS Income-Exp and Assets-Liab sheet example)

Refer to **Exercise 5-1: List PFS Assets and Liabilities** below, which will help you identify your assets and liabilities to prepare to enter your data into the PFS Assets, Liabilities, and Net Worth sheet. Refer to Appendix B for a summary listing of all the personal financial indicators (PFIs) used in this book.

Chapter 5 Exercise

Exercise 5-1: List PFS Assets and Liabilities
In this exercise, you will list your assets (Part A) and liabilities (Part B) to prepare for entering them into PFS sheet Assets, Liabilities, and Net Worth. Even if you do not plan to enter your data into the Assets-Liab sheet at this time, go ahead and record your data in the tables. You can do the calculation manually if you wish. Make copies of Tables 5-3 and 5-4 before starting this exercise,

Part A: List Your Assets
Take a few minutes to think about and list your major assets and their approximate values in Table 5-3 below or copy of it. Review the assets in the sample data for the Assets-Liab sheet (Figure 5-1), and enter your information, starting with your most liquid accounts—like checking and savings—and ending with your least liquid, like your home. The important thing is to identify your key assets and write them down. Refer to Table 5-1, and Figure 5-1 for examples of assets. Enter those that pertain to your financial situation. Use a pencil to enter your assets into the table. This is an exercise to get you thinking about the assets you have

and starting to document them. You may be pleasantly surprised. The assets listed here can be transferred to the actual PFS sheet - Assets, Liabilities, and Net Worth (Assets-Liab Tab) later.

Table 5-3: Assets Listing (Form)

Owner	Asset Type/ Description	Institution	Notes	Appx Value

Part B - List Your Liabilities

Take a few minutes to think about your major liabilities and list them. Use Table 5-4 below, or a copy of it, to record approximately how much you owe for each one. You may want to start with your liability that has the highest balance or amount owed. As with assets, the important thing is to write them down. Refer to the examples of liabilities in this chapter and enter those that pertain to your financial situation. Figure 5-2 shows examples of liabilities in the Assets-Liab sheet. Use a pencil to enter them into the table or write them on a piece of paper. You can also use a smartphone or spreadsheet software to record them. This is an exercise to get you thinking about your liabilities and starting to document them. The liabilities listed here can be transferred to the actual PFS sheet Assets, Liabilities, and Net Worth (Assets-Liab Tab) later.

Table 5-4: Liabilities Listing (Form)

Owner	Liability Name/Type	Institution	Notes	Appx Amt Owed

Chapter 6
Banks and Checking Accounts

Chapter Overview:
Part 1 of this chapter describes different types of banking and related financial institutions. It identifies the personal banker and their role as a key member of your Professional Advisor Group. The Certified Financial Planner (CFP), another a key member, and other potential group members are also introduced. Part 2 describes the characteristics of different checking accounts as well as mobile banking apps. Information is provided to increase one's basic understanding of banking and checking and the safeguards they provide, as well as what to expect from a bank. Many notes and tips are provided as well as best practices regarding checking accounts. Also covered are the benefits and processes of automating standard financial transactions, such as payroll deposit, online bill paying, AutoPay, automated savings, and investment transfers. Information on how to minimize fees and charges is provided. This chapter also introduces some of the available banking products and services. Additional information is provided regarding these topics in Chapter 7: Savings and Banking Services.

- **Part 1: Banks, Bankers, and Professional Advisors**
- **Part 2: Checking Accounts**

Chapter PFS and PFI Integration:
The PFS components in this chapter that relate to banking and checking accounts are found on the PFS Sheet - Income, Expenses, and Cash Flow (Tab Income-Exp). Also refer to the Assets-Liab sheet, which includes assets like checking and savings accounts. There are no specific Personal Financial Indicators (PFIs) associated with this chapter. However, it is important to keep track of the degree to which you are able to automate your checking account transactions (Payments, Deposits, and Transfers), which is referred to as your account automation ratio.

Chapter Exercises:
- **Exercise 6-1: Compare Banking Features**
- **Exercise 6-2: Automate Bank Accounts (Payments, Deposits, and Transfers)**

Chapter Notable Quote:
Quote 6-1: "That which you want to do least, do that first." - Anonymous

The quote above can be applied to many aspects of our lives. If you have a list of things you need or want to do, rank them in order, starting with the one you would least like to do and ending with the one you would most like to do. It does not always work out, but if nothing else, it may help you prioritize your list of tasks and get started rather than procrastinate. If you can, try to do this on a daily or weekly basis, and you may be surprised at how fast you can get through distasteful tasks when you focus on them and tell yourself "I can do this, and I'll be happier when I do!" If you do the least desirable thing first, the rest of your day or week could be pleasanter knowing you have already gotten the least desirable thing(s) out of the way and can look forward to the more enjoyable things you would rather do. However, you might be one of those people who have a long list of undesirable things to do and few desirable things to do, and you might find that you seem to be always doing things you would rather not do. This is not necessarily a bad thing because, eventually, as you work through the undesirable tasks on the list, you will probably get to a point where you are feeling a little better about yourself, and your life may be looking a little brighter over-all because you are "taking care of business." This is also related to the concept of "delayed gratification," whereby you put off the things you want or things you want to do until later and then enjoy them more.

Moving in the Right Direction Financially

With personal finance and checking accounts in particular, the concept relates to balancing your check-book and paying your bills on time before spending money on nonessential items. Employing this concept can also help you get started on taking beneficial personal finance-related steps, like setting up Paycheck Direct Deposit and AutoPay for paying bills with your checking account. With savings it can mean putting money away for your Emergency Fund (EF) before spending it on other things. Adopting this philosophy can make your life a little easier, more enjoyable, and potentially more prosperous.

Note: If you don't read the whole chapter, at least skim it and read the Checking - Tips and Summary Notes section at the end.

Part 1: Banks, Bankers, and Professional Advisors

The first section of this chapter describes the characteristics of banks and banking, including some of the more common options available, and the role of the banker in your overall financial plan. Many notes and tips are provided on how to save money and make good decisions regarding checking accounts.

Traditional Banks

These are for-profit institutions, typically owned by shareholders (stock owners). They are the full-service banks and branches that you see on the Main streets in many communities. They are also referred to as "brick and mortar" banks. They can be small banking institutions with just a few regional branches or large major banks with hundreds or thousands of branches nationwide. The branch offices may be standalone buildings, or they may provide their services within another retail location, such as a supermarket. The Federal Deposit Insurance Corporation (FDIC) publishes an annual report listing the number of physical branch locations for each bank that operates in the USA. Almost all banks and other saving/lending insti-tutions are insured by the FDIC. Even with the trend toward online banking, they are still maintaining a consistent number of branches across the country and building new branches in growing communities. These branches offer the broadest range of services and other advantages, such as drive-up auto teller machines. Also, traditional banks offer services such as safe deposit boxes for storage of valuables and important documents. These banks offer a wide range of services and accounts.

You Need Professional Help

Some people prefer to go it alone regarding their finances, thinking they cannot afford professional help. However, by working with competent professionals, you can make better financial decisions that can actually save you money or help you make more money with prudent investments. Also, there are many nonprofit organizations and governmental agencies that can help people with financial needs and issues, such as debt management and credit rebuilding, at little or no cost. They can also provide a starting point for each of the major financial areas listed in Table 6-1.

Some people can be financially successful by going it alone, but most of us need help from our "Professional Advisor Group." This group is made up of people whose core competency is a specialty, and many times it's all they do, so they know the ins and outs. These professionals can include some or all of those listed in Table 6-1. It is common for a Certified Financial Planner (CFP) to be the captain of the ship, to help you navigate the shark-infested waters of personal finance. They can recommend other members of your financial support group, and in many cases, they can provide recommendations for products and services that may obviate the need for other specialists, such as life insurance, which is more of a commodity.

Bankers and Professional Financial Advisors

Many people like the feeling of being able to walk into a bank or financial institution and do business face-to-face with someone that they know, and who may live in their community. This is especially true of smaller communities and local banks and branches, where you can develop a personal relationship with your banker. Having a personal banker or primary contact at an alternative financial institution, such as a credit union, can sometimes allow for additional flexibility in obtaining loans or waiving fees. Working with a banker at a smaller financial institution in your community also allows you to help support the local economy. In addition, your banker may be able to recommend other key members of your core Professional Advisor Group. This group can include, but is not limited to, the five primary members/functions listed below. In addition to your banker, your primary Financial Advisor (usually a Certified Financial Planner or CFP) may also serve as an initial point of contact who can direct you to other advisors as necessary. You can add members to your Professional Advisor Group over time, but it is a good idea to start with a Banking Advisor and a Financial Advisor. Eventually you may need the services of all of the core group listed here, and perhaps other specialists. Although their services are not free, any of these advisors can provide valuable guidance, and potentially save you money in the long run. Additional specialists can be added depending on your needs. The core group consists of the following:

Table 6-1: Professional Advisors

Advisor	Function
Banking Advisor (BS/MBA)	Can be initial contact for other advisors. Provides advice on personal and business accounts, banking services, and products.
Financial Advisor (CFP)	The CFP or other credentialed professional financial advisor who is a fiduciary, can pilot your financial ship and be the initial contact for other advisors. Provides financial analysis and advice on short- and long-term financial planning including investments, savings, asset allocation, portfolio diversification, risk management, guidance on budgets and debt, retirement planning, and help with Social Security decision making.
Insurance Advisor (Licensed insurance broker)	Assists with basic insurance: Home/Auto/Life/Health. Can be the initial contact for other insurance specialists (Health, Vision/Dental, Medicare, etc.).
Legal Advisor (Attorney)	Assists with estate planning, business formation, etc.)
Tax Advisor (CPA)	Assists with short- and long-term tax planning as well as tax preparation. Can provide advice on investments, retirement tax implications and social security as well as personal and business-related tax issues.
Home Advisor (Licensed Realtor or Agent, CRS)	A knowledgeable real estate professional can save you thousands of dollars when buying or selling, and recommend home repair professionals.
Vehicle Advisor (SAE Certified Mechanic)	A good, certified auto mechanic can inspect potential auto purchases and provide repair estimates. Can also maintain your cars and other vehicles.
Other Advisor(s)	As necessary

Each of these professional advisors can serve as your primary point of contact for their main area of expertise. If you need advice that is outside that area, they can usually direct you to a specialist that can address your issues. For example, you may have a trusted Insurance Advisor who can handle most basic insurance needs (Life, Home, Auto, etc.) but you are retired and over sixty-five, and on a fixed income, so you might need help with Medicare, Parts B, C, and D to keep your healthcare costs down. Your primary insurance advisor might refer you to a specialist who deals mainly with older clients and focuses on Medicare and supplemental insurance as well as prescription drug plans. There are many plans available and comparing them can be very confusing. A good Medicare insurance specialist can compare all of the insurers and plans available in your state and can narrow your choices down to the top three that could be appropriate for your medical condition and the medications you take. They can assist with selection and enrollment in the most cost-effective plan that meets your needs, potentially saving you hundreds or even thousands of dollars. Our Medicare insurance specialist is a licensed Medicare advisor and has a master's degree in health services. He was recommended by my CFP about five years ago and he has been a big help to my wife and me in navigating the Medicare maze.

Figure 6-1: Traditional Bricks-and-Mortar Bank

Online Banking and Mobile Apps with Traditional Banks

Although they may be bricks and mortar, most major banks allow you to do much of your banking online via a computer browser interface or smartphone "app." Online banking is banking done remotely from any location other than the physical bank itself. With online banking you can do all of the following:

- Monitor account balances and pending transactions
- Monitor activity (deposits and payments)
- Pay bills
- Manage payees (Add/Change/Delete)
- Deposit checks
- Send money
- Transfer funds

Recently I checked my balance, paid some bills, and deposited a check, all from my iPhone, using my bank mobile app, while sitting in the library. With online banking, you can opt to receive banking documents and notifications of activity via email. These include statements, bills due, bills paid, addition of new payees, and deposits. Smart phone apps are mobile versions (iOS/Android) or computer-based (Desktop, Laptop, etc.)

Web-based apps are made available by many banks for free to their customers to enable them to do regular banking tasks remotely. The mobile apps usually have most of the normal banking functions available on the online Web-based apps, depending on the bank and app.

Using Unsecure Wi-Fi Networks to Access Your Financial Data

If you access your banking data remotely, never use an unsecured public Wi-Fi network like the one you might find at a hotel, library, or coffee shop. Make sure you are on a private home Wi-Fi network that requires a password and using the bank's Website with two-factor authentication, if it is available. Better yet, use a Virtual Private Network (VPN) over Wi-Fi or your provider's cell data network. Using the bank's mobile app over the cell data network (LTE or 5G) is pretty safe and relatively fast. If you use a VPN or cell data, your financial information is encrypted end-to-end from your device to the bank's network. However, even if you are on a private Wi-Fi network, anyone else on that internal network can snoop on your data, if they have the Wi-Fi password. On unsecured networks, login information, account numbers, and other financial data are transmitted in clear text and a hacker can see your financial data. For more information on securing your home network you can search the Web for "secure wi-fi network," or you can go to the FTC Website:

https://consumer.ftc.gov/articles/how-secure-your-home-wi-fi-network.

In the past, if you wanted to deposit a check, you had to go into the bank during banking hours, or you could use an ATM during or after banking hours. Now, smartphone mobile apps allow you to deposit a check into any of your accounts at any time. You just follow the prompts and take a picture of the front and back of the check using your smartphone's camera.

Note: After depositing a check with a mobile app, you should write the date of deposit on the check and hold on to it for a week or so and then tear it up, after you have verified that the amount of the check has been credited to your account.

Credit Unions

Credit unions and their branches are usually brick-and-mortar and offer many of the same services as traditional full-service banks. The main difference is that the credit union is a nonprofit, cooperatively owned organization. Credit unions are typically owned by their members instead of a banking corporation. Credit union membership is usually based on affiliation with a business, union, or group. Examples include public employee credit unions such as education and law enforcement, as well as most Fortune 500 companies, who also offer credit unions to their employees and affiliates.

Credit unions have some advantages over traditional banks. One advantage is that as a depositor and owner, you are generally able to obtain higher interest rates on your savings. You may also be able to borrow money for things such as auto loans at a lower rate with more flexible borrowing guidelines than a traditional bank. A disadvantage is that there may be only a few branches, limiting where you can bank. In addition, services such as checking accounts typically have restrictions on the number of checks written. There are thousands of credit unions in existence. Ask around in your community, and you may find that you very well qualify for membership in one or more credit unions. For information on the products and services available as well as rates for savings and loans, go to the credit union's Website.

Savings and Loan (S&L) Companies

S&L companies, sometimes referred to as "thrifts," offer many of the same services as traditional banks, including deposits, loans, mortgages, checks, and debit cards. S&Ls tend to be more locally oriented and focus more on residential mortgages, whereas banks tend to focus more on commercial accounts and credit cards. S&Ls are more like credit unions in that they can be owned by their depositors and borrowers.

Online Savings Banks

Online or Web-based savings banks represent a major trend in banking, and there are quite a few of them. They do not have some of the expenses associated with traditional brick-and-mortar banks and may offer a higher interest rate on your savings. Some provide a limited number of checks, but they are not oriented toward checking or a high volume of transactions. They are more focused on taking deposits and holding them for longer periods of time. Online bank savings accounts can be linked to a regular bank checking account so that money can be transferred back and forth occasionally. Online banking institutions are becoming more lenient with their policies to draw more customers, with some offering a checking account with no fees, no minimums, and no overdraft charges.

Non-bank Options and Negative Account Activity

Some people may be unable to open a bank account due to factors such as a poor credit history or previous negative bank account activity. They may have to do their "banking" at a non-bank and are usually charged a fee for doing so. Large retailers and grocery stores can provide some services such as money orders for paying bills and check cashing services at the customer service desk. You can usually cash a paycheck at these retailers (for a fee). Avoid check cashing stores if possible. They charge a fee for each check cashed and a fee for each money order to pay a bill. They offer "consumer loans" and landlord rent payment, but be prepared to pay high fees and very high interest rates. Some banks are now offering a secure banking option with a low fee checking account (around five dollars per month). They don't charge for each check or money order. Some of these banks also offer no-fee early access to your paycheck (usually two days) if you have auto-deposit. A check cashing store may be a viable option for some people who cannot open a bank account, but you can go to the bank manager and ask what options you may have to establish an account.

Banking Options

A small community bank or credit union may serve your needs. Others may want the size and diversity of services provided by a larger bank with more branches available in more locations. If you are concerned about the solvency of a bank, you can check its rating online at https://www.bankrate.com and/or look up its "Texas Ratio." I am not concerned about a banking institution failing, as I consider the likelihood of this happening very low. All banks doing business in the U.S. are insured by the FDIC for $250,000 per depositor. If you have a larger monetary amount than that, you should consider opening multiple accounts with other traditional banks or online savings banks.

By opening an account with an online savings bank, you can provide a safe place to put your "rainy day" fund and frequently obtain higher interest rates on your savings in the process. A rainy-day or emergency fund is typically money set aside in a savings account for emergencies or in case you lose your job, etc. This is an important step toward becoming financially stable and helps to keep your savings out of sight and out of mind. I have a checking account with two different nationwide "brick-and-mortar" banks as well as an online savings account. This allows me to take advantage of special offers, spread my assets between banks, and move money between them. I can also take advantage of higher interest rates on savings with the online savings account.

Note: Suggestions and tips are provided here for checking accounts, and in the next chapter the focus will be on savings.

Part 2: Checking Accounts

Most people have a checking account, although the need to write checks is becoming less important these days. It is still very worthwhile from a personal finance management perspective to have a central clearing house for your finances. Also, some small businesses only accept cash or checks and do not accept credit cards. So, it's not a bad idea to keep one or two checks and some cash in your wallet, just in case. This chapter assumes you have a checking and savings account and can properly write a check to make a payment and receive a check for payment and deposit it. And that you know what the preprinted parts of a check are, including Account Number, Routing number, and Check number. If you are unsure of any of these or other parts of a check, or how a check should be filled out, do a Web search for "parts of a check."

A Safe Place to Keep Your Money
Having a checking account and a savings account is a good idea for several reasons. You can take care of pretty much all your banking needs in one place that is easily accessible, without having to handle cash or pay fees (depending on the type of account and balance requirements). A checking account allows multiple payment options, including checks, debit card, AutoPay and Auto Transfer, ATM cash, and Tap/Pay. While you probably won't make much, if anything, in the way of interest, you will have a relatively safe and highly liquid place to park your cash. Bank account deposits are insured by the Federal Deposit Insurance Corporation (FDIC). If your checking account is at a credit union, deposits are insured by the National Credit Union Association (NCUA). An insurance amount of up to $250,000 per individual depositor per financial institution is provided by both the FDIC and NCUA and is backed by the U.S. government.

Basic Checking Accounts
A basic account typically charges fees for overdraft protection transfer (e.g., twelve dollars), stop payment on a check (e.g., twenty-five dollars), or returned deposit items (e.g., twenty-five dollars). The bank may also

charge a monthly service charge of ten dollars or more for the account. A typical basic checking account provides the following:

- Internet banking and bill payment
- Mobile banking, mobile deposit, and alerts
- Access to fee-free ATMs (only for your bank)
- Access to identity theft protection (for a fee)

Enhanced Checking Accounts
Other features may be available with enhanced checking accounts. If you have more than one type of account and/or keep a combined deposit amount at a certain level (e.g., $20,000), you may be entitled to additional features. Some banks offer additional benefits for military personnel. Benefits of an enhanced account can include these:

- Complimentary personal checks
- No monthly fees
- No fees for overdraft protection transfer, stop payment, or returned deposit items
- Non-Bank ATM fees rebated (usually two per month)
- No fees for cashier checks and money orders
- Better rates on CDs, loans, and lines of credit
- Special brokerage discounts
- Access to identity theft protection (for a reduced fee)
- Account management and spending analysis apps (e.g., virtual wallet)

Additional banking features and services can include but are not limited to the following:
- Notary services
- Number of and location of branches and ATMs
- Non-bank ATM fees
- Any checking account-related information, such as number of free checks per month, cost of new checks, etc.

Refer to **Exercise 6-1: Compare Banking Features** at the end of this chapter, which will help you identify those banking characteristics and features that are important to you.

Balancing Your Checking Account
The main hassle with a checking account, other than potential fees, is the need to balance it. With today's computerized online real-time banking tools, it is extremely rare to find a bank error in the transactions of a regular checking account. However, if you write a check and don't record it or fail to verify that a check has cleared, your account can get out of control and start accumulating overdraft fees, which can eat up your balance very quickly. To help with balancing your account, most banks provide step-by-step detailed

instructions, printed on the back of your monthly statement. The instructions provide a simple three-step process on how to use your check register and your checking account statement to balance your account.

Reviewing Your Checking Account Statement - Debits and Credits
When reviewing one of your monthly bank statements, or online bank accounts, pay particular attention to the Debits and Credits. These are two old accounting terms that still apply today and are the two main "transaction" types that you will see on an account statement. A transaction is simply an entry to the account that is either an addition to the account balance (credit) or a subtraction from the account balance (debit). The bottom line, literally, is that any transaction will either increase (credit) or decrease (debit) the account balance. On your checking account statement, Withdrawals/Debits are listed first followed by Deposits/Credits.

Printing Statements at the End of the Month (well worth your time)
Printing and reviewing your bank statement may be on the list of those things you'd rather not do. But trust me, it can really pay off in terms of your awareness of your finances and understanding of the Debits/ Credits hitting your account. You will not likely find any banking errors, but you may well find an invalid charge from a payee or a valid fee that could be waived with a phone call to your personal banker. Reviewing your monthly statement could be a real eye-opener, especially if you are not the person who pays the bills. At the end of the month, I log in to my main online checking account, the one that I pay most of my bills from (automatically or manually). I also print off a copy of last month's statement so I can make notes and highlight any transactions I want to follow up on. Doing so can help with your budgeting process and can provide some real insight into what's happening in your checking account. The statement usually covers a date range from the middle of one month to the middle of the next month so you may have to print off a couple of statements to track with your monthly budget. If you do this each month, you can put together a nice little paper trail that tracks most of your income and outgo (expenses). You can use this paper trail to make and verify the entries in your Personal Financial Spreadsheet (PFS) and confirm that your AutoPay entries and other transactions are taking place correctly.

Once you've reviewed your checking account online and printed off the statement a couple of times, this will get easier to do because you'll be more familiar with the format and the entries. You are not doing this to catch bank errors; you are doing it to get a handle on your finances and provide input to your monthly budget. The whole process should take only about thirty minutes, so it's time well spent, especially if you catch an error like an invalid transaction, an incorrect debit from your account, or a fee the bank has charged you that don't think is valid. For example, remember that subscription (for whatever) that you signed up for a while back with the thirty-day free trial that would automatically go to monthly billing of $39 if you didn't cancel within the first thirty days? It could be costing you real money each month that you might not even know about unless you review your statements on a monthly basis.

Credits on your statement are additions to your balance and will usually have the word "Deposit" in the description of the transaction and will display in green on your screen or printout (green means more $$

in the account). Examples of credits or deposits include personal checks to you, payroll Direct Deposits, Social Security checks, 401K and pension disbursements, refunds (returned product), and adjustments (fee waiver) to the account. If the credit or deposit is listed under the heading PENDING at the top of the statement, it means it has been received but has not been credited to the account yet. And it will display in black rather than green. Debits on your statement are subtractions from your balance and will usually have the check number (Check # 103) or the word "Withdrawal" in the description of the transaction and will display in red on your screen or printout (red means less $$ in account.). Examples of debits or withdrawals include personal checks you've written, ATM withdrawals, online bill payments, automatic payments to creditors, transfers to your other accounts (including checking, savings, or investments), and any debit card purchases. If the deposit is listed under the heading PENDING, it means it has been received but has not been credited to the account yet. And it will display in black rather than green.

Automating Financial Account Transactions
By selecting a good bank or other comparable financial institution and maintaining a couple of basic accounts, you can automate a significant portion of your financial activity (especially bill paying) and remove much of the potential for human error from many of your important transactions. By automating those financial transactions that make sense for your situation, you can avoid missed payments, late payments, and associated penalty fees. This can save time and money, reduce stress, and potentially improve your credit rating. Banks and creditors like customers that automate, and they frequently offer benefits such as early access to funds deposited and discounts for setting up AutoPay for payments. With a basic checking account, you can automate many routine but important financial transactions such as these:

- **Automatic Payroll Deposit** (Paycheck Direct Deposit)
- **Automatic Payment of Recurring Bills** (AutoPay)
- **Automated Transfers to Savings** (Emergency Fund, Short/Long term savings)
- **Automated Transfers to Investment Accounts** (See Chapter 13: Investing Basics)

Automatic Payroll Deposit of Your Paycheck (Direct Deposit)
Some people like to receive their paycheck personally (from their employer or through the mail) and hold it in their hand before depositing it. Or perhaps they don't have a bank account in which to deposit it and have to take it to a store or check cashing service. Either way, it can add time, gas, and hassle to the process and can cost a percentage of the check amount just to cash it. If you have a checking or savings account, most employers allow you to choose to deposit your check automatically, saving time and money. You typically just fill out a request form and wait a week or two. With Direct Deposit, you never have to remember to deposit your check or worry about losing the check! Without Direct Deposit, your bank may put a hold on the funds, even if you deposit the check by the cutoff time. With Direct Deposit, the bank usually allows early access to your funds of up to two days sooner, reducing the possibility of NSF (Non-Sufficient Funds) or "bounced checks" and the associated fees. People who are retired frequently receive their Social Security, Pension, and 401K payments via Direct Deposit. Direct Deposit is the first step of automating your basic income and outgo financial transactions.

Manually Paying Bills Online using a Bank Bill Paying Service (O/L Bill Pay)

Many banks offer this service for free, along with a mobile smartphone app to manage it. With online bill pay, you can login online to your bank's Website using any browser-enabled device. You can then set up regular payees for categories such as rent or mortgage, utilities, loans, and credit cards. Paying bills online helps reduce paper, clutter, and stamps and saves considerable time in the long run. It also provides a secure centralized location for storing payee information (phone numbers, account numbers, etc.) as well as payment activity. Although it takes a little while to set up the payees, it is well worth it, and you save on postage! You can access your bank accounts to pay bills, deposit checks, and transfer funds, among other things, from a regular PC, tablet, or smartphone. Once you set up online bill paying, you will never go back to "Checks and Stamps." In addition, by focusing most of your income and outgo financial activity through a bank, you improve the accuracy of your finances in general and can track transactions, as compared to using cash, money orders, checks, or even credit cards.

Online Bill Pay - How Paid and When Paid

When using online bill-pay, be sure to take note of how the bill will be paid and when, both of which display when you are reviewing a payment to be made. This information also shows up in the Scheduled Payments section after you've made the payment. For most payments to banks and credit card issuers, payment will be sent electronically (EFT), which typically takes one to two days. If paying a utility bill and some other payees (even some banks), payment may be sent by mail, which typically takes five (working) days. If payment is sent via check, it may be debited from your account prior to the scheduled payment date.

You can run into delays with electronic payments as well. For example, I was making a payment to a credit card company and the due date was four days away. That should have allowed enough time for an electronic payment to reach the credit card company. However, the bill-pay date is based on the number of business days (workdays). When I entered the payment amount, the pay date showed as being five days away. That was because it was over the weekend and Monday was a holiday. If I had made that payment to the credit card company through my bank's online bill pay system, my payment may have been late, and could have cost me a lot in fees and interest. I called the card issuer (the payee), spoke to a customer service representative, and paid the balance over the phone by allowing them to debit the amount due from my checking account. They did not charge me to do this, and my payment was posted immediately, and I didn't have to worry about it arriving late. My bad for waiting till the last minute to pay my credit card bill. If I had paid a week before, it would not have been an issue.

Manual Payment of Bills - Using Mobile Quick Pay QR Code

Creditors want to make it as easy as possible for you to pay your bills whether you set up automatic bill payment or not. Increasingly creditors are sending out bills and statements with "Quick Response" or "QR" codes on them. The QR code is a little square digital code that you see on just about everything now, from product packaging to billing statements to TV commercials on screen to menus in restaurants. The QR code allows you to use the camera in your smartphone to take a picture of the code automatically which then directs you to a Web URL where you can find out more information or pay your bill or whatever.

When used by a legitimate organization, the QR code allows you to make an instant payment from your smartphone or other Web-enabled device. I just did this for a bill that was from a healthcare provider organization for a copay in the amount of $20.

Caution: There are potential scams and security issues when using QR codes to pay bills, so exercise caution if you choose to pay your bills this way. Usually, if you get an official-looking statement from one of your known creditors that has a preprinted QR code on it (not a sticker), chances are you are pretty safe. Just remember not to pay the bill on an unsecured public network. Refer to Chapter 18: Scams and Rip-Offs, for additional information on QR codes and related security issues.

Automatic Payment of Bills - Using an Automatic Bill Paying Service (AutoPay)

The AutoPay service is one of the best tools available to help you get a handle on your finances and build a good credit rating by preventing missed and late payments. Many banks and other financial institutions offer it to their customers, although the exact name of the service may vary. If you are a customer and have a checking or savings account with a bank, they usually don't charge you to make automated payments to creditors through them. Using AutoPay, you can set up regular monthly payments to payees you've defined using your bank's online bill payment system. As mentioned, these can include rent, mortgage, utilities, loan payments, and insurance premiums. Paying bills automatically with AutoPay helps organize your monthly payments, and you can save a lot of time over other methods of paying bills, including regular online bill pay, which is still basically a manual process. AutoPay puts bill paying on autopilot, and you decide which bills get paid automatically, how they get paid, for what amount, and when. Because it can provide automatic payment of many of your bills, AutoPay greatly reduces the chances of being late on or missing a payment to a creditor. This can improve your "on-time payments" rating (a major factor in your credit report) which can improve your credit score (over time).

Ways to Pay with AutoPay - Pros and Cons

Creditors like AutoPay because there is no need for an invoice or statement, and the process virtually guarantees your full payment will be received on time. I used to depend on the mailed paper invoice or statement from a creditor as a trigger to pay a bill, but sometimes the mail would be late or get lost. Sometimes I received the invoice but misplaced it. This was not a very surefire system with which to pay bills. Another good reason to use AutoPay is that some payees and creditors offer discounts to their customers if they use it as their payment method, especially if the payment is drafted from the customer's checking account or charged to a debit card. The payee usually doesn't pay a fee if you use either of these two methods. You may also use a cash-back credit card as your method of payment. You may or may not have to pay a fee, but you can get cash-back rewards for using that credit card to pay your bill. For example, my cell phone provider will take $20 a month off your bill if you AutoPay using your checking account or a debit card. Or you can use the credit card that the provider company sponsors to get the discount. When you AutoPay a bill with a checking or savings account instead of a credit card, you will generally pay lower service fees. If you use AutoPay with a credit card to get cash back (say 2 percent) and do not pay off the credit card balance every month, your payment can sit on your credit card, accumulating high interest that can easily negate any cash back you might receive. Another advantage to AutoPay using your checking or savings account (or debit card) is that checking, and savings accounts don't expire, as a credit card would, so you don't have to update your payment method.

To get the benefits of AutoPay, some payees require that you also sign up for paperless correspondence and statements. In addition, be sure to set up email notification so that you are made aware when automatic payments are to be made and when they have been made. You can specify email notification for AutoPays that you set up using online bill pay or by logging into the creditor's Website with your account. As you begin automating your bill payment to creditors, be sure they have a good email address, and pay close attention to your inbox. You can potentially run into problems with AutoPay when you think you've got it all set up, and the creditor you are trying to pay automatically thinks otherwise.

Setting Up Automatic Bill Paying (AutoPay)

Most AutoPay methods use Electronic Funds Transfer (EFT) to draw from your checking account on a predetermined date or within a date range each month. Once you've set up AutoPay, you might receive a letter from your insurance company stating that your "policy premiums are being paid by automatic monthly bank draft," which is a form of EFT. Or you may receive a statement from your utility company stating the "The total amount due is $250 and Autopay will occur on 06/25/2023." Inter-bank transfers use another form of EFT called Automated Clearing House (ACH), which is the network that connects all U.S. financial institutions so they can transfer money between banks.

There are basically four ways to set up AutoPay depending on your goals and the needs of the payee. Refer to Table 6-2.

Table 6-2: AutoPay Options and Methods

Method	From > To	Via	Pmt. Method Code
1 - EFT-1	Checking > Payee	Login Bank Online set up *A/P	A/P & EFT Chkg Acct X9999
2 - EFT-2	Checking > Payee (draft acct)	Payee authorized (Website or Ph.)	A/P & EFT Chkg Acct X9999
3 - Check/Mail	Checking > Payee	Login Bank Online set up A/P	A/P & Mail Check Chkg Acct. X9999
4 - Credit Card	Payee > Charges your Credit Card	Payee authorized (Website or Ph.)	A/P & Charge CC# X9999

Abbreviations:
A/P = AutoPay, **EFT** = Electronic Funds Transfer, **Chkg** = Checking, **Sav** = Savings, **CC** = Credit Card, **X9999** = last 4 digits of Chkg or CC acct #, **Ph** = Phone

Example Using Method 3, Check/Mail (A/P & Mail Check Chkg Acct. X9999)

The bill/payee will be paid automatically each month a set amount (determined by you), and will be mailed a check drawn on your checking account. Allow five days for the check to arrive.

Use the Personal Financial Spreadsheet (PFS) sheet Income-Exp to enter how you pay each bill in the "Payment Method" column and, if it is AutoPay, indicate the account paid from (last four digits) and whether it is paid by EFT, check, or credit card. For EFT-based methods of payment, you may also include the day of the month (or range) when it is drawn (debited). See "How Paid Code" entries above. Also make a note of how the AutoPay transaction that you've set up will appear on your bank statement. It is not always obvious that the name imbedded in the transaction code is the one you've authorized. Be sure to take note of the pay date when using online bill pay or AutoPay.

AutoPay Setup Example
Let's say you want to AutoPay the premium for your life insurance. You have implemented a policy with a consistent payment for a ten-year term. This example is the perfect candidate for an AutoPay bill. The payment is the same from month to month for 10 years and the penalty for missing a payment is policy cancellation, so you don't want to miss a payment. To setup AutoPay, you can login to your online banking Website or use a mobile banking app. Specify the following information to AutoPay your life insurance policy premium (example):

- Payee you wish to pay
- Recurring Payment
- Account (checking or savings) you wish to pay from
- Amount you wish to pay
- Date you wish to start
- Frequency (monthly, bi-weekly, quarterly, etc.)
- Duration (e.g., "Until I cancel" or "Specified number of transactions").

You can experiment with the settings and options if you don't finalize the selections you've made and any information you may have entered. These are generic guidelines, and the required steps for your bank will likely vary. In addition to setting up AutoPay, you can also set up an e-mail reminder to be sent to you to remind you to make a payment. When setting up AutoPay, be sure and take note of how the payment will be made (electronic or mail) and how many days from the current date the pay date is. The due date may be a problem if your payment is mailed, and it takes five days to reach the payee.

AutoPay Setup Verification
After setting up AutoPay with a creditor, it may take a few weeks until you see the results. Pay close attention to your billing statements (mailed or paperless) for that creditor over the next month or so to verify that AutoPay is in effect. You should see some wording on the first page of your statement that indicates that the bill is being paid by AutoPay (e.g., "Total Due by Auto Pay"). You may not see a "Payment Due Date" but instead a date on which AutoPay will be processed. For example, on a utility bill, it might say

"$200 will be automatically drafted from your designated account on 6/25/23." Also, be sure to check the statement for your bank checking account being debited or the credit card to which the auto payment is being charged. Make sure that the AutoPay debit (deduction) or the credit card charge is showing up on your statements.

Note: Getting a bill from a creditor that I know I've set up on AutoPay is actually kind of a pleasurable experience. I open the envelope and it tells me that the bill has already been paid or will be paid on a given date and all I have to do is review the bill to make sure it's accurate and then file it. It also helps to make sure I've got enough money in the account to cover the bill.

AutoPay Account Selection and Overdrafts
There are a couple of things to be aware of with AutoPay. If you specify a checking account to be debited for payment of a bill and the funds are insufficient, it could overdraw the account, unless you have overdraft protection and a backup account linked so that funds can be transferred to cover the overdraft. Some types of payee accounts are better candidates for AutoPay than others. In general, you want to automate payment of accounts that are mandatory (required) and fixed payment (same amount) or variable (varies a little):

Monthly mandatory/fixed payments (the payment is required and does not vary)
• Home Mortgage (Incl: Principal, Interest, Property taxes, Homeowner's Insurance)
• Rent payment
• Vehicle loan payment
• Personal loan payment
• Student loan payment
• Insurance premium (Auto, Life, Health, Long-Term Care)
• Home Security payment
• Homeowners' Association (HOA) Dues

Monthly mandatory/variable payments (The payment is required and varies, but not much.)
• Utilities: Gas and Electric
• Utilities: Water and Sewer
• Trash and Recycling
• Cell phone bill
• Internet/TV

Some people might recommend automated payment of credit card bills but the amount owed and paid each month can be as little as the minimum payment due to the full balance. Since the payment amount can vary considerably, it may lead to over drafting an account. Your handling of credit card statements and payments is critical to maintaining a great good credit rating and avoiding unnecessary penalties and fees. So you may want to get more involved when paying a credit card bill in order to have more visibility and direct control and ensure that you are paying what you intend to pay and have budgeted for.

Note: Setting up a creditor for AutoPay assumes that you have adequate funds in your chosen payment account to avoid overdrafts.

Opening a Checking Account

The requirements for opening a checking or savings account can vary from bank to bank. But, in general, you must have the following:

- **Proof of ID** (driver's license, passport, or other photo ID)
- **Social Security Number (**or Employee Identification Number)
- **Proof of address** (showing name and address of current residence, e.g., utility bill)
- **Initial deposit (**if required)

ChexSystems and the Fair Credit Reporting Act (FCRA)

If you have difficulty opening a checking account due to past financial issues, you can contact the nationwide specialty consumer reporting agency called ChexSystems, which operates under the Fair Credit Reporting Act (FCRA). This agency tracks problem consumer checking account activity and reports it to U.S. banks and credit unions. People with significant checking account difficulties and account closures are reported by ChexSystems to banks to assist them in making decisions on opening new accounts. As an example, if you have had an account closed for writing too many NSF (non-sufficient funds) checks, you will likely have a negative entry in your ChexSystems records. Many people don't even know they have a ChexSystems file. However, the FCRA allows consumers to access their ChexSystems report for free once every twelve months. You can request a copy of your ChexSystems report online at: https://www.chexsystems.com

If negative account activity is reported in your file, you may be able to contest it. If you've not had any issues opening accounts, your report will likely show no negative activity. In addition to obtaining your report, you can access a lot of good financial educational information.

Automated Transfer to Savings (See Chapter 7: Savings and Banking Services)

Just as you can set up automatic payments of bills, you can (and should) set up automatic payments to yourself (Emergency Fund, Short/Long term savings) (See Chapter 7). You can also set up regular transfers to one or more investment accounts, either with your bank or external organizations.

Automated transfer to investments (See Chapter 13: Investing Basics)

Just as you can set up automatic transfers to multiple savings accounts, you can also set up regular transfers to one or more investment accounts, either with your bank or external organizations.

Account Automation Ratio

With a basic checking account, you can automate important financial transactions to save time and money and potentially improve your credit rating (See Chapter 8: Credit Scores and Credit Reports). It is important to keep track of the degree to which you have been able to automate your checking account transactions

(Payments, Deposits, and Transfers). This is sometimes referred to as Account Automation Ratio (AAR) with respect to your checking account and includes the following types of transactions.

- **Automatic payments to creditors**
- **Automatic deposits of payroll checks**
- **Automatic withdrawals for savings/investments**

The focus here is mainly on the number of monthly bills you have set up for AutoPay. Take the number of AutoPay monthly payments you currently have set up and divide by the number of current payee accounts that potentially could be set up on AutoPay. So, if you currently have twelve regular payees (fixed and variable), and you have set up six of them on AutoPay, your account automation ratio is 50 percent, which is a good initial goal. Your long-term goal is to have AutoPay, Auto deposit, and Auto deduction for your payees and accounts where it is appropriate. It takes time to set up AutoPay for regular payments to your payees, but it is worth it because it saves you a lot of time down the road. It can also improve your on-time payment record with the three credit bureaus (Equifax Experian and TransUnion). Over time this can improve your credit rating. Try setting up one or two payees per week to spread it out into smaller, more manageable chunks. Refer to **Exercise 6-2: Automate Bank Accounts (Payments, Deposits, and Transfers)** at the end of this chapter, which will help you identify those checking account transactions that can be automated.

Checking - Tips and Summary Notes
Note: The use of actual checks is declining rapidly in favor of more convenient payment methods. However, there are still a lot of check-based transactions going through our banking systems and a few cautionary notes are still warranted. Whether you use checks or not, it still comes back to your checking account and how to best manage it.

- **Check your bank account daily.** It's a good idea to get into the habit of logging on to your account once a day to check your balances and transactions and avoid surprises. With today's online banking apps, it only takes a few minutes. This may seem a little extreme, but it keeps you tuned in to your money, helps to spot unusual transactions, and may help you sleep better at night. You can also check your main bill paying account to verify that the bills you've paid previously are queued for payment. A good example of how logging in daily helped me was when I had paid a credit card balance on one day and then accidentally paid it again the following day. Normally the bank's online system would warn you, and let you know that you were about to pay the same payee the same amount twice. However, the first transaction was on one day and the second transaction was on the next day, so they allowed the duplicate payment, even though the payment amount was identical. Since I log into my account once a day, I spotted the error and called the credit card company. They reversed the second payment, and it didn't cause a problem with an overdraft. This little mistake could have cost me several fees had I not caught it.
- **Do not allow yourself to be on another person's account (joint).** This applies especially to family members, except (perhaps) your spouse or possibly a parent and teenage child. With a joint

account, if the account is overdrawn (goes negative) and the primary account holder does not cover it, the bank can tap into any other accounts that you or the primary account holder has with the bank. This "right to offset" gives the bank the right to apply "other" deposited funds to cover the overdraft. Even though it may not be your account, they can report your information to a consumer reporting agency and/or to a third-party debt collection agency, which can harm your credit rating.

- **Do not keep checks in your wallet.** Well, maybe one or two checks is OK. Some small businesses do not accept credit cards, and you may not have enough cash to cover the purchase. If you do keep a check in your wallet, be sure to write the check number and date in your check register so that you can update the register with the date, payee, and amount. If you lose your wallet, you should contact the bank and request a "stop payment" for the check in your wallet. Unfortunately, there may be a fee ($30 or more) to do this.

- **Do not keep your check book in your organizer or purse.** I used to keep mine in my organizer, but I lost the organizer and had to close the account and open a new one. Fortunately, no checks had been written on the account before I closed it.

- If someone takes one or more of your checks, they can impersonate you, writing a check that may not clear your account, but you will be held responsible. In some states, writing bad checks is a misdemeanor or a felony depending on the amount and number of checks written. The authorities may come after you to make them good, even if you say you did not write them. Thieves of personal or business checks may take a few checks from the back of the check book, so they won't be noticed. It could take weeks before it is discovered that the checks are missing.

- **Always enter checks written into your checking account register.** This may seem obvious, but it is a common mistake, especially if you carry one or more in your wallet. It is best to enter each check at the time it is written. It is easy to forget that you wrote a check, who it was written to, or the exact amount. Also, be sure to enter online payments, deposits, and transfers in the check register as you make them. Tips on how to use your account register are usually included in the register itself.

- **Be sure to review your banking statement each month.** It is easy to just file these away and ignore them. You might be surprised that some unauthorized charges have shown up, or you were charged some banking fees that you were unaware of. You can always call the bank and contest (argue with them over) questionable fees. They may not waive the fees but at least you will be aware of what's going on and perhaps avoid them in the future. If you are balancing your account on a monthly basis, you will generally spot these types of questionable charges.

- **Balance your checking account once a month.** By doing this, you are not trying to catch banking errors but trying to monitor your balance and outstanding checks that you have written but which haven't cleared the bank. Instructions on how to balance your account are usually included on your monthly statement.

- **When reordering checks, select the cheapest ones available.** If your account provides complimentary checks, this is not an issue.

- **Open a student account if you are going to school full-time.** Student accounts can help to establish credit and may have reduced fees.

- **Consider not including your phone number on your checks**. For privacy purposes.
- **Check the balance in your account online before writing a check.** Of course, if you are checking your account daily, this may not be necessary. But always make sure you have enough to cover any checks written and, if checking your balance account online, be sure to take into account any other checks written in your check register that may not be posted to your account yet.
- **If someone writes you a check, cash it at their bank**. If possible, take the check to their bank and cash it, rather than deposit it into your account. If they do not have sufficient funds to cover the check, you will find out immediately. If they do have sufficient funds to cover the check, you will have the cash in hand. Otherwise, if you deposit it into your account and the check fails to clear, you will be charged a return check fee by your bank!
- **Avoid using a debit card with your checking account**. If possible, use a debit card for ATM cash withdrawal only. This is addressed further in Chapters 8 and 9, the credit card chapters. If you lose your debit card, someone can drain your checking account very quickly.
- **Do not allow overdrafts with a debit card and checking account.** It's best to not use a debit card with your checking account, but if you do, be sure to opt out of the "overdraft coverage" service for your checking account. It sounds good but can cost you a lot of money as described in the "bad check" scenarios that follow. Be sure to check how much the overdraft coverage will cost if you overdraw on your account. Also, find out how long you have to correct the overdraft.
- **Use caution when allowing a company to set up auto-withdrawal (drafting) from your checking account**. Once they start, it can be difficult to get them to stop and it's easy to forget the withdrawals are coming out of your account unless you are checking your statements regularly. Although most organizations are reputable, once they have your authorization, they can take pretty much what they want from your account. For example, you could join a fitness club and allow them to deduct the monthly membership fee from your account. However, if they go out of business, they can still debit your account. Additionally, if you close the checking account, you may not remember the auto-deduction that was being taken out, and it will be treated as if you wrote a bad check.
- **Note:** If you do allow auto-deduction from your checking account (like for a monthly insurance payment), be sure to add a note for the account in your PFS Income-Exp sheet. When paying bills using online bill pay, it's easy to forget the auto-deductions and accidentally overdraft an account, triggering an overdraft (OD) fee. I just had this happen and got charged $37, even though I had a deposit the same day. Luckily, I called the bank, and they waived (reversed) the OD fee because I was a good customer.
- **Request an ATM only card (if available).** This is not a debit or credit card and can only be used to withdraw cash from ATMs and requires a Personal Identification Number (PIN). It cannot be used to drain your checking account unless the thief knows your PIN.
- **Avoid the "Early Access" paycheck feature if there is a fee.** Some banks offer a service that allows you to request an advance on your next paycheck direct deposit into your checking account. This sounds good but can result in a very rapid increase in debt. The interest charged with an advance can be as much as 10 percent of the amount you borrow (a dollar for every ten dollars borrowed each time you take an advance). Early access that charges a fee can turn out to be a very expensive

form of credit and should only be used in situations where you need funds quickly and do not have access to less expensive forms of credit. It is only available in certain states. That said, there are banks that now provide an early access service for free as long as you have your paycheck auto deposited.

- **Avoid "Immediate Funds" check deposit feature if there is a fee.**
- When depositing a check using a mobile banking app, the deposit normally goes into a "pending" state, and you must wait a couple of days for the funds to become available. Some banks offer an option during the deposit process that allows you to have immediate access to the funds, but you may be charged a fee to do this of usually about 1 percent. As an example, I just received a check in the mail for my state income tax refund. The amount of the check was about $1,000 (appx). I took pictures of the front and back of the check using the app on my smartphone, and when I was about ready to submit the deposit, it gave me an opportunity to get immediate access to the funds for a fee of 1 percent or ten dollars. I did not use this option and when I checked the account balance a few minutes later, it showed the mobile deposit I just made as "pending." I could have had immediate access to the $1,000, but it would have cost me ten dollars to do so. It is not likely that the State of Ohio would write a bad check, so I chose to wait for the check to clear and it cleared the next day.
- **Avoid Non-Sufficient Funds (NSF) Fees.** These overdraft (OD) or "bounced check" fees can be substantial and can also apply when using a debit card that is declined. The merchant can charge you a fee, and your bank will charge you an NSF fee. The bank's fees will immediately lower your account balance so that when a small check you wrote hits your account, it could also bounce, triggering another NSF fee. It's a vicious cycle, and the banks make a lot of money off people who do not manage their bank accounts well enough to avoid NSF and associated fees.
- **Consider a bank that gives you a twenty-four-hour "grace" period on overdrafts.** Various banks and other financial institutions are increasingly offering this service to their customers that have checking accounts. It is basically "overdraft forgiveness". Check with your bank to see if they offer the service and find out what the conditions and limits are. An overdraft grace period allows you to transfer or deposit money to cover the overage, if less than a certain dollar amount (usually $50). You are usually allowed until the end of the following day to make a deposit. If you can make a deposit the bank may waive the overdraft fee (currently about $35). This does not apply to returned check fees, however. Check with your bank to find out what their policies are. They may also offer checking with no fees or minimum balance.
- **Try calling the bank to waive fees for overdrafts and late payments.** If you are a good customer and do not have a history of overdrafts, you may be able to contact the bank or other creditor on missed payments or overdrafts and request that they waive the late fees. Some banks will do this for you, so it's worth a call. What have you got to lose? I missed a house payment and called the bank and asked them to waive the late fee. Since I had been a customer for a long time and did not have any bad marks on my record, they waived the late fee. If you frequently overdraft your account, or miss payments, they will likely not work with you.

Chapter 6 Exercises

Exercise 6-1: Compare Banking Features

To assist you in researching banks, you can set up a comparison table. Look through the services and checking account and other features, listed here, that banks can offer in addition to basic checking and savings accounts. These can include interest rates for auto and home loans, and other features that may be of value to you. Select several banks and/or credit unions to see which ones have the best features. Make a copy of Table 6-3 and use it as an example of what to look for and to record your findings.

Table 6-3: Banking Features Comparison (Form)

Banking Feature	Bank 1	Bank 2	Bank 3
Smartphone mobile banking app (Free)			
Checking acct fees			
Free online bill paying (Web/Mobile)			
Cashier's check fee			
New auto loan interest rate			
1-year CD rate			
Cost for personal checks			
Credit APR, fees and cash back			
ATM Fees (non-bank)			
Account types (checking, savings, MMA)			
Access to free credit score/report			

Exercise 6-2: Automate Bank Accounts (Payments, Deposits, and Transfers)

With a basic checking account, you can automate important financial transactions to save time and money while reducing the possibility of late or missed payments. This exercise will help you identify those checking account transactions that can be automated, such as: payments, deposits, and transfers. There are three parts to the exercise, and it is recommended to do each part in a separate session.

Part A: Set up Automatic Payroll Deposit (Paycheck Direct Deposit)

If you are working and receive a paycheck and have a checking account, consider setting up direct deposit if you have not already done so. Check with your bank to see what benefits this may afford you, in addition to early access to funds.

Part B: Set Up Automatic Payment (AutoPay) of Recurring Bills

The goal for Part B is to set up at least one of your required fixed amount "payee" accounts for automatic payment (e.g., Auto loan, Insurance premium, Utility bill, or HOA dues). Make a copy of your PFS Income-Exp sheet (Chapter 3) and highlight those expenses/payees that are required and have a fixed or relatively consistent monthly payment amount. These are the best candidates for AutoPay. Use one of the following methods discussed in the chapter (See Table 6-2):

1. **Fixed Payment AutoPay:** Login to your account on your bank's Website to set up online bill pay to automatically draft your checking account and send the monthly payment to the payee (electronic or check). Be sure you have enough funds in your account to cover the payment amount, and select a payment date accordingly.
2. **Variable Payment AutoPay** (if payment is fairly consistent): Login to your account on your payee's Website to set up AutoPay and authorize them to draft (debit) your checking account for the monthly amount or charge the monthly bill to a specified credit card.

Try to reach an Account Automation Ratio of 50 percent. Your long-term goal is to have AutoPay for fixed expenses, Auto Deposit for income sources, and Auto Deduction for regular transfers to savings and investment accounts.

Part C: Set Up Automated Transfers to Savings
The goal for Part C is to set up and/or add to a savings account. If you do not have an emergency fund, take this opportunity to set one up. If you have one, you can set up an automatic monthly transfer to it from your checking account or through automatic payroll deduction, if available. If your emergency fund is already at the level you need (like six times your monthly required expenses), you can allocate a portion of the emergency fund account that is over your desired level to a secondary short- or long-term savings goal (you can use the same account but just track the secondary savings separately).

Notes:

_____
_____
_____
_____

Chapter 7
Savings and Banking Services

Chapter Overview:

This chapter describes the different types of savings accounts and various services and products that banking institutions can offer. Part 1 of the chapter focuses on savings in general and "regular" savings accounts with a few variations, and useful tips on savings are included. Alternatives to regular savings accounts, such as certificates of deposit (CDs), money market accounts (MMAs), and savings bonds are covered as well. Automated savings and Automatic Savings (round-up) apps are also introduced as passive, painless ways to save. Part 2 focuses on banking services and explains some of the most common supplemental products and services offered by banks and other financial institutions. Many notes and tips as well as best practices regarding savings accounts are provided.

- **Part 1: Savings Accounts and Cash Equivalents**
- **Part 2: Banking Services and Products**

Chapter PFS and PFI Integration:

The Personal Financial Spreadsheet (PFS) components in this chapter that relate to savings are found primarily on the Assets, Liabilities and Net Worth sheet (Tab Assets-Liab) and consist mainly of savings assets like Emergency Funds (EF) savings accounts, CDs and MMAs, as well as the 401Ks, and 403B retirement accounts that can be with your bank or other financial institutions. Personal Financial Indicators (PFIs) that pertain to this chapter include the following, which were introduced in Chapters 3, 4 and 5. These key savings related PFIs are included here for review along with the chapters in which they were introduced.

Savings-Related PFIs Review:

- **PFI 3-4: Personal Cash Flow (PCF) ($)** (Chapter 3)
  Total Monthly Net Income minus (-) Total Monthly Expenses = PCF ($)

- **PFI 3-5: Potential Saving Ratio (PSR) (%)** (Chapter 3)
  Total Monthly NI minus (-) Total Monthly Exp) / Monthly NI = PSR (%)

- **PFI 4-1: Saving-to-Income (STI) Ratio (%)** (Chapter 4)
  Saving/Invest Monthly Contrib. divided by (/) Monthly Gross Income = STI (%)
  (Incl. savings accts, 401Ks, IRAs, CDs, MMAs, etc. Exclude EF)

- **PFI 4-2: Emergency Fund Goal (EFG) ($)** (Chapter 4)
  Monthly Required Expenses x 6 = EFG ($)

- **PFI 5-1: Personal Net Worth (PNW) ($)** (Chapter 5)

Total Assets (Equity) minus (-) Total Liabilities (Debt) = PNW ($)

- **PFI 5-2: Emergency Fund-to-Expenses (EFE) (%)** (Chapter 5)
  Current EF Balance divided by (/) (Monthly Required Expenses x 6) = EFE (%)

- **PFI 5-3: Liquid Assets-to-Expenses Projection (LAE) (%)** (Chapter 4)
  Total Liquid Assets divided by (/) (Monthly Required Expenses = LAE (#Mo.)

Chapter Exercises:
- **Exercise 7-1: Compare Automatic Savings Apps**
- **Exercise 7-2: Compare Banking Products and Services**
- **Exercise 7-3: Compare HELOC Lenders**

Chapter Notable Quote:
Quote 7-1: "The habit of saving is itself an education. It fosters every virtue, teaches self-denial, cultivates the sense of order, trains to forethought, and so broadens the mind." - T. T. Munger

Part 1: Savings Accounts and Cash Equivalents

There are several forms of savings available from banks and other financial institutions. These are sometimes referred to as "Cash equivalents" and can include the following:

- **Regular Bank Savings** - More liquidity, lower interest, no penalties, FDIC insured.
- **Online Bank "high-interest" Savings** - Less liquidity, higher interest, no penalties, FDIC insured.
- **Certificates of Deposit (CDs)** - Less liquidity, higher interest, timed, potential penalties, FDIC insured.
- **Money Market Accounts (MMAs)** - More liquidity, higher interest, potential penalties, FDIC insurance varies.
- **U.S. Savings Bonds** - Less liquidity, higher interest, potential penalties, FDIC insured.

Keep in mind that the interest earned on savings accounts (any of the above) is usually taxable. The interest paid on an investment such as a CD or savings bond is referred to as Annual Percentage Yield (APY). The interest rate you pay on money borrowed is expressed as Annual Percentage Rate (APR). So APY applies to the money you invest (yield), and APR applies to the money you borrow (loans).

Savings and Your Emergency Fund ("Rainy Day" Fund)
Many Americans would not be able to handle a $1,000 unexpected emergency expense, unless they were able to charge it to a credit card or possibly sell some valuables. This is due largely to the fact that they do not have much, if any, cash reserves in an emergency fund or "rainy-day" fund. The importance of the emergency fund has been stressed in previous chapters, but we will review it here, along with savings in general, in the "savings chapter." A major benefit to saving is the associated peace of mind. Any savings are

better than none. The best approach for most people is to set aside a certain amount from each paycheck or have it automatically deducted and transferred to a savings account. Also transfer a set amount to an investment account, like a 401K, if possible, although this money would not be considered part of your rainy-day fund. Most people who save, especially with automated methods, say they do not miss the money, and they tend to forget it is there until they need it.

How much savings should you have for rainy days? Some financial advisors recommend that you calculate your required fixed and variable expenses per month and multiply them by six to cover six months' worth. So, if you have $2,000 of monthly expenses, you should try to build your rainy day or emergency savings up to about $12,000 of cash reserves. That might seem like a tall order, so maybe you want to set a goal of three months' savings, then maybe five months, and finally, six months. Six months may seem too daunting for some people, and they will not even attempt to start saving, so the abovementioned strategy makes sense. Chapter 13: Investing Basics, and Chapter 14: Retirement Requirements, provide additional information on the rainy-day emergency funds and their importance in helping to protect your retirement nest egg.

Figure 7-1: Your Rainy-Day Emergency Fund

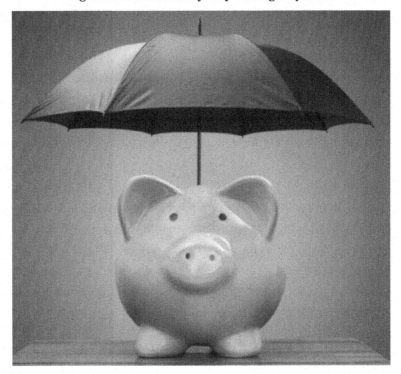

Regular Savings Accounts

A regular savings account is a highly liquid asset that is an essential part of your financial portfolio. Note that some bricks-and-mortar banks charge a monthly service fee unless you have a checking account with them or maintain a certain level of deposits. Monthly service fees can eat away at your savings, especially with the low interest rates currently paid by most bank savings accounts. Check with your bricks-and-mortar bank and ask how much interest, if any, they are paying on a regular basic savings account (what used to be called a "passbook" savings account in the old days). You might be surprised. Regular savings accounts are insured for up to $250,000 per depositor, per account ownership, per financial institution account by the FDIC. You may not make any money but will not likely lose any either. It's just a safe place to park your cash. I keep a regular savings account with a small amount with the same bank as my checking as a backup for my emergency savings and for quick transfers if needed.

Online High-Yield Savings Accounts

The two main things to remember with savings accounts are 1) save regularly and 2) make sure you are getting a competitive interest rate. Also make sure the money in the account is safe and readily available. Online savings accounts typically pay higher interest rates for savings than bricks and mortar banks and are commonly referred to as "high-yield" savings accounts. However, it is usually easier to access the regular bank savings account since the funds are immediately available. You can stop in at a branch and get cash from your savings from a teller or an ATM. With online high-yield savings accounts, you generally need to request a transfer to one of your linked bricks-and-mortar bank accounts, which can take a couple of days for the funds to be available. As an example, I have my rainy-day savings in a reputable high-yield account that pays a relatively high interest rate. I have linked this account to one of my regular checking accounts and can transfer money when I need to with about a day or two's delay. You can check with Bankrate or other source to see which banks are paying the best rates on savings accounts. If your online bank lowers its rate, or another bank offers a higher rate, you can move your savings from one account to the other with no fee. You can set up multiple savings accounts to keep track of different buckets of money. However, rather than setting up multiple accounts, you can use a simple spreadsheet to keep track of the money you put into a single savings account. As you put money into the savings account, you can enter amounts on the spreadsheet and separate it into different buckets, like "rainy day," "vacations," or "new car."

Automated Savings

A variation of the regular savings account is Automated Savings, where you have a set amount of money transferred to a savings account on a regular basis (usually monthly), which basically puts your savings on autopilot. You can have money transferred to an existing savings account (such as your emergency fund) from a checking account or other account. You can also have a set amount transferred from an auto-deposit paycheck or other source. Once you set up the "from" and "to" accounts, the automated transfer takes place behind the scenes, and before you know it, you can have a substantial amount put aside. Most people forget that it's happening and don't even miss the money.

Automatic Savings Apps (Round-Up)

Increasingly, banks are paying little or no interest on regular savings accounts. Some banks have stopped offering regular savings accounts altogether. Most banks still offer timed savings accounts like CDs and MMAs. These can pay reasonable interest, but they require you to park your money for a set period (usually one to five years), or you may get less interest and may incur a penalty. Automatic savings apps are becoming increasingly popular as an alternative to the regular savings account and can be a fairly painless means of saving while earning some interest on the money you set aside.

An automatic savings app is a smart phone app tool known as a "robo-advisor" or "round-up" app. It provides an automated way to save loose change. The app rounds up your purchases on linked credit or debit cards, then moves the change into a savings account or investment account. There are several of these apps available for download. They can provide hands-free behind-the-scenes savings and investment by automatically rounding up to a predetermined dollar amount when you make a purchase. For example, you can set the round-up amount to five dollars for linked credit cards using the app. If you make a purchase for four dollars, it is rounded up to five dollars, and one dollar is deposited into your account. Be aware that there may be fees and minimums associated with these automated saving tools. Do a search for "automatic saving apps," and you will find various apps and reviews/ratings of apps done by companies such as Bankrate, Forbes, NerdWallet, and others.

Budgeting and Savings with Bank Apps

Budgeting and savings are closely related. Budgeting is basically a form of cash flow management with a focus on savings, how much you spend, and in what areas. Many banks offer smart phone apps that help you plan and keep to a budget. Using the app, you can track your monthly spending in various categories and identify areas where you may need to reduce spending to achieve your savings goals. There are a number of low-cost and no-cost budgeting calculators that you can download to create a **budget** plan. Refer to Chapter 4: Budgets and Frugal Living for more information on budgeting and related financial apps. Also, check with your bank to see what they have in the way of budgeting and savings apps.

Mobile Financial App Types

It is important to understand the different types of mobile financial (smartphone) apps that are available and that are covered in this book. Although there is some overlap in functionality between the different products available, there are three distinct categories of mobile smartphone financial apps.

1) **Mobile Banking Apps** (See Chapter 6): Smartphone versions (iOS/Android) of computer-based Desktop and Laptop applications for online Web-based banking. Most major banks have developed these apps and provide them free to their customers to do regular banking tasks remotely. I use a banking app on my iPhone to monitor my accounts, pay bills, make deposits, send money, and transfer funds (on a secure network).

2) **Automatic Savings Apps** (See Chapter 7): Independently developed software "round-up" apps for automated (background) saving and investing. Three of the more popular apps of this type are Acorns, Chime, and Quapital. All these apps run on iOS and Android and are listed in alphabetical order. Their appearance here is not an endorsement. Refer to **Exercise 7-1: Compare Automatic Savings Apps** at the end of this chapter, which will help you identify and compare those automatic savings apps that are of interest to you.

3) **Budgeting/Financial Apps** (See Chapter 4): Independently developed software apps for setting up and managing budgets to track expenses and manage debt. They can also provide centralized management for bank accounts and investment accounts as well as basic retirement planning.

Certificates of Deposit - CDs (Timed Savings)

Another major product offered by most banks is a form of timed savings known as the Certificate of Deposit or CD. A CD is a form of savings where a specific dollar amount is deposited for a specific period of time. CDs have a fixed maturity date and a fixed interest rate. Access to the funds is limited until the maturity date. CDs are subject to early withdrawal fees that can be quite substantial. Also, the CD may auto-renew at a lower rate if you allow the maturity date renewal period to lapse. Check with your banking institution to see what time periods and rates are available. To see which banks are offering the highest yields or rates, you can go to https://www.bankrate.com or another Website. CDs are not a very liquid form of asset. The time period or "term" for a CD is typically six months to five years. If you choose to buy CDs, be sure you can leave the money alone for the required time period. Note that all CDs impose penalties for early withdrawal. CDs are insured for up to $250,000 per person, per account ownership type, per financial institution, by the FDIC. Also, the longer time period CDs that pay higher rates usually require a higher minimum deposit to open the CD.

Features to look for in a CD purchase include these:
- Competitive Annual Percentage Yield (APY)
- Low minimum deposit ($1,000 or less)
- Term options from 60 to 120 months (five to ten years)
- Interest compounded daily and credited monthly
- Automatic notifications prior to maturity
- FDIC insured to the maximum allowable

Money Market Accounts – MMAs (Timed Savings)

A money market account (MMA) is another form of timed savings (usually six months to five years) that falls into the "cash equivalents" category. It has moderate liquidity and usually earns higher interest than a regular savings account. A money market fund is a mutual fund that invests in money market securities that are mostly short-term debt securities. Money markets can be volatile and are not FDIC insured, so you could lose money (although not very likely). MMAs can also provide limited check-writing ability. The minimum deposit and minimum balance for this type of account is normally considerably higher than those for a basic savings account.

U.S. Savings Bonds (Timed Savings)

Savings bonds are debt securities issued by the U.S. Department of the Treasury to help pay for the U.S. government's borrowing needs. U.S. savings bonds are considered one of the safest investments because they are backed by the U.S. government. Savings Bonds can be purchased directly from the federal government at https://www.treasurydirect.gov.

There are two main types: Series "EE" bonds with a fixed interest rate, and Series "I" bonds with an inflation-adjusted interest rate. Bonds are normally kept for a minimum of one year to normal full maturity of five years, with less interest if redeemed early. When redeemed, the interest gained is federally taxed by the IRS; however, they are exempt from state and local taxes. I Bonds are thirty-year bonds with a variable interest rate that changes every six months based on the Consumer Price Index (CPI). Check with your financial advisor and ask if "EE" or "I" bonds could be a worthwhile addition to your portfolio.

Health Savings Accounts (HSA) and Flexible Spending Accounts (FSA)
Both HSAs and medical FSAs are special tax-deferred savings accounts that allow you to put aside money to be used for qualified medical expenses. The main difference is that an FSA is established by an employer, whereas the HSA can be established by an individual. Talk to your employer's human resources representative to see what options may be available. There is a wealth of information on the Internet comparing the HSA and FSA. Search the Web for information regarding eligibility and setup requirements as well as what is covered and what happens to the money set aside if it is not all spent on health care costs.

Savings - Summary Notes and Tips
- **Download a savings/budgeting app to help you save and manage your expenses.**
- **Establish a savings account with a higher interest rate.**
- Online savings institutions and credit unions typically offer higher interest rates than a regular bank savings account. In addition to your higher interest savings account, it's OK to have a regular bank savings account that is linked to your checking account as a backup for overdraft protection. You can put a small amount of money in this account and most of your money in the high interest account.
- **Invest your money if you can. If you cannot invest, at least save a percentage of each paycheck, with a high-yield online savings account.** Many banks allow you to set up an automatic transfer to a savings account. If you save regularly, it can build into quite a few dollars over time.
- **Put money into a savings account instead of the lottery.** Although playing the lottery can be fun, and you might actually win some cash, you'll probably have more money in the long run if you put it into savings.
- **For fun, put a dollar bill (or a five- or ten-dollar bill) into a bill changer at the car wash.** At least you know you will break even, and it makes you feel like you hit the jackpot! Do a video of you getting the coins while saying "I won! I won!"
- **Do not stash cash in your home.** Do not put it under a mattress or other hiding place, especially if people know where it is. Most home-item theft is by people you know, including family.
- **Feed the pig.** Provide a traditional piggy bank or other type of creative/fun container to encourage young people to save and get them used to handling money. They could take the money they earn from helping around the house and put it in the piggy bank, and you could allow them to keep a percentage to buy something. A large coffee tin with a plastic top also works well. They can paint it or paste stickers or decoupage it to personalize it and make it theirs. They could set a savings goal and take the money out periodically and count it. If they have achieved their goal, they can spend some of the money.
- **Take the spare change from your pockets at end of day and stash it.** Put the change in a mason jar or other container. If you think you might be tempted to tap into it, put it out of sight; otherwise, you

c

can watch it fill up. When full, take it to a store that has a change counting machine (many grocery stores do). It is amazing how much it can add up to over time. The machines will count your change and spit out the "rejected" coins (damaged or foreign). Most machines will charge about 10–15 percent of the value of the coins. You can avoid this fee if you count the coins yourself, put them into coin wrappers, and take them to a bank. However, this can be very tedious and time-consuming. I recently took a jar of coins that I had been collecting to a local grocery store change counting machine and cashed them in. It charged me 12 percent, and some of the coins were rejected (a few Canadian coins). The machine printed out a receipt for about a hundred dollars (not bad), which I took to the customer service counter and exchanged for cash. This same store offers banking-type money services such as check cashing, money orders, bill paying, and money transfer. Fees are charged, but they are less if you have a store card.

- **Take the one-dollar bills from your wallet at the end of the day and stash them.** If you want to be more aggressive than just stashing your spare change, at the end of the day, take the dollar bills from your wallet and put them in a cigar box or other container. We used to do this and called it the "Box-o-Bux." Each year, when our girls were young, we would take the money out at the start of summer and let them count it. It helped them to appreciate savings and how much it could add up to over time. In addition to the dollars from the box, we let them count the change from the jar and put it into coin wrappers. We would allow them to keep a certain percentage, and they could use it for spending money when we went on vacation.
- **Take the money that you would have spent or have saved on a purchase and stash it.** If you are thinking of buying something and decide you can do without it or you find it somewhere else cheaper, take the money you saved and stash it in your Box-o-Bux or somewhere.
- **When you've paid off a car, put the monthly payment in a savings account.**
- Continue making the same payment but put it into a savings account. You can use the money for auto maintenance or apply it to your next car purchase. Your budget will remain pretty much the same, since you are used to not having that money to spend.
- **Designate a month to be "Family Frugal."** Each year, establish a particular month as a month to be frugal, e.g., "Frugal February." During this month, try to use up the food in your refrigerator and your pantry, some of which you might have ended up throwing away. Try not to buy anything that is not necessary or spend money on things you do not really need. Avoid eating out if possible.
- **Do not be penny wise and pound foolish.** Although you can save a substantial amount over time, try not to focus on saving tiny amounts while spending large amounts. Another way to put it is "pinch dollars, not pennies."
- **A penny saved is a penny earned!** Although is hardly worth it to bend over and pick up a penny these days, it still helps to condition your thinking about money, and you can always throw it into the change jar!
- **Interest on most savings is taxable.** Keep this in mind when filing your taxes. Although you may not be getting much interest, the interest earned on most regular savings accounts is taxable. Banks are required to send the IRS a statement on interest and dividends.

- **Develop "Cash Awareness" by sorting the paper money in your wallet**. After you buy something, take the bills out of your wallet and sort them by denomination ($1, $5, $10, etc.), As you handle each bill, turn it over so that the president's face (the good side) is up and the back side is down. This helps develop an appreciation of the cash and increases your awareness of how much money you have. It also makes it easier to find the right bill for your next purchase.
- **Play a game with your friends called "Who's on the Bill,"** and see how many of the presidents you can name for each denomination, ($1, $2, $5, $10, $20, $50 and $100). Hint: For the hundred-dollar bill, it's all about the Benjamins!

Part 2: Banking Services and Products (in alphabetical order)

In addition to checking and savings accounts, most banks and financial institutions also offer other money-related products and services. The most common ones are listed here along with a brief description. These are included here to increase your financial vocabulary and awareness of the types of banking services available. They may or may not be applicable to your financial situation. They are listed here in alphabetical order. Refer to **Exercise 7-2: Compare Banking Products and Services** at the end of this chapter, which will help you identify and compare those products and services that are of interest to you.

Auto Loans

Most banks offer loans for new and used automobiles. Interest rates and the term of the loan vary depending on whether the car is new or used and the age of the car. The lowest rates can be obtained if you have an account with the bank. Also, the better your credit rating, the lower the interest rate. A down payment (10-20 percent) is also typically required. Go to the bank's Website or call them to find out what rates are available for new and used cars. Alternatives to bank car loans are available from credit unions, credit card companies, or loan companies, which the auto dealer can put you in touch with. These sources may have lower rates than banks.

Cashier's checks

A cashier's check is one obtained from a banking institution and is guaranteed. It is drawn on the bank's owns funds and is signed by a cashier. It is usually paid from an account you have with the bank. You may be charged a fee, depending on the type of checking account or other accounts you have with the bank. A cashier's check is treated as guaranteed funds by the recipient. Cashier's checks are similar to money orders but are backed by the bank.

Check Cashing

Most banks, credit unions, and other financial institutions offer check cashing services, although they may charge a fee. If you have an account with them, the fee may be waived or lowered. Remember, if someone writes you a personal check, take it to their bank to cash it, if possible, rather than deposit it.

Currency Exchange - International

Many banks offer currency exchange for a fee. For example, let's say you are planning on taking a trip from the U.S. to a European country. You could go to your bank and give them a number of U.S. dollars in exchange for some number of euros. The number of euros you would receive would be based on the current exchange rate and minus the bank's fee for the transaction. When you return from your trip, you may be able to exchange your euros for dollars, if you have enough left over. Note that not all banks or branches offer this service.

Financial Advisor Services

Many banks offer financial advice to their customers and may have a certified financial planner (CFP) available that you can meet with. They can help assess your financial needs and risk tolerance and recommend various investment options and portfolio diversification. As with any financial advisor, when working with bank financial advisors, ensure that they are a fiduciary, who is required by law to offer financial products that are appropriate and, in the client's best interest. Verify that they offer a wide range of investment options and not just their own products.

Home Mortgages

Most banks and many other financial institutions offer various types of mortgages for home purchase or refinancing. These include traditional fixed-rate mortgages of various terms (typically fifteen or thirty years) as well as three- or five-year Adjustable-Rate Mortgages (ARMs). They also can arrange for appraisals as well as closing and escrow services. Home mortgages are closely related to home equity loans and home equity lines of credit.

Home Equity Line of Credit (HELOC)

A HELOC (pronounced "HEELOCK") is a revolving line of credit, somewhat like a credit card, except that it is secured by your home as collateral. Not everyone can take advantage of a HELOC since it requires that you have a home, have built up enough equity (ownership) to qualify, and have good credit. Equity build-up can happen when you pay down your mortgage. It can also happen if you live in an area where home prices are increasing. With a HELOC, the lender approves you for a maximum amount you can borrow based on the amount of equity you have in your home and other factors. Strictly speaking, home equity is the appraised value of your home minus the mortgage balance. It is basically how much of your home you actually own. The bank or a mortgage lender owns the rest.

Home Equity = Appraised Value (-minus-) Mortgage Balance

Your home must be worth more than you owe to be considered for a HELOC, and one lender may approve you for a certain amount while another lender will approve you for less (or more), depending on the appraisal, your credit score, and other factors. Some lenders use more conservative home appraisers than others. You may think your home is worth $200,000, but if a certified real estate appraiser says it's worth $180,000, that's probably the number the bank will use, and the maximum amount you can borrow for the line of credit may be less than you thought.

You can typically borrow up to 80 percent of the equity in your home (appraised value minus the mortgage balance), although some lenders will go up to 85 percent. The example in Table 7-1 uses 80 percent. For example, let's say your home is worth $100,000 (AV = Appraised Value), and you owe $60,000 on the mortgage (MB = Mortgage Balance), you have $40,000 in equity (HE = Home Equity). Some people would think, I have $40,000 equity, I should be able to borrow 80 percent of that or $32,000 (HA = HELOC Amount). Some lenders will see it that way, but others may have a different way of calculating the maximum HELOC amount they will loan. Upon closing the loan, you can borrow up to the maximum HELOC amount with a variable interest rate and a negotiable repayment period of up to thirty years. Refer to Table 7-1 for a simple HELOC example.

Table 7-1: HELOC Calculation Example
(Formula: (AV – MB) = HE * 80%) = HA)

(AV) Appraised Value (of home)	$100,000
(MB) Mortgage Balance (minus)	-$60,000
(HE) Home Equity	= $40,000
(80 percent of Home Equity)	(.80 x 40,000)
(HA) HELOC Amount (Max)	= $32,000

In addition to ordering the appraisal, the lender commonly reviews your credit score, credit history, employment, and Debt-to-Income (DTI) ratio, as well as your Debt-to-Credit (DTC) and Housing-to-Income (HTI) ratios. You could talk to three different lenders and get differing requirements and maximum HELOC amounts for the same house. Be sure you understand how your lender calculates the HELOC amount for your home and compare it to other lenders. Contact your banker or other lender and ask them to explain how their HELOC works and what their requirements are.

Refer to **Exercise 7-3: Compare HELOC Lenders,** which is at the end of this chapter. You can use Table 7-2 to compare HELOCs from multiple lenders using the criteria listed. Exercise 7-3 includes a form with lender information blanked out.

Table 7-2: HELOC Lender Comparison with Sample Data

Comparison Criteria	Lender A	Lender B	Notes
Home Appraisal Value:	$100,000	$100,000	
Mortgage Balance:	$60,000	$60,000	
Home Equity:	$40,000	$40,000	
Max HELOC %:	85%	80%	
Max HELOC Amt:	$35,000	$30,000	
Interest Rate (APR):	9%	9.5%	
Variable Rate:	Yes	Yes	
Rate Lock/Cost:	$100	$0	
Closing Costs:	$200	$0	
Time to close:	45 days	45 days	
Annual Fee:	$75	$60	
Credit Score Required:	700	700	
Bank Account Required:	No	No	
Other Loan Fees:	0	0	
Draw Period:	10 yrs	10 yrs	
Payment Period:	20 yrs	20 yrs	

Usually, there are minimal closing costs with a HELOC, as compared to a regular mortgage or home equity loan, but small fees can add up. These issues are usually offset by lower interest rates and flexible borrowing options, as well as possible tax benefits for interest paid (if used for home improvement). Refer to Table 7-3 for a comparison between a HELOC, home equity loan, and personal loan.

Table 7-3: Comparing a HELOC, Home Equity Loan, and Personal Loan

Loan Type	Principal Amount	Term of Loan	Interest Rate	Monthly Payment	Collateral	Flexibility	*Tax Adv?
HELOC	Varies	Varies	Varies	Varies	Home	High	Varies
Home Eq Loan	Fixed	Fixed	Fixed	Fixed	Home	Low	Varies
Personal Loan	Fixed	Fixed	Fixed	Fixed	Varies	Low	Varies

* Interest may be tax deductible if the loan is used for home improvements.

Note: You can do a Web search for "free heloc calculator" and use the identified results to try different scenarios.

You can use a HELOC revolving credit line for just about anything, now and in the future, up to the credit limit and draw period. Or you may not use it at all, keeping it available as a backup in case of emergency. Let's say you have a $10,000 line of credit. You could use it to buy a used car for $7,000 and a high-end TV for $1,000, and you would still have $2,000 left on your line of credit to buy or pay for other things. If you borrow against the line of credit, there is a variable interest rate (usually relatively low). With a variable payment, you could pay interest only or interest plus principal. A HELOC is very flexible. Once the line of credit is established, you can write checks, transfer money online to a checking or savings account, get a cash advance, or use a Visa credit card tied to the HELOC. Note that the interest you pay on the money spent from a HELOC may be tax deductible if the money is used for home improvements.

Home Equity Loan

A home equity loan is similar to a second mortgage and is related to the HELOC in that it is based on the equity you have in your home. The main difference is that you are borrowing a specific amount, as a lump sum, with the stability of a fixed rate, term, and monthly payment. As with the HELOC, a home appraisal is required, and usually there are more closing costs associated with a home equity loan. Since this is actually a loan for a fixed amount, once it is paid off, you must reapply for another loan if you want more funds. Or you could apply for a HELOC to have more flexibility.

Note: A home equity loan and home equity line of credit are both loans against your home as collateral. They are essentially a second mortgage behind the primary mortgage. As such, if you sell your house, you must pay off the loan or line of credit as well as the primary mortgage.

Caution: A HELOC or home equity loan can be a very useful and cost-effective tool in the world of personal finance, but keep in mind that in both cases, your home is collateral, and if you are unable to make the monthly payment, you could lose your home!

So, if you take out a HELOC for $50,000 and you use the money to upgrade your home's kitchen, add a garage, or purchase reliable primary transportation, that's probably worth the risk. If you are planning on using the money to buy a boat or pay off some credit cards, that may not be worth putting your home at risk. That said, there are people who take out a HELOC and don't actually use it. They keep it open as a backup plan in case of emergency. Or they might see a bargain price (say $20,000) for a particular used car they've been shopping for. With the pre-approved line of credit, they can just write a check for the car using the line of credit and still have $30,000 available. You don't have to use the HELOC, but you will typically have to pay a yearly fee (usually less than $100) to keep it open and available. That's a small price to pay for a $50,000 line of credit and peace of mind.

IRA - Traditional Individual Retirement Account

A traditional IRA is a defined benefit investment account that can reduce taxable income for the current tax year. An IRA can be set up for you by your bank or other financial institution for withdrawal when you retire. It is a low-liquidity retirement asset that you can put contributions (pre-tax money) into, tax deferred. You do not pay income tax until cash is withdrawn (distributions), at which time it is taxed as ordinary income at your current tax rate. Money put in an IRA is usually invested in stocks but can be any form of investment. Tax on gains from your IRA is also deferred until you start taking distributions from it at retirement. Withdrawing money from the IRA early results in a significant penalty, and the amount withdrawn is subject to income tax at your current tax rate. Additional information on Traditional IRAs is presented in Chapter 13: Investing Basics, and Chapter 14: Retirement Requirements.

IRA - Roth Individual Retirement Account

A Roth IRA is also a defined benefit investment account, primarily for withdrawal when you retire. It is a low liquidity retirement asset that you can put money into. Unlike a traditional IRA, you put after-tax money into it, and it is not tax deferred. You don't pay tax on the contributions or gains from a Roth IRA, regardless of how much it may have appreciated. Money put into a Roth IRA is usually invested in stocks but can be any form of investment. As with a traditional IRA, withdrawing money early results in a penalty. Also, there are stricter limits to the amount that can be contributed based on income. Additional information on Roth IRAs is presented in Chapter 13.

Money Orders

A money order is a payment certificate for a specified amount of money. It is required that the funds for the amount on it be prepaid and that it is made out to a specific payee. It is a more trusted method of payment than a personal check. It is usually issued by banks, post offices, and some retail stores. A money order functions much like a check in that the person who purchases the money order may stop payment.

Money Transfer Wire Services

Most banks and other financial institutions, including some retail stores, offer national and international wire (electronic) money transfers for a fee.

Online Money Transfer Services

Many banks offer various pay/receive (send/request) services, as part of their online banking services, to transfer money. Examples include Zelle, Venmo, and others. Using these services, you can send and receive money with trusted individuals without the need to write a check.

Safe Deposit Box (SDB)

Most brick-and-mortar banks offer safe deposit boxes for rent. They come in various sizes, and depending on the bank and size of the box, the associated yearly fees can range from twenty-five to a hundred dollars. They are an excellent place to store important documents as well as small valuables such as jewelry outside the home. They are usually kept in a safe with a large and heavy bank vault door. Documents to be put in an SDB for safe keeping can include, but are not limited to, the following:

- **Passports**
- **Copies of credit cards (front and back)**
- **Copies of driver's licenses (front and back)**
- **Vehicle titles**
- **Savings bonds**

- **Copies of wills**
- **Powers of attorney**
- **Videos/photos of home interior items for insurance purposes**

Important Note: Be sure to have your spouse's signature on the authorized safe deposit box access list as well as anyone else's you wish to give access to it. Make sure trusted individuals know where the SDB is kept (bank name and address) and where the keys are. Also, do not lose the keys (usually two), as banks can charge twenty-five to fifty dollars to replace a safe deposit box key.

Chapter 7 Exercises

Exercise 7-1: Compare Automatic Savings Apps

In this exercise, you will research Automatic Savings apps. To assist in selecting an app, you can make a copy of Table 7-4. Do a Web search for "best saving apps" or "best round-up apps," or you can search for each one individually by name and compare the features to determine which ones best serve your needs.

Table 7-4: Automatic Savings Apps Comparison (Form)

App Name	Cost	Notes

Exercise 7-2: Compare Banking Products and Services

To assist you in researching banks, you can set up a comparison table. Look through the products and services that banks can offer from Part 2 of this chapter. Select several banks and/or credit unions to see which ones have the widest range and best products available. Use Table 7-5 as an example and list the banks across the top and the features to be compared down the left side. Before starting this exercise, make a copy of Table 7-5.

Table 7-5: Banking Products and Services Comparison (Form)

Banking Product/Service	Bank 1	Bank 2	Bank 3
Auto loan (new/used) APR			
Cashier's check fee			
Checking account fee			
Financial planner services (CFP)			
30-year home mortgage rate			
CD rate (12-60 month)			
HELOC interest rate (Avg/range)			
Notary fee			
Safe Deposit Box yearly fee			
IRA (traditional and Roth)			
SEP and SIMPLE IRA setup			

Exercise 7-3: Compare HELOC Lenders

To assist you in researching HELOCs and the lenders that offer them, you can set up a comparison table. Select one or more banks and/or credit unions to see which ones have the best terms and least requirements for a HELOC. This exercise assumes that you have a home and that you have some equity in it. The exercise can be done instead of, or in addition to, Exercise 7-2. Before starting this exercise, make a copy of the Table 7-6 Form and list the lenders across the top.

Table 7-6: HELOC Lender Comparison (Form)

Comparison Criteria	Lender A	Lender B	Notes
Home Appraisal Value:			
Mortgage Balance:			
Home Equity:			
Max HELOC %:			
Max HELOC Amt:			
Interest Rate (APR):			
Variable Rate:			
Rate Lock/Cost:			
Closing Costs:			
Time to close:			
Annual Fee:			
Credit Score Required:			
Bank Account Required:			
Other Loan Fees:			
Draw Period:			
Payment Period:			

Chapter 8
Credit Scores and Credit Reports

Chapter Overview:
Chapter 8: Credit Scores and Credit Reports, and Chapter 9: Credit and Credit Cards, are two of the most important chapters in this book. The content is applicable to a very large segment of the population. In previous chapters we have referred to a person's credit score as it relates to their finances affected by it. This chapter describes what a credit score is, its importance, how it is determined, and who determines it. You will also learn how to find out what your current credit score is without having to pay for it. The chapter lists some things you can do to help improve (raise) your score and things that can have a negative impact (lower it). In addition to your credit score, the chapter also describes credit reports and what they contain. Exercises are provided to create an account with one of the three nationwide credit reporting bureaus and obtain your credit score and report at no cost. This chapter is divided into three parts.

- **Part 1: Credit Scores**
- **Part 2: Credit Reports**
- **Part 3: Credit Assistance**

Chapter PFS and PFI Integration:
The chapter introduces PFS Sheet - Credit and Credit Cards, with a tab label of "Cred-Cards." The Cred-Cards sheet provides a way to record information about your credit rating and report which you will obtain using exercises in this chapter. You will also record your credit card information in the PFS Cred-Cards sheet. The important PFI Debt-to-Credit (DTC) ratio is introduced, along with a brief review of the related and equally important PFI Debt-to-Income (DTI).

Chapter Exercises:
- **Exercise 8-1: Create Credit Bureau Account**
- **Exercise 8-2: Obtain Your Credit Score and Report**

Chapter Notable Quote:
Quote 8-1: "It's not where you start but where you finish that counts." - Zig Ziglar

Part 1: Credit Scores

The quote above is particularly appropriate when applied to your credit score. Many people don't know if they have a credit score, let alone what their score is. You may currently have a low credit score, which is not uncommon and nothing to be ashamed of. Your credit score can range from a low of 300 to a high of 850. As you can see in Table 8-1, 34 percent of Americans have a score that is considered "Fair-to-Poor." After reading this chapter and the next, you will know what your credit score is and how you can improve it. Regardless of where you start, it's where you finish that counts. Many people these days have a credit score that is based on the Fair Isaac Corporation system and is known as their "FICO score." It is a number between 300 and 850. Table 8-1 shows credit score ranges from the Experian credit bureau Website, based on U.S. consumer debt research. In 2022, the average FICO score in the U.S. was 714, which is considered "good" according to Experian data. A more detailed explanation of the credit score is provided later in this chapter. If you know your credit score, you can see how you compare to the rest of America.

Table 8-1: Ranges for FICO Credit Scores

Score Range	Rating Description	% of Americans
800-850	Exceptional	20%
740-799	Very Good	25%
670-739	Good	21%
580-669	Fair	18%
300-579	Very Poor	16%

The Benefits of a High Credit Score

The benefits of having a score in the 800–850 (Exceptional) range are many, and this score can affect other areas of your life, not just your finances. The bottom line (literally) is that, if you have worked diligently for the last five years to improve your score to 820, which is considered "Exceptional," that's something to be proud of. When you are at the bank and they run the "hard inquiry" credit check on you, it comes up as 820! Nobody knows or cares that five years ago your score was 660. As Zig says, "It's not where you start but where you finish that counts."

Most people who have a score over 800 have been relatively responsible financially to have achieved that score. And once they reach that level, they rarely drop by much, and even when they do, it is due to some financial activity, like a major purchase, and their score usually goes back up to where it was. It's nice to be able to go to a lender if you need to borrow money, for whatever reason, and know you will not only get approved for the loan but will get the best terms available (e.g., lowest interest rate or APR). It also means you can go to any number of other lenders and shop around for the best rate.

Credit Rating and Reporting

In the U.S., if you have a Social Security number and have ever applied for credit, you probably have a credit score and a credit report (three of each). Your credit score can change depending on how your credit history changes. Your credit score is largely derived from one or more of your credit reports. Your credit score can affect whether you can get a loan and how much you'll have to pay for that loan. Your credit score is a numeric value associated with you personally that helps lenders determine your creditworthiness. The higher your score, the better your creditworthiness and the more the likelihood that you will be extended credit. The combination of your credit score and report is sometimes referred to as your credit profile, which is a good indicator of your credit health and financial health overall.

Your Credit Report + Your Credit Score = Your Credit Health

Taking Control of Your Credit

Getting your credit under control starts with an awareness and understanding of your credit score and what's in your credit report. Your credit score is calculated and determined by your financial activity over time and is based on the information contained in your credit report, which is a record of your credit history. Major factors include how much you borrow, how much you owe, and how regularly you pay your debts on time. Your credit score is based on your credit report, which is a record of your borrowing and payment history. Your credit report contains an entry for nearly every loan you have ever taken out, every credit card you have ever had, and whether the account is open or closed. In the U.S., credit scores and reports for individuals are kept and maintained by three main nationwide consumer credit reporting agencies or credit bureaus: Equifax, Experian, and TransUnion. The terms "credit reporting agency," "credit bureau" and other variations all refer to the three nationwide consumer credit reporting companies "The Big Three" and are used in this book. Whether you are aware of it or not, you probably have a credit score and report kept by each of the credit bureaus. These three are the major ones recognized by the Federal Trade Commission (FTC) and the Fair Credit Reporting Act (FCRA). There are other Websites and sources for credit scores and reports, but most of them obtain their information from one or more of the three nationwide credit reporting bureaus whose logos are shown in Figure 8-1.

Figure 8-1: Nationwide Consumer Credit Reporting Bureaus

You can obtain your credit score and report directly from any or all of these bureaus or from other third-party organizations. The contents of and the process for obtaining your credit information is described in this chapter.

Note: For more information about credit reports and your rights under federal law, visit the Website for the Consumer Financial Protection Bureau (CFPB) at: https://www.consumerfinance.gov/learnmore

Refer to **Exercise 8-1: Create Credit Bureau Account** at the end of this chapter for instructions on creating an account with one or more of the three main credit-reporting bureaus (Equifax, Experian or TransUnion). In this exercise you will research and select one of the three credit bureaus and create a login account on the credit bureau's Website. There is a wealth of good credit information on all three Websites, and specific ways you can improve your credit score and report.

Lenders/Creditors and Your Credit Score

Companies that extend credit to consumers for loans or purchases (banks, credit unions, mortgage companies, retailers, etc.) check with one or more of the credit reporting companies (bureaus) to obtain your credit score and credit report. When you apply for a credit card or buy something on credit (e.g., auto or home), the creditor requests your credit score and a copy of your credit report from one or more of the three credit reporting bureaus. This helps them to determine your creditworthiness, whether they will extend you credit, and, if so, how much they will loan and what interest rate they will charge. Typically, the better your score, the more you can borrow and the lower the interest rate.

Insurance Companies and Your Credit Score

When you buy insurance (car, home, etc.), the carrier will check your credit rating. It is used to determine your "insurance score," which is one of the factors that determines whether they will insure you and what your premiums will be. Other factors can include your claims history, driving record, and moving violations. If they do insure you, they will periodically contact one of the credit bureaus to obtain your credit information and update your insurance score. A change in your insurance score can increase or decrease your premiums. Also note that it is important to keep adequate insurance coverage for auto and home to protect you from catastrophic events. It is important to have a licensed insurance agent that can help you determine the proper coverage and type of insurance you need. When buying an insurance policy, ask your agent if your credit score is a factor in determining the monthly premium. If your core increases will the premium go down?

Landlords, Job Applications, and Your Credit Score

Even when you rent an apartment or apply for a job, the landlord or potential employer can (and frequently does) run a credit check on you to see how creditworthy you are. A person's creditworthiness is generally a pretty good indication of their overall trustworthiness and character. Creditworthy people are generally more trustworthy. They are generally more likely to pay their debts on time, less likely to skip town owing rent, and more likely to come to work on time. Years ago, the average person could not even see what their score was or what was contained in their credit report. Only creditors had access to your scores and report. So, you could apply for a loan and be turned down without even knowing why. There could well have been inaccurate information in your report, but you could not see it in order to potentially correct the information.

The bottom line is that a low credit score can result in one or more of the following:

- Higher home and auto loan interest rates
- Higher credit card interest rates and lower credit limits
- Declined credit applications (credit cards, loans, etc.)
- Higher home and auto insurance premiums
- Denied rentals and higher security deposits required
- Impact on employment potential

What is a Credit Score?

In the simplest terms, a credit score is a three-digit number that represents your creditworthiness. A person's credit score is frequently based on the Fair Isaac Corporation (FICO) system scoring model. It is a number between 300 and 850. A score of 500 or lower is considered "poor" whereas a score of 800 or higher is considered "excellent." The "Big Three" credit reporting bureaus (Equifax, Experian, and TransUnion) have their own rating system (model) for your credit score, known as the VantageScore 3.0, which also uses a scoring range of 300-850. Note that in Figure 8-2, the scores shown on the meters on the Credit Karma Website indicate they were calculated using VantageScore 3.0. Also note that the scores are slightly different because one uses the report history from TransUnion and the other uses the report history from Equifax. You could average the two scores for a reasonably good estimate of your creditworthiness. You could also receive a FICO score from two different sources, and they could be different since the score from any given source is derived from the credit history file or credit report, that they use to generate the score.

The three consumer credit reporting bureaus are independent companies and may have slightly different information in their credit history files for a particular person. Hence there will likely be slight discrepancies regarding personal information as well as credit history. Whenever you check your credit score or report, it's a good idea to check your report from all three credit bureaus. This way you can compare the reports, identify errors and correct the discrepancies by contacting all three bureaus. The credit report generated by each credit bureau is determined by whatever credit account data is reported to that bureau by your creditors. Your resulting credit score is calculated by the bureau based on the credit scoring model they use. If you request your score from Experian, it will likely be calculated using the FICO Score 8 model based on the data that Experian has in your credit file (credit report). If you request your score from Equifax or TransUnion, you will likely get a score calculated using the VantageScore 3.0 model based on the data that each of those companies has in their credit file (credit report for you. If you are financially active with various types of credit accounts, your credit scores from each of the bureaus will tend to change from one month to the next. Your report contents and scores usually lag behind your purchasing and payment activity. Most creditors report your account activity to the credit bureaus once a month.

Refer to Table 8-2 to see how an application for a credit card, and its subsequent use, generates entries in your credit report for each bureau, which then recalculates your credit score based on the activity.

Table 8-2: How a Credit Event Can Affect your Credit Report and Score

Consumer Credit Event >	Creditor Credit Action >	Bureau Credit Report Action >	Bureau Credit Score Action
You apply for a new credit card online and get approved for $5,000 limit.	Credit card issuer (creditor) reports your new credit line to 3 credit bureaus	New account and credit limit added to your credit report. Your Debt-to-Credit (DTC) ratio decreases (good).	Credit score increases with increased credit available.

You make purchases for $1,000 charged to the new credit card.	Creditor reports purchase(s) to 3 credit bureaus	Purchase and credit use are added to your credit report. Your debt-to-Credit (DTC) ratio decreases. (bad)	Credit score decreases with increased credit utilization.
You pay the $1,000 statement balance by due date	Creditor reports statement balance paid in full to 3 credit bureaus	Payment on time to creditor added to credit report. Your debt-to-Credit (DTC) ratio increases. (good)	Credit score increases with payment on time and increased credit available.

FICO and VantageScore Models

Although the VantageScore uses a slightly different algorithm, the three consumer credit bureau's ratings are pretty much comparable to FICO, which has become the de facto standard of the financial credit world. Your FICO score is the credit score many lenders use to determine your credit risk. Your credit score is one of the main things that banks look at to decide whether to extend you credit, how much to lend, and what interest rate they will charge. Depending on which credit bureau you request your credit score from you may get a FICO score or a VantageScore, but the two scores should be fairly close as they are both based on your credit report history. Either one or both scores and reports could be used by your lender. The next lender might use a different combination. In some cases, the credit score is free with the report and in others there is a small fee. If the lender requests your score and report when you apply for a loan, they usually share the information obtained with you since it is a major factor in the approval process.

Note: There are two main versions of the FICO credit-scoring model currently in use. The most common scoring model used in lending decisions is FICO Score 8, though FICO Score 9 was released in 2014, and lenders are migrating to it. Both scores are widely used and effective at determining creditworthiness. According to FICO's Website, 90 percent of top lenders use FICO scores for lending decisions, and more than twenty-seven million scores are requested each day.

Note: There are other types of FICO scores available that may be used by specific lenders such as home mortgage and auto loan, but they are beyond the scope of this book.

Where to Get Your Credit Score

You can get your score from a number of sources, but you may have to pay for it, and depending on the source, it could be FICO or VantageScore3.0. You can get your score and report from several online financial services without paying for it by just doing a search for "free credit score". These companies can also provide credit monitoring, financial tools and education. And of course, you can also get your free credit report and/or score from the three credit bureaus (Equifax, Experian and TransUnion). Credit card issuers, banks and credit unions are increasingly allowing customers to check their credit score and report for free. When comparing banks and credit cards, be sure to include this as one of your criteria. Web sources such as CreditCards.com, Credit Karma, Forbes, NerdWallet, SoFi, and others can help you find credit cards that offer free credit scores and reports, as well as other features and benefits.

For example, one of the major banks offers the following benefits at no cost, if you have their credit card:
- Access to your FICO Score 9 credit rating
- Free credit report from one of the three credit bureaus
- Tips to help improve your score
- Monthly score history to track your score over time
- Zero fraud liability

One of the credit bureaus offers the following benefits for creating an account and registering.
- Free credit report and FICO Score 8 credit rating
- Report and score refreshed monthly
- FICO score monitoring
- Credit monitoring and alerts
- Free personal privacy scan

Some credit card issuers now include your score with your monthly statement. You can also do a search for "free credit scores" but if you are asked to enter credit card information, the score is not free. Many of the free credit score sources will also give you information on ways to improve your score and prevent it from getting worse. Some of the budgeting/financial apps, such as Mint, which were discussed in Chapter 4, can also provide your credit score for free. With today's options for obtaining free personal credit information, you can easily obtain three different scores from three different sources and just average them for a pretty good idea of where you stand regarding your creditworthiness rating. You could also request your credit report from each of the three credit bureaus for a more complete picture. Whatever you do, you should not have to pay for your credit score or report! In fact, you can get your FICO credit score and a credit report directly from FICO at no cost. Visit the FICO Website: https://www.myfico.com

Refer to **Exercise 8-2: Obtain Your Credit Score and Report** at the end of this chapter, which provides some guidance on ways to obtain your free credit score and credit report. Part A focuses on the credit score. Part B focuses on the credit report.

Figure 8-2 shows a sample credit scoreboard screenshot from Credit Karma, which includes a score from both TransUnion and Equifax. As previously discussed, the scores are slightly different because each is based on information that the credit company has in their credit reporting file on you. There are usually minor differences between the three credit reporting companies (Equifax, Experian, and TransUnion), and your score from any of them can fluctuate up or down a few points from one check to the next. The scores in the figure are calculated using the VantageScore 3.0 scoring model which uses the same scoring scale as FICO (300-850). Note that this is a generic example.

Figure 8-2: Credit Score Dashboard Example

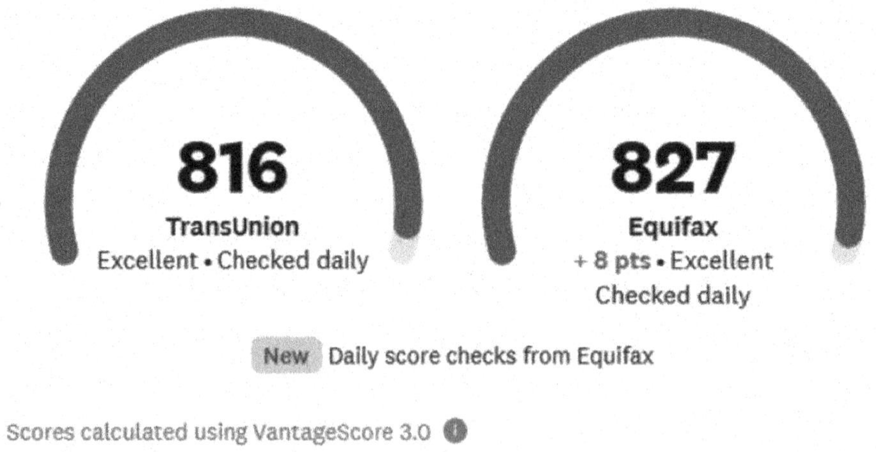

816
TransUnion
Excellent • Checked daily

827
Equifax
+ 8 pts • Excellent
Checked daily

New Daily score checks from Equifax

Scores calculated using VantageScore 3.0 ⓘ

FICO Score Credit Factors

Payment history and credit utilization are the main factors that determine your credit score. There is a wealth of information available on the FICO Website at:

https://www.myfico.com/credit-education

According to FICO, your score is made up of five weighted categories, listed below in order of their weighting or percentage of the total when calculating your credit score. The weighting is an indicator of how important the category is in determining your credit score. If all five categories were weighted equally, each one would be worth 20 percent of the total (20/100). However, the first category that determines your FICO score is Payment history with a weight of 35 percent. The second category is Credit currently being used and is weighted at 30 percent. So, your payment history, in combination with the amount of your available credit you are using, represents 65 percent of your credit score. You can see that it pays to pay your bills on time and not max out your credit cards. The FICO credit score categories are listed in order of their weighting. Additional details about factors that affect your credit score can be found on the FICO Website.

1. Payment history - 35 percent

The most important factor in determining your FICO score is whether you pay your bills on time. Missed or late payments for various types of loans can bring your score down. These include credit cards, mortgages, and car loans. Most creditors don't report missed payments unless they are over thirty days late.

2. Credit currently being used - 30 percent

Another major factor that impacts your credit rating is how much of your available credit you are using (credit utilization), mainly with credit cards or revolving credit. This is usually referred to as your Debt-to-Credit

(DTC) ratio and includes the number of cards you have and whether they are at or near their charge limit. Lenders usually recommend keeping the balance on any one card and on all cards combined to less than 30 percent of the maximum and ideally below 20 percent. Keeping your balance low or, better yet, paying off the balance each month is best. Using credit cards and not carrying a balance improves your FICO credit rating. In addition, you avoid paying interest on the balance, which can run from 15 percent to 25 percent APR or higher. Carrying high credit card balances and paying high interest is not good money management but may be necessary at times. It's also OK to occasionally make a large purchase, that pushes you close to the limit on one or more credit cards, assuming you have or will have the money to pay off the balance before the due date of the next statement.

3. Length of credit history - 15 percent

This is determined by how long your accounts have been open and how long it has been since their last use. When our daughters started college, we helped each of them obtain a "starter" credit card when they were eighteen years old. They were allowed to use them occasionally but had to pay the balance at the end of each month since they were both working part-time. By the time they finished college, they each had two credit cards with a three- to four credit history, which helped their credit ratings. Both girls had a FICO rating of 700+ by the time they graduated.

4. Credit mix - 10 percent

This is determined by how many different types of accounts you have. Examples include revolving accounts such as credit cards and installment loans such as auto, mortgage, or student loans. Maintaining different types of credit is good for your overall FICO score. Sign in to check your credit mix rating.

5. New credit - 10 percent

This is determined by how many credit inquiries are made and how many new credit lines are opened in a period of time. It is generally recommended to have fewer credit cards (three to four) and no more than two new accounts opened over a one-year period. It may be tempting to apply for credit when shopping at a store, and store employees are rewarded for the number of applications they have customers fill out. However, it does not reflect well on the consumer to open a lot of new accounts, especially if they carry balances.

The Dynamic Duo of Credit Decisions: DTI and DTC
Recall from Chapter 3 that Debt-to-Income (DTI) is considered one of the most critical Personal Financial Indicators (PFIs). It is determined by taking your total monthly Debt Payments (excluding utilities and discretionary expenses) and dividing them (/) by Monthly Gross Income and should not exceed 40 percent. An equally important indicator that creditors use to evaluate your credit application is the Debt-to-Credit or DTC ratio. These two measures (DTI ratio and DTC ratio) combine to form the basis of millions of credit decisions and transactions daily. Your DTC ratio focuses on "revolving" credit, which usually refers

to credit cards but can include things like a home equity line of credit (HELOC). Your DTC ratio is some-time referred to as "credit utilization" or "credit card use." Whereas your DTI ratio indicates how much of your monthly income (what percentage) you are using to pay monthly debts, your DTC ratio indicates how much of your available credit (what percentage) you are currently using. DTI ratio is a major factor in home buying but does not directly impact your credit score. Unlike your DTI ratio, your DTC ratio can and frequently does affect your credit score. Your credit score then factors into your overall creditworthiness and your ability to obtain a mortgage or qualify for a car loan.

More on Debt-to-Credit (DTC) Ratio

DTC is determined by taking the amount of revolving credit (mainly from credit cards) you are using and dividing (/) by the total of revolving credit limits and should not exceed 30 percent. Creditors don't like to extend more credit to people who have "maxed out" their credit cards. Unfortunately, for a lot of people, charging their credit cards up to their limits and paying only the minimum payment is all too common. So, let's say you have one credit card with a $5,000 credit limit and your current balance is $1,000, your DTC ratio is 20 percent (1,000/5,000 * 100). If you pay off the balance on this statement, your DTC utilization is zero. In general, a ratio of 30 percent or less is considered good, but the lower the better. If you carry a balance from one month to the next, it's easy to go over 30 percent credit utilization, without even realizing it; plus, you will pay more interest on the balance carried over.

PFI 8-1: Debt-to-Credit (DTC) Ratio - Formula/Calculation
Personal Financial Indicator (#PFI-11)

Total Revolving Credit Used (/divided by/) Total of Revolving Credit Limits = DTC (%)

$1,000 / $5,000 = .20 (*100) = 20%

(PFS Cred-Cards sheet example)

If you have multiple credit cards, you can just add up the credit limits for all your credit cards. Next, add up the balances and then divide the total of your balances by the total of your card credit limits. The result is your overall DTC ratio, which should be less than 30 percent. Keep in mind that you also want to limit the credit utilization on any one card to less than 30 percent. As a quick refresher, according to FICO, your credit score is made up of the five categories shown below, in order of priority. As you can see, Credit currently being used (your DTC ratio), is No. 2 on the list, second only to No. 1. Payment history (paying your bills on time). As with its cousin DTI, it's hard to overstate the importance of keeping your DTC ratio below the recommended limits (30 percent for DTC and 40 percent for DTI). For a potential creditor it is an indicator that says you have your credit use under control.

1. **Payment history**
2. **Credit currently being used (DTC ratio)**
3. **Length of credit history**

4. **Credit mix**
5. **New credit**

How to Quickly Improve Your Credit Score

One of the most important things you can do to rapidly improve your credit score is to pay down the balance or pay off one or more of your revolving credit (credit card) accounts. This rapidly decreases your DTC ratio or credit utilization (lower is better) and directly affects your credit report/score. This also assumes you don't make a bunch of charges on other credit cards at the same time, which would negate your efforts to pay down a high-interest credit card. Your credit score from each of the three credit reporting bureaus (Equifax, Experian, and TransUnion) is derived from the credit report that each of the bureaus keeps on you. These reports are fed by updates from your creditors on the status of your account. It may take days or even weeks for the updates from your creditors to reach each of the bureaus. But when they do, they will update your DTC ratio(s). This should improve your credit rating, all else being equal.

Let's look at a simple example. Say you have two credit cards.

- Card 1 has a credit limit of $4,000.
- Card 2 has a credit limit of $6,000.
- Your total credit limit is $10,000.

If you have a $2,000 balance on Card 1 and a $3,000 balance on Card 2, you are using 50 percent of the available credit on Card 1 and 50 percent on Card 2. If you add the Card 1 and Card 2 balances, you are at $5,000, with a maximum credit limit of $10,000 for both cards, and so your DTC for each card and for both cards combined is 50percent. The recommended DTC should not exceed 30 percent. If you pay off the Card 1 balance of $2,000 its DTC goes to 0 percent. Card 2 DTC stays the same, but the total DTC goes down to 30 %percent (3,000/10,000).

Note: Refer to PFS Sheet – Credit and Credit Cards, which you will use to enter your credit card data, with **Exercise 9-1: Record PFS Credit and Credit Card Info**. The PFS Cred-Cards sheet calculates DTC utilization based on the credit cards, limits and balances you enter.

The Importance of Credit Utilization and DTC

Here is a real-world example of how DTC affects your credit and how important credit usage is. Ted recently charged the cost of a vacation cruise to one of his credit cards that gives 3 percent cash back for travel-related charges. He called the credit card company to request an increase of his credit limit to do this. That charge put him very close to his credit limit for that card and his DTC ratio for that card went to about 80 percent! And his overall DTC went up to 30 percent. As a result, his credit score dropped eighty points, going from 820 (excellent) to 740 (good) in two days! He was not too concerned because he planned to pay off the credit card balance with money from his savings, and his score would go back up within a matter of days. In the meantime, he received 3 percent cash back on the amount charged to his credit card.

Credit Scores and Credit Applications

A high credit score alone may not be enough in certain credit situations. For example, a twenty-two-year-old may be doing everything right, like having a couple of starter credit cards and paying regularly, but still get turned down for an auto lease or mortgage. If they have few paid-off loans and a short borrowing history that is not varied, they may have what is known as a "thin file," and creditors are less likely to approve credit for large amounts. They may need to negotiate with the dealer about why they were turned down, select a less expensive (or used) auto to lease, or possibly have a cosigner. Remember that if you are turned down for credit, you are entitled to a free copy of your credit report to help you understand why you were declined.

Note: If you get turned down for a loan application or a credit card, you are entitled to a free copy of your credit report. You may find some errors in your report that could affect your score and ability to obtain a loan.

Borderline Credit and Thin Files

Buying a home or leasing a car requires the buyer to have a very good credit rating and longer credit history. People who have a thin file will have greater difficulty qualifying for credit and getting the best terms, especially for leases and mortgages. Thin files are fairly common for younger people and people who, for whatever reason, haven't borrowed much money. According to Experian, a thin credit file typically refers to a credit history with fewer than five credit accounts on a credit report maintained by one of the three national credit bureaus. An unfortunate paradox for consumers is that the more they need credit, the less likely they are to get it, and the less they need credit, the more likely they are to get it. Fortunately, there are steps you can take to improve the chances of getting approved, even if you have less than stellar credit and/or a thin file. The following suggestions may help.

- Work to increase your credit rating to 700 or higher (See Table 8-3 for factors).
- Have at least two credit cards (Visa, MasterCard, Store) with regular payment history.
- Have at least two installment loans paid off with no late payments, within the last two years.
- Take out a small personal loan, even if you could pay cash, and pay it off to help build a credit history.
- Have two or more open account installment loans that you are currently paying on.
- Obtain a copy of your credit report showing regular payment on all entries.
- Verify that your credit report shows accurate information.
- Work to improve your Debt-to-Income (DTI) and Debt-to-Credit (DTC) ratios.
- Save up adequate down payment (at least 20 percent) money that is not borrowed.
- Have at least two years in a full-time job with steady income (especially if you are self-employed.)

Things that Affect Your Credit Score

There are many Websites and sources of information that give advice on specific things you can do to improve your score and caution you about things that can worsen your score. Do a search for "improve credit score" or "hurt credit score" or "affect credit score" and you can then research the results to see which ones might apply to your situation. Sources can include those identified in this book, such as Creditcards.com, Credit Karma, Forbes, Intuit, NerdWallet, Sofi, USA.gov, the big three consumer credit bureaus (Equifax, Experian, and TransUnion) and many others.

Hard and Soft Inquiries

Anytime your credit score is checked, for whatever reason, it creates an inquiry event with one or more of the national credit reporting bureaus (Equifax, Experian, or TransUnion). The inquiry is classified as either hard or soft, depending on why it was requested. If you check your own score or if a company does a background check on you, it will generate a soft inquiry, which normally does not affect your score. This can happen when you apply for a job or rent an apartment. However, if you apply for an auto loan or a credit card, the lender or credit card company will need to decide whether to extend you credit. This generates a hard inquiry, which could lower your credit score, especially if you already have several credit cards with balances and multiple recent hard inquiries.

There are many things that can affect your credit score. The following three tables contain lists of some of the most important and most common things that can affect your score and tell you whether they are likely to improve, worsen, or typically have no effect on your overall score. Table 8-2 lists some things you can do that usually help to improve your score, while Table 8-3 lists things you should avoid doing because they usually hurt your score. Table 8-4 lists things that usually do not normally affect your score, although you might think they would. More information on factors that can help and hurt your credit score can be found on the FICO Website, the three main credit bureau Websites, and many others. Keep in mind that the single most important thing you can do to build and maintain a good credit rating is to pay your bills on time over time!

Note: Refer to www.myfico.com/credit-education for more information, including videos on credit scores and related issues.

Table 8-3: Things That Can Help Credit Scores

Paying your bills on time every month consistently	Number 1 factor in credit score! Setting up automatic bill payment (AutoPay) can help here.
Developing a mix of "good" credit to show you can handle multiple types of credit.	A combination of revolving (credit card) with low utilization, installment (car) and mortgage (home) loans is best. (Rent payment can substitute for home mortgage)
Reducing the amount of credit used compared to credit available.	Improves Debt-to-Credit (DTC) ratios. Don't charge over 30% of your credit limit on any one card and on all cards combined.
Requesting a credit limit increase but not using it.	Increases maximum credit available and improves your DTC ratios. Call and ask if it will generate hard or soft inquiry. Hard inquiry may lower score short term.
Paying off your credit card balances each month.	Keeps your debt-to-available credit (DTC) very low and avoids high credit card interest.
Keeping your credit cards for a long time. The longer the better.	Establishes a longer credit history for each card and average history for all cards combined. As long as you do not overuse them.
Paying off an installment loan (auto or personal loan)	Improves Debt-to-Income ratio (DTI) by reducing debt and is recorded as a positive "Closed" entry on your credit report.
Renting a residence and paying utility bills on time	The VantageScore scoring model, created by the three major credit bureaus now weights rent and utility payment records.
Being an authorized user on someone else's "good" account	Can help build good credit for authorized users on revolving credit card accounts.
Checking your credit reports regularly. (Equifax, Experian or TransUnion)	By itself, this won't help your score but will alert you to errors so you can contest them and get them corrected.

Table 8-4: Things That Can Hurt Credit Scores

Applying for a lot of credit in less than 1 year (mortgage, loan or credit card)	Two or three applications for new credit within a year can bring your score down. However, if you are approved, it can increase your credit limit. As long as you don't overuse your new credit lines by charging them to 30% or more of their maximum, it can reduce your credit utilization or Debt-to-Credit (DTC) ratio over time.
Maintaining a high balance close to the credit limit for one or more credit cards	Maxing out a credit card is bad and can also result in over-limit fees.
Maintaining a high balance close to the credit limit for all credit cards combined	Maxing out your credit over multiple cards is very bad. It also creates heavy interest debt that is difficult to pay down, especially if paying the minimum monthly payment on each card.
Being more than 60 days late with a revolving credit or installment loan payment	If the credit issuer reports your past due status, it can negatively affect your score. Call them to discuss your situation. You should make at least the minimum monthly payment.
Declaring bankruptcy	Major factor that negatively affects your credit score. Stays on your report for 7-10 years. If you declare bankruptcy, you can get a secured credit card to help rebuild credit.
Allowing an account to be turned over to a debt collection agency	Major factor that negatively affects your credit score. If you pay off a debt that went to collections, it may improve your credit rating.
Having no credit cards (debit cards don't count)	Shortens your credit history which could result in a "thin file". May appear to a lender that you cannot handle credit as opposed to being frugal and paying cash for everything.
Refinancing an installment loan (mortgage, student, or car loan)	Can hurt your score since it usually generates a hard inquiry when you apply for a new loan (which increases your indebtedness). It may appear to a lender that you couldn't make the payment.
Being an authorized user on someone else's "bad" account	Applies to co-signers on loans and bank accounts, as well as harming primary and authorized users' credit on revolving credit card accounts
Hard inquiries resulting from a credit check. (Does not apply to soft inquiries)	Inquires that result from credit checks due to a car loan, mortgage, or new credit card. Hard inquiries can lower your score but only stay on your credit report for a couple of years.
Closing paid off accounts and unused credit cards.	Does not help your score and can hurt it, since it reduces your available credit. Applies mostly to credit cards and other revolving lines of credit.

If your credit score has decreased, you can find information on some of the possible reasons by looking through the actions mentioned in Table 8-3 that can hurt your score or by checking the three credit bureau Websites for more details. In general, the most common reasons for a drop in your credit score include the following:

- Late or missed payment(s)
- Application for new credit (mortgage, loan, or credit card hard inquiries)
- Increase in your credit utilization
- Decrease in one of your credit limits
- Closing a credit card account or line of credit
- Inaccurate information on your credit report
- Foreclosure or bankruptcy

Table 8-5: Things That Don't Affect Credit Scores

Being late on a home mortgage or rent payment	If less than 30 days late and if the mortgager or landlord does not report you to the credit bureaus.
Disputing a charge or other erroneous information on your credit report	Does not affect score
Being late on a credit card payment	No effect if less than 30 days late and if the credit issuer does not report you to the credit bureaus. If 60 days or more, could be reported and sent to collections.
Checking your credit score or requesting a copy of your credit report.	Results in a soft inquiry. No effect.
Checking account overdraft	No impact to credit score, although the banks may charge fees.
Having 10 or more credit cards	No effect unless you are maxed out on one or more of them or unable to make minimum payments
Soft inquiries	Results from credit score and report inquiries. No effect.
Shopping for installment loan rate (home/auto/personal) or apartment hunting	Minimal effect. Treated like a single hard inquiry if done in a short time period window such as 30-45 days.
Losing your job	No effect unless you start missing payments
Enter a debt management plan	Proactive measure to help get high-interest debt under control. Can improve Debt-to-Income (DTI) and Debt-to-Credit (DTC) ratios which can improve credit rating. No negative impact on credit score.
Not using a credit card	No affect as long as the balance is 0 but the credit card company may cancel your card due to lack of use.

Part 2: Credit Reports

A credit report is a record of your credit history. It contains personal information and information on whether you pay your bills on time and how much you owe your creditors. It looks at employment history and payment history but does not consider a person's age, occupation, sex, or criminal record. Your credit score is based mainly on the information in your credit report(s). Table 8-6 is an example of the type of summary information contained in a typical credit report from one of the credit bureaus.

Table 8-6: Credit Report Accounts Summary Example

Account Type	Open Accounts	Accounts with a Balance	Balance	Available Balance	Credit Limit	Monthly Payment Amount
REVOLVING	13	4	$5,000	$95,000	$100,000	$150
MORTGAGE	1	1	$100,000	$50,000	$150,000	$1,500
INSTALLMENT	2	2	$10,000	$30,000	$40,000	$300
OTHER	0	0	0	0	0	0
TOTAL	16	7	$115,000	$170,500	$290,000	$1,950

You can get a free credit report from each of the three major credit reporting bureaus (Equifax, Experian, and TransUnion) by going to the annualcreditreport.com Website. As with your credit score, you should not have to pay for your credit reports. The reports are usually provided in an online form so you can review them from a PC or any device with Internet access. You can also request a hard copy. Depending on your credit history, credit reports can be lengthy.

****

Important Note: As of this writing, due to economic uncertainty and the fact that managing your financial health is important, all three credit bureaus are offering free weekly credit reports. The bureaus may also be offering free credit scores. You can go to each bureau's Web site and log in to your account (or create one) to check credit score availability and request a single report or you can go to annualcreditreport.com and request all three.

****

Knowing your credit score and checking your credit report are important parts of managing and controlling your finances. You can learn more about credit monitoring, identity theft, and ways to improve your credit score on the Annual Credit Report Website.

Refer to **Exercise 8-2: Obtain Your Credit Score and Report** at the end of this chapter for instructions on obtaining your credit score and report. In Exercise 8-1, you created an account with one or more of the three nationwide credit reporting bureaus (Equifax, Experian, and TransUnion). In Part A of this exercise, you will obtain your credit score from one of the credit bureaus or another source of your choice. You may be able to contact an officer at your bank, if you have done business with them previously, to obtain your score or, you can register with another company such as Credit Karma. In Part B you will access your credit report from one of the three nationwide credit reporting bureaus using the annualcreditreport. com Website. Figure 8-3 shows the initialannualcreditreport.com screen from which you can select the report(s) you want.

Figure 8-3: Federally Authorized annualcreditreport.com Website

AnnualCreditReport.com
The only source for your free credit reports. Authorized by Federal law.

| Home | All about credit reports | Request yours now! | What to look for | Protect your identity |

FTC Credit Report Information
The following is an excerpt from the Federal Trade Commission (FTC) Website, Credit Report section, (some paraphrased). The above "Important Note" supersedes some of the information that the FTC excerpts provide below, and credit report availability and requirements may change. Visit the federally authorized annualcreditreport.com Website to get the latest information regarding credit reports.

< Begin Excerpts: FTC Credit Report Information >
The Fair Credit Reporting Act (FCRA) requires each of the nationwide credit reporting companies (Equifax, Experian, and TransUnion) to provide you with a free copy of your credit report, at your request, once every twelve months. The FCRA promotes the accuracy and privacy of information in the files of the nation's credit reporting companies. The Federal Trade Commission (FTC), the nation's consumer protection agency, enforces the FCRA with respect to credit reporting bureaus.

What is in a Credit Report? A credit report includes information on where you live; how you pay your bills; and whether you've been sued, have liens against you, or have filed for bankruptcy. Nationwide credit reporting companies sell the information in your report to creditors, insurers, employers, and other businesses that use it to evaluate your applications for credit, insurance, employment, or renting a home. The FTC Website describes in plain English the details about your rights under the FCRA, which established the free annual credit report program.

There are three credit bureaus that compile your credit history: TransUnion, Equifax, and Experian. These bureaus are the entities that provide your credit report. A credit report provides all the details on any loans you have now or have had in the last seven to ten years, depending on the type of account and its status. Credit histories also list certain public records such as judgments against you, bankruptcies, and tax liens.

154

Your credit report will list all credit activity associated with each account. Your lenders report the following information to the bureaus:

- The date the account was opened
- Type of account: An "installment" loan with a fixed payment, such as a car loan; or a "revolving" line of credit such as a credit card
- Whether the account is joint or individual
- Your balance
- When the last payment was made
- Any past due information
- The credit limit on your account
- Any additional terms of the loan
- The status of the account: Current/open, closed, charged-off, sent to collections

How to Get Your Free Credit Report
To order, visit **annualcreditreport.com** or call 1-877-322-8228.

Note: The three nationwide credit reporting companies do not share information and you could have the same or different errors on each of the three. If you find errors, be sure to send an information change notification to all three in order to contest and get the errors corrected.

A Warning About "Imposter" Websites
Only one Website is authorized to fill orders for the free annual credit report you are entitled to under law; annualcreditreport.com. Other Websites that claim to offer "free credit reports," "free credit scores," or "free credit monitoring" are not part of the legally mandated free annual credit report program.

Annualcreditreport.com and the nationwide credit reporting companies will not send you an email asking for your personal information. If you get an email, see a pop-up ad, or get a phone call from someone claiming to be from annualcreditreport.com or any of the three nationwide credit reporting companies, do not reply or click on any link in the message. It's probably a scam, and never provide any personal information over the phone. Forward any such email to the FTC at spam@uce.gov.

Information You Provide to Get Your Free Report
You need to provide your name, address, Social Security number, and date of birth. If you have moved in the last two years, you may have to provide your previous address. To maintain the security of your file, each nationwide credit reporting company may ask you for some information that only you would know, like the amount of your monthly mortgage payment.

identityTheft.gov can help you report and recover from identity theft.

Why You Want a Copy of Your Credit Report

Your credit report has information that affects whether you can get a loan, and how much you will have to pay to borrow money. You want a copy of your credit report to do the following:

- Make sure the information is accurate, complete, and up-to date before you apply for a loan for -a major purchase like a house or car, buy insurance, or apply for a job.
- Help guard against identity theft. That's when someone uses your personal information like your name, your Social Security number, or your credit card number, to commit fraud.

< **End Excerpts: FTC Credit Report Information** >

Part 3: Credit Assistance

Credit Counseling Organizations

There are public and private organizations that can help you manage your debt and put you on a plan. Talk to a credit counselor if you are in trouble with debt. Using legitimate, nonprofit credit counseling can help you manage your debt and won't hurt your credit score. Contact the National Foundation for Credit Counseling (NFCC) at https://www.nfcc.org for more information on debt management. NFCC provides many free services including counseling on credit and debt, bankruptcy, student loans, and more. They can also provide form letters to lenders and the credit bureaus that you can use to dispute errors and fraudulent activity in your credit reports. In addition, they provide online credit education and financial tools.

Also, your credit card statement provides a toll-free 800 number that you can call for more information about credit counseling services. These contact numbers can be found in the Payment Information section as part of the warning information regarding late payments and minimum payments. By calling one of these numbers, you can get a list of credit counseling agencies approved by the Department of Justice. You can also go to https://www.justice.gov and search for "credit counseling."

Almost every day you can hear commercials promising to eliminate or reduce your credit card debt and enticing you to take advantage of various programs. The fact that they advertise on radio and TV gives you an idea of how many people are in trouble with credit card debt. Some of these programs are legitimate and can help you, but you may have to pay for the services they provide. Some advertise that they can reduce or eliminate your debts while not affecting your credit or you having to declare bankruptcy. Some of these companies take advantage of people who are in trouble and need help.

There are some good private debt assistance and counseling companies. Most of them provide help in improving your credit score, managing your dept and help in repairing your credit report but typically charge for the services. Some companies provide free services up front and charge for them later. If you see an advertisement for a credit assistance company on TV or hear a radio ad, be careful and check their reviews and consumer affairs as well as their BBB rating (should be A or A+). You can do a search for the company name and reviews. Unfortunately, there are unscrupulous companies that take advantage of people who are in trouble financially. If you are considering enlisting the help of a credit counseling company, ask the following questions:

- Are they asking for cash up front?
- Are they promising unrealistic credit score increases?
- Do they have a money back guarantee?
- Do they say they can wipe bankruptcy from your credit history?

If any of the answers is yes, reconsider your choice and walk away.

Protecting Your Credit: Credit Monitoring and Credit (security) Freeze
There are two main methods available to help protect your credit: credit monitoring and a credit (security) freeze. The NFCC and other sources provide information on both.

Credit Monitoring
This is typically a monthly subscription service that scans all three of your credit reports daily. Potential fraud and questionable charges are reported to you for investigation and resolution. Some services will work with you to help resolve issues that are identified. The following summarizes the main characteristics of credit monitoring:

- Passive service monitors credit report changes (daily)
- Most services monitor all three credit reports (Equifax, Experian, and TransUnion)
- Looks for and reports suspicious activity (after the fact) to be investigated
- Potentially fraudulent activity can include address changes, new accounts, hard inquiries, and public records
- Weekly reports are emailed that state whether there were critical credit changes to report.
- Typical monthly charge is $10-$20

Credit (Security) Freeze
You can also "freeze" your credit so that no one can open a new account in your name (identity theft). This is a good idea if you do not plan on applying for credit soon (next six months or so). You must create an online account with the three credit bureaus to freeze your credit. You can unfreeze your credit if you plan on opening a new line of credit or buying a home or car. Existing creditors can still access your credit information. The following summarizes the main characteristics of a credit freeze:

- Prevents credit and loan applications in your name.
- Active method that requires you to "freeze" each of your three credit report files.
- Requires you to create a basic account with each of the three credit bureaus.
- Credit freezes are free based on a federal law that went into effect in September of 2018.

- No monthly monitoring subscriptions required.
- Creditors checking your credit reports will see that they are frozen and will not open new accounts.
- If you want to apply for credit, you must unfreeze each of your reports from the three credit bureaus and then refreeze them.

The Freeze and Thaw Process
Search the Web for "*bureau-name* credit freeze" and just replace "*bureau-name*" with one of the three credit bureaus (Equifax, Experian, or TransUnion). You can set up a basic login account with each bureau at no cost, and freeze or unfreeze your credit file whenever you need to for free. Keep in mind that you must contact all three credit bureaus and place the freeze on all three of your credit reports at the same time. Once you log in to each bureau, the process only takes a few minutes. You must do the same to unfreeze or "lift" the freeze on all three of your credit report files. Visit https://www.usa.gov for more information on how to place or lift a freeze on your credit report.

Fraud Alerts
A fraud alert notifies lenders to take extra steps to verify your identity and can be added to your credit report file with or without a credit freeze in place. For maximum protection you can apply both a credit freeze and fraud alert, but the alert is most often applied when you know of or suspect a data breach or fraudulent activity involving your identity. As with the credit (security) freeze, you can place an alert for free, but you only need to contact one of the bureaus and they are required to notify the other two. The initial basic fraud alert time period is one year which will expire automatically but can be extended to 7 years if you have been a victim of ID theft or fraud, and have completed an FTC identity theft report, or filed a police report. According to the FTC, "Credit freezes and fraud alerts can protect you from identity theft or prevent further misuse of your personal information if it was stolen." You can find more information about what they do and how to place them at:

https://consumer.ftc.gov/articles/what-know-about-credit-freezes-fraud-alerts

Credit Protection and Identity (ID) Theft Protection
When you have an account with one or more of the three credit bureaus, they can monitor your credit file as do Credit Karma and others. There is also a wealth of credit information available, including how to improve your credit score. In some cases, there is a monthly fee, depending on the level of monitoring and protection you choose. Each of the credit bureaus offers some form of enhanced protection for your identity and credit with ID theft protection alerts and multi-bureau credit monitoring. Some offer basic coverage for free, or you can try their premium level for free and then pay a monthly fee thereafter, usually around twenty dollars/month. Premium level credit monitoring usually includes lost wallet protection, ID theft insurance coverage of $1 million per year, and fraud assistance in the event of ID theft. Also, check with your homeowner's insurance, as they may have a provision that can assist you with fraud resolution.

Mistakes, Disputes, and Fraudulent Activity in Your Credit Report(s)

By comparing the data between the three credit bureau reports you can take corrective action as necessary if you find errors or activity that may be fraudulent. According to the Federal Trade Commission (FTC), it is estimated that about 20 percent of credit reports have errors in them. Some of the errors are relatively benign while others can be very damaging. For this reason, check your credit reports annually (all three of them). It is very important that you do this about six months before applying for an auto loan or home mortgage. It can take months to get errors corrected. If you find a fraudulent entry, such as an account that you know you did not open, report it to the creditor, the three credit bureaus, and the FTC.

I check each of my credit reports quarterly and have found minor errors and discrepancies in all three over time. The worst one was a negative entry reported (ninety-day late) from a creditor I had never done business with. They also had a home address for me in New York where I had never lived. I had one entry that was a legitimate creditor that could not locate me, and the bill had gone to collections. I contacted the creditor, settled the account, and requested (in writing) that they notify each of the three credit bureaus. The correction was posted within one month. By itself, checking your report won't help your score but will alert you to errors so you can contest them and get them corrected. Keep in mind that not all creditors will send updates to the three credit bureaus. The FTC requires that each of the three credit bureaus must do the following:

- Make sure that the information they collect about you is accurate
- Provide you with a free copy of your credit report annually
- Allow you to correct any mistakes

A Federal Trade Commission study of the U.S. credit reporting industry found that 5 percent of consumers had errors in one of their three major credit bureau reports that could lead to them paying more for products such as auto loans and insurance. Overall, the congressionally mandated study on credit report accuracy found that one in five consumers had an error on at least one of their three credit reports. To dispute errors, contact the credit reporting bureau whose report you found the mistake in, and follow the procedure they recommend.

Negative Report Information

A frequently asked question is how long information stays on a credit report. In general, negative information stays on credit reports for seven years and bankruptcy stays on a credit report for seven to ten years. Positive information, such as accounts being paid as agreed, can stay on indefinitely if the account is open and is being reported by the lender. Hard inquiries can stay on your credit report for up to 2 years and are not necessarily bad unless you have several within a short period of time. Home mortgage and auto loan shopping are the exceptions. Negative information examples include the following:

- Late payments
- Collection/or charge-offs

- Bankruptcy
- Repossessions
- Foreclosures
- Hard inquiries

ChexSystems and the Fair Credit Reporting Act (FCRA)

As a reminder from Chapter 6, if you have difficulty opening a checking account due to past financial issues, you can contact the nationwide specialty consumer reporting agency called ChexSystems, which operates under the Fair Credit Reporting Act (FCRA). This agency tracks problem consumer checking account activity and reports it to U.S. banks and credit unions. People with significant checking account difficulties and account closures are reported by ChexSystems to banks to assist them in making decisions on opening new accounts. The FCRA allows consumers to access their ChexSystems report for free once every twelve months. You can request a copy of your ChexSystems report online at https://www.chexsystems.com. If negative account activity is reported in your file, you may be able to contest it. If you've not had any issues opening accounts, your report will likely show no negative activity. In addition to obtaining your report, you can access a lot of good financial educational information.

Chapter 8 Exercises

Exercise 8-1: Create Credit Bureau Account

In this exercise, you will research and select one of the three nationwide credit reporting bureaus (Equifax, Experian or TransUnion) and create a login account on its Website. You may create an account for each of them if desired. If you wish to freeze your credit file you must create an account with each of the three bureaus. If you already have an account with one of the bureaus, you can skip this exercise. There is a wealth of good information on credit in general and how to improve your credit score and report on all three credit bureau Websites. Each of the three credit bureaus has a consumer information section that explains credit scores and reports.

Exercise 8-2: Obtain Your Credit Score and Report

There are several ways to obtain your score and report. In Exercise 8-1, you created a login account for one or more of the big three credit reporting bureaus (Equifax, Experian, or TransUnion). In Part A of this exercise, you will obtain your credit score from one of the credit bureaus or another source of your choice. These can include a bank, credit card issuer or another financial company. Or, you may already know your score, having checked it recently. In Part B you will access your credit report, either from annualcreditreport.com or through one of the credit bureaus.

Part A: Free Credit Score Options
- Use your account created with one of the three credit reporting bureaus (Equifax, Experian, and TransUnion).

- Check with each of your credit card issuers to see if they provide this service, as it is becoming increasingly common. Create an account and put up with some advertising.
- Search for "free credit scores" on the Web. If you are asked to enter credit card information, the score is not free.
- Check with your banker to obtain your score and/or report.
- Access your score and report through myFICO.

Part B: Free Credit Report Options
- Use your account created with one of the three credit reporting bureaus (Equifax, Experian, and TransUnion).
- Access https://www.annualcreditreport.com/index.action for your report(s).
- Search for "free credit report" on the Web.
- Check with your banker to obtain your score and/or report.
- Access your score and report through myFICO.

Chapter 9
Credit and Credit Cards

Chapter Overview:

Chapter 8 focused on your credit score and credit report, two of the most critical factors in determining your financial well-being. Chapter 9 focuses on how to manage credit in general and credit cards specifically and is probably the single most important chapter in the book. It provides information on credit behavior and offers some specific suggestions and tips on what to do and what not to do to help keep your credit healthy. It covers general-purpose credit cards— such as Visa and Mastercard—as well as retail store credit cards, debit cards, and lines of credit. The chapter is divided into four parts and covers a wide range of credit and credit card topics.

- **Part 1: Credit Concepts and Issues**
- **Part 2: Credit Card Statements and Bill Paying**
- **Part 3: Credit and Debit Card Types and Use**
- **Part 4: Credit and Credit Card Tips and Notes**

Part 1 provides an overview of credit and identifies the problems associated with using credit cards. Part 2 focuses on billing and credit card transactions and explains each section of the billing statement and what to look for as an informed consumer. Part 3 describes the various types of credit and debit cards available and the features of each. Exercises are provided to record your credit card information and enter it into the PFS Cred-Cards sheet. A credit card feature comparison exercise is also provided. Part 4 provides many tips and notes on credit in general as well as credit card dos and don'ts to increase awareness and avoid being taken advantage of. Tips are provided to help you obtain credit, get the most out your credit cards, and keep your spending under control.

Chapter PFS and PFI Integration:

The chapter covers PFS Sheet – Credit and Credit Cards with a tab label of "Cred-Cards." The Cred-Cards sheet provides a way to record information about the credit bureau account you created in Chapter 8, Exercise 8-1, as well as your credit rating and credit report obtained from Exercise 8-2. You can record your credit cards and credit lines with Exercise 9-1 and enter your credit card information into the PFS Cred-Cards sheet. The first section of the Cred-Cards sheet is for your credit score and credit report information. Section 2 lists your credit cards and other lines of credit, such as a Home Equity Line of Credit (HELOC), with pertinent information and utilization. Section 3 of the Cred-Cards sheet provides summary calculations for credit limit and card balances and averages the APR for all your revolving credit lines. Cred-Cards sheet Section 4 calculates your combined Debt-to-Credit (DTC) ratio for all credit cards/lines entered. See Figure 9-3 for a screenshot of the Cred-Cards sheet with sample data.

PFS Cred-Cards Sheet Sections:
- **Section 1: Credit Scores and Reports** (from credit bureaus)
- **Section 2: Revolving Credit Lines** (credit cards and lines of credit)
- **Section 3: Credit Card Calculations** (total credit limit, total CC balance, average APR)
- **Section 4: Debt-to-Credit (DTC) Ratio** (revolving credit utilization rate)

Chapter Exercises:
- **Exercise 9-1: Record PFS Credit and Credit Card Info**
- **Exercise 9-2: Compare Credit Card Features**

Refer to **Exercise 9-1: Record PFS Credit and Credit Card Info** at the end of this chapter, which will help you record credit scores and credit report information using a blank form of the PFS sheet Credit and Credit Cards to enter your credit data. You will also list your credit cards and record important information about each card such as primary user, card issuer, card number (Last four digits), credit limit, credit used, APR, and notes regarding card perks and fees. Perks can include cash back and airline miles, etc. Card fees can include annual fees and foreign transaction fees (FTF). Annual fees can be as much as $100 or more, and FTF fees are usually 3%. This PFS sheet calculates your Debt-to-Credit (DTC) ratio based on the credit cards, credit limits, and card balances (utilization) you enter.

Chapter Notable Quotes:
Quote 9-1: "It is a great and powerful feeling to pay off your credit cards on your way to being debt free."
- Anonymous

Quote 9-2: "Compound interest is the eighth wonder of the world. He who understands it earns it; he who doesn't, pays it." - Albert Einstein

Part 1: Credit Concepts and Issues

What is Credit?
There are many definitions of credit, and many variations on those definitions, which is an indication of how important this concept is in our vocabulary and our lives. With respect to personal finance, credit most often refers to borrowing money from a lender for a set time period with a specified rate of return (fixed or variable interest). The process starts when a potential borrower approaches a lender to borrow money. The lender extends credit (a level of monetary trust) to the borrower. This can be in the form of a loan for a specific amount (principal) and time period (term), or it can be a "line of credit," which is a more open-ended agreement with a "not-to-exceed" limit on how much can be borrowed. In either case, the loan or credit line is a contract between the borrower and lender where the borrower receives an amount of money (debt obligation) that they are expected to pay back with interest.

Credit Types

From the credit reporting bureau (Equifax, Experian, and TransUnion) perspective, there are three main types of personal credit that they track (revolving, real estate, or installment). The information tracked is based on updates received from creditors you do business with. These credit categories form the basis of your credit report and are shown in Table 9-1, summarized from one of the Big 3 credit bureaus. This is a simplified version of Table 8-6 in Chapter 8. The table below contains data for a fictitious household member and is a snapshot of the credit status for that individual. It shows the type of account, the number of accounts of that type (both open and closed), the current balance for all open accounts of that type, and the current payment amount for all accounts that are open with balances. Notes were added showing an example of that account type.

Table 9-1: Credit Bureau - Personal Credit Type Summary

Type of Account	Count (#)	Balance	Payment	Notes/Examples
Revolving	16	$4726	$122	Credit card, HELOC
Real Estate	3	$145770	$1236	Mortgage
Installment	2	$8752	$471	Auto loan

Most loans can be classified as one of three categories: Amortized (installment) loans, Revolving credit loans (lines of credit and credit cards), and securities or bonds (loans to municipalities and governments). The most common types of amortized installment loans are listed here:

- **Home loans (mortgages)**
- **Auto loans (vehicle)**
- **Student loans**
- **Personal loans**

From an accounting perspective, a credit is a deposit to a monetary account, whereas a debit is a withdrawal from an account. There are many aspects of credit that will be covered in this chapter and the book as a whole. These include credit cards, credit scores, credit ratings, credit reports, credit history, credit profile, credit health, credit counseling, credit account, credit line, credit monitoring, and credit freeze.

The Credit Card Epidemic

Credit cards are a relatively new financial concept made viable and widespread by the development of modern-day computers. Bank of America launched the BankAmericard card in the late 1950s. This was one of the first modern credit cards. Today, there are thousands of credit cards available, and Americans carry more credit card debt than the population of any other country. According to Experian, the average credit/loan balances in the U.S. are as follows, based on 2022 data:

- Average Credit Card Balance: $6,000
- Average Personal Loan Balance: $18,000
- Average Auto Loan Balance: $23,000
- Average Student Loan Balance: $39,000
- Average Mortgage Balance: $236,000

(Amounts are rounded and approximate)

Credit card use is ubiquitous, and overuse is a common problem. Credit cards are not bad as long as you play by the rules and use them responsibly. To help you get your credit card use under control, this chapter provides many tips on how to use your credit cards to your advantage and get the most out of them while paying the least amount of interest and fees. It also provides suggestions to help you reduce and virtually eliminate credit card debt, which can be a major accomplishment for a lot of people, me included.

The Value of Good Credit

Having good credit can make your life a lot easier, not to mention less costly. By the same token, having poor credit can make your life harder and more miserable.

As mentioned previously, your creditworthiness can affect many aspects of your life including these:
- How much you can borrow for a home or car loan
- What interest rate you will pay for any loan or credit application
- What interest rate you will pay for credit card purchases, transfers and cash advances
- Whether you can obtain a credit card and what your credit limit will be
- Whether you will be considered for a job you apply for
- Whether you will be able to rent an apartment and deposit amounts required
- Whether you will be able to obtain home utility accounts (water/gas/electric/phone/Internet)
- Whether you will be able to rent a car
- Whether you will be able to make airline reservations
- And much more ...

To demonstrate the importance of good credit, refer to Bullet Point 3 above and the following example. Amy just received a solicitation in the mail for a credit card that offered 0 percent interest for purchases and transfers for a specific promotional time period (about one year). She would be charged 3 percent of any amount transferred. She would also get a check for $200 if she charged $1,000 or more in purchases during the time period. After that period, the Annual Percentage Rate (APR) for purchases would be adjusted to either 15 percent, 21 percent, or 25 percent, based on her creditworthiness. If she did not have good credit, the credit card company would not have even sent her the offer. You can see that her credit rating could make a big difference in the interest rate they would charge her for regular purchases after the promo period ended.

If you have poor credit, you are viewed as a higher risk than people who have good credit, and creditors are less likely to want to deal with you. And, if they do, you will pay a penalty in some form, usually higher interest rates and/or lower credit limits. If you have a good credit history with credit cards and installment loans, your credit scores and reports will reflect this, and creditors will want to deal with you.

Note: To learn more about factors to consider when applying for or using a credit card and many other financial subjects, visit the Website for the Consumer Financial Protection Bureau (CFPB) at

https://www.consumerfinance.gov/learnmore

Unauthorized Credit Card Purchases and Your Liability

The rules are different for Credit cards, Debit cards, and ATM cards, but the focus here is on credit cards. Most credit card companies do not go after you as the card holder to recover illegitimate charges. However, based on the Fair Credit Billing Act (FCBA), you may be liable for a small fee, which most card issuers waive. The bottom line is, if you have a Visa or Mastercard or any other legitimate credit card, and you report the theft, loss, or illegitimate use of the card as soon as you know its missing, you basically have little or no liability for unauthorized charges. The credit card company will typically send you a new card. If you see a charge on your credit card statement you feel is incorrect, you can contest the charge in writing by sending a letter to the credit card company within thirty days, explaining the situation. If you can do it in less than thirty days, that's even better, or you may be able to file the dispute online. You may also send a dispute letter to the individual or company that made the invalid charge. In many cases, the credit card company will go to bat for you and contest the charge with the company. This happened to me when I returned an item to a company, expecting a credit for about $200. The company said they never received the returned product. I called the credit card company and contested the charge. They opened a dispute case and contacted the company directly. It turned out that the company had received the item, but it had not been placed in the returned items bin on the shipping dock.

Adding an Authorized User to a Credit Card

Use caution when allowing another person as an authorized user, such as a spouse, on your credit card. The terms can vary from one card issuer to another, but this can be a way to help someone build their credit. It allows them to charge on the account, and their charge activity will be reported to credit bureaus as an authorized user. However, the authorized user is not contractually responsible for the payment of the account. As the primary account holder, you are still responsible for paying all charges made on the account.

The Boiled Frog Syndrome

The biggest problem with credit cards is that they insulate you from the actual money-spending experience or process of handling money. Many people tend to just whip out the plastic and deal with the bill later, whether they have the money to pay for the purchase or not. This is a huge area of importance for personal financial awareness. Some people just continue to charge their cards until they reach their limit, which, as we know, harms their credit rating. That which you do not monitor, you cannot control. The Boiled Frog

Syndrome refers to the fact that if you put a frog in water and slowly increase the temperature, before the frog notices it, it's too late. This is what happens to people who slowly overuse their credit cards and do not monitor their credit and credit use.

Credit cards can be very useful when used properly. They simply provide a convenient way to spend money and are nearly indispensable in today's world. Try buying a plane ticket or reserving a rental car without one. As discussed previously, having multiple credit cards can help your credit score because it increases your overall credit limit, as long as you are not using too much of it. People who have no credit cards and pay cash for everything are viewed as a worse credit risk. People who have a couple of credit cards, are viewed as a better credit risk, as long as they don't max out their credit limit and pay their bills on time because they have demonstrated that they can handle credit (borrow money and pay it back as agreed).

Mindful Awareness and Credit Card Use

Try to consciously be aware whenever you are paying for something using a credit card. It may help you decide to put the card back in your wallet and pay cash or decide you really don't need what you were going to buy. If you do use a credit card, be mindful that you are borrowing money from the credit card company (the issuer, lender, or creditor). The creditor pays the merchant at the point of sale on your behalf and effectively "loans" you the money at an interest rate of 15 percent to 25 percent. It may be a small loan, but it is a loan none the less, and it's easy to let multiple small loans accumulate to add up to a large amount of debt. Over time, the total of the small loans begins to approach the credit limit of the credit card (maybe $5,000), and your credit score goes down due to high debt and high credit utilization. The debt can easily grow to a point where you cannot pay off the loan(s) when due, and you begin to carry a balance from one month to the next. Worse yet, you may start paying minimum payments, which barely cover the interest, let alone the balance or principal of the original purchase. This is when the debt snowball begins and the balance from one month to the next continues to grow. You are on your way to being a boiled frog! Fortunately, you are a human and can observe, notice, and correct the excessive heat problem before you become boiled. All kidding aside, this is the most serious and most common financial issue facing most people.

Compound Interest and Revolving Credit

Compound interest can work for you or against you. It can be your friend if you are an investor, or your enemy if you are a debtor. Remember the quote from Albert Einstein about compound interest: "He who understands it, earns it. He who doesn't, pays it." If you have a savings account that pays interest, you are the one who earns it. If you carry a balance on your credit cards you are probably the one who is paying it. The negative effect it can have on credit card debt, if you carry a balance, is one of the most common reasons people feel out of control with their finances. This is especially true if you make only the minimum payment each month. You are basically paying interest (which is compounded daily) on previously unpaid interest and not just the previous principal balance. Unpaid interest is added to and becomes part of your new balance each month. This is mainly a problem with credit card debt and overused credit lines. Both are forms of revolving credit, and your payment can vary considerably from one month to the next, but you must make at least the minimum due or incur late payment fees. Carrying a balance and compound interest are not a concern with installment loans (e.g., auto and personal loans) where the payment is set for the term of the loan. Each payment pays a certain amount to the principal and a certain amount to interest, and you don't have the option of paying a partial or minimum payment (well, they might let you get away with it once or twice).

Note: Additional information on compound interest can be found in Chapter 10: Buying, Borrowing, and Debt, as well as Chapter 13: Investing Basics.

Those Are the Rules!

The credit card rules are set up so that if you can pay back the loan resulting from purchases on credit from the card issuer by the due date of your next statement, you will not have to pay any interest. That's pretty cool, since you are essentially getting an interest free loan for about twenty-five days depending on the card issuer. See note on Payment Due Date below. If you can pay your balance in full by the due date with every credit card you have, you will never pay any interest on the purchases charged on those cards! However, if you carry a balance from one month to the next, you will pay interest on the balance until it is paid off. And you will pay interest on interest in many cases (compounded daily). This is especially true if your balance is increasing from month to month. **Those Are the Rules!**

Key Credit Card Billing Statement and Payment Terminology

- **Closing Date:** End of billing cycle (cutoff date after which transactions will go on next statement). This is also the online availability date and frequently the mail date.
- **Payment Due Date:** Payments received after this date incur late fees and other penalties. Must occur on the same day every month and must allow at least 21 days from the statement Closing Date, by law. Ranges from federally mandated minimum of 21 days to around 28 days, with the average being about 25 days.
- **New Balance:** Statement balance reflecting new charges and payments, within the statement billing cycle, since the last closing date.
- **Minimum Payment Due:** Required payment amount by payment due date to avoid fees and keep account in good standing. Refer to Table 9-2 for Minimum Payment Warning.
- **Days in Billing Cycle:** Typically, 30 days but can vary.
- **Grace Period:** Time between current statement closing date and next statement closing date. Purchases made during this period are not subject to interest if the last statement balance and the current state balance were paid in full (PIF) by the Payment Due Date.

Notes on Grace Period

The majority of card issuers allow you a window of time (usually around twenty-five days) where you can charge purchases on your card and not have to pay interest. This is the case for many card issuers long as you have paid your previous statement balance in full and pay the current statement balance in full. If you pay only a partial payment, even if by the due date and carry a balance from one month to the next, some card issuers will rescind this so called "grace period". Also, some card issuers do not consider this a grace period, but simply a benefit to their customers and an incentive to pay their bill in full, and not carry a balance. Typically, the term "grace period" refers to a period of time after something is officially due that allows you to go beyond that date and not be penalized with a late fee or derogatory credit report remarks. A good example of a true grace period is a home mortgage. With most mortgages there is a set date when the payment is due. But lenders typically allow a fifteen-day grace period before considering the homeowner past due on their payment, and possibly reporting them to the credit bureaus. Let's say my actual mortgage due date is the first of the month. If I have a fifteen-day grace period, as long as my payment is received by the fourteenth, it would not be considered late. Sometimes even when you're within the grace period you may be considered past due and may be charged a late fee, which might subsequently be waived on your behalf. If you are making a mortgage payment using online bill pay from your bank, be sure to take note of the method of payment and the date the payment will be received. I just made a payment for my mortgage on the 1st of the month (which happens to be a Saturday) using my bank's online bill paying system, and it said the method of payment would be "sent by mail." And the actual date it showed was the 10th of the month! Still it was well within the grace period, but it was an eye opener when you think about how long it would take for the payment to be received.

Credit Card Use Affirmation

So, try to develop a mindset of saying this affirmation whenever you are using a credit card: "I am borrowing this money, and I will pay it back within thirty days, or I will have to pay a lot of interest. And I may get cash back just for using the card for the purchase as long as I can pay it off." With a little self-control and mindful awareness, you can have your cake and eat it too, and build good credit in the process! Keep in mind that using a credit card builds your credit history (positively or negatively), whereas using a debit card does not.

Part 2: Credit Card Statements and Bill Paying

Credit Card Statement Sections and Important Information

There are six main sections to most credit card statements. It is very important with regard to financial awareness to know what kind of information is available in each section and what to look for. The wording of the section titles may vary a little, and there may be additional sections depending on the card issuer, but the six primary sections you will see on nearly every statement are listed below in the order they appear on most statements. Additional details as well as specific information on what to look for are provided in the following text and in Tables 9-1, 9-2, and 9-3.

1. **Payment Information** - New balance, Minimum payment due, and Payment due date. Late payment warning and Minimum payment warning (see below for explanation)
2. **Account Activity Summary** - Previous balance, Payments, Credits, Purchases, Cash advances, Fees (like late fees), Interest (on previous balance), and New balance
3. **Credit Line/Limit** - Total revolving credit line (includes cash advance line) and available credit.
4. **Rewards Summary** - Total cash or points. May include detail by category (gas, dining etc.)

5. **Transaction Detail** – List of each transaction (purchases and credits) to account
6. **Interest Charge Calculation** – If you are paying your credit card balance in full before the statement due date, interest charges should be zero.

Payment Information Section - Late Payment Warning and Minimum Payment Warning

I received a statement for one of my credit cards. The balance was almost exactly $1,000. On the statement there was a "Late Payment Warning" and a "Minimum Payment Warning," which are part of the Payment Information section. Card issuers now include these warnings on every statement to help increase awareness of problems associated with late and minimum payments.

Example: Late Payment Warning

The late payment warning says that, if I am late on a payment, I may have to pay a $37 late fee. They will also probably raise my interest rate (APR) from an already high 20 percent to as much as 25 percent or more. Remember that, if you pay off the balance each month, your interest rate is effectively 0 percent.

Example: Minimum Payment Warning

On your statement, it states that "If you make only the minimum payment each period, you will pay more in interest, and it will take you longer to pay off your balance." It tells you how long it will take to pay the balance (in my case $1,000) and how much your total payback will be. They present the information as shown in Table 9-2, which is an actual example.

Table 9-2: Credit Card Statement - Minimum Payment Warning - Example
(Balance of $1,000 and APR of 16 percent)

If you make no additional charges using this card and each month you pay:	You will pay off the balance shown on this statement in about:	And you will end up paying an estimated total of:
Only the minimum payment ($25 in this case)	5 years	$1,480
$36	3 years (two years less)	$1,280 (Savings=$200)

So, if your balance is currently $1,000, and you don't charge anything else to this credit card and pay only the minimum each month, it will take you about **FIVE YEARS** to pay it off and you will pay almost $500 in interest. As the table shows, if you just increase the amount you pay per month from $25 to $36, you reduce the time from five years to three years and reduce the interest paid by about $200.

Credit Card Statement – Interest Charges Section

Another important part of your statement is the Interest Charges section. It tells you the interest rate (APR) you are paying or will pay for (1) Purchases, (2) Cash Advances and (3) Balance Transfers. The information is usually presented as shown in Table 9-3. If you are paying your balance off each month and have not done any cash advances or balance transfers, the amount in the last two columns should be zero. If you see anything other than zeros, you should investigate by calling the credit card company to find out what they are charging you for and why. It is nice to see the zeros because it means you are not paying any interest. Also, as you can see in the table, cash advances carry a much higher APR than regular purchases and balance transfers. So only use the cash advance option in emergencies. If you take a cash advance, not only will you pay a very high interest rate on whatever you borrow, you will also likely pay a cash advance fee of 5 percent of the amount for each cash advance. And cash advance can negatively impact your credit rating.

Table 9-3: Credit Card Statement - Interest Charges Section - Example 1
(Typical entries when balance is paid in full each month)

Balance Type	Annual Percentage Rate (APR)	Balance Subject to Interest Rate	Interest Charges
Purchases	18.49%	- 0 -	- 0 -
Cash Advances	26.49%	- 0 -	- 0 -
Balance Transfers	18.49%	- 0 -	- 0 -

Table 9-4 Shows another example of the Interest Charges section where the credit card was used to purchase a computer, for $2,000 as an example, using a promotional interest rate (APR) and a set time period for repayment. In this case, the purchaser has taken advantage of a "deferred interest promotion," which is basically a zero (0) interest (same as cash) loan as long as the purchase is paid off within the promotional time. Notice that the table shows the Plan Type as "twelve months no interest if paid in full by" and then shows the Promotion Expiration Date. This is the date that you must keep track of, and it will show up on every statement until you pay off the promotion amount. The Promo Plan Deferred Interest Charges amount shows the amount that will be owed by buyer if the purchase is not paid off within the promotional time, and it will continue to increase from month to month, but the buyer will not have to pay it if they pay off the purchase within the allotted time period.

This example statement is the first one the buyer received after making the initial purchase. If the buyer fails to pay off the purchase within the designated time frame (twelve months), all the deferred interest is added to the balance and the buyer must pay all of the differed interest. Also, if the buyer is late with a payment or if they pay less than the minimum amount due shown, in any given month, they will be in violation of the terms of the promotion and the same thing will happen and the APR will likely go up.

Table 9-4: Credit Card Statement - Interest Charges Section - Example 2
(Deferred Interest Promotion entries - some columns omitted)

Plan Type	Promotion Expiration Date	Balance Subject to Interest Rate	Interest (APR)	Interest Charges	Promo Plan Deferred Interest	Deferred Interest Balance	Min. Amt. Due
12 Mo No Int if paid in full by	01-16-24	- 0 -	18.50% (v)	- 0 -	$12.09	$1,500	$45

Annual Percentage Rate (APR)

Most credit cards carry an interest rate of 15 percent to 25 percent for regular purchases, with the national average being around 18 percent. The credit card example in Table 9-4 carries a variable APR of 18.50 percent for regular purchases. Keep in mind that this is an Annual Percentage Rate (APR). Interest for credit card balances is calculated monthly to coincide with your statement. However, the number of days in each month varies, so the interest is calculated using a daily periodic rate or DPR. The DPR is calculated by dividing the APR by the number of days in a year or 365. The card issuer multiplies the daily rate times the account balance and by the number of days in the month to come up with your monthly statement amount. Divide the APR by twelve to get an approximate monthly rate or about 1/12th of the APR. So, a card with a 24 percent APR will cost you about 2 percent per month on the balance.

Variable APR Example

Note that the 18.5 percent APR for the credit card statement example in Table 9-4 is a variable (instead of fixed) rate indicated by the "(v)" after the rate. This means that the rate can go up or down from whatever it is currently. The variable rate is usually calculated using the U.S. Prime Rate (U.S. interbank lending rate) + margin or the LIBOR (London Interbank Borrowing Rate) + margin. A code after the APR usually indicates which rate is used.

Bill-paying Errors

I tend to be somewhat dyslexic when paying bills online, so I verify every account number and amount paid twice. Just the other day, I paid a bill and entered the amount $358.56 instead of the correct amount of $385.56. When I verified it in scheduled payments, I noticed and corrected the error. If I had not, I would have been short of the actual amount and would not have paid the balance in full as I'd intended. In addition, on the next statement, I would have been charged 20 percent interest (the normal interest rate for purchases on this particular card) on the whole balance instead of 0 percent interest. Another potential error source to pay attention to is this: if you have multiple cards from the same issuer, be sure to verify the correct payee and sixteen-digit account number on the card. Check the last four digits of the account, the amount, and the date paid, so you don't accidentally pay the wrong bill. Also check the last amount paid to the payee, as you may find that you've already paid the bill.

Bill Paying and Credit Card Billing Statements

Try to pay your bills when you get them, using your bank's online bill paying app if possible. This avoids having to set aside a bigger chunk of time to pay bills and lessens the chances that you will be overdue on a payment. It also forces you to be more aware of how much you are spending on a daily basis and how much you have in your checking/savings online accounts.

I have found the easiest way for me to manage bills is to maintain a simple IN/OUT box. As the bills come in, I separate the advertising and promotional material (especially checks) from the actual bill and tear it up or shred it. (I get at least two or three offers a month from credit card companies asking if I want to transfer a balance from another credit card. They usually include a couple of checks and encourage me to use up my credit and further increase my indebtedness. It's very tempting and convenient but does not make financial sense.)

As I open and process each bill, I highlight or circle the balance owed, the minimum payment, and the due date. I sort the bills with the nearest or soonest due date on top and latest due date on the bottom. I try to pay all bills when they are received or at least once a week, but this is not always possible. I put all of them in the top or IN basket. Sorting them puts the bill with the nearest due date on top. I can see which bills are due and when, and I am less likely to be late with a payment. This is especially important if you are using online bill pay through your bank, as most payments are delayed by a couple of days. It can also help you avoid late payment fees.

If paying by USPS mail, allow at least five days for the payment to arrive to the creditor. For online bill payment, allow at least three days. If a bill is due in less than two days, I call the company and pay the bill over the phone (if possible) using a credit card (if possible). Most companies do not charge a fee for this unless you talk with a representative over the phone. Some companies offer no-fee automated payment systems accessible via the Web or phone. If paying a credit card bill by phone, most companies have automated phone systems that can take checking account information. There is usually no charge for paying by check over the phone with an automated system.

Why Read Every Bill (especially credit card bills)?

Read every loan and credit card statement (phone bills, etc.) and bank statement you get in the mail or by email. This helps to become familiar with the format and where the information is. Some people just open the bill, assume the charges are valid, and go ahead and pay the bill. There could be small charges lurking there, but they can get lost. Be sure to focus on the new charges to verify that they look legitimate. You might spot unauthorized charges made by someone else or even charges authorized by you that you've forgotten about, like perhaps you forgot to cancel a recurring charge.

Note: If you do pay bills automatically with a credit card (like an insurance premium), or you use AutoPay from your checking account, be sure to note the method of payment on the PFS Income-Exp sheet.

Credit Card Statement Transactions Example 1

Credit card statements list each transaction (purchase or charge to card). For each transaction, there is an entry for the date, description, and amount charged. There is usually a phone number embedded in the transaction description so you can call them, if necessary. The description contains the company name, what you bought (product), an 800# to call them, and the city and or state where they are located. A while back I purchased a monthly subscription to a software package. A close look at the statement about six months later revealed that the software company was charging $14.75 monthly to my credit card. That's not a whole lot of money but it adds up. I called the company and cancelled the monthly charge. Note that the Description entry below has been changed to be generic.

Date	Description	Amount
Jun 11	SOFT-CO *SOFT-PROD XYZ 800-999-9999CA	$14.75

Part 3: Credit and Debit Card Types and Use

Using the Right Credit Cards the Right Way (What's in your wallet?)

There are a number of factors that can determine the desirability of a credit card. But the four main ones are these:

- **Low interest rate for purchases**
- **No annual fee**
- **Cash back rewards**
- **Promo zero APR offer**

There are a lot of these cards available, but you must have good credit to get them. If you pay your balance each month, the interest rate is not that important. The annual fee can range from zero to as much as a hundred dollars or more per year. There are several different types of rewards cards. Some give airline miles, while others allow you to accumulate points that can be used to redeem various consumer products. Some only accumulate cash back points for certain categories, which may change each month. Some cards accumulate cash back points for everything you buy and have a fixed percentage amount that you get back but specify a purchase limit. With others a charge/cash back limit is not specified. I have a card with no cash-back limit and once, while building a home, I charged $10,000 for a driveway that I had paved. I got 1.5 percent cash back or $150 on the purchase!

Get Paid to Use Credit Cards

If you have the right kind of credit cards and pay off your balance each month, you can actually get paid to use your credit cards. I just requested my "cash rewards" for the three cards I use most over the year and received a "cash back" check from each of them. The three checks together totaled over $100 (your mileage may vary)! At 2 percent cash back you would have to spend $5,000 to get $100 cash back. Admittedly, you must spend a fair amount to get that much cash back. But if you have budgeted to spend the money for a purchase anyway, using funds from your savings, check to see if you can charge it to a credit card that pays cash back. Or you may be able to apply for a credit card you can charge the purchase to that has an introductory promo at zero interest as well as cash back. Mindful awareness pays.

Cash back cards are great, but they increase the likelihood of charging. If you can pay the balance when due, they can be very beneficial. However, if you carry a balance, you are fighting a losing battle. The card pays you about 1.5-2 percent cash back on your purchases and, if you carry a balance, you pay them 15-20 percent interest or more on your balance. What's wrong with this picture?

Credit Card Rewards and Perks
Most rewards cards (those with perks) fall into one of three categories:

- **Miles** (airline and hotel points)
- **Merchandise** (catalog of stuff you can buy with points)
- **Money** (cash back - varying categories and percentages)

There are advantages and disadvantages to each. The most flexible reward is money. If you fly a lot, you can do well with a "miles" reward. However, there is no substitute for cold, hard cash. You can buy merchandise, a plane ticket, or a hotel room with cash, so that is my first choice. The credit card company can take back your airline miles if they expire or if the airline merges with another or goes out of business.

Some credit cards offer fixed cash rewards on multiple fixed categories, like 3 percent for gas, 2 percent for groceries, and 1 percent for all other purchases. There may be a limit to the total cash back, so be sure to verify this. Also, some cards offer differing percentages for rotating categories that you must selectively activate online periodically. This can be somewhat of a hassle. I prefer to use credit cards that have fixed cash rewards for fixed categories because they run on autopilot, and I do not have to make decisions from month to month. A particular card may offer cash back rewards for some combination of these fixed categories:

- 5 percent on travel related expenses (airfare, hotels, rental cars, etc.)
- 4 percent on groceries and gas (may be some exclusions)
- 3 percent on restaurants (includes fast food)
- 2 percent cash back rewards on grocery stores and drug stores
- 1.5 percent unlimited cash back rewards on everything else

Note: Be sure you are getting the percentage cash back that you think you are. Call the card issuer and ask them what kinds of gas stations or other types of purchases qualify for each cash back level and if there are limits. I have a card that pays 4 percent cash back for gas and groceries, 3 percent for dining out, 2 percent for purchases at the provider's store, and 1 percent for all other purchases. I bought gas at a big-name grocery store gas station and expected to get 4 percent but only got 1 percent because it was not a brand name independent gas station.

Check with bankrate.com or other reputable source to see which credit cards pay the best cash back rates and have the best features. For example, one possible card you could apply for offers unlimited 2 percent cash back on all purchases, with no limit, no annual fee, and a $200 intro reward if you spend $1,000 in the first three months. You also get a 0 percent intro APR for fifteen months on qualifying balance transfers. Although it says the recommended credit score ranges from 670 (good) to 850 (excellent), you would probably need a score of at least 700 to qualify for this card. That said, the card issuer may approve the card but with a lower maximum credit limit and a higher interest rate on regular purchases.

Note: Some cards also provide other perks, such as cellphone protection. The card described above covers your cellphone against damage or theft for up to $600 per claim (subject to a twenty-five-dollar deductible) each month you pay your cellphone bill with the card.

I recently applied for a credit card with benefits that included no annual fee, a high unlimited cash back percentage on all purchases, as well as fifteen months zero interest on balance transfers. In addition, it provided free credit scores and reports. I really didn't need more credit, but the card had a lot of benefits, including coverage for my cell phone. When I activated that card, I signed up for the "FICO Score" option and received free access to the following:

- FICO Credit Score 9 and score history
- Full credit report from one of the major credit bureaus
- Key factors that might impact my score
- Monthly score updates.

Figure 9-1: Credit Cards - The Power of Plastic

Credit Card Features and Benefits Overview

The following bullet points list various credit card features and examples of what to look for in terms of desirability. Some of these benefits or features, such as contesting or disputing a charge, are pretty much standard and common to nearly all credit cards. Other benefits such as no foreign transaction fees, are not as common. When comparing credit cards, consider the following and make sure the card you choose provides most or all of them.

- Cash back (or other) reward points (common - varies with limitations and categories)
- No annual fee (can be as high as a hundred dollars or more per year)
- Low interest rate (Less than 15 percent) and high credit limit (over $5,000)
- Transfer of high interest balances to a lower interest card (usual fee 3 percent of amt transferred)
- No interest if you pay off the balance each month (standard)
- No foreign transaction fees when used abroad (not so common, can be 3 percent)
- Extended factory warranties on electronics and other items (not so common)
- Automatic car rental insurance if used to pay for rental (more common)
- Fraud protection and zero liability for unauthorized charges (more common)
- Identity (ID) theft protection
- Free credit score and credit report (more common)
- Right to contest (dispute) questionable charges (standard)
- Building of credit history and credit rating if paid regularly (common - if card is in your name or you've added an authorized user.)
- Provision to help build credit history of authorized user (less common)
- Borrowing money using cash advance option (common, although higher interest).

Note on Extending Factory Warranties: Not all credit cards will extend factory warranties just for using them to buy an item such as electronics or appliances. Even if they do, there may be conditions that apply. Be sure to call the card issuer and tell them what you intend to buy before you make your purchase and verify that they will extend the manufacturer's warranty and ask about any other special conditions there may be. I assumed when I bought a laptop computer that the card I used would extend the warranty. When I called the card company, I found that they did not provide this benefit. If I had called and verified first and used a different card to buy the laptop, it would have doubled the warranty.

Refer to **Exercise 9-2: Compare Credit Card Features** at the end of this chapter, which will help you identify those credit card features that are important to you. Table 9-5 contains some of the most important features and benefits of those listed above. A blank form, Table 9-6 is used to record the information for each credit card being compared.

Retail Cards (Store Credit Cards)

Many retail stores, gas stations, and other businesses offer a type of credit card that is limited to use at the store. Some offer a 5 percent discount if you use their card at the checkout counter. The biggest problem with these in-store cards is that their interest rate (APR) is very high - like in the 27 percent range. If you pay the balance when the statement comes, the interest rate is not a big deal. If you do not, you are losing money big time. I used to think store cards were a waste of time, but they can save you a lot if you use them properly and don't carry a balance.

When using a store credit card, if you charge additional purchases on the card after you have already made a purchase and charged it using their "0 percent " or "same as cash" promotional offer, payments will be applied to the zero-interest (actually deferred interest) offer balance instead of the higher-interest more recent charges. You will also be charged high interest on new charges until the lowest-interest purchases are paid off.

Retail Store Credit Card Deferred Interest Example

Most "Big Box" stores offer a discount (usually 5 percent) if you use their credit card, or you can opt for deferred interest, but you can't opt for both. With deferred interest purchases, if you pay off the balance within a specific "promotional" time period (usually six, twelve, or eighteen months), there is no interest. The actual interest (a very high rate, like 27 percent) will be calculated from the beginning, but it will be "deferred," meaning it is being put off until the end of the promotional period. You do not have to pay the interest if you have paid off the original amount borrowed within the promotional period and were not late on a payment. This requires some diligence, and the buyer must pay off the purchase much faster than the minimum payment, but it saves a ton of interest (money!). If you follow the rules, you can basically get an interest-free loan for up to eighteen months.

If you do not pay off the purchase within the promotional period time allowed, ALL of the deferred interest is due and is added to your balance at the end and you begin compounding and paying interest on interest. In my case, I would have been charged 27 percent APR on the original special offer amount ($15,000), which would have added THOUSANDS of dollars to my balance! Also, if you miss a payment or are late on a payment, the deferred interest becomes due, and the APR can increase to a "penalty" rate (29 percent or more).

Bank Credit Card Using Zero Interest Promo APR Period Example

The zero-interest "promo" period credit card option is offered by some banks and credit card issuers and is a good option for some people. If you have good credit and a zero balance on your card, you may be able to take advantage of one of these offers. You can also call the credit card issuer and ask if they have any promos. You can use the checks provided to pay for college tuition, home improvement, or medical bills. You can usually get a low APR (0-2 percent) for a promotional period (usually twelve to eighteen months) but at the end of the promo period, the rate can go up to 20 percent or more. You are not required to pay off the balance, but you must still make minimum payments even during the promo period. For each transaction you will be charged a fee of 3-4 percent. If you pay off the total amount charged over the promo period (and do not charge any new purchases), you pay zero (0) interest. After the promo period, the APR will go up, depending on whether you did a balance transfer, direct deposit, or cash advance. If you still have a balance on your credit card at the end of the promo period, your APR will go to the new rate, but there is no accrued interest, as with the store deferred-interest cards. Regular purchases charged during the promo period will carry the normal APR of 15–25 percent and will not be paid off until the original zero-interest promo charge amount has been paid off.

This option is not like a HELOC, where you can have an open line of credit for an extended period. With the zero-interest promo APR option, you have a limited time to complete the transactions (one to two months).

Zero-Interest APR Promo Scenario - Factoring in the Transfer Fee

Let's say you have a credit card with a zero balance and a $10,000 credit limit, and your bank is running a promo whereby you can charge the $5,000 cost of your kitchen upgrade to the credit card for a 3 percent transfer fee of $150 ($5,000 x .03). The promo APR is 0 percent interest for twelve months. If you pay off the balance before the promo period ends (with no late payments), you pay zero interest. After the promo period ends, you are charged interest on the balance, if there is any, and future purchases at the regular purchase APR of 19.9 percent. Some people might think of the 3 percent transfer fee ($150 in this scenario) as an interest rate. With a personal loan amount of $5,000 for 12 months at an APR of 5.5 percent the payment and interest paid would be about the same as with the zero-interest promo and transfer fee of 3 percent. If the personal loan APR turns out to be higher than 5.5 percent, it would cost less to do the transfer fee. If the loan APR is lower than 5.5 percent, it would be cheaper to do the loan. If there are origination fees associated with the personal loan, it would cost less to do the balance transfer with the 3 percent transfer fee. If the transfer fee were 4 percent that would tip the scales in favor of the personal loan.

Note: With the above scenario, your Debt-to-Credit (DTC) ratio for the credit card used will go to 50 percent (Using $5,000 of a $10,000 credit limit) and your overall DTC ratio will increase, which may affect your credit score.

Figure 9-2: Comparing a Promo Transfer Fee and a Personal Loan APR
(https://www.calculator.net/amortization-calculator.html)

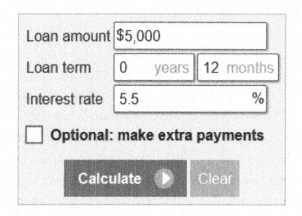
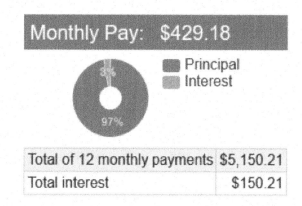

Secured/Prepaid Credit Cards (Help build credit)

Secured cards can be useful for people who do not have much of a credit history, or poor credit, to help improve their credit rating. These prepaid cards are called "secured" cards because you secure the card by giving the bank money to keep as backup collateral. You can go to many banks and apply for a secured card with a limit of, for example, $500. As an example, you give them $500 (in cash or through money order or cashier's check), and they will open a savings account for you in which to deposit the money that backs up the card. They will give you a plastic card (usually with a Visa or MasterCard logo) that can be used as a credit card as long as you stay below the limit (do not exceed 50 percent of the maximum limit, if possible). Like a regular credit card, you receive a statement and must pay at least the minimum payment each month, if you have a balance.

You cannot withdraw from the savings account as long as you have the card. There is usually an annual fee (like twenty-five dollars) for the card. Your use of this card is reported to the three credit bureaus and can help build your credit and improve your credit score. There are many such cards available from banks and credit card issuers, with varying guidelines and requirements. The bottom line is, you can have no credit and still get a legitimate credit card. Search the Web for "secured credit card" to learn more.

Secured cards can be useful for people who do not have much of a credit history, or poor credit, to help improve their credit rating. These prepaid cards are called "secured" cards because you secure the card by giving the bank money to keep as backup collateral. You can go to many banks and apply for a secured card with a limit of, for example, $500. As an example, you give them $500 (cash, money order or cashier's check), and they will open a savings account for you in which to deposit the money that backs up the card. They will give you a plastic card (usually with a Visa or MasterCard logo) that can be used as a credit card as long as you stay below the limit (do not exceed 50 percent of the maximum limit, if possible). Like a regular credit card, you receive a statement and must pay at least the minimum payment each month, if you have a balance. You cannot withdraw from the savings account as long as you have the card. There is usually an annual fee (like twenty-five dollars) for the card. Your use of this card is reported to the three credit bureaus and can help build your credit and improve your credit score. There are many such cards available from banks and credit card issuers, with varying guidelines and requirements. The bottom line is, you can have no credit and still get a legitimate credit card. Search the Web for "secured credit card" to learn more.

Debit Cards

Consider not using bank debit cards except for getting cash from a teller machine, where you must enter a personal identification number (PIN). Some of these cards have a Visa or Mastercard logo, but they are tied directly to your checking account. With a debit card, the amount spent is deducted immediately from your checking account. If you lose your card and someone uses it at a-point-of purchase checkout, they can drain your account with their purchases. That said, debit cards do have some advantages over credit cards. They are easy to get and do not charge fees to you or the retailer. Using a debit card is safer than using cash, and you don't pay interest. However, this is also a disadvantage since using it does not help you build a credit history.

Prepaid Debit Cards

Some major retail stores offer these cards and will service them for a fee. With a prepaid card, you give the store a certain amount of money and they "load" or apply it to the card. The card usually has a Visa or Mastercard logo and you can use it to pay for things like you would a debit card. However, it is not a credit card. The store usually charges a fee or percentage, depending on the amount the card is loaded with. When the limit is reached, you can "reload" or "recharge" the card for an additional fee. We did this with our daughters when they were still in high school to help them learn how to use a "plastic" card to pay for things. However, we got tired of paying the "load" fees, so we canceled the cards and obtained secured credit cards. When you use a prepaid debit card, it is not reported to the credit bureaus and has no effect on your credit score.

Gift Cards

Gift cards are a form of prepaid card that are usually tied to a specific store. You can go to many grocery stores and buy a gift card of a certain value for a particular store. You usually pay cash for the card. The disadvantage of these cards is they can only be used at the store that the card is from. Also, the dollar amount on cards for some stores can expire, if not used within a specific period of time. In addition, many people who receive these cards do not spend the whole amount. If you receive a gift card for a hundred dollars from store XYZ and only spend ninety, the store will receive an interest-free loan from you for ten dollars until the balance is spent. So, try to be sure you buy something or spend more than the amount the card is for to bring the balance to zero. If you still want to give a gift card, consider giving a prepaid Visa or Mastercard that can be used at any store. (These usually carry a fee for purchase.) That said, I just bought a fifty-dollar gift card at a nice nursery for my wife as a Mother's Day present. Sometimes, it's nice to get a gift card and go to the particular store the giver intended, instead of getting a generic Visa/MasterCard or cash.

Table 9-5 compares the features of various credit cards and shows examples of what to look for in terms of desirability. The first entry is the Issuer (bank or other) and Type of Card (Visa, Mastercard, or other). Refer to **Exercise 9-2: Compare Credit Card Features** at the end of this chapter, which uses Table 9-5 and provides an opportunity to compare the features of various types of credit cards using the Table 9-6 form.

Note: Most credit card issuers charge very high fees for late payment, returned payment, or going over the limit, as you can see in the examples in Table 9-5. These can add up very quickly, and the penalty APR 29.99 percent may be applied to the account in the event of a late payment and can continue to apply until six consecutive minimum payments are made when due. Paying at least the minimum due by the due date avoids high penalty APRs and late payment fees, and it will keep the account in good standing, but it takes forever to pay off the balance on the credit card.

Table 9-5: Credit Card Features Comparison

Comparison Feature	Card 1	Card 2
Credit Card Issuer/Type	Bank ABC / Visa	Bank XYZ / Mastercard
Annual Fee	0	$49
Cash Back Rewards	1.5% all purchases	5% Gas, 3% Dine, % Other
Credit Limit	$5,000	$5,000
Cash Back Purchase Limit	Unlimited	First $2,000 spent only
Purchase Interest Rate (APR)	14.9%	15.9%
Cash Advance APR	26.9%	27.9%
Cash Advance fee	5%	4%
Zero/Low APR Promo/Period	12mo/0%	18mo/2%
Balance Transfer fee	4%	3%
Convenience Check Fee	4%	4%
International Transaction Fee	0	3%
Late Payment Fee	$40	$40
Returned Payment Fee	$39	$39
Over Limit Fee	$39	$39
Penalty APR	29.99%	29.99%
Fraud Protection	Yes	Yes (for fee)
Extended Factory Warranties (Call to verify)	Yes	No
Free Credit Score/Report	Yes	No
Mobile Banking (secure app to manage acct)	Yes	Yes

Prescreened Credit Offers and Options

According to the Fair Credit Reporting Act (FCRA), the credit bureaus (Equifax, Experian and TransUnion) are allowed to include your name on mailing lists. These lists can be used by creditors and insurers to make "Firm Offers" for credit or insurance, that you did not initiate. The FCRA also allows you to request that your name be excluded from lists used for firm offers of credit or insurance. By opting out you prevent the credit bureaus from providing your credit file information for Firm Offers. If you receive an offer for a new credit card that says you've been "preselected," preapproved," or "prequalified," you can opt out for five years by calling toll-free 1-888-5-**OPT-OUT** (1-888-567-8688) or visit the Website https://www.optoutprescreen. com or you can opt out permanently by mailing your request, using the form available on the Website. A friend of ours recently received an offer in the mail for a credit card with no annual fee and free credit score. The mailing said they had been preselected but the addressee's name on the envelope was that of a deceased relative. The interest rate (APR) for standard purchases was variable and started at 30 percent, if you were to be approved for this credit card,

The PFS Sheet Credit and Credit Cards Entries

The Personal Financial Spreadsheet has a sheet dedicated to credit scores and credit cards. Refer to **Figure 9-3**. The standard entries for each credit card include the following:

- **Primary Card Holder Name** (e.g., Ted or Amy)
- **Credit Card Issuer/Card Type** (e.g., Bank ABC /Visa)
- **Card Number Last 4 digits** (use the x9999 format so that only the last four digits show). There could be multiple card numbers from the issuer, if there is more than one card user.)
- **Credit Limit** (max dollar amount that can be charged)
- **Current Balance** (appx-rounded to nearest ten or hundred dollars)
- **Annual Percentage Rate** (APR)
- **Yearly Fee** (if there is one)
- **Notes / Rewards** (e.g., 2 percent cash back on all purchases, no limit, no foreign transaction fees - FT Fee=0)

Figure 9-3 shows sample entries for PFS Sheet - Credit and Credit Cards (Tab/sheet name Cred-Cards). Note that credit scores and reports were covered in Chapter 8, and this information can be entered into the PFS Cred-Cards sheet as part of **Exercise 9-1: Record PFS Credit and Credit Card Info.**

Figure 9-3: PFS Sheet - Credit and Credit Cards (sample entries)

	A	B	C	D	E	F	G
1	CREDIT and CREDIT CARDS		Book Build: Ch. 9				Updated: MM-DD-YYYY
2							
3	<<< Sect 1: Credit Scores and Reports >>>						
4				Date Run	Source		Credit Reporting Bureau
5			Credit Score:	750	mm-dd-yy	ABC CC Co.	(Equifax / Experian / TransUnion / Other)
6			Report (Y/N):	Y	mm-dd-yy	XYZ CC Co	(Equifax / Experian / TransUnion / Other)
7							
8	<<< Sect 2: Revolving Credit Lines >>>						
9	(Credit Cards & Lines of Credit)						
10	Card Issuer / Sponsor / Brand	Prim / Auth User	Last 4 Digits	Credit Limit	Balance	APR %	Rewards / Notes
11	Bank Company ABC Amex	Amy	x9999	10,000	0	15.70%	Double Airline miles, free luggage
12	Bank Company DEF Visa	Ted / Amy	x9999	5,000	500	19.20%	3% Travel, 2% Dine, 1% Else
13	Bank Company GHI Mastercard	Amy / Ted	x9999	5,000	1,000	18.50%	4% Gas, 3% Groc., 1% Else
14	Bank Global Business M/C	Ted	x9999	10,000	750	14.90%	2% All purchase, No Foreign TX fee
15	Big Box Store Card	Amy	x9999	10,000	1,500	25.00%	6 Mo deferred interest
16	Bank Home Equity Line of Credit (HELOC)	Ted / Amy	x9999	20,000	3,000	8.00%	(Variable APR)
17	Other			0	0	0.00%	
18	Other			0	0	0.00%	
19							
20	<<< Sect 3: Credit Card Calculations >>>						
21	Credit Card Summary Totals (All Cards)						
22							Formulas / Notes
23	Total Credit Limit			$60,000			=SUM(D11:D19)
24	Total CC Balance				$6,750		=SUM(E11:E19)
25	Average APR					12.7%	=AVERAGE(F11:F19)
26							
27	<<< Sect 4: Debt-to-Credit (DTC) Ratio >>>					11.3%	=E24/D23
28	(DTC = Revolving credit utilization rate)						(DTC Ratio < 10% is OK)
29	(DTC = Credit Used (Balance) / Credit Avail (Credit Limit)						DTC applies to all cards combined
30							

< > ··· Income-Exp   Assets-Liab   Cred-Cards   Home-Info   Auto-Info   Insure-Pols   Fin-Plan   Income-Exp-F   Assets-Liab-F   Cred-Cards-F   Home-Info-F   Auto

Part 4: Credit and Credit Card Tips and Notes

General Wallet and Credit Card - Summary Tips and Notes

- **Add your credit card information to your PFS Sheet – Credit and Credit Cards**. Refer to the section at the end of this chapter for what to include. (Be sure to password protect your spreadsheet.)
- **Keep a copy of front and back of credit cards, driver's license and other important cards that are in your wallet in a safe place** (e.g., safe deposit box).
- **Keep a copy of your passport (front and back) in your wallet/and or suitcase if you are traveling internationally and in a safe place at your home.** (If your passport is stolen while you are traveling, you will have a copy of it.)
- **Keep your proof of auto insurance card in your wallet.** If you are stopped by the authorities, you will have two of the three things they will want to see handy: driver's license and proof of insurance. You will also have the policy number, the VIN, and roadside assistance number handy.
- **Do not keep your Social Security card in your wallet.**
- **Carry credit cards instead of checks.** You are not liable for stolen credit card charges if you report them within thirty days, and you have the right to dispute or contest incorrect or questionable charges.
- **Keep two credit cards in your wallet.** This provides a backup in case you have a problem with one of the cards when you go to use it.
- **Log in to your online bank accounts and credit card accounts periodically.** Do this at least once a month. With the up-to-date online data available today, there is no excuse for going over on bank accounts and credit limits, if you have the money, of course.
- **Beware of paying for magazine and software subscriptions with a credit card.**
- They can automatically renew subscriptions in accordance with an agreement in fine print.
- **Beware of "try before you buy" offers.** They say you can "cancel at any time," but most people forget. Set a reminder to help you remember to cancel.
- **Beware of buying anything where your credit card can automatically get charged each month.** Examples include weight loss programs and health club memberships. They might offer a free three-month trial and then automatically charge a set dollar amount each month for membership unless you cancel.
- **Do not borrow against your home to pay off credit cards.** If possible, do not take out a home equity loan or line of credit to reduce your credit card debt. Many people have done this and, before they knew it, the balance on the credit card(s) had returned to what it was before they took out the home equity loan and now, they have credit card debt AND increased debt against their home as well as a higher mortgage.
- **Do not borrow against your employer 401K or other retirement plan to pay off credit cards.** The same reasoning applies here as to borrowing against your home. Also, if you lose your job, you must pay the entire balance owed of the original amount borrowed within a short period of time as determined by your employer.

- **Avoid using store credit cards.** They charge very high interest. An exception is, if you can get a discount on a purchase and you pay the balance when you receive the statement.
- **Keep billing addresses current with all creditors.** This applies especially to credit cards. Fill out a post office change of address (COA) to have your mail forwarded. You can do this at any post office at no cost, or you can do it online for one dollar at: https://moversguide.usps.com/mgo/disclaimer?referral=UMOVE
- The COA is usually good for six months, and you may need to renew it. My wife's credit score dropped because we had forgotten to let the issuer of one of our store credit cards know about our new address when we moved. We missed two payments, and they reported it to the three credit bureaus. We called the company and explained what had happened and they wrote to the credit bureaus and had the record of the missed payments removed.
- **Stop pre-approved credit cards by opting out.** If you receive an offer for a new credit card that says you've been "preselected," "preapproved," "prescreened," or "prequalified," you can opt out for five years by calling toll-free 1-888-5-**OPT-OUT** (1-888-567-8688) or visit www.optoutprescreen.com.
- **Try to limit the total number of credit cards you have to no more than three or four.** This can help simplify your finances. However, if you already have five or more credit cards, closing one of the accounts can reduce your credit limit and affect your credit score.
- **Call your credit card company and ask for a lower interest rate.** You can also ask for an increased credit limit.
- **If you are charged a late fee, call the credit card company and ask to have it waived.** If you have no history of being late, they may waive the fee and credit your account.
- **You can possibly have late fees waived for other bills.** For example, if you go over on a data plan with your wireless provider, call them and they may waive the fee, if you have been a long-time customer with a good payment record.
- **Pass on the "credit protection" insurance.** Some companies will try to get you to sign up for credit protection when you obtain a new card or even after you've had it for a while. They say it will make the payment if you can't (due to life events such as job loss, illness, injury, LT disability, and death). They will bill your account for the insurance based on your balance. As an example, one such card charges eighty-five cents per hundred dollars of new balance. Another charges 1 percent of your balance each month.

Specific Credit Card Tips and Notes

- **When possible, try to obtain and use cash back rewards credit cards that have no annual fees or rotating categories.**
- **Don't put all of your charges on one particular credit card just because it pays a high cash back.** If you get the statement, and you have to come up with the balance or pay interest, it could cause a cash flow problem for you. It's better to spread your charges around on different cards to maintain activity on those cards and reduce the payoff to a more manageable amount, even if the card pays less cash back.

- **Pay bills over the phone with a credit card**. These can include utility bills such as electric, gas, phone, and Internet, as well as some medical bills and insurance premiums. You can ask to do this with any bill, and, in many cases, you can get cash back rewards. Note that some creditors will charge up to 3 percent to do this, which negates the 1.5 or 2 percent cash back that you might get. Also, be careful you don't charge too much to any one card since your intention is to pay the balance off when you receive the statement at the end of the monthly cycle.

- **Rotate credit card usage to keep them active.** This helps prevent the issuer from cancelling them. If you have three or more cards, keep two cards in your wallet and rotate or switch them out every six months or so. Credit card companies can cancel the card for disuse. This can reduce your available credit limit by thousands of dollars, which can lower your credit rating.

- **Pay more than the minimum monthly payment on credit cards.** Paying only the minimum payment will require years for you to pay off the balance and the interest and total paid will be considerably more than the original charge.

- **Pay your credit card bill in full each month**. If you pay your bill in full each month, it does not make any difference what the interest rate is. If you carry a credit card balance from one month to the next consistently, you are fighting a losing battle, unless you have a 0 percent interest rate for a specific time period.

- **Do not charge more on a credit card than you can afford to pay back within thirty days**. This will help you keep to a budget and reduce the amount of interest you have to pay.

- **Use a credit card to purchase appliances and electronics to extend the factory warranty.** Contact the credit card company first to verify that they will do this.

- **Don't use credit cards for cash advances except in emergencies.**

- **Avoid balance transfers from one credit card to another, if possible.** Unless you can get a substantially lower interest rate for six to twelve months, and plan to pay off the balance within that time.

- **Do not allow other authorized users on your credit card, if possible.** They could misuse the card, and it will affect your credit rating. One exception may be your spouse.

- **Freeze credit cards in a clear zip-lock bag to make it harder to use them.** If you choose to defrost them, you will have some time to think about it.

- **Use payoff strategies to reduce credit card balances and create a feeling of progress.** Pay lowest balances first to get them paid off quickly, or pay balances with the highest interest rate first to reduce the interest paid. Refer to Chapter 10: Buying, Borrowing, and Debt, for additional information on strategies to reduce debt.

- **Review all charges on your credit card statement.** Most people don't pay much attention to the charges on their statement and can end up paying for something they did not want for months.

- **Contest bogus charges on your statement.** You can call the credit card provider and contest them within thirty days. They will usually credit your account and investigate the charge on your behalf.

Chapter 9 Exercises

Exercise 9-1: Record PFS Credit and Credit Card Info

In this exercise, you will enter your credit card information into a blank form (copy of Figure 9-4) based on sample entries shown in Figure 9-3: PFS Sheet - Credit and Credit Cards. Even if you do not plan to enter your data into the spreadsheet at this time, go ahead and enter your data in Figure 9-4, the Credit and Credit Cards form. You can do the calculations manually if you want to.

Note: Before starting this exercise, make a copy of the blank Figure 9-4: PFS Sheet - Credit and Credit Cards (Form), and use Figure 9-3 as a guide for data entry. Be sure to record all your credit cards, including retail store credit cards. You may also want to record your debit cards even though they do not have an interest rate or credit limit, so you have them all in one place, with codes and expiration dates.

Figure 9-4: PFS Sheet - Credit and Credit Cards (Form)

	A	B	C	D	E	F	G
1	CREDIT and CREDIT CARDS		Book Build: Ch. 9				Updated: MM-DD-YYYY
2							
3	<<< Sect 1: Credit Scores and Reports >>>						
4					Date Run	Source	Credit Reporting Bureau
5			Credit Score:				(Equifax / Experian / TransUnion / Other)
6			Report (Y/N):				(Equifax / Experian / TransUnion / Other)
7							
8	<<< Sect 2: Revolving Credit Lines >>>						
9	(Credit Cards & Lines of Credit)						
10	Card Issuer / Sponsor / Brand	Prim / Auth User	Last 4 Digits	Credit Limit	Balance	APR %	Rewards / Notes
11							
12							
13							
14							
15							
16							
17							
18							
19							
20	<<< Sect 3: Credit Card Calculations >>>						
21	Credit Card Summary Totals (All Cards)						
22							Formulas / Notes
23	Total Credit Limit			$0			=SUM(D11:D19)
24	Total CC Balance				$0		=SUM(E11:E19)
25	Average APR					#DIV/0!	=AVERAGE(F11:F19)
26							
27	<<< Sect 4: Debt-to-Credit (DTC) Ratio >>>					#DIV/0!	=E24/D23
28	(DTC = Revolving credit utilization rate)						(DTC Ratio < 10% Is OK)
29	(DTC = Credit Used (Balance) / Credit Avail (Credit Limit)						DTC applies to all cards combined
30							

Exercise 9-2: Compare Credit Card Features

To assist you in researching credit cards, Table 9-6 has features listed to compare two credit cards. Refer to Table 9-5 in this chapter for example values. These criteria show what to look for in terms of credit card desirability. The first entry is the issuer (bank or other) and type of card (Visa, Mastercard, or other). Select two or more credit cards to see which ones have the best features. Use Table 9-5 as an example and make a copy of the Table 9-6 form to list the credit cards across the top and the features to be compared down the left side.

Table 9-6: Credit Card Features Comparison (Form)

Comparison Feature	Card 1	Card 2
Credit Card Issuer/Type		
Annual Fee		
Cash Back Rewards		
Credit Limit		
Cash Back Purchase Limit		
Purchase Interest Rate (APR)		
Cash Advance APR		
Cash Advance fee		
Balance Transfer APR		
Balance Transfer fee		
Zero/Low APR Promo/Period		
Convenience Check Fee		
International Transaction Fee		
Late Payment Fee		
Returned Payment Fee		
Over Limit Fee		
Penalty APR		
Fraud Protection		
Extended Factory Warranties (Call to verify)		
Free Credit Score/Report		
Mobile Banking (secure app to manage acct)		
Other		
Other		

Chapter 10
Buying, Borrowing, and Debt

Chapter Overview:
Your home is typically the most expensive thing you will purchase in your lifetime and is covered in Chapter 11. An automobile (or other vehicle) is probably the second most expensive thing you will buy, and is covered in Chapter 12. Home purchase and auto purchasing options are discussed in their respective chapters. This chapter covers a range of major expenditures, such as home improvements (garage addition, deck, fence, etc.), furniture, electronics, power equipment, and appliances. These other types of purchases are big-ticket items that many of us spend money on, in addition to homes and autos. This chapter offers suggestions as to the most cost-effective ways by which these items can be acquired, along with some debt-management strategies and general buying tips. The chapter is divided into four parts:

- **Part 1: Buying and Borrowing Options**
- **Part 2: Big Ticket Buying and Borrowing**
- **Part 3: Borrowing and Debt Management Strategies**
- **Part 4: Buying, Borrowing, and Debt Tips**

Chapter PFS and PFI Integration:
The Personal Financial Spreadsheet (PFS) components in this chapter that relate to home maintenance and improvements are found on the Home-Info and Fin-Plan sheets and consist mainly of entries for home improvements as well as maintenance. The PFS Cred-Cards sheet is also referenced. The Personal Financial Indicators referenced in this chapter include Debt-to-Income (DTI) and Debt-to-Credit (DTC) ratios.

Chapter Exercise:
- **Exercise 10-1: Compare Loan Amortization Calculators**

Chapter Notable Quotes:
Quote 10-1: "Buy quality. It may cost more in the short run but costs less in the long run." - Anonymous
Quote 10-2: "Neither a borrower nor lender be, especially within the family." - Anonymous

Quote 10-1 above, on buying quality, can be applied to almost anything you buy but is directly related to the big-ticket items covered in this chapter. Buying quality can save you money over the long run and extend the life of your possessions, most of which are simply liabilities (cash outgo). However, if you really want something, do some research, comparison shop, and get the best one for the money. Consumer Reports magazine is a good place to start for product ratings. And remember that you frequently get what you pay for. A good example of buying quality is when we shop for furniture, let's say a TV cabinet or a bookcase. With my family, we usually end up buying something from one of the many craftsman furniture stores in the area. The prices are not as high as you might think, considering the quality. And it's made in America! When you are buying something that you will be using and looking at every day it pays to spend a little more.

Instead of shopping for a quality product, many people go shopping for a price. After the product breaks down or wears out, they don't even remember they paid only nine dollars for that item instead of ten dollars for a better one. The dollar they saved is gone and they may still need a new product because they also saved on quality. Sometimes they lament that they wished they had bought the better-quality item and paid the extra dollar. It really does pay off in the long run, and frequently in the short run, for a number of reasons. When you buy quality, you also increase the chances of getting a better price if and when you sell an item. This can amount to quite a bit of money over a cheaper item and can sometimes make the difference whether you can sell the used item at all.

Part 1: Buying and Borrowing Options

Quote 10-2: "Neither a borrower nor lender be, especially within the family." - Anonymous
This quote may seem a little harsh, but it can reduce angst among family members (and friends). Family members who loan money to other family members create a dependency between the borrower and the lender. Within our family, I have been both the borrower and lender, and neither was a comfortable situation. The borrower is indebted to the lender, and the lender may feel they have something over the borrower, whether consciously or not. People who borrow, especially to make ends meet, may not repay the loan, or they may take longer than intended to repay it. Once they know they can get money from a friend or family member, they may come back to the source again. If lending money to a family member or anyone else, make sure its money you can spare and consider it a gift, as you may not get it back. Just remember, the lender is in charge (has the power). Keep loans between people and institutions, not family members.

The "I want it all now" mentality has created new financial diseases such as "Consumeritis" and "Affluenza," from which many of us in Western society suffer. They may be fictitious, but they can be very real in terms of their effect on our finances. These "first world diseases" have reached near-epidemic proportions as we strive to keep up with our neighbors. Regardless of our financial situation, most of us are faced with a multitude of options for acquiring "things."

Note: For many of us, our retirement plan is probably the single most expensive thing we might buy during our lives. Chapter 13: Investing Basics and Chapter 14: Retirement Requirements cover retirement-related investments and retirement plans specifically,

Acquisition Things (Stuff): The four main "Big Ticket" acquisitions categories, in order of cost are these:
- Home/Residence
- Automobile (can include motorcycles, boats, and campers/trailers)
- Home Improvements/appliances
- Electronics/Furniture

Acquisition Methods: For each acquisition type, there are three main ways to acquire them (and things in general).

- Purchase outright (cash)
- Borrow money (loan)
- Rent (lease)

For the purposes of this book, these methods apply primarily to the financial situations of Western cultures. For each item to be acquired, we usually have three options: buying outright (cash); borrowing the money as a loan to be paid off over time (including credit cards); or by renting the item for some, usually predetermined, time period. For each type of acquisition, and method of acquisition, there are advantages and disadvantages. This chapter describes some of the pros and cons of various acquisition methods for the "big ticket" items.

Renting and Leasing

Depending on the item to be acquired and your financial circumstances, renting may be the best choice. Pretty much anything can be rented, big and small ticket items. These include a residence (home or apartment lease) and a car (auto lease). You can also rent power tools, appliances, home electronics, or furniture (rent-to-own). Home rental is covered in Chapter 11, auto rental is covered in Chapter 12, and appliance/ furniture rental is covered in this chapter.

Purchasing with Cash

For smaller purchases such as home electronics or home improvements, paying cash may be the best approach, especially if you have the money available. Be careful though, because spending too much cash outright can deplete cash reserves set aside for your rainy-day fund. That said, paying cash for an item, even something as expensive as a car, puts you in the driver's seat (literally and figuratively). You can frequently negotiate discounts and get a better deal if you don't have to depend on your bank or the seller to provide financing. In addition, you may be able to avoid paying hundreds or thousands of dollars in loan interest by paying cash. On the other hand, you may be able to obtain a loan with a very low interest rate and spread the debt out over time.

Secured (Good) Debt) vs Unsecured (Bad) Debt)

Taking out a loan or borrowing is the most common way to purchase certain items, especially items such as a home or a car. Paying cash for these types of items is not generally a good idea unless you have a lot of cash and can afford to take the hit to your cash reserves.

Money borrowed toward purchasing a home (home mortgage) or a car (auto loan) is known as a "secured" loan or secured debt. It is also referred to as "good" debt because it is taken for what might be termed "essential purchases" since the majority of Americans who buy a home or car will need to obtain some financing. A secured loan is for a specific item, and the item purchased becomes collateral for the loan and can be repossessed by the lender, if you fail to make payments. These loans and others, such as student loans, may also be referred to as "installment" loans, as there is a set payment due each month. Smaller installment loans, wherein the item being purchased does not serve as collateral for the loan, are known as personal loans and are considered "unsecured" debt. For reference, nearly all credit cards and other revolving lines of credit are unsecured debt. Credit card debt, in particular, is considered "bad debt."

Amortized Loans and Calculators

Most installment loans are generally categorized as "Amortized loans," which means they have fixed payments that are paid periodically until loan maturity. The amount borrowed (principal) is set, and the annual percentage rate (APR) for the loan does not vary. Figure 10-1 shows an online Amortized Loan Calculator, which can be used to calculate common loan types such as mortgages, auto loans, student loans, and personal loans. If you do a Web search, you will find there are several to choose from at no cost. Note that you can enter all necessary loan variables, and you can also view the Amortization Table, which shows every monthly payment for the life of the loan. Doing so, you can see exactly how much of your payment is applied to the principal and how much is applied to interest, for any given payment. Using one of these calculators with a three-year loan, for example, you can compare the first payment to the thirty-sixth payment and can see that most of the interest is paid at the beginning of the loan while most of the principal is paid at the end.

Refer to **Exercise 10-1: Compare Loan Amortization Calculators** at the end of this chapter, which can assist you in selecting a simple general purpose amortization calculator for use with installment loans, such as auto and personal loans.

Figure 10-1: Amortized Loan Calculator Example

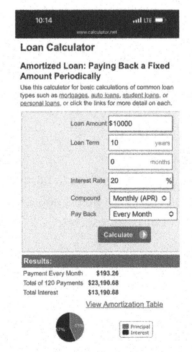

Credit cards and lines of credit at stores are unsecured loans and are referred to as "revolving" credit loans since the amount borrowed and the payment can vary from month to month. A home equity line of credit, HELOC, however, is secured by your home as collateral. Buying an expensive sound system or TV using a credit card or store financing is essentially an unsecured loan. The seller could, theoretically, come after you for the item if you fail to make the monthly payments, but they really don't want to come pick up your used TV, take it back to the store, and try to resell it. Instead, they would more likely report you to the three credit bureaus and damage your credit. As previously mentioned, secured loans such as home or auto or other installment loans are considered to be "good debt." Unsecured loans and revolving credit card debt are "bad debt," and this unsecured credit card debt decreases your net worth.

For personal loans, financing can be obtained by borrowing from the following, more or less in order of desirability:

- Installment loan from a bank at a fixed rate and term
- Loan from a bank or credit card issuer using low promotional APR, for a given term
- Loan against your home equity (using a HELOC, covered in Chapter 7.)
- Loan from a credit union
- Charge to a major credit card (Visa, Mastercard, etc., especially if you get cash rewards)
- Charge to a store credit card (from retail outlet)
- Loan from an online or Web-based lender
- Loan from a relative or friend
- Loan from short term loan company (loan shark – payday or predatory lender)

Part 2: Big Ticket Buying and Borrowing

Home Improvements and Maintenance Expenditures

The next biggest expenditure after a home and car is typically home improvements. These types of improvements usually cost thousands of dollars but can add thousands to the value of the home. Also, apart from increasing resale, the value of these improvements can be substantial in terms of livability, functionality, convenience, and home comfort.

Home improvements can be anything from installing vinyl siding to adding a deck or upgrading a kitchen. Other types of home improvements include upgrading bathrooms and replacing flooring/carpeting. Maintenance can include repainting the house and replacing a water heater or air conditioning system. Any of these can cost a considerable amount, and many people tap into their savings account. Others may finance the purchase using a home equity line of credit (HELOC) or by charging the purchase to a cash back or deferred interest credit card.

Using Savings to Buy

If you have the cash available (checking or savings), and the cost of the improvement is not too great, you can pay as you go. Many people do this, especially if they have been saving over time for a specific purpose. If it does not significantly decrease your Emergency Fund (EF), this is a great way to do it. You have basically deferred the purchase until you've saved enough. Most savings accounts do not pay more than 2 percent interest (as of this writing), so, you are not losing much interest. Many people prefer to use savings so that the purchase is paid for upfront. The interest you save over borrowing can be substantial, especially if you buy the item with a credit card and don't pay off the balance.

Promo Option 1: Using Deferred Interest Credit "Promo" to Buy

If you do not have much equity in your home but have fairly good credit, you can apply for a store credit card account and charge expensive home improvements using the store's deferred interest plan. Most "Big Box" stores offer a discount if you use their credit card or you can opt for deferred interest, but you can't opt for both. With deferred interest purchases, if you pay off the balance in full within a specific "promotional" time period (usually six, twelve, or eighteen months), there is no interest.

The regular interest APR for a store credit card (usually around 25 percent) will be calculated from the beginning, but the interest will be accrued and "deferred," meaning it is being accumulated but not charged. If you do not pay off the original promo amount charged by end of the promo period or if you default on the agreement by missing or being late on a payment, interest will be imposed from the date of purchase at the APR that applies to new purchases at the time of the original purchase. In some cases, the interest rate can be as high as 27 percent APR! If you missed or were late on a payment or if you do not pay off the purchase within the time allowed, all of the deferred interest is due. This deferred interest is added to your balance and the interest rate on the card can increase to a "penalty" rate. Using the deferred interest option requires the buyer to pay the purchase off much faster than paying the minimum payment but saves a ton of interest. It also requires you to have a substantial positive monthly cash flow and requires some diligence to make sure you pay it off before the time period expires.

Note: Be wary of taking the discount (usually around 5 percent) and just charging the purchase. If you carry a balance and it takes you a while to pay off the purchase, the regular interest rate is applied which is around 25 percent. That can wipe out your 5 percent discount on the initial purchase pretty fast!

Promo Option 2: Using Zero (0) Interest Promo APR Period Credit Card to Buy

An alternative to the store credit card deferred interest option is the zero-interest APR promo period credit card option offered by some banks and credit card issuers. This option was introduced in Chapter 9 and is provided here as a review and an alternative to the deferred interest option. If you have good credit, and a zero balance on your card, it is not uncommon for a bank to send you a couple of blank checks to use as you see fit. Even if they do not send you blank checks you can call the credit card issuer or the bank and ask if they have any promos. You can use one or both checks to pay for home improvement at a low APR (0-2 percent) for a promotional period (usually twelve or eighteen months). For each transaction you will be charged a fee of 3-5 percent. If you pay off the total amount charged within the promo period, you pay zero (0) interest.

After the promo period and depending on the bank and the specifics of the promo offer, the APR can go to a variable rate of 20 percent or more. In some cases, the rate is based on the type of transaction and use of the promo APR money and can depend on whether you did a Balance Transfer (e.g., from higher rate card), Direct Deposit (e.g., to your checking account to pay for home improvements), or Cash Advance (e.g., used for whatever). If you still have a balance on your credit card at the end of the promo period, your APR will go to the new rate. However, unlike the deferred interest credit card option, you are not charged for the deferred interest that would have accrued. Regular purchases charged during the promo period will carry the normal APR of 15-25 percent and will not be reduced until the original zero interest promo charge amount has been paid off.

As mentioned, in order for you to take advantage of this zero-interest promo period, you must pay an up-front fee per transaction, which is normally 3-4 percent of the amount charged. You have a limited time to complete the transactions (about one to two months). Let's say you have a credit card with a zero balance and a $10,000 credit limit. You could use one of the bank checks to pay for a bathroom upgrade of $5,000 for a 4 percent fee of $200 ($5,000 x .04). If you got a regular personal loan of $5,000 for twelve months, you would pay about 7.5 percent APR to cover the cost of the 4 percent fee. If you still have a balance after the promo period, you will pay interest going forward, typically at a balance transfer APR of about 18-20 percent (varies based on the prime rate).

Using a HELOC to Buy

If you have lived in your home a while and have some equity built up, you may be able to use a line of credit against your home (a secured variable interest loan). This is known as a home equity line of credit or HELOC (pronounced "HEELOCK"). It's like a revolving line of credit with a credit card, except it is secured by your home as collateral. It is simpler than a home equity loan and generally requires less or no closing fees, although the interest rate may be a little higher.

A HELOC can be used to buy almost anything, but it is best to use it for home improvements. Also, if you borrow against your home, you will need to pay it back at a regular rate and will have a minimum monthly payment based on the amount you borrowed. HELOC interest may also be tax deductible if used for home improvements. Refer to Chapter 7: Savings and Banking Services, for additional information on HELOCs as well as a chapter exercise to help you compare HELOC lenders and loans.

Note: A home equity loan and home equity line of credit are both loans against your home as collateral. They are essentially a second mortgage behind the primary mortgage. As such, if you sell your house, you must pay off the loan or line of credit as well as the primary mortgage.

Over the last ten years we have made some major improvements to two of our homes. We added a garage to one of them (House 1) and added a deck and fencing to the other (House 2). We paid for these improvement projects in very different ways. With the House 1 garage addition, we used a HELOC, and with the deck/ fence addition, we charged the cost to a store credit card with deferred interest. Let's look a little closer at each of these home improvements.

Example House 1: Garage Addition (using a HELOC)

House 1 lacked a garage when we bought it. When we'd lived in the home long enough, and the value was such that we had built up some equity (ownership) we were able to obtain a HELOC. We built a two-car garage that cost about $30,000, using the line of credit. The HELOC used the home as a secured loan, and we got a relatively low interest rate. In addition to our regular mortgage, we paid a small monthly payment for the HELOC garage addition. Over time, we made many small improvements, such as landscape and an integrated backup power generator. These small investments added value to the home. When we sold House 1, we had to pay off the HELOC. It was a loan against the home and was paid off from the proceeds of the sale.

Example House 2: Deck/Fence Addition (using deferred-interest store credit card)

We sold House 1 and bought a newer two-story home, House 2, in a residential neighborhood. This house had a backyard, but it did not have a deck or patio, which would be a nice extension of the living area. Since we had just purchased the new home and put 20 percent down, we did not have much equity. We went to a builder's store and opened an account. We could have used some savings, but that would have depleted our rainy-day fund. We applied for a credit card account with the store and received a $20,000 line of credit, mostly due to our good credit rating and the fact that we would be spending our money at their store, using their credit card.

We decided on a deck and fence combination for the back yard and charged it to the store credit card. The deferred interest promotional offer was 0 percent for eighteen months. If you paid it off in less than eighteen months, and had no missed or late payments, you paid no interest. If not, the accrued interest would be added to the loan at a rate of about 27 percent. We got the deferred interest promotion for eighteen months with no interest. If we'd paid only minimum payments each month, we would have paid several thousand in interest over several years. By paying off the loan balance within the agreed-upon time period (eighteen months), we basically got an interest-free loan.

Note: One important catch to be aware of is that if you charge anything else to the credit card, your payments will go to the main 0 percent interest loan, and you will be charged interest at the normal rate (about 25 percent) on any purchases that are not part of the original deferred interest promotion.

To take advantage of a deferred interest credit promotion requires that you pay the purchase off much faster than the minimum payment, but you will save a ton of interest (thousands of dollars in our case). It also requires considerable diligence. If I had missed or been late on a payment, the deferred interest would have been due and would have increased the card's APR to a "penalty" rate. We were able to pay off the loan in seventeen months, but it took some active budgeting and serous belt tightening to get it done. Paying off a $20,000 loan in 18 months requires a payment of just over $1,000 per month (and that's without interest!)

Many people have good intentions when opting for deferred interest offers, but they are unable to pay off the balance within the allotted time. They end up paying deferred interest on the purchase, which can be thousands of dollars. And they frequently carry a high balance at high interest for much longer than the original promotional period.

Figure 10-2: High-Tech Big Screen TV

Electronics and Furniture

This category or grouping includes several different items such as TVs, home entertainment systems, appliances like washers and dryers, and furniture such as sofas and the like. It can also apply to other major purchase items including power equipment such as generators and lawn mowers. The cost of most of these items can often be in the thousands of dollars range.

There are many ways to acquire these types of items, but some are more cost effective than others. Let's look at a few of the more common options. The list starts with the most desirable method (least expensive, lowest interest) and ends with the least desirable method (generally most expensive in the long run). It also assumes that you have a good credit rating (at least 700), otherwise some of these offers would not be available, or you would have to pay higher interest for money borrowed.

- **Cash back credit card** (assuming you pay it off each month): If you have a cash-back credit card, such as a Visa or Mastercard you can get the following benefits, among others.
  - **Cash back** - Up to 3.0 percent or more of your purchase as cash, credit, or points.
  - **Zero percent loan** - (for about a month). This assumes you can use savings or regular income to pay off the credit card balance when the bill comes. Even if it takes two or three months to pay it off, you will still not have paid much interest.

- ◦ **Extended warranty** - Some credit cards provide an extended warranty for some items. For example, if you use the card to buy a TV with a one-year manufacturer warranty, the card provider may double the warranty. Call the card issuer to verify that they will do this and to find out what other benefits they can provide.
- **Credit card – zero/low interest promo period:** Many new and existing card offers can be used to pay for big-ticked items using low/no-interest introductory promo periods from 12 to 18 months. Many of the offers don't have accrued interest, even though you may still have a balance at the end of the promo period. The balance is then subject to the current APR for regular purchases.
- **Credit card – deferred interest:** Many stores offer a credit card where you can charge the item with no interest for a specified period, such as six months or a year. However, if you are unable to pay off the amount borrowed within the allotted time, accrued deferred interest may be added to your balance.
- **Cash from savings:** If this will not impact your rainy-day fund substantially, this can be the least expensive method, and you can have the item immediately. One downside is that you are forfeiting a small amount of interest that the savings could make, but you may also avoid significant interest that you could incur by charging it to a credit card and carrying a balance.
- **Lay-away:** If you do not need the item soon, many stores offer what is essentially a zero-interest loan. This is a low cost deferred gratification method of acquiring something since you will have paid for it before you take possession. You can select the item (e.g., large screen TV), and the store will hold it for you as you pay it off over a period of time.
- **Short-term personal loan:** This is unsecured debt from a bank or other institution and is generally a more expensive way to purchase something. The interest rate is usually high (5-10 percent) but not nearly as high as that incurred while using a credit card and carrying a balance. Most credit cards are in the 15-20 percent APR range.
- **Peer lending:** There are several well-known online lending consortiums. The members have the money to lend and are willing to take a risk for a profit. If you need money for whatever reason and have reasonably good credit, you may be able to use one of these services. An online bidding process can allow you to borrow money at a fairly reasonable rate.
- **Borrow against your home:** If you have a home equity line of credit, this is an option but not a very good one, since it adds to the secured debt against your home. The interest rate may be low, but it might not be deductible unless the money is used for home improvements.
- **Rent to own:** There are a number of nationwide companies that will allow you to take delivery of an item, such as a TV or a piece of furniture, and pay a monthly rental amount that can be applied to the purchase price. The advantage of this method as compared to layaway is that you can obtain the item immediately and pay it off over time. The disadvantage is that you end up paying much more for the item than you would if you put it on layaway. With layaway, you have a set price for the item and will pay no interest, but you can't take the item with you. Rent-to-own companies tend to cater to people with lower credit ratings, who may not have a credit card or other financing option. If you intend to go this route, be sure to check out the quality of the items offered, especially furniture. This is less of an issue with appliances and electronics.

- **Borrow against your retirement plan:** Many people have a 401K or 403B retirement plan that they can borrow against. This is not a good idea. It takes the money that was invested and uses it for an unsecured personal loan. You pay it back to your plan with interest, but you lose the gains that you could have had if you'd left it in the retirement plan. Also, if you leave the company, you have to pay off the loan balance in full even though you may not have the money to do so. If you leave the company and are unable to pay off your loan balance, your employer's retirement plan will cancel the debt with what is called a "deemed distribution," whereby they will send you a 1091-R at the end of the year showing the unpaid portion of the loan as a distribution to you. This distribution will be subject to income tax and will also more than likely carry a 10 percent early withdrawal penalty on your income tax return. This combined "tax hit" could easily be 35 percent or more, a situation you should really try to avoid.
- **Payday loan:** Companies making these loans are sometimes referred to as "predatory lenders" or "payday lenders." They usually give out very short-term loans (thirty days) and charge very high interest rates (30 percent and up). The loans are sometimes secured by your auto title. These types of lenders are regulated in most states with regard to how much interest they can charge.

Note: Consumer's Union, the Consumer Reports' consumer financial protection bureau, monitors predatory mortgage, payday and student loan practices as a watchdog.

Part 3: Borrowing and Debt Management Strategies

Balance Transfers to Lower Interest Rate
It is very common these days for people to transfer a high-interest-rate credit card balance to a card with a lower rate. This can be a good strategy if you have a good credit rating and are disciplined. Many new cards, and some you may already have, offer promos with six to eighteen months at low or zero interest, if you make the payment according to the agreement. If you can transfer a high-interest balance, don't make the mistake of charging to the card that you transferred from for a while (since it now has a zero balance). If you do, before you know it, you may charge it back up to where it was before you did the balance transfer to the lower-interest-rate card. Also, don't charge anything to the new card (card you transferred to) until you pay off the high-interest balance that you transferred. Any new charges to that card will carry the current high APR (perhaps 20 percent or more), and any payments you make will be applied to the low-interest transfer amount.

Pay Down High-Interest Debt or Put It in Savings?
If you have credit card debt, or have a loan with a high interest rate, it makes sense to pay down the higher interest rate debt first. The exception is if you are trying to build your emergency fund which is very important, even though the interest rate may be relatively low. A friend of mine had a $50,000 HELOC and purchased a car with it for $20,000 at 8 percent APR. He was paying the minimum due (interest only) on the HELOC and putting money into a savings account that was paying 4 percent, a fairly good rate for savings in this day and age. However, they were paying 8 percent interest on the HELOC loan balance

and getting 4% interest their savings. Unless you're building your emergency fund, it makes financial sense to pay off high interest debt first (Avalanche method). Or, you may be using the Snowball method of debt pay down, where you pay off the debt with the lowest balance first. Avalanche and Snowball methods are covered below.

Freeze Your Cards or Cancel Them?

If you're overusing your credit cards, you can freeze them (literally). Put the high interest rate card in a baggie with some water in it and put it in the freezer! Do NOT cancel a line of credit (especially if in good standing), as this will reduce your available credit. As a result, your credit utilization or Debt-to-Credit (DTC) ratio will go up, which is bad for your credit rating (refer to DTC ratio in Chapter 9).

Freeze your credit files

If you're tempted to use your credit card(s) or apply for a new credit card or other credit, you can freeze your credit file with each of the three credit bureaus. No one (including you) will be able to initiate credit in your name if the files are frozen. You can unfreeze them, but it requires some time to unfreeze your file with all three bureaus. So, it forces you to stop and think if you want to take on more credit/debt or not. More information is provided later in this chapter on how to freeze and unfreeze your credit file with each of the three credit bureaus.

Avalanche vs. Snowball Debt Paydown Method?

Two commonly used methods of paying down debt are referred to as the "Avalanche" method and the "Snowball" method. These methods can be applied to revolving credit accounts, such as credit cards (variable term and rate) as well as installment loans (fixed term and rate). So, let's assume you've got the following loans and lines of credit (as shown in Table 10-1), and your goal is to pay off all of them off within a specific time frame (e.g., two or three years, based on cash flow). After checking your cash flow and your budget, you see that you should be able to accomplish this if you can remain diligent.

Table 10-1: Loans and Credit Lines Debt Paydown - Avalanche vs. Snowball

Loan Description	Loan/Credit Type	Interest (APR)	Balance	
Auto Loan	Installment	10%	**$4,000**	<<< **Snowball**
Student Loan	Installment	6%	$5,000	
Credit Card 1	Revolving	16%	$7,000	
Credit Card 2	Revolving	**18%**	$8,000	<<< **Avalanche**
		Credit Balance:	**$24,000**	

Avalanche Debt Paydown Method

Using the **Avalanche** method, you would start paying the highest-interest-rate loan or debt first, which is Credit Card 2 at 18 percent Annual Percentage Rate (APR), and pay the minimum payments on your other debts. You would continue to pay on the highest-interest-rate debt until it is paid off and then go on to the next highest APR debt (Credit Card 1 at 16 percent). Then you would pay off the third-highest-APR debt, which is your auto loan at 10 percent APR, and so on. With this method, you would pay the loans off sooner and pay less interest because you would be focusing on the highest-interest-rate debts first. Financially speaking, the avalanche is the most prudent way to go, but it can take longer to see tangible results, and progress is less visible. The avalanche method is so named because paying off the highest interest first gets the biggest results in terms of interest saved which is similar to an avalanche, in which there is a lot of snow coming down the mountain at once.

Snowball Debt Paydown Method

Using the **Snowball** method, you start by paying off the debt with the lowest balance first (auto loan with balance of $4,000), regardless of the interest rate. You keep paying on it until it is paid off while paying the minimum due on the other loans. When it is finally paid off, you might want to have a little party to celebrate your accomplishment. Then you go on to the debt with the next highest balance due and pay on it until it's paid off. You can see that the snowball method yields more tangible or visible results early on. It makes you feel like you're making progress and helps to motivate you to keep going until you reach your goal of being debt free. You are paying more interest, but studies have shown that people using the snowball method are more successful at paying down their debt.

The snowball method is so named because paying off the lowest balance gets the quickest visible results. And after you pay off the first debt you roll on to the next biggest debt, and your snowball keeps getting bigger as you pay off your larger debt balances. Note that this example includes multiple loan types and not just credit cards. However, focusing on credit cards is smart because they typically carry the highest interest rates. If you use the avalanche method and stay vigilant, you can save interest. Using the snowball method may improve your chances of succeeding at paying down your debt. Either method will accomplish your goal if you stick with it.

Debt Consolidation

With debt consolidation, you can pay off higher-interest-rate loans and lines of credit by combining balances. You may be able to have only one monthly payment that is less than the combined payment of the loans you consolidated. You may be able to refinance high-interest credit card balances with a lower-interest personal loan (depending on your credit rating). Multiple high-interest loan and revolving credit balances can be consolidated, thus enabling you to move from a high APR of 25 percent or 26 percent to a lower interest rate of perhaps 12 percent or 13 percent. That's still high interest but much better than what you had. You can benefit from consolidating if you have the discipline to pay off the consolidation loan and not open more credit lines, or immediately start charging your credit cards back to where they were.

Windfalls and Debt Payoff

A few years back, when I was an instructor and textbook author in the field of network technology, I received a rather large royalty check, which was for book sales that I had not been paid for. At the time, I had some large balances on my credit cards and was not managing my finances very well. This accumulated royalty back pay was totally unexpected. We could have taken the money and gone on a vacation or spent it on something extravagant. Or we could have just deposited it in our checking account and "frittered it away" as my mother used to say, with nothing to show for it. But we decided to apply it to our credit card debt, and that was probably the smartest thing we could have done, and it allowed me to pay off significant portions of my credit card debt. This was the single most important step we could have taken toward reducing our overall debt load and improving our credit scores. It also contributed significantly to an improvement of my overall outlook and attitude. That royalty check was kind of a windfall for us and allowed us to pay off our credit cards versus carrying a 25 percent APR with high balances for an indefinite period. People receive windfalls in the form of inheritances and other sources. Maybe that's an opportunity for them to apply at least some of those monies to their debt so they can become closer to being debt free at some point.

You don't have to budget for and track everything in all categories. Just focus on the top five repeat offenders that have the most impact on cash flow. Most of these will be variable discretionary expenditures that fall into categories such as entertainment, personal care, and food (and drink), etc. You need to take note of and minimize all expenses, but you don't have much control over mandatory (required) fixed expenses such as housing and taxes. Review the categories listed above and refer to Chapter 3 for a review of types of expenses in the PFS Income-Exp sheet.

Awareness Note: With awareness and knowledge comes motivation to take steps to improve our situation. Make good choices!

Debt Collectors (Sent to Collections)

Some people cannot pay their debts for one reason or another, and their account may "go to collections" or "go delinquent." Creditors sometimes sell the "bad debt" accounts to a debt collector. They may also report the bad debt to the three credit bureaus, which can damage a person's credit rating. The Fair Debt Collection Practices Act (FDCPA), established by the Consumer Financial Protection Bureau (CFPB), is a federal law that defines some rules and limitations that debt collectors must abide by to help reduce the harassment of debtors. Debt collectors must follow these rules when contacting you about a debt that was sent to collections. Note that the law only applies to third-party debt collectors (not the original creditor). Debts covered under this law include auto loans, medical bills and credit card bills. Do a Web search to find out more about what debt collectors can and cannot do under the FDCPA.

Third-party debt collectors buy bad debt from creditors for pennies on the dollar and then start calling to locate the debtor (or a relative) and try to get them to pay the debt. If they are successful, they get to keep the money paid or a portion of it. However, some debt collectors use badgering and unscrupulous tactics to accomplish their goal. Their goal is to call people and try to convince them to pay. If you do not believe you owe the debt and have proof of the same, you can respond in writing with the proof and ask them to stop contacting you, which they must do by law. However, they can still report you to the credit bureaus.

Debt-Collection Example

If you are contacted by a debt collector, you can dispute their claim, but you only have thirty days to send a dispute letter. I was contacted by a debt collector representing a hospital and was told I owed them for some physical therapy that I'd received two years prior. It turned out that I did owe the money, but they did not have my current address. They had been sending it to my old address, and it was not getting forwarded. I called the hospital, gave them my new contact information, and worked it out directly with them. I paid the bill to the hospital over the phone, and they pulled my file from the debt collector. I also requested a receipt from them to prove I had paid the debt in case it showed up on my credit report. Fortunately, it did not affect my credit rating.

Do a Web search for "credit card answers," and you will find many resources to help you deal with aggressive creditors and bad debt issues.

Declaring Bankruptcy

Let's say you have heavy debt and are unable to pay it down. You are being hounded by creditors and are behind on your auto loan and mortgage payments. You might consider filing for personal bankruptcy, depending on your financial situation. There are various types of bankruptcy, but the details are beyond the scope of this book. Filing for bankruptcy may cancel much of your debt and enable you to keep your car and your home (assuming you can make the payments). However, doing so will negatively affect your credit rating and will stay on your credit report for up to ten years. Even though you declare bankruptcy, some types of debts cannot be discharged. These include alimony, student loans and some types of taxes. Suffice it to say that you should only consider bankruptcy as a last resort. I declared bankruptcy when I was much younger, but it took a long time to get it removed from my credit reports and reestablish my credit.

It should be noted that a bankruptcy can be a fresh start, and it is appropriate for some people. And there are some creditors who will help you when you are recovering from a "BK" since they know that you can't re-file for another eight years. There is much information available on the Web regarding bankruptcy. Just search for "Who should declare bankruptcy?"

Declaring bankruptcy should not be taken lightly. Talk it over with a financial advisor that you can trust. If you feel strongly that your situation warrants filing for bankruptcy, get in touch with a good attorney that specializes in the U.S. bankruptcy code. As with other legal and financial professionals, check references, reviews, and the Better Business Bureau (BBB) for an A or A+ rating. Be aware that there are unscrupulous types out there offering to help you declare bankruptcy, but you may end up owing even more debt that cannot be discharged.

Compound Interest and Credit Cards – More Information

Compound interest could, arguably, be the eighth wonder of the world, as the quote from Einstein says, but that depends on your perspective and whether you are a lender or a borrower. If you are a lender (bank, mortgage company, credit card issuer, or a bond holder), it can be your friend and works in your favor.

However, if you are the borrower, it can work against you, especially if you carry a balance from one month to the next with revolving credit accounts. So, we cover compound interest from the buyer's or borrower's perspective here in this chapter, because it is about borrowing and debt. Compound interest and the problems it poses were introduced in Chapter 9: Credit and Credit Cards. We will cover compound interest and the Rule of 72 from the perspective of the lender (or the investor) in Chapter 13: Investing basics.

Pay Off Your Credit Card Balance Each Month (if possible)

Interest on a credit card balance is compounded daily using your average daily balance. So, if you have a credit card with a 24 percent annual percentage rate (APR) any balance will accrue interest at the rate of approximately 2 percent/month. (1/12 of the APR). If you make a charge on your credit card and don't pay it off by the due date of the current statement and carry a balance over to the next month you will pay more interest on the unpaid balance, and any unpaid interest will be added to the new principal. If you carry a balance from one month to the next, you will be charged interest on interest, which is the compounding effect. This can add up very quickly!

Note: The compound "interest-upon-interest" issues relative to carrying a balance on your credit cards or other revolving lines of credit do not apply to installment loans, where there is a fixed payment each month. Additional information on this can be found in Chapter 8 and chapter 12.

Pay Down or Pay Off Installment Loans Early (if possible)

Let's say you just bought a car with an installment loan of $10,000 for five years (sixty months). You have a fixed interest rate (APR) of 7 percent and a monthly payment of about $200. A portion of each payment is applied to the principal, and a portion is applied to interest. If you pay additional dollars toward principal earlier in the term rather than later, you will save a substantial amount of interest. For example, if you could afford to pay an extra $50 per month in year two you will save a more interest than paying the extra in year four. This is because the interest calculated in each payment is determined by the principal balance, assuming regular monthly payments. If you start paying extra at the beginning of the loan, that extra amount over your regular monthly installment loan payment is applied to and reduces principal, which reduces the amount of interest owed. This is assuming you don't have a prepayment penalty clause in your loan agreement.

In other words, if you pay extra with your payment during the first and second year, that benefits you finically more than paying extra in years four and five. The extra you pay above your normal payment goes to the principal and reduces your balance more quickly. This is why installment loans—including auto loans and mortgages—are "front-end loaded," If you run an amortization table for a five-year car loan—like the one described above—from an interest standpoint, look at the amount of principal and interest paid with the first payment as compared to the last payment. With a five-year installment loan the first payment is the same amount as the last (payment sixty). However, the first payment is mostly interest with a little bit of principal and the last payment is mostly principal with a little bit of interest.

Setup a Budget to Control Discretionary Spending
Refer to Chapter 3: Income, Expenses, and Cash Flow, for ways to increase income and decrease expenses. Also review Chapter 4: Budgeting and Frugal Living for ways you can use a budget to help manage your income and reduce outgo. Focus on the top five heaviest spending categories that have the most impact on cash flow. As mentioned previously, most of these will be variable discretionary expenditures that fall into categories such as entertainment, personal care, and food (and drink), etc.

Other Debt-Reduction Options
- Use cash instead of plastic. The money spent is more visible than when using a credit card.
- Call the credit card issuer and ask if they can reduce your interest rate (many will).
- Contact a debt counseling agency such as **nfcc.org,** and get help working out a payback plan.
- Go to the U.S. Department of Justice Website https://www.justice.gov and search for "credit counseling."

Part 4: Buying, Borrowing, and Debt Tips

- **Use Consumer Reports (CR:** Check ratings before buying new consumer items. CR tests and rates many items, including TVs, washers, dryers, lawn mowers, snow blowers, vacuum cleaners, tires, etc. Copies of the annual Consumers Reports Buying Guide are available at most public libraries.
- **Get the best one for the money:** Whatever you are buying, new or used, do the research and get the best one you can afford. Spending a few extra bucks up front will pay off over the life of the item.
- **Buy quality:** You frequently get what you pay for. Buying quality can save you money in the long run and extend the life of your possessions. Also, when you go to sell the item, you will likely get more for it.
- **If buying/selling used items:** Choose a reputable, highly rated online service. I've had good luck with Craig's List, but there are many others. I sold my four-year-old Craftsman mower and three-year-old snow blower quickly and got a good price for them. I'd maintained them well, and they were in good condition. I posted a couple of photos of each one. The online interface is easy to use. If you are selling, accept only cash, money order, or cashier's check from the buyer.
- **Check seller ratings:** When buying from an online service, read customer reviews (good and bad), and check the Better Business Bureau (BBB) for ratings and complaints.
- **Check referrals when hiring a company for a service:** (painting, tree removal, roof repair, etc.). Get three quotes, read customer reviews, and check the BBB ratings.
- **Skip the extended warranty:** When buying new electronics and appliances, skip the extended warranty when offered. It overlaps with the manufacturer's warranty and costs a lot.
- **Use the preferred sources for borrowing list:** The previous section lists possible sources for funds from lowest cost to highest. Use the first choices on the list if possible.
- **Strive to improve your credit score:** It is interesting to note that, if you have good credit and don't need to borrow, creditors want to lend you money. If you have bad credit and need to borrow, creditors don't want to lend you money. It may be unfortunate, but it makes sense; those with bad credit

are less likely to pay the loan back. The better your credit rating, the lower the interest rate you will pay.

- **Neither a borrower nor a lender be, especially with family:** The lender is in charge and has the power. They have the money, and you want the money. Keep loans between individuals and institutions. Try to avoid lending to and borrowing from family members and friends. It frequently results in a soured relationship.

- **Check/Track your Debt-to-Income (DTI) and Debt-to-Credit (DTC) ratios:** Compare your secured debt (e.g., mortgage, HELOC, or auto loans versus unsecured debt (credit cards, personal loans. etc.). How much of each do you have? How does your outgo compare to your income? That which you do not monitor, you cannot control (use PFS worksheets).

- **Never be a cosigner on loans:** If the primary borrower fails to pay off the loan, the lender or collection agency will come after you!

- **Don't borrow against your home to pay off credit cards:** Many people do this, but studies show that, within about a year, they have charged the credit cards back up to where they were, and now they have a secured loan against their house.

- **Live within your means:** Seems obvious but most people don't. Spend less than you make. It's as simple as that but hard to do. When I was younger, I got a bi-weekly paycheck and spent it like I had that money entirely at my disposal (on movies, dinner, entertainment, etc.). What I did not take into account was that the rent was due in ten days, my car payment was due in fifteen days, I had no groceries, and my gas tank was empty. So how much money did I really have that was unspoken for?

- **Get on the savings bandwagon:** There is a growing trend in the U.S. to save more. After years of "consumeritis" and trying to keep up with the neighbors, Americans are beginning to see the benefits and security of keeping a savings account.

- **Work toward being debt free:** It is a liberating and powerful feeling. It's OK to have some "good debt" but try to reduce "bad debt," especially unsecured debt like credit cards.

- **Get three quotes:** For a large purchase or services, the third time's the charm. If possible, get three estimates for anything, such as buying a TV or getting car work done. Be sure to compare apples to apples.

- **Use delayed gratification:** As often as possible, when you want something, try to delay the purchase (the longer the better, usually). Frequently, a better deal will come along. This is a good use of procrastination! I am a guy who wants it now. A while back, I was in the market for a new truck. I found one I liked, but it was not exactly what I was looking for. I decided to wait, and two months later, I found an almost-new previously leased truck that had a bigger engine, more options, and only twelve thousand miles on it. I saved $11,000 compared to the new one I had been looking at. Delayed gratification paid off!

General "Small Item" Buying Notes and Frugality Tips

- **Always negotiate:** This is especially true if you have been a good customer.

- **Always ask Is that the best you can do?"** When you receive a price or quote, always ask this question. You never know; they may give you a better deal.
- **Take advantage of "No/No/No" offers:** No down payment, No interest, and No payment until mm/dd/yy.
- **Take advantage of "Same as cash" (SAC) credit purchases.** SAC offers can save you a lot of money if you can pay them off within the allotted time.
- **Take advantage of BOGO offers.** Buy One Get One (BOGO) offers are usually a good deal, but only if you need or can use two of something.
- **Shop at Warehouse Clubs.** (Sam's, Costco, etc.)
- **Shop at local small businesses if prices are comparable.** It's good to support your community and your neighbors when you can.
- **Pay cash.** Offer to pay cash and take it with you.
- **Be willing to walk** – If you don't get the deal you want, make an offer and be willing to leave. You will frequently get a counteroffer.
- **Ask for store discount coupons.** Don't be afraid to ask if they have any you can use. They usually have a newspaper or ad insert section. Ask if they can give you one.
- **Use credit cards that extend warranties**. Many credit cards will extend the manufacturer's warranty if you use them. Call the credit card issuer and ask them. While on the phone, you can ask them to increase your credit line and decrease your interest rate!

Chapter 10 Exercise

Exercise 10-1: Compare Loan Amortization Calculators

In this exercise, you will research amortization loan calculator apps and use them to compare various loan types, such as home mortgages, auto loans, and personal loans. To assist you in selecting an app, you can copy Table 10-2. Do a Web search for "Amortized Loan Calculator," or search for one individually and compare the features to determine which one best serves your needs.

Table 10-2: Amortized Loan Calculator Comparison (Form)

(Compare mortgages, auto loans, student loans, and personal loans)

App Name	Features / Notes

Chapter 11
Buying or Renting a Home

Chapter Overview:

This chapter focuses specifically on your residence, the most expensive purchase most of us will ever make. Whether a house or apartment, and whether buying or renting, relevant terminology and topics are presented. The emphasis is on factors that impact your credit rating and mortgage loan terms. The financial indicator Housing-to-Income (HTI) ratio is reviewed, and the Income-to-Housing (ITH) projection indicator is introduced to help determine the home price affordability range for a prospective buyer. The chapter contains many notes and tips as well as best practices regarding home buying, selling, and renting. Exercises are provided to help gather home-related information and enter it into your PFS Home-Info sheet. An exercise is provided to help research, select, and use an online mortgage calculator. The chapter is divided into five parts:

- **Part 1: Home Buying, Credit, and Mortgages**
- **Part 2: Housing Personal Financial Indicators (PFIs)**
- **Part 3: Buying and Selling a Home**
- **Part 4: Buying vs. Renting a Home**
- **Part 5: PFS Home Info and Maintenance Sheet**

Chapter PFS and PFI Integration:

This chapter covers PFS Sheet - Home Info and Maintenance, with a tab label of "Home-Info" and the home-related entries of the Income-Exp sheet from Chapter 3. The Home-Info sheet provides a way to record information about your residence, whether you are buying or renting. The first section is Home Information, which includes home and property specifications as well as mortgage, taxes, insurance, and sales history information. The second section of the sheet is Home Maintenance and Improvement, which provides a way to record work done and maintenance performed as well as upgrades. The PFI Housing-to-Income (HTI) ratio, which compares mortgage payment to monthly income, is reviewed, and a new PFI is introduced, Income-to-Housing (ITH) projection, which estimates home price affordability range based on annual income.

Chapter Exercises:
- **Exercise 11-1: Compare Home Mortgage Calculators**
- **Exercise 11-2: Record PFS Home Info**

Chapter Notable Quote:
Quote 11-1: "Home Sweet Home - It's a Blessing and a Curse" - Anonymous

A home is the most expensive item most of us will acquire during our lifetime. For past generations, it was not uncommon to buy a home and live in it for most of their lives and in many cases, to pay off the mortgage. For these folks, it was also not uncommon to get a job with one company and stay with them for most of their working life or until they retired.

In our modern job-hopping world, a person is likely to hold many jobs with multiple companies and even have multiple careers over their lifetime. By the same token, a person may also buy and sell many homes over a lifetime. When my wife and I built our first home, we took out a construction loan and then obtained a thirty-year mortgage to finance it. We sold our first home, built another, and sold it. Since then, we have moved five times and have bought and sold five homes. I was primarily a tele-worker during that time and could do my work pretty much anywhere I had a high-speed Internet connection.

Part 1: Home Buying, Credit, and Mortgages

Figure 11-1: Home Sweet Home (Tiny home trend)

Home Buying and Borrowing

For some things it is better to buy and for others it may be better to borrow. Given the cost of most homes, it is not likely someone would purchase it outright with cash, although there are certainly exceptions. Most people who opt to purchase a home are actually taking out a secured loan, known as a mortgage. A person with a home and mortgage is known as a homeowner, but in reality, they usually own a small portion of the home and the lender, who holds the mortgage (loan), owns the rest. To "buy" a home, you usually must come up with a down payment of about 10-20 percent and finance the rest for ten to thirty years. This chapter assumes that you would be buying a home as a primary residence and not as a vacation home, investment, or rental property.

We won't present all the various types of home loans available here but instead will focus on some basic principles and the most common types of loans. There are many variables and options for home financing, and there are thousands of lenders. The requirements vary depending on your situation (e.g., first-time home buyer, military), your credit qualifications, your Debt-to-Income ratio, and the type of loan. Conventional fifteen and thirty year fixed-rate and Adjustable-Rate Mortgages (ARMs) are the most common. Other types include Federal Housing Administration (FHA) loans, Veterans Administration (VA) loans, and Refinances (REFIs). Some of these, such as VA loans, can require as little as zero down payment. Refer to Table 11-1 for criteria to consider based on your real estate needs, your personal financial status, and the types of mortgage loans available. Be sure to check with your go-to real estate person from your Professional Advisor Group as discussed in Chapter 6.

Table 11-1: Common Mortgage Loan Terminology and Comparison Criteria

Mortgage Criteria	Examples and Notes
Home/loan purpose	Primary residence, vacation, rental property, investment, refinance
Home type	Single family, condo, town house
Loan type	Conventional, FHA, VA, ARM, etc.
Buyer type	Average, first time homebuyers, military, low-income, investor
Creditworthiness	Debt-to-Income (DTI), Debt-to-Credit (DTC) Housing-to-Income (HTI)
Credit profile	Determines interest rate. Credit score (700+) and credit history
Interest rate	Determined by credit profile. Fixed or variable
Qualifications	Household income, employment status, cash flow, net worth
Loan amount	FHFA sets a limit each year. Limit for 2023 is $726,200 (varies)
Down payment	0-20%, Will you require assistance?
Private Mort. Insurance	PMI Required if less than 20% down, based on loan type
U.S. Govt backed	Based on loan type (e.g., FHA, VA)

The Impact of Your Credit Rating on Home Buying

The first thing to do before contemplating a home purchase is to check your credit report and credit rating. Generally speaking, the better your credit rating, the lower your interest rate will be for the mortgage. A good credit rating is normally considered to be 700 or higher. A rating of 750 or higher is considered excellent (the range is 300-850). The difference in interest paid for the mortgage between a buyer with a good credit rating and a buyer with a poor one can be hundreds of dollars in monthly payment and thousands of dollars over the life of the loan. A person with a poor credit rating may not be able to get financing at all. Credit scores and credit reports were covered in Chapter 8.

Bob's and Ted's Home Buying Experience

To demonstrate the impact your credit score has on home financing, consider the following example. Bob and Ted each apply for a conventional thirty-year fixed rate loan to purchase a home for $200,000. They each put 20 percent down (to avoid PMI) and financed $160,000 for thirty years. Refer to Table 11-2 for information on the two loans that they took out. Bob has a "Very Good" credit score of 780 (according to FICO), and Ted's credit score is considered "Good" at 680. All else being equal, Bob's credit rating gets him a fixed Annual Percentage Rate (APR) of 5 percent from his lender. Ted's lender will finance his home purchase but at a higher fixed interest rate of 7 percent. Bob and Ted both live in their homes for thirty years until they pay off their loans. How does Bob's monthly payment compare to Ted's? How do their totals compare for principal and interest combined for the life of the loan? And, more importantly, how much more did Ted pay than Bob for his home purchase at the end of the mortgage term? The difference is due to increased interest that resulted from Ted's lower credit rating.

Table 11-2: Comparing Bob's and Ted's Mortgages

Mortgage Loan Information	Bob	Ted	Notes
Credit rating (score)	780 (Very Good)	680 (Good)	
Home price	$200,000	$200,000	
Down payment	$40,000	$40,000	
Mortgage amount	$160,000	$160,000	
Interest rate (APR)	5%	7%	
Loan term	30 years	30 years	
Monthly payment	$860	$1,065/Mo.	
Total payback (principal and interest 360 pmts.)	$310,000	$383,000	
Total Interest paid	$150,000	$223,000	Ted paid $73,000 more interest than Bob!

Note: Dollar amounts are rounded and approximate. Property taxes and homeowner's insurance are not included.

Home Mortgage Calculators

You can use a mortgage calculator to compare various loan amounts, time periods, and interest rates. Many of them provide a wide range of entries that can accommodate various types of mortgages. They can allow you to enter the down payment, property taxes, and homeowner's insurance, as well as Private Mortgage Insurance (PMI) and other variables. By including taxes and insurance, you will get a more realistic monthly payment, assuming you know approximately how much they will be and plan to include them in your monthly payment (property taxes and homeowner's insurance are kept in an "escrow" account). Do a Web search for mortgage calculators, and you will see many—as well as smart phone apps—available for use online or download. Some are free and do not require you to enter personal contact information. Figure 11-2 shows an example of a free online mortgage calculator from https://www.calculator.net.

Refer to **Exercise 11-1 Compare Home Mortgage Calculators** at the end of this chapter. With this exercise you can research and try various free online mortgage calculators and select one that best suits your needs.

Figure 11-2: Mortgage Calculator Example (Principal and Interest Only)

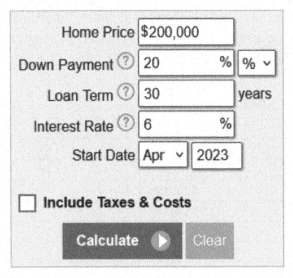

House Price	$200,000.00
Loan Amount	$160,000.00
Down Payment	$40,000.00
Total of 360 Mortgage Payments	$345,341.10
Total Interest	$185,341.10
Mortgage Payoff Date	Apr. 2053

Prequalification

Before purchasing a home, most people will contact one or more potential mortgage lenders to compare the types of loans available, interest rates, and borrowing requirements. Upon selecting a lender, you will usually be given a checklist that identifies the documents you must provide to get "prequalified" or preapproved. These documents typically include copies of recent pay stubs, previous income tax returns with W2s, and current statements from checking and savings accounts. A list of assets, expenses and liabilities must be provided so the lender can determine your Debt-to-Income (DTI) ratio and total debt obligations. After providing the required documents, the lender will then come up with a maximum dollar amount that you can borrow for a home based on how much of a down payment you will need. The lender will provide you with a preapproval letter stating how much you have been approved for. You can show this to home sellers to let them know that you are a serious potential buyer.

Important Note: Keep in mind that just because a lender might say you have been approved for a certain amount does not necessarily mean you can afford the monthly payment. Be sure to factor in other costs such as homeowner's insurance, association fees, maintenance, and repairs. Consult your budget to see if you can really afford the home. Many people take on too much debt when buying a home and become "house poor," meaning that you can afford the house payment, but that's about it because you don't have much discretionary income leftover.

Note: When you apply for a loan or line of credit secured by your home, the lender is required by the Consumer Financial Protection Bureau (CFPB) to provide you a list of approved housing counselors nearby so that you can discuss your situation, get a second opinion, and hopefully make a more informed decision. This applies to every customer who applies for a home-related loan or line of credit. For more information, visit the CFPB Website at:

https://www.consumerfinance.gov/mortgagehelp

They also offer free foreclosure help if you're behind on your mortgage, or having a hard time making payments, and can get you in touch with a Housing and Urban Development (HUD)-approved housing counselor.

Part 2: Housing Personal Financial Indicators (PFIs)

Mortgage Expenses and Income Ratios – HTI and ITH

There are two home-related Personal Financial Indicator (PFI) ratios based on the current or expected mortgage amount, if applying for a mortgage.

Figure 11-3: PFS Housing Required Monthly Expenses Section of Income-Exp Sheet

	A	B	C	D	E
24	<<< Sect 2: Expenses >>>				
25					
26	< Housing Required Monthly Expenses >	Institution	Monthly Payment	Payment Method	Notes
27	Housing Expense Name / Type				
28	(Required Housing Expenses)				
29					
30	Home - Mortgage PITI (or Rent)	Anytown Mortgage	1,800	O/L Bill Pay	Bank X9999 (Escrow Tax/Ins)
31	Home - Homowners Assoc, Dues (HOA fees)	Subdivision HOA	100	O/L Bill Pay	O/L: www.xyzprop.com - Qtrly
32	Home - Water/Sewer/Trash/Recycle	Anycounty Services (Avg)	175	O/L Bill Pay	CC x9999 (one bill)
33	Home - Electricity/Gas	Anytown Electric/Gas (Avg)	250	Auto-Pay	CC x9999 (one bill)
34					
35	(Optional Housing Expenses Included)				
36	Home - Security/Smoke alarm	XYZ Security	50	Auto-Pay	Auto Pay CCx9999
37	Home - TV Cable	Anytown TV	85	Auto-Pay	Auto Pay CCx9999
38	Home - High Speed Internet	Anyprovider Internet	50	Liquid Assets-Exp (LAE)	No. of Months
39	Home - Pest Control	Anytown Pestsbegone	40		Billed Qtrly CCx9999
40	Other			Auto-Pay	
41	Total Housing Required Monthly Expenses		$2,550		=SUM(C30:C40)
42					
43	Housing-To-Income Ratio (HTI %)		28.7%		=(C41/C21)
44	= (Required Housing Expenses / Gross Income)				(HTI Ratio < 30% is OK)

- **Housing-to-Income (HTI) Ratio:** Compares required housing expenses to monthly income.
- **Income-to-Housing (ITH) Ratio:** Home price affordability range based on annual income.

With HTI, you can determine what percentage of your income you are currently (or will be) spending on your home and directly related expenses (formula is built into the PFS Income-Exp sheet). See entries at the bottom of the screenshot in Figure 11-3. You can use ITH to project a rough estimate or approximate price range for how much home you can afford based on your gross annual income. Monthly household income is also found on the Income-Exp sheet and can be used to calculate annual gross income for use with ITH.

Housing-to-Income (HTI) Ratio Personal Financial Indicator (PFI)

The Housing-to-Income (HTI) financial indicator ratio was introduced in Chapter 3 and is widely used by real estate professionals and mortgage lenders. It is sometimes called Housing Expense Ratio or HER. The Figure 11-3 screenshot shows the PFS Housing subsection of the Income-Exp sheet and the HTI ratio financial indicator, with sample entries. In addition to totaling home-related fixed monthly expenses, this section of the spreadsheet calculates the HTI percentage, which is a formula embedded in the Income-Exp sheet. Refer to PFI 11-1 below for the formula and example to calculate the HTI ratio. The HTI ratio is determined by taking the monthly expenses that make up your mortgage payment (PITI = Principal + Interest + Property Taxes + Homeowner's Insurance), plus any homeowner's association dues, and then dividing that total by your Monthly Gross Income. Most lenders like to see an HTI ratio of less than 30 percent (less is better). This means you spend less than 30 percent of your gross income on your mortgage or rent plus other required housing-related expenses. The following is an example of HTI ratio.

PFI 11-1: Housing-to-Income (HTI) Ratio - Formula/Calculation
Personal Financial Indicator (#PFI-12)

Housing Required Monthly Expenses (/divided by/) Monthly Gross Income = HTI (%)

$2,550 / $8,900 = .287 (*100) = 28.7%

(PFS Income-Exp sheet example)

Note that the HTI ratio formula in the PFS Housing subsection includes the mortgage payment and HOA dues as well as all utilities (water/gas/electricity) plus security system, Internet, TV, and pest control. Many lenders only include mortgage payment and HOA fees as home expenses, to keep things simple. But by including these other housing costs (or at least utilities), you get a more realistic estimate of your actual home-related expenses. If we include the utilities and the other "optional" homeowner expenses listed in Figure 11-3, the total home-related expenses increase to $2,550/month. And the HTI ratio is .287 or 28.7 percent, which is still good but higher than using the mortgage amount and HOA dues alone and getting closer to the generally accepted limit of 30 percent.

You can check with your realtor to determine whether they include the utilities and security or any of the other "optional" housing expenses in the HTI ratio. We have included all housing expenses listed, both required and optional, for a total of $2,550/month, and that is the number used in the HTI ratio calculation above. If you choose not to include them in the HTI ratio calculation, you still must account for them elsewhere as expenses. So, it's best to include them all in the housing section and know that your HTI ratio with all major home expenses included is actually better than it looks. Note that the "Home - Mortgage PITI" entry amount of $1,800/month includes Principal, Interest, Taxes (property), and Insurance (homeowner's).

The Housing-to-Income (HTI) ratio (PFI 11-1) was introduced in Chapter 3 and is widely used by real estate professionals and mortgage lenders. PFI 11-2 shows how the Income-to-Housing (ITH) affordability range is calculated to estimate how much home you can afford.

The Income-to-Home (ITH) Affordability Range - How much home can you afford?

As a general rule, a prospective home buyer or household should be able to afford about two to three times their annual salary, assuming other aspects of their finances are in balance. Some real estate people and especially first-time buyers use this calculation to get an approximate range that the buyer can afford. To calculate your ITH range, multiply your annual gross income times two to three to determine the range for the approximate amount you can afford. Multiply by two and then by three to come up with the lower and upper limits for the range. Keep in mind that everyone's financial situation is different, and this is just a general guideline. So, if you make $60,000/year, multiply it times * 2 = $120,000 and then * 3 = $180,000. If the mortgage for the home you are looking to buy is over $180,000, you may not be able to afford it or you could be "house poor" if you do purchase it. Keep in mind that if you're unable to come up with a 20 percent down payment when purchasing a home (conventional mortgage), you will likely have to pay private mortgage insurance (PMI). If you borrow part of the down payment (not recommended but not uncommon), this is a separate loan for which the monthly payment also needs to be accounted. PMI alone can add $200 a month or more to your mortgage payment.

Refer to PFI 11-2 below for the formula to calculate your ITH range. We start by multiplying the monthly gross income by twelve to get the annual income. You can adjust the calculation as necessary to reflect your own personal situation (e.g. weekly gross times fifty-two = annual gross income) or to include household income rather than just individual. To determine the ITH range, multiply your annual Gross Income times two and then times three to determine the approximate home price range (*2-*3) you can theoretically afford. Note that these calculations make use of the Total Monthly (Gross) Income calculated in the PFS Income-Exp sheet, which is $8,900/month.

Note: PFI 11-2 Income-to-Home ratio is just one of many tools like this. There are various online home affordability calculators available on the Web. Some are more accurate than others. Use this one with caution, as it assumes your other financial PFI ratios, such as Debt-to-Income (DTI), are relatively healthy. DTI as it relates to home buying is covered next.

PFI 11-2: Income-to-Housing (ITH) Affordable Range ($x-$z) - Formula/Calculation
Personal Financial Indicator (#PFI-13)
Monthly Gross Income (*times*) 12 = Annual Gross Income
Annual Gross Income (*times*) 2 = ITH ($) Range Lower Limit
Annual Gross Income (*times*) 3 = ITH ($) Range Upper Limit

$8,900 * 12 = $106,800 (Annual Gross)

$106,800 * 2 = $213,600 (Lower Limit)

$106,800 * 3 = $320,400 (Upper Limit)

Income-to-Housing (ITH) Range: $213,600 - $320,400

(PFS Income-Exp sheet example)

Home Buying and Your Debt-to-Income (DTI) Ratio

A major factor that determines how much home you can afford and whether you will get a loan is your Debt-to-Income (DTI) ratio. Recall that DTI is the percentage of your income that you use to pay your bills, and most lenders are looking for a DTI ratio of 40 percent or less. Mortgage lenders use the DTI ratio along with your credit history and other factors to determine your creditworthiness. You may have a lot of income, but if you also have a lot of debt (especially credit card debt), you may not get financing. If your DTI ratio is too high, you may have to buy a less expensive home, put more money down, or pay a higher interest rate for the loan, or all the above. To calculate your DTI ratio, add your monthly debt payments and divide the total by your gross monthly income. So basically, you are dividing verified debt by verified income. (Refer to Chapter 3 for additional DTI information.)

Table 11-3 shows a simple example of a DTI ratio for a prospective homebuyer. The lower the ratio (percentage of debt to income), the better chance you have of obtaining a mortgage at a good interest rate. The better (lower) your DTI ratio, the more likely you will be able to handle the mortgage payment and other expenses associated with home ownership. Refer to Figure 11-3, the PFS Income-Exp sheet, for the built-in DTI ratio calculation. Or you can do a Web search for "DTI calculator" and use one of the apps available to calculate your DTI ratio.

Note: The Personal Financial Spreadsheet (PFS) calculates your DTI ratio automatically as you enter income and expenses. It is built-in to the Income, Expenses, and Cash Flow sheet.

Table 11-3: Simple Debt-to-Income (DTI) Example for Homebuyer

Monthly Expense	Amount	Notes
House Payment or Rent	$950	
Student loan	$600	
Auto loan	$500	
Credit cards	$300	
Monthly Debt Total	**$2,350**	
Gross Monthly Income	**$6,500**	

Monthly Debt (/divided by/) Gross Monthly Income = DTI Ratio

($2,350 / $6,500 = .36 (rounded) x 100 = appx 36%)

Opinions vary, but, as a general rule, your combined monthly debts should not be greater than about 38 percent of your gross monthly income (GMI), and your rent or mortgage payment alone should not be greater than 28 percent of your GMI. When you apply for a mortgage, the lender will calculate your DTI ratio, along with your current debt as well as the debt with your new estimated mortgage payment. Your mortgage payment includes principal, interest, taxes, and insurance (PITI). While it is a very important credit indicator, DTI does not directly affect your credit scores. This is because the credit reporting bureaus don't track your income, which is a key component of the DTI.

Part 3: Buying and Selling a Home

Home Buyer Requirements

Purchasing a home has the most stringent requirements for buyers in the credit industry, followed closely by auto leasing. Mortgage lenders require the buyer to be well qualified, with a very good credit rating and adequate credit history. It is common for young people and people who pay cash for everything to have what is called a "thin file," which is a credit history with few accounts (loans or credit cards) and/or short credit history. First-time and younger home buyers may be able to improve their chances of getting a mortgage by paying attention to some basic guidelines. The following suggestions can help people who are planning on applying for a lease or mortgage with the thin file problem. If you can meet the following requirements, your chances of being approved and receiving favorable rates increase significantly. Bear in mind that it can take some time for these actions to take effect.

- Work to increase your credit rating to 700 or higher, if possible.
- Have at least three credit cards (applied for over a one- to two-year period), each with at least a year of regular payment history.

- Have at least two installment loans (auto, furniture, or other) paid off with no late payments, within the last two years.
- Have two or more open account installment loans (even small ones) that you are currently paying on.
- Obtain a copy of your credit report showing regular payment on all entries (can include utility bills, loans, etc.).
- Verify that your credit report shows accurate information (personal and accounts).
- Work to improve your debt-to-income (DTI) ratio to be less than 35 percent.
- Work to improve your debt-to-credit (DTC) ratio to be less than 20 percent.
- Save up adequate down payment (at least 20 percent) money that is not borrowed.
- Eliminate student loans, if possible.
- Show at least two years on a full-time job with steady income (especially if you are self-employed).

The Monthly Payment (PITI)

When buying a home, your monthly mortgage payment usually consists of four parts: Principal, Interest, Taxes, and Insurance (referred to as PITI).

- **Principal** (P): Amount borrowed for the home per month for term of loan
- **Interest** (I): Interest for the amount borrowed per month for term of loan
- **Taxes** (T): Property taxes (if included in monthly payment)
- **Insurance** (I): Homeowner's insurance (if included in monthly payment)

Note that property taxes and homeowner's insurance can be paid separately and may not be included in the monthly mortgage payment. Also note that the principal and interest portions of the monthly payment for a conventional mortgage is fixed for the life of the mortgage (typically fifteen or thirty years). However, taxes and insurance can vary from one year to the next. Since the principal goes down (admittedly very slowly) with each payment, you can build equity (ownership value) over time, when buying a home. If the home appreciates (increases in value), you can also benefit from increased equity.

PMI and MPI

If using a conventional mortgage with less than 20 percent down payment, the lender may require that you carry Private Mortgage Insurance (PMI), which is a separate premium that adds to your monthly payment. A PMI policy protects the lender and ensures that they will get paid should you miss payments or default on the mortgage. If the lender requires it, the PMI policy is typically paid for by the home buyer for the benefit of the lender. It does not prevent a home from going into foreclosure. The homeowner can cancel PMI if they are able to get their equity up to 20% or greater.

Some people get Private Mortgage Insurance (PMI) confused with Mortgage Protection Insurance (MPI), which protects the buyer in case they're unable to make payment due to death. Some MPI policies also cover disability that prevents the owner from being able to work and make the payment. An MPI policy is more like a life insurance policy that helps ensure that the payment on a home is made due to the death of the homeowner. Mortgage protection insurance is optional for the buyer depending on what other insurance they may already have (life, disability). An older home buyer with no dependents may not carry life insurance, but may have a house payment, and could opt for MPI insurance. Check with your insurance advisor to determine if MPI is a policy that is appropriate for your financial situation.

Conventional Mortgages: Fifteen-Year and Thirty-Year Considerations

Conventional home mortgages are typically either fixed thirty-year or fixed fifteen-year mortgages, with the thirty-year mortgage being most common. Some financial advisers recommend you take out a thirty-year mortgage, even if you can afford the higher payment for a fifteen-year mortgage. The reasoning is that, although the thirty-year mortgage typically has a higher annual percentage rate (APR), it has a lower required monthly payment for the life of the loan (albeit for twice as long!). The main advantage of the thirty-year loan is that it can provide added (and sometimes much needed) flexibility during difficult financial times.

Many people like the idea of a fifteen-year mortgage, which typically carries a lower APR than a comparable thirty-year loan. It also allows them to pay the mortgage off much more quickly and save a considerable amount in interest. This sounds good, but it also locks the buyer into a significantly higher fixed monthly payment. If your financial situation changes, it could become more difficult to make the payment.

With a thirty-year loan and a lower monthly payment, you may be able to weather a financial storm without missing a payment or defaulting on the loan, which could result in a major hit to your credit score. As with most any conventional home mortgage loan, you can always pay it off more quickly if you have the monthly cash flow to spare. Any extra you pay over the set thirty-year payment goes directly to reduction of the principal and bypasses the interest. You can make the determination regarding how much extra you want to pay on your home loan. You may also decide for any given month that you can't or don't want to pay any extra over the basic payment. Of course, with a fifteen-year loan, you could also decide to pay extra toward principal. You could cut the term of the loan from fifteen to ten years if you have the cash flow!

With our thirty-year fixed conventional scenario, you determine when and how much extra you want to pay. Some months you could pay extra, but you don't have to. By paying more each month, you can effectively shorten the length of the loan and achieve the same time period as a fifteen-year loan while saving about the same amount of interest. And, if you are a little strapped for cash, you can drop back to the basic PITI payment of the original thirty-year mortgage to which you agreed.

Scenario: Paying Thirty-Year Mortgage Off Early

For example, let's say you have a thirty-year fixed mortgage of $150,000 at an interest rate of 7 percent. Your regular monthly payment (principal and interest) would be about $1,000 per month (excluding property taxes and homeowner's insurance, which would be paid separately). Instead of the regular payment, you could decide to pay $1,100 per month. The extra hundred dollars is normally applied to the loan principal. This is about the same as paying an extra payment each year. At this rate, you could pay the thirty-year loan off in about twenty-two years, just by adding an extra 10 percent to the regular principal and interest payment. If you wanted to pay the loan off in fifteen years, you could pay an extra $350 a month. Keep in mind this is a simple example, and these numbers are approximate. The bottom line (literally) is that interest paid over the life of a loan can be significantly reduced by paying even a small amount of extra principal each month.

Note: If you do pay more than the regular monthly payment on your thirty-year mortgage each month, verify with your mortgage company that the extra amount you are paying is being applied to the loan principal. You can include a note with the payment coupon that tells them you want the extra applied to the principal. As with many of my financial lessons, I learned this one the hard way.

Prepaying Your Mortgage vs. Investing in the Stock Market

Some financial advisors recommend making the least possible down payment on a home purchase, extending the loan for as long as possible, and investing the amount you would save on the monthly payment over a fifteen-year mortgage. And, instead of adding extra to your monthly payment to pay down a thirty-year mortgage, taking that extra money and investing it also. The logic is that paying down a thirty-year mortgage with a 4 percent APR is like getting a fixed return at 4 percent. Every extra dollar you add to the mortgage payment goes to the principal, and you avoid paying 4 percent interest on it. However, if you can get a 4 percent APR by prepaying your mortgage, and you can get 7 percent by investing in your 401K (e.g., stock mutual funds), that is a viable alternative. On the other hand, if your mortgage APR is 8 percent and you can get 7 percent in your mutual fund investments, it may make more sense to prepay the mortgage, as you are virtually guaranteed an 8 percent ROI (not factoring inflation and taxes for either). In addition, interest paid on a mortgage may be tax deductible (as of this writing). All this said, it's a personal decision, and paying off your mortgage is still worthwhile, and many people like the feeling of "owning your home."

Note: All this assumes you have the extra money to prepay your mortgage or to invest in the market. If you have a thirty-year fixed mortgage at 4 percent and struggle to make the payment, just be thankful that you have a mortgage at a relatively good rate. If you have extra cash flow, you and your financial advisor can decide what to do with it.

Mortgage Interest Rate vs. Annual Percentage Rate (APR)

When taking out a mortgage and comparing rates, there are two numbers to be aware of. For example, a mortgage for a home through a particular lender may be advertised at an interest rate 6.75 percent (6¾ percent) but an APR of 6.89 percent. Interest rate is the actual rate for the mortgage principal being borrowed, whereas APR can include additional fees and is usually the greater of the two. More information is available at the bankrate.com Website:

https://www.bankrate.com/mortgages/apr-and-interest-rate

Note: When comparing loans and lenders, be sure you are comparing apples to apples (interest rate vs. APR).

Closing Costs and Commissions - Buyer and Seller Considerations
An important factor that many people do not consider when buying a home is that a typical home purchase/ sale includes several closing costs and fees that have to be paid by the buyer and/or seller. The home buyer typically pays 2–5 percent of the purchase price in closing fees, though some of these can be negotiated. Seller costs are typically 5–10 percent since the seller normally pays the commission to the realtor/agent (about 6–7percent). The commission paid by the seller when selling a $100,000 home can be as much as $7,000 or more. If you do not have much equity in your home, closing costs and commissions can eat up your equity and/or profits quickly, leaving you with little money to put down on your next home. This is one of the major problems with a mortgage that requires little or zero down payment. You basically have no equity, unless the home values in your housing market are increasing rapidly. If you have no equity in the home (via a down payment), you will go negative if you have to sell soon, due to closing costs and commissions. In slow home markets it is not uncommon for sellers to have to come up with money (write a check) at closing, in order to sell their home. This happened to me due to decreases in home values in our area. As the sellers, by the time we paid fees and the commission, we barely broke even after three years of living in the home.

Note: If you are considering selling your home, keep in mind that the seller usually pays the agent commissions (around 6 percent) and other closing costs. Also be sure to factor in the closing costs you paid to buy your home. When calculating net profit from the sale of a home don't forget to deduct the commission and closing costs from gross profit, as well as other closing costs you may have paid.

Contingent Home Sales
Some buyers will make an offer on a home they wish to purchase that is "contingent" on the sale of their current home. If the seller accepts their offer, the buyer has a certain amount of time to sell their own home. The proceeds of their current home sale usually make up the bulk of the down payment on the new home. Potential buyers can also make their offer contingent on whether the home they wish to purchase passes inspection or some other requirement(s). Buyers who purchase a home contingent on the sale of theirs typically put down a deposit of $500-$1,000 as earnest money for the seller. If the buyer cannot sell their home, they forfeit the earnest money.

Payment Coupon Book
Upon closing, the mortgage company usually sends the buyer a payment coupon book that lists the following:

- Amount of principal loan balance
- Interest rate in effect for the loan (e.g., 3.8750, which equals 3 7/8)
- Proper lender contact address and phone number
- Coupons (twelve) with exact payment due, including PITI and due date (e.g., March 1st)
- Late payment amount including late fee ($40–$50), due if payment is made after due date (e.g., March 15th)

Online Home Buying and Selling Guides

There are many online guides that outline the steps and provide recommendations for purchasing a home. One of these is Zillow, which identifies the following ten steps and provides an excellent source of information related to home buying and selling. Additional details and tools are provided at:

https://www.zillow.com/learn/10-steps-to-buying-a-home

> Step 1: Check your credit report and score (annualcreditreport.com).
> Step 2: Figure out how much you can afford (use your budget and a mortgage calculator).
> Step 3: Find a real estate agent.
> Step 4: Get preapproved by a lender.
> Step 5: Start looking at homes.
> Step 6: Make an offer.
> Step 7: Have home inspected.
> Step 8: Get insurance and establish utilities.
> Step 9: Close on the home.
> Step 10: Get the keys and move in.

Homeowner's Insurance

Homeowner's insurance is required by the lender when you purchase a home with a mortgage. The cost is frequently included in the monthly payment of PITI (Principal/Interest/Taxes/Insurance). If included with your monthly payment, it is paid out of an escrow account maintained by the lender. It may also be paid separately by the homeowner. If paid as part of the mortgage payment, the insurance company usually bills the lender semi-annually, and the lender collects from the homeowner as part of their monthly payment.

Homeowner's insurance provides coverage for major events that may damage your home, such as fire, theft, or flood (if included in the policy). Smaller damage claims such as a tree branch falling on the roof may be claimed against homeowner's insurance. However, if too many small damage claims are filed, often this increases your monthly premium and, in some cases, results in the insurance company cancelling your policy. It is best to file only major claims against your homeowner's insurance. It is suggested that you walk around your home and take pictures or, better yet, videos of your belongings. This will help you keep an accurate record of your major belongings in case you need to file a claim. If you take a video, consider narrating as you go, describing items and their cost.

Note: The discussion of insurance in this chapter deals primarily with home purchases and rentals. Refer to Chapter 16: Insurance and Risk Management, for a more comprehensive view of the various types of insurance available. Also refer to PFS sheets Insure-Pols and Home-Info for additional insurance-related information.

Note: Be sure to save your home video on a flash drive that you keep in a safe deposit box or other location outside your home.

Umbrella Insurance

Many financial advisors recommend that homeowners have an "Umbrella" personal liability policy in addition to Homeowner's and Auto liability insurance. An umbrella policy with $1,000,000 of coverage is typical. This type of policy can help to protect you against major claims related to your home or auto, such as lawsuits for damages as well as defamation, slander and libel lawsuits. For example, if a neighbor's son runs through a plate glass window in a sliding glass door in your home and they sue you. The umbrella policy gets its name from the fact that it covers liability over what your standard home and auto would cover and starts when those coverages are exhausted. In order to buy an Umbrella policy, you must have homeowner's and auto policies in place. With a million-dollar Umbrella policy, you are covered for up to $1,000,000 in damages in addition to your home and auto coverage. Without the policy, you may be liable and have to liquidate your assets to pay the damages. The premium for an umbrella policy is generally paid separately from PITI and is a combination policy based on your home and autos. The premium is usually a small amount, considering it can save you thousands of dollars in the event of an accident on your property or a major auto accident, if you are at fault.

Real Estate (Property) Taxes

Nearly every municipality (county and/or city) collects property taxes from its homeowners. The tax is frequently included in the monthly payment of PITI (Principal/Interest/Taxes/Insurance). It is paid out of an escrow account maintained by the lender. It may also be paid separately by the homeowner. Real estate taxes vary from one area to the next and are based on the valuation of your home. Valuation is usually done by the county tax assessor's office. For example, relatively low taxes of, say $2,400 per year may be charged in one county, and an adjacent county could charge $4,000 per year. When shopping for a home, pay close attention to the property taxes you will have to pay, as it can increase your monthly house payment significantly. Taxes can, and usually do, go up, which will automatically increase the monthly payment. Many homeowners choose to include the tax in the monthly payment so that they don't have to worry about saving money, receiving the semi-annual tax bill, and submitting it themselves. Property taxes represent the "T" in "PITI."

Online Property Tax Lookup

Most states and counties have a Web-based online search tool that you can use to determine what the real estate taxes are for a particular property. Information is also available regarding home sale price, property valuation, and ownership. The property in question can be looked up by parcel number, address, or owner. Visit the Website for the state/county where the property is located. You can also use the provided online tools to look up sales tax rates for state, county, city, and school districts for a particular property.

A New Home Appraisal Can Increase or Decrease Property Taxes

Property taxes for most municipalities are based on home assessed value, which is established using an appraisal, and in many areas, values generally appreciate, but in some regions, values can decrease over time, and the property tax should be adjusted accordingly. This happened to me when I moved to a small town where, during the five years that I owned the home, the home values in the area decreased by about 20 percent. We contacted the local county auditor's office and did an update appraisal. Our property taxes were adjusted after we showed the new appraisal compared to the one that we'd used to buy the home originally. We actually received a small rebate for the prior year's taxes paid, and going forward, our taxes decreased.

Home Warranties

Home buyers can usually request a home warranty to be paid for by the sellers. It generally costs about $500 for a one-year policy. This insurance covers breakdowns and failures related to most major systems in the home, such as plumbing, electrical, air conditioning, etc. This insurance may be required by the lender. It is different than homeowner's insurance and does not cover damage to the home, such as by fire, theft, or flood. If you are the buyer, this is a good thing, since the seller typically pays for it. If you are the seller, it is also a good thing, since it demonstrates that you are willing to pay for an insurance policy that sort of guarantees the main systems in the home are in good shape, to help put the buyer at ease.

We had a home warranty with our current home, and we called them several times to have things fixed, even though it was a fairly new home. When the policy expired, we did not renew it, preferring to handle the cost of repairs as needed instead of prepaying. It's a chance you take. Sometimes the policy provider can be pretty picky as to what is covered and what isn't. We had purchased a previous home with a warranty and were not too happy with it. For one reason or another, they denied every claim we made. Be sure to read the fine print, and call the warranty company before you do anything or attempt any repairs yourself. In one case, we actually paid for a repair person to come out, and it did not fix the problem. The warranty company did not cover the expense since they determined it was not covered once they got there. Also, the company providing the coverage can go out of business, leaving you with no coverage, even though it was already paid for.

Note: One option is to save a certain amount each month and budget for a "home repair fund." If there is a home repair or appliance replacement that needs to be made, you can save enough money ahead of time to pay for it or at least part of it. If you set aside a hundred dollars/month in a savings account over the course of a year, and you don't have any repairs required for the home, at the end of the year you've saved $1,000. You can either continue to build your home repair fund with it or spend it on something else.

Home Title Insurance

Home title insurance is a legitimate part of buying a home and is a title search that is done to protect the lender, seller, and buyer. It helps to ensure there are no claims or liens on the property from the previous owner or other parties. There are also products that offer a service that monitors your home title or deed, which usually resides at your local county auditor's office, by checking on it regularly, for a monthly fee.

While they may not provide insurance, they do provide monitoring and after-the-fact notification so you can take action. Home title fraud is a legitimate concern, and it is possible for someone to change ownership of your home title and file it with the auditor's office without your knowledge. Basically, they are committing identity fraud, and they can apply for lines of credit against your home. You can monitor the status of your home title yourself by checking on it regularly, and if you detect it early, you can notify the appropriate authorities to deal with it. Call your local county auditor's office where your home title is kept and ask them about this issue and find out what course of action they recommend. A Web search for "home title insurance" will also yield some useful information from various reputable sources, to learn more about home title fraud, home title insurance, and whether it's appropriate for you. Steps you can take can be found at the Better Business Bureau:

https://www.bbb.org/article/news-releases/22679-bbb-alert-home-title-fraud

Home Refinancing Options and Scenarios (reasons a homeowner may wish to refinance a mortgage):
- **Lower interest rate:** If you have been in a home less than five years and expect to stay there another five years and are able to reduce your APR by 2 percent percentage points or more, it may be worthwhile to refinance at a lower rate and lower payment (e.g., 6 percent > 4 percent). Be sure the amount to be saved offsets the closing costs and hassle.
- **Cash-out Refi(nance):** If you have been in the home long enough to build up some equity, you may be able to do a cash-out refi (short for refinance) and take some equity out of the home, while reducing your interest rate at the same time. You could use the money for debt consolidation to pay off high-interest-rate debt such as credit cards. You may also be able to accomplish the same thing using a home equity line of credit (HELOC), although the original mortgage would remain intact. Also, the cash-out refi establishes a new mortgage for another fifteen or thirty years.
- **Home improvements:** You could use a cash-out refi or HELOC.
- **Empty-nester downsize:** With today's market, homes are selling above the asking price. You could take advantage of this, reaping a sizable nontaxable gain by selling your home and moving to a smaller one that fits your needs. You may also be able to take advantage of lower interest rates.
- **Reverse Mortgage:** This is an option for retirees that own their home and wish to turn it into an income stream. It is also called an Equity Conversion Mortgage. Check with the Federal Housing Administration (FHA) and/or Housing and Urban Development (HUD) for more information at the FHA Website: https://www.fha.com/fha_reverse

Part 4: Buying vs. Renting a Home

Buy or Rent?
Purchasing a residence (with a mortgage) may be a good idea if you can say "yes" to most of the following home ownership questions. Consider these when comparing the advantages and disadvantages of buying a residence vs. renting.

- Do you have the money for the down payment (estimated 10–20 percent of purchase price)?
- Do you have the money for the closing costs?
- Are you a first-time home buyer?
- Is it likely you will be able to sell your current home?
- Do you think you will live in the new home for five or more years?
- Do you have a stable job where you have worked for two or more years?
- Do you have a good credit rating (700 or higher)?
- Can you afford to maintain the property and the home (if major systems fail)?
- Is there a home warranty on the major items, such as appliances and plumbing?
- Can you afford to pay the property taxes and homeowner's insurance?
- Can you pay the monthly Homeowner's Association (HOA) fees (if applicable)?
- Do you really want to be a homeowner?
- Do you want to build equity in your residence? Note that the value of a home can decrease.
- If you are moving into a new area or state, would you consider renting for a year?

Home Renting

When renting (home, apartment etc.), your monthly rental payment is fixed for the term of the lease, with no equity build up, but you are not paying PITI, the landlord is. Some landlords may offer a "rent-to-own" option, wherein you can build some equity by being able to apply a portion of your rental payment to the potential purchase of the home.

If you responded "no" to most of the previous home ownership questions, especially those related to how long you would stay in the home, renting a residence may be a better choice. Consider the following rental factors when comparing renting to buying a home.

- You will need money for the first and last month's rent, plus security/cleaning deposit.
- You will need to sign a lease for six months, a year, or more.
- Do you have a stable job where you have worked for a year or more?
- Is it likely you or the landlord could sublet the residence if you have to move?
- The landlord is usually responsible for home maintenance and repairs.
- If you lose your job, you won't have to worry about foreclosure but just about finding a place to live!
- If you want to move, there is usually less financial liability (although you may have to pay off the lease).
- No liability of existing home to sell (usually).
- Monthly rent can be less than a mortgage payment.
- No property taxes or homeowner's insurance to pay.
- Do you have a pet or intend on getting one? Note that some landlords do not allow pets.

Renters Insurance

This type of insurance is very worthwhile for those who rent, as it protects the renter from theft and other damages. The landlord is generally not responsible for the loss or the cost of the insurance in these cases. Renter's insurance is not very expensive; however, many people who rent do not carry it. This may be because they think it is more expensive than it is, or they may not even know about it.

Housing-to-Income (HTI) Ratio for Renters

If you are renting, add up your monthly rent + renter's insurance + parking and any monthly maintenance fees. Include utilities such as water and electricity if they are part of your monthly rent payment. Do not include deposits or Internet access fees. Divide your monthly housing rental expense by your monthly gross income (before deductions) to get your HTI ratio or percentage. So, if you make $4,000 per month, and you pay $1,000 per month for rental expenses, divide $1,000 by $4,000 and your ratio is .25 (multiply by 100 to get the percentage) or 25 percent. Opinions vary, but your HTI ratio should be below 30 percent. So basically, you spend 25 percent of your gross monthly income to pay your rental expenses, which is a good ratio. Keep in mind that the landlord will normally require a security deposit for damage and cleaning, some of which will be nonrefundable. They will also require first and last month's rent. These expenses are not included in the HTI ratio for renters. although they will impact your budget. So, when you go looking for a place to rent, be sure you have enough for the first and last months and better yet, three months plus whatever deposits the landlord may require.

Part 5: PFS Home Info and Maintenance Sheet

PFS Sheet - Home Info and Maintenance (Home-Info Tab)

Refer to Figure 11-4 For a screen shot of the PFS Home-Info tab, which contains sample information related to your home or rental. This sheet of the PFS provides a central reference for basic home information such as date of purchase, parcel number, lot size, property tax, and homeowner's insurance policies, as well as a place to record major repairs and maintenance, such as pressure washing, driveway paving, painting, window cleaning/replacement, water heater and carpet replacement, and more. Figure 11-5 is a form with no data, based on Figure 11-4, and is used with Exercise 11-2 (gather home data).

Refer to **Exercise 11-2: Record PFS Home Info** at the end of this chapter, which will help you identify and record important information about your home and property specifications, as well as mortgage, taxes, insurance, and other information related to maintenance projects. Note that this sheet is primarily focused on a purchased home. You can add rental information if you choose to.

Figure 11-4: PFS Sheet - Home Info and Maintenance (sample entries)

	A	B	C	D	E	F
1	**Home Info and Maintenance**			Book Build Ch. 11		Updated: MM-DD-YYYY
2						
3	**<<< Home Information >>>**					**Notes**
4						
5	**Address:**	1234 Home Rd., Anytown, ST		**Mortgage Co.:**	MortCo, Inc.	
6	**Description:**	2-Story, 3 Bdrm, 2 Bath, 2-car garage		**Payment (PITI):**	1,200/mo	Incl. Prop Tax & Ins.
7	**Year Built:**	2010		**Loan Number:**	1123456789	
8	**Living Area:**	2,500		**Mortgage Bal:**	$125,000	
9	**Lot Size:**	60x90		**Home Owner Ins:**	FGH Ins Co.	
10	**Parcel No:**	1234567890		**HO Policy No:**	123456789	
11	**Market Value:**	$250,000	2023 assess	**HO Coverage:**	$300,000	Incl. Prop Tax & Ins.
12	**Taxable Value:**	$150,000		**HOA Dues:**	$200/Year	AutoPay Qtrly, CC#9999
13	**Prop Tax/Year:**	$2,400	County Treasurer	**Renters Ins:**	N/A	
14	**Last Sale Date:**	mm-dd-yyyy		**Other:**		
15	**Last Sale Price:**	$220,000		**Other:**		
16	**Other:**					
17						
18	**<<< Home Maintenance and Improvement >>>**					
19						
20	**Est Start Date**	**Act Start Date**	**Project Description**	**Amount**	**Company**	
21	99/99/9999	99/99/9999	Landscape	$1,000	Various nurseries	
22	99/99/9999	99/99/9999	Gutter guards	$500	Roofing Contractor	
23	99/99/9999	99/99/9999	Outdoor Electrical	$900	Contractor	
24	99/99/9999	99/99/9999	New Toilets (2x)	$500	ABC Plumbing	
25	99/99/9999	99/99/9999	Finish Basement	$2,000	Contractor	
26						
27			**Total Home Projects**	$4,900		=SUM(D21:D26)
28						

< > ···   Income-Exp   Assets-Liab   Cred-Cards   **Home-Info**   Auto-Info   Insure-Pols   Fin-Plan   Income-Exp-F   Assets-Liab-F   Cre

Figure 11-5: PFS Sheet - Home Info and Maintenance (Form)

	A	B	C	D	E	F
1	**Home Info and Maintenance**			Book Build Ch. 11		Updated: MM-DD-YYYY
2						
3	**<<< Home Information >>>**					**Notes**
4						
5	**Address:**			**Mortgage Co.:**		
6	**Description:**			**Payment (PITI):**		
7	**Year Built:**			**Loan Number:**		
8	**Living Area:**			**Mortgage Bal:**		
9	**Lot Size:**			**Home Owner Ins:**		
10	**Parcel No:**			**HO Policy No:**		
11	**Market Value:**			**HO Coverage:**		
12	**Taxable Value:**			**HOA Dues:**		
13	**Prop Tax/Year:**			**Renters Ins:**		
14	**Last Sale Date:**			**Other:**		
15	**Last Sale Price:**			**Other:**		
16	**Other:**					
17						
18	**<<< Home Maintenance and Improvement >>>**					
19						
20	**Est Start Date**	**Act Start Date**	**Project Description**	**Amount**	**Company**	
21						
22						
23						
24						
25						
26						
27			**Total Home Projects**	$0		=SUM(D21:D26)
28						

Chapter 11 Exercises

Exercise 11-1: Compare Home Mortgage Calculators

A mortgage calculator can compare different types of mortgage factors. They are tailored to mortgage requirements and can accommodate many other mortgage variables such as property taxes and homeowner's insurance. Do a Web search for "free mortgage calculator" and identify two or three of them you like. Some examples are included in Table 11-4. You can make a copy of the table and use it with this exercise.

Table 11-4: Home Mortgage Calculator Comparison
(Alphabetical order)

Source Name	Cost	Notes
Bankrate		https://www.bankrate.com/calculators
Calculator.Net		https://www.calculator.net/mortgage-calculator.html
Mortgage Calculator Org		https://www.mortgagecalculator.org

Exercise 11-2: Record PFS Home Info

In this exercise, you will enter your home information into a blank form (Figure 11-5) created from Figure 11-4, the Home-Info sheet. You will then enter the data you've collected into your PFS sheet Home Info and Maintenance. Even if you do not plan to enter the data into the spreadsheet at this time, go ahead make a copy of Figure 11-5 and use Figure 11-4 as a guide for data entry. You can transfer the data to your PFS sheet later. The only calculation in this sheet is a summary of home project costs, which you can do manually now if you want to.

Chapter 12
Buying or Leasing a Vehicle

Chapter Overview:
This chapter deals with the second most expensive thing most people acquire: their car or other primary mode of transportation, such as a truck or motorcycle. Although they can represent major expenditures, boats, motor homes, trailers, and other recreational vehicles are not covered. The purchase, ownership, and maintenance of multiple vehicles is a major part of many people's lives. The chapter compares the advantages of purchasing and leasing. Information is also provided on how to shop wisely for new and used vehicles, as well as tips on trade-ins and maintenance. The chapter provides a high-level view of some of the more important things to consider when acquiring a vehicle. Exercises are provided to research auto loan calculators and gather auto-related information for entry into your PFS Auto-Info sheet. The chapter is divided into six parts:

- **Part 1: Auto Purchasing Guidelines**
- **Part 2: Auto Loans and Financing**
- **Part 3: Buying a Car**
- **Part 4: Auto Maintenance**
- **Part 5: Auto Lease and Purchase**
- **Part 6: Auto Insurance**

Chapter PFS and PFI Integration:
The chapter covers PFS Sheet – Auto Info and Maintenance, with a tab label of Auto-Info. The Auto-Info sheet provides a way to record information about your vehicle whether you are buying or leasing. The first section is Vehicle Information, which includes auto description and specifications and VIN, as well as loan, license, registration, insurance, warranty, and purchase information. The second section of the sheet is the Maintenance Record for the vehicle, which provides a way to record work done and maintenance performed as well as upgrades. Personal Financial Indicator PFI 12-1: Transportation-to-Income (TTI) Ratio (percent) and the "Auto 20/4/10 Rule" are introduced. Together they provide guidelines for purchasing a car and budgeting of transportation expenses.

Chapter Exercises:
- **Exercise 12-1: Compare Auto Loan Calculators**
- **Exercise 12-2: Record PFS Auto Info**

Chapter Notable Quote:
Quote 12-1: "An ounce of prevention equals a pound of cure." - Anonymous

This old adage applies to vehicles of all types! It means that if you deal with potential problems early, you may be able to avoid them or save time and money. However, if you wait until later, the problem could become much worse, and it may cost more to fix. It can be applied to many aspects of our lives, including home repairs, autos, health, and others. Regarding auto maintenance and repairs, it means that if you see or hear something strange about your vehicle and have it diagnosed early, it may require only a minor repair or adjustment. If you ignore the problem and let it go, it may require more time and money to correct the problem. This quote applies especially to auto maintenance and primarily to used cars.

Part 1: Auto Purchasing Guidelines

It's a Personal Choice

What we drive is a reflection of our personality and values. For some people, a car is a way to get from point A to point B at a minimum cost. Style and looks are not important to them, and they have no need for frills; they simply want basic transportation functionality. For other people, a car is a way of life. Some people are focused on the luxury aspect or exclusivity of a particular brand, and the options and features are important to them. Others may subscribe to the philosophy of "Life is too short to drive boring cars," or they may have "the need for speed," or both. Some might opt for a utilitarian vehicle such as a pickup truck or van, especially if they use it for work, while others are focused on practicality, frugality, fuel efficiency, and eco friendliness. Some have a combination of needs and wants when it comes to car buying.

Buying a New or Used Vehicle

Regardless of the type of "car" person you are, you have a lot of options when acquiring a vehicle. You can buy new or used, or, if you have very good credit, you can lease. You may get a better deal if you buy a used car (without a trade in). You will also have more leverage when buying new if you can sell your old car rather than trade it in. Some people really like the new car smell and do not like the idea of driving a car that someone else has owned. If you decide to buy new, you can save time and money on your next car by using an online buying service like that provided by Consumer Reports. The CR Build & Buy Car Buying Service is intended to help make car buying cheaper and easier, with less stress and anxiety. If you are a member of the AARP, they also have an Auto Buying Program.

Online buying services have arrangements with dealers that can sell you a car at a better price than you might ordinarily get. You can create an account to subscribe and use the service by going to this link: www.cr.org/buildandbuy. If you buy new at a dealership, try to purchase at the end of the month and at the end of the model year (typically between October and December). The sales staff may have more flexibility to give you a better deal during these times.

My wife and I have two cars, a small SUV that we bought used (it was three years old and had forty thousand miles on it). It is comfortable, gets relatively good mileage, has a great repair record, and a lot of cargo capacity, so it's pretty functional too. We also have a pickup truck that we bought used (three years old with thirty thousand miles on it). It's great for hauling large or heavy loads or pulling trailers. As you would expect, it does not get very good mileage, but it's functional. It also has an excellent repair record.

Auto Purchase Guidelines: The 20/4/10 Auto Buying Rule

Whether buying new or used, a good **financially aware** rule of thumb is the "**Auto 20/4/10 Rule,**" which is highly recommended by automotive sales experts. Here's how the rule is applied:

- **20 = Make a 20 percent down payment (or more)**
- **4 = Four-year car loan maximum (or less)**
- **10 = 10 percent maximum of gross monthly income (or less)**

Let's say you are looking at buying a five-year-old used car. For the price of $10,000 (excluding tax), you would need to put 20 percent down or $2,000. You plan to finance the car for no more than four years (forty-eight months) and try to keep your total vehicle and transportation expenses under 10 percent of your gross monthly income. Refer to the Personal Financial Indicator TTI ratio explanation below for what to include in your "transportation expenses." The Transportation-to-Income (TTI) Ratio (%) is used to see where you are currently regarding your transportation expenses as a percentage compared to your income. The TTI ratio can also be used to determine where you might be if you purchase a particular vehicle. The Auto 20/4/10 Rule works with the TTI Personal Financial Indicator to give you some clear guidelines that can help you to avoid going "underwater" (owing more than your car is worth). Following these guidelines can significantly reduce the amount of interest you might otherwise pay by limiting the loan term to four years or less. And, doing so can help to ensure you don't go over budget on your car expenses by limiting the overall transportation cost to no more than 10 percent of your gross income. Recall from Chapter 11 that home-related expenses should be no more than 30 percent of gross income. These percentages are all general guidelines to increase awareness and to help with making sound financial decisions.

PFI 12-1: Transportation-to-Income (TTI) Ratio (%)

A good way to determine how much car you can afford is to use the Transportation-to-Income (TTI) Ratio (%). TTI is determined by adding up your monthly expenses related to transportation and then dividing that total by your Monthly Gross Income. Most lenders like to see a TTI ratio of less than 10 percent (less is better). This means you spend less than 10 percent of your gross income on transportation-related expenses. Let's say your monthly transportation expenses include the following, and your total transportation expense per month is $600. If your gross monthly income is $4000 then divide $600 by $4000 and you get .15 (*100) = 15 percent so your TTI is higher than recommended. You can use the PFS Income-Exp sheet with your data to calculate your own TTI ratio. But we'll use the numbers in the PFI 12-1 example below.

- **Loan payment (fixed)**   **$250**
- **Insurance premium (fixed)** **$150**
- **Monthly maint. (varies)**   **$100**
- **Fuel cost (varies)**   **$100**
-    **Total trans. cost/mo.**   **$600**

PFI 12-1: Transportation-to-Income (TTI) Ratio (%) - Formula/Calculation
Personal Financial Indicator (#PFI-14)

Transportation Required Monthly Expenses (/divided by/) Monthly Gross Income = TTI (%)

$600 / $4,000 = .15 (*100) = 15%

(Generic PFI example)

The Repair Record and Transportation Expenses

Something our SUV and truck have in common is that they were both purchased used (three years old), and both have very good repair records. One of the most important car-buying tips, regardless of what kind of car it is or whether it's new or used, is to buy a car that has a good repair record for reliability. The repair record rating is a good indicator as to how much repair and maintenance a vehicle will require over time and what subsystems are more likely to fail or have problems (electrical, A/C, transmission, etc.). Many cars have excellent reliability records (few reported repairs), and some have terrible reliability records (high number of reported repairs). It stands to reason that a car with a good repair record will have fewer things go wrong and cost you less to maintain and repair over time than one with a poor repair record. As an example, Bob bought an older European sports car with high mileage. It looked great but had a poor repair record and a poor reliability rating. In addition, the cost of parts and repairs was much higher than for other cars. He ended up getting rid of it and lost money in the process.

Consumer Reports and Buying Guide

One of the best tools I have found to help with buying cars, new and used, is Consumer Reports (CR) magazine. I have a subscription to Consumer Reports, which has been an independent, nonprofit product testing organization since 1936. CR tests and rates all sorts of products, from cars and TVs to vacuum cleaners and lawn mowers. They try to be unbiased (impartial) and do not accept advertising. They also do not allow the manufacturers of the products they rate to use their rating in the manufacturers' advertising as testimonials. Consumer Reports rates new car models based on predicted reliability. They classify older model used cars and trucks based on the most reliable models and list the ones to avoid. They survey thousands of subscribers and rate cars based on reliability by year, make, and model, and identify common trouble areas that owners report. It is easy to compare various brands and model years to see which ones are generally more dependable. Consumer Reports also publishes a yearly Buying Guide, which is available at most public libraries. With a subscription to the magazine, you get the latest Buying Guide for free and online access to ratings of various products, including cars, trucks, SUVs, etc.

One nice feature of the annual Buying Guide is the "Best of the Best" section for used cars. You can decide how much you want to spend and on what type of vehicle (truck, sedan, SUV, etc.), and they list some of the most reliable cars and the range of model years. For example, you could decide you want to spend $15,000–$20,000 and want to buy a good used SUV. They list the best models and years that would fit your budget. You can then go looking for used SUVs for sale that match their recommendation. In the Buying Guide, they also list used cars to avoid in the "Worst of the Worst" section. These cars have had multiple years of worse than average reliability and will likely cost you more to maintain over time.

Note: Consumer reports develops the repair history records for various cars by polling actual owners of the cars and collecting thousands of surveys each year.

Part 2: Auto Loans and Financing

Auto Depreciation and Loans

Almost all new cars, and most new things we buy, depreciate, or decrease in value after we buy them. Buying a two- or three-year-old newer used car lets someone else take the depreciating hit! If you buy a new car, as soon as you drive it off the dealer's lot, it decreases in value from what you paid by 10–20 percent or more, depending on the make and model. Let's say you buy a new car and finance it for five years, then need to sell the car within the first two years. You will likely be what the industry calls "upside down." This means that you owe more on the loan than the car is worth. The longer you keep a car, the more principal you pay with each payment. This alone is a good reason to take out the shortest-term loan you can afford (ideally five years/sixty months or less) and then keep the car until you pay it off.

Auto Loan Types

Most auto loans are simple interest loans and are similar to a home mortgage. You pay the interest rate, calculated monthly, based on the amount of principal owed, so the loan is "front-end loaded," meaning that at the beginning of the term of the loan, your monthly payment goes to pay a higher percentage of interest. As you pay more of the loan off and reach the end of the loan period (e.g., five years or sixty months), more of your monthly payment is going to principal and less to interest. This ensures that the loan company gets their interest up front, even if you sell the car in a few years and can pay off the loan. Also, make sure that you are getting a "simple interest" loan with no prepayment penalty and not a "precomputed" loan, which sets the loan amount and interest when the loan is initiated.

Buying a Monthly Payment vs. Buying a Car - Monthly Payment vs. Term of Loan

The term of an auto loan is determined largely by the amount of principal to be financed and whether the car is new or used. Certainly, the creditworthiness of the buyer and down payment are also considered. Many car buyers will finance a car for as long as the lending institution will allow, thinking they don't care what the loan interest rate is as long as they can get the payment down to some budgeted level. Table 12-1 shows the difference in monthly payment and total interest paid for a typical auto loan with a 20 percent down payment and with a four-year (forty-eight month) term and the same loan with a five-year (sixty month) term. Down payment, APR, credit, and other factors are the same. Only the term of the loan changes from four years to five years. Note the difference in monthly payment and total interest paid back over the life of the loan. Taxes, title, registration, and other fees are not factored in.

Table 12-1: Auto Loan Payment and Interest Based on Term of Loan

Auto Loan Information	4-Year Term	5-Year Term	Notes
Auto Price	$20,000	$20,000	
Down payment (20%)	$4,000	$4,000	
Loan amount financed	$16,000	$16,000	
Interest rate (APR)	10%	10%	
Loan term	**4 years (48 mo.)**	**5 years (60 mo.)**	
Monthly payment	**$405**	**$340**	$65 Decrease per Mo.
Total payback (principal and interest)	**$19,500**	**$20,400**	
Total Interest paid	**$3,480)**	**$4,400**	5-yr term cost $920 more interest than 4-yr term

Note: Dollar amounts are rounded and approximate.

In Table 12-1, the buyer with the five-year (sixty month) term was able to decrease his monthly payment by $65 (from $405 to $340) but had to make payments for an additional twelve months. In exchange for a slightly lower monthly payment, he paid more than $900 in additional loan interest than the four-year (forty-eight month) term buyer.

Credit Rating Impact on Auto Loan Terms

Your credit rating can have a major impact on how much car you can qualify for as well as an impact on the interest rate and term of the loan, which determines your monthly payment. Table 12-2 shows an example of an auto loan and the impact that your credit score can have on the terms of your loan. A buyer with an excellent score (e.g., FICO score of 800 or higher) may be offered a loan with an 8 percent APR as compared to 12 percent APR for a buyer with good credit (e.g., FICO score of 700). The dealer or lender will look at your credit score and credit history as well as your Debt-to-Income (DTI) ratio to decide how much you should be able to borrow for an auto, as well as how much of a down payment will be required, what the interest rate charged will be, and what the maximum term of the loan will be (e.g., thirty-six or forty-eight months). All these factors combined determine your monthly payment. Note that this same credit information also applies to insurance rates and monthly premiums. In Table 12-2, the amount financed, down payment, and term of loan are all the same. Only the APR changes, based on the buyer's credit rating. Note the difference in monthly payment and total interest paid back over the life of the loan. Taxes, title, registration, and other fees are not factored in.

Table 12-2: Auto Loan Payment and Interest Based on Credit Rating and APR

Auto Loan Information	Credit Score 800 (APR 8%)	Credit Score 680 (APR 12%)	Notes
Auto Price	$20,000	$20,000	
Down payment (20%)	$4,000	$4,000	
Loan amount financed	$16,000	$16,000	
Interest rate (APR)	**8%**	**12%**	
Loan term	4 years (48 mo.)	4 years (48 mo.)	
Monthly payment	**$390**	**$420**	**$30 Increase Monthly**
Total payback (principal and interest)	**$18,750**	**$20,200**	
Total Interest paid	**$2,750**	**$4,220**	**12% APR cost $1,470 more interest than 8% APR (over 4 yrs)**

Note: Dollar amounts are rounded and approximate.

In Table 12-2, the buyer with the lower credit score (680) and resulting higher interest rate (APR of 12 percent) was able get financing with only a thirty-dollar increase in his monthly payment ($390 to $420) as compared to the buyer with a higher credit score (800) and lower interest rate (APR 8 percent). However, because of his lower score and higher APR, he paid almost $1,500 in additional loan interest than the higher credit score buyer.

Auto Loan Calculators

You can use an auto loan or lease calculator to compare various types of auto acquisition methods, payment amounts, and time periods. Many of them provide a wide range of entries, which includes down payment, taxes, license, title, registration, and trade-in allowances that can accommodate most any type of auto loan. Several calculators are available online to help you estimate your payment. Avoid those that ask for a lot of up-front personal information. You will see many available for use online or download, as well as smart phone apps. Some are free and do not require you to enter personal contact information. Figure 12-1 shows an example of a free online auto loan calculator.

Figure 12-1: Auto Loan Calculator Example

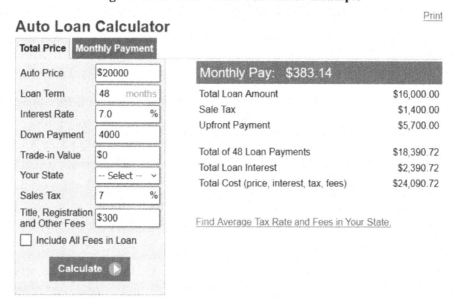

Refer to **Exercise 12-1: Compare Auto Loan Calculators** at the end of this chapter for some guidance on finding an online auto loan calculator that meets your needs. Three online calculators are listed in Exercise 12-1. There are many good ones available. This screenshot is from calculator.net.

Part 3: Buying a Car

Prequalification

As with a home purchase, before purchasing a vehicle (car, truck, motorcycle, etc.), contact one or more potential lenders (banks, credit unions) to compare the types of loans available along with their interest rates and borrowing requirements. Upon selecting a lender, you may be given a checklist that identifies the documents you must provide to get "prequalified" or "preapproved." If your credit score is high enough, you may not need to provide much in the way of documentation. The lender will then come up with a maximum dollar amount that you can borrow for a car based on how much of a down payment you will need. The lender will provide you with a preapproval letter stating how much you have been approved for. You can show this to dealerships or private party sellers to let them know that you are a serious potential buyer.

Used Car Dealers

Dealerships sell new and used cars. They refer to used cars as pre-owned and frequently have newer vehicles available. Used car dealers usually sell used cars, which are usually fairly old (ten years or more) and may be in need of repairs. This does not mean they are mechanically unsafe. You can get a good deal at a used car dealer, especially if you are mechanically inclined and have cash or your own prearranged financing. But exercise caution because they may charge very high interest rates if you obtain financing through them. Also, they may be "here today and gone tomorrow." You may think you have a warranty, but if they go out of business, there's not much you can do. Used car dealerships that advertise "buy here, pay here" usually have high interest rates and may have prepayment penalties. That said, I bought one of the cheapest and most dependable cars I've ever owned at a small used car dealer. You've just got to be mindful and aware when shopping for a car. It's a good idea to take a mechanically savvy friend along and buy them lunch.

New vs. Used
The average person cannot tell the difference between a new car and one that is three years old. This is due, in part, to the fact that it costs manufacturers a lot to make changes from one model year to the next, so the changes tend to be relatively minor. A friend recently bought a 2015 Camaro SS with twenty thousand miles on it, and it looks like a new car. My truck is ten years old as of this writing. I take good care of it, and a number of people have asked me if it is new. It only has fifty thousand miles on it, and based on the excellent Consumer Reports repair record, it will probably last two hundred thousand miles or more!

Manufacturer Certified Pre-Owned (CPO)
A couple of years ago, we bought a used late model SUV with forty thousand miles on it from a dealer. It was three years old and was a one-owner lease car. It was a "Certified Pre-owned" (CPO) car and was in nearly perfect condition. As a CPO car, it came with an extended sixty-thousand-mile bumper-to-bumper warranty. In addition, we did not have to pay for the next four services up to sixty thousand miles. The car looked new, yet we paid much less than what it would have cost new. It currently has ninety thousand miles on it and will easily last two hundred thousand miles or more with proper care and maintenance. The main benefit to buying a CPO vehicle is that it has been inspected thoroughly and must pass an extensive examination checklist. CPO usually means an extended warranty is included with the asking price of the vehicle and the manufacturer stands behind it. The CPO program varies from one manufacturer to the next. The average price of a CPO vehicle is typically higher than that of a comparable non-CPO used car. However, they offer the protection of an extended manufacturer's warranty, and may include roadside assistance as well as complimentary oil changes.

Note: If you plan to buy a CPO vehicle, be sure to ask at the dealership exactly what is covered with the manufacturer's CPO warranty, and how it works with the existing vehicle warranty. Be sure to get a copy of the CPO warranty and the Carfax report for the vehicle.

Buying a Used Vehicle – Reliability Ratings
If you choose to buy a used car, especially an older one (five to six years old), be sure to check the Consumer Reports Buying Guide reliability ratings. This section of the guide goes back up to six or seven years from the current year for each manufacturer/model. It lists seventeen of the major potential "trouble spots" for each car (engine, electrical, suspension, paint, etc.). Each potential trouble spot or area is rated based on reliability as compared to all the other cars of the same year. The following reliability "codes" are used by Consumer Reports when rating vehicles. So, you could look up the engine or transmission reliability rating for a particular year, make, and model to see how it compares to other similar models. If the engine or drivetrain is rated "much better than average," chances are you're not going to have a problem with that

part of the vehicle. However, this doesn't mean your power windows won't stop working or problems with other subsystems on the vehicle won't develop.

- **Much better than average**
- **Better than average**
- **Average**
- **Worse than average**
- **Much worse than average**

Cost of Maintenance and Repairs

Try not to buy a car that has a poor repair record, especially one that has high mileage (of over a hundred thousand). They are prone to failure, and repairs can be very expensive. For example, let's say that someone buys a ten-year-old, expensive sports car with 125,000 miles on it. The car may look good, but within a couple of months, it might develop so many mechanical problems that it might not be worth fixing due to the high cost. The body and interior might look great, and the car might run well, but if the engine and transmission need a lot of work, it could turn into a real money pit. All the more reason to take the used car you are considering buying to a trusted mechanic to check out the parts of the car that are hard to see.

Total Cost of Ownership (TCO)

They say that when buying a used car, you are buying another person's problems. Be sure to budget a certain amount per month for repairs. The monthly payment might be only $300, but maintenance and repairs could average out to be another $200/month. Most people only look at the monthly payment and may not consider the "Total Cost of Ownership." This includes other necessary car-related expenses, such as those listed below. These peripheral expenses can easily add up to as much as or more than the car payment. Depending on your age, driving record, and other factors, you can pay $200/month for auto insurance alone. More about auto insurance later.

- **Insurance** (liability or comprehensive)
- **License/registration** (can be expensive depending on price of car)
- **Maintenance** (oil change, tires, brakes, wipers, air filter, battery)
- **Repairs** (funny noises or something breaks)
- **Fuel** (can be very expensive unless you have an electric or hybrid)

Sales Tax

Some people neglect to take into account sales tax when determining how much they want to spend on a car, new or used. Vehicle sales tax can be a significant factor and varies from state to state. It can be anywhere from 0 to10 percent, depending on the state and city where you live. In Ohio, the state and local tax combined are about 7 percent, and every time a car is sold, sales tax is collected. I did not really think about this when I bought a used car in Illinois. I did not have to pay Illinois tax at the time of purchase, but when I went to register in Ohio, I had to pay over $1,000 in Ohio sales taxes.

Factory and Extended Warranties

When buying a new or used car, you may have the option of buying an extended warranty. Depending on the year, make, and model these can cost thousands of dollars. The goal is to be able to buy relatively inexpensive insurance now to avoid potentially very expensive repairs down the road after your existing warranty is over. If you have a 3-year/36,000-mile factory warranty and buy an extended warranty, you are getting no additional coverage until the original factory warranty expires. However, if you are at year four (year one of the extended warranty) and something major goes wrong, you may be covered and not have to pay for the repairs. People who buy an extended warranty may choose to roll the cost into the loan for the vehicle. This allows them to finance the extended warranty and pay interest on it. If you are interested in an extended warranty, check to see if there is one available from the manufacturer.

The Auto Repair Fund

Consider setting aside an amount each month for possible repairs . Today's late model cars are built extremely well as compared to those from twenty or even ten years ago. For example, if you buy a good five-year-old, high-dependability car that's in good condition and with average mileage on it, the chances of anything major going wrong with it are low. Take the $1,200 or whatever you would have spent on an extended warranty and put it in a high-yield savings account over the course of a year. Divide the cost of the extended warranty by twelve and put $100/month into savings. If a major repair is needed let's say at month eight, you will have about $800 available to apply to the repair cost. At the end of a year, you may still have $1,000 or more in your savings account. You could continue to put a hundred dollars per month into your "Auto Repair Fund" savings account in case you have to use it for bigger repairs down the road. You could even add the fund contributions to the PFS Income-Exp sheet as a budgeted monthly expense and to the Assets-Liab sheet as an asset. You should also add any warranty information to your Auto-Info sheet

Have It Checked Out by a Mechanic

If you are buying a used car, especially an older one with higher mileage, ask if you can take the car to a reputable certified mechanic to have it checked out. If the mechanic does spot some problems, ask how much they estimate it would cost to have them fixed (ballpark). It still may be worth buying the car if it's a minor fix. Many dealerships will allow you to take a car overnight or for a day or more to see if you like it and want to buy it. That should give you an opportunity to have a mechanic look it over.

The Used Car History Report

Ask the dealership if they can run a CARFAX (www.carfax.com) or AutoCheck (www.autocheck.com) vehicle history report on the used vehicle in question. They likely have already done this and should be able to show it to you. CARFAX was one of the first companies to offer this service, and AutoCheck is part of Experian, one of the big three credit reporting companies. The vehicle history report can help to minimize the risk of buying a used vehicle with unknown problems or issues. Several reputable Websites offer vehicle history reports. Some of these services also have tips for buyers and sellers. Some services can provide a score, based on their rating system, for a particular auto. Select the one that provides the information you need for the least cost. Using the online Website, you can run a report yourself if you have the vehicle identification number (VIN). However, there is usually a fee of twenty to forty dollars for a single vehicle, depending on the type of report you want. Many dealerships will run the report for free since they pay a monthly subscription fee for an unlimited number of reports. The report will show previous ownership and maintenance history. A Carfax or AutoCheck report can answer the following types of questions about a used car you may be considering buying. Be sure to have them run the check before you buy the car.

- How many previous owners has the car had?
- Has it been in the shop for repairs multiple times?
- Has it been reported in an accident?
- Has it been in a flood or some other major disaster?
- Has it been branded a "lemon"?
- Has it been stolen or repossessed before?
- What was the vehicle used for (taxi, rental, lease)?
- Are there manufacturer safety recalls for this brand, model, and year?

The Test Drive

Be sure to take a good, long test drive that puts the vehicle through its paces (in town and highway). A friend was looking at buying a used diesel pickup truck with high mileage (over two hundred thousand miles). Mileage of 200,000 miles or more is not uncommon with diesel trucks. High mileage may not be much of an issue if the vehicle has been well maintained. The typical diesel engine can last for 300,000 to 500,000 miles, but the peripheral systems—such as transmission, steering, suspension, and air conditioning—can fail. These peripheral systems can be very expensive to repair. When they took the truck for a test drive, it ran fine around town, but when driven on the highway, it would not shift to fourth gear! It had a Six-Speed automatic transmission. It's a good thing they tested it on the highway. They did not buy the truck. It's possible it had been used to tow a trailer or something heavy, and the transmission may have been overloaded.

Vehicle Values – What's My Car Worth?

You can get an idea of what your car is worth by looking it up with one or more of the online car valuation Websites. It's easier if you have the Vehicle Identification Number (VIN) before you start. You can check the wholesale, trade-in, and retail values of a car manufacturer, model, and year. The values will vary based on the Website you use and the mileage and condition of the car. Check more than one to get an average of the values for your used car. Some of the sources you can use to establish vehicle values are listed below (in alphabetical order). These companies are the big three auto valuation companies that many of the car dealerships use. They may also be interested in buying your car and will give you a quote based on the information, as well as photos, you provide them.

- Edmunds (www.edmunds.com)
- Kelly Blue Book (www.kbb.com)
- National Automobile Dealers Association (www.nada.com)

Part 4: Auto Maintenance

Throwing Good Money After Bad

With an older car, how do you determine when to stop fixing it and get rid of it? Opinions vary on this, but as a general rule, if the estimated cost of repairs is greater than half the value of the car, consider selling it or trading it in. So, if the car is worth approximately $3,000, and you have repair estimates that total nearly $1,500, it is probably time to get rid of the car. Keep in mind that with many older cars, major repairs can happen in rapid succession, as one repair can lead to another. Soon you are throwing good money after bad into a large money pit.

Maintenance Recommendations

If you take care of your car, it will take care of you! A car today is generally considered a necessity (unless you live in a large city with a good public transit system). Your car takes you shopping, to work, and to visit friends. Keeping it in good shape can help you avoid breakdowns and more expensive repairs later.

Pay Me Now or Pay Me Later

The "an ounce of prevention equals a pound of cure" quote is especially applicable when dealing with auto repairs. I remember a TV commercial from a while back from a transmission repair company in which the mechanic says to the customer whose transmission is shifting poorly, "Pay me now or pay me later." If the problem is taken care of now, the transmission might be rebuilt, or it may only be necessary to change the fluid and filters (ounce of prevention). If the problem is ignored, the transmission may need to be replaced (pound of cure), which could cost a lot more. Another good example of this is brake problems. When you hear a screeching noise coming from the front end near the wheels, take it to a mechanic and ask them to check the brakes (or check them yourself). It may be something as simple as needing a new set of brake pads. If you let it go, you may need a new set of rotors, which costs a lot more. Taking care of the problem early on can save a lot of money in the long run. It is especially important to maintain the safety-related components of your vehicle—such as tires, brakes, and wipers—as these items, when in good working order, can prevent accidents and injury. If you have a flat tire and must use a space-saver spare tire, get it replaced with a regular tire as soon as possible. Performing regular preventive maintenance can help you avoid getting stranded on the side of the highway when it's ninety degrees out, and the nearest exit is a mile away (been there done that!). To keep your car looking good and increase resale value, it is recommended that you have it professionally detailed at least once a year and have a good coat of wax put on it. This is especially important if it's kept outside. Just doing this can add hundreds or even thousands of dollars in value to the car if you sell it or trade it in.

Some people will wait until something major goes wrong to have repairs done, even when they have had clear warning signs. As another example, let's say your car is getting progressively harder to start. Instead of taking it to have it checked, you keep driving it until you come out on a cold night from a restaurant, and it won't start. You could have taken it to pretty much any auto parts store, and they would normally have run a charging system check at no cost. If the problem is the battery (which it is frequently), and you buy it from them, many of them will install the new battery at no cost and dispose of the old one. The same is true of wiper blades. If you buy them from the auto parts store, frequently they will install them for free. All you need to do is ask.

Check and Maintain Correct Tire Pressure

And one final important maintenance suggestion: Check your tire pressure once a month and keep it at recommended factory settings. Note that tire pressure tends to decrease in the winter because of the lower temperatures. See the label on the inside of the driver's door jamb for the proper pressure (e.g., 36 PSI). Your tires will last longer, the car will ride better, and you will get better gas mileage! You can go to an auto repair facility that you have done business with, or a tire store, and they will usually check and adjust the tire pressure for free and will let you know if there are any problems with the tires. Refer to Figure 12-2 for a screenshot of the information related to auto maintenance that is found on the Auto-Info tab of the Personal Financial Spreadsheet. This sheet of the PFS provides a central reference for basic auto information such as date and milage when purchased, serial number, warranty information, insurance policies, and a place to record important repairs and maintenance such as tire rotation, wiper, battery replacement, and more. Figure 12-3 is a blank form based on Figure 12-2 and is used with Exercise 12-2 to prepare for entry of your auto info data into the Auto-Info Sheet.

Refer to **Exercise 12-2: Record PFS Auto Info** at the end of this chapter, which will help you identify and record important information about your vehicle(s) such as specifications, insurance, warranty, and other information related to autos and maintenance. If you have more than one vehicle you can add a PFS sheet (Auto-Info-2) for it and make another copy of Figure 12-3 to record its information.

Figure 12-2: PFS Sheet – Auto-Info and Maintenance (sample entries)

	A	B	C	D	E	F	G	H
1	**Auto Info and Maintenance**		Book Build Ch. 12				Updated: MM-DD-YYYY	
2								
3	**<< Vehicle 1 Name >>**	**Purch Miles**	**Curr Miles**	**Batt Repl**	**Oil Chg**	**Tires Repl**	**Tire Rotation**	**Wipers**
4	Year/Make/Model/Trim	99,999	99,999	99,999	99,999	99,999	99,999	99,999
5	Purchase/Lease Date:	Mo/Year	Mo/Year	Mo/Year	Mo/Year	Mo/Year	Mo/Year	Mo/Year
6	Dealership Name:	XYZ Auto Sales						
7	Financing Through & Moly Pmt	QRZ Finance Co. $999						
8	Amt. Financed/No. Mos. @ APR	ABC Auto Ins.						
9	Serial # (VIN):	12345678911						
10	Warr/Service Contract:	XYZ Ext Warr. Co.						
11	Warr/Service Date Init/Expire:	Mo./Year, Mo/Year						
12	Insurance Carrier:	ABC Auto Ins.						
13	Insurance Policy #:	123456789						
14	License Plate #:	MFS-1234						
15								
16	CarFax report?	Y						
17	Factory recalls?	N						
18								
19	**<< Maintenance Record >>**	(Optional if most/all work is done at the same facility and records are kept)						
20								
21	Company	Date	Mileage	Work Done			Cost	Formula / Notes
22	Svc Co. A	Mo/Year	99,999	XXXXXXXXXXXXXXXXXXXX			0	
23	Svc Co. B	Mo/Year	99,999	XXXXXXXXXXXXXXXXXXXX			0	
24	Svc Co. C	Mo/Year	99,999	XXXXXXXXXXXXXXXXXXXX			0	
25	Svc Co. D	Mo/Year	99,999	XXXXXXXXXXXXXXXXXXXX			0	
26	Svc Co. E	Mo/Year	99,999	XXXXXXXXXXXXXXXXXXXX			0	
27								
28							0	=SUM(G22:G27)

Income-Exp | Assets-Liab | Cred-Cards | Home-Info | Auto-Info | Insure-Pols | Fin-Plan | Income-Exp-F | Assets-Liab-F | Cred-Cards-F | Ho

Figure 12-3: PFS Sheet - Auto-Info and Maintenance (Form)

	A	B	C	D	E	F	G	H
1	**Auto Info and Maintenance**		Book Build Ch. 12				Updated: MM-DD-YYYY	
2								
3	**<< Vehicle 1 Name >>**	**Purch Miles**	**Curr Miles**	**Batt Repl**	**Oil Chg**	**Tires Repl**	**Tire Rotation**	**Wipers**
4	Year/Make/Model/Trim	99,999	99,999	99,999	99,999	99,999	99,999	99,999
5	Purchase/Lease Date:	Mo/Year	Mo/Year	Mo/Year	Mo/Year	Mo/Year	Mo/Year	Mo/Year
6	Dealership Name:							
7	Financing Through & Moly Pmt							
8	Amt. Financed/No. Mos. @ APR							
9	Serial # (VIN):							
10	Warr/Service Contract:							
11	Warr/Service Date Init/Expire:							
12	Insurance Carrier:							
13	Insurance Policy #:							
14	License Plate #:							
15								
16	CarFax report?							
17	Factory recalls?							
18								
19	**<< Maintenance Record >>**	(Optional if most/all work is done at the same facility and records are kept)						
20								
21	Company	Date	Mileage	Work Done			Cost	Formula / Notes
22							0	
23							0	
24							0	
25							0	
26							0	
27								
28							0	=SUM(G22:G27)

Part 5: Auto Lease and Purchase

Automobile Leasing

Auto leasing is a relatively new way to acquire a vehicle that is becoming increasingly common. When you lease a car, you are basically renting it for a specific time period. A lease is essentially a long-term rental agreement between you (Lessee) and the dealer (Lessor). A lease has very little in common with a purchase, other than these facts:

- You usually put some money down
- They checked your credit rating
- There is a set monthly payment for a certain period of time (term)
- You drive away in a new car (although you can buy or lease a used car)

A lease usually has a term of two to three years. There is no equity buildup (ownership), and some people who lease cars typically get a new one every three years. When the lease is up, they just turn in the old car and start another lease on a new car or renew the lease on their current car for another three years. Dealers like to offer leases because they usually get the car back when the customer reaches the end of their first lease. They can be fairly sure they will have a good quality, late model, low mileage used car to sell that is often certified by the manufacturer. They make money on the lease and then on the sale of the car when it comes back from the lease as a used car. Leasing is fairly common if the car is used primarily for business, as the lease payment can typically be written off as an expense when filing taxes. The purchase of a car for business use can also be written off, but it's a little easier and more straightforward with a lease. A lease is a way of driving a more expensive car with a lower payment. However, you must not exceed the allowable mileage, or you will pay a penalty when the lease is over, and you turn the vehicle in. These days it is common to see auto dealers running TV ads that focus on the low monthly lease payment for specific models.

Ad for Auto Lease Example:

"Make/Model new car lease, $209 per month for thirty-six months. Cash due at signing: $2,700. Excludes taxes, title, and license fees. Not all buyers will qualify. Low mileage lease. Payments may vary. Dealer determines price. Residency restrictions apply."

The advertised low lease payment may entice you to visit the dealership. But the "not all buyers will qualify" part means you must have excellent credit, and this will disqualify some potential lease customers. However, even if you don't qualify for a lease, you are in the dealership, and they might be able to sell you a used car and possibly get you financing even though your credit rating may not be that great.

Lease and Purchase Comparison - Food for Thought

If you are a person that normally does not keep a car for more than three years and does not put a lot of miles on the car, leasing may be a good option for you (assuming you have excellent credit). If, on the other hand, you normally keep a car for five years or more, purchasing the car might be the best choice.

Some people like leasing because it allows them to drive a more expensive car than they can afford to buy, and their main goal is to get the monthly payment down as low as possible. Lease payments are typically less than the monthly payment when buying. For example, the monthly payment when purchasing a car (financed for five years) might be about $600/month. The lease payment for the same car for a three-year lease might be around $450/month. With a lease there is no "down payment," but you must pay an "amount due at signing" fee, usually in the $2,000 to $4,000 range, depending on the car. You can further reduce the monthly lease payment by paying more at signing in the form of a "cap reduction." For a businessperson, leasing keeps the monthly outgo down and can help with cash flow. The biggest difference between a purchase and a lease is that at the end of a purchase loan (typically five years), you own the car. With a lease (typically three years), you normally return the car and have no equity (ownership) in the car. Many people who lease will start a new three-year lease on another car when they return the first lease car.

Most dealers offer a closed-end lease, where there is a predetermined lease term, mileage limits, and a residual value. The monthly payment is based on the depreciation, rental cost, sales tax, and fees. When you sign a lease, the lessor (dealership) establishes a retail value that they think the car will be worth at the end of the lease, known as the residual value. If the car is worth more than the residual value, you may be able to sell the car and pay off the lease. However, if it is worth less, you can just turn it in and walk away, assuming it is in good condition and has less than the agreed upon maximum mileage (usually twelve thousand to fifteen thousand miles/year). You may have the option of buying the car and keeping it, selling it, or just terminating the lease and giving it back to the dealership. The value of the car is determined by the auto value tables used by the dealership.

Low Mileage Lease

With a lease, you are limited as to the number of miles you can put on the car per year and for the life of the lease (usually three years). If you go over the limits, you pay a (stiff) penalty. As an example, you might sign a three-year low-mileage lease that requires you not exceed forty-five thousand miles (fifteen thousand per year). The term "low mileage" or "ultra-low mileage" may sound like a "good" thing at first, but if you go over the limit, you pay a penalty for each mile. Penalties can be as high as twenty-five cents per mile when you turn the car in at the end of the lease. So, if you go a thousand miles over the maximum, you will pay another $250 at the end of the lease. Ultra-low mileage leases may specify the maximum number of miles per year to be as low as ten thousand or twelve thousand. As mentioned, leasing requires that you have excellent credit. This is why the TV commercials advertise a low monthly payment for a new car for a "low mileage" lease for "highly qualified lessees" This means you may be able to get a relatively low monthly lease payment if you have excellent credit and don't put too many miles on your car per year. Table 12-3 summarizes the basic characteristics of a car purchase as compared to a lease. Taxes and license are not considered.

Lease or Buy – A Personal Choice

This question of lease or buy can only be answered by the specific individual. They simply must weigh the pros and cons of such a decision. Those that prefer the lease option will argue that they keep the big down payment in their pocket (or bank or investment) so that their money can continue to work for them. Also, due to the length of the lease term, they will very rarely, if ever, have to replace a set of tires, muffler, or brakes, or any bigger ticket maintenance item that is encountered with vehicles as they age. However, they will always have a car payment, but because that payment is typically lower since they're not buying the entire vehicle (they're only buying the years that they will use the vehicle), they are able to afford a more expensive vehicle than they normally would with a purchase. For those that prefer the purchase option, they will argue that they will continue to own the vehicle long after their payments have stopped, which means no car payment for several years. Many will view the idea of no car payment as a huge plus in regard to their budget, being able to keep that payment in their pockets each month rather than have the outlay. However, if you keep a vehicle long enough, major maintenance items (tires, mufflers, brakes) are sure to need replacing. There is also the potential of a major repair should the transmission or computer stop working properly. A purchase typically requires a larger down payment, but there is also the potential to pay it off and thus have no payment for several years.

Table 12-3: Comparing New Car Purchase vs. Lease - Example

Comparison Item	Purchase	Lease	Notes
Credit score level required	Medium-High	Very high	
Car retail price	$50,000	$50,000	
Down payment	$5,000		
Due at signing		$4,000	
Term of loan/lease	5 years	3 years	
Monthly payment (appx)	$600	$450	
Ownership at end of term	You own car	Residual value owed	Option to buy, renew or walk away

Auto Summary Tips - Buying/Leasing/Maintenance

- Buy rather than lease unless you have a good reason to lease.
- Be sure to test drive a similar model.
- You may get a better deal if you are not stuck on a particular color or options.
- If you buy a new car, check out online buying services, such as Consumer Reports.
- Never pay the invoice/sticker price for a new car.
- Purchase at the end of the month and/or at the end of the model year.
- Don't finance a car (new or used) for more than five years, preferably four years.
- Use the "Auto 20-4-10 Rule" for purchasing a vehicle (20 percent down, four-year max loan term, transportation budget not to exceed 10 percent of your gross income).
- Avoid buying an extended warranty unless it's from the manufacturer.
- Avoid after-sale extended warranty offers in the mail.
- Put money in a savings account for repairs.
- Buy a dependable car that is three to five years old with low mileage that will hold its value.
- Buy a used car that has a good repair record according to Consumer Reports.
- Take a used car to a reputable certified mechanic to have it checked out before you purchase it.
- Obtain a history report (CARFAX or other) from the seller if purchasing a used car.
- Buy used from a private party to get a better price.
- Beware of "Buy here, pay here" used car dealers and those that advertise "good credit, bad credit, no credit, we can get you financed." The interest rates can be very high.
- Do not buy a more expensive car than you can afford (new or used).
- Be willing to walk (leave the dealership) if they will not give you a deal.
- Arrange financing with a bank or credit union before going to a dealership.
- Be sure you are getting a simple interest loan.
- For new/late model used cars, try to keep the car for five to ten years.
- Buy a new/used car that has a good repair record (Consumer Reports Buying Guide).
- Sell your old car rather than trade it in.
- If trading in your old car, look up the trade in value (Edmunds, Kelly Blue Book, etc.).
- Budget a certain amount for monthly maintenance, insurance, and gas.
- When shopping for auto insurance, talk with an agent to determine the type and amount of coverage you want/need.
- Create a simple insurance spreadsheet to compare car insurance company costs.
- Have your car professionally detailed at least once a year with a good coat of wax.
- Keep your tire pressure at recommended factory settings (e.g., 36 PSI). Your tires will last longer, and you will get better gas mileage.
- If you take care of your car, it will take care of you!

Part 6: Auto Insurance

Auto Insurance

Auto insurance is a requirement in all fifty U.S. states. If you are stopped by the police while driving, you will be asked for three things: your driver's license, vehicle registration, and proof of insurance (current). If you don't have proof of insurance, you may get a warning and have to prove it later, or they may cite you immediately.

Note: The discussion of insurance in this chapter deals specifically with vehicles. Refer to Chapter 16: Insurance and Risk Management, for a more comprehensive view of the various types of insurance available. Also refer to the Personal Financial Spreadsheet (PFS) sheets Insure-Pols and Auto-Info, for additional insurance-related information.

Note: Remember, when comparing auto insurance (and other types) from one company to another, you are comparing apples to apples, and the coverage is the same.

At a minimum, most states require you to carry basic liability and uninsured motorist insurance.. This means that the repairs to the other person's vehicle will be covered if an accident is your fault. If the accident is their fault, and they do not have insurance, your uninsured motorist insurance will cover bodily injury but not property damage to your vehicle. You need uninsured motorist property damage coverage if you carry just liability.

If you have a newer car (less than five years old), you will probably want collision to cover damage to your car if the accident is your fault. If you have a car that is between five and ten years old, you may decide not to carry collision, depending on the value of the car.

If you specify a high deductible (e.g., $500) you can keep premiums down, but you must pay the first $500 for repairs. Some insurance companies will increase your premium, or not renew your policy, if you have multiple accidents within a short period of time. You may get reduced premiums if you have multiple cars, a good driving record, no drivers under twenty-five years of age, or if one of your cars is considered a leisure (low use) vehicle. You also may get a multi-policy discount if you have homeowner's or renter's insurance with the same company. Your credit score also plays a major part in how much you pay for auto insurance. Generally speaking, the better your score, the lower your premiums. Your credit score is factored in with your age, driving record, and type of car(s) you own, along with other demographic information.

Note: Car rental insurance may be covered with your basic policy, so you may not need to purchase insurance when renting a car. Be sure to verify this with your insurance agent in advance, especially if you will be renting an auto in a foreign country.

Roadside Assistance Auto Insurance

Most auto insurance policies include basic roadside assistance (aka towing and labor coverage) on each vehicle you insure for a nominal premium. If you are stranded, you can call qualified roadside assistance for help, whether it's to fix a flat, bring you gas, or unlock a door. Some people choose to decline the coverage to save money, but I think this is mistake. If your policy does not provide it, consider adding it, as it is typically not expensive. This is a very valuable service and can come in handy if you need it and get you out of a bind relatively painlessly. If you have roadside assistance coverage, be sure to let family members who drive your cars know how to contact the insurance company to report a roadside problem to get help. Read your policy or contact your agent to verify your coverage. Roadside assistance usually includes the following 24 x 7:

- **Car won't start** (jump start)
- **Out of gas** (you pay for the gas they bring)
- **Keys locked in car** (police may need to be contacted)
- **Flat tire** (change/repair)
- **Towing** (may charge extra for longer distance)

Note: The manufacturer's extended warranty that you get with a Certified Pre-owned (CPO) vehicle frequently covers roadside assistance for a limited time (usually one year). Your current auto policy may also cover it. If you have double coverage, you might consider canceling it with your auto policy and possibly save some money on the premium. Verify this with your insurance carrier.

My auto insurance covers roadside assistance, and I had to use it recently. It was the middle of winter, and my truck was parked in my driveway with icicles hanging off it and would not start. It appeared the battery was dead or close to it, so I called the Roadside Assistance number on the back of my insurance card. A service truck was dispatched, and they were there in about an hour. A nice young man pulled his truck up next to my truck and connected a portable booster box to my battery. That should have done the trick. My truck cranked over but did not start, so he connected the jumper cables from his truck to mine. Again, my truck cranked over but would not start. The problem was more serious than a dead battery. I thanked the young man for his valiant effort and gave him a tip for being prompt, courteous, and doing his best, and then he left.

I called the Roadside Assistance number again, this time to have my truck towed to the dealership to have the problem diagnosed and repaired. The tow truck got there in about an hour, and he drove off to the dealership with my truck on his flat bed. The dealership called me about an hour later but had not yet determined the problem. It could have been the engine computer, lack of fuel, or lack of ignition. I just hoped it wouldn't cost too much. Oh well, I figured, I have my rainy-day cash reserves fund to cover it. The next day, the service manager called and let me know what the problem was. Mice, looking for food and a place to make a nest, had gotten into the truck since it was parked outside. They had chewed through multiple sections of the wiring harness. Since I had comprehensive coverage on the truck with a $250 deductible, I was covered. Otherwise, I would have had to pay over a thousand dollars to replace the wiring harness.

Auto Accidents

Note: The Roadside Assistance app lists the things you need to do if you have an accident, and they are usually printed on the back of your proof-of-insurance card, which you should carry in your wallet.

Note: Be sure to keep a copy of the insurance card for each vehicle in your car and in your wallet. Also, you can look up your auto information, including insurance and VIN, on the PFS Auto-Info sheet.

SMOG Tip

Whenever driving, remember the "**SMOG**" and use it when you are getting ready to make a lane change. SMOG is a memory jogger and a defensive driving technique that is taught in some driving courses. Before making a lane change, ensure you do all of these:

S =   **Signal** (Turn **SIGNAL** or hand signal)

M =   **Mirrors** (Check your **MIRRORS**)

O =   **Over the shoulder** (Look **OVER** your shoulder)

G =   **Go** (**GO** for it! Make your lane change)

Note: If I had remembered to use the SMOG technique, I would have avoided an accident not too long ago. Hopefully just putting it in this book might help someone remember it and avoid an accident.

Chapter 12 Exercises

Exercise 12-1: Compare Auto Loan Calculators

An auto loan calculator is a basic loan calculator with specific extensions and options for autos. It can compare various factors related to vehicle purchase, leasing, and financing options, as well as trade-ins, vehicle registration, and sales tax. Do a Web search for "free auto loan calculator" or "free auto lease calculator," and you will see many available. Identify two or three of them and decide which one you like the best by ranking them according to your preference. Some good examples include the following (in alphabetical order). Make a copy of Table 12-4 and use it as a starting point for Exercise 12-1.

Table 12-4: Auto Loan Calculator Comparison
(Alphabetical order)

Source Name	Cost	Notes
Calculator.Net		www.calculator.net/auto-loan-calculator.html
Calculators.org		www.calculators.org/auto
Cars.com		www.cars.com/car-loan-calculator/

Exercise 12-2: Record PFS Auto Info

In this exercise, you will locate your vehicle information to prepare for entering it into PFS Sheet - Auto Info and Maintenance. Even if you do not plan to enter your data in the spreadsheet at this time, go ahead and write your information in the Figure 12-3 form. The only calculations are for summing up repair costs, which you can do manually if you want to. Before starting this exercise, make a copy of the blank Figure 12-3, PFS Sheet - Auto Info and Maintenance (Form) and use Figure 12-2 as a guide for data entry. If you have more than one vehicle you can add a PFS sheet for it (Auto-Info-2) and make another copy of Figure 12-3 to record its information.

Chapter 13
Investing Basics

Chapter Overview:

Investing wisely, especially when you are young, can go a long way toward making your life and especially your retirement years more enjoyable and less stressful. This chapter integrates some basic retirement planning with investing information. It focuses mainly on general investing concepts and low-risk forms of long-term investing. You can make these investments on your own or with the help of a financial advisor, more specifically a Certified Financial Planner (CFP). An overview of the services provided by a CFP is described in this chapter. The chapter additionally provides a high-level discussion of investing concepts, as well as an overview of the types of investments to be aware of, and related terminology. It offers some suggestions as to what types of investments you might want to consider based on risk and taxation factors. Tips on investing and retirement are also provided. Exercises are provided to help calculate your personal financial indictor (PFI) status and current investments. An optional exercise is available to help research, select, and use an online ROI calculator. The chapter is divided into eight parts:

- **Part 1: Investing Goals and Checklist**
- **Part 2: Investing Assistance and Options**
- **Part 3: Securities (Stocks, Bonds, or Cash)**
- **Part 4: Investing in the Stock Market**
- **Part 5: Mutual Funds and Investment Strategies**
- **Part 6: Bonds and Investment Strategies**
- **Part 7: Alternative Investments**
- **Part 8: The Ultimate Investment**

Note: This chapter contains a significant amount of valuable information. If you find yourself getting bogged down or confused, consider skimming the chapter headings and read through the text without doing the exercises

Chapter PFS and PFI Integration:

Investments can be assets and at the same time, provide income. On the Personal Financial Spreadsheet (PFS) sheets, they might be listed as both Assets and Income. The PFS components in this chapter that relate to investments are found on the Assets, Liabilities, and Net Worth sheet and consist mainly of assets like IRAs, 401Ks, Stocks, Mutual funds, Annuities, CDs, MMAs, and various others. Refer to Figure 13-2 for examples of investment assets that could be entered on the Assets, Liabilities, and Net worth sheet. Refer to Figure 13-3 for examples of income sources entered on the Income-Exp sheet. Table 13-1 lists various types of investments and retirement accounts. This is not a complete list but covers the more common ones that are available. Personal Financial Indicator PFI 13-1: Return on Investment (ROI) and PFI 13-2: Investment-to-Income (ITI) Ratio (%) are introduced. PFIs for PCF, PNW, DTI, DTC, HTI and TTI are reviewed along with ITI and ROI to determine overall financial health. Together they provide guidelines for planning and implementation of a comprehensive savings and investment strategy.

Chapter Exercises:

- **Exercise 13-1: Personal Investment Survey Questionnaire**
- **Exercise 13-2: Compare ROI Calculators**
- **Exercise 13-3: Evaluate Your PFI Status Using the Investing Checklist** (optional)
- **Exercise 13-4: Record Investment Assets, Income, and Options**

Chapter Notable Quotes:
Quote 13-1: "You miss 100 percent of the shots you don't take." - Wayne Gretsky
Quote 13-2: "The quickest way to double your money is to fold it in half and put it back in your pocket." - Will Rogers
Quote 13-3: "Whether you think you can or you can't, you're right." - Henry Ford

Part 1: Investing Goals and Checklist

Investing and Saving – ROI and Risk

Chapter 7 dealt with various types of savings. Investing is different from saving but is similar in that you are putting aside money for future use. While saving is generally considered very low risk, investing can be anywhere from low risk to high risk, depending on the quality of investment, timing horizon, and market volatility. For our purposes, savings is money put aside for a future use/purchase or rainy day (emergency) fund. Savings are typically kept in a regular bank savings account, a credit union account, or online savings account. An important factor that distinguishes savings accounts from investments is that savings accounts are highly "liquid". Savings is an asset that allows you to access your money very quickly without impacting your retirement accounts (e.g., 401K) or paying much, if any, penalty. Most savings vehicles (and cash equivalents) provide a relatively stable interest rate and a modest return on investment (ROI). Investments (e.g., stocks and bonds) on the other hand, are not very liquid and are expected to provide a higher ROI but with higher volatility, especially stocks. Savings accounts usually bear a certain amount of interest that can vary, known as Annual Percentage Yield (APY). However, just because a savings account is stable does not mean it is risk-free. The risk with savings accounts is the very real chance that you will lose buying power over time, due to inflation and taxes. And just because you have an investment in the stock market, which can be volatile, does not mean it is risky. The risk is very low with an investment vehicle such as a stock-based index mutual fund. Both savings and stocks are plagued by inflation and gains are subject to tax.

If we define risk as the possibility that you may lose principal in an investment, there is very little risk associated with a savings account, and virtually zero chance that you will lose any of your initial capital. However, the low interest (ROI) paid by most savings accounts can result in a net loss in purchasing power when factoring in inflation, taxes, and fees. The same could be said about other cash equivalent investments (e.g., CDs, MMAs), and also fixed income sources such as bonds. The interest yields paid may not keep up with inflation and taxes. On the other hand, investing in stocks has historically provided an ROI, on average, that exceeds inflation and taxes. Based on that, we could say that savings provides stable, consistent, non-volatile growth, but not without risk. Investing in stocks comes with some volatility, but there is really little risk that you will lose your capital investment over the long haul, unless you sell. Even then you could write off part of the loss from the sale of stock. Savings accounts are not inherently risk free and stocks are not inherently risky. That said, I currently have an online "high yield" savings account that pays a higher APY than most CDs and MMAs, and it's relatively liquid. I also have several retirement accounts that are invested in various high-quality stock mutual funds. However, investing in speculative investments like cryptocurrencies, penny stocks, or junk bonds can be risky, and should be avoided for the average investor, as there is a real possibility of losing principal. More on ROI and risk later.

Note: You can go to https://www.bankrate.com or other source to see a list of institutions and the interest rates yields (APY) they offer. Bankrate also provides minimum deposit requirements for various savings, CD and money market accounts.

Investments Status, Baseline, and Goals
Reading through this chapter will help you define your investing goals and increase your awareness and understanding of the types of investment that exist and that you might be interested in. Of course, any discussion of potential investing assumes that you have an income stream that you can redirect and/or existing investments/savings that you could repurpose.

Personal Investment Survey Questionnaire
You can begin to home in on or refine your investing goals by asking some questions like those in **Exercise 13-1: Personal Investment Survey Questionnaire** listed at the end of the chapter. The questions are food for thought and can serve as a starting point for discussions with a financial advisor. The questions in the survey will be addressed in this and subsequent chapters by using the four exercises listed at beginning of the chapter:

More on Risk
Nearly all investments have some level of risk associated with them. As previously discussed, risk relates to the security of the investment and the likelihood that the investor may lose principal. Included with risk assessment is the volatility of the price of the investment, or the likelihood it will fluctuate significantly. This can greatly impact retirement timing and investment horizons. Also, considered is how the investment has traditionally performed over time, with respect to various performance indicators such as Return on Investment (ROI) and ratios such as Price-to-Earnings (PTE). When comparing investments' performance, it is important take into account taxes and inflation.

With investing you are basically buying something that you think (hope) will increase in value, although there is no guarantee that it will. The increase in value of an investment, as compared to what you paid for it, is referred to as profit or gains or return on investment (ROI). Usually, the higher the risk of the investment, the greater the potential for making money (gains) with it. Lower risk investments will likely pay less in gains, but you are also less likely to lose your initial investment. Additional information on risk is presented in Chapter 16: Insurance and Risk Management.

Investment ROI vs. Inflation and Taxes

The primary goal with any investment is that the return on investment (ROI) or gains will beat (compensate or offset) taxes and inflation. You want to own investments where the returns cover or exceed the costs and expenses. The interest you make on savings and CDs as well as dividends, and profits (gains) from the sale of stocks are all taxable. The amount of tax varies with your tax bracket, where you live, the type of investment account, and how long it is held before you sell. If inflation is around 3 percent, your investments need to provide a combined ROI of 3 percent to break even. Also keep in mind that the ROI must factor in investment (fund) management fees, which can be as high as 2 percent. Many traditional no-load index mutual funds from reputable companies are free of commissions. So, a fund that averages 7 percent ROI per year may just be keeping up with inflation and taxes, not to mention management fees. The "Basic ROI" calculation does not take time, inflation, taxes, or fees into account. So, if someone says they got a 10 percent ROI on some investment, but it was over a two-year time span, that is actually closer to 5 percent annualized, and chances are they were not accounting for inflation, taxes, and transaction or management fees. Here is an example of "Basic ROI." Amy invested $5,000 (net after fees) in a promising stock two years ago. Today the stock is worth $5,500. If we do not factor in inflation and taxes, her ROI is calculated thus: Current stock value minus purchase price or cost of the investment ($5,500 - $5,000 = $500) divided by stock cost ($500/$5,000 = .10). Multiply times hundred to get the percentage = 10 percent gain. Refer to the ROI calculator shown in Figure 13-1, where Amy's investment had an ROI of 10 percent but an annualized ROI (over two years) of only 4.88 percent and that does not take into account inflation or taxes.

Refer to **Exercise 13-2: Compare ROI Calculators** at the end of this chapter for some guidance on finding an online ROI calculator that meets your needs. There are many good ones available. The screenshot in Figure 13-1 shows a basic ROI calculator (from calculator.net). Some ROI calculators, such as Forbes Advisor's ROI calculator, allow you to enter the expected inflation rate and other variables. The inflation rate is the annual average percent increase in the cost of living based on the Consumer Price Index (CPI). The CPI is based on the combined prices of a wide range of goods and services and is used to track inflation for a particular country. You can access the Forbes ROI Calculator at: https://www.forbes.com/advisor/investing/roi-calculator/

Figure 13-1: ROI Calculator Example with Annualized ROI

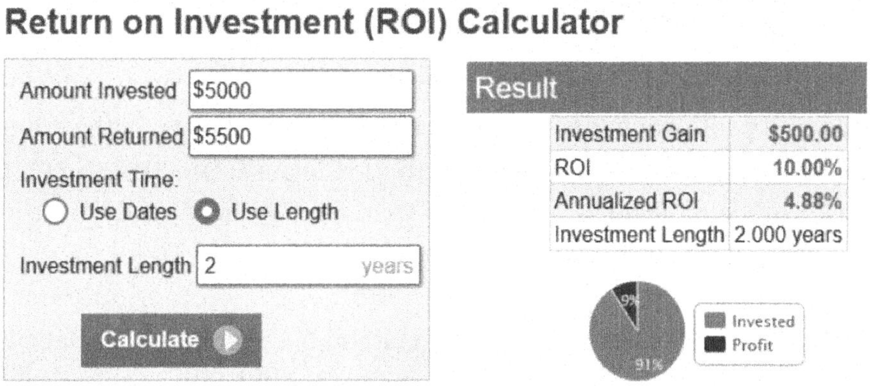

Return on Investment (ROI) Calculator

In addition to using the manual PFI 13-1 calculation (below), you can use an online ROI calculator, some of which account for time, inflation, taxes, and other ROI variables and that allow you to determine Real ROI. Personal Financial Indicator (PFI) 13-1 shows the formula to determine basic return on investment (ROI) that can be applied to nearly any form of investment. The example below uses the basic ROI formula and does not account for inflation or taxes. In the example, the investor bought some stock three years ago at a price of $5,000 and sold it for $5,500. The ROI is 10 percent, but that "profit" or "gain" is misleading as it is not annualized and does not account for taxes, inflation, or fees. It is important to be aware of this so you can compare apples to apples when it comes to investments. Most people do not take these variables into account when determining the value of their invested assets. Most people do not know the basic ROI of their investments, let alone annualized, and do not factor in inflation and taxes. We have included ROI for your current investments in the "Investing Checklist." Be sure to take into account the length of time you have held an investment or asset so you can determine the annualized rate of return.

PFI 13-1: Return-on-Investment (ROI) Ratio (%) - Formula/Calculation
(Personal Financial Indicator #PFI-15)

(Investment Gain (-minus-) Investment Cost) (/divided by/) Investment Cost = ROI (%)

($5,500 - $5,000 = $500) / $5,000 = .10 (*100) = 10% ROI (over 3 years)

(Generic example)

Investing Checklist Steps and Investment-to-Income PFI
You most likely have some kind of investment(s), even if it's just a savings account or perhaps a 401K through your employer. However, it's a good idea to review the Investing Checklist Steps presented here to evaluate the investments you are already making before considering additional investments. If you are currently making one or more monthly investments, you can use PFI 13-2 Investment-to-Income (ITI)

below to determine your monthly investment percentage as compared to your gross monthly income. The range is 0–100 percent but 10–20 percent is normal. The ITI ratio calculation is provided below for use in **Exercise 13-3: Evaluate Your PFI Status Using the Investing Checklist** (optional). The formula is Total Monthly Investments divided by (/) Gross Monthly Income. Investments can include stocks, mutual funds, 401Ks, IRAs, bonds, and pension contributions but do not include savings. In the example, your monthly investments total $750, which is divided by your monthly gross income ($6,000) = .125 * 100 = 12.5 percent. So, in this case, you are investing about 12.5 percent of your monthly income, which is a reasonable amount, especially if you are contributing to a savings account too.

PFI 13-2: Investment-to-Income (ITI) Ratio (%) - Formula/Calculation
(Personal Financial Indicator #PFI-16)

Monthly Investments (/divided by/) Monthly Gross Income = ITI (%)

$750 / $6,000 = .125 (*100) = 12.5%

(Generic example)

Refer to **Exercise 13-3: Evaluate Your PFI Status Using the Investing Checklist** (optional) at the end of this chapter for instructions on using PFI Appendix B to determine where you stand on key PFIs that have been introduced. The main purpose of this exercise is to consolidate all your personal financial indicator (PFI) information, provide a review, and to assist you in recording your PFI information. This chapter also introduces two new ratio PFIs, one for Investment-to-Income (ITI) and one for Return on Investment (ROI). Refer to Table B-1 in Appendix B: Personal Financial Health Indicators, which lists the PFI name (e.g., DTI), Chapter number, and PFI Number (e.g., 3-1); PFS Sheet (e.g., Income-Exp); and formula for each indicator. Make a copy of and use Table B-1 in Appendix B as a form to enter your indicator values and notes. By calculating these PFIs based on your current financial situation, you may be able to identify monies with which you can fund additional investments. The more thorough you are in completing the checklist, the better your awareness and understanding of your finances.

Note: The PFI results from this exercise will be used in Chapter 19, Exercise 19-1 for PFS Sheet - Financial Planning and Projects.

Investing Checklist Time Considerations
Refer to Exercise 13-3 at the end of the chapter for the **INVESTING CHECKLIST STEPS.**
Completion of the Investing Checklist can require a significant time investment, depending on how much of your information is readily available. So, be sure to plan ahead and split the checklist steps up into three or four sessions. Exercise 13-3 is optional but is recommended, and can largely be completed with the chapter 19 end-of-book exercises.

Part 2: Investing Assistance and Options

Investing - Where to Start

Investing, whether short term or for retirement, can be very confusing and intimidating for some people, and many people do not even know where to start. Unfortunately, a lot of people put off doing something about investing until late in life, or worse yet, do nothing. Many of us are financially illiterate when it comes to investing, having little understanding of what to invest in and how. They say it takes money to make money, which is generally true, but in some cases, it's not the lack of money to invest; people just don't know which investments might be appropriate for them and who they can trust to make recommendations. In addition, they simply don't know how to actually make or execute the investment. This is where a good Certified Financial Planner (CFP) can make a big difference. As discussed in Chapter 6, a CFP is a key member of your Professional Advisor Group.

Certified Financial Planners

Some people decide to do their own investing, but this can be risky, especially if they have limited knowledge of investment types and how to invest wisely for their future. Many people elect to do their investing with the help of a Certified Financial Planner or CFP. A good CFP has a fiduciary responsibility to the client, meaning that they should advise the client toward investments that are in the client's financial best interests. Keep in mind that not all people who offer financial advice are CFPs. That said, a good CFP is well worth what they are paid if they can help you successfully build a solid financial portfolio.

A CFP designation is a professional certification for financial advisors/planners conferred by the Certified Financial Planner Board of Standards, Inc. (CFP Board) in the U.S. (www.cfp.net). There are other financial industry certifications, but CFP is the de facto standard and is the one that most people recognize and are familiar with. Also, consider working with a "fee-only" CFP. The National Association of Personal Financial Advisors. NAPFA is the main professional association for fee-only financial advisors in the U.S. To find out more about fee-only financial advisors or find one in your area, you can visit their Website https://www. napfa.org. All CFPs are registered investment advisors with a fiduciary responsibility to act in their clients' best interest. Fee-only CFPs do not accept any fees, commissions, or other compensation based on product sales. That said, there are many good CFPs and financial advisors that are not exclusively fee-only CFPs. Important things to consider, when choosing a professional financial advisor include:

- Select and interview two or three of them
- Ask what they charge for a financial plan and what it includes
- Ask how they get paid
- Ask how long they've been a CFP
- Ask for and review references
- Trust your intuition

Services and advice that a CFP provides can include these (partial list):

- Financial analysis surveys – Needs assessment and risk tolerance
- Guidance on budgets, debt, and taxes
- Investment advice – Financial plan, investment types, asset allocation, portfolio diversification
- Retirement planning – When you may be able to retire and how much you will need
- Insurance recommendations – Type and amount of life insurance, long-term care insurance, and umbrella insurance.
- Help with Social Security decisions

Refer to Figure 13-2 for examples of potential liquid investment assets previously entered into the Assets-Liab sheet. Refer to Figure 13-3 for examples of potential investment income sources previously entered into the Income-Exp sheet.

Figure 13-2: PFS Assets Section of Asset-Liab Sheet (sample entries)

	A	B	C	D	E	F	G
1	**ASSETS, LIABILITIES and NET WORTH**		Book Build: Ch. 5			Updated: MM-DD-YYYY	
2							
3	**<<< Sect 1: Assets >>>**						
4	Owner	< Liquid Assets (Name / Type) >	Institution	Notes	Curr. Value	Monthly Contrib.	Beneficiary / Formula
5	Joint	Bank Checking Acct 1	Bank	Cash	1,000	0	Joint
6	Joint	Bank Checking Acct 2	Bank	Cash	5,000	0	Joint
7	Joint	Emergency Fund (EF) - Online Savings Acct	Savings-Co	EF Goal = $27,000	13,700	300	Emergency Fund Acct. - Joint
8	Joint	Savings Acct. - Short-Term (Ass./Inc.)	Anytown Bank	Savings	15,000	200	Joint
9	Joint	Money Market Acct (MMA)	Anytown Bank	Savings	5,000	200	Joint
10	Joint	5-Yr Certificate of Deposit (CD)	Anytown Bank	Savings	10,000	200	Joint
11	Ted	Pension (Ass./Inc./Ret.)	Pension Co.	Retire: Defined benefit	60,000	0	Amy
12	Ted	401K (Ass./Inc./Ret.)	Mgmt Co.	Retire: Stock Funds	75,000	0	Amy
13	Amy	403B Retirement Plan (Ass./Ret.)	Mgmt Co.	Retire: Stock Funds	35,000	500	Ted
14	Ted	IRA Invest (Stocks/Bonds) (Interest/Dividends)	Invest-Co.	Retire: Stock Funds	45,000	300	Amy
15		Other liquid asset			0	0	
16		Other liquid asset			0	0	
17		Other liquid asset			0	0	
18				Total Liquid Assets:	264,700		=SUM(E5:E17)
19							
20		< Non-Liquid Assets (Name / Type) >					
21	Joint	Home Value (Appraised)	Mortgage Co.	Appraised value	250,000	Ref. Sect 2: Liabilities for Mortgage balance	
22	Joint	Auto values (total) (Car and truck)	Cars Paid for	Estimated values (10k+20k)	30,000		
23	Joint	Jewelry & Other	Other Assets	Appraised values	10,000		
24		Other Non-liquid asset			0		
25		Other Non-liquid asset			0		
26				Total All Major Assets:	$554,700		=SUM(E5:E26)-E18

Figure 13-3: PFS Income Sources Section of Income-Exp Sheet (sample entries)

	A	B	C	D	E
1	**INCOME, EXPENSES and CASH FLOW**	Book Build: Ch. 3			Updated: MM-DD-YYYY
2					
3	**<<< Sect 1: Household Income >>>**				
4	< Income Source (Who/Type/Asset/Income/Retmt.) >	Institution	Monthly Gross	Monthly Net	Notes / Formulas
5	Ted - Social Security (Inc.)	US Govt	1,500	1,300	DD Chkg: X9999
6	Ted - Pension (Inc./Ret.)	Pension Co.	750	600	DD Chkg: X9999
7	Ted - 401K (Ass./Inc./Ret.)	Mgmt Co.	1,000	800	DD Chkg: X9999
8	Ted - Part time job at Hardware store (Inc.)	Anytown Hardware	800	600	Regular income (1040 wages)
9	Ted - Small furniture repair business (Ass./Inc.)	Ted's Furniture Repair	500	500	
10	Ted - Rental Property (Ass./Inc.)	Anytown Mortgage Co.	750	600	Rental income less maint exp.
11	Amy - Full-time Instructor Salary (Inc.)	Anytown College	3,000	2,600	
12	Amy - 403B Contribution (Ass./Ret.)	Mgmt Co.	0	0	For retirement
13	Joint - Money Market Acct (MMA) (Ass./Inc./Ret)	Anytown Bank	100	70	
14	Joint - Savings Acct. - Emergency Fund (Ass./Inc) - Interest	Anytown Bank	100	70	
15	Joint - Savings Acct. - Short-Term (Ass./Inc.) - Interest	Anytown Bank	100	70	
16	Joint - Savings 5-Yr.CD - Long-Term (Ass./Inc.) - Interest	Anytown Bank	100	60	
17	Joint - Invest IRA Acct Income (Stocks/Bond Interest and Dividends)	Invest-Co.	200	150	
18					
19					
20					
21	**Total Monthly (GROSS) Income:**		**$8,900**		=SUM(C5:C20)
22	**Total Monthly (NET) Income:**			**$7,420**	=SUM(D5:D20)

Your Emergency Fund

In previous chapters we covered the Emergency Fund (EF), and the benefits of having adequate cash reserves, but its importance in your overall financial plan cannot be overstated. Note that the EF and the PFI Emergency Fund Goal (EFG) play an important part in the Investing Checklist. Financial experts may disagree, but most recommend that you set aside enough in savings as an emergency fund (rainy-day fund) to cover about six months' worth of fixed (major) expenses if you are still working, and twelve months if you are retired. The emergency fund is a critical component of your financial portfolio. It helps protect the rest of your financial plan. It also helps you sleep better, knowing you have a cushion in case of an unexpected expense or loss of your job. It's a personal decision as to how much you set aside for an emergency fund. It needs to be an amount you are comfortable with and should be based on several factors. Ask yourself the following questions to help you decide:

- Is the emergency fund shared between partners?
- Are you and your partner in good health?
- Do both of you currently work?
- How quickly could you get another comparable job if you lost your current one?
- Do you have other forms of liquid funds available? (That you would not be penalized if you tapped into them)
- Do you have or could you obtain a home equity line of credit (HELOC) that you could tap into, if necessary, to supplement your savings?

Note: You should have the HELOC established prior to an emergency, especially if the emergency is a job loss. Also keep in mind that when times get rough, lenders and creditors tend to get backed up, and they might also be more selective in their lending practices.

So, add up your non-discretionary (required) monthly expenses, such as house payment, car payment, insurance payments, utilities, and an amount to cover at least minimum credit card payments, etc. Be sure to include some money for food, gas, and other necessities and then multiply the total by six. This means that, if you are still working and have $5,000 of non-discretionary monthly expenses, you should try to build up an emergency fund of about $30,000. This may seem like a lot, but it is realistic, and it doesn't have to happen overnight. The main thing is to be consistent and contribute as much as you can each month to reach your goal. Refer to Chapter 6 for information on various types of savings accounts.

Part 3: Securities (Stocks, Bonds, or Cash)

Investment and Securities Terminology

There are many types of investments available, but most of them fall into a single huge category called "Securities." This term includes a wide variety of investments, consisting mainly of three subgroups: Equity instruments (stocks); Debt instruments (bonds); and "Money Market" instruments that are "Cash Equivalent" instruments, such as CDs, MMAs, and short-term notes. The three securities subgroups represent the major types of investments you can purchase on the open market, usually from a bank, investment company, or broker. The sales of publicly traded securities are regulated by the Securities and Exchange Commission (SEC).

For simplicity, we are grouping securities investments into one of three basic types: Stocks, Bonds, or Cash. A fourth category is called "Alternative Investments," which is a catchall term for anything that is not securities stocks, bonds, or cash. Real estate and commodities are good examples of alternative investments. However, most investments that are in the alternatives category are variations on equities or ownership types of investments. Often-used industry terminology refers to stocks as "Equities," bonds as "Fixed Income," and cash as "Cash Equivalents," which are broader categories. Commodities can include raw materials like oil, lumber, gold, steel, corn, and livestock. Investment advisors often use the three categories shown below as a general guideline for client portfolio diversification.

Assets can be categorized in various ways, such as Asset Class, Tangibility, Liquidity, and Tax Status. Asset classes are groups of similar types of investments that are subject to the same regulations. Financial advisors often use asset class to diversify portfolios across multiple types of investment assets. They are generally grouped into one of three main assets classes or categories:

- **Equities** (Stocks and other Ownership Investments)
- **Fixed Income** (Bonds and Securities)
- **Cash Equivalents** (Cash, Savings, CDs, MMAs)

The previously mentioned **Alternative Investments** category is sometimes listed, which can include real estate, commodities, and other equity-based "ownership" types of investments. Most of the alternative investments are variations on equities. Real estate is a major investment type that could be considered a category on its own as it can represent a significant portion of the portfolio for some investors.

Stocks, Bonds, Cash, or Other - Expanded
Building on the three basic categories above, many financial advisors like to break investment types into six distinct groups as shown below, with some examples and elaboration. In general, most investments fall into one of these six basic categories of investment (asset classes). They all have pluses and minuses as described in this chapter. The first three listed here—stocks, bonds, and cash equivalents—are the ones this chapter is most concerned with. Along with real estate, they represent the most common types of major investments for most people.

- **Stocks** (shares of a company - also called equities)
- **Bonds** (loan/note to a company, organization or municipality, or government)
- **Cash Equivalents** (variations on highly liquid savings accounts)
  - Savings accounts (regular, non-emergency)
  - Money market accounts (MMAs)
  - Certificates of deposit (CDs)
  - U.S. Federally Issued securities (Treasury Notes, Bonds, and Bills)
- **Precious Metals** (gold/silver, etc.)
- **Real Estate** (Land and residential/commercial property)
- **Collectibles** (art/cars/coins/stamps, etc.)

You can invest in any or all of these investment types directly or indirectly by buying mutual funds (with the exception of collectibles). You can also invest in tax-deferred options such as an IRA or annuity.

Refer to **Exercise 13-4: Record Investment Assets, Income, and Options** at the end of this chapter, which will help you record investment information related to your assets and income. You will also select a couple of investments that you are interested in to do some research, using form Table 13-3.

Common Financial Portfolio Investments
Table 13-1 contains some of the more common types of investments that people are likely to have in their financial portfolio. It also includes a brief description of these investment types and shows their estimated risk level and tax status. These topics are the subject of much discussion, and there are differing opinions on them. The investments listed in the table are mostly considered "mainstream" and have relatively low risk levels. With respect to ROI, all investments should be adjusted for inflation and taxes.

Risk Level
For our purposes in Table 13-1, risk is designated as High (H), Medium (M), or Low (L), and is mostly related to volatility. Few of the investments listed actually have much real risk or potential of losing any of your original investment. Risk was covered previously in this chapter and risk management is discussed

further in Chapter 16: Insurance and Risk Management. For information regarding the liquidity of these types of assets, refer to Chapter 5: Assets, Liabilities, and Net Worth.

Tax Status

Tax-deferred investments (such as a 401K) are usually focused on the longer-term horizon and are considered retirement investments. Tax status refers mainly to how the gains on these investments are treated by the IRS and state governments. There are always exceptions, but in general, the gains can be classified as follows:

- **Taxable**
- **Tax Deferred**
- **Free of Tax**
- **Variable**

Qualified Retirement Plans

Qualified Retirement Plans—such as IRAs, 401Ks, 403Bs, and pensions—make up the largest portion of the investment options available, as shown in Table 13-1. A qualified retirement plan is one that meets the requirements defined in Section 401(a) of the U.S. tax code. Contributions to a qualified plan by the employer and employee are tax deductible. Most employers sponsor one or more of these plans as part of the employee benefits package, along with paid vacation and tuition reimbursement and other perks. To be considered "qualified," a retirement plan must also comply with the requirements of the Employee Retirement Income Security Act (ERISA). This federal law ensures that qualified plans follow the rules in place regarding the conduct of plan fiduciaries and their management of plan assets. It also covers employee health plans. Qualified retirement plans can be employer-sponsored or self-directed. For example, if the employee does not have a qualified plan available through their employer or if they are self-employed, they can set up one for themselves and their employees using a SEP IRA or a Simple IRA. These tax-deferred plans allow the investor to reduce their taxable income by contributing to the plan, and any contributions or gains are not taxed until retirement. Investments that are qualified are indicated in the Type and Description in Table 13-1. Rollovers from a qualified plan must go into another qualified plan to retain their tax-favored status.

Note: Refer to Chapter 14: Retirement Requirements, for additional information on qualified defined contribution and defined benefit retirement plans such as 401Ks and IRAs, which are shown in Table 13-1.

Any or all of the assets in the table can be part of an investor's financial portfolio. This is not intended to be a complete list of investment types. In this chapter, we will go into some investments in greater detail than others. The common types of savings accounts, such as Money Market Accounts (MMAs) and Certificates of Deposit (CDs), were covered in Chapter 7. They are also described briefly here as a review. The investments in Table 13-1 are not in a particular order but are grouped with other similar types. The descriptions and discussions of these investments that follow are in the order they appear in the table.

Table 13-1: Types of Investments and Retirement Accounts

Investment Type	Description / Notes	Risk Level	Tax Stat
Individual Stock	Stock shares or equities of a specific company – Can purchase on one of the stock exchanges.	**M-H**	**Taxable**
Mutual Fund (mostly stocks)	Mainly equities (stocks) – Groups of Individual stocks for diversification. Mutual funds can also be invested in multiple bonds and precious metals.	**M**	**Taxable**
Exchange-Traded Fund (ETF)	Investment fund, similar to a mutual fund, except they are traded on the stock market exchange. Most ETFs are index. An ETF is a bucket that holds various assets like stocks and bonds.	**M**	**Taxable**
U.S. Treasury Securities - Treasury Bonds, Notes and Bills	Loans to U.S. government, that bear interest (free from Fed tax but not state). Various maturities and yields. (backed by U.S. government.)	**L**	**Varies**
Municipal ("Muni") Bonds	Loans to municipalities such as cities and states, that bear interest (free from fed and state tax).	**M**	**Free**
Corporate Bonds	Loans to corporations, that bear interest (Taxed by Fed and state).	**M**	**Taxable**
Traditional IRA (Individual Retirement Account) (Qualified)	Usually, stocks but can be various types of investments. Contributions are tax deferred and deductible. You pay income tax on contributions and gains when cash is withdrawn at retirement.	**M**	**Deferred**
Roth IRA (Qualified)	Tax-free retirement investment. Usually stocks but can be any form of investment. No deduction for contributions up front. Contributions can grow tax free with no tax on withdrawals, regardless of gains.	**M**	**Free**
SEP IRA (Qualified) (Simplified Employee Pension)	An easy-to-setup employer sponsored IRA. The employer or self-employed person can make tax deferred contributions for themselves and employees. Employees cannot contribute.	**M**	**Deferred**
SIMPLE IRA (Qualified) (Savings Incentive Match Plan for Employees)	A simple employer sponsored IRA. The employer or self-employed person can make tax deferred contributions as well as employees. Only for businesses under 100 employees.	**M**	**Deferred**

401K Plan (Qualified)	Tax deferred investment retirement account for employees of private companies and self-employed individuals Usually made up of stock funds.	L	Deferred
403B Plan (Qualified)	Tax deferred investment retirement account for public employees (schools, churches and non-profits) Usually made up of stock funds.	L	Deferred
457B Plan (Qualified)	Tax deferred investment retirement account for public employees (government and municipal). Similar to 401K/403B. Not widely available compared to 403B. Usually made up of stock funds.	L	Deferred
Pension (Qualified)	Tax deferred retirement account provided by tax exempt and public organizations (schools, police depts, etc.) and some private companies. Usually invested in stocks.	L	Deferred
Certificate of Deposit (CD)	Purchased timed money savings accounts. (6 mo., 12 mo., 5 yr, etc.)	L	Taxable
Annuity (Fixed/Variable) Individual Retirement Annuity (IRA) is qualified)	Usually, tax deferred retirement investment offered by many insurance companies. Immediate annuity can provide income stream.	L	Deferred
Money Market Account (MMA)	Long term savings account. Typically, higher interest yield than a regular savings account but usually requires a higher minimum balance.	M	Taxable
529 Plan (college and other education)	State sponsored college savings/ investment account. Usually invested in stocks. Gains not taxed if used for college and other qualified education expenses.	M	Varies
Healthcare Savings Account (HSA)	Savings account that allows the individual to set aside savings that are tax deferred and non-taxable if used for personal or family health care. Contributions are also tax deductible. An HSA can be established by an individual.	L	Varies

Flexible Spending Arrangement (FSA)	Savings account that allows the individual to set aside savings that are tax deferred and non-taxable if used for personal or family health care. Contributions are also tax deductible. An FSA is typically established by an employer.		
Precious metals	Purchased gold/silver in various forms. Can be direct purchase or in an IRA. Precious metals are not FDIC insured or bank or government guaranteed, and may gain or lose value. Not interest bearing.	**M**	**Taxable or Deferred**
Real Estate (Equity REIT)	Options include purchase of primary or secondary residence, purchase of fixer-upper, purchase of rental property or purchase of land. Also, may include Real Estate Investment Trust (REIT)	**L**	**Varies**
Collectibles (Cars, Coins, Stamps, Art, etc.)	Investments that can appreciate in value. (e.g., 1969 Chevy Camaro SS 396)	**M**	**Taxable**
Commodities (e.g., Agriculture, Energy, Metals)	Raw materials used to produce finished goods. Separate market from securities. Can be hedge against inflation.	**M**	**Varies**
Cryptocurrency	Type of digital currency that generally only exists electronically. Search the FTC Website for more information.	**H**	**Varies**

Figure 13-2 shows the PFS - Asset, Liabilities, and Net Worth sheet with sample entries. In the Notes column, it indicates whether a particular asset is designated for retirement or college. Bonds and other types of investments like stocks can provide an income stream if they pay dividends. Check with your financial advisor if you need investments that can provide income.

Part 4: Investing in the Stock Market

Investing in Stocks

Stocks are publicly held shares of ownership issued by a company. Stocks are also referred to as "equities" or "securities." Corporations sell shares of their stock to raise money. If you buy stocks for an investment, you own a small part of the company and are referred to as a "shareholder." Start-up companies issue shares in an "initial public offering" or IPO. Existing companies also offer stocks for sale for expansion. Shares are typically bought on one of the major stock exchanges (through a human or online discount broker). The combination of these exchanges and a bunch of financial firms is generically referred to as "Wall Street."

Wall Street is actually a street in New York City where the financial district is located. The term "Wall Street" is often used when referencing the financial markets in the U.S.

Brokers may charge a commission to buy and sell stocks. However, there are online discount brokers that charge a low set fee per trade, or in some cases no fee. Many of them have no account minimums and frequently run promotions for new accounts. Do a Web search for "discount broker" and you will find many options. Brokers are overseen and regulated by the Financial Industry Regulatory Authority (FINRA). You can check the credentials of a particular broker or brokerage firm using the free online tool called "BrokerCheck," which is provided by FINRA. BrokerCheck can tell you whether a person or firm is registered—as required by law—to sell securities (stocks, bonds, mutual funds, etc.); offer investment advice; or both.

Financial Securities Markets

The three major U.S. financial securities markets are these:

- **NYSE** - New York Stock Exchange (actually on Wall Street)
- **NASDAQ** - National Association of Securities Dealers Automated Quotation
- **AMEX** - American Stock Exchange

Note: Although somewhat volatile, stocks have consistently increased in value on average over time at an annual rate of return of about 7 percent, adjusted for inflation and dividends. This is an average and does not apply to individual stocks.

What is a Stock Market Index?

Stocks are typically categorized based on how large the company is. Based on how much capital (cap) or worth they have, companies are often referred to as "Large Cap," "Mid Cap," and "Small Cap." A stock market index is a way to group specific stocks and track them, based on their value at a given point in time. The four main stock market indexes (indices), or benchmarks, that are tracked daily are listed here:

- **Dow Jones Industrial Average (DJIA)**
- **Standard and Poor's 500 (S&P 500)**
- **NASDAQ composite**
- **Russell 2000**

The Dow Jones Industrial Average (DJIA)

Often referred to as "The Dow," this is the oldest and most widely known indicator of how the U.S. stock market is doing. It is an index that tracks the average value of thirty of the largest publicly owned companies from the NYSE and NASDAQ. The DJIA was created in 1896 by Charles Dow and Edward Jones. Examples of companies included in the DJIA include IBM, Boeing, Home Depot, and Apple Computer.

The Standard and Poor's 500 (S&P 500)
Often referred to as "The S&P," this is another major indicator of how the U.S. stock market is doing. It is an index that tracks the value of the five hundred largest U.S. publicly traded companies. The S&P index is one of the best gauges of large-cap U.S. stocks.

The NASDAQ Composite
The Nasdaq Composite Index is the market benchmark for over three thousand companies (small-, mid-, and large-cap equities) listed on the Nasdaq stock exchange.

The Russell 2000
The Russell 2000 index is a benchmark that measures the performance of the two thousand smallest-cap U.S. companies. It is not as well known or commonly referenced as the other three indexes.

Buying Individual Stocks
Many people purchase individual stocks or shares of companies they think will do well and increase in value, as well as pay them dividends. The stocks purchased become part of the investor's portfolio, which can include other types of investments. People who wish to buy or sell stocks must go through a broker, who charges a small commission. Billions of stocks are bought and sold daily. Companies issue a set number of stocks or shares for startup or growth. The value of a stock is determined by how many people want to buy it and how many want to sell in a given trading day. If more people buy than sell, the value of a share of stock goes up. If more people sell than buy, the value goes down. It is basically driven by supply and demand. Buying and selling stocks is a little like gambling. When you buy a stock, you are betting that it will go up, but it might go down. You have about as much control over stock prices as you have over picking the winning horse at the racetrack. However, some stocks are considered "sure bets" as long as you hold onto them for the long haul. As a general rule, don't invest in individual stocks unless it is money you can afford to lose, or you just really like the company for some reason. The value of a stock can be determined by its price/earnings (P/E or PTE) ratio.

People who buy and sell individual stocks try to buy and sell shares based on any number of "indicators" that they think will help them predict what the market or a particular stock will do (go up or down). Their main goal is to "time" the market to buy when a stock's value is low and sell when it is high. They are also referred to as "market timers." The problem with individual stocks and market timing is that if they time the market wrong, they can lose a lot of money. The goal with buying stocks is to "buy low" and 'sell high," thus making money. Unfortunately, the average investor tends to "buy high" and "sell low."

Example: Buy High and Sell Low
A casual investor might see a stock they are interested in for ABC Company that is increasing in value. They watch it for a while and finally decide to buy it. By then many of the potential buyers have already jumped on the bandwagon, and the stock may top out and begin to drop. Early investors that bought low might decide to sell and make some money (capital gains). This brings the stock price down. Our investor

sees the stock price dropping and decides to sell so as to not lose any more money. Our guy bought high and sold low and lost money. Unfortunately, this is all too common, and it is quite possible that the stock could go back up. If our investor had kept the stock and not sold it, he might have made money in the long run. One of the biggest mistakes you can make when investing is following the lead of emotional investors. Keep in mind that stocks are more volatile than the corporations that issue them, but investor emotions are even more volatile than stocks. If a person buys an individual stock and holds onto it for a long time, the problems associated with market timing are not as important. The stock may go up or down in value many times, but as long as the stock continues to increase in value on average over time, the shareholders can make money on the stock over the long haul. Even if the shares go down over a long period and lose value "on paper," the investor only loses money if they actually sell the stock. As long as they hold onto the stock and do not sell it, there is always the possibility that it can go back up. If they sell, they make the loss real; however, they may be able to declare the loss when they file their income taxes.

Blue Chip Stocks
Often referred to as "Blue Chips," these are large, expensive stocks from stable, well-known corporations that have high value and have been in the market for a long time. With a solid track record of consistent performance and growth, their stocks are often a key component in the portfolios of serious, long-term investors. They are household names that are usually recognized by most people. If you invest in Blue Chips, you may not make a lot, but you can be pretty sure you will not lose money. Examples of Blue Chips include Apple, Boeing, Cisco, IBM, and Walmart. They are large-cap companies that are market leaders and are usually part of the Fortune 100. They are also frequently included in the Dow Jones Industrial Average (DJIA), a composite index that tracks the stock market performance of thirty of the most prominent U.S. companies.

Credit Rating Agencies and Stock Rating Services
There are several agencies that rate companies and governments as to solvency and credit strength on a worldwide basis to help retail and institutional investors make informed investing decisions regarding securities, including stocks and bonds. Three companies which are known as the "Big Three" credit rating agencies together provide over 90 percent of the corporate and governmental credit ratings used worldwide. The Big Three Credit Rating Agencies include:

- S&P Global Ratings (S&P)
- Moody's Investors Service
- Fitch Group

You can check with one or more of these companies, as well as other stock rating services, such as Morningstar. Just do a Web search for "stock rating service" or "stock rating system". For people who want to pick their own stocks, there is a ton of information available, such as stock ratings, dividends, earnings, company profiles, and more. As with many things, you have to consider the source.

Do not confuse the "Big three" Credit Rating Agencies (above) with the "Big three" Credit Reporting Agencies or Bureaus (See Chapter 8: Credit Scores and Reports.):

* Equifax
* Experian
* TransUnion

Whereas the Big three nationwide consumer credit reporting companies or agencies focus is on creditworthiness or individuals, the Big three" Credit Rating Agencies focus is on creditworthiness of companies and governments.

Investing During Turbulent Times in a Volatile Market

As this book is nearing completion, we're going through some difficult circumstances as a country affected by multiple worldwide crises and the stock market going up and down. What do wise financial advisors recommend you do with your equities (stocks) investments in these turbulent times? Should you sell all your stock and get out of the market so as to minimize your losses and protect your money? What will you put your money into from the sale of your stocks, cash equivalents, and bonds? If you sell all your stock, you will likely incur brokerage fees and tax ramifications, and you will have converted a potential loss on paper into a real loss. Perhaps this as an opportunity to buy shares of new promising stocks and more of current good-performing stocks, while the market is down. Continuing to invest using proven techniques like Dollar Cost Averaging (DCA), as described in Part 5 of this chapter, is a good strategy. And remember, buy low and sell high, not the other way around! If you and your financial advisor have a sound long-term plan, stay the course and ride it out (if you can), as the market will inevitably get back to where it was and then some. Historically, no investment has done as well as the U.S. stock market, having increased about a 10 percent in value per year over the last hundred years (not inflation adjusted). That does not mean you shouldn't sell some of your poor-performing stocks and do some tax loss harvesting (see Chapter 14). Refer to Figure 13-4 showing the average growth of the stock market based on the Dow Jones Industrial Average (DJIA) for over a hundred years up to 2022, based on the Dow index.

Figure 13-4: Dow Jones Index - Stock Market Performance over the Last 100 Years
(https://www.macrotrends.net/1319/dow-jones-100-year-historical-chart)

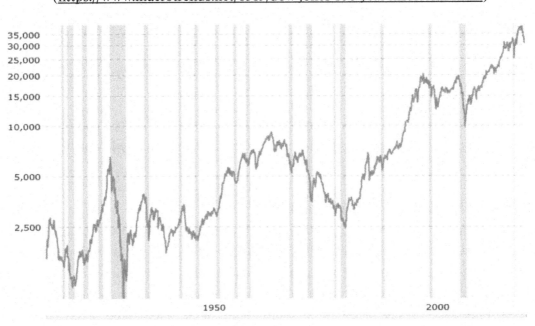

Bull and Bear Markets

Bull and Bear markets are terms used by financial people to describe market trends that go up or down significantly for an extended period. A Bull Market is characterized by stocks increasing more than 20 percent in value from previous highs. The term "stocks" refers to individual stocks, mutual funds, or other investment vehicles that are stock-based. A Bull Market generally fosters an optimistic mood, and is considered a good thing, with more investors inclined to get into the market. But a market trend like Bull (and Bear) Market can be like a "self-fulfilling prophecy." If people think the market is going up, they tend to buy more stock, which makes the prices of stocks go up, because there are more buyers than sellers. The more the stock values increase, the more people want to buy. This can go on for quite a while until there is a "market correction or adjustment." Another real world example of a self-fulfilling prophecy is when somebody says "Hey, I think that grocery store is going to be running low on toilet paper." Anyone hearing that goes to the grocery store and buys a bunch of toilet paper so that they don't run out, and guess what? The grocery store runs out of toilet paper! On the other hand, you have a Bear Market, which is basically the opposite of a Bull Market, and is characterized by stocks decreasing more than 20 percent in value from a previous peak. It is generally considered a bad thing for most investors, with more people inclined to get out of the market.

A Bear Market fosters a pessimistic mood, and people view the market as risky. As with the Bull Market, a self-fulfilling prophecy also applies to a Bear Market, only in reverse. If people think the market is going down, they tend to buy less stock, and many sell off perfectly good quality stocks at a loss. This makes the prices of stocks go down. Because there are more sellers than buyers, the stock values continue to decrease, and the less people want to buy. This can go on for quite a while until there is a "market correction or adjustment." The great stock market crash of 1929 didn't happen because people were investing in bad companies but because people were able to buy stocks on a 10 percent margin and didn't have the money to back up the purchase. So, when the market was good and stocks were going up, people could make money, but when the market started to decline, people backed out and sold their stocks to cut their losses and couldn't pay their debts.

A savvy investor probably sees it the other way around. The slow Bear Market is probably the best time to buy (prices are down), and the Bull Market is the time to sell (prices are up). Remember when it comes to stocks and many other things, BUY LOW and SELL HIGH, not the other way around.

Note: An easy way to remember which market is the **Bear** and which one the **Bull** is to think of the Bear hibernating (low energy) and then contrast this with an image of the Bull charging (high energy). Some financial institutions use the bull as an icon in their advertising, signifying strength and market growth.

Figure 13-5: Bear vs. Bull Market

Stock Sales and Long-term vs. Short-term Gains

If an investor sells a stock after holding it for a while, they might make some money, but it is taxable as capital gains. If they have kept the stock for more than a year, it is considered "long-term gains" and is taxable at a lower capital gains rate. If they kept the stock for less than a year and sold it, it is considered "short-term gains" and is taxable at a higher regular income rate.

Most financial planners advise against buying and selling individual stocks, although I certainly wish I had bought Microsoft stock a few years back! There is nothing wrong with buying stock in one or more companies you like and holding onto it for a while, knowing that it might go up or down. Over the long haul most stocks will likely go up, although at different rates. Reasons for buying individual stocks vary with each investor.

- Some people like an established company that has a strong track record of gains
- Perhaps they like a particular company's products or management team
- Perhaps they like small startup companies in a fast-growing industry

- Perhaps they like large companies that pay dividends
- Some people like to invest in what are called "penny stocks"

Dividends are a share of a company's profits that are distributed, typically quarterly, to shareholders. Penny stocks are from very small companies that trade for less than five dollars a share. The penny stocks are so named for their low price, but it may also indicate what they will be worth down the line.

Part 5: Mutual Funds and Investment Strategies

Buying Groups of Stocks for Diversification

Groups of stock shares from various companies can also be purchased in what is known as a "mutual fund." Financial companies such Vanguard decide which stocks to include in a particular fund and then sell them to investors. The groups of individual stocks usually have something in common. You can invest in any or all three investment types (stocks, bonds, or cash equivalents) as well as alternative investments such as a REIT or commodities, by buying mutual funds.

When buying stocks through the use of mutual funds, you can invest in many different types, such as Small Cap, Mid Cap, Large Cap, International, and Emerging Markets. There are thousands of mutual funds available from financial companies. The major benefit to investing in mutual funds is diversification. Many people build their retirement portfolio by investing in various mutual funds using tax-deferred options such as a 401K, IRA, or annuity, which are covered later.

Another benefit of buying a mutual fund is that the fund manager can seek to limit the number of transactions, which can reduce the taxable gains generated. This is especially true of index funds, which are covered later. If you buy individual stocks, you may not only pay a brokerage fee, but you may also be putting all your eggs (dollars) in one or a couple of baskets (individual stocks). If an individual stock you purchase goes up in value, you win. If it goes down, you lose. Stock mutual funds are invested in a group of usually similar-type stocks. Some will go up and some will go down, but the average is more stable. The highs (gainers) balance out the lows (losers).

If you invest in more than one type of mutual fund, they can provide additional diversification. A diversified and well-balanced equities portfolio will likely have investments in multiple index funds such as the Dow Jones, the S&P 500, and the NASDAQ. There are some important concepts and terms you need to keep in mind when investing, especially with mutual funds:

- **Asset Allocation** - This is the mix and percentage of investment types that make up your portfolio. For example, you might have 80 percent invested in various stock-based mutual funds, 10 percent in U.S. and municipal bonds (bond funds), and 10 percent in a precious metal (e.g., gold) mutual fund.

- **Buy-and-Hold** - The "Buy and Hold" philosophy of investing has been around probably since the birth of the stock market. It is a passive strategy that fits well with my strategy of investing in no-load index mutual funds that are bought using dollar cost averaging (DCA). It is basically buying good quality stocks (or other securities, not necessarily blue chips) and holding onto them for the long haul (usually three or more years) through the ups and downs. Once the investment is made, it is pretty much on autopilot. It is a strategy used by Warren Buffet and other successful investors.

- **Diversification** - Diversification in your portfolio means that you have a mix of different investment types and/or a mix within a particular type. Mutual funds by their nature are somewhat diversified as they contain several different stocks or other types of investments, each of which can go up or down. If you buy several different types of mutual funds, you can further diversify your portfolio.

- **Index Funds** - (Note that a part of this paragraph is paraphrased from https://www.investopedia.com). An index fund is a type of mutual fund made up of a group of stocks that is associated with a particular financial market index. These funds are a passive (vs. active) investment that track a particular market benchmark, such as the S&P 500 index. Index funds are considered a relatively cheap and safe method of investing in stocks and do not require much, if any, active management. An index mutual fund can provide broad market exposure, low operating expenses, and low portfolio turnover. Many of them are basically indexed to the activity of the overall stock market, which historically has increased at an average rate of about seven percent per year. As mentioned previously, a diversified portfolio will likely have investments in multiple funds that track the major market indexes.

- **No-load Funds** - Many companies offer what are known as "no-load" mutual funds, some of which are also index funds. No-load funds do not pay a commission or may pay a minimal commission when purchased and require little broker involvement. There are hundreds of these no-load funds available through companies such as Vanguard, Fidelity, Schwab, TD Ameritrade, and T-Rowe Price, as well as many others. Some funds have minimum investment requirements to open an account (like $1,000). Some companies offer starter funds for minors (under age eighteen). Some funds do better than others, but in general, it is pretty safe to invest in no-load index funds from a well-known company that has a strong track record. You can also buy these funds directly from the company that creates the fund. Keep in mind that true no-load funds do not pay a commission (load) on the front end (at time of purchase) or back end (at time of sale). That said, managed loaded funds may do better than true no-load funds, so load is not the only factor to consider.

Compound Interest

Some of this is a review but the importance of compound interest cannot be overstated. Compound Interest can work for you or against you. It can be your friend if you are an investor or your enemy if you are a debtor. Recall from Chapter 9: Credit and Credit Cards, the negative effect carrying a balance can have on credit card debt, especially if you make only the minimum payment each month. You are basically paying interest (which is compounded daily) on previously unpaid interest and not just the previous principal balance. Each month, unpaid interest is added to and becomes part of your new balance. This is mainly a problem with credit card debt because your payment can vary considerably from one month to the next. It is not an issue with installment loans (e.g., auto and personal loans), where the payment is set for the term of the loan. Each payment pays a certain amount to the principal and a certain amount to the interest, and you don't have the option of paying a partial payment (well, they might let you get away with it once or twice).

Remember what Einstein said regarding compound interest: "He who understands it, earns it. He who doesn't, pays it." Just as compound interest can work against you if you carry a lot of credit card debt, it can work in your favor if you have money invested in bonds, savings, and other fixed interest investment vehicles. Compound interest is a concept that has helped many ordinary people become millionaires by using regular savings/investing strategies such as Dollar Cost Averaging, as described in the text following Table 13-2. By reinvesting interest and dividends, compound interest is basically interest on interest, which works in your favor if you are the investor (stocks or bonds). If you put a hundred dollars as the principal in a savings account at 1 percent interest (APR), at the end of a year you will have $101 in the account. The 1 percent interest for the following year will be applied to the new account balance of $101, and at the end of that year, you will have $102.01. Over time, and with larger dollar amounts, the account balance can grow substantially. There are several compound interest calculators on the Internet that you can use to enter a dollar amount, interest rate, and time period to see how much an investment can grow over time. It is important to know how often the interest is compounded, and with an APR, it is usually monthly.

Rule of 72 and Compound Interest

The Rule of 72 has been around for a long time in the financial world. It is a formula based on compound interest that can determine how long it would take (in years) for your principal amount invested to double, based on a given fixed interest rate or yield. In reverse, it can tell you what interest rate you would need for your investment to double your principal, given a set time period. It really doesn't matter what the principal amount of the investment is, but it is included here for clarity. Refer to Table 13-2 for examples of how the Rule of 72 formula with compound interest works. The first example uses the formula to determine the amount of time (in years) for the investment ($1,000) to double (to $2,000) given an Annual Percentage Rate (APR) of 10 percent. Admittedly, a 10 percent rate of return may not be realistic by today's standards, but it better illustrates how the formula works. Calculations in the table are approximate. You can perform the calculations manually or with an online compound interest calculator.

Table 13-2: Rule of 72 Formula and Compound Interest - Examples

Examples	Variables	Calculations	Notes
Example 1 (Known APR)	Principal amount:	$1,000	
	Interest rate:	10%	
	Time Required to Double:	**72/10 = 7.2 (years)**	
Example 2 (Known APR)	Principal amount:	$1,000	
	Interest rate:	5%	
	Time required to double:	**72/5 = 14.4 (years)**	
Example 3 (Known Time)	Principal amount:	$1,000	
	Time target in years	8 yrs.	
	APR required to double:	**72/8yr = 9%**	
	(APR required to double invest-ment in time target 8 years)		

Here's an alternative and humorous point of view from Will Rogers:

Quote 13-2: "The quickest way to double your money is to fold it in half and put it back in your pocket." - Will Rogers

Dollar Cost Averaging (DCA)

Dollar cost averaging is one of the most important concepts of investing. In essence, it means investing a set amount of money at regular intervals (usually monthly) over time. So, let's say you contribute a hundred dollars per month to your 401K to invest in certain stock-based mutual funds. Stocks shares (and the value of the mutual fund share they are in) inevitably go up and down in price over time. If you invest a hundred dollars this month (Month 1) and the price of a mutual fund share is ten dollars, you've just bought ten shares at ten dollars/share. If the mutual fund share price goes up the next month (Month 2) to twelve dollars, your hundred dollars will buy about 8.3 shares ($100/12). The following month (Month 3), the price may drop to eight dollars/share, and your hundred dollars will buy about 12.5 shares ($100/8). So far you have invested three hundred dollars over three months. You have invested the same amount (hundred dollars) each month, but the number of shares you purchased each month was different because the share price was different. If you had invested the whole three hundred dollars in Month 2, when share prices were at twelve dollars per share, you would only have twenty-five shares. If you invested the whole three hundred dollars in Month 3, when share prices were at eight dollars per share, you would have 37.5 shares. If the mutual fund stock price goes up, your hundred dollars buys fewer shares. If the mutual fund stock price goes down, your hundred dollars buys more shares. With DCA, if you invest the same amount each month, some months you will buy more shares, and other months you will buy fewer shares. If you buy (invest) the same dollar amount at the same time each month, the cost to you to buy shares of a stock or a mutual fund is averaged over time. This is what dollar cost averaging is all about. With DCA, you should actually be happy when a Bear Market occurs (market goes down over time) as compared to a Bull Market (market goes up over time). This is because you are using DCA, and when the market does down, your dollars buy more shares, which will most likely go back up in value eventually. That said, it may be difficult to get excited by a Bear Market if you are close to retirement, and you see your nest egg decreasing in value.

DCA and Market Timing

One highly touted goal of stock purchasing is to "buy low" and "sell high." However, no one knows if the price per share of a stock will go up or down, from one day to the next, although chances are most stocks, especially proven performers, will increase in value over time. With DCA, you are basically in it for the long haul. The market can go up or down over months and years, and as long as you stay the course, you will probably do OK in the long run. I've talked with people who brag that they have "made" a bunch of money with XYZ stock this week, and then the next week they "lost" money. This is all "on-paper" because they did not buy or sell stock. Remember, even if you "make" money when you sell, you still have to pay capital gains tax (depending on how long you hold the stock), which comes out of your "profits." You don't realize a loss in the stock market until you sell. If you lose money from a stock sale, you can actually write off the loss over a period of years. This does not mean you should never sell a poor-performing stock or mutual fund, but you should discuss it with your financial advisor. Rather than try to predict what the economy will do or the best time to buy a stock, you can use DCA to even things out and do some pretty solid investing over time, with minimal involvement on your part.

(Buy-and-Hold) + (DCA) + (No-Load) + (Index) = Proven Investment Strategy

The Buy-and-Hold passive investment strategy in combination with dollar cost averaging (DCA) is a relatively brainless and painless way to invest and not have to worry about what the stock market is doing. Investing in diversified no-load and index funds using DCA is a relatively low-risk, powerful strategy for basic investing. Although somewhat boring, DCA has proven successful over the years and created many millionaires. Following these principles, people with relatively little market experience or investing knowledge have consistently done well over time, even as compared to the market experts or market timers.

Part 6: Bonds and Investment Strategies

Bond Investing

Bonds are one of the most prolific forms of investing available. This is mainly because they are also one of the most popular forms of capital generation for companies of all types and sizes as well as governments, local, state, or nationwide. For the investor, they are one of the safest ways to make some money (unearned income interest) while preserving their capital investment (principal). Along with stocks, cash equivalents, and some alternative investments like real estate, bonds (fixed income) can be a worthwhile component in a diversified financial portfolio. Millions of bonds are bought and sold daily.

Bond Ratings

Bond investors have a wide variety of offerings to choose from, at all risk levels, from junk bonds to AAA-rated quality corporate bonds and government securities (Savings Bonds). When you buy a bond, you are lending a set amount of money (principal) to the borrower for a specified time period (maturity) and at a specific interest rate (coupon rate). Bonds are rated based on a variety of factors but mainly on the creditworthiness of the bond issuer and their ability to pay back the investor their principal with interest. There are multiple bond rating organizations, but perhaps the best known is Moody's Investor Service. Moody's rating scale evaluates Investment Grade, Speculative Grade, and other securities prior to issue and rates them for the benefit of institutional investors and individuals. John Moody introduced ratings to the U.S. bond market in 1909. Moody's rating scale runs from a high of "AAA" to a low of "C." It is divided into two sections, investment grade and speculative grade. For more information, visit https://www.moodys.com.

Bond Terminology

There are three main terms or characteristics used to describe bonds:
Face Value, Interest Rate, and Maturity.

Par value - Par Value is the face value of the bond when issued, as stated by the issuer. Par value shows the bond's maturity value and dollar value of the coupon (interest) payments the bond holder will receive.

Coupon rate - Most bonds today are purchased and redeemed electronically. The term coupon is from the old days when the bond holder would receive a coupon book and redeem the coupons periodically. Coupon rate is essentially the bond interest rate or coupon yield (annual interest yield or APY) the bond holder receives over the maturity period of the bond.

> Let's say you bought a corporate bond with the following characteristics:
> - Maturity: ten years
> - Par value: $500
> - Coupon rate: 4 percent
>
> You would receive 4 percent of its par value ($500 * .04 = $20) each year for a period of ten years.

Maturity - The bond's maturity is the time from initial issue until its maturity end date.

A bond's maturity is usually referred to as short-, medium-, or long-term. Opinions may vary, but a short-term maturity period is generally one to three years, medium-term is four to ten years, and long-term is ten or more years. Shorter-term bonds (one year and less) are sometimes referred to as "cash equivalent," and medium to long term can be classified as "fixed income."

Whatever the duration of a bond, the borrower fulfills their debt obligation when the bond reaches its maturity date, and the final interest payment and original sum you loaned (the principal) are paid to you.

Note: For more information on bond rates and yields, search the Web for "corporate bond rates" or "treasury bond rates."

Fixed Bonds - These are long-term fixed income securities with a maturity of greater than one year. Fixed bonds are debt instruments (loans) to governments and other organizations that bear a fixed interest rate that is paid to the bond purchaser or holder. They can also pay dividends. Issuing bonds is the primary way that governments borrow money to build roads and schools and fund other major projects. Bonds are a relatively stable low-risk form of investing, and they typically do not have a very high return. Investors frequently buy bonds, either directly or through a financial advisor, to help diversify and balance their portfolio. There are four main groups of bonds issued.

U.S. Government Bonds – Issued by the U.S. Department of the Treasury.

These are loans from you to the U.S. government that bear interest (free from federal tax but not state). Issued in various maturities. Yields can vary daily.

- T-Bill – one year or less
- T-Note – From two to ten years (ten-year T-Note is a major tracked financial indicator)
- T-Bond – From ten to thirty years

Securities can be purchased directly through https://www.treasurydirect.gov. You can set up an account and buy all forms of government bonds with no transaction fees. You can also determine the value of a given bond and cash it in if desired. You can currently buy two types of U. S. savings bonds:

E Series Bonds - Pay a fixed interest rate for up to twenty years (current rate: 2.1 percent). They are all electronic and can be cashed in after one year. EE bonds earn interest monthly, and interest is compounded semiannually, meaning that every six months they apply the bond's interest rate to a new principal. The new principal is the sum of the prior principal and the interest earned in the previous six months. Thus, your bond's value grows both because it earns interest and because the principal gets bigger.

I Series Bonds - Protect against inflation. Earn both a fixed rate of interest and a rate based on inflation. The overall rate is reset twice a year (current rate: 6.89 percent).

U.S. Government Agency Bonds - Issued by a Government Sponsored Enterprise (GSE) and affiliates or agencies of the U.S. government such as the Federal National Mortgage Association (FNMA) or Fannie May.

Municipal Bonds - Issued by municipalities.

These are loans to municipalities, such as cities and states, that bear interest (free from federal and state tax in some cases). Municipal bonds (sometimes referred to as "Munies") are rated by one or more of the three major rating agencies: Fitch Ratings, Moody's Investors Service, and S&P Global Ratings.

Corporate Bonds – Issued by private-sector organizations

These are loans to corporations that bear interest (taxed by federal and state governments). There are quality corporate bonds that are more conservative, with lower risk and lower yields. Another riskier category of corporate bonds, referred to as "junk bonds," Note that some bonds have tax advantages for the municipality in which you live (e.g., city or county).

Bond Diversification

Within any category of investment in a diversified portfolio, the investments can be further diversified to mitigate risk. In the case of bonds, this means having a good mix of different types of bonds, including corporate and government. The bond mix should ideally have bonds with short, medium, and long maturities, and various risk levels, including Investment Grade and Speculative Grade. It is also possible to purchase various bond funds for further diversification.

Portfolio Mix - Stocks and Bonds

Many financial advisors recommend a portfolio that comprises a mix of stocks and bonds. When the client is younger, the portfolio is mostly made up of more volatile (and arguably riskier) stocks (perhaps 80 percent stocks and 20 percent bonds). As the client reaches retirement age and beyond, conventional wisdom suggests moving a higher percentage of the investments toward (arguably less risky) bonds to protect against market fluctuations and give the client a more conservative portfolio. Bond prices and interest rates have an inverse relationship, and when interest rates increase (usually due to an increase of the prime interest rate by the Federal Reserve Board), bond prices decrease, and when interest rates decrease, bond prices increase. This is because bonds have a specific yield (payout to the holder), and if interest rates in general go up (the cost to borrow money), the value of existing bonds will go down because new bonds will be issued at a higher yield rate. If you are holding bonds with a lower yield, they will become less desirable, fewer investors will want to buy them, and they will decrease in value. There will be less demand for bonds that have a lower yield as interest rates are going up. These are general guidelines, and as times change, so could the market, and bonds could become more attractive. Also note that some people buy bonds because they can pay dividends and provide a regular source of income.

The movement of large portions of a person's investment portfolio into less risky investments based on age alone assumes that an investor in his retirement years is totally risk-averse, which is not the case. If you move a high percentage of your investment portfolio into a low yield but stable investment like bonds, as you enter your retirement years, you may be investing too conservatively. In the long run, you may miss out on some potential stock market gains, even though stocks are inherently riskier. With people living twenty, thirty, or more years into their retirement, older investors are now keeping a higher percentage of their investment portfolio in stocks than in previous years.

Stock and Bonds – Retirement Income

Many people like the security of a fixed income stream in retirement. When you buy stocks or mutual funds that invest in stocks, you become a part-owner of the company or companies issuing the stock. With stocks, you are taking more risk, but with increased risk can come increased reward (not always). In addition to price increase, stocks can pay a dividend to the investor. Dividends are a share of a company's profits that are distributed, typically quarterly, to shareholders. When you buy a bond, you are loaning money to a company or government for a specified interest rate and time period. When a company issues bonds, it is looking to raise capital quickly and is betting that it will do well and be able to pay off the bonds with interest to its bond holders, while growing in stature and increasing net profit. When a company issues stocks, the investor becomes a part owner and may be able to take part in the company growth through increases in its stock price. Bonds provide a revenue stream to the investor through the interest they bear. Stocks can provide a revenue stream similar to bonds by paying dividends to their investors. When comparing stocks to bonds, ask yourself if you would you rather be an owner (stocks) or a loaner (bonds)? There are benefits to both.

Part 7: Alternative Investments

529 Plans (educational savings plan)

A 529 plan is a state-sponsored tax-advantaged college savings/investment account that helps encourage people to save for future education costs. All fifty U.S. states sponsor at least one type of 529 plan. Most of them can now be applied to various types of educational expenses, and not just college. For example, the Ohio 529 plan can be used to pay K-12 tuition, as well as student loan debt. These plans are usually invested by the state plan administrator in various portfolios, such as mutual funds. Although the contributions to a 529 are not tax deductible, the gains are not taxed if used for qualified educational expenses. The Tax Act of 2017 expanded the coverage from college expenses to include primary and secondary educational expenses as well. People can put money in a 529 for a family member (child, grandchild, nephew, niece, etc.) to help with educational expenses. Account earnings grow tax-free, and qualified withdrawals are free from federal and state income tax. You cannot deduct your contributions from federal income tax, but most states' 529 plans offer state income tax advantages for in-state residents. Nearly all states have 529 plans that offer a standard investment portfolio, and some allow you to pick and choose from other investments. You can also have accounts in multiple states, as there are differences between the various state plans. Most states also offer a prepaid tuition 529 option that allows you to buy future college credits at today's cost. When filing income tax, large contributions can be exempted for the gift tax. For more information on 529 plans, visit the U.S. Securities and Exchange Commission (SEC) at:

www.sec.gov/reportspubs/investor-publications/investorpubsintro529htm.html

Healthcare Savings Account (HSA)

An HSA is a savings account that allows the individual to set aside an amount each year that is tax deferred and nontaxable if used for personal or family health care. The HSA may be employer sponsored or you can buy an eligible health insurance plan and open a health savings account with any provider you want. They are portable and convenient but have some drawbacks.

Flexible Spending Account or Arrangement (FSA)

Both HSAs and medical FSAs are special tax-deferred savings accounts that allow you to put aside money to be used for qualified medical expenses. The main difference is that an FSA is established by an employer, whereas the HSA can be established by an individual. Both accounts allow you to invest the money put into the account. FSAs are usually funded through voluntary salary deduction agreements with your employer. No employment or federal income taxes are deducted from your contribution.

Note: For more information on HSAs, FSAs, and other tax-favored health plans, including definitions, requirements, and qualifications, go to the IRS Website at:

https://www.irs.gov/publications/p969

Precious Metals

In addition to stocks, bonds, and cash equivalents, there is another class of investments referred to as "precious metals." These include primarily gold and silver but also platinum. Gold is by far the most popular and can be purchased in the form of coins or gold bars of various values. You can keep your gold with a bank or other institution in a secure safe, or you can have it delivered to your home and put it in your own safe. You can also put gold into an IRA. Gold and silver are traded (bought and sold) on the New York Stock Exchange (NYSE), and prices vary day-to-day, similar to stocks. However, precious metals like gold have no intrinsic value (although this is debatable), which is very different from stocks issued by companies, which have value.

Some investors and financial advisors recommend including gold or silver as a small percentage (like maybe 10 percent maximum) of a client's portfolio. You can purchase gold or silver directly or through a broker. Some people like to have a percentage of some precious metals in their portfolio as a "hedge," which means they think gold will hold its value or increase when the rest of the stock market goes down. Historically, gold has done fairly well as compared to the stock market as a whole.

Although you can buy gold and keep it in your home, do you really want to have a pile of gold or silver in a safe in your house? Sounds like an incentive for a thief to rob you. It is common to see gold and silver advertised on TV. It is not necessary to keep precious metal investments close by so you can touch them. I can't physically touch the money in my IRA or CD, but it would not make me feel any more secure if I could.

Note: Precious metals are not FDIC insured or bank- or government-guaranteed. Precious metals are not interest bearing and may gain or lose value.

Real Estate Options for Investing

Real estate can be a lucrative investment if you have the right temperament and can be an important component of a diversified portfolio. Options for investing in real estate include but are not limited to the following:

- **Purchase primary or secondary residence** - If the home is in an area where home values are appreciating, you can make money. If you live in the home as a primary residence for two or more years (of the last five), before selling it, you can make up to $250,000 gains if you are single and $500,000 if you're married, without having to pay capital gains tax. A homeowner can deduct mortgage interest and property taxes up to a point.

- **Purchase fixer upper to flip** – If you are handy and willing to put in some sweat equity, you can do well fixing up homes and reselling them. Keep in mind that you must live in the home as your primary residence for two of the last five years, or you will have to pay capital gains. If you can sell the home yourself, you can avoid real estate commissions.

- **Purchase rental (leased) property** - If you own a rental property, you can depreciate it and write off maintenance expenses, management costs, property taxes, and mortgage interest. However, managing a rental property involves potential tenant headaches, which some people don't want to deal with. Also keeping the property occupied can be an issue.

- **Home rental to vacation or overnight travelers** - An increasingly popular sideline business for homeowners is renting out the use of their home, or some portion of it, on a part-time or periodic basis through avenues such as VRBO and Airbnb.

- **Purchase Real Estate Investment Trust (REIT).** - A REIT is an exchange-traded fund similar to a mutual fund that invests in commercial and residential real estate.

- **Purchase land to build on** – Buying land on which to build a future residence can be a good way to get the home of your dreams. For example, you could buy a piece of property in a growing area and do utility improvements. You might decide to build a home on the property for yourself or build on speculation (spec) to sell. Or you might decide to keep the property for a while, let it appreciate, and then sell if land values are increasing.

Collectibles

Collectibles are basically groups of things that can be bought and sold with the assumption that they will increase in value over time. Many people collect things as a hobby, with the potential benefit that they could appreciate in value. Examples of collectibles can include vehicles (cars, trucks, and motorcycles) as well as antiques, artwork, coins, and stamps. The main problem with collectibles is that they are only worth what someone will pay for them.

As a funny side note, my wife and I went to see a standup comedian a while back who told a joke about investing in collectibles. He said he was preparing for his retirement by investing in collectibles such as Beanie Babies and Pokémon cards. Laugh if you will, but these can appreciate in value more than some of the more traditional investments! We bought some Beanie Babies for our girls when they were little. We did some research recently, and some of them are worth thousands of dollars if in perfect condition. Also, take a look at how much some of the older baseball cards and comic books are worth!

Commodities

Commodities are raw materials that are used to produce finished goods. In general, commodities remain consistent with regard to characteristics and quality, irrespective of the source or production location. There are hundreds of commodities, but they are grouped into three main categories: Agriculture (wheat, sugar, and lumber); Metals (gold, copper, and steel); and Energy (Natural gas, crude oil, and uranium). Livestock is also considered a separate category. Commodities are physical goods that are traded (bought and sold) in markets. The commodities markets are not part of the securities markets, which consist mainly of stocks and bonds that are financial contracts. Commodities are a huge part of the world economy and can be a worthwhile addition to an investor's portfolio, as a small percentage, to increase diversification and act as a hedge against inflation.

Cryptocurrency (e.g., Bitcoin and Ethereum)

Cryptocurrency is a digital currency that does not have a central issuing or regulating authority. It is mentioned here as an example of the many digital currencies that exist because the subject sometimes comes up when discussing investments. Cryptocurrency is an idea and somewhat theoretical concept that is gaining acceptance; however, it is somewhat risky and probably not for the average investor. To find out more about cryptocurrencies and potential scams, go to the Federal Trade Commission's Consumer Website at https://consumer.ftc.gov/articles/what-know-about-cryptocurrency-and-scams. The following is an excerpt from the FTC Website:

< Begin Excerpts: FTC Cryptocurrency information >

"Cryptocurrency is a type of digital currency that generally only exists electronically. There is no physical coin or bill unless you use a service that allows you to cash in cryptocurrency for a physical token. You usually exchange cryptocurrency with someone online, with your phone or computer, without using an intermediary like a bank. Bitcoin and Ether are well-known cryptocurrencies, but there are many different cryptocurrency brands, and new ones are continuously being created."

< End Excerpts: FTC Cryptocurrency information >

Part 8: The Ultimate Investment - Yourself

Pursue your passion! This is most likely where you currently put your time and money or would like to. Have faith in yourself regardless of what others might say, and remember, nothing succeeds like perseverance. Also be sure to enjoy the ride and the moments along the way!

Quote 13-3: "Whether you think you can or you can't, you're right." - Henry Ford

This quote refers to the importance of self-confidence and perseverance in determining your success when taking on projects and pursuing goals. Also be sure to practice the four Ds for success:

- **Desire**
- **Determination**
- **Dedication**
- **Diligence**

Investing in Yourself

Examples of investing in yourself include starting a small business or writing a book. Rather than just working a regular job and exchanging X hours for X dollars of pay, investing in yourself can leverage your time spent working. These self-investments can result in a significant multiplication of your efforts. As an example, while I was teaching at various colleges, I worked on several textbooks for use in their computer and network certification training programs. I worked on most of these books in my spare time and was not paid directly for the hours I worked. Instead, I received monthly royalty payments once the books were published. The amount of the royalty I received was based on the number of books sold. The long-term financial benefits of the royalties far outweighed the hourly rate I might have been paid. In fact, I continued to receive royalty checks for the sale of some of the books for up to three years after I wrote them. In addition to the royalty income, I did some custom network training development and network consulting. I was also able to rent office space and write off some of the expenses on my taxes.

Putting yourself through college or technical school or just taking classes is a form of investing in yourself. I took several programming courses at UCLA to get into a computer programming job and was able to switch careers and make more money. Starting a small business is another good way to invest in yourself. As an example, our daughter started an Internet online sales business and has done very well with it. It was initially just a part-time effort, but the business has grown to the point that she has enough orders to warrant hiring some help. As with most forms of self-employment, she is also able to write off some of her living expenses to the business (e.g., mortgage payment, utilities, insurance, etc.). Entrepreneurship is an excellent way to multiply your efforts so that you are not just trading an hour of your time for an hour of pay working for someone else. Another possible avenue for investing in yourself is to develop a smart phone app or start a Web log (blog).

If you are really handy and have some home building and/or renovation experience. You might consider buying fixer upper homes, mentioned previously. By doing the most important "bang for the buck" renovations and reselling the homes or "flipping," you can make a decent living. There are lots of ins and outs to doing this, but I know a few people who are quite successful. Based on the number of home improvement TV programs, this can be a pretty lucrative business if you play your cards right. The truth is you are always working for yourself, whether you realize it or not and regardless of who is paying you, or if you are being paid at all. If you perform your current job well, and learn all you can, you might get promoted, get a raise, or qualify yourself for another better-paying job, or even start your own business. If you perform your current job poorly and begrudgingly, you may get demoted or lose your job. In either case, your diligence and quality of work will be reflected in your success or failure. Either way, you will draw to yourself what you deserve, whether you realize it or not. You reap what you sow. Some people don't believe they have what it takes to start a small business and that may be true. In any case, whether you think you can or think you can't, you are probably right!

Investing/Saving – Summary Notes and Tips
- Develop a habit of regular saving, even if it is just small amounts.
- Try to save 10 percent of what you earn (15–20 percent if you can) in a high-yield online savings account.
- Give 10 percent to charity or your religious organization (tithe) and live on the remaining 80 percent.
- Whatever you do, don't do "nothing" just because it all sounds so complicated!
- Start investing and saving early and invest for the long haul.
- Hire a certified financial planner (CFP) to help develop your investment options and strategy.
- Read a basic investment guide to increase your knowledge. There are many, like Clark Howard's Online Investment Guide and Investing for Dummies (check with your local library).
- Build your emergency savings fund (top priority) to protect your other investments.
- Put away cash for your emergency savings fund until you have accumulated at least six months of expenses.
- Buy mutual funds that are invested primarily in stocks.
- Buy no-load and index stock funds (like S&P 500), if possible.
- Diversify by buying different types of stock mutual funds (e.g., small cap, mid cap, international, etc.).
- Invest a small part of your portfolio in cash equivalents such as CDs and MMAs.
- Diversify your investments between stocks, bonds, and cash equivalents.
- Use dollar-cost averaging to buy a set amount of investments at regular, consistent (monthly) increments over time.
- Invest in a 401K or other tax-advantaged account using dollar-cost averaging.
- Resist the temptation to sell if the market dips. You do not realize a loss unless you sell.
- Beware of financial/investment scams. Like the email from the Nigerian Prince that has a million dollars he cannot access unless you help him by giving him your bank account number and password, at which time he will transfer the million to your account so you can split it. If it sounds too good to be true, it probably is.
- Beware of TV ads for gold and silver.
- Evaluate the performance of your financial portfolio and rebalance annually.
- Max out your tax-deferred and tax-free options (401K, IRAs, etc.), especially those with an employer match, before investing in anything else (except for your emergency fund).
- Buying no-load indexed mutual funds may not be exciting, but that's OK. Good investing for the long haul should be boring!

Chapter 13 Exercises

Exercise 13-1: Personal Investment Survey Questionnaire

1. Do you have a professional financial advisor? _____
2. Do you have a personal financial plan (short- and long- term)? _____
3. Do you know your credit score? _____
4. Do you know what's in your credit report? _____
5. Do you have an account with one of the three major credit bureaus? _____
6. Do you have a fully funded emergency fund? _____
7. What savings accounts do you currently have? _____
8. Do you have automated savings set up? _____
9. What investments do you currently have? _____
10. Do you have automated investing set up? _____
11. Are you participating in your employer's retirement plan? (e.g., 401K) _____
12. What is your risk tolerance level for investments in general? _____
13. Do you know what the annualized ROI is for each of your investments? _____
14. Are there types of investments you prefer? _____
15. Are there types of investments you want to avoid? _____
16. What percentage of your current investment is liquid? _____
17. Are your current investments diversified? _____
18. Do the ratios (%) or percentages for your Personal Financial Indicators (DTI, DTC, HTI, etc.) fall into an acceptable range? _____
19. How much cash flow do you have available each month to invest? _____
20. Do you know what your net worth is? _____
21. Do you need an income stream from your investments? _____
22. Do you have proper insurance and adequate coverage for your life situation? _____

Exercise 13-2: Compare ROI Calculators

An ROI calculator is a basic calculator with options for Real ROI as well as Rate of Return (ROR). Do a Web search for "free ROI calculator," and use Table 13-4 to find an online ROI calculator that meets your needs. There are many good ones available. The Figure 13-1 screenshot is from calculators.net. Make a copy of Table 13-4 and use it as a starting point for Exercise 13-2.

Table 13-4: ROI Calculator Comparison
(Alphabetical order)

Source Name	Notes
Bankrate.com	https://www.bankrate.com/retirement/roi-calculator/
Calculator.net	https://www.calculator.net/roi-calculator.html
Calculators.org	https://www.calculators.org/investing/

Exercise 13-3: Evaluating Your PFI Status Using the Investing Checklist (instructions follow).
Exercise 13-3 is a post-midway book checkpoint to determine where you stand on key PFIs. You will use the Investing Checklist steps (below) as a guide along with the PFI definitions in Appendix B. It is an optional exercise but highly recommended. The main purpose is to consolidate all your personal financial indicator (PFI) information, provide a review, and assist you in recording your PFI information.

Copy Table B-1 in Appendix B. Use Table B-1 for a reference on how to calculate the PFIs and as a form to enter your indicator values and notes. By calculating these PFIs based on your current financial situation, you will be able to identify monies (capital) with which you can fund additional investments.

Note: Completion of the Investing Checklist and PFIs can be a significant time investment, depending on how much of your information is readily available. So, be sure to plan ahead and split the checklist steps up into three or four sessions. The more thorough you are in completing the checklist, the better your awareness and understanding of your finances.

Copy the **Investing Checklist Steps** given below, which is part of Exercise 13-3. These are steps that you can take at this time to get a current picture of your overall finances and investment status. As you complete each step, check it off and make notes on a separate note pad or smartphone. Each step is associated with one or more of the PFIs that were introduced in previous chapters. If you do not have these PFI calculations available, you can recalculate them at this time. Refer to Appendix B for a complete list of all PFIs and information on how to calculate each of the PFIs listed below.

Exercise 13-3 Investing Checklist Steps
(Refer to Appendix B, Table B-1, for PFI Calculations)

1. Determine your current **Gross Income and Net Income** (monthly or annual)
2. Determine your current **Cash Flow** using **PFI 3-4** for Personal Cash Flow (PCF).
3. Determine your current **Net Worth** using **PFI 5-1** for Personal Net Worth (PNW)
4. Evaluate your current **Savings** (Non-EF) ratio using **PFI 4-1** for Savings-to-Income (STI).
5. Evaluate your **Emergency Fund** Goal (EFG) and progress toward it using **PFI 4-2**.
6. Evaluate your current **Debt** levels ratios based on loans relative to income.
   a. **Debt-to-Income** (DTI) using **PFI 3-3**
   b. **Housing-to-Income** (HTI) using **PFI 11-1**
   c. **Transportation-to-Income** (TTI) using **PFI 12-1**
7. Evaluate **Debt-to-Credit** (DTC) ratios using **PFI 8-1** (Use PFS sheet Cred-Cards for input)
8. Identify **high-interest debt** that can be reduced to free up capital for investment.
9. Evaluate current **Investment** financial position using **PFI 13-2** Investment-to-Income (ITI).
10. Determine annualized **Return-on-Investment** (ROI) for current investments using **PFI 13-1**.
11. Evaluate your available **investing options**.
   a. Employer sponsored (e.g., 401K)

   b. Self-directed (e.g., IRA)
   c. CFP-directed (e.g., mutual funds)
12. Evaluate current personal and property insurance coverage (Auto/Home/Life, etc.)

Exercise 13-4: Record Investment Assets, Income, and Options

In Part A of this three-part exercise, you will review your assets that you listed from Chapter 3, Exercise 3-1. In Part B you will review any income sources that you listed in Chapter 3, **Exercise 3-1: List PFS Income and Expenses**. You will view them as investments, determine if any of them are paying dividends or possibly paying out distributions, and record them in Part A and Part B of this exercise. In Part C, you will select Investments (Perhaps two or three of them) from Table 13-1 that are of interest to you and that you don't currently own. Record them in Part C of Table 13-3.

Note: Before starting this exercise, make a copy of Table 13-3.

Part A: Identify Investment Assets

Review your assets listed in Chapter 3, Exercise 3-1. If they can be considered investments, record them in the Part A section of Table 13-3. This information and your entries should be on PFS Sheet - Assets, Liabilities, and Net Worth (Assets-Liab Tab).

Part B: Identify Investment Income Sources

Review your income sources listed in Chapter 4, Exercise 4-1, that pay dividends or if you are taking distributions. If they can be considered income-producing investments, record them in the Part B section of Table 13-3. This information and your entries should be on PFS Sheet - Income, Expenses, and Cash Flow (Income-Exp Tab).

Part C: Identify Investment Options

Review the various investments listed in Table 13-1. Select one or more investments from the table, or another source of your choice, that are of interest to you and that you don't currently own. Record them in the Part C section of Table 13-3.

Note: For Part C, if you pick a stock or other investment of that nature, record the price at the time you make the selection, and monitor it over a period of time. Or you can review the past performance of the desired stock or investment.

Table 13-3: Investment Assets, Income, and Options (Form)

Part A	Investment Asset Type/ Description	Owner/Institution	Notes	Appx Value
Part B	Investment Income Source (Div/Dist)	Owner/Institution	Notes	Appx Value
Part C	Investment Options Type/Description	Owner/Institution	Notes	Price

Chapter 14
Retirement Requirements

Chapter Overview:

Investing, Insurance, and Estate Planning are huge topics, and each of them can have a major impact on your retirement. As a result, this chapter focuses on each of these areas but primarily as they relate to retirement. It identifies some steps you can take and provides tips to help make it a long and happy one. It covers the key concepts and terminology for these very important subjects. You can dig deeper into the topics that are of interest to you. Think of this chapter as food for thought regarding retirement, essential insurance, and estate planning with accompanying cautionary notes, rather than recommendations. Additional information on investments is covered in Chapter 13: Investing Basics, and additional information on insurance is covered in Chapter 16: Insurance and Risk Management. This chapter is divided into four parts:

- **Part 1: Retirement Investments – Your Nest Egg**
- **Part 2: Retirement Plans (401Ks, Pensions, and Annuities)**
- **Part 3: Insurance for a Secure Retirement**
- **Part 4: Estate Planning and Estate Documents**

Chapter PFS Integration:

This chapter covers some fields of the PFS Sheet - Insurance Policy Info, with a tab label of "Insure-Pols." The Insure-Pols sheet provides a centralized location to record key information for your retirement-related insurance policies, such as life, health, and long-term care, as well as home- and vehicle-related policy information. This PFS sheet is dedicated to insurance policies of all types based on monthly expenses. PFIs Emergency Fund-to-Expenses (EFE) and Liquid Assets-to-Expenses (LAE) can be used with this chapter and adapted to retirement scenarios.

Chapter Exercise:
- **Exercise 14-1: Compare Retirement Calculators**

Chapter Notable Quotes:
Quote 14-1: "Today's preparation determines tomorrow's success." - Anonymous
Quote 14-2: "If you have enough and you've had enough, it's time to retire." - Anonymous

Introduction

Part 1 of the chapter focuses on investments and investing in your retirement years. Part 2 of the chapter describes the various types of qualified retirement plans such as 401Ks, Pensions, and Annuities that were introduced in Chapter 13. Part 3 of the chapter deals with various types of insurance that will help protect you and your nest egg and that are related to retirement and estates. Part 4 deals primarily with the documents required for estate planning and the professional services that are available to help with this planning. Part 4 also provides a brief overview of the reverse mortgage as a retirement/estate option for homeowners and their heirs. Regarding insurance, the chapter is not meant to provide comprehensive coverage, especially since home and auto insurance were covered in Chapters 11 and 12, respectively. Chapter 16 deals more generally with all types of insurance to increase awareness of what's available and what kinds of insurance might be appropriate given a person's situation or circumstances. This chapter provides a high-level discussion and review of some important things to consider when acquiring insurance. The inclusion of coverage here helps ensure that having the right kind of insurance is not overlooked, since it is a major factor contributing to a successful retirement.

Background: Ted and Amy's Investments

The sample financial data shown in the **PFS** screenshots throughout this book belongs to a fictitious couple named **Ted** and **Amy**. Ted retired at age sixty-seven and has Social Security income and a couple of other retirement sources that he is drawing on. These include a 401k and a pension, which is an annuity, both from former employers. He is taking small retirement distributions from his 401K and is receiving monthly payouts from his pension. Amy plans to retire in about five years and is contributing to her employer-matched 403B plan. Ted is on Medicare and Amy has health and life insurance through her employer. In addition to their qualified retirement plans, they have an emergency fund, a short-term savings account, and a Certificate of Deposit (CD), as well as some stocks and bonds that pay dividends and interest.

Part 1: Retirement Investments – Your Nest Egg

Investing for Retirement – Overview and Perspective

It takes money to make money, but that doesn't mean that inheriting a bunch of money is the only way you can become wealthy. By following the guidelines outlined in Chapter 13 on investing and the information presented in this chapter, you will see that by employing some very basic rules and principles and starting early, you'll be able to build a pretty substantial nest egg by the time you retire. If you can take the money you make through a normal salary and put away a little bit of it with each paycheck (like automatically investing 10 percent of your gross pay in a 401K), you will have quite a bit accumulated when you are ready to retire. Just by making some basic smart investments and letting the market do what it does, you should be OK, assuming you don't take from your investment accounts along the way. The biggest problem is that most of us don't think about retirement until it's pretty late in the game. When you're in your thirties or forties and tied up with the activities and turmoil in your current situation, it's hard to think about putting money away so you'll have it in thirty to forty years. In the U.S., according to the Government Accounting Office (GAO), nearly half of the people fifty-five or older do not have any form of retirement savings, such as a 401K or IRA. In many cases, they have access to a 401K or similar retirement plan through their employer but do not contribute to it. In the U.S., many of these people will rely solely on Social Security and Medicare (or Medicaid) or may end up working much longer than they would like. Social Security is based on how much you and your employers have paid into the program over your working years. If you were not employed for several years, your social security check may be lower than expected. On the other hand, the Social Security Administration recently increased payouts to recipients by 8.7 percent as a cost-of-living adjustment (COLA) due largely to inflation. Three of the most important factors in building a sizable nest egg for retirement are listed below. If you start putting a percentage of your income into quality investments at around thirty years old, you could be a millionaire by the time you retire, although a million dollars by then will be worth significantly less, due to inflation. The earlier you start, the easier it will be to achieve this goal.

- **Start investing and saving early.** (Even small amounts. The earlier the better.)
- **Invest in stocks regularly.** (No-load index funds using dollar cost averaging.)
- **Pay yourself first.** (Set a goal to invest 10 to 15 percent of your gross income.)

Hire a Professional Financial Advisor

If you don't already have one, obtain the services of a professional financial advisor, preferably a CFP, to help in determining your goals and plans for retirement and to help you achieve your investing and retirement goals. Be sure they are a fiduciary who is legally obligated to put your interests first. Refer to Chapter 13: Investing Basics for the important things to consider and questions to ask, when choosing a qualified professional financial advisor. The chapter also covers the services and types of advice that a CFP can provide. They can help develop your investment/retirement options and a strategy for implementation, as well as factoring in tax implications. They can also help you determine how much accumulated wealth is enough for you to retire comfortably and help you decide when you may be able to retire. In addition, they should be able to help develop a withdrawal/distribution plan for which investments you will tap into and in what order to maximize funds during your retirement years. As a brief review from previous Chapter 13, the services a CFP can provide may include the following (partial list).

- **Financial analysis with needs assessment**
- **Guidance on budgets, debt, and taxes**
- **Investment and portfolio advice**
- **Retirement planning**
- **Insurance recommendations**
- **Help with Social Security**

Retirement in a Volatile Market

With all the stuff happening in the world, a lot of people are concerned, scared, and worried, or all the above. If the stock market goes down over time and stays down for a while (as can happen with a recession), it can have a major impact on people who are nearing retirement as they watch the value of their nest egg portfolio decrease from one month to the next. Depending on how long a recession lasts, they may be able to hold on and not deplete their retirement savings too rapidly, and hopefully, they can ride out the storm. Although it goes up and down, the stock market is one of the few investments that have weathered these global catastrophes over the last hundred years.

As shown in Chapter 13, the Dow Jones Industrial Average Index (DJAI or "the Dow") is a key market indicator that tracks the stock market performance of U.S. companies. The S&P 500 is another major index that reflects the health of the mainstream U.S. stock market and is perhaps an even better indicator of overall market health, as it tracks the top 500 U.S. publicly traded stocks. The graph in Figure 14-1 shows the performance of the S&P 500 Index over the last 90 years. Regardless of how low the stock market has gone, as indicated by the Dow and the S&P, it has historically recovered and exceeded previous highs. It may have taken some time, but it always has (at least in my lifetime), and it does this (on average) regardless of what worldwide catastrophes are occurring. The market has averaged about a 10 percent increase in value (growth rate) per year over the last ninety to hundred years. As previously mentioned, the great stock market crash of 1929 didn't happen because people were investing in bad companies or the market was flawed but because people were able to buy on 10 percent margin and didn't actually have the money to back up the purchase. The performance of the stock market could have been even better, were it not for this fact.

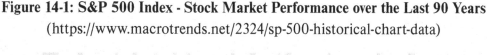

Figure 14-1: S&P 500 Index - Stock Market Performance over the Last 90 Years
(https://www.macrotrends.net/2324/sp-500-historical-chart-data)

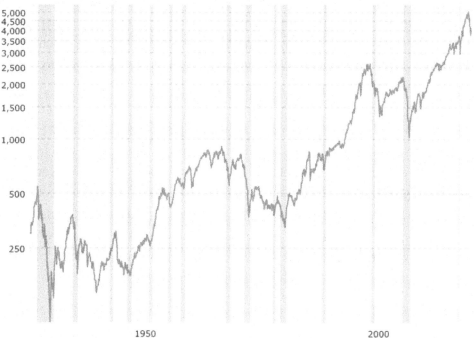

Many retirees are living longer and are keeping large portions of their portfolios in stocks for growth and adding to their securities (stocks) holdings. They are increasingly, with guidance from their financial advisors, taking on a higher level of risk inherent with stocks for a potentially higher level of return. Retirees in general are taking a more long-term perspective even though they are retired or nearing retirement, and you would normally expect them to be more conservative with their investment by holding a higher percentage of low-risk investments such as bonds and cash equivalents. But like I said at the beginning of the book, it really doesn't make a difference whether the stock market, interest rates, unemployment, or the price of gold goes up or down; the principles in this book are the same. You don't change key sound principles just because there's a crisis of some kind. There will always be a crisis of some sort somewhere in the world.

Investment Mix, Diversification and Rebalancing

Depending on your age and when you plan to retire, a financial planner might recommend an investment mix of 80 percent in stocks, 10 percent in bonds, and 10 percent in cash equivalents. This will vary based on your financial situation and tolerance for risk. A CFP can also evaluate the performance of your investments and rebalance your financial portfolio annually. Another option is to contact one of the investment companies and open a targeted retirement fund. These funds typically automatically rebalance at intervals by shifting some of your investments from higher-risk stock funds to lower-risk bond funds and cash equivalents (CDs and MMAs) as you approach retirement.

Rebalancing is typically done annually and is based on keeping your asset mix percentages consistent as the market changes over time. Let's say you and your financial advisor have invested in assets according to your financial plan. Based on your risk tolerance, you decided on a portfolio investment mix of 60 percent in stocks, 20 percent in bonds, 10 percent in real estate, and 10 percent in precious metals. Over the course of the year, the value of some of your holdings in each category increased while others decreased. So, you decide to increase or decrease various holdings based on altered asset values and market performance, to rebalance your portfolio. This typically means buying or selling your portfolio assets to periodically readjust asset allocation to the level defined in your financial plan.

As an example of a portfolio, a financially successful retired couple may have the following sources to support them in their retirement years. These are a mix of different types of investments and income sources, all of which have been described here and in Chapter 13 (with the exception of Social Security and Medicare). These are listed here to give you an idea of what a realistic diversified financial portfolio could look like. This would be considered a well-planned and well-financed retirement nest egg that probably took some time and diligence to achieve. Your list will vary but may include some of the following ways to fund your retirement. Of course, you could also continue to work, if you desire, and many people do.

- 401K
- Variable Annuity
- Traditional IRA
- Roth IRA
- Pension
- Social Security
- Medicare

Note: Social Security and Medicare are beyond the scope of this book. Your financial advisor may be able to direct you to someone who specializes in these areas. You can also go to the Social Security Website (ssa.gov) to get answers to any questions you may have and get an estimate of the amount you will receive, depending on when you plan to retire.

Retirement - How Much is Enough?

When it comes to retirement, a common question people ask is, "How much do I need to retire comfortably?" The book *The Number* by Lee Eisenberg addresses this question. The bottom line is that the answer depends largely on your life expectancy and your desired lifestyle in retirement. Most people scale back their lifestyle when they retire. They may downsize to a smaller home or apartment, take fewer vacations, or reduce discretionary spending. Review your required expenses and discretionary spending and work with your CFP to come up with a retirement and disbursement plan that does not deplete your nest egg too rapidly. Most CFPs recommend limiting the disbursement or amount you can take from your investments to no more than 5 percent per year on a monthly basis. This allows your remaining investment to continue to grow. Assuming you largely have equities (stocks) and investments that grow at 6-7 percent per year on average (adjusted for inflation), you may be able live on the gains from your investments. As an example, let's say you have investment assets of $1,000,000. At the point you wish to retire, you could take a disbursement of $50,000 per year. Keep in mind that you will have to pay taxes on the principal and gains unless you have a Roth IRA. There are retirement calculators on the Web that you can use to play with the numbers. One is at Bankrate:

https://www.bankrate.com/retirement/retirement-calculator

Refer to **Exercise 14-1: Compare Retirement Calculators** at the end of this chapter to help you select one that meets your needs. Here is an example using the BankRate calculator. You enter the following variables:

- Annual income required: **40,000**
- Number of years until retirement: **10**
- Number of years required after retirement: **25**
- Annual Inflation: **0**
- Annual Yield on Balance (average): **7.5**
- Amount needed when you wish to retire: **Appx $480,000.**

Retirement and General Investing Mistakes and Obstacles

There are many variables involved with investing, and each investor has their own set of requirements. Here are some of the more common mistakes people make with regard to retirement and investing in general. These are grouped as "A" and "B" priorities or issues. Although they are all important, the Group A category of mistakes is more critical and potentially more damaging to financial health in the long run. There are many opinions on this issue, and financial experts may disagree with the mistakes I'm listing here.

Group A Mistakes:
- Not having a rainy-day emergency savings fund
- Not hiring a financial planner
- Not having a plan
- Not having safety net insurance (long term care, disability, etc.)

- Buying individual stocks (instead of no-load index mutual funds)
- Not using dollar-cost averaging (trying to time the market)
- Not diversifying (too many eggs in one basket)
- Not considering spouse (when making financial decisions)
- Borrowing against retirement accounts (e.g., IRA, 401K, 403B)

Group B Mistakes:
- Counting on Social Security (and taking it early)
- Not factoring inflation, taxes, and management fees with ROI
- Investing in poor quality assets (junk bonds, penny stocks)
- Investing in get-rich-quick scams
- Investing too conservatively (bonds and cash)
- Investing based on emotional factors or politics.
- Taking distributions early from retirement accounts
- Taking excessive distributions from retirement accounts

Part 2: Retirement Plans - (401Ks, Pensions, and Annuities)

Qualified Retirement Plans

Qualified Retirement Plans, such as IRAs, 401Ks, 403Bs, and pensions, make up the largest portion of the investment options available, as was shown in Table 13-1. Most employers sponsor one or more of these plans as part of the employee benefits package, along with health insurance, paid vacation, tuition reimbursement, and other perks. To be considered "qualified," a retirement plan must comply with the requirements of the Employee Retirement Income Security Act (ERISA). This federal law was enacted in 1974 and ensures that qualified plans follow the rules regarding conduct of plan fiduciaries and plan assets. It also covers employee health plans. Qualified retirement plans can be employer-sponsored or self-directed. For example, if the employee does not have a qualified plan available through their employer or if they are self-employed, they can set up one for themselves, such as a Simple IRA. These tax-deferred plans allow the investor to reduce their taxable income by contributing to the plan, and any contributions or gains are not taxed until retirement. Investments that are qualified are indicated in the Type and Description in Table 13-1. Rollovers from a qualified plan must go into another qualified plan to retain their tax-favored status.

Qualified retirement plans can be classified as either **Defined Contribution** plans (e.g., 401K, 403B, IRA) or **Defined Benefit** plans (e.g., pension). Defined Contribution plans are largely employee-directed whereas Defined Benefit plans are largely employer-directed.

Defined Contribution Qualified Retirement Plans - 401K and 403B

Traditional 401K plans are tax-deferred retirement accounts for employees of private sector (for-profit) companies. If you are self-employed, you can invest in an Individual 401K plan, which has many of the same benefits as a traditional 401k. 403B plans are tax-deferred retirement accounts for nonprofit organizations and public employees such as police, firefighters, and teachers. Both 401K and 403B plans are usually invested in stocks in the form of multiple diversified mutual funds. Contributions to the plan are tax deferred, so the employee does not pay taxes on the contributions or gains until they retire and begin taking distributions. They are then taxed at their retired income tax rate (usually lower). Although an employee may take money out of their 401K before retirement (generally before age 59-½) or borrow against it, this is strongly discouraged as it can greatly affect their retirement income in the long run. In addition, if the money is withdrawn, it is taxed at their ordinary income rate and severe penalties are applied (like 10 percent). With the 401K, the amount of income you can defer is set by the IRS and can vary from one year to the next. For a particular year, the maximum income you can defer is set. However, if you're age fifty or over, you may be able to contribute additional monies per year. Check with your plan administrator for contribution limits.

Defined contribution 401K plans have largely replaced private company defined benefit pension plans (see description of pensions below). A financial management company hired by the company or organization administers the plan and usually offers several options that the employee can invest in, such as various stock-based mutual funds and bonds. They also allow the employee to determine how much they want to invest or contribute. It is surprising that, even with a 401K plan available, many employees have no retirement savings. Some companies have begun requiring a certain percentage of a new employee's pay (like 3 percent) to be contributed to the retirement plan as a way of ensuring that the employee contributes to his or her retirement. Most employees will forget that a percentage of their pay is being deducted and do not miss the money. However, when they get ready to retire, they can have quite a nice nest egg built up. Contributing to a 401K or 403B is a relatively painless way to invest and provide for your retirement. And before you know it, that little monthly defined contribution to your qualified retirement plan has grown to a substantial amount and is the cornerstone of your financial foundation, not to mention being the biggest chunk of your personal net worth! For example, if you start with $1,000 at age thirty and put just a hundred dollars per month into a 401K or 403B S&P 500 index fund, assuming a modest average growth of the market at 7 percent and retirement at age seventy, you could easily have over $250,000 in your retirement fund. And that just assumes normal growth in the stock market. Some may say, well, it took you forty years! However, if you didn't do it, you could be sitting here forty years from now and have zero dollars in your fund!

The Employer Match
The employee may select the 401K investments on their own or use a financial advisor to help them decide which of the offered 401K funds to invest in. Many 401Ks and other defined contribution plans (like 403Bs) allow for an employer match for a certain percentage of the employee's pay based on what percentage the employee contributes, up to a specified limit. So, if the employee contributes 4 percent of their gross pay, their employer may match that with another 4 percent of the employee's gross pay. This is effectively increasing your investment without investing your own money. If you do not contribute to your 401K, the employer matches nothing, so you would be foolish to not contribute at least the percentage of your salary that the company matches, as this is like doubling your investment for free. You may be able to contribute more than 4 percent, but the employer might choose to only match up to 2 percent or not match it at all.

In today's job market, a 401K with employer match is like getting a raise and can make a huge difference in your retirement income. In some cases, the employer will dictate that a portion of your investment goes into company stock. Generally speaking, this is to be avoided since it is kind of like putting too many of your eggs into one basket. It is the opposite of diversification. If the company's stock goes down or the company goes out of business, it can significantly affect the employee's overall portfolio. That said, it's still probably not a bad idea since it may inspire you to work harder to help the company do better financially.

401K Employer Match Summary

With a 401K (or other) match plan, contributing up to the employer match amount (if offered) is a no-brainer. As part of their benefits package, many companies are now matching what the employee contributes up to 8 percent of the employee's salary. So, if the 401K plan allows the employee to contribute up to 10 percent of their gross pay, the employer will match them dollar for dollar up to 8 percent. After that, you can continue to contribute up to the max allowed (possibly 10 percent or more) if you can afford it. Although non-matched, these contributions are still a tax-deferred investment in most cases. Follow these steps if you have a 401K available and if your situation warrants it.

1) **Enroll in your company's 401K** (or other qualified plan, using payroll deduction). Set it up on your first day of employment, if possible, or soon thereafter. Time marches on!
2) **Select Funds and other investments** (with help from your financial advisor).
3) **MAX OUT YOUR EMPLOYER MATCH CONTRIBUTION FIRST! (Before you invest any money anywhere else.)** Be sure to set aside and contribute the amount or percentage of your gross income that your employer matches so you can get the full match. If the match is 5 percent and your monthly gross income $5,000, that amounts to $250 per month you would contribute, and the employee match is another $250, so you just doubled your investment at no cost to you!
4) **Contribute additional employer non-matched funds** (if you have the extra money, up to the limit allowed by your plan). Even without the company match, any additional contributions you make are being invested using dollar-cost-averaging into a diversified stock mutual fund (in most cases).
5) **Feel good**. You are making some smart long-term financial moves to help secure your retirement.

401K – Current Real-World Example

A young friend of ours started a new job recently and she called to let us know how the 401K plan worked and for some advice as to what she should do. It turns out that the company has a great 401K plan whereby they will match 6 percent of her gross pay, whether she participates in the plan or not, for the first five years of employment. And they will match up to 3 percent of her gross pay for any contributions she makes to the plan, up to 20 percent of gross pay. So, she gets 6 percent of gross pay in company money invested in her 401K by the company, right off the bat. And if she contributes 10 percent of gross income to the plan, the company will match 3 percent of that. The remaining 7 percent she contributes will be an investment (probably in mutual funds) and will be deferred income since it is in a qualified defined contribution plan. Pretty decent retirement!

Note: It is important to limit investments when you have high-interest credit card debt eating up your monthly income, but a 401K is a special circumstance. Take advantage of the opportunity, if you can afford to, while you can. Can you afford not to?

IRA Rollovers

Although you can have a 401K with more than one company, there are limits to the amount you can contribute. In addition, the investment options may be better for one company as compared to another. When you leave a company, it is common to transfer (roll over) your 401K to another qualified (tax-deferred) plan, usually an IRA of some type. This gives you more flexibility for investment options. Also, some companies require you to roll over your 401K if you leave.

Individual Retirement Accounts (IRAs)

An IRA is similar to a 401K and is a "tax-advantaged" bucket into which you can put many different types of investments, such as cash, CDs, stock mutual funds, and even precious metals (like gold). If you do not have a 401K or 403B option available through your employer, you can open and contribute to an IRA. Even if you do have one available, you may still be able to contribute to an IRA. There are four basic types of IRAs: Traditional, Roth, SEP, and SIMPLE. All IRAs offer a tax-deferred growth of your investment dollars. With traditional IRAs, you can deduct the money you put into the account from your taxable income for a given tax year. The amount you can contribute is limited, based on your income and other plans you may be contributing to. Although the amount put into an IRA can be deducted from your current taxable income (deferred), it is taxed as ordinary income when you do take it out, and any gains (profits) are also taxed. Another benefit of a traditional IRA is that you can add money to it until April 15 and reduce your taxable income for the previous year. In other words, you could contribute $5,000 to your IRA on April 14th of 2022 and apply it to your 2021 income.

With a traditional IRA, you can begin withdrawing money as early as age 59½, at which time your contributions and any gains are taxed at your current rate, as ordinary income. If you take money out early (before 59½), you will also pay a penalty of 10 percent. When you reach age seventy-two, you are required to start taking distributions or you may have to pay an additional penalty of 50 percent of the shortfall. For example, if your annual required minimum distribution (RMD) is $10,000 and you take only $8,000, your shortfall is $2,000 and, at 50 percent, your penalty is $1,000. Work with your financial advisor to ensure that you are taking proper RMDs from your IRAs and other affected accounts. More information on RMDs is available from the IRS at:

https://www.irs.gov/retirement-plans/retirement-plan-and-ira-required-minimum-distributions-faqs

Note on Social Security Retirement Age

As of this writing, you can start taking Social Security benefits as early as age 62, but you won't receive full benefits until you reach full retirement age. Social Security currently defines full retirement as age 66 or 67, depending on when you were born. If you delay taking your benefits from your full retirement age up to age 70, your benefit amount will increase. As time goes on, full retirement age changes, depending on when you were born. Retirement age and how much you will receive is based on governmental decisions regarding Social Security and its future. So, it's kind of a moving target.

More on Qualified Retirement Plans

Roth IRAs

A Roth IRA is another type of tax-advantaged bucket into which you can put various types of investments. It is a tax-free retirement account that is usually invested in stocks but can be other forms of investment. You contribute to a Roth with after-tax dollars. You contribute to a Traditional IRA with pre-tax dollars, which are tax deferred. Roth contributions are not tax deferred. You do not get a tax deduction for the money contributed because it is assumed you have already paid tax on the income you are contributing. However, you do not pay tax on withdrawals, as you would with a traditional IRA, assuming you meet the minimum holding period. The amount put into a Roth IRA can grow over time, and neither the contributions nor gains are taxed when you take it out. With a little luck and some good investments, a Roth IRA can outperform other types of investments because the gains can grow substantially, and still not be taxed when withdrawn. Many people have both a Roth IRA and a traditional IRA. The amount you can contribute to either type of IRA per year is limited by the IRS and is based on your age and income. With a Roth, although there is no deduction for contributions up front, contributions can grow tax free with no tax on withdrawals, regardless of how much gains there are. Also, there is no penalty if you do not take distributions at age seventy, as with the traditional IRA. Some employers now offer a Roth 401K option. Many people have both a traditional IRA and a 401K (see below). However, if you or your spouse has a 401K savings plan at work, the amount you can contribute tax deferred to an IRA may be reduced, if you file jointly. If your and/or your spouse's Modified Adjusted Gross Income (MAGI) is above a certain level, IRA contributions may not be tax deductible. You can still contribute to the IRA, but the contributions will not be tax deferred.

SEP IRAs

A Simplified Employee Pension Individual Retirement Arrangement (SEP IRA) is a type of IRA for sole proprietors, self-employed people, and business owners. A person can open a SEP IRA to provide retirement benefits for themselves and their employees. The owner and employees can contribute tax-deferred dollars to a SEP IRA. As with traditional IRAs, they can deduct the money they put into the account from their taxable income for a given tax year. The amount you can contribute is limited based on your income and other plans you may be contributing to. Although the amount put into an IRA can be deducted from your current taxable income, it is taxed as ordinary income when you do take it out (usually at retirement age), and any gains (profits) are also taxed.

Defined Benefit Qualified Retirement Plans - Pensions

A pension is a qualified tax-deferred defined benefit plan, as opposed to a 401K defined contribution plan. Pensions are retirement accounts primarily for public employees (teachers, firefighters, police, etc.) as well as private companies. They may be invested in a fixed annuity or other form of investment. In the past, they were widely available to employees of private organizations. My wife and I both draw a pension from a company we previously worked for. With a defined benefit pension plan, the employee contributes to the account over time, as does the employer. Upon retirement, the employee receives a monthly check based on their salary and years of service. Pensions are still available to employees of some private companies, but their use is declining in favor of defined contribution plans like 401Ks (private sector) and 403Bs (public-sector). Pensions put more of the investment responsibility on the employer, whereas 401Ks and 403Bs put more of the responsibility on the employee to oversee their own plan. Plans like the 401K allow the employee to determine how much to contribute and into which investments. If you have a pension in combination with a balanced financial portfolio, it can go a long way toward helping you to achieve a more comfortable retirement. However, it is a good idea to have some type of self-funded IRA as a backup, if you are eligible and have the money. With pensions, when you retire you can receive a pension for life, based on the stability of the company that you worked for, and fund performance. With the 401K, the amount you've invested over the years is a limited amount, and you can run out of money. Of course, this depends on how much you invested, how much those investments have grown, and how much you take in distributions at retirement.

Annuities Overview

Annuities are a special type of investment/retirement account that are offered by many insurance companies, either directly or through banks and brokers. They are insurance contracts, although they are not insurance policies. As such, they can have "riders" attached to the contract that alter the terms of the annuity and can be tailored to the needs of the client. The primary goal of an annuity is to provide a regular income stream in retirement for the "annuitant's" lifespan.

Annuities can have many variables and implications regarding investment security, risk, return, cost, payout, fees, operating expenses, and early withdrawal penalties. It is not the intent of this book to go into all the various types of annuities. There are several ways annuities can be classified or grouped. The more common ones are by interest rate as "Fixed," "Variable," or Fixed-indexed and by payout method as "Deferred" or "Immediate." There are many annuities invested in diversified stock-based funds that perform very well. My wife and I have variable deferred annuities that have done well over the years. Annuities can be a valuable tool in the mix of investments in your portfolio. There are three main types of annuities: fixed annuities, fixed-indexed annuities, and variable annuities. Variable annuities can be immediate or deferred. The immediate and deferred classifications indicate when you will begin receiving your annuity payments. Understanding your financial goals is critical in deciding the best type of annuity for your situation.

Annuity Terminology

The following terminology is useful in describing the characteristics of various types of annuities.

Annuity Contract Plan Types:
- **Individual Retirement Annuity (IRA)** - Deferred variable annuity that is invested in various securities. Provides an income stream. You start receiving annuity payments at a future date. Contributions and gains are taxed at retirement.
- **Roth IRA** - Deferred variable annuity that is invested in various securities. Provides an income stream. You start receiving annuity payments at a future date. Contributions and gains are not taxed at retirement.
- **Non-qualified** - Variable annuity that is invested in various securities. Provides an income stream. Not tax advantaged.

Payout Method:
- **Immediate** - Provides an income stream. Annuitant begins receiving payments after funding the annuity. Oriented toward people at or nearing retirement. Also referred to as an Income annuity.
- **Deferred** - You start receiving annuity payments at a future date, usually after funding the annuity during an accumulation period. Payments funding the annuity and gains can be tax deferred and taxed at distribution.

Payout time:
- **Lifetime** - Guarantees an income stream for the rest of the annuitant's life or a set period.
- **Fixed-period** - Payments are over a fixed period, usually twenty or thirty years.

Interest Rate:
- **Fixed** - You receive a set interest rate on annuity funds and set payments based on annuity contract.
- **Variable** - You receive varying interest and payments based on the performance of underlying annuity investments (mostly securities).
- **Fixed-indexed (equity-indexed)** - Payouts from fixed-index annuities are based on a market index, like the S&P 500 or Nasdaq. May have a capital/growth preservation option for investments.

Phase:
- **Accumulation** - Buildup of the annuitant's funds in preparation for the payout phase (lump sum for immediate payout annuities, periodic investment with deferred annuities).
- **Payout (Annuitization)** - Distribution of annuity payments to the annuitant.

Note: To see if an annuity or a particular type of annuity is right for you and for more information on annuity types, advantages, disadvantages, and tax implications, talk with your financial advisor.

Annuity Calculator (Accumulation/Payout Phase)
Just as there are home loan calculators, auto loan calculators, ROI calculators, and retirement calculators, there are annuity calculators available, many of which are free. There are frequently two calculators-in-one or two separate calculators from a given online source. One calculator is for the annuity "accumulation"

phase, and one for the annuity "payout" phase. Do a search for "free online annuity calculators" to see what's available, and experiment by inputting various contribution amounts, payout amounts, years to receive payouts, and interest rates.

Part 3: Insurance for a Secure Retirement

The discussion of insurance in this chapter deals primarily with retirement and preparation for it. Refer to Chapter 16: Insurance and Risk Management, for a more comprehensive view of the various types of insurance available. Each of the major types of insurance is explained and PFS sheet Insurance Policy Info standard entries are described in Chapter 16.

In addition to financial services, a financial advisor may be able to make recommendations for some types of insurance or direct you to a specialist who can provide cost-effective services to help you choose. These can include life insurance, umbrella insurance, long-term care insurance, and health insurance. These types of insurance can help protect your investments. When doing retirement planning, failure to buy adequate insurance to protect your nest egg can result in rapid depletion of your retirement dollars.

Health Insurance and HSAs

Health insurance is as important, if not more so, than any other type of insurance in helping to protect you and your retirement nest egg. However, it is a complicated subject, and private health insurance and Medicare are beyond the scope of this book. There are many people making a living these days by helping other people sort through the options available and selecting a plan that can be cost effective. Visit https://www.healthcare.gov if you or someone you know is having difficulty obtaining health care.

If you are still working and are covered by an employer-sponsored health plan, good for you. Depending on your employment status, you may also be able to participate in a tax-advantaged plan such as a Healthcare Savings Account (HSA) or Flexible Spending Account (FSA). These are discussed briefly in Chapter 13: Investment Basics, and Chapter 15: Income Tax Basics.

If you are sixty-five or older, you can use Medicare for your health and prescription needs. You must register with Medicare before you turn sixty-five. Your financial advisor can help you find a knowledgeable professional who can help you select healthcare providers and plans that work with Medicare. Medicare is managed by the Centers for Medicare and Medicaid Services (CMS). Social Security works with CMS by enrolling people in Medicare when they reach age sixty-five. Go to their Websites for more information:
https://www.ssa.gov/medicare
https://www.medicare.gov

Life Insurance

The main purpose of life insurance is to provide replacement income for your family should you (or your spouse) meet an untimely demise. This is especially true for young people who have a family and a home, and even more so if the spouse is not employed. If you are working and your employer provides life insurance, that's a nice benefit. However, the amount of insurance may be less than you need, and if you leave the company, you may lose your insurance, unless you can take it with you. If your employer provides life insurance, you may still need a supplemental policy. If not, you will need a primary portable policy.

If you are an empty-nester and/or nearing retirement, consider not carrying life insurance. Do you have anyone that depends on your income? If not, you may be able to save the cost of the premium and improve your cash flow if you cancel the policy. If the policy is a Whole Life or Universal Life, it should have a cash value. If you have had the policy long enough, you may be entitled to some of the cash value, minus fees and penalties. If you are retired or retiring soon and have an existing policy, talk to your financial advisor and consider canceling it to eliminate the premium and reduce monthly outgo. Retirees typically do not have to worry about income replacement as do younger workers. By the same token, it does not make a lot of sense to buy life insurance for children, although some parents and grandparents do. The child has no income to replace or family to support, so there is really no compelling reason to buy life insurance for them. Additional details about life insurance are covered in Chapter 16: Insurance and Risk Management.

Note: Be sure to discuss the ramifications of any changes to insurance policies with your financial advisor and insurance advisor. Also refer to PFS sheet Insure-Pols for additional insurance-related information.

Umbrella Insurance

Many financial advisors recommend that homeowners have an "Umbrella" policy in addition to homeowner's insurance. An umbrella policy with $1,000,000 of coverage is typical. This type of policy protects you against major claims related to your home or auto, such as lawsuits for damages including defamation, slander and libel. With an umbrella policy you can be covered for up to $1,000,000 in damages. Without the policy, you may be liable and may have to liquidate your assets to pay the damages. The premium for an umbrella policy is generally paid separate from your house payment. It is usually a small amount considering it can provide peace of mind and might save you hundreds of thousands of dollars. The premium amount is based on your home and the vehicles you have.

Long-Term Care Insurance

Long-Term Care (LTC) is the single most important type of insurance to help protect your nest egg. If you are unable to care for yourself, this insurance will pay some or all the costs of living in an assisted living facility or nursing home. The cost for staying in one of these facilities can be VERY expensive and can deplete your retirement nest egg rapidly. The premium for an LTC policy is usually a small amount, considering what it covers. As with life insurance, the earlier you buy it, the less expensive it will be.

Long-Term Disability Insurance

Long-term disability is worthwhile for anyone who depends on their earned income. If you become disabled by injury or illness, this insurance pays about 60 percent of your salary, excluding commissions and bonuses, until you recover or reach the age of sixty-five. This insurance is often provided to an employee by their employer at little or no cost.

Part 4: Estate Planning and Estate Documents

Estate Planning

Estate planning deals with issues related to your assets and your heirs, including wills, trusts, and tax issues. Estate planning can be complicated and is beyond the scope of this book. However, we will provide some basic information here. Your financial advisor should be able to help or recommend someone who specializes in this area based on your financial situation.

Essential Estate Planning Documents

Everyone should have at least a basic last will and testament or "will" that has been notarized and stored in a safe place, such as a safe deposit box at a bank.

Important Note for People that Use a Bank Safe Deposit Box

Make sure your heirs know where the bank safe deposit box is (bank and branch address), and where the keys to it are kept. Also, anyone you want to have access to the safe deposit box must be listed on the signature card along with your signature and that of your spouse, or they will not be able to get into the box to retrieve your notarized will and other estate documents, even if they have the key. For example, you and your spouse may have to go to the bank with your daughter or son to record all three signatures.

Powers of Attorney (POA)

For most people with simple finances and minimal likelihood of family members contesting, a simple will can probably suffice. For people with multiple homes, more complex finances, and high net worth, a living trust, drawn up by an attorney, may make more sense. In addition to a will, you should also have a Financial Power of Attorney (POA) or Durable POA, and a Health Care POA (with directives). Note: The POAs are equally as important as the will since they determine who can conduct your affairs, regarding your health finances, if you are not able to.

DIY Will Software

There are several will-making software packages available for a cost, such as Quicken WillMaker, and there are some free ones online that are pretty good. Using one of these packages, you can create wills and powers of attorney for yourself and spouse by simply answering a few questions. For example, Quicken WillMaker allows you to create the following estate planning documents for you and your spouse. You can use this as a checklist and also talk with an attorney or other knowledgeable estate planning person.

- **Last Will and Testament**
- **Health Care Directive (Living Will and POA)**
- **Durable POA for Finances**
- **Final Arrangements**
- **Information for Caregivers and Survivors**
- **Living Trust**

Hire an Estate Lawyer?

For many people, a simple will and other estate-related documents created using Do-It-Yourself (DIY) software may suffice. However, as with other services such as a CPA for tax advice/preparation or CFP for financial planning, it may be prudent to hire a licensed professional. For more complex estates you may want to enlist the services of an attorney that specializes in estate planning issues such as wills and probate documents as well as DPOA, HPOA, etc. An attorney obviously costs more than DIY, but if you can afford it, it could be money well spent. This is especially true if there is strife among family members and heirs and there could be a contested will and probate involved. Hiring an attorney may cost more in the short run, but you can end up with a more tailored set of documents that can better meet your needs and the needs of your family, as well as saving money in the long run. In addition, a good lawyer can provide some peace of mind and reduce the burden on your heirs. Recently, my wife and I had to deal with the unexpected passing of a family member who did not have a will. I was the designated estate administrator, and we enlisted the help of an estate attorney to help us get through it. My sanity is still intact (more or less) and dealing with the courts and lack of a will would have been much more difficult without his help. We have moved on from that stressful period and have since hired this attorney to develop a new set of wills and other estate planning documents for us. They store digital copies, which makes it easier to make changes to the documents and distribute them.

Reverse Mortgage (Home Equity Conversion Mortgage (HECM)

The following is an excerpt from the U.S. Department of Housing and Urban Development Website: https://www.hud.gov/program_offices/housing/sfh/hecm/hecmhome

< Begin Excerpt: HUD Home Equity Conversion Mortgage (HECM) Website >

Reverse mortgages are increasing in popularity with seniors who have equity in their homes and want to supplement their income. The only reverse mortgage insured by the U.S. Federal Government is called a Home Equity Conversion Mortgage (HECM) and is only available through an FHA-approved lender. The HECM is FHA's reverse mortgage program that enables you to withdraw a portion of your home's equity. The amount that will be available for withdrawal varies by borrower and depends on age, interest rate and appraisal.

< End Excerpt: HUD Home Equity Conversion Mortgage (HECM) Website >

This is a complex subject, but here it is in a nutshell. The "Reverse Mortgage" is an estate (home) option for people 62 and older, that own or have substantial equity in their home, and wish to turn it into a regular income stream. In general, the goal of a reverse mortgage is to allow the homeowner to stay in their home for the rest of their life. There is a loan against the property that provides the retiree a set income per month that is non-taxable, and that becomes due when they sell, move out or pass away. While the borrower is in the home, and receiving monthly payments, interest is added to the loan balance. The interest is tax deductible but not until the loan is paid off.

The FHA typically insures the reverse mortgage so, you have a federally backed mortgage, if you follow the FHA guidelines and meet the requirements for the Home Equity Conversion Mortgage (HECM). If you cannot take advantage of the FHA HEMC program, you may have to go with a proprietary lender. From an estate perspective, the borrower's heirs have some options in dealing with the home and the loan against it. Based on the excerpt above from HUD above, the HEMC version of the reverse mortgage is becoming increasingly popular, and it may be appropriate for some retirees. If you think you may be a good candidate for a reverse mortgage, talk with your financial advisor and get in touch with a HUD counselor that can advise you on reverse mortgages at their Website:

> https://answers.hud.gov/housingcounseling/

Additional information on reverse mortgages can be obtained from the FTC Website:

> https://consumer.ftc.gov/articles/reverse-mortgages

Retirement, Investments, Insurance, and Estates – Summary Notes and Tips

Retirement and General Investments

- Keep a positive outlook on money and its importance in your life.
- Hire a Certified Financial Planner to help identify your investment/retirement goals and options and develop a strategy.
- Start saving and investing early.
- Read a basic retirement guide to increase your knowledge. There are many, including **Retirement for Dummies** (check with your local library).
- Pay yourself first. Set aside 10 percent of your gross income until you retire. You will never miss it.
- Contribute to a 401K and/or IRA/Roth regularly and often.
- Invest in a 401K or other tax advantaged account using dollar-cost averaging.
- Max out your tax-deferred and tax-free options (401K, IRAs, etc.), especially those with an employer match.
- Build your own retirement nest egg first. Contribute to college for your heirs, if you choose, second.
- Consider adding to a 401K/403B/IRA instead of paying off your mortgage.
- Consider an Immediate Payout Annuity to provide steady income.

- If considering a reverse mortgage, be sure to work with an FHA-approved lender.

Retirement and General Insurance

- Buy umbrella insurance to protect your estate and finances against major liability.
- If you are still working and have a spouse or dependents, buy term life insurance to protect your family from loss of income.
- Some types of non-term life insurance (like "whole life") have a cash value if you cancel the policy after a certain period.
- When comparing types of life insurance and premiums, the saying goes "buy term and invest the rest."
- The earlier you buy life insurance, the less expensive it will be.
- When buying life insurance for children, there is typically no income to replace.
- Buy Comprehensive Long-Term Care (LTC) insurance to protect your nest egg.

Retirement and Estate Planning

- Create a will and other estate planning documents as listed in the chapter.
- Be sure your heirs know about your will, your finances and other estate documents.
- Keep your will and other estate planning documents in a safe deposit box and let family members know where it is and where you keep the keys to it.
- Be sure to add signatures to the safe deposit box card for those you want to have access to it.
- Live a happy and comfortable life in retirement that your retirement income affords. You do not have to save your retirement for your heirs' inheritance. Live your retirement years to their fullest!

Figure 14-2: Retirement Options Cartoon - Bill Abbott

"I've crunched the numbers in your
retirement account. It's time to figure out
who will be wearing the mask and who
will be driving the getaway car."

Chapter 14 Exercise

Exercise 14-1: Compare Retirement Calculators

Do a Web search for "online retirement calculator," and select one that meets your needs. There are a number of retirement calculators available that you can use to play with the numbers and do what-if scenarios. One such calculator is from BankRate.com: https://www.bankrate.com/retirement/retirement-calculator

Here is an example of the entries that the BankRate calculator uses. Make a copy of Table 14-1 to record your findings and notes.

- Annual income required: **40,000**
- Number of years until retirement: **10**
- Number of years required after retirement: **25**
- Annual Inflation: **0**
- Annual Yield on Balance (average): **7.5**
- Amount needed when you wish to retire: **Appx $480,000**

Table 14-1: Retirement Calculator Comparison

Comparison Criteria	Calculator #1	Calculator #2	Calculator #3
Name / Source:			

Chapter 15
Income Tax Basics

Chapter Overview:

This chapter is an overview of U.S. taxes in general and focuses on the highlights of personal income tax for working people and retirees. Complex tax code, business issues, and state tax are beyond the scope of this book. The chapter deals primarily with personal federal income taxes and starts by explaining the basic IRS Form 1040 and its key elements. There is a focus on terminology and some straightforward legitimate ways to reduce your tax burden. The chapter also provides an overview of tax preparation software and services, as well as some tax tips. Other types of taxes—such as property tax, estate tax, and sales tax—are also discussed briefly in this chapter. The chapter is divided into six parts:

- **Part 1: Income Tax Form 1040 - Information and Terminology**
- **Part 2: Calculating Income Tax Using the IRS Tax Brackets**
- **Part 3: Calculating Income Tax - Filing Status and Deductions**
- **Part 4: Tax Preparation Options and Services**
- **Part 5: Tax-Advantaged Plans and Options**
- **Part 6: Other Taxes**

Chapter PFS Integration:

The **PFS** components in this chapter that relate to taxes may be found on **Sheet - Home Info and Maintenance** (Tab **Home-Info**) and consist mainly of property taxes.

Chapter Exercise:

- **Exercise 15-1: Calculate Income Tax and Effective Tax Rate**

    In this exercise, you will determine taxable income and taxes owed using your own 1040 form from last year and the standard deduction. If you do not have last year's form, use the sample data provided. Using the IRS tax brackets you will determine your marginal bracket and then calculate your taxes owed and effective tax rate.

Chapter Notable Quote:

Quote 15-1: "The hardest thing in the world to understand is the income tax." - Albert Einstein

If Albert Einstein, the developer of the theory of relativity, thinks the income tax code is hard to understand, then that really says something! Perhaps this chapter will help a bit.

Part 1: Income Tax Form 1040 - Information and Terminology

Graduated System

The U.S. income tax is a graduated system where the more you make, the higher tax percentage you pay up, to a limit. Your tax increases based on the bracket you fall into. So, if your adjusted gross income (AGI or taxable income) is at a certain level, that dictates the bracket you are in and the taxes you pay. A common misconception is that if you are in, let's say, the 5th marginal bracket at 32 percent, you pay 32percent of your AGI in taxes, but that is not the case. You pay less tax on the first dollars you make and more tax on the last dollars, so it is an average, and your effective tax rate may actually end up being 28 percent. Refer to **Exercise 15-1: Calculate Income Tax and Effective Tax Rate** in Part 2 of this chapter, which takes you through the brackets and necessary calculations.

Income Tax Form 1040

The 1040 has many pieces of data or information, such as your last name and wages. Tax calculation fields on the 1040 all have a "location identifier" or line number. The non-number fields do not. In this chapter we will refer to the fields on the 1040 as 1040L99, where 99 is the line number (or location identifier) on the 1040 form. But what fields on the 1040 are most important for an overall understanding of personal income tax? For the purposes of this chapter, we will limit our discussion of income tax mostly to key fields on Page 1 of the 1040 and a few fields on Page 2. Page 1 focuses on personal information and income sources, as well as deductions. Page 2 focuses on the taxes you have already paid for the year and either tax owed or tax refund due (if you overpaid). As an example, Field 1040L12b refers to the charitable contributions data field form 1040, Page 1. Field 1040L25a refers to the federal income tax withheld from your W2. Refer to Table 15-1 for descriptions and examples of the other income-related fields on Form 1040, Page 1. For a simple single filer, the most important lines/fields in Figure 15-1 are 1040L1, 1040L12a, and 1040L15. Look them up on Figure 15-1 and Table 15-1 to see what data they contain. Lines 35a and 37 on 1040 Page 2 are also important. Refer to Figure 15-2 and Table 15-2 to see what data they contain as well. To begin with, obtain a copy of your most recent federal tax return 1040 form (Pages 1 and 2), and refer to it as you review the explanations of the various income and tax-related terms shown in Tables 15-1 (1040 Page 1 fields) and 15-2 (1040 Page 2 fields). After you have reviewed the terminology and definitions, you will calculate your effective tax rate based on your income and tax bracket. A sample blank 1040 form (Pages 1 and 2) is provided here for reference.

Note: If you do not have access to last year's 1040, refer to the blank forms provided here. Blank copies of IRS Form 1040, Pages 1 and 2, are available at irs.gov/forms. Instructions for filling these forms can also be found there.

Table 15-1: IRS Form 1040 Page 1 - Income-Related Fields

(Page 1, Items 1-15)

Loc.	Income Field Name	Notes / Examples
1	**Earned income**	W2 wages, salaries, tips (Ordinary income)
2a	**Tax-exempt interest**	
3a	**Qualified dividends** (from stocks)	
4a	**IRA distributions**	
5a	**Pensions and annuities**	
6a	**Social Security benefits**	
7	**Capital gain or loss**	
2b	**Taxable Interest**	
3b	**Ordinary dividends**	
4b-6b	**Taxable amount(s) from 4a-6a**	
8	**Other income**	
9	**Total Income** (Add Lines 1+2b+3b+4b+5b+6b+7+8)	
10	**Adjustments to income**	
11	**Adjusted Gross Income** (Line 9 minus Line 10)	AGI
12a	**Standard deduction or**	From Form 1040 or Table 15-5
	Itemized deduction	From Schedule A or Form 1040
12b	**Charitable contributions** (if you take standard deduction)	Applicable 2020 & 2021 only. Max deduction $300/individual and $600/couple
12c	Add Lines 12a and 12b	
13	**Qualified business income deductions**	From Form 8995
14	Add Lines 12c and 13	
15	**Taxable Income** (subtract Line 14 from Line 11)	

Figure 15-1: IRS Form 1040 Page 1 – Income-Related Entries

Form **1040**   Department of the Treasury—Internal Revenue Service
U.S. Individual Income Tax Return   2022   OMB No. 1545-0074   IRS Use Only—Do not write or staple in this space.

Filing Status
Check only one box.

☐ Single ☐ Married filing jointly ☐ Married filing separately (MFS) ☐ Head of household (HOH) ☐ Qualifying surviving spouse (QSS)

If you checked the MFS box, enter the name of your spouse. If you checked the HOH or QSS box, enter the child's name if the qualifying person is a child but not your dependent.

Your first name and middle initial	Last name		Your social security number

If joint return, spouse's first name and middle initial	Last name		Spouse's social security number

Home address (number and street). If you have a P.O. box, see instructions.		Apt. no.	**Presidential Election Campaign**
City, town, or post office. If you have a foreign address, also complete spaces below.	State	ZIP code	Check here if you, or your spouse if filing jointly, want $3 to go to this fund. Checking a box below will not change your tax or refund.
Foreign country name	Foreign province/state/county	Foreign postal code	☐ You ☐ Spouse

Digital Assets At any time during 2022, did you: (a) receive (as a reward, award, or payment for property or services); or (b) sell, exchange, gift, or otherwise dispose of a digital asset (or a financial interest in a digital asset)? (See instructions.) ☐ Yes ☐ No

Standard Deduction Someone can claim: ☐ You as a dependent ☐ Your spouse as a dependent
☐ Spouse itemizes on a separate return or you were a dual-status alien

Age/Blindness You: ☐ Were born before January 2, 1958 ☐ Are blind Spouse: ☐ Was born before January 2, 1958 ☐ Is blind

Dependents (see instructions):
If more than four dependents, see instructions and check here . . ☐

(1) First name Last name	(2) Social security number	(3) Relationship to you	(4) Check the box if qualifies for (see instructions):	
			Child tax credit	Credit for other dependents
			☐	☐
			☐	☐
			☐	☐
			☐	☐

Income

Attach Form(s) W-2 here. Also attach Forms W-2G and 1099-R if tax was withheld.

If you did not get a Form W-2, see instructions.

Attach Sch. B if required.

Standard Deduction for—
• Single or Married filing separately, $12,950
• Married filing jointly or Qualifying surviving spouse, $25,900
• Head of household, $19,400
• If you checked any box under Standard Deduction, see instructions.

1a	Total amount from Form(s) W-2, box 1 (see instructions)	1a	
b	Household employee wages not reported on Form(s) W-2	1b	
c	Tip income not reported on line 1a (see instructions)	1c	
d	Medicaid waiver payments not reported on Form(s) W-2 (see instructions)	1d	
e	Taxable dependent care benefits from Form 2441, line 26	1e	
f	Employer-provided adoption benefits from Form 8839, line 29	1f	
g	Wages from Form 8919, line 6	1g	
h	Other earned income (see instructions)	1h	
i	Nontaxable combat pay election (see instructions) . . . 1i		
z	Add lines 1a through 1h	1z	
2a	Tax-exempt interest . . . 2a	b Taxable interest	2b	
3a	Qualified dividends . . . 3a	b Ordinary dividends	3b	
4a	IRA distributions 4a	b Taxable amount .	4b	
5a	Pensions and annuities . . 5a	b Taxable amount .	5b	
6a	Social security benefits . . 6a	b Taxable amount .	6b	
c	If you elect to use the lump-sum election method, check here (see instructions) . . . ☐		
7	Capital gain or (loss). Attach Schedule D if required. If not required, check here . . . ☐	7	
8	Other income from Schedule 1, line 10	8	
9	Add lines 1z, 2b, 3b, 4b, 5b, 6b, 7, and 8. This is your **total income**	9	
10	Adjustments to income from Schedule 1, line 26	10	
11	Subtract line 10 from line 9. This is your **adjusted gross income**	11	
12	**Standard deduction or itemized deductions** (from Schedule A)	12	
13	Qualified business income deduction from Form 8995 or Form 8995-A	13	
14	Add lines 12 and 13	14	
15	Subtract line 14 from line 11. If zero or less, enter -0-. This is your **taxable income**	15	

For Disclosure, Privacy Act, and Paperwork Reduction Act Notice, see separate instructions.   Cat. No. 11320B   Form **1040** (2022)

Table 15-2: IRS Form 1040 Page 2 - Taxation-Related Fields
(Page 2, Items 16-38)

Loc./Section	Taxation Type / Source	Description / Examples	Notes
16	Tax		
24	Total Tax		
25a	Federal income tax withheld from: Form(s) W2	Tax deducted from paycheck for W2 employees	
25b	Federal income tax withheld from: Form(s) 1099		
26	Est. tax payments & amts applied from 2020 return	Estimated tax from 1099 employees	
33	Total Payments		
Refund	Direct deposit?	For Electronic filing	
34	Overpaid		
35a	Refunded to you		
35b	Routing number	Account routing number	
35c	Account type	Checking or Savings	
35d	Account number	Account number	
36	Applied to 2022 tax		
Amount You Owe			
37			
38	Estimated tax penalty		
Third Party Designee	Any person designated as IRS interface	Often the tax preparer	
Sign here	Your signature		
Paid Preparer Use Only	Preparer information	Tax preparer name	

Figure 15-2: IRS Form 1040 Page 2 – Taxation-Related Entries

Form 1040 (2022)   Page **2**

Tax and Credits	16	**Tax** (see instructions). Check if any from Form(s): 1 ☐ 8814 2 ☐ 4972 3 ☐ _____	16
	17	Amount from Schedule 2, line 3	17
	18	Add lines 16 and 17	18
	19	Child tax credit or credit for other dependents from Schedule 8812	19
	20	Amount from Schedule 3, line 8	20
	21	Add lines 19 and 20	21
	22	Subtract line 21 from line 18. If zero or less, enter -0-	22
	23	Other taxes, including self-employment tax, from Schedule 2, line 21	23
	24	Add lines 22 and 23. This is your **total tax**	24
Payments	25	Federal income tax withheld from:	
	a	Form(s) W-2	25a
	b	Form(s) 1099	25b
	c	Other forms (see instructions)	25c
	d	Add lines 25a through 25c	25d
If you have a qualifying child, attach Sch. EIC.	26	2022 estimated tax payments and amount applied from 2021 return	26
	27	Earned income credit (EIC)	27
	28	Additional child tax credit from Schedule 8812	28
	29	American opportunity credit from Form 8863, line 8	29
	30	Reserved for future use	30
	31	Amount from Schedule 3, line 15	31
	32	Add lines 27, 28, 29, and 31. These are your total **other payments and refundable credits**	32
	33	Add lines 25d, 26, and 32. These are your **total payments**	33
Refund	34	If line 33 is more than line 24, subtract line 24 from line 33. This is the amount you **overpaid**	34
	35a	Amount of line 34 you want **refunded to you**. If Form 8888 is attached, check here ☐	35a
Direct deposit? See instructions.	b	Routing number ⬚⬚⬚⬚⬚⬚⬚⬚⬚ c Type: ☐ Checking ☐ Savings	
	d	Account number ⬚⬚⬚⬚⬚⬚⬚⬚⬚⬚	
	36	Amount of line 34 you want **applied to your 2023 estimated tax**	36
Amount You Owe	37	Subtract line 33 from line 24. This is the **amount you owe.** For details on how to pay, go to *www.irs.gov/Payments* or see instructions	37
	38	Estimated tax penalty (see instructions)	38

Third Party Designee

Do you want to allow another person to discuss this return with the IRS? See instructions . . .   ☐ **Yes.** Complete below.   ☐ **No**

Designee's name	Phone no.	Personal identification number (PIN)

Sign Here

Under penalties of perjury, I declare that I have examined this return and accompanying schedules and statements, and to the best of my knowledge and belief, they are true, correct, and complete. Declaration of preparer (other than taxpayer) is based on all information of which preparer has any knowledge.

Joint return? See instructions. Keep a copy for your records.

Your signature	Date	Your occupation	If the IRS sent you an Identity Protection PIN, enter it here (see inst.)
Spouse's signature. If a joint return, **both** must sign.	Date	Spouse's occupation	If the IRS sent your spouse an Identity Protection PIN, enter it here (see inst.)
Phone no.		Email address	

Paid Preparer Use Only

Preparer's name	Preparer's signature	Date	PTIN	Check if: ☐ Self-employed
Firm's name			Phone no.	
Firm's address			Firm's EIN	

Go to *www.irs.gov/Form1040* for instructions and the latest information.   Form **1040** (2022)

Table 15-3 contains many of the important and useful terms to know when discussing income taxes. This list is not intended to be exhaustive, but these terms made our "Top Forty" and are the ones you are more likely to run across. Browse through the table and see how many of the terms you are familiar with. Could you define them? Descriptions and examples are provided for some of the more common terms. For the ones you don't know, do a Web search and fill in some of the blanks and add notes to Table 15-3 or copy of it.

Table 15-3: The Top Forty Tax Terms
(IRS Income and Taxation Terminology)
(Listed Alphabetically)

Tax Terminology	Description / Examples	Notes
Bracket creep		
Capital gains	Profit from sale of item(s) – stock, collectibles	
Capital gains – Long term	More than a year	
Capital gains – Short term	Less than a year	
Child tax credit		
Contract employee		
Dependent		
Effective tax rate		
Estimated Tax payments	1099 Employees: Quarterly payments, Possible penalties if estimated payments are less than actual owed	
Filing status	Single, Joint, Head of household, etc.	
Free lance workers		
Full-time employee		
Inflation		
Interest earned 1099	1099-INT	
Investment Asset Allocation		
Itemized Deduction	Mortgage interest, property tax, medical expenses, charitable contributions	
Marginal tax rate		
Non-Qualified investment	Not Tax deferred – Ex: Sale of stocks	
Part-time	More than/less than 30 hrs/wk	
Post-tax dollars	After tax	
Pre-tax dollars	Before tax	
Qualified investment (plan)	Retirement, Tax advantaged (deferred) plan - IRA, 401K, 403B etc. (HSA??, 509??)	
Regular (W2) Employees		
Self-employed worker	1099-MISC	
Self-employment tax	(Appx 15%) in addition to income tax at whatever tax bracket you are in.	

Standard Deduction	Amount based on filing status (single, Joint)	
Tax advantaged (plan)		
Tax bracket	Or tax rate	
Tax credit	Certain purchases – reduces tax dollar for dollar.	
Tax deduction	Reduces taxable income	
Tax deferred	Pre-tax dollars to qualified investments	
Tax exemption		
Tax loss harvesting		
Tax refund		
Taxable event	e.g., Buy/sell stock	
Taxable income		
Form W2	Wages and withholding	
Form W4	Withholding Certificate	
Form 1040	IRS Income tax form	
Form 1040-EZ	Short form for very simple taxes (Obsolete)	
Form 1098	Mortgage interest paid reported by lender	
Form 1099-MISC	Miscellaneous Non-W2 working income, dividends, interest, and capital gains.	
Form 1099-INT	Interest income form	

Part 2: Calculating Income Tax Using the IRS Tax Brackets

Your IRS Account

If you are a taxpayer and have an IRS username and password, you can go to https://www.irs.gov and log in to your IRS account and see what information is there and what resources are available to you. You can also pay estimated taxes and avoid penalties. If you don't have an account, you can create one. On the IRS Website, you can do all of the following:

- Get your refund status
- Get your tax record
- Find forms and instructions
- File your taxes for free
- Make a payment

IRS Tax Brackets

For 2023, there are seven tax brackets or rates for the U.S., as shown in Table 15-4. Do you know what bracket you are in currently? Some people might say "I'm in the 35 percent bracket" and may think their tax bracket percentage in Table 15-4 is their actual or effective tax rate, when it is actually their marginal tax rate. For most people, their income falls into multiple brackets, so the effective tax rate is more like an average of the brackets percentage. Refer to Table 15-4 for the IRS brackets for 2022 to determine your tax bracket or marginal tax rate, based on your taxable income from 1040-L15. You can then calculate your effective tax rate based on your income and filing status. For example, let's say you are a single filer with $70,000 of adjusted gross income (AGI) and are taking advantage of the generous standard deduction. From this you can determine taxable income and find that you are in the 22 percent bracket (3rd bracket), which is your marginal tax rate. Exercise 15-1 takes you through the tax brackets and rates for a given income level of $60,000 (AGI). So, if you're a single person with an AGI of $60,000, you would pay 10 percent on the 1st $10,275 (Bracket 1); 12 percent on the amount between $1,275 and $41,775 (Bracket 2); and then 22 percent on the amount from $41,775 up to $60,000 (Bracket 3).

Note: Due to the 2017 Tax Cuts and Jobs Act (TCJA), the standard deductions were raised significantly, making it harder to come up with enough itemized deductions to justify itemizing.

Refer to Figure 15-1 field 1040L12a and Table15-5 for the standard deductions (single, married, etc.) associated with each filing status.

Chapter 15 Exercise

Exercise 15-1: Calculate Income Tax and Effective Tax Rate

In this exercise, you will go through the process to determine taxable income, taxes owed, and effective tax rate using the sample data provided. You will then repeat the process by calculating your own taxable income, taxes owed, and effective tax rate using your own 1040 form from last year, the IRS income tax tables, and the standard deduction. If you do not have last year's form, just complete the exercise using the sample data provided. Referring to the IRS tax brackets in Table 15-4, you will determine which marginal bracket you are in, and which lower brackets apply to you based on your taxable income (AGI - Standard Deduction). With taxable income and marginal tax bracket (rate), you can then calculate your taxes owed and effective tax rate.

Note: This example uses $60,000 taxable income, which is the adjusted gross income (AGI) minus the standard deduction (single status). Calculations are approximate and rounded.

Optional: You can substitute your own AGI and standard deduction. See 1040L12a for amount to deduct depending on your filing status.

1. Take your AGI and deduct the standard deduction to get taxable income (Example: $60,000)
2. Income up to the limit for Bracket 1 ($10,275) is taxed at 10 percent = (10,275 x .10 = 1,030)
3. Take the Bracket 2 rate (12 percent) times $31,500 ($41,775 - $10,275) = (31,500 x .12 = 3,780)
4. Income above $41,775 is taxed at Bracket 3 rate (22 percent). (Assumes taxable income $60,000.)
5. Calculate Bracket 3 tax ($60,000 - 41,775 = 18,225) = (18,225 x .22 = 4,010)
6. Add Bracket 1 tax ($1,030) + Bracket 2 tax ($3,780) + Bracket 3 tax ($4,010)
7. Your tax owed: approximately $9,000
8. Your effective tax rate is the tax owed divided by taxable income: 9,000/60,000 = 0.15 or 15 percent

Example Summary:

Taxable income: $60,000
Marginal tax rate: 22 percent
Actual tax owed: Appx $9,000
Effective tax rate: Appx 15 percent

Table 15-4: IRS Tax Brackets/Rates (2023)
(https://taxfoundation.org/2023-tax-brackets/)

Tax Rate/Bracket	Single Filer	Married Filing Jointly	Head of Household
10%	$0-to-$11,000	$0-to-$22,000	$0-to-$15,700
12%	$11,000-to-$44,725	$22,000-to-$89,450	$15,700-to-$59,850
22%	$44,725-to-$95,375	$89,450-to-$190,750	$59,850-to-$95,350
24%	$95,375-to-$182,100	$190,750-to-$364,200	$95,350-to-$182,100
32%	$182,100-to-$231,250	$364,200-to-$462,500	$182,100-to-$231,250
35%	$231,250-to-$578,125	$462,500-to-$693,750	$231,250-to-$578,100
37%	$578,125 or more	$693,750 or more	$578,100 or more

(Source: Internal Revenue Service)

321

Part 3: Calculating Income Tax - Filing Status and Deductions

Table 15-5: Standard Deductions Based on Filing Status
(Refer to 1040 12a Text Box for Amount)

Filing Status	Amount	Notes
Single	$12,550	
Married filing jointly (MFJ)	$25,100	
Married filing separately (MFS)	$12,550	
Head of Household (HOH)	$18,800	
Qualifying widow(er) (QW)	$25,100	

Tax Refunds and Withholding

If you receive a large refund or if you owe a lot of tax at the end of the year, you should review your withholding and possibly make some changes. IRS Form W4 is used to tell your employer how much tax to withhold from your paycheck. The goal with income tax is to have an amount withheld that matches the amount you owe at that end of the year. Having more withheld so you can get a big refund is not financially sound. It may feel good to get a big check from the IRS, but you have effectively loaned the federal government money at zero interest. If you receive a $1,000 refund, you could have put that money into savings or an investment account and made a return. On the other hand, if you have too little withheld, the IRS may charge a penalty and/or require you to make estimated tax payments quarterly during the next tax year. A link is provided here to an online withholding estimator from the IRS. https://www.irs.gov/individuals/tax-withholding-estimator

Part 4: Tax Preparation Options and Services

Tax Preparation Chains

There are a number of tax preparation services available, and many people have used them over the years. H&R Block and Jackson-Hewitt are a couple of the better-known ones. They fill a niche and can process most straightforward returns. They have a staff of trained tax preparers with varying degrees of experience. Most of these services provide an early refund option whereby you receive a portion of your refund as an advance loan based on the amount of your expected refund. You could e-file your return and possibly get your refund in ten days (but maybe not).

Tax Accountant Professional

As with other professionals (CFP, estate attorney), employing a CPA or other accounting professional that specializes in taxes can be beneficial to your bottom line. The cost of having a CPA do your taxes can be comparable to the cost of a chain tax preparation service and may save you money as well as reduce the chances of being audited.

DIY Tax Prep Software – Apps and Online

These do-it-yourself (DIY) tax preparation options are very popular and can get the job done for people with simple returns. However, they are only as good as the person inputting the information. That person may misinterpret instructions or enter the wrong data or enter incorrect data and may miss deductions and credits, thus reducing their refund. Professional tax preparers make a lot of money each year correcting mistakes in returns that the IRS rejects. Also, the DIY software package being used may not have the most current tax tables or the right information for your state. DIY tax returns have a higher audit rate than returns prepared by professional tax preparers. Do a search for **"best tax prep software"** to see what is available, read its reviews, and evaluate its cost and features. Examples of DIY tax software include Intuit TurboTax and TaxAct. H&R Block has a DIY online tax preparation option. Also, the IRS Website allows you to self-file and provides instructions on how to submit your own tax return.

Free Tax Calculators/Refund Estimators

These online and mobile apps are free and can help you get an idea of whether you will get a refund or owe taxes. They prompt you for your filing status, income, deductions, dependents etc. and then provide an estimate of taxes owed. Just remember the old **GI-GO** principle: Garbage In-Garbage Out. The estimates are only as good as the data you input. Some examples of free tax calculators are listed here.

- **H&R Block:** https://www.hrblock.com/tax-calculator
- **Intuit TaxCaster:** https://turbotax.intuit.com/tax-tools/calculators/taxcaster/
- **NerdWallet:** https://www.nerdwallet.com/taxes/tax-calculator
- **SmartAsset:** https://smartasset.com/taxes/income-taxes

Part 5: Tax-Advantaged Plans and Options

There are various legitimate ways to reduce your tax burden. Most of them are elective and assume you have the available cash to take advantage of them. For example, you could put some extra money in an IRA at the end of the current tax year to reduce your taxable income. Some of the more common tax reduction methods are listed in Table 15-6.

Table 15-6: Federal Tax-Advantaged Plans and Options

Category	Reduction Option	Options/Examples	Taxation / Notes
Home Ownership	Tax deduction	Mortgage interest	Reduces taxable income (if itemizing on schedule A).
		Property tax	Reduces taxable income (if itemizing on schedule A).
Retirement	Tax deferral	Conventional IRA	Defers tax on contributions and gains until retirement until April 14th next year.
		401K, 403B	Defers tax on contributions and gains until retirement.
		Annuities (deferred)	Defers tax on contributions and gains until retirement.
	Tax exempt	Roth IRA	Gains never taxed.
Education	Tax avoidance	529 plan	State sponsored. Gains not taxed if used for education.
		Coverdell	Education savings account similar to 529 plan
Health Care	Tax avoidance	Healthcare Savings Account (HSA)	Contributions and gains not taxed if used for healthcare expenses.
		Flexible Spending Account (FSA)	Contributions and gains not taxed if used for healthcare expenses.
Charitable donations	Tax deductions	Tithing, Goodwill, Colleges, Humane society	Contributions to non-profit organizations are tax deductible, up to a point. Reduces taxable income.
Gifting	Tax avoidance	Could reduce assets	No tax to giftee, or gifter in general. Depends on whether cash or stocks, options and amounts.
Loans to governments and corporations	Tax avoidance	Municipal Bonds (bonds issued by cities and states, etc.)	Municipal bonds not taxed at federal or state level (usually).
		US treasuries, T-Bills	US Treasury bonds not taxed by state or local governments.
Tax related	Tax deductions	State income tax paid	Reduces taxable income.

Part 6: Other Taxes

Income Tax Plus

Although the income tax takes the biggest bite out of our budget, we pay a lot of other smaller taxes that can really add up. We've covered most of these elsewhere, but it's worth mentioning them here just to see them all in one place and fully appreciate their impact. Still, despite the substantial taxation here, I wouldn't want to live anywhere else but in the U.S.A. And, over the years, I contributed a lot to some of the public financial and health programs listed here—like Social Security and Medicare—as did my employers (e.g., unemployment), but I am glad I did, since I have also benefited from them. In addition to state and federal and frequently city income tax, other taxes, many of which come straight out of our paychecks to create "Net Pay," are included here. After factoring in 401K contributions, etc., it's a wonder there is anything left!

From Gross to Net and Beyond

- Federal Income Tax
- State Income Tax
- City Income Tax
- Social Security Tax
- Medicare Tax
- Unemployment Tax
- Investment proceeds Tax
  - Interest
  - Capital Gains
  - Dividends
- Sales Tax
- Gas Tax

Estate Taxes

In some states, the estate (assets) tax, sometimes called the "death tax," and its cousin, the inheritance tax, can take a substantial chunk of an estate when someone passes on. Both of these taxes have been eliminated in the state of Ohio, as a result of legislation passed in 2013. Twelve states in the U.S. still tax a deceased person's assets (Estate Tax). Six states still tax recipients' inheritances (Inheritance Tax). Even if you live in a state with no Estate Tax, if you have a relative who passes away and that lived in a state that does, and you are a beneficiary, that state can impose an inheritance tax on your proceeds.

Property taxes

Real estate or "Property" taxes were covered in Chapter 9: Buying or Renting a Home. They are usually included in the monthly mortgage payment as part of "PITI"—Principal, Interest, Taxes, and Insurance—but can be paid separately, as with homeowner's insurance. Local municipalities depend on property taxes to function and provide services. Property taxes can increase or decrease depending on the assessed value. If they decrease, you may be able to get a credit from your county assessor's office.

Homeowner's Online Real Estate Lookup

Most states and counties have a Web-based online search tool that you can use to determine what the real estate taxes are for a particular property. Other information is also available regarding home sale price and property valuation. Using these online tools provided by the county auditor, you can search and view real estate/appraisal information, property tax information, and tax levy information. Visit the Website for the state/county where the property is located. You can also use the provided online tools to look up sales tax rates for state, county, city, and school districts for a particular property.

Chapter 16
Insurance and Risk Management

Chapter Overview:

Insurance is a huge topic, as is risk management, and both can have a major impact on your life. This chapter is divided into four parts: Part 1 covers various types of personal insurance and Part 2 covers types of property-related insurance. Part 3 deals with information contained in the PFS Insurance Policy Info sheet and entry of your insurance data. Part 4 addresses financial risk and how to manage or mitigate it through the use of insurance, investment diversification, and other measures.

- **Part 1: Personal and Related Insurance**
- **Part 2: Property and Related Insurance**
- **Part 3: PFS Insurance Policy Info Sheet**
- **Part 4: Financial Risk Management**

Chapter PFS and PFI Integration:

This chapter covers Personal Financial Spreadsheet (PFS) Sheet - Insurance Policy Info with a tab label of "Insure-Pols." The Insurance Policy Info Sheet provides a centralized location to record key information for your insurance policies—such as life, health, and long-term care—as well as home- and vehicle-related policy information. This PFS sheet is for insurance policies of all types. There are no specific Personal Financial Indicators (PFIs) for this chapter.

Chapter Exercises:
- **Exercise 16-1: Compare Life Insurance Calculators and Policies**
- **Exercise 16-2: Record PFS Insurance Policy Info**

Chapter Notable Quote:

Quote 16-1: "Insurance: You may not ever need it, but you can't afford to not have it." - Anonymous

Regarding insurance, the chapter is meant to provide more generalized coverage, especially since home and auto insurance were covered in Chapters 11 and 12, respectively. This chapter provides a high-level discussion and review of some important things to consider when acquiring insurance. By including an overview of insurance in this chapter, it helps ensure that you are aware of the general types of insurance available, and you will be better able to identify and select the most appropriate insurance for your particular situation.

Financial Advisor Insurance Assistance and Your Personal Financial Plan

In addition to financial services, a certified financial advisor may be able to make recommendations for some types of insurance or direct you to a specialist who can provide cost-effective services to help you choose. These can include life insurance, umbrella insurance, long-term care (LTC) insurance, and health insurance. These types of insurance can help protect you and your investments. When developing your financial plan (Refer to Chapter 19) be sure to include adequate insurance as a major component of the plan. Many common life, retirement, and general investing mistakes are insurance related, resulting from the lack of safety net insurance—especially LTC—health, and disability. Insurance in general helps to protect your financial world. Some types of insurance are products you can shop for and buy on your own (e.g., Life, LTC, Health, Dental, Vision). These can be supplemented by the employer as part of their benefits package. Others, like the Healthcare Savings Account (HSA), are a combination of tax-favored savings accounts and self-funded health insurance. Additional information is presented in Table 16-1 and Chapter 13 regarding HSAs and related plans. Be sure to talk with your financial advisor if you have questions regarding the type of insurance and coverage that would meet your needs.

Verify AM Best Insurance Carrier Rating

The AM Best Company has been rating insurance companies of all types for financial strength since 1899, and is considered by many to be the De Facto standard of the industry. Whatever type of insurance you need, be sure the insurance carrier is listed by AM Best with a Financial Strength Rating (FSR) and Issuer Credit Rating (ICR) of A or A+ (highest rating). The AM Best rating is a good indicator of the insurance company's ability to satisfy claims and applies to all types of personal and property insurance, including Home, Auto, Life, Long Term Care, and many others. Also make sure your insurance provider is a licensed insurance agent in the state where you live. Recall that an insurance advisor is one of your Professional Advisors group, identified in Chapter 6. You can create an account with AM Best and look up a carrier's rating at their Website.

https://ratings.ambest.com

Part 1: Personal and Related Insurance

Table 16-1: Personal Insurance Types and Terminology

Insurance Type	Description / Notes
Life Insurance – Term	Level term periods (typ.): 10, 15, 20, or 30 years (renewable), no cash value, level premiums, Fixed death benefit.
Life Insurance - Whole Life	Permanent policy length, cash value, level premiums, and fixed death benefit. Premiums typically higher than Term. A portion of premium goes to investments.
Life Insurance - Universal Life	Permanent policy length, cash value, variable premiums, fixed/variable death benefit. Premiums typically higher than Term. A portion of premium goes to investments.
Long Term Care (LTC)	Critical nest egg protection - buy it early. Covers services provided by assisted living and Alzheimer's facilities.

Workman's Compensation ("Comp")	Required employer-provided disability insurance for workers who are injured on the job.
Long Term Disability (LTD)	Insurance for persons with disabilities and unable to work. Can be covered by Social Security Disability Insurance (SSDI), your employer or personal policy.
Health Insurance	Healthcare coverage provided by employer or individual for family. Typically, high deductibles. Contact www.healthcare.gov for help obtaining health care.
Healthcare Savings Account (HSA)	Special pre-tax savings account that allows you to put aside money to be used for qualified medical expenses.
Flexible Spending Account (FSA)	Tax deferred savings account that allows you to set aside savings that are tax deferred and non-taxable if used for personal or family health care. Contributions are also tax deductible. An FSA is typically established by an employer.
Dental/Vision	Many employers provide healthcare benefits which include dental and vision. Individuals can also buy dental and vision separately.
Medicare	Government program to provide healthcare services to individuals aged 65 and over. www.ssa.gov/benefits/medicare www.mymedicare.gov
Unemployment	Government program to provide temporary income to individuals who are out of work.

Health Insurance and HSAs

Health insurance is as important, if not more so, than any other type of insurance in helping to protect you and your retirement nest egg. However, it is a complicated subject, and private health insurance and Medicare are beyond the scope of this book. There are many people making a living these days by helping others sort through the options available and select a plan that can be cost effective.

If you are still working and are covered by an employer-sponsored health plan, good for you! Depending on your employment status, you may also be able to participate in a tax-advantage plan such as a Healthcare Savings Account (HSA) or Flexible Spending Account (FSA). These are also discussed briefly in Chapter 13: Investing Basics, and Chapter 15: Income Tax Basics.

If you are sixty-five or older, you can use Medicare for your health and prescription needs. You must register with Medicare before you turn sixty-five. Your financial advisor can typically help you find a knowledgeable professional who can work with you to select healthcare providers and plans that work with Medicare. Medicare is managed by the Centers for **Medicare** and Medicaid Services (CMS). Social Security works with CMS by enrolling people in **Medicare when they reach age** sixty-five. Go to their Websites for more information:

www.ssa.gov/benefits/medicare

www.mymedicare.gov

Life Insurance

The main purpose of life insurance is to provide replacement income for your family should you (or your spouse) meet an untimely demise. This is especially true for young people who have a family and a home, and even more so if the spouse is not employed. If you are working and your employer provides life insurance, that's a nice benefit. However, the amount of insurance may be less than you need, and if you leave the company, you may lose your insurance, unless you can take it with you. If your employer provides life insurance, you may still need a supplemental policy. If not, you will need a primary portable policy. If you are nearing retirement and do not have someone that depends on your income, consider not carrying life insurance.

Term Life Insurance

If you are still working and have a spouse and/or dependents, most financial advisors recommend buying "term life" insurance to protect your family from loss of income if you (or your spouse) pass away. Term Life provides a certain amount of coverage for a specified "term" or period of time, typically in five-year increments. For example, the primary wage earner in a family might purchase a $750,000, thirty-year term policy for a specific monthly premium, depending on their physical condition, medical history, and life expectancy. The amount and term of the insurance policy needed varies but can be roughly estimated by multiplying the annual wages for the insured person by ten with a term based on their expected remaining working years. So, let's say your gross income is $50,000 per year, and you are forty years old, and expect to work another twenty years. You might look for the best price on a $500,000 policy that would cover you for a term of twenty years. It is likely that the insurance underwriters will require you to take a physical. Talk to your financial advisor to discuss other factors you might want to consider. Note that we are not talking about disability insurance, which is discussed below.

Who Should have Life Insurance and What Type?

If you are retired or retiring soon and have an existing policy, talk to your financial advisor and see if it makes sense to maintain the policy and continue paying premiums. Retirees typically do not have to worry about income replacement, as they are retired and not dependent upon a job for income. By the same token, it does not make a lot of sense to buy life insurance for children, although some parents and grandparents do. The child has no income to replace or family to support so there is really no compelling reason to buy life insurance for them. Life insurance is mandatory if you have a family with children and you are the primary bread winner. Refer to the example scenarios following Table 16-2.

Financial advisors generally recommend term life insurance as it is more targeted, and you are just paying for life insurance with the premium. There are other types of non-term life insurance that are sometimes referred to as "permanent" policies. Examples included: "whole life" or "universal life." In general, these policies are a life insurance policy combined with an investment vehicle of sorts. These types of policies can insure you for life, and they can accumulate cash value over time as you pay the premiums. The amount of cash value depends on the types of investments they can provide for the policy holder. If you terminate the policy after a certain number of years, you will often receive a check for whatever the cash value is. However, the premiums are usually higher than term life, because a portion of every premium goes to investment. Table 16-2 shows some possible ways to compare life insurance policies. Table 16-1: Personal Insurance Types and Terminology provides some additional information about Whole Life and Universal Life. Most impartial insurance professionals would agree that a term life policy can provide the most coverage at the lowest cost for a young family.

A saying in the industry goes: "Buy term and invest the rest." The problem is most people who buy term life don't invest the rest. There are benefits to a whole or universal life policy, in that they accumulate cash value over time since they are an investment vehicle, in addition to being a life insurance policy. Also, the renewable term policy may require another physical at the end of the renewal period. Universal and whole life generally do not since they are not a renewable policy. They are typically in effect until the insured reaches a specific age or passes away. If you buy a whole life or universal life policy, try to buy it when you're young, as the rates increase the older you are. This is also true for term life policies.

Refer to **Exercise 16-1: Compare Life Insurance Calculators and Policies** at the end of this chapter. Exercise 16-1, Part A has you search for and select a life insurance calculator to estimate how much coverage you need for 10-year term life insurance. Part B provides guidance in selecting a term policy from various providers or carriers. Make a copy of Table 16-4 to compare various types of life insurance using Table 16-2 as a guide. You can also use Table 16-4 to compare other types of life insurance such as Whole Life and Universal Life by adding investment options as comparison criteria. When comparing policies be sure to use the same criteria to ensure an apples-to-apples comparison.

Table 16-2: Life Insurance Policy Comparison

Criteria	Policy 1	Policy 2	Policy 3
Insurance Company:	ABC Ins. Co.	DEF Ins. Co.	XYZ Ins. Co.
Policy Type:	Term	Term	Term
Policy/Term Length:	10-year	10-year	10-year
Cash Value?	No	No	No
Premium (monthly):	Level, $50/Mo	Level, $70/Mo	Level, $60/Mo
Death benefit:	Fixed, $500,000	Fixed, $500,000	Fixed, $500,000
Policy Holder Age:	40	40	40
Medical Exam?	Y	Y	Y
Renewable?	Yes	No	No
Portable?	No	Yes	No

Real World Life Insurance Scenario Examples

As people's financial situations change, so do their life insurance requirements. Here's a couple of examples:

Life Insurance Scenario #1: Ted had a $100,000 term life policy that he cancelled recently because the premiums were increasing, and he was retired. If he got hit by a bus, there was no need to replace income since it was derived from social security and retirement plan distributions, which Amy would get if the bus got Ted. Also, by cancelling his policy they added the $250/month they paid for the premiums to their discretionary income, thereby improving their cash flow.

Life Insurance Scenario #2: Amy had a term life insurance policy with a relatively low set premium that was good for another two years. In addition, there was no requirement for her to take a physical. She elected to keep that policy active, at least for a couple of years. This would allow her to see what the new premiums and medical requirements would be at that time. Amy was still working and had a small life insurance policy through her employer. In two years, if the premiums were still low, she would keep the insurance, otherwise she could cancel.

Life Insurance Scenario #3: When Ted and Amy got married in their late twenties, neither of them had life insurance. They bought a home, they both worked, and they had no kids at the time. They were DINKs (Dual Income No Kids). In a few years they had two children, and Ted stopped working to take care of the kids. They still had no life insurance. Ted and Amy were the perfect example of when to make sure you have life insurance. Since Amy was the sole breadwinner at the time, what if something happened to her? Bob, unemployed, would be left taking care of the kids and unable to pay the mortgage. At a minimum, Amy should have obtained at least a basic "term" policy, whether through her employer or an independent licensed insurance agent. Amy's situation was the perfect example of someone who should have had life insurance. Since she and Ted were both in their early thirties and healthy nonsmokers, they should have been able to get a good policy for a reasonable monthly premium. They should have comparison shopped for a policy, and perhaps a $500,000 policy for a ten- or twenty-year term for Amy (and possibly Ted) would have done for the time being. They should have checked with their financial advisor first for a recommendation.

Long-Term Care Insurance

Long-Term Care (LTC) is the single most important type of insurance to help protect your nest egg. If you are unable to care for yourself, this insurance will pay some or all the costs of living in an assisted living facility or nursing home. The cost of staying in one of these facilities can be VERY expensive and can deplete your retirement nest egg rapidly. The premium for an LTC policy is not cheap, but most advisors recommend it, considering what it covers. As with life insurance, the earlier you buy it, the less expensive it will be. Some policies specify that the premium will not change more than a certain amount over a given time span. If you are between forty and sixty years old and in good health, talk with your financial advisor about LTC insurance and consider obtaining quotes to see how much a policy would cost you and your partner.

Long-Term Disability Insurance

Long-Term disability is worthwhile for anyone who depends on their earned income. If you become disabled by injury or illness, this insurance pays about 60 percent of your salary, excluding commissions and bonuses, until you recover or reach the age of sixty-five. This insurance is often provided to an employee by their employer at little or no cost.

Part 2: Property and Related Insurance

Property Insurance Types and Terminology

Property insurance is usually grouped as related to home or auto. The following lists the most common types of property-related insurance. Homeowner's, Home Warranty, Home Title, and Renter's insurance are covered in Chapter 11 and this chapter. Auto insurance is covered in Chapter 12. Umbrella insurance is covered in this chapter.

- **Homeowner's**
- **Umbrella**
- **Renter's**
- **Home Warranty**
- **Home Title**
- **Auto**

Homeowner's Insurance

Homeowner's insurance is required by the lender when you purchase a home with a mortgage. The cost is frequently included in the monthly payment of PITI (Principal/Interest/Taxes/Insurance). If included with your monthly payment, it is paid out of an escrow account maintained by the lender. It may also be paid separately by the homeowner. If paid as part of the mortgage payment, the insurance company usually bills the lender the full year's premium annually, and the lender collects from the homeowner as part of their monthly payment. Homeowner's insurance provides coverage for major events that may damage your home, such as fire, theft, or flood (if included in the policy). Smaller damage claims such as a tree branch falling on the roof may be claimed against homeowner's insurance. However, if too many small damage claims are filed, often this increases your monthly premium and, in some cases, results in the insurance company cancelling your policy. It is best to file only major claims against your homeowner's insurance. It is suggested that you walk around your home and take pictures or, better yet, videos of your belongings. This will help you keep an accurate record of your major belongings in case you need to file a claim. If you take a video, consider narrating as you go, describing items and their cost.

Umbrella Insurance (Personal and Property)

Many financial advisors recommend that homeowners have an "Umbrella" personal liability policy in addition to Homeowner's and Auto liability insurance. An umbrella policy with $1,000,000 of coverage is typical. This type of policy can help to protect you against major claims related to your home or auto, such as lawsuits for damages. Another major area of coverage that Umbrella provides is personal liability regarding defamation, slander, and liable suits that might be filed against you. For example, if a neighbor's son runs through a plate glass window in sliding glass door in your home and they sue you. The umbrella policy gets its name from the fact that it covers liability over what your standard home and auto would cover and starts when those coverages are exhausted. In order to buy an umbrella policy, you must have home-owner's and auto policies in place. With a million-dollar umbrella, you are covered for up to $1,000,000 in damages in addition to your home and auto coverage. Without the policy, you may be liable and have to liquidate your assets to pay the damages. The premium for an umbrella policy is generally paid separately from PITI and is a combination policy based on your home and autos. The premium is usually a small amount considering it can save you thousands of dollars in the event of an accident on your property or a major auto accident, if you are at fault.

Business Liability Insurance

Home and Auto insurance in combination with a good umbrella policy can help protect you from most of the likely personal liability suits or claims that you might encounter. However, if you have a small business, your home, auto and umbrella personal liability policies do not protect you regarding business issues or liability claims. Consider buying business liability for the extra protection that it may afford you, in addition to your personal liability coverage.

Renter's Insurance

This type of insurance is very worthwhile for those who rent, as it protects the renter from theft and other damages. The landlord is generally not responsible the loss or the cost of the insurance in these cases. Renter's insurance is not very expensive; however, many people who rent do not carry it. This may be because they think it is more expensive than it actually is, or they may not even know about it. Talk to a licensed insurance agent and see if you can bundle your auto, umbrella, and renter's insurance.

Home Warranty Insurance

Not to be confused with homeowner's insurance, a home warranty policy is optional insurance, usually purchased by the seller of a home to give prospective buyers some peace of mind. It is usually a one-year policy that covers repairs and replacement for Heating, Ventilating, and Air Conditioning (HVAC) systems, as well as electrical systems, plumbing, water heater, and other major appliances. Read the policy to verify what is covered.

Home Title

Home title insurance is a policy, usually paid for by the seller, that protects the buyer against unforeseen claims or liens against the property that didn't show up on the title search. Home title insurance is not a requirement when purchasing a home but is recommended by most real estate professionals.

Auto Insurance

Auto insurance is a requirement in all fifty U.S. states. If you are stopped by the police while driving, you will be asked for three things: your driver's license, registration, and proof of insurance (current). If you don't have proof of insurance, you may get a warning and have to prove it later, or they may cite you immediately.

Note: The discussion of insurance in this chapter deals with multiple types. Insurance specifically for vehicles is covered in Chapter 12.

Roadside Assistance Auto Insurance

Most auto insurance policies include basic roadside assistance (aka towing and labor coverage) on each vehicle you insure for a nominal premium. If you are stranded, you can call qualified roadside assistance for help, whether it's to fix a flat, bring you gas, or unlock a door. Some people choose to decline the coverage to save money, but I think this is a mistake. If your policy does not provide it, consider adding it as it is typically not expensive. This is a very valuable service and can come in handy if you need it, and it can get you out of a bind relatively painlessly. If you have roadside assistance coverage, be sure to let family members who drive your cars know how to contact the insurance company to report a roadside problem to get help. Read your policy or contact your agent to verify your coverage. Roadside assistance usually includes the following 24 x 7:

- **Car won't start** (jump start)
- **Out of gas** (you pay for the gas they bring)
- **Keys locked in car** (police may need to be contacted)
- **Flat tire** (change/repair)
- **Towing** (may charge extra for longer distance)

Part 3: PFS Insurance Policy Info Sheet

The PFS Sheet – Insurance Policy Info Entries and Guidelines

The Personal Financial Spreadsheet has a sheet dedicated to Insurance Policy Info (Insure-Pols Tab). Refer to Figure 16-1. The standard entries for each insurance policy include the following:

- **Who (insured) and Type:** (e.g., Ted or Amy) (Life, LTC)
- **Carrier and AMB Rating.** (Insurance Co. Name and AM Best rating)
  - **Financial Strength Rating (FSR):** (preferably A or A+)
  - **Issuer Credit Rating (ICR):** (preferably A or A+)
- **Phone:** 999-999-9999
- **Policy No.:** 999999999999
- **Coverage:** (e.g., $500,000)
- **Premium:** (monthly payment)
- **Payment Method:** (Online, auto-deduct from checking or charge to credit card x9999)

- **Formula / Notes:** (e.g., Renewal 1/1/24 Exam)

Figure 16-1 shows sample entries from PFS Sheet - Insurance Policy Info. Note that home and auto insurance information were covered in Chapters 11 and 12, respectively, and can be entered into the PFS sheet as part of **Exercise 16-2: Record PFS Insurance Policy Info**, which is at the end of this chapter. The Insure-Pols sheet is a centralized location where information on all of your policies, both personal and property, can be kept for quick reference. (Insure-Pols Tab). Refer to Figure 16-1.

Figure 16-1: PFS Sheet - Insurance Policy Info (sample entries)

Who / Type	Carrier & AMB Rating	Phone	Policy No.	Coverage	Mo. Premium	Paymt Method	Formulas / Notes
Insurance Policy Info		Book Build Ch. 16				Updated: MM-DD-YYYY	
Amy Life	Ins Company, A/A+	999-9999	99999999	500,000	125	AP CC X9999	
Amy Long Term Care	Ins Company, A/A	999-9999	99999999		125	AP CC X9999	
Ted Life	Ins Company, A+/A	999-9999	99999999	250,000	80	AP Chkg	
Ted Long Term Care	Ins Company, A/a	999-9999	99999999		125	AP CC X9999	
Ted Health - Medicare Part B (Doctor)	Medicare	999-9999	99999999		240	Auto ded SS Dep	
Ted Health - Medicare Part D (Drug)	Ins Company, A/A+	999-9999	99999999		40	Auto ded SS Dep	
Ted Health - Medicare Supplem. (N)	AARP or other	999-9999	99999999		110	AP Chkg	
Joint - Home Owners	Ins Company, A/A+	999-9999	99999999	300,000	200	Incl. mort pmt	
Joint - Umbrella	Ins Company, A/A	999-9999	99999999	1,000,000	100	AP CC X9999	
Joint - Auto (2 cars)	Ins Company, A+/A	999-9999	99999999		300	AP CC X9999	Billed $3,600/yr
		Total Insurance Monthly Expense			$1,445		=SUM(F4:F16)
		(Also listed on the Income-Exp tab)					

Tabs: Income-Exp, Assets-Liab, Cred-Cards, Home-Info, Auto-Info, **Insure-Pols**, Fin-Plan, Income-Exp-F, Assets-Liab-F, Cred-Cards

Refer to **Exercise 16-2: Record PFS Insurance Policy Info** at the end of this chapter. Refer to Figure 16-1 for sample entries for various types of insurance. Make a copy of Figure 16-2 (Form) to record your entries.

General Insurance – Summary Notes and Tips
- Buy umbrella insurance to protect your estate and finances against major liability.
- If you are still working and have a spouse or dependents, buy term life insurance to protect your family from loss of income.
- If you are retired or retiring, consider canceling your life insurance policy to eliminate the premium.
- Some types of non-term life insurance (like "whole life") have a cash value if you cancel the policy after a certain period.
- When comparing types of life insurance and premiums, the saying goes thus: "buy term and invest the rest."
- The earlier you buy life insurance, the less expensive it will be.
- Avoid buying life insurance for children since there is no income to replace.
- Buy Comprehensive Long-Term Care (LTC) insurance to protect your nest egg.

Part 4: Financial Risk Management

Risk Overview

Most personal finance problems can be grouped into one of four major areas: Income/Expenses, Assets/Liabilities, Credit/Debt, and Insurance/Risk. Listed here are some of the more common types of risks within the Insurance/Risk category. With regard to investments, we previously defined risk as the likelihood of losing your initial investment or principal. However, some people consider investment volatility (major price fluctuations) a risk and seek to avoid volatile types of investments (mostly stocks). Keep in mind that, if you take a long-term view, asset price variation is to be expected. Some people can handle more volatility in their investments than others.

Financial Risk Examples

- Lack of critical insurance (life, health, or auto)
- Inadequate insurance
- Increased risk due to lack of coverage
- Using life insurance for investment
- Lack of diverse and balanced financial portfolio
- Financial data exposure – unsecure Wi-Fi and easy to crack passwords
- Third-party online money management services that consolidate your accounts can be risky. Exercise caution when using these apps.

Financial Risk Mitigation Options

- **Risk Sharing** - Buying Insurance
- **Risk Avoidance** - Low-risk investments; Cash equivalents
- **Risk Balancing** - Diversification of portfolio, hedges with investments
- **Risk Prevention –** Limits on types of investments. Proactive data security measures (refer to Chapter 18: Scams and Rip-Offs)
- **Risk Acceptance** - Acknowledging that there is a risk and that you are accepting responsibility for dealing with it

Risk Sharing

Insurance is critical in preserving wealth, whether in the form of actual insurance policies or investments that can act as a hedge against inflation. Examples of critical insurance include life insurance, umbrella insurance, long-term care insurance, auto insurance, and health insurance. These types of insurance can help protect your investments.

When doing retirement planning, failure to buy adequate insurance and make proper investments to protect your nest egg can result in rapid depletion of your retirement dollars. The biggest insurance-related mistake of investing is lack of safety net insurance as listed above. Essential insurance for a secure retirement and insurance in general helps to protect your financial world. You may never need it, but you can't afford to not have it.

Put another way: Some people say they can't afford the insurance premiums, but somehow, they can come up with the money to fix whatever the insurance would have covered. It's a risk some people are willing to take. Buying insurance of any kind is risk sharing since it puts part of the financial responsibility on the insured in the form of premiums and deductibles in exchange for coverage and assurance the insurance company will pay the bills if something bad happens. So, it is a shared burden.

Note: An important step that investors can take to ensure their savings, checking, and investments remain safe at no cost to them is to make sure their financial institutions are FDIC insured. And they need to make sure the balance for each account stays under the $250,000 Federal Deposit Insurance Corporation limit.

Risk Avoidance
The best way to remove risk from the equation is to avoid it altogether. If you don't want to take a chance on drowning in the ocean, then don't swim in the ocean. However, by not doing so, you will also miss out on the benefits, just like the gains you could miss out on that might be achieved with higher-risk investments. That said, there is wisdom in not taking chances with speculative investments like cryptocurrencies, penny stocks, and junk bonds, unless you have money you can afford to lose. The problem with low-risk investments is low returns. Some might argue they are preserving their capital, but they are fighting a losing battle. A savings account is very low risk and might carry a 2 percent or slightly better annual percentage yield (APY). But with inflation averaging around 3 percent, the buying power of the dollar goes down every year. And that does not even take into consideration the fact that any interest you make is taxed.

Risk Balancing
Rather than avoiding risk and volatility altogether, and also losing out on the potential rewards, you can spread the risk around between multiple investments. Diversification of holdings in portfolio based on investment type is a common risk management strategy employed by financial advisors. There are thousands of mutual funds that invest in multiple companies within a given fund category. For example, you might buy shares in a mutual fund that invests in large cap stocks (equities). With each share you buy of the mutual fund, you are purchasing a small piece of each company that is in the fund. Mutual funds can be invested in virtually anything, including stocks, bonds, precious metals, and real estate. By investing in a mutual fund, you are investing in multiple companies simultaneously. Buying multiple mutual funds allows you to further diversify your investment portfolio.

Certain types of investments are considered "hedges," which counterbalance other types of investments. This usually means that if the stock market goes down, the hedge holds its value or can actually go up. If the inflation rate goes up, the hedge can increase in value faster than the rate of inflation. Real estate and commodities are examples of hedges. Hence the term "hedging your bets." Chapter 13: Investing Basics goes into greater detail on various types of investments as well as what types of holdings could go into a well-balanced, diversified portfolio.

Risk Prevention

Have you ever heard the saying "A fool and his money are soon parted"? Being taken in by a financial scam or scheme can nullify decades of hard work and nest egg building. It is unfortunate how many people are duped into giving away millions each year to people they don't know, and the scammers are getting smarter and craftier every day. Just remember, if something sounds too good to be true, then it probably is! There are many proactive measures we can take to help reduce exposure to scams and prevent scammers from taking our money. There are simple things we can do, like not accessing financial accounts when on an unsecure Wi-Fi network and not carrying a bank debit card. You can educate yourself as to the types of scams that are being perpetrated so that you can spot and avoid them before being taken advantage of. You can help prevent ID theft by "freezing" your credit file with the three credit reporting agencies or bureaus (Equifax, Experian, and TransUnion). This is a simple yet powerful measure you can take to prevent anyone other than you from opening new credit in your name. Remember, you must "unfreeze" your account with all three bureaus to apply for new credit (e.g., a new credit card or auto loan). You can put a freeze on your account with all three credit bureaus for free. To learn more about how to place or lift a freeze on your credit report, refer to Chapter 9: Credit and Credit Cards. Also, visit the U.S. Government Website at: https://www.usa.gov/credit-freeze

Note: Proactive data security measures, including how to spot scams, are covered in this book in Chapter 18: Scams and Rip-Offs.

Chapter 16 Exercises

Exercise 16-1: Compare Life Insurance Calculators and Policies

Part A: Compare Life Insurance Calculators

A good life insurance calculator can help you determine how much life insurance you need based a variety of factors including salary, age, assets, and liabilities as well as age and family support situation. Do a Web search for "term life calculators" and you can compare several that are available. There are good free ones available from BankRate, Forbes, Fidelity, NerdWallet, and others. Try them out using the same inputs and compare the results. Select one that will meet your needs and use it to calculate the amount of term life insurance you will need based on your personal, financial, and family situation. Use Table 16-3 to compare features and capabilities of the various calculators available. Note the one you used as well as the amount of Life insurance recommended.

Table 16-3: Life Insurance Calculator Comparison (Form)

Comparison criteria	Calculator 1	Calculator 2	Calculator 3
Calculator source			
Ease of use			
Functionality			
Cost			
Features			
Amount of insurance recommended			
Term of policy			

Part B: Compare Life Insurance Policies

To assist you in researching life insurance policies, refer to Table 16-2 which compares characteristics of term life policies. Table 16-4 below is a form to enter your findings. You can replace the criteria in Table 16-2 with your own if you wish. Select two or three policies of a similar or different type to see which ones have the lowest premium with the fewest drawbacks. Use Table 16-2 as an example and make a copy of Table 16-4.

Table 16-4: Life Insurance Policy Comparison (Form)

	Policy 1	Policy 2	Policy 3
Insurance Company:			
Policy Type:			
Policy/Term Length:			
Cash Value?			
Premium (monthly):			
Death benefit:			
Policy Holder Age:			
Medical Exam?			
Renewable?			
Portable?			

Exercise 16-2: Record PFS Insurance Policy Info

In this exercise, you will enter your insurance information into a blank form (Figure 16-2) based on Figure 16-1 to prepare for entry into PFS sheet Insure-Pols. Even if you do not plan to enter your insurance data into the spreadsheet at this time, go ahead and gather the data and enter it in the form. You can do the calculations manually if you want to.

Note: Before starting this exercise, make a copy of the blank Figure 16-2: PFS Sheet - Insurance Policy Info (Form) and refer to Figure 16-1 for a description of each field, as a guide for data entry, if needed.

Figure 16-2: PFS Sheet - Insurance Policy Info (Form)

	A	B	C	D	E	F	G	H
1	**Insurance Policy Info**		Book Build Ch. 16				Updated: MM-DD-YYYY	
2								
3	Who / Type	Carrier & AMB Rating	Phone	Policy No.	Coverage	Mo. Premium	Paymt Method	Formulas / Notes
4								
5								
6								
7								
8								
9								
10								
11								
12								
13								
14								
15								
16								
17			Total Insurance Monthly Expense			$0		=SUM(F4:F16)
18			(Also listed on the Income-Exp tab)					

Chapter 17
Education, Jobs, and Student Loans

Chapter Overview:
This chapter deals with another major money-related and potentially very expensive part of some people's lives. Some college students end up spending more on their education than they do on a home, and many of them spend more than they might pay for a late model car. The chapter is a high-level review of different types of jobs/careers and identifies various types of institutions of higher learning. It also discusses employment as it relates to your purpose in life. The chapter is divided into six parts:

- **Part 1: Jobs and Careers - Passion and Purpose**
- **Part 2: Education, Colleges, and Degrees**
- **Part 3: College Value and Cost**
- **Part 4: College Jobs and Alternatives**
- **Part 5: College Cost Containment**
- **Part 6: College Payment Options and Tips**

Chapter Background:
I spent over thirty years of my career teaching at and developing educational materials for various institutions of higher learning, both public and private. This chapter provides an overview of higher education (beyond high school) based on my experience teaching at technical schools and community colleges and attending four-year universities. The chapter also includes some insights and a discussion of the advantages and disadvantages for various types of institutions and payment options.

Note: If you do not read the whole chapter, I highly recommend you browse the chapter; read the following Part 1: Jobs and Careers - Passion and Purpose; and review the two tables included in this chapter regarding types of degrees and ways to pay for college.

Chapter PFS Integration:
The PFS components in this chapter that relate to education, jobs, and student loans may be found on the Assets, Liabilities, and Net Worth Sheet and consists mainly of liabilities such as student loans, and assets such as savings accounts and 529 plans. Income sources such as part-time jobs can be recorded in the Income, Expenses, and Cash Flow sheet of the PFS. Any college-related financial data can be recorded in the optional college sheet as described in the note below, if you choose to create one.

Consider Adding a PFS "College" Sheet:
Many people who have college-bound family members will add a "College" sheet to their Personal Financial Spreadsheet (PFS), just for college-related expenses and payment sources. With this optional PFS sheet, they can centralize and track college expenses such as tuition, room, board, books, and other related costs.

In addition, they can use the sheet to monitor the status of student loans and other expenses for multiple students. Funding sources can include student loans, part-time jobs, gifts, 529s, scholarships, and other sources as described in Table 17-2. The chapter includes two optional research exercises that will help you identify and compare colleges and expenses using the online Web-based tools that are available. In Exercise 17-1 you will research college cost estimating tools and, in Exercise 17-2 you will research online tools that allow you to compare colleges based on characteristics that are important to you.

Chapter Exercises:
- **Exercise 17-1: Research College Cost Calculators (optional)**
- **Exercise 17-2: Research College Comparison Tools (optional)**

Chapter Notable Quotes:
Quote 17-1: "To Live, To Love, To Learn, To Leave a Legacy. That's what we all want." - Dr. Stephen Covey

Quote 17-2: "You can only become truly accomplished at something you love. Don't make money your goal. Instead, pursue the things you love doing, and then do them so well that people can't take their eyes off of you." - Maya Angelou

Quote 17-3: "What we obtain too cheaply, we esteem too lightly." - Thomas Paine

Quote 17-4: "Genius is 1 percent inspiration and 99 percent perspiration." - Thomas Edison

Part 1: Jobs and Careers - Passion and Purpose

It's Not Just a Job
Whatever our lot in life, financially or otherwise, most of us are pretty similar as human beings, and in what we want out of life. The first quote above, by Dr Stephen Covey, author of *The 7 Habits of Highly Effective People*, puts it very simply, and it accurately describes my overall desires.

As we go through life, many of us ask ourselves, "Who am I?" "What do I really want?" "What is my purpose?" Some people know what they want to do or be at an early age. Most of us, however, struggle, working at multiple unsatisfying jobs for years before discovering our passion or purpose. Some people never do find their calling or niche. There are many books written to help you determine your strengths and weaknesses and what direction or career might best suit you. The book *What Color is Your Parachute* by Richard Nelson Bolles is the world's most popular and best-selling career guide, having sold over ten million copies. The most important thing with any job or career, however, is that you enjoy what you are doing. This is not always possible, and sometimes you just have to suck it up and make the best of an unpalatable situation. The sooner you accept a job for what it is and just resign yourself to doing your best, the sooner you will be able to move on to a better job.

Some (most) jobs are probably stepping stones to your ultimate ideal job. By the same token, there are people who have landed what they thought would be their dream job only to find that it wasn't as great as they thought it would be. Many people go through multiple unsatisfying jobs over their lifetime before they find a job or career path where they can really enjoy meaningful work and be of service to others. Do what you like, like what you do! Life is too short to work at a job that you hate. Many people stay in jobs they dislike for the security, good pay, and benefits. But you must have the courage to let go of what you have in order to pursue your dreams. If you enjoy what you do and do it well, the money will come, almost as a by-product. Maya Angelou puts it very well:

Quote 17-2: "You can only become truly accomplished at something you love. Don't make money your goal. Instead, pursue the things you love doing, and then do them so well that people can't take their eyes off of you." - Maya Angelou

You can recognize people who are doing what they love because you can see it in their face. It's a look of pure enjoyment. All of us have the potential to achieve this in our lifetimes if we really want to. What is your vision of success, wealth, and fulfillment? Follow your inner wisdom and dreams. There will certainly be detours on your path, and it's easy to come up with reasons and excuses why you cannot or should not do something. If you pursue your purpose with passion, are enjoying yourself, and begin to lose track of time, those are good signs to let you know that you are on the right track. Do that which gets you out of bed in the morning. If you make a list of things you are good at and a list of things you love to do and then merge the two, it may help you discover your purpose in life or your *dharma*, as it is referred to in some wisdom traditions. That which you want to put your time and energy into will be a good indicator of your purpose. If your work is meaningful and interesting and contributes to your personal growth, you may be in your *dharma*. Some spiritual teachers say that you may be able to tap into a supernatural creative intelligence flow as you discover your purpose in life, but it may take you ten thousand hours of practice to reach critical mass and tap into the flow. The vehicle (you) needs to be ready with focused application of practice. Writers write even when they have writer's block. If they don't write, they can't make it through the blockage.

Quote 17-3: "What we obtain too cheaply, we esteem too lightly." - Thomas Paine

The meaning of this quote is that if we are given things without having to work for them, we do not value them as much. And things that we struggle with, work hard for, or pay more for are naturally more highly valued. This quote is especially appropriate when applied to paying for college. When I graduated from high school, it was assumed that I would go to college. My family lived in a college town where a major state university is located. I was expected to attend this well-known in-state public college and get good grades, and my parents would pay for my tuition to obtain a four-year bachelor's degree. Since I would be living at home, they would not have to pay for my room and board.

Both of my parents and my two older sisters had obtained master's degrees and placed a high value on post-secondary education. I dropped out of college in my junior year and went to work as an instructor at a private mechanics training school. My younger brother stayed in college and ended up getting two master's degrees. I enrolled at the university and started out my first semester with decent grades. I got through my freshman first year with a "C+" average. But it went downhill from there. I barely squeaked by my sophomore year and did so poorly my junior year that I dropped out of school. I didn't get my bachelor's degree until thirty years later. Better late than never, I guess. I am convinced that if I had had to work part time to pay for a portion of my own college tuition, I would have done better because I would have had some "skin in the game," so to speak. More on this later.

Part 2: Education, Colleges, and Degrees

Life-long Learning
I am a big believer in life-long learning. This does not mean obtaining an advanced degree. It does not even mean going to college. It simply means that we always have opportunities to continue learning throughout our lives, whether it be through self-study, on-the-job training, or life experience. It can also mean taking work-related seminars (continuing education), obtaining industry certifications, a college certificate, an associate degree, or a bachelor's degree. Volunteering is another way to further your education and life-long learning.

Higher Education - Colleges and Universities
The term "higher education" refers generally to any post-secondary (after high school) education, but more specifically, college or university education. This can include education at community colleges as well as vocational or trade schools. There are basically three types of colleges or universities in the U.S.: community colleges, four-year colleges, and vocational schools. Many communities have one or more of these. These institutions can be public or private, and non-profit or for-profit. Public colleges and universities get their funding primarily from the state government, whereas private colleges receive their funding primarily from private donations and tuition. Our oldest daughter attended Wright State University, an Ohio state public school. Our youngest daughter attended Ohio University, a public school as well. There are a number of other public and private schools in Ohio that they could have attended. Since obtaining their bachelor's degrees, they have both obtained their master's degrees. By attending in-state public schools, both daughters kept the cost of their college education down as compared to out-of-state and/or private schools.

Community Colleges (two-year)
These are sometimes called Junior Colleges. They typically offer two-year associate degrees and one-year certificates in various disciplines. In some cases, they may be referred to as technical colleges. Enrollment requirements are usually minimal (high-school degree or GED), and tuition is very low as compared to other types of colleges. Many community colleges have agreements with four-year colleges for students who plan on transferring to a four-year college. They offer two-year transfer degrees to substitute for the first two years of the four-year college. These schools have flexible schedules, offer evening classes, and many also offer online or distance learning courses. They cater to working adults who are part-time and full-time students online and on campus. The cost of tuition for public community colleges is usually quite

low as compared to private colleges. I am more familiar with the community college environment. I am a big fan of community colleges, having taught computer and networking classes at colleges in Arizona, California, and North Carolina.

Four-Year Colleges and Universities
These offer four-year bachelor's degrees and advanced degrees (master's and doctorate) in various disciplines. The focus of the college typically is Liberal Arts, Business, Engineering, Agriculture, or a combination of these and others.

Technical/Vocational Schools
Some people do not wish to go on to college after graduating from high school and choose to not go to college at all. Some may want to enter the job market directly as an apprentice or other entry-level position. In the U.S. and many developed countries, there is a shortage of qualified skilled workers in technical fields and technical/vocational schools are a good way to prepare for these positions. They offer two-year technical degrees in various subjects, such as Information Technology and Auto Mechanics. Community colleges also offer vocational degrees and certificates in technical fields. Vocational schools cater to students who do not wish to attend a traditional four-year college or who may want to get a degree more quickly for entry into the job market.

Note: Be sure that any institution you attend is accredited.

Accredited and Non-accredited Institutions
It is important to make sure that any institution you wish to attend is "accredited." Accreditation is used by colleges and universities to let applicants know they provide a quality education and that they are officially recognized by the U.S. Department of Education (USDE). There are many non-accredited schools that will be happy to take your money, but a degree from one of these schools may be of dubious value.

Nearly all public colleges and private nonprofit colleges are accredited, which means their curriculum is approved by the USDE and meets certain standards. Be wary of non-accredited, for-profit institutions as they may offer substandard education at high tuition prices and make unrealistic promises of employment after graduation. Also, some have been known to go out of business, for one reason or another, before you complete your degree. This is a real concern and is especially true of non-accredited, for-profit vocational schools. In addition, a diploma from one of these schools may not be recognized by other schools or when applying for a job. Unscrupulous schools that charge high tuition and focus on enrolling as many students as possible are sometimes referred to as "diploma mills." That said, there are many accredited private institutions and technical schools that are reasonably priced and offer a good quality education. For more information, visit the USDE Website at https://www.ed.gov/accreditation. For more information on selecting a college or university, search the Web for "selecting a college or university." There are many good sources of information that describe colleges and rate them based on various criteria. You can also search the Web for "choosing a college."

Four-year colleges and universities offer Bachelor of Arts (BA) or Bachelor of Science (BS) degrees, or both, depending on the college and major. BA degrees emphasize the social sciences and humanities, whereas BS degrees focus more on math and science. For example, you might attend a four-year university, majoring in Business Administration, which is part of the university's college of business. You could obtain a Bachelor of Arts (BA) in Business Administration (BABA). Or you might obtain a Bachelor of Science (BS) degree from the college of Engineering (BSE), in one of the engineering specialties such as Mechanical, Electrical, or Aerospace Engineering.

Table 17-1 lists generic degree names that are offered by public and private colleges in the U.S. Also shown is the typical number of years required to complete the degree while assuming the student is taking a full load of courses/credits each semester. Entries in the table are examples, and abbreviations can vary from one school to another.

Table 17-1: Types of College Degrees

Type of Degree	Example Abbrev	Avg # Years	Colleges / Notes
College Certificate (one-year degree)		1	Offered by many community colleges in various technical subjects or disciplines. Can provide focused knowledge in a field without the need to take general education courses required with a degree. Examples include nursing, programming, networking, and physical therapy.
Associate degree (two-year degree)	AA, AS, AAS	2	Offered by community colleges in various technical subjects or disciplines and gen-ed course programs. Can sometimes transfer to 4-year college.
Bachelor's degree (four-year undergraduate degree)	BA or BS	4	Basic undergraduate degree offered by 4-year colleges in various disciplines.
Master's degree (graduate degree)	MA or MS	5-6	Advanced degree offered by many 4-year colleges in various disciplines.
Doctor's (Doctoral or Doctorate) Graduate Degree	PhD: Doctor of Philosophy	6-8	Advanced degree offered by many 4-year colleges in various disciplines. Obtained after Master's degree.
Online Degrees	Any of the above	varies	Many reputable colleges now offer online Bachelor's, Master's and Doctoral degree programs in various subjects.

Do you need a degree?

For some jobs/careers, a basic or advanced degree is either desired or required. For example, most schools (K-12 and colleges) require a master's degree in education to teach at their institution, although a doctor's degree is desirable. This does not mean that you cannot be successful and prosperous without a degree. There is no substitute for dedication and hard work. Some of the world's most successful entrepreneurs have no more than a high-school diploma or a partial college degree. Many people who have a good work ethic, and put in the hours, are doing quite well financially with two-year degrees and one-year certificates, especially in technical fields. This doesn't mean you have to work your tail off to the exclusion of all other aspects of your life but there usually is no substitute for time devoted to something you want to get good at. There is a direct correlation between hours spent and proficiency (practice makes perfect).

Quote 17-4: "Genius is 1 percent inspiration and 99 percent perspiration." - Thomas Edison

It used to be that a high-school degree was the minimum requirement for a lot of good-paying jobs. However, that is changing, and in today's world, an associate (two-year) degree is becoming the minimum requirement. Other options short of a post-secondary four-year degree include one-year certificates and technical degrees from public and private institutions. A person with an Associate of Applied Science (AAS) two-year degree in a technical subject such as Computer Programming or Diesel Mechanics is very employable and can make as much or more than a person that graduates with a four-year liberal arts degree. It is not uncommon for a person with an associate technical degree and four or five years of experience to be able to make a six-figure salary. At the time of this writing, it is estimated there are over a hundred thousand unfilled positions in the U.S. alone for Information Technology (IT), which includes jobs in the areas of Application Programming, Network Security, Server Administration, and Database Management. Apprenticeships, volunteering, and networking with personal contacts are other ways to get your foot in the door. It should also be noted that hands-on experience in a given field can be very valuable in applying for jobs and may be viewed as equivalent to a degree, especially in technical fields.

> **Comic Relief:** Ted was sitting on a park bench, feeling dejected, when his friend Bob came up and asked why he was down. Ted told him that he didn't get much respect from people. Ted whipped out a business card and showed it to Bob. Ted said "Why don't you do what I did? I had these business cards printed up with my name and the letters BS, MS, and PhD after my name. Ever since then, when I give them to people I meet, I get a lot more respect than I used to. Ted asked what BS, MS, and PhD meant. Ted responded, "Well, we all know what BS means, right?" Ted said, "Yeah, I know what BS means." Ted said, "Well MS means "more of the same," and PhD means "piled higher and deeper!"

Part 3: College Value and Cost

Value of a College Degree

There is a lot of discussion these days about the value of a college degree and, with rising tuition costs, whether it's even worth it to pursue one. So, what is a college degree worth in real dollars? That depends on the person, the degree, and the job market. Some four-year degrees like a BS in Engineering are valued for their earning potential as well as the joy of doing the work. Other degrees, such as Art History, may not pay as much but can bring great satisfaction to the recipient. Some will say that a degree is not really that important in this day and age, and that may be true in some cases, depending on the degree and the institution. However, a degree can be worth millions in earning potential over the span of a person's working lifetime, as compared to a person who has only a high-school degree.

According to research by the Social Security Administration, there are significant differences in lifetime earnings based on educational level. For example, men with bachelor's degrees earn around $900,000 more in average lifetime earnings than high-school graduates. Men with graduate degrees (master's or higher) earn about $1.5 million more in median lifetime earnings than high-school graduates. People with four-year degrees can generally make more than someone with a two-year degree, unless the two-year degree is in a technical field. Automation may eliminate some jobs, making them obsolete, but it makes the assembly line more productive and the manufacturing equipment more complex. This requires more people with a higher degree of skill. An automated assembly line still requires qualified technicians to program and maintain the equipment. People who take technical training to keep up with technological advances will always have good-paying jobs in today's world.

A person who obtains a four-year degree in a low-demand job market area, such as Philosophy, may have trouble finding a job, let alone making a lot of money at it. If that same person has a lot of college loan debt, they can be fighting an uphill battle for years. On the other hand, a person who obtains a four-year degree in a high-demand job market—such as Physics, Engineering, or Computer Science—is virtually assured of finding well-paying employment and may have multiple job offers. These types of jobs and the requisite schooling are often referred to by the acronym "STEM," which stands for Science, Technology, Engineering, and Mathematics. The U.S. currently has a shortage (in the millions) of qualified job applicants in these areas.

Cost-Benefit and Break-even Analysis

One way to see if a post-secondary degree is worth the time, effort, and money invested is to do a cost/benefit analysis. Cost benefit adds up all the estimated costs and expected benefits of making a decision to see if the benefits outweigh the costs. However, some benefits are somewhat intangible. For example, you can put a value on increased earning potential as a result of obtaining a degree, but it is more difficult to assign a value to the networking potential and personal relationships that you would establish while attending a four-year college. By doing a simple break-even analysis, you can estimate the total cost of a degree at a particular institution (cost for one year * number of years for the degree) and then estimate how much additional income you could reasonably expect per year to determine how many years the payback would take. Costs should include tuition, room and board, books, transportation, and living expenses, as well as principal and interest on loans. Also be sure to account for lost income during the time you are attending college. Next, estimate the increase in salary per year that you realistically could expect, based on a study of the job market. Calculate the number of years to break even So, let's assume your costs for the degree total $40,000. If your current salary is $40,000 per year and after getting the degree you can make $50,000, that's another $10,000 per year, so you should be able to break even in four years.

Non-Monetary Reasons to go to College

Keep in mind there are many jobs, such as teaching, that require an advanced degree and don't pay that much. However, these types of jobs can be very gratifying and may come with some benefits, such as a relatively long summer break and many paid holidays, not to mention contributing to students' personal and educational development. I was a full-time faculty member at a community college and experienced this first-hand. At that time, the average starting salary of a community college teacher in the U.S. was about $40,000 for a nine-month year. I wasn't making that much money, but the benefits offset the lower pay. Money is not everything, and there are other nonmonetary reasons to go to college, although all the reasons mentioned here can also apply to non-college situations.

- **Developing critical thinking skills**
- **Expanding awareness**
- **Honing communication skills**
- **Learning how to learn**
- **Discovering your purpose and what you want to do in life**
- **Meeting people, building relationships, and networking contacts**
- **Pursuing knowledge beyond the courses you take**
- **Participating in collegiate activities—life works to the extent you participate.**

Part 4: College Jobs and Alternatives

The Trades

There are other technical skill jobs whereby a person can make a good living and that may not require a degree. By working in one of the traditional construction "trades," many people do quite well financially as tradesmen, a category that includes welders, plumbers, electricians, carpenters, and HVAC (Heating/Ventilating/Air Conditioning) workers. Applicants can obtain the requisite knowledge through self-study and by working as an apprentice. Of course, they can also attend classes at a community college or vocational/trade/tech school. In addition to working for an existing business, a tradesman may choose to start their own business, which can afford them other benefits. A gentleman who lives in our neighborhood works as a handyman and stays very busy, doing a variety of jobs. He makes a good income and seems to enjoy what he is doing.

Job Interview Tips

This is not a book on how to get a job, but it's worth mentioning a few insights and pointers I've gleaned in my years as an employee, supervisor, and manager in corporate America. Here are some tips that might help on how to prepare for and conduct yourself in a job interview.

- Dress nicely, but don't overdo it. Dress codes are not as important as they once were.
- Prepare for the interview by doing some research on the company/institution to which you are applying, and come up with a few questions for the interviewer(s).
- If they ask why you want this job, tell them the truth, and be truthful throughout the interview.
- Try to maintain an aura of competence and confidence, but do not be cocky.
- Companies hire people not because they know everything but because they are willing to take on responsibility and grow personally.
- Ask what the advancement opportunities are from the position you are interviewing for.
- If you are interested in furthering your education, like pursuing a master's degree, ask if they have a tuition assistance program.
- You are interviewing the company and potential managers just as they are interviewing you.
- If unemployment is low and it is currently a job-seekers market, you may be able to negotiate better terms of employment.
- When presented with an offer that includes salary and benefits, it doesn't hurt to ask if they can sweeten the pot. Can you work from home one or two days a week? Is there a sign-on bonus? Is there a 401K with employer matching?

Compensation and Types of Pay

- **Full-time or Part-time** – Full-time jobs usually have benefits like health insurance, a 401K plan, tuition reimbursement, and paid time off. Part-time jobs generally do not, although the hourly pay rate may be the same.
- **Salary vs. Hourly** – Salaried jobs are based on a yearly rate and usually do not pay for overtime.
- **Self-Employed Contract work vs. Regular Employee.** A regular employee will receive a W2 IRS wage statement, showing taxable income, at the end of the year, whereas a contract employee that is self-employed would receive a 1099 form stating the amount paid to the employee during a tax year. The employer typically takes taxes out of each paycheck for the regular employee. The employer does not take taxes out of the paycheck for a self-employed contract employee, who is expected to pay estimated taxes quarterly to the IRS. The contract employee also must pay self-employment taxes, which are sometimes overlooked and can result in penalties.

Tip: Converting Salary/Hourly wages

You can convert salary dollars per year to dollars per hour for an hourly rate and vice versa very quickly. Assume the average full-time working person works about two thousand hours per year or fifty weeks (actually 52 X 40 hours/week = appx 2,000 hours). You can easily convert an hourly rate to salary dollars per year and vice versa. Let's say you know the hourly rate. Multiply it times two and tack on three zeros. So if someone makes fifteen dollars/hour, multiply 15 x 2 = 30, add three zeros, and you have the approximate equivalent annual salary of $30,000 per year. If you are given the annual salary of $70,000 per year and want to convert it to an hourly rate, just reverse the process. Divide the thousands number by 2. So, 70/2 = 35 and discard the three zeros. A salary of $70,000/year = thirty-five dollars/hour (appx.). If someone makes an hourly rate of sixty dollars/hour, that's $120,000 per year assuming they work full time for the entire year. If someone makes a salary of $200,000 per year, that's a hundred dollars/hour.

Part 5: College Cost Containment

Borrowing for College
According to federal data, the average student has accumulated over $35,000 in student loan debt by the time they graduate from a four-year college. The total outstanding federally sponsored student loans amount is over a trillion dollars. Of course, students can work part time through college and can significantly offset the amount they have to borrow if they work evenings and during the summer months.

I met a young man a while back who had just graduated with a degree in sociology and had almost $80,000 in student loan debt. He tried to obtain a job in his field of study but didn't have much luck. He was very discouraged and began a self-study program of computers and networking. Eventually, he landed an entry level job in the computer/networking field. Over a three-year period, he worked his way up to the position of an IT Manager and was finally able to pay off his student loans. Some students are not so lucky and spend many years after graduation paying off their student loans. More on this later. If you must take out a student loan, apply only for a federally backed (lower interest) one and only for the minimum you need to get through the semester.

Note: Student loans are not forgiven even if you declare bankruptcy!

The Cost of College – Tuition Options
The cost of going to college, for the average student, is made up primarily of tuition, books, and room and board. Tuition is by far the biggest chunk or expense and, at most schools around the country, continues to rise without showing any signs of decreasing. There is a big difference in cost between attending an in-state public college as compared to an out-of-state private college for the same degree. The four major factors that determine tuition costs are these:

- Whether the student's residence is in-state or out-of-state
- Whether the college is a public or private institution
- Whether the student attends a community college for the first two years
- Whether the student obtains a scholarship

In-state vs. Out-of-state

The tuition alone for a four-year undergraduate degree at the Ohio State University (OSU) was about $10,000/year for in-state students, for the year 2020. For an out-of-state student, the tuition was closer to $30,000/year. For many schools, to be considered "in-state," a student must have lived in the state for at least one year prior to applying for admission. Tuition costs vary considerably even between public institutions in the same state. Whereas in-state tuition at the OSU main campus is about $10,000/year, tuition at the Kent State main campus is about $12,000/year, and at a satellite OSU campus, tuition averages about $6000 (however, course offerings may be limited).

Public or Private institution

In addition to in-state and out-of-state tuition differences, costs also vary depending on whether the institution is public or private. In general, a private institution's tuition is about 30–40 percent more expensive than a public institution's, although some private schools offer generous scholarships to help offset the difference.

Community College Option

Another very cost-effective option for reducing tuition costs, although perhaps not as glamorous, is to attend a community college for the first two years when pursuing a four-year degree. Students who want the traditional "college experience" (e.g., with fraternities and sororities, the social aspects, and a sense of independence) associated with the freshman and sophomore years may not be interested in this option. However, it allows the student to take the required general education (gen-ed) courses that normally would be taken at the four-year school but at a much lower tuition cost. Many community colleges offer two-year transfer degrees that can substitute for the first two years at a four-year college. The community college and four-year college typically negotiate an agreement to allow students to do this, depending on the degree being sought.

As previously mentioned, the average in-state tuition for a student at Ohio State is about $10,000 per year, or $20,000 for the first two years. By comparison, in-state tuition at Columbus State Community College is about $4,000 per year, or $8,000 for the first two years. A student taking the first two years at Columbus State would save about $12,000 in tuition costs by attending the community college for the first two years and then transferring to Ohio State for years three and four. When the student graduates, the college name on their degree is that of the four-year school, with no indication that they attended a community college for the first two years and saved a ton of money on tuition.

Private/Nonprofit College Costs

The cost of a four-year degree at a private nonprofit college can be over $150,000 (includes tuition, room, and board). Although many of these institutions offer generous scholarships, a student who insists on attending a particular private college in another state will end up paying higher private school tuition as well as extra out-of-state tuition. This can double the cost of attending one college versus another. However, if their parents or grandparents are paying for everything, why should the student care?

Alternative College Degree Options

There are several accredited alternative college degree options you might consider that could reduce your tuition costs and help you avoid on-campus attendance of classes. In addition to their traditional bricks-and-mortar classrooms, major universities are offering distance learning online degree programs. These are becoming increasingly popular, with online classes saving travel expenses, parking and commute time, as well as reducing pollution. For example, Ohio State Online, Purdue University Global, and Penn State World Campus offer bachelor's degrees and other programs in various fields of study that are entirely online. Some colleges offer degree assistance in technological fields for people who pass high-level industry certification exams, such as Cisco Certified Network Professional (CCNP). There are also various accredited colleges around the U.S. that give credit for approved practical experience in various disciplines, and some allow students to customize degree programs using alternative study methods with online distance learning.

Split the Bill and Set Expectations/Limitations

Many parents feel they need to "put their kids through college." Some do this at the expense of their own retirement. This can be a mistake in households where money is tight. Students can pay for college by obtaining scholarships, working part time, and obtaining student loans, and they have the rest of their life to catch up. Parents, especially those closer to retirement, do not have many options to fund or supplement their retirement nest egg.

Studies have shown that students who work part time (up to twenty hours per week), especially at college-related jobs, do better in school (they do not have as much free time to screw around). Those that pay a portion of their own tuition and college expenses do even better since they are invested in their own success. If you are a parent of a college-bound kid, consider paying 50 percent of their tuition if they contribute the other 50 percent. Also consider limiting the schools that they can attend to two or three good quality in-state public colleges. By paying for part of their own college education, students are more likely to take their coursework seriously, and it will foster ownership and responsibility in them. Some people refer to this as "having some skin in the game." With our daughters, while they were still very young, we set the expectation that they would (1) go to college, and (2) they would pay for half of the cost. Our daughters' college bachelor's degrees were paid for using a combination of 529 plans and savings from us, part-time work by them, and some federal student loans. In addition, one of our daughters got her master's degree through an employer that paid for her courses. Our other daughter used student loans to pay for her masters' degree. Table 17-2 lists some of the ways by which you can help pay for college.

Refer to **Exercise 17-1: Research College Cost Calculators**, at the end of this chapter, which will help you identify and make use of college cost estimating tools.

Refer to **Exercise 17-2: Research College Comparison Tools**, at the end of this chapter, which will help you identify and make use of college comparison tools.

Table 17-2: Ways to Pay/Offset/Reduce College Costs - Summary

Method	Notes
Attend community college for first two years	One of the best ways to reduce costs substantially. Get degree from two-year school and transfer to four-year school as a junior. Your degree will be from the four-year school.
Attend in-state college/university vs. out-of-state	Attending in-state school is still expensive but much cheaper than paying out-of-state tuition.
Attend public college/university vs. private college	Attending public school is cheaper than paying private school tuition.
Attend "commuter" in-state college to reduce room and board	Some public schools cater to working adults who can commute from home or apartment to avoid the cost of living on campus. They also offer distance learning classes via the Internet.
Student works part time	Students can do better in school and can help pay for tuition, etc. to help reduce the amount of student loans.
Parents and student split college costs (50/50 or 60/40)	Students appreciate schooling more and it reduces financial load on parents. Students have "skin in the game".
Tuition reimbursement from employer	Many employers will help pay for schooling (Associate, Bachelor's, Master's.) in exchange for commitment to stay with the company for a specified number of years.
Obtain scholarships (academic or sports)	Many scholarships are available that students could qualify for but might not be aware of. Awarded dollar amount is usually split over multiple semesters.
Obtain grants	Federal Pell Grants, SMART and LEAP grants. State and local grants. Check with school Financial Aid Office for options.
Gifts from parents/family	These can be tax deductible if under certain limits. Check with your tax preparer.

Invest in state-sponsored 529 savings plan (All states have them.)	Contributions are deductible for some state's income tax. Earnings are typically tax free if used for college and other qualified educational expenses. Some states offer tax advantages.
Take distance learning (online) courses offered by community colleges.	Can take through community college at much less tuition and avoids commute time, gas, environmental impact.
Take distance learning (online) courses offered by major universities and colleges	Major universities are offering entirely distance learning online degree programs. You can probably find a public one in your state with a Web search.
Shorten/Compress time in college	Take college-level dual credit courses in high school, Take CLEP exams. Take more than full-time class load. Go year round.
Take out Federal (Stafford) student loan (instead of private student loan sources.)	As a last resort, take out student loans only for the short comings from part time work and other sources. Only borrow what you need.
Tuition assistance	Some students can qualify depending on family income and other factors.
Credit card cash back with savings backup. Use cash-back credit card to charge tuition each semester. Assumes you have savings or 529 you can use to pay the balance in full.	If you can pay off the balance using a backup savings account, you can get about 2% cash back and only lose about ½% you would have gotten from leaving the money in savings. If you use a 529 college savings plan to pay the balance, you can use the contribution and gains tax free assuming you use the money for college expenses and track it on a spreadsheet.
Credit card balance transfer offer using bank check to pay for tuition at low APR (0-2%) for promotional period (12 or 18 mo.). If you pay it off within the promo period, you pay zero (0) interest.	The fee per transaction is normally 3-4% and you have a limited time to complete them (about 1-2 mo.)
Home Equity Line of Credit (HELOC) If you have equity in your home, you can borrow against it at a competitive rate and pay it off over time.	Assumes you have substantial equity in your home as the home is used as collateral. You can usually borrow against the home equity at a relatively low interest rate and the interest you pay may be tax deductible.

Join military or National Guard reserves.	In most states, a student can sign up with the National Guard reserves which offers educational assistance including tuition reimbursement. Must get passing grade. The GI bill is an option for some students.

A Plan to Get Your Master's Degree and Graduate With NO Debt!

Phase 1:

- Go to community college for two years at low cost, working toward a transferable two-year degree.
- Work part time (twenty hours/week) while attending community college to pay for tuition, books, expenses, etc. Community college tuition is very low, so you might be able to put a few bucks into savings for Phase 2.

Phase 2:

- Transfer to a bachelor's degree program at a university and graduate with a four-year degree.
- Continue to work part time at the university.
- Having completed your four-year degree, look for a job with a company or public sector employer that will pay for you to go to college part time to obtain your master's degree or forgive a portion of your student loans.

Part 6: College Payment Options and Tips

Student Loans

It is estimated that over 80 percent of students who earn a bachelor's degree borrow money in the form of federally subsidized and private student loans. Student-loan debt for federally backed loans alone is currently well over $1 trillion. Many students take out loans for at least part of their tuition and college expenses. Some borrow only for the shortfall from part-time work and other sources each year. Other students borrow the entire cost of tuition, books, and room and board for four years of college, leaving them with a huge debt and big monthly payments shortly after they graduate.

For federal student loans, payments are deferred until after graduation. Once a student ceases to be enrolled in at least four credit hours (part time), their student loans begin accruing interest and monthly payments are due. If they have taken out student loans and are ready to graduate, they need to complete exit counseling at studentloans.gov.

Avoid private student-loan sources (e.g., banks, credit unions), if possible. Federal student loans usually offer lower interest rates and have more flexible repayment terms and options than private student loans.

Personal Financial Awareness

Do not borrow the maximum a lender will loan you. Borrow only what you need from one year to the next. This is especially true if you are dealing with private third-party lenders.

College loans cannot be forgiven, even through bankruptcy. Do not cosign on a college loan. It can lead to serious family strife and financial problems! However, as of this writing, there are some members of Congress who are seeking to forgive existing student loans, which amounts to billions of dollars. As a general rule, don't borrow over 50 percent of your expected gross pay for your first job. For example, if you expect to make $50k/year when you graduate, try not take out more than $25k in student loans for an undergraduate (bachelor's) degree.

The FAFSA (Free Application for Federal Student Aid) is the application students fill out in order to determine their financial aid eligibility. Regardless of family income, the FAFSA should be completed to apply for federal student aid. The FAFSA needs to be filled out each academic year. Contact the financial aid office at your college or go to this Website for more information: https://studentaid.gov/h/apply-for-aid/fafsa

Additional Notes on 529 Plans (educational savings plan)
This information is provided here as a review from chapter 13 where the 529 was covered as an investment. A 529 plan is a state-sponsored tax-advantaged college savings/investment account that is designed to encourage saving for future education costs. All fifty U.S. states sponsor at least one type of 529 plan. The gains from a 529 are not taxed if used for qualified educational expenses for college, as well as primary and secondary education. Ohio's "CollegeAdvantage" plan (and most other 529 plans) can be used to pay for four-year, two-year, trade or regular vocational schools, certificate, graduate, and apprenticeship. Or you can use it to pay for K-12 tuition, student loan debt and more. Account earnings grow tax-free, and qualified withdrawals are free from federal and state income tax. You can't deduct your contributions from federal income tax, but some states' 529 plans offer state income tax advantages for in-state residents. Most states that have 529 plans offer a standard investment portfolio, and some allow you to pick and choose from other investments. You can also have accounts in multiple states, as there are differences between the various state plans. Many states also offer a prepaid tuition 529 option, which allows you to buy future college credits at today's cost. When filing income tax, large contributions can be exempt for the gift tax.

Actual Real World 529 Example
Mary and I started putting money into a 529 plan for each of our girls when they were about ten years old. We contributed about $10,000–12,000 into each of their accounts over an eight-year period. By the time they were ready to go to college, each of the accounts had increased in value to about $20,000 for each of our girls. The gains or earnings for each account had accumulated to a substantial amount over that time frame (your mileage may vary). When we withdrew money from the 529s for college expenses, we paid no tax on the earnings (tax free) or the original investment contributions (it had already been taxed as ordinary income). Valid college expenses included tuition, books, and room and board, as well as some other college-related expenses. I kept track of all the financial information by semester in a separate spreadsheet for each girl. The spreadsheet included the following:

- How much the tuition/books/room and board was for each semester
- How much was coming from our 529s
- How much the girls contributed from their part-time jobs and scholarships
- How much was coming from the student loans they had borrowed

College and Jobs - Summary Notes and Tips

- A two-year associate degree is becoming the entry-level requirement for many jobs.
- Jobs in Science/Technology/Engineering/Mathematics (STEM) are in high demand.
- "Keep interested in your own career, however humble. It is a real possession in the changing fortunes of time." (From the Desiderata)
- Do what you like, like what you do. If you enjoy what you do and do it well, the money will come.
- When you get a job, you are not working for someone else. You are working for yourself to develop skills, improve your mind, build your resume, and improve your promotability and employability for the future.
- Consider attending a community college for the first two years of a four-year degree to reduce costs.
- Attend in-state college/university in favor of out-of-state to keep costs down.
- Attend public college/university in favor of private college to keep costs down.
- As a student, work part time to reduce the need for student loans.
- Split the tuition college cost equally between student and parents.
- Investigate tuition reimbursement from employer.
- Investigate available scholarships (check with counselors).
- As a parent, invest in a state-sponsored 529 college savings plan when your kids are young.
- Take distance learning (online) courses when possible.
- Consider attending an online university that is accredited.
- If you must borrow to cover tuition and expenses, take out only federal student loans.
- Avoid private student loan sources (e.g., banks, credit unions).
- Regardless of family income, the FAFSA should be completed in order to apply for federal student aid.
- FAFSA needs to be filled out each academic year. You can submit a FAFSA at https://studentaid.gov/h/apply-for-aid/fafsa.
- College loans cannot be forgiven, even through bankruptcy.
- Don't borrow over 50 percent of your expected gross pay for your first job.
- Do not cosign on a college loan.
- Once a student ceases to be enrolled in at least four credit hours (part time), their student loans begin accruing interest, and monthly payments are due.
- Buy course books online through discount sources. Some offer free shipping for college students with a .edu email account.

Chapter 17 Exercises

Exercise 17-1: Research College Cost Calculators (optional)

In this exercise you will do a search for "college cost estimators," look through the choices available, and select a couple of them to do additional investigation. You will be looking for tools that are from objective sources and that allow you to enter the estimated tuition and other costs per year as well as sources for funding, such as savings and 529 plans. Figure 17-1 shows an example of a college cost estimating tool from https://www.calculator.net.

Figure 17-1: College Cost Calculator Example

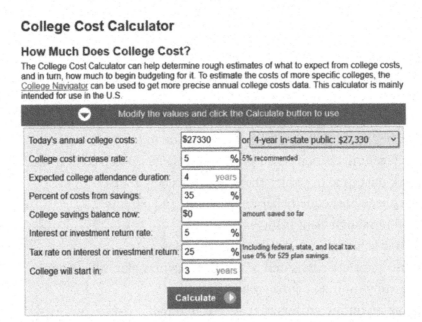

Exercise 17-2: Research College Comparison Tools (optional)

In this exercise, you will do a search for "college comparison tools," look through the choices available, and select a couple of them to do additional investigation. You will research online tools that allow you to compare colleges based on characteristics that are important to you. These types of tools allow you to compare multiple colleges based on various criteria and allow you to rate them to help you decide which one to attend. Be sure to select a reputable and objective source. The following screen shot is from U.S. News and World Report Website. By signing up for a free account, you can compare multiple schools and save your results.

Figure 17-2: College Comparison Tool Example
(https://www.usnews.com/best-colleges/compare/)

Compare Colleges

Find the college that's the best fit for you by using our college compare tool. See how they stack up against one another by ranking, alumni salary, tuition and financial aid, and admissions data.

School Name	Add to Compare

Chapter 18
Scams and Rip-offs

Chapter Overview:
This chapter provides information for what to do and not do to help avoid being duped and losing money through scams. Millions of dollars a year are handed over willingly to scam and rip-off artists by unsuspecting people. Take a look at the scams listed here to see if you may have been the target of any of them. New scams and rip-offs show up every day, so the information presented here is largely generic. However, it does provide some specific examples that I have seen. The chapter describes different types of scams and how they can be used to take advantage of people. It also provides information regarding end-user device security measures that you can take.

Various types of security apps are available to help protect you from scams and protect almost any end-user device such as a desktop, laptop, tablet, and smart phones from virus and malware attacks. Apple and Android smart phone devices should also be protected with a smart phone antivirus. User education and awareness and back up methods are also discussed. When you finish the chapter you will know about different types of phishing scams, robocalls, unsolicited text messages, identity theft, ransomware, browser trojan scams, and QR code scams.

Chapter PFS Integration:
The chapter does not cover a specific PFS Sheet.

Chapter Exercise:
  - **Exercise 18-1: Compare Computer and Smartphone Security Apps (optional)**

Refer to Exercise 18-1 at the end of this chapter. This is an unstructured exercise that can help you identify and compare virus and threat protection software apps that can help protect you from some types of scams and protect your devices from virus and malware attacks. As part of the exercise, you can evaluate your current security software to determine if the features and functionality meet your needs.

Chapter Notable Quotes:
Quote 18-1: "If something sounds too good to be true, then it probably is!" - Anonymous

Quote 18-2: "It's morally wrong to allow a sucker to keep his money." - W. C. Fields

Regarding the first quote above, most people can sense when something is a scam, but they want to believe it's legitimate, so they override their own gut feeling or suspicions and get duped anyway. A recent "acquaintance" says they can double your money in six months but there is a minimum investment of $1,000 that is required now since the deal may go away soon. What could go wrong? If you have a feeling that something is too good to be true, then honor that feeling and walk away. This is your intuition talking. Listen to it! Many people every year are tricked into investing in schemes by convincing and charismatic con artists. They are promised unrealistic returns, but they still hand over the money, and most never see it again.

Regarding the quote from W. C. Fields, unfortunately, some thieves probably believe it justifies taking advantage of people who often are clueless. Knowledge and awareness are the keys to not being yet another unsuspecting mark!

How Scams are Delivered

Most rip-off schemes are email-based or phone-based, although the number of scams via text message is increasing. They are becoming more prevalent, and scammers are becoming increasingly conniving and aggressive. Scams can also be perpetrated through regular mail, the Internet, phone (text and voice), or in person. Most phone/text scams are based on fear and try to scare targets into taking immediate action before they've had a chance to think things through. Knowledge of various types of scams and how they can be delivered can help us thwart many of them and avoid being taken advantage of.

Phishing Scams and Rip-offs - Notes and Tips:

If you encounter any of the following via phone, email, text, or any other delivery method, you are probably dealing with a scam of some type. If it's a phone call, you can just hang up. If it is email or text, just delete it without clicking or tapping any links.

Beware of these Phishing Ploys:

- Any caller that uses hostile or threatening language.
- Any caller you do not know or someone pretending to be someone you do know.
- Any caller identifying themselves as a relative (grandchild, niece, nephew) saying they are in trouble financially and asking you to send them money. Also, many scam artists prey on the elderly, so alert your parents or grandparents.
- Any caller that threatens to close your bank account if you do not send personal information immediately.
- Any caller requesting you to transfer money or pay a fee to renew a license, etc.
- Any caller requesting you to provide personal information like Social Security number, account numbers, PINs, etc. Just the fact that they called you indicates they are probably a scammer, even if the caller ID displays what appears to be normal company. Hang up and call the company to see if the call you received was legitimate.
- Any caller identifying themselves as being from a major company like Microsoft or Verizon, or identifying themselves as being from the Windows technical or Windows cancellation department.
- Any caller identifying themselves as being from the Social Security Administration and saying that your Social Security card has been suspended for "some reason."
- Any caller identifying themselves as being from the IRS, especially if they say you owe back taxes and will be sued if you do not at least pay a partial payment, wire money, or send them gift cards.

- A text message telling you to call an area code outside the U.S., especially 900 numbers. Fees as high as ten dollars/minute can be charged.
- Telemarketers - if it sounds too good to be true, it probably is.
- Mail, email, or phone offers where you can be a "secret shopper" or "secret buyer." My daughter received a letter with lots of legitimate looking company logos on the page, telling her how she could be a secret buyer. They wanted her to wire money to evaluate the service provided by Western Union. She was supposedly going to be reimbursed and would be paid a fee for her time. She did not take the bait.
- Any offer that involves you wiring money through Western Union or other wire transfer service.
- Any offer that involves a Nigerian (or other country's) prince who needs you to help him claim a million-dollar inheritance. Of course, you will be paid well for your assistance!
- Scams telling you that you are a sweepstakes winner, especially if you do not recall entering the sweepstakes.
- Calls from unusual area codes. Unless you were expecting the call, it's probably a scam artist. If they are a legitimate caller, they will usually leave a message. If it is a robocaller, they will not leave a message, and if they do, it is usually a partial message asking you to call a number.
- Email that comes from a .com.xx domain email address, where xx is a foreign country code. I just received one recently that only said, "I meant to send you this earlier," followed by a link to click. The "from" email address had my name, but the real source URL address, in parenthesis, was from a domain in Brazil (.com.br.).

Avoiding Scams when Buying and Selling (Tips and Notes from Craig's List)
- **Deal locally, face-to-face** - Follow this one rule and avoid 90 percent of scam attempts.
- **Do not extend payment to anyone you have not met in person.**
- **Beware of offers involving shipping** - Deal with locals you can meet in person.
- **Never wire funds (e.g., Western Union)** - Anyone who asks you to is probably a scammer.
- **Do not accept cashier/certified checks or money orders** - Banks will cash fakes, then hold you responsible.
- **Transactions are between users only** - No third party provides a "guarantee."
- **Never give out financial info** (bank account, social security, PayPal account, etc.).
- **Do not rent or purchase sight-unseen** - That amazing "deal" may not exist.
- **Refuse background/credit checks** - Until you have met landlord/employer in person.
- **Can you spot a scam?** (Tips from Bank of America)
- You are told to act immediately or something bad will happen.
- They ask for personal information or codes. (Never share codes or personal information when contacted unexpectedly by phone, text, email, computer alert, or social media.)
- You are asked to pay in an unusual way, such as wire transfer, gift cards, or payment apps.

Robocalls

It is estimated that in the month of January 2021, there were over five billion robocalls in the U.S. alone. I used to receive about three to five a day. Most of them appeared to be from legitimate area codes in Ohio. There is little you can do except not answer and let it go to voicemail, or you can just hang up. Telemarketers can use spoof apps that allow them to insert a bogus source phone number and any message they want into the calls so that it displays on your phone as the caller ID for the incoming call. You cannot access the real number that made the call. If you try to call the displayed number back, you get a message that the number is not in service. You cannot even block the caller because the actual number they are calling from is not known.

Recent legislation helps protect citizens from nuisance and illegal calls. The law imposes fines of up to $10,000 for illegal calls and encourages the Federal Communications Commission (FCC) and telecom providers to develop better laws and methods to help prevent unwanted calls. Nuisance calls are those that may try to sell you something—like an extended warranty for your car—or they might try to get you to switch to another electrical power company to lower your utility bills. Illegal calls are those that try to scam you and break FCC regulations.

What you can do about robocalls:

- Sign up for the federal "Do not call" registry to limit the number of sales calls you get. Go to their Website at https://www.donotcall.gov
- Sign up for a third-party robocall blocking app or service, such as a Robokiller or Truecaller. The cost of the software ranges from free to about five dollars/month.
- Use the "Silence Unknown Callers" option on your smart phone to screen calls and automatically send calls from unknown callers to voice mail. On an iPhone, this is done under Settings>Phone. If the call is important, they will usually leave a message. Calls from your contacts list and recent outgoing calls will not be screened.
- Contact your service provider to see what services they may be able to offer. I enrolled in Call Filter for Free with my provider.

Phishing Scam Phone Example 1

I received a phishing (phone/fish) call from a guy who said his name was "Jake Green" and he was from the tech support department of the Microsoft Operating System. He informed me that an intrusive virus software had infiltrated my PC, and they were getting error messages sent to their server at Microsoft. He asked me if I was the primary user. He wanted me to go my PC and type some keystrokes that he was going to tell me. Microsoft would never do this. I hung up.

Phishing Scam Phone Example 2

I received another phishing call, this one supposedly from the IRS. It was a recorded message in a heavy European accent. It said "You are being sued by the IRS. Please call this number ASAP to prevent legal action: 999-999-9999. I repeat, call 999-999-9999."

If you call the number, they will try to get personal information such as credit card number, name on the card, expiration date, and security code. The IRS does not notify people of tax issues by phone unless they have sent multiple written communications. And they will not threaten you with a suit over the phone.

Phishing Scam Email Example

I got this email, supposedly from my wife Mary, but it was actually from some email address in Germany (.de). If you get one like this, be sure you don't click the imbedded "www" link. They try to entice you by saying things like "Just wondering if you know the couple in this picture . . ."

> **From:** Mary <2ab17rav4@xyz.de>
> **Sent:** Monday, February 22, 2021 12:16 PM
> **To:** you <abcdef99@emailco.com>
> **Subject:** Fwd: Message for Mary
> (De-personalize? On Monday, February 22, 2021 10:08 AM, Mary Lorenz wrote:
> **Just wondering if you know the couple in this picture – I'm pretty sure you must be familiar** http://www.abcd.efgh.ijlkmn.com/

Ransomware Email Scams

These are some of the most dangerous scams. They can infect your computer when you open an email attachment or click a link from an unknown source or a source that may look familiar. When you click on the link, the virus is activated and displays a message telling you to pay some amount of money or your hard drive will be wiped clean, and you will lose all your data. In some cases, this is not an idle threat. To protect yourself, run antivirus software on a regular basis, don't open emails from an unknown source, and back up your important files to an external drive or cloud-based service such as Microsoft OneDrive. Refer to the Computer and Phone Security section at the end of this chapter for more on cloud-based backup services.

Protecting Your Identity (See Chapter 8 and Chapter 9 for additional information)

Identity theft is becoming increasingly common. This can occur when someone obtains personal information about you, such as your Social Security number, and attempts to take out a loan or open a credit account in your name. Unless you've had it happen to you, you don't fully appreciate how it can affect your life. Horror stories abound from people who have gone through the painful and laborious process of trying to clean up and purge credit activity records that don't belong to them. This chapter plus Chapter 8: Credit Scores and Credit Reports, and Chapter 9: Credit and Credit Cards, provide the information and precautions you need to take to protect your identity and thwart would-be identity thieves. Steps you can take that are covered in this book include the following:

- Credit monitoring
- Reviewing your credit reports
- Freezing your credit file
- Being suspicious of anyone who contacts you to talk about money.

Identity Theft Credit Card Scam

Identity theft can be something as simple as just losing a credit card and someone using it unlawfully. An easy way for someone to steal your identity is for them to take your credit card to process a payment and then keep a copy of the card (or transaction slip) or just record the information from the card. I went to a restaurant in New York City and paid with a credit card. Within a week, I got a call from the credit card company asking if I had authorized purchases of over $1000 from the Eastern European country of Estonia. When I told them no, the card company denied the charges, and I was not liable for anything. Be sure to review your credit card bills carefully. If you notice charges that you know you did not make, contact the credit card company (within thirty days to be safe), contest the charges, and you will likely not be liable. For more info about identity theft, visit the Federal Trade Commission (FTC) Website at https://consumer.ftc.gov/features/identity-theft or https://www.identitytheft.gov. Did someone steal or use your personal information? Act quickly to limit the damage.

Identifying and Dealing with Scams:

- If you suspect that a call, a mailed piece, an email, or a text is a scam, search for XYZ (name of company) plus the words "scam," "rip-off," or "complaints." You may get lots of hits from other unhappy people reporting the scammers.
- If you are notified of anything you supposedly "won" that requires you send money first, it is a scam (I saw this warning on a poster in the post office).
- If you receive an email or regular mail that looks suspicious, look for strange sentence structure or incorrectly used or misspelled words. Usually these are scams and are often foreign in origin. English is likely not the scammer's first language. Do not click on any links.
- Beware of phishing phone calls trying to trick you into providing personal information, like Social Security number, bank account numbers, login ID, password, or access codes.
- Beware of job sites posting bogus help wanted ads. They can gather your personal information and rip you off.

Cell Phone Text Scam Example 1

I recently received a text message to my cell phone number that read: "You are the lucky beneficial of one million two hundred thousand dollars in the Mega Millions May international online jackpot draw. Payment Code: USUKMEGA81092508. As soon as you receive this message, Email our claim representative at: powerballlottery@abcde, 999-999-9999." I did a search on "abcde" (actual domain name not shown), and it came back with a URL in Romania (RU). Note the incorrect use of the word "beneficial." The sentence should read: "You are the lucky beneficiary . . ." The text was probably sent by someone whose primary language was not English.

Cell Phone Text Scam Example 2

I recently received a popup message on my cell phone that said it was from Apple Security and informed me that I had a trojan virus on my iPhone that had been installed at one of the Websites I had just visited.

I was instructed to click on the button to remove the virus and then update my operating system. Instead, I turned the phone off and then back on. I looked up the wording on the popup message and found several entries describing this supposed virus alert as a scam. Whatever you do, DON'T call a number, press a button, or click on a link.

Cell Phone Text Scam Example 3
Here's another example of a phishing attempt I faced. It was pretty sneaky but believable. I might have fallen for it except I had not applied for unemployment! They also made a grammatical error by using the word "purpose" when it should have been "purposes." This scam could also have been an email scam. I did a search on the domain of ".ly," and the link they wanted me to click on was from the country of Libya. Here's the text from the scam.

"Your Ohio unemployment insurance claim is currently on hold for verification purpose. Please verify your claim by clicking the link provided below to sign in and activate your account."
https://xyz.ly/abc123

Cell Phone Text Scam Example 4
Here's another recent example of attempted phishing. The text message says your Amazon account has been compromised and provides a link to click on to log in and verify your account credentials. If action was not taken, the account would be cancelled. There were errors in the text, and the Web link was from another country. Once again, no matter how tempted you may be to, don't click links in texts or emails!

Browser Trojan DLL Scam Example 1
This is a trojan malware virus that attaches itself to your browser and pops up several windows with bogus error messages stating that it has detected a dangerous virus file, and it appears to be from Microsoft with very realistic-looking warning graphics. It tries to convince you to call a number in order to receive support. It says that if you don't call the phone number shown, it will remove the virus and disconnect you from the Internet to protect the Microsoft servers from your computer. There are several legitimate guides on the Internet that can help you remove the Trojan virus. Just enter the name of the xxxxxx.dll file on the fake virus screen and look through the links available to find one from a known source. This trojan is obviously a scam. A legitimate organization would not threaten you if you did not call a phone number.

QR Code Scams
QR codes are everywhere and can be very handy for consumers. By simply scanning the square digital code with your smart phone camera, it opens a Web link or URL that can provide additional information for restaurants and other businesses, from products on sale to beers on tap. Just the other day I was watching a TV show, and a QR code popped up on the screen as part of a commercial. I scanned the code from my phone, and it took me to Web link where I downloaded the free app for the program. That all sounds great, but scammers are rapidly developing ways to take advantage of these handy codes. A common ploy is to use a fake QR code to direct consumers to illegitimate Websites to try and take advantage of them.

Do a search for "QR code scams," and you will see many warnings about them and information on how they work, including YouTube videos.

Another QR code scam technique is done at local shops and establishments where a sign is posted with a QR code, and you are encouraged to scan the code to get points, set up an account, etc. Beware! Scammers can create a QR code with peel-off adhesive on the back and apply it to an existing valid code without the business owner's knowledge. Scammers are just waiting for customers to scan the code so they can take them to a Website to collect vital personal information, all unbeknownst to the customer.

To help thwart these scammers, when you hold your phone up to the code, look carefully at the URL Web address displayed. This is the Internet location you will access when you take a photo of the QR code. If it looks suspicious, don't click the code. People have had their bank account drained by scanning fake codes.

To minimize chances of getting scammed, refer to the following:
- Check to see if a sticker has been applied and avoid scanning sticker codes.
- Codes in printed magazines are usually legit.
- Read the URL/Web address (take note of the Website where you will be sent).
- Verify the Web page source. Does it look legit?
- Avoid short links. They can hide the real Web link and turn into long links if you click them.
- Download a QR code scanner that also validates Web page URL links. Do a Web search for "QR code scanner" to see apps that are available.

Do not pay for anything using a QR code. Go online to make your payment to verify the payee.
Some municipalities use QR code technology to let drivers pay for parking online. Scammers put fake QR code stickers over the real ones, and when motorists scan the fake QR codes, instead of being taken to the municipalities' authorized Website or app, they are redirected to a fake Website that collects their credit card information.

Phishing Example – Bank email response to me when I notified them of phishing email.

      From: Abuse <abuse@chase.com>

      Date: December 17, 2022 at 4:42:37 PM EST

      To: James Lorenz <email address>

      Subject: We received your message

Thank you for forwarding us the suspicious email you received. We will review it and let you know if you need to do anything else. If you responded to this or any other "phishing" email, call us immediately. You can also visit bankname.com/contactus to find the best phone number based on your accounts. In the future, you should continue to look out for any email that does the following:
- Asks you to confirm, verify, or give out account numbers, Social Security numbers, or other personal information.
- Threatens to close your account if you do not send personal information immediately.

- Says there are unauthorized charges on your account and asks you to enter or confirm your account information.

These emails are designed to look like we sent them, so be careful and report any that you receive. We work relentlessly to shut down sites that generate fraudulent email. For more information and advice, visit bankname.com/security. Thank you for choosing bank-name.

Warning from the Social Security Administration - When you sign up for Social Security, on the back of the welcome packet, is the following warning:

!SCAM ALERT!
Scammers are pretending to be government employees. They may threaten you and demand immediate payment to avoid arrest or other legal action. Don't be fooled! If you receive a suspicious call, hang up. Do not give them money or personal information. Report the scam to OIG.SSA.GOV

Figure 18-1: Scammer Sam

Fraud and Scam Information from the FTC and AARP
AARP works with the Federal Trade Commission (FTC) to help thwart scams and rip-offs. An AARP membership provides access to many benefits, including the AARP Fraud Watch Network. You can create a free account and do a search for money scams and frauds. You can obtain a lot of useful information as well as the tips and tools that are available. The elderly are a favorite target of scamsters. For example, the FTC reported that over $1 billion had been lost to cryptocurrency scams over the previous fifteen months, as of this writing. They said the median loss for crypto victims aged sixty and older was more than $8,000. Talk to your parents and grandparents about scams, and let them know what to look out for. Any urgent request for payment in gift cards, wire transfers, or cryptocurrency is more than likely a scam. Fraud involving cryptocurrency is becoming increasingly common. Also, be sure to review with Web-savvy family members the sections above on identifying and dealing with scams and phishing scams and rip-off notes and tips. If you adhere to the cautionary suggestions of what to do or not to do, you can greatly reduce your chances of getting scammed. However, new scams are coming out all the time. The list of suggestions given here should be considered only a partial list.

The FTC consumer Website https://consumer.ftc.gov provides lots of tips and information on scams and how to avoid them for the following areas:

- **Shopping and Donating**
- **Credit, Loans, and Debt**
- **Jobs and Making Money**
- **Unwanted Calls, Emails, and Texts**
- **Identity Theft and Online Security Scams**

Computer and Phone Security

Whether you have a desktop, laptop, tablet, smart phone, or all of the above, security should be your number one priority and should be applied in multiple ways as follows:

Protective and Preventive AntiXware

These can include antivirus, anti-malware, anti-ransomware, and privacy measures for email and browsers. This software can help prevent attacks before they occur and neutralize them before they do damage. Install a good quality virus/malware protection software package that can alert you to malicious intruders and potentially avoid many lost hours of work, especially if you do a full scan on a nightly basis. A good antiXware package can fend off most viruses and malware and quarantine the offending files(s). Be sure to do the research, read the reviews, and ask around as to what others are using. Cost should not be the most important factor in selecting the product. Many companies and organizations have multiuser license agreements, and their employees or members are allowed to install virus software for free. You should have security software installed on any PC/Windows-based computers as well as Mac OS devices. PC Magazine and other reputable sources do frequent reviews of these types of products, and you should be well protected with one of the top candidates. Windows Defender comes with newer versions of Windows, but there are also many good packages out there.

Apple and Android smart phone devices should also be protected with a smart phone antivirus app, although it is less likely that these devices will get infected. There are free and inexpensive apps available. Do a search for "smart phone antivirus apps" or do specific searches for Android or Apple (iOS) antivirus apps to see products and reviews.

User Education and Awareness

One of the most important things you can do is not opening or clicking on suspicious links in emails or text messages. An educated user community can go a long way toward thwarting rip-offs, scams, and malware. Many companies and organizations publish weekly or monthly newsletters letting people know about the latest scams. Included with a discussion on security software are password management apps, which were covered in Chapter 2 with the Personal Financial Spreadsheet (PFS).

Backup Methods

If your PC or smart phone is attacked and compromised in some way and you have lost access to your data or files, backups can help you recover access. Make sure to do regular backups of individual files daily and entire drives full of data weekly or monthly. Some common and relatively easy ways to back up files are listed here:

- **Use cloud-based backup service** - Software such as **Windows "OneDrive"** automatically backs up and syncs Office and other files to the cloud for access if the PC is damaged or otherwise unable to access the files. You can get 5GB (gigabytes) of storage for free and 1TB (terabyte) with a subscription to Microsoft Office. OneDrive comes bundled with Microsoft 365. If you don't have or choose not to use OneDrive, there are other backup/sync services available.
- **Copy files to an external drive.** Copy important files from the local hard drive to an external USB hard drive or USB flash drive. These external drives are inexpensive and provide a lot of storage that can be kept offsite.
- **Email important files as an attachment**. When you've finished working on an important file, you can email it to yourself at an alternate account. If the main device is damaged or you cannot access the file locally, you can get to the email attachment from virtually any other device with access to the secondary account via the Internet.

Using Unsecure Wi-Fi Networks to Access Your Financial Data

If you access your banking data remotely, never use an unsecure public Wi-Fi network like you might find at a hotel or coffee shop. Make sure you are on a private home Wi-Fi network that requires a password, and use the bank's Website with two-factor authentication, if it is available. Better yet, use a Virtual Private Network (VPN) over Wi-Fi or your provider's cell data network. Using the bank's mobile app over the cell data network (LTE or 5G) is pretty safe and relatively fast. If you use a VPN or cell data, your financial information is encrypted end-to-end from your device to the bank's network. However, even if you are on a private Wi-Fi network, anyone else on that internal network can snoop on your data. On unsecure networks, login information, account numbers, and other financial data are transmitted in clear text, and a hacker can see and capture your financial data.

Chapter 18 Exercise

Exercise 18-1: Compare Computer and Smartphone Security Apps (optional)

This is an unstructured exercise that can help you identify and compare virus and threat protection software apps that can protect you from some types of scams and protect your devices from external attacks. If you already have one of these apps (likely), you can also take this opportunity to investigate the security software currently installed on your computer (laptop or whatever) and/or smart phone. If you do not want to keep the current security software, you can do some research and choose the one that better meets your needs. You may want to deinstall the old security software.

Chapter 19
Personal Financial Planning

Chapter Overview:

This chapter provides information and tools to help you develop a plan to get your financial house in order, based on where you are currently. It focuses on the Personal Financial Spreadsheet (PFS) Financial Planning and Projects (Fin-Plan) sheet, which was developed for this chapter. The chapter also addresses the key Personal Financial Indicators (PFIs) covered in the book. The PFS in combination with the PFIs can help determine your current financial status. Together they can help establish a framework for savings and investments as well as budgeting and maintenance of key personal indicators. The chapter offers a structured approach for moving forward and building your Personal Financial Plan.

Chapter PFS and PFI Integration:

This chapter focuses on the Personal Financial Spreadsheet (PFS) Financial Planning and Projects sheet with a label of "Fin-Plan" to consolidate key financial indicators and investing goals from Chapter 7 (Savings), Chapter 13 (Investments), and Chapter 14 (Retirement). The top ten Personal Financial Indicators (PFIs) introduced in previous chapters are incorporated into the Fin-Plan spreadsheet, along with savings and investments. For each goal and action item, you can enter the Start Date, Completion Date, Current Dollar Amount or Percentage, Target Goal, and Actual Values, as well as Notes. Refer to Figure 19-1 for a screenshot of Fin-Plan sheet, Section 1.1.

Chapter Exercise:

- **Exercise 19-1 (Fin-Plan Section 1): Gather Personal Financial Planning Data**
- **Exercise 19-2 (Fin-Plan Section 2): Gather Major Purchases and Projects Data**

Chapter Notable Quotes:

Quote 19-1: "Success is not final. Failure is not fatal. It is the courage to continue that counts." - Winston Churchill

Quote 19-2: "Learn from the past, plan for the future and live in the present." - Anonymous

Personal Financial Goals and Plans

Your personal financial goals and plans to achieve them are based on various factors such as your age, life stage, lifestyle, current financial situation and attitude toward money. The goals and financial plan for an 18-year-old, who has no credit history, and wants to buy their first car will be very different as compared to a retired couple who have built their nest egg and have excellent credit. Or, when compared to a middle-aged person who is in their prime working years and making good money but has serious financial problems and bad credit.

The Personal Financial Spreadsheet (PFS) is a key tool for managing your finances and setting goals. There are many factors contributing to an overall financial plan that draw on information from multiple chapters in this book. These areas have been identified as you have progressed through each chapter and here we are, at the end of the financial content. If you haven't done so already, this is an opportunity to put together a comprehensive personal financial plan that addresses the areas of greatest interest and importance to you. You can develop short (one-year), intermediate (two- to three-year), and longer-term (three- to five-year or more) financial goals through retirement, if appropriate for your situation. Some of the goals shown in the PFS Fin-Plan sheet are short term and some are longer term. These are suggestions and you can replace them or add your own. You can discuss with your financial advisor, if you have one, the order in which you want to attack them. For anyone to be very successful financially over the long run, they must have goals and a plan to achieve them. Refer to PFS Sheet - Financial Planning and Projects (Tab: Fin-Plan) for ideas on financial planning and examples of goals and plans. Figures 19-1, 19-2, and 19-3 show screenshots with sample entries for financial goals.

Be S.M.A.R.T.

Setting goals and developing plans can be helpful in any aspect of your life, but the goals must be realistic and achievable, and the results must be measurable within a given timeframe. Many financial professionals like to use the "SMART" criteria when setting goals. My wife and I use this technique at our annual financial offsite meetings. **SMART** is an acronym that can be applied when defining goals and objectives. It helps you remember the essential characteristics of any goal. To be a "SMART" goal, it must be all of the following:

- Specific
- Measurable
- Achievable
- Relevant
- Time-bound

Listed below are some examples of SMART goals from people with differing financial situations. Notice that in each case, they are statements almost like affirmations, that specify exactly what goal is to be achieved, how it is to be measured, and when. These goals can be short term or long term, big or small, aggressive or conservative. The important thing is that they move you in the right direction financially, and that you have a backup plan if the goal is not satisfactorily achieved.

"I will improve my credit score from 700 to 750 by the end of this year by paying down the balance on my high-interest credit cards, which will improve my Debt-to-Credit (DTC) ratio."

"I will build my emergency fund savings account to be $3,000 over the next six months by working another part-time job and reducing my nonessential discretionary spending by $200 per month."

"Over the next two weeks, I will comparison shop auto insurance providers' policies and reduce my monthly premium by 20 percent."

"In five years, by the time I am fifty years old, I will work to have a diversified financial portfolio worth $50,000 by investing monthly into multiple equity-based mutual funds through the use of dollar cost averaging."

Certified Financial Planner (CFP) Assistance
When you finish reading this chapter and entering data into PFS sheet Fin-Plan for Exercise 19-1, consider seeking the assistance of a professional financial advisor if you have not already done so. A Certified Financial Planner (CFP) can help you analyze your financial situation, help you establish appropriate financial goals, and help you devise a plan to achieve them. Take your spreadsheet with you and review it with them. Many financial advisors do not charge for an initial visit. You could gain quite a lot of information from that meeting. It could also be worthwhile to pay a small fee for a follow-on meeting, to help point you in the right direction and help you develop your comprehensive personal financial plan. Selecting and acquiring the services of a CFP for financial advice was described in Chapter 13: Investing Basics.

PFS Financial Planning and Projects Worksheet Information
The PFS Financial Planning and Projects (Fin-Plan) sheet is divided into two main sections, and each main section is divided into three subsections, as indicated below. See Figures 19-1 through and 19-4.

Section 1: Personal Financial Planning Goals (Figures 19-1 through 19-3)
    1.1 Personal Financial Indicators
    1.2 Savings and Investments
    1.3 Financial Action Items

Section 2: Major Purchases and Projects (Figure 19-4)
    2.1 Home-Related Plans
    2.2 Vehicle-Related Plans
    2.3 Other/Big Ticket Plans

The first Subsection (1.1) contains the ten key financial indicators covered in the book with suggested "not-to-exceed" (NTE) values to help keep your credit healthy and avoid lowering your score. Five of the indicators are key dollar amounts (e.g., Cash Flow) and five are ratio or percentage indicators (e.g., Debt-to-Income). The second subsection (1.2) is for savings and investment goals. And the third subsection (1.3) is for financial action items (e.g., reduce discretionary spending or verify adequate insurance). Refer to **Exercise 19-1 (Fin-Plan Section 1): Gather Personal Financial Planning Data** and **Exercise 19-2 (Fin-Plan Section 2): Gather Major Purchases and Projects Data**, at the end of this chapter.

In these exercises, you will collect data for the Fin-Plan sheet in two parts. The first part of the sheet is for your financial plan. The second part assists in documenting big ticket project items for home, auto, and other. This is the concluding exercise of the book and will hopefully bring it all together. Refer to Figures 19-1, 19-2, and 19-3 for sample entries you can use in your financial plan and projects, or customize the spreadsheet to outline your own goals.

Note: Make a copy of these figures to assist you in collecting data for the Fin-Plan sheet.

> **Figure 19-1: Fin-Plan Sect 1.1 Personal Financial Indicator (PFI) Goals**
> **Figure 19-2: Fin-Plan Sect 1.2 Savings and Investments Goals**
> **Figure 19-3: Fin-Plan Sect 1.3 Financial Action Items Goals**
> **Figure 19-4: Fin-Plan Sect 2.1-2.3 Major Purchases and Projects Goals**

Chapter 19 Exercises - Overview and Screenshots

Note: Exercises 19-1 and 19-2 assume you have completed **Exercise 13-3: Evaluate Your PFI Status Using the Investing Checklist** from the prior Chapter 13. If not, you can still complete this exercise, although it may take longer.

You will start by collecting Exercise 19-1 data for Fin-Plan Section 1 (Personal Financial Planning Goals). Fin-Plan Section 1 focuses on your main financial plan goals (PFIs, investments/savings, and action items), and Section 2 is for major project plans and expenditures. It is recommended that you complete Section 1 to develop your personal financial plan. Section 2 is independent from Section and is optional.

Note: This exercise may be a bit overwhelming or seem complicated at first, but explanations will be provided to help simplify things and offer guidance along the way. Make a copy of ALL Figures in this chapter to assist you in collecting data for the Fin-Plan sheet and make notes on them. Take time to brainstorm with your significant other and try to pick your **top five financial goals** and your **top five projects** before starting Exercise 19-1.

Figure 19-1: Fin-Plan Sect 1.1 Personal Financial Indicator (PFI) Goals

	A	B	C	D	E	F	G
1	**Financial Planning and Projects**		Book Build Ch. 19				Updated: MM-DD-YYYY
2							
3	**<<< Sect 1: Personal Financial Planning Goals >>>**						
4							
5	**< 1.1 Personal Financial Indicators >**	**Start Date**	**Compl. Date**	**Currently**	**Target Goal**	**Actual**	**Notes**
6	Gross Income (GI-$$) (Before taxes)	mm-dd-yy	mm-dd-yy	$0	$0	$0	
7	Net Income (NI$-$$) (After taxes)	mm-dd-yy	mm-dd-yy	$0	$0	$0	
8	Personal Cash Flow (PCF-$$)	mm-dd-yy	mm-dd-yy	$0	$0	$0	
9	Personal Net worth (PNW-$$)	mm-dd-yy	mm-dd-yy	$0	$0	$0	
10	Emergency Fund (EF-$$)	mm-dd-yy	mm-dd-yy	$0	$0	$0	
11							
12	Debt-to-Income (DTI-%) (max 40%)	mm-dd-yy	mm-dd-yy	0.0%	0.0%	0.0%	
13	Debt-to-Credit (DTC-%) (max 20%)	mm-dd-yy	mm-dd-yy	0.0%	0.0%	0.0%	
14	Savings-to-Income (STI-%) (max 20%)	mm-dd-yy	mm-dd-yy	0.0%	0.0%	0.0%	
15	Housing-to-Income (HTI-%) (max 30%)	mm-dd-yy	mm-dd-yy	0.0%	0.0%	0.0%	
16	Transportation-to-Income (TTI-%) (max 10%)	mm-dd-yy	mm-dd-yy	0.0%	0.0%	0.0%	
17	Other						
18	Other						

Auto-Info | Insure-Pols | **Fin-Plan** | Income-Exp-F | Assets-Liab-F | Cred-Cards-F | Home-Info-F | Auto-Info-F | Insure-Pols-F | Fin-Plan-F

Figure 19-2: Fin-Plan Sect 1.2 Savings and Investments Goals

	A	B	C	D	E	F	G
20	**< 1.2 Savings and Investments >**	**Start Date**	**Compl. Date**	**Currently**	**Target Goal**	**Actual**	**Notes**
21	Employer 401K or 403B Plan	mm-dd-yy	mm-dd-yy	$0	$0	$0	
22	Regular IRA	mm-dd-yy	mm-dd-yy	$0	$0	$0	
23	Roth IRA	mm-dd-yy	mm-dd-yy	$0	$0	$0	
24	Stocks (Equities)	mm-dd-yy	mm-dd-yy	$0	$0	$0	
25	Bonds (Fixed Income)	mm-dd-yy	mm-dd-yy	$0	$0	$0	
26	Cash Equivalents (CD or MMA)	mm-dd-yy	mm-dd-yy	$0	$0	$0	
27	Savings - Short term	mm-dd-yy	mm-dd-yy	$0	$0	$0	
28	Savings - Long term	mm-dd-yy	mm-dd-yy	$0	$0	$0	
29	Other						
30	Other						

Figure 19-3: Fin-Plan Sect 1.3 Financial Action Items Goals

	A	B	C	D	E	F	G
34	**< 1.3 Financial Action Items >**	**Start Date**	**Compl. Date**	**Currently**	**Target Goal**	**Actual**	**Notes**
35	Build Personal Financial Spreadsheet (PFS)	mm-dd-yy	mm-dd-yy	$0	$0	$0	
36	Seek assitance of a financial advisor	mm-dd-yy	mm-dd-yy	$0	$0	$0	
37	Make payments to creditors on time	mm-dd-yy	mm-dd-yy	$0	$0	$0	
38	Create and monitor a monthly budget	mm-dd-yy	mm-dd-yy	$0	$0	$0	
39	Decrease discretionary spending	mm-dd-yy	mm-dd-yy	$0	$0	$0	
40	Review and reduce monthly fixed expenses	mm-dd-yy	mm-dd-yy	$0	$0	$0	
41	Reduce high-interest credit card debt	mm-dd-yy	mm-dd-yy	$0	$0	$0	
42	Add to an emergency fund savings account.	mm-dd-yy	mm-dd-yy	$0	$0	$0	
43	Add to an investment account (401K or IRA)	mm-dd-yy	mm-dd-yy	$0	$0	$0	
44	Check credit score and credit report	mm-dd-yy	mm-dd-yy	$0	$0	$0	
45	Review credit card and bank statements	mm-dd-yy	mm-dd-yy	$0	$0	$0	
46	Review insurance types and coverage	mm-dd-yy	mm-dd-yy	$0	$0	$0	
47	Shop insurance costs for savings	mm-dd-yy	mm-dd-yy	$0	$0	$0	
48	Other	mm-dd-yy	mm-dd-yy	$0	$0	$0	
49	Be Mindfully Aware and Be Here Now!	Every Day!					
50							

Figure 19-4: Fin-Plan Sect 2.1-2.3 Major Purchases and Projects Goals

	A	B	C	D	E	F
51	<<< Sect 2: Major Purchases and Projects >>>					
52						
53	< 2.1 Home Related Plans >					
54	Project Description	Start Date	Compl. Date		Amt. Budget	Amt. Spent
55	Gutter guards	mm-dd-yy	mm-dd-yy		$0	$0
56	Outdoor Electrical	mm-dd-yy	mm-dd-yy		$0	$0
57	New Toilets (2x)	mm-dd-yy	mm-dd-yy		$0	$0
58	Fence	mm-dd-yy	mm-dd-yy		$0	$0
59	Countertops	mm-dd-yy	mm-dd-yy		$0	$0
60	Replace stairs carpet	mm-dd-yy	mm-dd-yy		$0	$0
61						
62						
63	Total Home Projects Budget/Spent				$0	$0
64					=SUM(E55:E62)	=SUM(F55:F62)
65						
66	< 2.2 Vehicle Related Plans >					
67	New car	mm-dd-yy	mm-dd-yy		$0	$0
68	Car tires	mm-dd-yy	mm-dd-yy		$0	$0
69	Pontoon House boat	mm-dd-yy	mm-dd-yy		$0	$0
70						
71					$0	$0
72	Total Vehicle Projects Budget/Spent				=SUM(E67:E70)	=SUM(F67:F70)
73						
74						
75	< 2.3 Other / Big Ticket Plans >					
76	New bed	mm-dd-yy	mm-dd-yy		$0	$0
77	Refrigerator	mm-dd-yy	mm-dd-yy		$0	$0
78	Summer vacation	mm-dd-yy	mm-dd-yy		$0	$0
79						
80						
81	Total Other / Big Ticket Budget/Spent				$0	$0
82					=SUM(E76:E80)	=SUM(F76:F80)

<u>Chapter 19 Exercises</u>
Concluding Financial Planning Exercises 19-1 and 19-2

PFS Sheet: Financial Planning and Projects (Tab Fin-Plan)
(Preparation and Background Information)

- **Review Chapter 13 Exercise: 13-3** - Assumes you have completed **Exercise 13-3: Evaluate Your PFI Status Using the Investing Checklist.** If not, you can still complete this exercise although it may take longer.
- **Make Copies of PFS Screenshots** - Before starting Exercise 19-1, make a copy of screenshot Figures 19-1, 19-2, and 19-3 to assist you in collecting and filling out the corresponding Financial Planning Spreadsheet Subsections 1.1, 1.2, and 1.3.
- **PFS sheet Fin-Plan Goals - Section 1** - Provided for use in developing your personal financial plan. It includes financial indicators, savings and investments and financial action Items.
- **PFS sheet Fin-Plan Goals - Section 2 (optional)** - Provided for planning and tracking projects and major expenditures based on estimated/actual dates and money budgeted and spent. The sample entries in the Fin-Plan sheet are just a starting point. Customize Section 1 by adding your own financial goals as you see fit. Section 2 is optional and can be used to record and track any major projects or expenditures.
- **Brainstorm financial goals and projects** - Before you start Exercise 19-1, take some time to think about and establish some "SMART" financial goals. Meet with your partner or significant other, and brainstorm ideas related to financial goals. You might do this at your "offsite meeting". Each of you should jot down notes and then get together and compare notes. Start with short term goals and then develop some longer-term goals. Do the same before starting Section 2 of this exercise for major planned projects. But this time write down your major personal goals for home improvement or vacations and/or other major projects.

Exercise 19-1 (Fin-Plan Section 1): Gather Personal Financial Planning Data
In this exercise you will collect data and enter it into the copies you made of screenshot Figures 19-1, 19-2, and 19-3, for the spreadsheet sections listed below.

- **Personal Financial Indicators (PFIs)** - Use copy of Figure 19-1
- **Savings and Investments** - Use copy of Figure 19-2
- **Financial Action Items (AIs)** - Use copy of Figure 19-3

Your working copy of Figure 19-1 has entries for the Top Ten Personal Financial Indicators (section 1.1 of the PFS Fin-Plan sheet), Figure 19-2 has Savings and Investments (section 1.2), and Figure 19-3 has Financial Action Items (section 1.3). It is recommended that you make a separate copy for each subsection (1.1, 1.2, and 1.3) so you have more space for notes. Or you can make a single copy with all three sections on it.

Objectives: Use the generic financial planning entries in the Fin-Plan sheet, Section 1 as a starting point from which to develop your own personal financial plan. Highlight/record all data that applies to you or add any other financial goals you may have. If your financial goals are different than the ones in the Fin-Plan sheet, add, change or delete as you see fit.

Financial Goal Progress Tracking Data

For each PFI, Save/Invest Goal, or Action Item, you can enter the following data:

- Start Date
- Completion Date
- Current Dollar Amount (or Percentage)
- Target Goal
- Actual Value
- Notes

Refer to Figures 19-1, 19-2, and 19-3 for screenshots of Section 1 of the Fin-Plan sheet. See details below for instructions on each subsection.

PFS Fin-Plan Section 1 Instructions

Subsection 1.1 - Personal Financial Indicators (PFIs)

Review your PFI results from the prior Chapter Exercise 13-3, if available, and enter the dollar amounts and ratios data in Subsection 1.1 that correspond with your PFIs in your copy of Figure 19-1. If your previous data is not available or has changed, you can recalculate the ten PFIs for Subsection 1.1 (See Figure 19-1 for list), if necessary. Refer to Appendix B: Personal Financial Health Indicators, for help with formulas.

Subsection 1.2 - Savings and Investments

Review your savings and investment data from the prior Chapter Exercise 13-3, if available, and enter the data that corresponds with your current savings and investments in Subsection 1.2 of your copy of Figure 19-2.

Subsection 1.3 - Financial Action Items (AIs)

Review your financial action items' status from the previous exercises and enter them into Subsection 1.3. Refer to Table 2-1: The Top Twelve Financial Action Items (A/Is), which were presented as a preview in Chapter 2. Take a good look at the A/Is listed in this subsection (refer to your copy of Figure 19-3, a variation of the Table 2-1 A/Is) and use a code (from zero to five) to indicate your status/progress on each of them. A code of zero means you haven't started (for whatever reason), and a code of five means you have implemented it as a core financial value and/or "good habit."

Exercise 19-2 (Fin-Plan Section 2): Gather Major Purchases and Projects Data

In this exercise you will collect data for Section 2 of the Fin-Plan sheet which includes home improvements and related plans, vehicle projects, and other big-ticket items such as vacations. Figure 19-4 is a screenshot of all three subsections in Section 2.

2.1 Home-Related Plans

2.2 Vehicle-Related Plans

2.3 Other/Big Ticket Plans

1. Talk with your partner to develop a list of plans and projects for your home, autos, and other things such as vacations. This would be an excellent exercise for couples who are engaged or planning to get married—or for any couple for that matter!

2. Make a copy of Figure 19-4, which has three subsections for home/auto/other projects and purchases planning.

3. Record any short-, medium-, or long-range family projects, plans, or goals you may have on this sheet. You can also enter an estimated start date as well as estimated and actual costs.

Chapter 20
Attitude of Gratitude and Prosperity

Chapter Overview:

I have included this chapter to wrap up the book because it sort of embodies my personal holistic philosophy and builds on the concepts of mindfulness and awareness that were introduced in Chapter one. It is my strong belief that physical, mental, spiritual, and financial health are all critical for a balanced and harmonious life (not that it will always be that way). Most of the content in this chapter reflects my personal philosophy when it comes to money and life in general. While some of the content may sound critical or judgmental, I do not intend it in that way. I simply want to offer a perspective for consideration. Like many people as they age, I am more aware of my mortality and have pursued a more spiritual path in recent years. I meditate daily and practice gratitude and appreciation as part of my daily ritual. This book has become a mission for me, my "purpose in life", as described in Chapter 17: Education, Jobs, and Student Loans. I hope you, the reader, consider the content of this chapter in the way I have intended.

The bottom line for me is the belief that your thoughts and attitude can and do have a major impact on your life and financial success. Your attitude toward money can go a long way in determining your success and happiness in life. This chapter focuses on attitude and how it can affect your wealth (not just financial). It provides some guidance on how to have a healthy relationship with money. It also introduces some tools you can use to help develop a better attitude and more awareness regarding money. Several key concepts are introduced, including Mindful Awareness, Positive Mental Attitude (PMA), the Gratitude Stone, the Abundance Mentality, and the Law of Attraction. I have also included some "food-for-thought" quotes related to attitude, work, money, and life in general. There are attitude and money notes and tips, as well as some miscellaneous quasi-spiritual stuff that might help improve your thoughts and overall mood. When reading this chapter, it is important to be willing to entertain new concepts, approaches, and ideas.

Chapter PFS Integration:

The chapter does not cover a specific PFS sheet.

Chapter Exercise:

The chapter does not specify an exercise. However, exploring the practice of meditation would be a good one.

Chapter Notable Quotes (The Grand Finale!):

Quote 20-1: "Keep an open mind, but don't let your brain fall out." - Bazooka Joe

Quote 20-2: "Your attitude, not your aptitude, will determine your altitude." - Zig Ziglar

Quote 20-3: "A bad attitude is like a flat tire. You can't go anywhere until you change it." - Anonymous

Quote 20-4: "A mind is like a parachute. It doesn't work if it is not open." - Frank Zappa

Attitude of Gratitude

Positive thinking contributes to a successful life and good relationships with people as well as money. I believe the single most powerful concept that contributes to your success, financially and otherwise, is gratitude. Research has shown that people who are thankful and express gratitude are happier and live longer and fuller lives. A gratitude mindset improves physical and mental health while reducing stress and increasing happiness. The more grateful you are, the more hopeful you become. Appreciate and focus on what you have and not on what you do not have. People who are grateful are more aware and appreciative of their surroundings as compared to those that take everything for granted. Gratitude can help you transition from anger, criticism, and blame in favor of acceptance, forgiveness, and tolerance. On the other hand, if you are not appreciative of what you have and always worry about how much money you have, the less you will have. There is a saying that goes like this: "What you think about, you will bring about." They also say, "A fool and his money are soon parted." This does not mean you are a fool if you struggle with money matters. Most people do. Fortunately, you can begin to change that by employing the principles described in this book and this chapter.

People who have been taught to handle and manage money will probably always have money and may be referred to as having a "rich" mentality or wealth consciousness. People who have not been exposed to money and how to manage it may develop a "poor" mentality or poverty consciousness. Even if they come into some money, they may not have it for long. Poor people who win the lottery sometimes mismanage their winnings because they are not used to having money. They may spend it extravagantly or put the money into poor investments. Before long, they are right back where they started before they won the money. Another example of this could be the college athlete who signs a million-dollar contract with a pro team and, not having been taught how to manage money, ends up being taken advantage of by "friends," family members, and unscrupulous agents. Financial education can foster a better money attitude and can go a long way toward a better life.

Money has a negative connotation for some people. Sayings such as "Follow the money!" "Money is the root of all evil," and "Money doesn't grow on trees" are examples. Money, by itself, is not bad or good, but how you view it and deal with it can be. It is important to have or develop a healthy attitude toward money. This book does not promote materialism and amassing great wealth, although that's OK. The intent is to provide encouragement to help you see money as a tool to achieve your goals and live the life of your dreams, whatever they might be. Having a good relationship with money does not necessarily mean having a lot of it. People who do not make a lot can be quite happy by living within their means. By the same token, there are many people who make a lot that are in terrible shape financially because they spend more than they make and are deep in debt. What it boils down to is that you need to spend less than you take in. If you dread paying the bills and view money as a necessary evil, you may not have much of it. There is another saying that goes thus: "You have as much money as you are willing to take responsibility for."

If you are working to reduce your debt, living within your means (budgeting), and doing some saving/ investing—even if you are still in debt—you are certainly moving in the right direction with money. Doing these things can help improve your physical and mental health and affects a multitude of other aspects of your life. In addition, if you maintain a positive attitude and are thankful for what you have, it will also influence every part of your life, from personal relationships to financial relationships. A grateful mindset can significantly improve your mental health.

Quote 20-5: "Acknowledging the good that you already have in your life is the foundation for all abundance." - Eckhart Tolle

Quote 20-6: "Gratitude opens the door to the power, the wisdom, the creativity of the universe." - Deepak Chopra, M.D.

The Gratitude Stone and Meditation
A gratitude stone is literally a small stone, of your choosing, that you can use to focus on and express gratitude. Any stone that fits into the palm of your hand can be a suitable gratitude stone. Examples can include specific *chakra* stones, crystals, polished stones, semi-precious gemstones, river rock stones, any stone with special meaning for you, or whatever you like. I use a small stone with a beautiful near-perfect fossil of an ancient sea creature imbedded in it. The fossil is that of a trilobite, one of the most prolific early invertebrates to ever exist on our planet. This little guy lived in the primordial oceans on our planet an estimated five hundred million years ago. This kind of helps me put things into perspective.

Figure 20-1: Trilobite Fossil

My wife and I use our gratitude stones to focus on the most wonderful and positive things that have happened to us during the day and to give thanks and acknowledge the many blessings and gifts we have in life. We try to give thanks every day for who we are and what we have. Every night, before we go to bed and while holding the gratitude stone, we list the things and people we are thankful for in our lives. Expressing gratitude helps to lift your mood and shuts out negative thoughts. You can use the gratitude stone to focus on the positive things that you are thankful for in your life. I use mine when I do my "gratitude affirmations" each night. These affirmations are included at the end of this chapter. We also use the gratitude stone when we meditate. We try to meditate for about twenty to thirty minutes per day and express gratitude for all we have. We have been meditating for the last couple of years and derive a lot of physical, mental, and spiritual benefit from it. There are several apps you can use for guided and/or independent meditation. We use the *Chopra* app, and the *Calm* app. We also subscribe to various works by Eckhart Tolle, including meditations. Books by Deepak Chopra and Eckhart Tolle that have influenced me are listed in the References and Resources section at the end of the book, and I have included some quotes by them in this book. To see what other meditations and apps are available, do a search on the Internet, and you will find many to choose from. You can also talk to friends and family about what meditation apps they might use.

Keeping Things in Perspective

In addition to thinking about a 500-million-year-old trilobite to help keep things in perspective, try visualizing yourself relative to our planet and solar system. As Michael Singer says, in his book *The Untethered Soul,* "You are living on a planet spinning around the middle of outer space, and you're either worrying about your blemishes, the scratch on your new car, or the fact that you burped in public." If you are standing at the Earth's equator, you are traveling at about 1,000 miles per hour (MPH) to rotate once in 24 hrs (one day). For the earth to orbit our sun in one year, it must hurtle through space at 67,000 MPH! It's amazing when you think where we fit in this cosmic puzzle. It seems like a miracle to me that we are even able to reflect on all this as sentient beings.

Abundance vs. Scarcity Mentality

Motivational speakers sometime characterize people as having an "abundance" or a "scarcity" mentality, and this influences their choices in life. People who come from abundance see the glass half full and expect it to get fuller. If it gets empty, they are certain it will be refilled. For these people, there is plenty to go around. They are not worried that someone

else will take what is theirs or that they will not get their fair share or piece of the pie. Instead of worrying whether they will get a big enough piece, people with the abundance mentality expect that the pie will get bigger. A rising tide floats all boats.

On the other hand, people who come from scarcity see the glass as half empty and feel certain it is going down. They worry there is not enough to go around, so they must get their share while they can. Scarcity people are generally pessimistic and expect that things will get worse. They may also begrudge people who have a lot. They often come from a victim mentality. They may feel that the world is not fair and that people are "doing it to them."

Quote 20-7: "Life may not be fair, but it beats the alternative." - Anonymous

Quote 20-8: "The pessimist complains about the direction of the wind; the optimist hopes it will change soon; the realist adjusts the sails." - William Ward

Sometimes it's not enough to just be an optimist. You must also be a realist and face the facts and educate yourself in order to make informed decisions, instead of just hoping for the best. In any case, beware of the pessimistic scarcity mentality and its potential effects on you and those around you. People who come from scarcity are generally not self-aware and do not take responsibility for their situation and instead blame outside influences. This attitude gives power to others and takes it away from the individual. They may feel the reason they are not successful is because of outside forces that are beyond their control, and therefore it is not their fault. Since their circumstances are beyond their control, this becomes their reason for not trying to improve their situation. The scarcity mentality can permeate every aspect of our lives and make us miserable, and it's not always easy to change. People with a negative, scarcity mentality tend to worry, blame, and complain about their situation. Positive, abundance-mentality people tend to accept and respond effectively to their situation. Giving is a statement of abundance. If you make contributions of services, goods, or money, you are promoting abundance and coming from an abundance awareness.

This is not a rich versus poor thing, and it's not even about money. People with an abundance mentality are aware that we are all surrounded by abundance, and we just need to be appreciative of what we have. The abundance or scarcity mentality is not determined by the amount of worldly goods or money you may or may not have. There are people who are poor by the world's standards, but because they express gratitude and give of themselves, they do live in abundance. Conversely, there are rich people who do not practice gratitude and are stingy with what they've been blessed with, so they live in scarcity. Even though they may have a lot of worldly goods or possessions, they live in fear that someone might try to take it from them, or the next time they are seeking something, they are afraid they might not get enough.

Do you take responsibility for your situation, good or bad, or do you blame your situation on other people? When I was younger, I was "unconscious" most of the time, meaning I was not very self-aware and acted very selfishly. I did not take responsibility for my situation, be it with money or relationships. My ego ran my life, and it was out of control much of the time. Unfortunately, people who do not take responsibility for their current situation are rarely able to improve it. If you take responsibility for your current dismal financial condition, you have the power and the right to take responsibility for improving it and for your resulting financial success. Focusing on paying down your debt, putting your money into savings, and improving your credit score are examples of taking responsibility for your financial situation.

Regarding work attitude, if you do your current assignment well, you may have a chance to do something you like more. Complaining about what you are doing and griping that you should have more responsibility and money is a recipe for being stuck where you are. Coworkers don't want to work with complainers. Remember, it is attitude, not aptitude that determines altitude. A fast-food order taker with a good attitude can go far.

Work Attitude Example: When I go to a restaurant, I am sometimes surprised at the number of waiters and waitresses that have an attitude. Some of them act like they are doing you a favor by serving you. Others act like they enjoy serving you and are glad you are their customer. Which one do you think will get the bigger tip? When I go to a restaurant, I am happy to see servers enjoying their job and glad to be serving me. While others may have a less-than-agreeable attitude, the happy servers are sure to get the bigger tip. People with an "abundance mentality" do their work with love, dedication, and commitment and are thankful for the opportunity. There are lots of people who would love to just have a job. The more appreciative you are for your job, whatever it may be, the more opportunities you will attract. Also, while you are on the job, take time to increase your knowledge and develop skills. Here are a few more advice quotes related to the importance of work attitude.

Quote 20-9: "The harder I work, the luckier I get." - Anonymous

Quote 20-10: "Luck is when opportunity meets preparedness." - Anonymous

Quote 20-11: "If a task has once begun, never leave it till it's done. Be the labor great or small, do it well or not at all." - Anonymous

Quote 20-12: "Opportunity is missed by most people because it is dressed in overalls and looks like work." - Thomas Edison

If you hear about someone receiving a lot of money, be excited and happy for them. This is saying yes to more money and prosperity in your own life. This is coming from abundance. If your reaction is disappointment and envy, you are coming from scarcity and saying no to more money. Do not focus on how little money you have. Mentally focusing on what we do not have, what is lacking, why we can't do things—this is a thought pattern coming from a scarcity mentality.

Attitude and Money – Summary Notes and Tips:
- Money cannot buy you love, but it can buy a reasonable facsimile.
- Give and you shall receive. Seems counterintuitive, but it works.
- 'Tis better to give than to receive.
- The more you give, the more you will have, and the better you will feel.
- Express gratitude for what you have; don't focus on what you don't have.
- Download a meditation app to help with attitude adjustment.
- The past is gone, and you can't do anything about it other than learn from it.
- Focus on the present. What you do now can help you to make a better future.
- Focus on what you can do within your sphere of influence.
- Try to make small improvements each day regarding money, even if it's just logging on to your online bank account to verify the balance and debits and credits.

- Remember, if you are facing the right direction, you just need to put one foot in front of the other until you reach your goal(s).
- Focus on paying down your debt and improving your credit score. It's a great feeling!
- If you carry a balance on multiple credit cards, pay down the card with the highest interest rate first. You will save a lot of money in interest.
- If you carry a balance on multiple credit cards, pay down the card with the lowest balance first. You will feel like you are making progress.
- Give yourself credit for paying off credit cards. Treat yourself to a reward!
- Set up a budget and live within your means to help develop a mindset of self-control.
- Practice deferred gratification. If you have the urge to buy something, hold it off. The item may go on sale, or you may decide you don't need it after all. It feels great to decide not to spend money frivolously. Don't spend money frivolously—practice deferred gratification.
- Maintain a healthy attitude about money.
- The better you manage your money, the better you will feel about money, and the more money you will have.
- Download money apps to help train yourself on becoming prosperous. Train yourself to have a prosperous mentality. Consider using a good money app to focus on a positive mental attitude toward money.
- Use positive money affirmations like these:
  ◦ "I prosper in all areas of my life"
  ◦ "I welcome wealth and abundance,"
  ◦ "My income exceeds my expenses."
  ◦ "Money is positive energy and allows me to be generous to others."
- Focus on your strengths, not weaknesses.
- Money is just a tool. It is not bad, but how and where you use or abuse it can be.
- Take responsibility for your current situation so you can take the credit when it improves. Take responsibility for your current attitude and situation and focus on improving it.
- Be a big tipper. You will never miss the money. Tipping contributes to your own prosperity mentality as well as the receiver's. Consider tipping the mail person and sanitation worker occasionally.
- Celebrate when people around you do well and are prosperous. It will rub off on you.
- Pay it forward (versus pay it back). When in line at a fast-food drive through, pay the bill for the customer behind you. It will change their day and your life.
- Throw small amounts of change (coins) out the window as a sign that money is not that important. For the person who picks it up, it might make their day.
- If a business/cashier makes a mistake in your favor, draw their attention to it. It may save their job and help to maintain your integrity.
- When you receive money, be grateful. Gratitude is a great multiplier.
- Try this game to help make you feel good about money: Pretend that the front of a bill is the positive side, and the back is the negative side. Every time you handle a bill, turn the positive side up.
- Read books about money and attitude.

- Listen to prosperity audio books and podcasts when you are in your car.
- Love yourself. Focus on the positive. Ask yourself, "What good is there in me?"
- Do not put money ahead of love. Money is just a tool.
- Donate to your favorite nonprofit organization. There are many good ones from which to choose. Do the background research and make sure their values align with yours.
- Tithe (give a percentage of your income) to your church or other organization.
- Expect that success is inevitable and do not take no for an answer.
- As Henry Ford used to say, "Whether you think you can or think you can't, you are right."
- Do not work for money: have it work for you.
- Invest in yourself!
- Do not trade one hour for x dollars for the rest of your life—Multiply yourself through investments.
- Life works to the extent that you participate.
- Cut smart phone usage by one hour a day and focus on your inner self and those around you.
- Do not let the "dowannas" (don't want to's) run your life. Just do it! Most of the time you will be glad you did.

The Secret Book and the Law of Attraction.
The law of attraction is described in the book *The Secret* by Rhonda Byrne. It is a key principle that many believe can help you achieve what you want in life, financially and otherwise. I am a firm believer in the Law of Attraction and attribute much of the success in my life to the concepts and practices outlined in this book.

Quote 20-13: "When the student is ready, the teacher appears." - Anonymous

This quote may apply to you. This quote may apply to you. It certainly has for me throughout my life. You may have decided to read this book because you were ready to take a hard look at your financial situation and wanted to increase your knowledge about money matters. I feel this is what happened when my wife introduced me to the spiritual and life skill teachings of Deepak Chopra and Eckhart Tolle. I began reading books that promoted mindful awareness and ways to improve my life. I was ready and open to some more spirituality in my life to help me give meaning to it all. At various times during my life, I have been the teacher and often, the student. Even when you are the teacher there is always something to be learned. One of the best ways to learn something is to study it as though you were preparing to teach it. When you decide you really want to do something and you are passionate about it, the universe seems to align with you and brings you resources to help you achieve your goals. This happened to me while writing this book. As I was collecting information and deciding on the content for the book, I would notice bits and pieces of related information to include. I grabbed a couple of folders and started filing information and ideas for future use as I ran across them. Sources of information and inspiration are everywhere, including Websites, money magazines, newspaper articles, radio talk shows, conversations with people, and inner wisdom and intuition. Perhaps it was coincidence or perhaps it was me drawing assistance to myself to help me achieve my goals.

When I retired and started formalizing and writing this book, all forms of support started to come my way, including information and concepts that I had not thought of. For example, my wife left the classic book *Think and Grow Rich* by Napoleon Hill on the dining room table. I picked up a couple of quick concepts from it. I was the student and many teachers appeared to help me along. As I was putting the content together, I kept running into financial situations and issues of my own. I encountered potential rip-offs that, if I had not been aware, would have caused me to lose money or get ripped off. I would tear out pages of money magazines and file them, thinking I would be able to use some of the concepts and topics mentioned in them as I developed the book. The universe was aligning with my goals. Maybe it is really just a function of heightened awareness (when the student is ready, the teacher appears). In any case, it is the universe assisting you to pursue your passion or at least to support you in achieving your goals. If you are driven to do something, you are tuned into the frequency that allows you to build toward that goal, and you notice resources as they present themselves, even though they may have always been there. My definition of luck is a variation of an earlier quote: "Luck is being prepared enough, and aware enough, to take advantage of opportunities that present themselves." In other words, it's not enough to just be prepared, unless you are also mindful and living in the present, so you can become aware of the opportunities that come along.

The Book: The Secret (and the Law of Attraction)

There have been many self-help books written over the years, money-related and otherwise. However, the one that has had a major influence on me, and my family, is a best-seller entitled *The Secret* by Rhonda Byrne. The book is based on a concept known as "The Law of Attraction," which says that your thoughts can directly change your life. What we think about, we bring about. The book has sold over thirty million copies worldwide. A film of the same name preceded the book. I highly recommend that you read the book and watch the movie. It will be time well spent. About ten years ago, at the recommendation of our niece, our family sat down together and watched the movie. It has had a profound effect on many aspects of our lives.

There is a chapter in the book called "Wealth and the Law of Attraction." When it comes to money, give attention to what you want. Visualize yourself as prosperous, with checks coming in and enabling you to pay the bills and take vacations. Give no attention to what you do not want. Do not give attention to negative thoughts—notice them and replace them with positive thoughts. What have you got to lose by thinking positively?

The Law of Attraction in Action

Example 1: I went to the mailbox and found a check from the state of North Carolina for $350. It was money from a deposit or something that was from years ago, when I lived there. They had been trying to track me down to reclaim it. Maybe this is a small example of the law of attraction. Or maybe not, who knows. Either way I had an extra $350 that I did not even know about, and it seemed to just come out of the blue.

Example 2: I was working on this chapter and had just come from an appointment. As I was leaving the building, a couple of things on a table caught my eye: a little ceramic piggy bank and a small antique book with a little sign that read "Free to a good home." I had just written something about teaching younger children about money, and we were working with our five-year-old granddaughter to identify coins. I was thinking about getting her a piggy bank, and there it was, and a free one no less! My wife is a big crafts person and is always looking for old books to use in her artwork. I took the piggy bank and the book, and the next time I went to that appointment, I brought a couple of nice things that someone might want (another antique book and an antique cobbler's child shoe form) and left them on the table with a small sign that said, "Free to a good home." We have used the piggy bank (See Figure 1-1 in Chapter 1) several times with our granddaughter, and the little antique book has been put to good use. As I am writing this chapter, I am reminded that you attract good things to yourself when you are passionate about what you are doing and believe in yourself.

Positive and Negative Thoughts

One technique I came across that can help you favor positive thoughts over negative ones is to imagine you have a giant **Delete** key and a giant **Volume** button in your mind. If you have a negative thought, press the delete key repeatedly and replace it with a positive thought. It doesn't matter what the negative thought is. Just the process of noticing it and pressing the giant delete key will help you develop an awareness, and the negative thought will lose energy. You can also visualize negative thoughts as clouds coming and going through your mind and observe them floating away and disappearing. If you have a positive thought, turn up the volume button to focus on the positive. If you worry about something, you are drawing that negativity to yourself by focusing on it. Imagine yourself physically healthy, in good relationships, and having plenty of money to do what you want. I've heard it said that when you focus on the negative or worry that things might turn out badly, it is like praying for what you do not want, most of which will never come to pass. Or put another way, you are paying interest on a loan you might not even need.

Say positive things to people (especially your partner and family) on a regular basis or whenever you can. You might give them a smile or a compliment or acknowledge them for a job well done. Every little bit helps and starts positive momentum. *The Secret* book teaches you to "Ask, believe, and receive." Just ask the universe (whoever or whatever you perceive it to be) for what you desire, believe that you have already received it, and you will be blessed with it. Whatever you are grateful for, you will feel good about, and you will bring more of it to you. Some spiritual scholars teach that you already have it, and you just need to become aware of it.

The Secret to Money App

This app is inspired by Rhonda Byrne's book *The Secret*. In the app you will develop a new perspective on your own personal finances and potential to live a life of abundance. The Secret to Money app is a highly-rated smartphone app that you can download for a small fee. It is very cool and can help you change the way you think about money. With this app you will receive instructions on various actions you can take regarding how you relate to money. It includes five practices that will help you develop a wealth mindset.

Menu selections in the app include **Purchases, Manifested Money, Daily Inspirations, Affirmations, Desires,** and **Giving**. If you do an Internet search, you will find details on the app and many positive reviews.

Miscellaneous Mood Lifters and Attitude Adjusters

Lots of people get into bad moods, and sometimes these can be hard to get out of. Sometimes it can lead to clinical depression. One technique to lift your mood is to get active and do something (from reading a book to running a marathon). Anything that takes your mind off your current situation can help. Even if you have the "don't wannas," do something that distracts you. Do something that requires your attention so you can't dwell on negative thoughts. It's hard to stay negative if you're focused on something positive. Even if it's something simple like complimenting your partner or friend or lending a helping hand. Doing something positive starts the mood shift that makes it easier to do the next positive thing and helps to promote the trend. Immersing yourself in some type of service can turn around a major negative mood. When upset or in a bad mood, ask yourself, "Is this situation really that bad? What is the worst that can happen? What is most likely to happen?" Maybe you shouldn't take it all too seriously. Be thankful for what you have and show appreciation for the many blessings you have. Try some of the following:

- To help reduce stress, stop and center yourself by closing your eyes, focusing on your heart at the center of your chest or your forehead, and taking several slow, deep breaths. Do this several times a day.
- Ground yourself by imagining you are a connection between the earth and the cosmos. And just the fact that you exist and are self-aware is a miracle.
- Keep things in perspective. Remember, you are walking around on a huge planet that is habitable by humans and is orbiting a giant fireball at a speed of 660,000 miles per hour.
- Time spent looking at the view is time well spent.
- Go outside and commune with nature and get some sun. Be a tree hugger!
- Stop and look at the sky long enough to see the clouds move.
- Practice abstinence from social media and/or the news for a day per week or better yet, for a whole week. For some people, this is very hard to do. Studies have found that avoiding social media and the news (whatever channel or source), for just one week significantly boosts well-being while reducing depression and anxiety.
- Practice the **5As** with your friends and family, or anyone else for that matter. This will lift your mood and theirs and improve your relationships. These are listed alphabetically:
  - **Acceptance**
  - **Acknowledgment**
  - **Affection**
  - **Appreciation**
  - **Attention**
- Practice patience and listen to your inner wisdom. Embrace and enjoy the search for your *dharma*, your calling, your purpose.

- If you take care of the present, the future will take care of itself! Your past and future are mental constructs that do not exist (or maybe they do!) The only thing that is real is the present (as of this writing), which is successive moments of the now. Reliving and regretting what has happened in the past and worrying about what may happen in the future (but probably won't) simply robs you of the now, and you lose the opportunity to be fully present in your current situation.

Quote 20-14: "A candle loses nothing by lighting another candle." - James Keller

And one final quote from Winnie the Pooh and Piglet:

Quote 20-15: "'What day is it?' asked Pooh. 'It's today,' squeaked Piglet. 'My favorite day,' said Pooh." - A. A. Milne

Make the most of it, even if it's just taking it easy to reduce your stress level! Thanks

The Gratitude Affirmations
by James Lorenz

Background:

This is a nondenominational combination of affirmations, meditations, and enlightenment concepts that have influenced my spiritual growth and awareness. It has evolved over the years and has increased my appreciation for the miracles that are everywhere in our universe. I have said these affirmations (or an earlier version) every day for over thirty years. Hopefully, you will get some benefit from these words, as I have. If you believe in a God, the references herein can represent a supreme being, higher consciousness, or whatever you conceive God to be.

The Gratitude Affirmations

- Thank you, God, for everything. I have nothing to complain about.
- Let me align with cosmic consciousness.
- Let me know the wisdom of the ages.
- Let me see the face of God in all that there is.
- Let me learn from the past, plan for the future, and live in the present.
- I come from love, abundance, honesty, understanding, kindness, optimism, gratitude, generosity, confidence, and faith.
- I love and accept myself as I am and am willing and able to improve myself in mind, body, and spirit.
- I love, accept, forgive, release, and respect myself and all those in my life.
- Thank you, Sister Water, Mother Earth, Father Sky, and Brother Sun for your life-sustaining powers.
- Thank you, God of the Universe, for the strength, courage, health, and wisdom to complete my life's work and live a long and happy life.

 I am thankful for (list people and things)

Note: There is no copyright on the Gratitude Affirmations.

Appendix A
Personal Financial Spreadsheet (PFS)
Screenshots of All 7 Sheets
(Tabs and Sample Entries/Input)

This appendix provides the following to help you build your PFS (optional):

- Information on how to construct each of the seven main sheets or tabs.
- Formulas, shown next to the cells where they are actually located.
- Generic cell entries and data as examples show how your spreadsheet could look.
- Screen shots taken with Row Numbers and Column Letters shown for cell entries.
- The following table lists the seven sheet Tab Names and Titles

Table A-1: Personal Financial Spreadsheet (PFS) Tab Names and Sheet Titles

Tab #: Name	Sheet Title (Cell A1)	Notes
Tab 1: Income-Exp	Income, Expenses, and Cash Flow	
Tab 2: Assets-Liab	Assets, Liabilities, and Net Worth	
Tab 3: Cred-Cards	Credit and Credit Cards	
Tab 4: Home-Info	Home Info and Maintenance	
Tab 5: Auto-Info	Auto Info and Maintenance	
Tab 6: Insure-Pols	Insurance Policy Info	
Tab 7: Fin-Plan	Financial Planning and Projects	

Table A-2: Personal Financial Spreadsheet (PFS) Figures - Screenshots
(Figure A-Chap#-Seq#: PFS Tab - Tab-Name - X of Y (Sect. #/Name)

Screenshot Figure #, Tab Name and Section #
Figure A-3-1: PFS Tab - Income-Exp - 1 of 4 (Sect. 1–Income)
Figure A-3-2: PFS Tab - Income-Exp - 2 of 4 (Sect. 2–Housing Exp)
Figure A-3-3: PFS Tab - Income-Exp - 3 of 4 (Sect. 2–Other Exp)
Figure A-3-4: PFS Tab - Income-Exp - 4 of 4   (Sect. 3–DTI, Cash Flow)
Figure A-5-1: PFS Tab - Assets-Liab - 1 of 2 (Sect. 1–Assets)
Figure A-5-2: PFS Tab - Assets-Liab - 2 of 2 (Sect. 2–Liab, Net Worth)
Figure A-9-3: PFS Tab - Cred-Cards - 1 of 1 (Credit Cards list)
Figure A-11-4: PFS Tab - Home-Info - 1 of 1 (Home Info)
Figure A-12-2: PFS Tab - Auto-Info - 1 of 1 (Auto Info)
Figure A-16-1: PFS Tab - Insure-Pols - 1 of 1 (Insurance Pols Info)
Figure A-19-1: PFS Tab - Fin-Plan - 1 of 4 (Sect. 1.1–PFI Goals)
Figure A-19-2: PFS Tab - Fin-Plan - 2 of 4 (Sect. 1.2–Save-Inv Goals)
Figure A-19-3: PFS Tab - Fin-Plan - 3 of 4 (Sect. 1.3–Action Item Goals)
Figure A-19-4: PFS Tab - Fin-Plan - 4 of 4 (Sect. 2.1-3–Purch-Plan Goals)

Appx. A, Figure A-3-1: PFS Tab - Income-Exp - 1 of 4 (Sect. 1 Income)
(Figure 3-1: Household Income Section of Income-Exp Sheet (sample entries)

	A	B	C	D	E
1	INCOME, EXPENSES and CASH FLOW	Book Build: Ch. 3			Updated: MM-DD-YYYY
2					
3	<<< Sect 1: Household Income >>>				
4	< Income Source (Who/Type/Asset/Income/Retmt.) >	Institution	Monthly Gross	Monthly Net	Notes / Formulas
5	Ted - Social Security (Inc.)	US Govt	1,500	1,300	DD Chkg: X9999
6	Ted - Pension (Inc./Ret.)	Pension Co.	750	600	DD Chkg: X9999
7	Ted - 401K (Ass./Inc./Ret.)	Mgmt Co.	1,000	800	DD Chkg: X9999
8	Ted - Part time job at Hardware store (Inc.)	Anytown Hardware	800	600	Regular income (1040 wages)
9	Ted - Small furniture repair business (Ass./Inc.)	Ted's Furniture Repair	500	500	
10	Ted - Rental Property (Ass./Inc.)	Anytown Mortgage Co.	750	600	Rental income less maint exp.
11	Amy - Full-time Instructor Salary (Inc.)	Anytown College	3,000	2,600	
12	Amy - 403B Contribution (Ass./Ret.)	Mgmt Co.	0	0	For retirement
13	Joint - Money Market Acct (MMA) (Ass./Inc./Ret)	Anytown Bank	100	70	
14	Joint - Savings Acct. - Emergency Fund (Ass./Inc) - Interest	Anytown Bank	100	70	
15	Joint - Savings Acct. - Short-Term (Ass./Inc.) - Interest	Anytown Bank	100	70	
16	Joint - Savings 5-Yr.CD - Long-Term (Ass./Inc.) - Interest	Anytown Bank	100	60	
17	Joint - Invest IRA Acct Income (Stocks/Bond Interest and Dividends)	Invest-Co	200	150	
18					
19					
20					
21	Total Monthly (GROSS) Income:		$8,900		=SUM(C5:C20)
22	Total Monthly (NET) Income:			$7,420	=SUM(D5:D20)
23					
24	<<< Sect 2: Expenses >>>				
25					

Income-Exp   Assets-Liab   Cred-Cards   Home-Info   Auto-Info   Insure-Pols   Fin-Plan   Income-Exp-F   Assets-Liab-F   Cred-Cards-F

Appx. A, Figure A-3-2: PFS Tab - Income-Exp - 2 of 4 (Sect. 2 Housing Exp)
(Figure 3-2: Housing Required Monthly Expenses Section of Income-Exp Sheet)

	A	B	C	D	E
24	<<< Sect 2: Expenses >>>				
25					
26	< Housing Required Monthly Expenses >	Institution	Monthly Payment	Payment Method	Notes
27	Housing Expense Name / Type				
28	(Required Housing Expenses)				
29					
30	Home - Mortgage PITI (or Rent)	Anytown Mortgage	1,800	O/L Bill Pay	Bank X9999 (Escrow Tax/Ins)
31	Home - Homowners Assoc. Dues (HOA fees)	Subdivision HOA	100	O/L Bill Pay	O/L: www.xyzprop.com - Qtrly
32	Home - Water/Sewer/Trash/Recycle	Anycounty Services (Avg)	175	O/L Bill Pay	CC x9999 (one bill)
33	Home - Electricity/Gas	Anytown Electric/Gas (Avg)	250	Auto-Pay	CC x9999 (one bill)
34					
35	(Optional Housing Expenses Included)				
36	Home - Security/Smoke alarm	XYZ Security	50	Auto-Pay	Auto Pay CCx9999
37	Home - TV Cable	Anytown TV	85	Auto-Pay	Auto Pay CCx9999
38	Home - High Speed Internet	Anyprovider Internet	50	Liquid Assets-Exp (LAE)	No. of Months
39	Home - Pest Control	Anytown Pestsbegone	40		Billed Qtrly CCx9999
40	Other			Auto-Pay	
41	Total Housing Required Monthly Expenses		$2,550		=SUM(C30:C40)
42					
43	Housing-To-Income Ratio (HTI %)		28.7%		=(C41/C21)
44	= (Required Housing Expenses / Gross Income)				(HTI Ratio < 30% is OK)

Appx. A, Figure A-3-3: PFS Tab - Income-Exp - 3 of 4 (Sect. 2 Other Exp)

(Figure 3-3: Other Required Monthly Expenses Section of Income-Exp Sheet (sample)

	A	B	C	D	E
46	< Other Required Monthly Expenses >	Provider Name / Desc	Monthly Payment	Loan Balance	Payment Method
47	Insurance - Ted Medicare Part B - Medical	Social Sec / Medicare	160	0	Auto deduct from SS Chk Dep
48	Insurance - Ted Medicare Part D - Drug Coverage	Large-Med-Co.	70	0	Auto-Pay EFT Chk Acct X9999
49	Insurance - Ted Medicare supplemental	XYZ-MediCo Supplem Plan	120	0	Auto-Pay EFT Chk Acct X9999
50	Insurance - Ted Vision & Dental	ABC-Medical	40	0	Auto-Pay EFT Chk Acct X9999
51	Insurance - Ted Long Term Care (LTC)	AnyInsCo LTC	200	0	Auto-Pay EFT Chk Acct X9999
52					
53	Insurance - Amy Health (Thru employer, incl. Life, Vis., and Dent)	Anytown College	230	0	Auto deduct from paycheck
54	Insurance - Amy LTC Long Term Care (LTC)	AnyInsCo LTC	210	0	Auto-Pay EFT Chk Acct X9999
55					
56	Home Property Tax	County Auditor (Yrly/12=$200)	0	0	(Incl w/ Mort Pmt - $9,999/YR)
57	Insurance - Home Owners	BigInsCo (Yrly Prem/12 = $50)	0	0	(Incl w/ Mort Pmt - $9,999/YR)
58	Insurance - Umbrella	BigInsCo (Yrly Prem/12 = $20)	20	0	Auto Yrly CC#9999 ($9,999/Yr)
59	Insurance - Auto (Car ABC and XYZ)	BigInsCo (Yrly Prem/12)	100	0	Auto Yrly CC#9999 ($9,999/Yr)
60					
61	(Loan and Credit Line Required Payments)	(Include Loans, Credit Cards, and Credit Lines if Carry Monthly Balance)			
62	Auto Loan - Ted - ABC Car	ABC Car Finance Co.	0	0	Paid Off!
63	Personal Loan - Ted	Personal Loan Bank	0	0	Paid Off!
64	Student Loan - Amy	Student Loan Bank	0	0	Paid Off!
65	Other Loan				
66					
67	Home Loan (Mortgage balance)	Anytown Mortgage Co,	0	170,000	(Pmt in Housing Section)
68	Home Equity Line of Credit (HELOC)	Anytown Bank	300	5,000	Open credit line $30,000
69	Credit Card - Amy - XYZ M/C	XYZ Credit Card	400	1,800	
70	Credit Card - Ted - QRS M/C	QRS Credit Card	100	600	
71	Other CC1				
72					
73	Total Other Required Monthly Expenses		$1,950		=SUM(C47:C72)
74	Total Loan and Credit Line Balances			$177,400	=SUM(D62:D72)

Appx. A, Figure A-3-4: PFS Tab - Income-Exp - 4 of 4 (Sect. 3–DTI, Cash Flow)

(Figure 3-4: DTI Ratio, Discretionary Expenses, and Cash Flow Sections - Income-Exp Sheet)

	A	B	C	D	E
76	Total Required Monthly Expenses (Used w/ DTI & EF)		$4,500		=C41+C73
77					
78	Debt-to-Income Ratio (DTI %)		50.6%		=(C76/C21)
79	= (Required Monthly Expenses / Gross Income)				(DTI Ratio < 40% is OK)
80					
81					
82	< Discretionary Monthly Expenses >				
83	Groceries	Various	400		
84	Dining out	Various	200		Need to track; incl fast food
85	Gas	Various	300		Varies, work miles, cost of gas
86	Auto maint	Various	100		All cars avg
87	Personal care (hair, massage, gym, etc)	Various	250		
88	House clean	Various	90		
89	Lawn mow / landscape / snow remov.	Various	50		
90	Vacations	Various	300		Try to keep under $3600/yr
91	Misc - other		300		Check CCs for avg / mo.
92					
93					
94	Total Discretionary Monthly Expenses		$1,990		=SUM(C83:C93)
95					
96	Total Monthly Expenses (outgo) - ALL TYPES		$6,490		=C76+C94
97					
98	<<< Sect 3: Cash Flow >>>				
99					
100	Monthly Personal Cash Flow (PCF) ($)	(Positive or Negative)	$930		=D22-C96
101	(Total Mo. Net Income minus (-) Total Mo. Expenses)				
102					
103	Potential Savings Ratio (PSR) (%)	% of PCF for Savings	12.5%		=(D22-C96)/D22
104	(or PCF-to-Net Income (NI) ratio)				
105	(Total Moly NI minus (-) Total Moly Exp) / Moly NI)				
106					
107	PCF ($$) x PSR (%) = Moly Dollars Avail. for Savings	$$ of PCF for Savings	$117		=C100xC103

Appx. A, Figure A-5-1: PFS Tab - Assets-Liab - 1 of 2 (Sect. 1–Assets)
(Figure 5-1: PFS Assets Section of Assets-Liab Sheet (sample entries))

	A	B	C	D	E	F	G
1	ASSETS, LIABILITIES and NET WORTH		Book Build: Ch. 5			Updated: MM-DD-YYYY	
2							
3	<<< Sect 1: Assets >>>						
4	Owner	< Liquid Assets (Name / Type) >	Institution	Notes	Curr. Value	Monthly Contrib.	Beneficiary / Formula
5	Joint	Bank Checking Acct 1	Bank	Cash	1,000	0	Joint
6	Joint	Bank Checking Acct 2	Bank	Cash	5,000	0	Joint
7	Joint	Emergency Fund (EF) - Online Savings Acct	Savings-Co	EF Goal = $27,000	13,700	300	Emergency Fund Acct. - Joint
8	Joint	Savings Acct. - Short-Term (Ass./Inc.)	Anytown Bank	Savings	15,000	200	Joint
9	Joint	Money Market Acct (MMA)	Anytown Bank	Savings	5,000	200	Joint
10	Joint	5-Yr Certificate of Deposit (CD)	Anytown Bank	Savings	10,000	200	Joint
11	Ted	Pension (Ass./Inc./Ret.)	Pension Co.	Retire: Defined benefit	60,000	0	Amy
12	Ted	401K (Ass,/Inc./Ret.)	Mgmt Co.	Retire: Stock Funds	75,000	0	Amy
13	Amy	403B Retirement Plan (Ass./Ret.)	Mgmt Co.	Retire: Stock Funds	35,000	500	Ted
14	Ted	IRA Invest (Stocks/Bonds) (Interest/Dividends)	Invest-Co.	Retire: Stock Funds	45,000	300	Amy
15		Other liquid asset			0	0	
16		Other liquid asset			0	0	
17		Other liquid asset			0	0	
18				Total Liquid Assets:	264,700		=SUM(E5:E17)
19							
20		< Non-Liquid Assets (Name / Type) >					
21	Joint	Home Value (Appraised)	Mortgage Co.	Appraised value	250,000	Ref. Sect 2: Liabilities for Mortgage balance	
22	Joint	Auto values (total) (Car and truck)	Cars Paid for	Estimated values (10k+20k)	30,000		
23	Joint	Jewelry & Other	Other Assets	Appraised values	10,000		
24		Other Non-liquid asset			0		
25		Other Non-liquid asset			0		
26				Total All Major Assets:	$554,700		=SUM(E5:E26)-E18
27							
28				Total Moly Save/Invest Contrib:		1,700	=SUM(F5:F26)
29							
30				Saving-to-Income (STI %):		19.1%	=F29/'Income-Exp'!C21
31							
32		EF Goal is $27,000		Emerg Fund-to-Exp: (EFE %):		50.7%	=E7/('Income-Exp'!C76*6)
33							
34				Liquid Assets-to-Exp:	No. Months:	59	=E18/('Income-Exp'!C76)

Income-Exp | **Assets-Liab** | Cred-Cards | Home-Info | Auto-Info | Insure-Pols | Fin-Plan | Income-Exp-F | Assets-Liab-F | Cred-Cards-F ⋯

Appx. A, Figure A-5-2: PFS Tab - Assets-Liab - 2 of 2 (Sect. 2–Liab, Net Worth)
(Figure 5-2: PFS Liabilities and Net Worth Sections of Assets-Liab Sheet (sample entries))

	A	B	C	D	E	F	G
36	<<< Sect 2: Liabilities >>>						
37							
38	Owner	Liability Name / Type	Institution	Notes	Amount		
39	Joint	Home Mortgage Balance	Mortgage Co.	Secured debt	170,000		
40	Joint	Auto Loans (balance owed)	Various	Secured debt	0		
41	Joint	Credit Card Debt (See Cred-Cards Tab)	Various	Unsecured debt	5,000		
42	Joint	Home Equity Line of Credit (HELOC)			5,000		
43	Amy	Credit Card - XYZ Visa			1800		
44	Ted	Credit Card - QRS M/C			600		
45		Other Liability			0		
46		Other Liability			0		
47				Total Major Liabilities:	$182,400		=SUM(E39:E46)
48							
49	<<< Sect 3: Net Worth >>>			Total Personal Net Worth (PNW$):	$372,300		=E26-E47
50	(Net Worth = Total Major Assets - Total Major Liabilities)			(Includes Home Equity)			

Appx. A, Figure A-9-3: PFS Tab - Cred-Cards - 1 of 1 (Credit Cards list)

(Figure 9-3: PFS Sheet - Credit and Credit Cards (sample entries))

	A	B	C	D	E	F	G
1	**CREDIT and CREDIT CARDS**		Book Build: Ch. 9				Updated: MM-DD-YYYY
2							
3	**<<< Sect 1: Credit Scores and Reports >>>**						
4					Date Run	Source	Credit Reporting Bureau
5			Credit Score:	750	mm-dd-yy	ABC CC Co.	(Equifax / Experian / TransUnion / Other)
6			Report (Y/N):	Y	mm-dd-yy	XYZ CC Co	(Equifax / Experian / TransUnion / Other)
7							
8	**<<< Sect 2: Revolving Credit Lines >>>**						
9	(Credit Cards & Lines of Credit)						
10	Card Issuer / Sponsor / Brand	Prim / Auth User	Last 4 Digits	Credit Limit	Balance	APR %	Rewards / Notes
11	Bank Company ABC Amex	Amy	x9999	10,000	0	15.70%	Double Airline miles, free luggage
12	Bank Company DEF Visa	Ted / Amy	x9999	5,000	500	19.20%	3% Travel, 2% Dine, 1% Else
13	Bank Company GHI Mastercard	Amy / Ted	x9999	5,000	1,000	18.50%	4% Gas, 3% Groc., 1% Else
14	Bank Global Business M/C	Ted	x9999	10,000	750	14.90%	2% All purchase, No Foreign TX fee
15	Big Box Store Card	Amy	x9999	10,000	1,500	25.00%	6 Mo deferred interest
16	Bank Home Equity Line of Credit (HELOC)	Ted / Amy	x9999	20,000	3,000	8.00%	(Variable APR)
17	Other			0	0	0.00%	
18	Other			0	0	0.00%	
19							
20	**<<< Sect 3: Credit Card Calculations >>>**						
21	**Credit Card Summary Totals (All Cards)**						
22							Formulas / Notes
23	Total Credit Limit			$60,000			=SUM(D11:D19)
24	Total CC Balance				$6,750		=SUM(E11:E19)
25	Average APR					12.7%	=AVERAGE(F11:F19)
26							
27	**<<< Sect 4: Debt-to-Credit (DTC) Ratio >>>**					11.3%	=E24/D23
28	(DTC = Revolving credit utilization rate)						(DTC Ratio < 10% is OK)
29	(DTC = Credit Used (Balance) / Credit Avail (Credit Limit)						DTC applies to all cards combined
30							

< > ⋯ Income-Exp Assets-Liab Cred-Cards Home-Info Auto-Info Insure-Pols Fin-Plan Income-Exp-F Assets-Liab-F Cred-Cards-F Home-Info-F Auto

Appx. A, Figure A-11-4: PFS Tab - Home-Info - 1 of 1 (Home Info)

(Figure 11-4: PFS Sheet - Home Info and Maintenance (sample entries)

	A	B	C	D	E	F
1	**Home Info and Maintenance**			Book Build Ch. 11		Updated: MM-DD-YYYY
2						
3	**<<< Home Information >>>**					**Notes**
4						
5	**Address:**	1234 Home Rd., Anytown, ST		**Mortgage Co.:**	MortCo, Inc.	
6	**Description:**	2-Story, 3 Bdrm, 2 Bath, 2-car garage		**Payment (PITI):**	1,200/mo	Incl. Prop Tax & Ins.
7	**Year Built:**	2010		**Loan Number:**	1123456789	
8	**Living Area:**	2,500		**Mortgage Bal:**	$125,000	
9	**Lot Size:**	60x90		**Home Owner Ins:**	FGH Ins Co.	
10	**Parcel No:**	1234567890		**HO Policy No:**	123456789	
11	**Market Value:**	$250,000	2023 assess	**HO Coverage:**	$300,000	Incl. Prop Tax & Ins.
12	**Taxable Value**	$150,000		**HOA Dues:**	$200/Year	AutoPay Qtrly, CC#9999
13	**Prop Tax/Year:**	$2,400	County Treasurer	**Renters Ins:**	N/A	
14	**Last Sale Date:**	mm-dd-yyyy		**Other:**		
15	**Last Sale Price:**	$220,000		**Other:**		
16	**Other:**					
17						
18	**<<< Home Maintenance and Improvement >>>**					
19						
20	**Est Start Date**	**Act Start Date**	**Project Description**	**Amount**	**Company**	
21	99/99/9999	99/99/9999	Landscape	$1,000	Various nurseries	
22	99/99/9999	99/99/9999	Gutter guards	$500	Roofing Contractor	
23	99/99/9999	99/99/9999	Outdoor Electrical	$900	Contractor	
24	99/99/9999	99/99/9999	New Toilets (2x)	$500	ABC Plumbing	
25	99/99/9999	99/99/9999	Finish Basement	$2,000	Contractor	
26						
27			**Total Home Projects**	$4,900		=SUM(D21:D26)
28						

< > ⋯ Income-Exp   Assets-Liab   Cred-Cards   Home-Info   Auto-Info   Insure-Pols   Fin-Plan   Income-Exp-F   Assets-Liab-F   Cre

Appx. A, Figure A-12-2: PFS Tab - Auto-Info - 1 of 1 (Auto Info)
(Figure 12-2: PFS Sheet - Auto-Info and Maintenance (sample entries))

	A	B	C	D	E	F	G	H
1	**Auto Info and Maintenance**		Book Build Ch. 12				Updated: MM-DD-YYYY	
2								
3	**<< Vehicle 1 Name >>**	**Purch Miles**	**Curr Miles**	**Batt Repl**	**Oil Chg**	**Tires Repl**	**Tire Rotation**	**Wipers**
4	Year/Make/Model/Trim	99,999	99,999	99,999	99,999	99,999	99,999	99,999
5	Purchase/Lease Date:	Mo/Year	Mo/Year	Mo/Year	Mo/Year	Mo/Year	Mo/Year	Mo/Year
6	Dealership Name:	XYZ Auto Sales						
7	Financing Through & Moly Pmt	QRZ Finance Co. $999						
8	Amt. Financed/No. Mos. @ APR	ABC Auto Ins.						
9	Serial # (VIN):	12345678911						
10	Warr/Service Contract:	XYZ Ext Warr. Co.						
11	Warr/Service Date Init/Expire:	Mo./Year, Mo/Year						
12	Insurance Carrier:	ABC Auto Ins.						
13	Insurance Policy #:	123456789						
14	License Plate #:	MFS-1234						
15								
16	CarFax report?	Y						
17	Factory recalls?	N						
18								
19	**<< Maintenance Record >>**	(Optional if most/all work is done at the same facility and records are kept)						
20								
21	**Company**	**Date**	**Mileage**	**Work Done**			**Cost**	**Formula / Notes**
22	Svc Co. A	Mo/Year	99,999	XXXXXXXXXXXXXXXXXXXXX			0	
23	Svc Co. B	Mo/Year	99,999	XXXXXXXXXXXXXXXXXXXXX			0	
24	Svc Co. C	Mo/Year	99,999	XXXXXXXXXXXXXXXXXXXXX			0	
25	Svc Co. D	Mo/Year	99,999	XXXXXXXXXXXXXXXXXXXXX			0	
26	Svc Co. E	Mo/Year	99,999	XXXXXXXXXXXXXXXXXXXXX			0	
27								
28							0	=SUM(G22:G27)
29								
30								

Income-Exp   Assets-Liab   Cred-Cards   Home-Info   Auto-Info   Insure-Pols   Fin-Plan   Income-Exp-F   Assets-Liab-F   Cred-Cards-F   Hoi

Appx. A, Figure A-16-1: PFS Tab - Insure-Pols - 1 of 1 (Insurance Pols Info)
(Figure 16-1: PFS Sheet - Insurance Policy Info (sample entries))

	A	B	C	D	E	F	G	H
1	**Insurance Policy Info**		Book Build Ch. 16				Updated: MM-DD-YYYY	
2								
3	**Who / Type**	**Carrier & AMB Rating**	**Phone**	**Policy No.**	**Coverage**	**Mo. Premium**	**Paymt Method**	**Formulas / Notes**
4								
5	Amy Life	Ins Company, A/A+	999-9999	99999999	500,000	125	AP CC X9999	
6	Amy Long Term Care	Ins Company, A/A	999-9999	99999999		125	AP CC X9999	
7	Ted Life	Ins Company, A+/A	999-9999	99999999	250,000	80	AP Chkg	
8	Ted Long Term Care	Ins Company, A/a	999-9999	99999999		125	AP CC X9999	
9	Ted Health - Medicare Part B (Doctor)	Medicare	999-9999	99999999		240	Auto ded SS Dep	
10	Ted Health - Medicare Part D (Drug)	Ins Company, A/A+	999-9999	99999999		40	Auto ded SS Dep	
11	Ted Health - Medicare Supplem. (N)	AARP or other	999-9999	99999999		110	AP Chkg	
12								
13	Joint - Home Owners	Ins Company, A/A+	999-9999	99999999	300,000	200	Incl. mort pmt	
14	Joint - Umbrella	Ins Company, A/A	999-9999	99999999	1,000,000	100	AP CC X9999	
15	Joint - Auto (2 cars)	Ins Company, A+/A	999-9999	99999999		300	AP CC X9999	Billed $3,600/yr
16								
17			Total Insurance Monthly Expense			$1,445		=SUM(F4:F16)
18			(Also listed on the Income-Exp tab)					

Income-Exp   Assets-Liab   Cred-Cards   Home-Info   Auto-Info   Insure-Pols   Fin-Plan   Income-Exp-F   Assets-Liab-F   Cred-Cards

Appx. A, Figure A-19-1: PFS Tab - Fin-Plan - 1 of 4 (Sect. 1.1 PFI Goals)

(Figure 19-1: Fin-Plan Sect 1.1 Personal Financial Indicator (PFI) Goals)

	A	B	C	D	E	F	G
1	**Financial Planning and Projects**		Book Build Ch. 19				Updated: MM-DD-YYYY
2							
3	**<<< Sect 1: Personal Financial Planning Goals >>>**						
4							
5	**< 1.1 Personal Financial Indicators >**	**Start Date**	**Compl. Date**	**Currently**	**Target Goal**	**Actual**	**Notes**
6	Gross Income (GI-$$) (Before taxes)	mm-dd-yy	mm-dd-yy	$0	$0	$0	
7	Net Income (NI$-$$) (After taxes)	mm-dd-yy	mm-dd-yy	$0	$0	$0	
8	Personal Cash Flow (PCF-$$)	mm-dd-yy	mm-dd-yy	$0	$0	$0	
9	Personal Net worth (PNW-$$)	mm-dd-yy	mm-dd-yy	$0	$0	$0	
10	Emergency Fund (EF-$$)	mm-dd-yy	mm-dd-yy	$0	$0	$0	
11							
12	Debt-to-Income (DTI-%) (max 40%)	mm-dd-yy	mm-dd-yy	0.0%	0.0%	0.0%	
13	Debt-to-Credit (DTC-%) (max 20%)	mm-dd-yy	mm-dd-yy	0.0%	0.0%	0.0%	
14	Savings-to-Income (STI-%) (max 20%)	mm-dd-yy	mm-dd-yy	0.0%	0.0%	0.0%	
15	Housing-to-Income (HTI-%) (max 30%)	mm-dd-yy	mm-dd-yy	0.0%	0.0%	0.0%	
16	Transportation-to-Income (TTI-%) (max 10%)	mm-dd-yy	mm-dd-yy	0.0%	0.0%	0.0%	
17	Other						
18	Other						

< > ⋯ Auto-Info | Insure-Pols | **Fin-Plan** | Income-Exp-F | Assets-Liab-F | Cred-Cards-F | Home-Info-F | Auto-Info-F | Insure-Pols-F | Fin-Plan-F ⋯ + ⋮

Appx. A, Figure A-19-2: PFS Tab - Fin-Plan - 2 of 4 (Sect. 1.2 Save-Inv Goals)

(Figure 19-2: Fin-Plan Sect 1.2 Savings and Investments Goals)

	A	B	C	D	E	F	G
20	**< 1.2 Savings and Investments >**	**Start Date**	**Compl. Date**	**Currently**	**Target Goal**	**Actual**	**Notes**
21	Employer 401K or 403B Plan	mm-dd-yy	mm-dd-yy	$0	$0	$0	
22	Regular IRA	mm-dd-yy	mm-dd-yy	$0	$0	$0	
23	Roth IRA	mm-dd-yy	mm-dd-yy	$0	$0	$0	
24	Stocks (Equities)	mm-dd-yy	mm-dd-yy	$0	$0	$0	
25	Bonds (Fixed Income)	mm-dd-yy	mm-dd-yy	$0	$0	$0	
26	Cash Equivalents (CD or MMA)	mm-dd-yy	mm-dd-yy	$0	$0	$0	
27	Savings - Short term	mm-dd-yy	mm-dd-yy	$0	$0	$0	
28	Savings - Long term	mm-dd-yy	mm-dd-yy	$0	$0	$0	
29	Other						
30	Other						

Appx. A, Figure A-19-3: PFS Tab - Fin-Plan - 3 of 4 (Sect. 1.3 Action Item Goals)

(Figure 19-3: Fin-Plan Sect 1.3 Financial Action Items Goals)

	A	B	C	D	E	F	G
34	**< 1.3 Financial Action Items >**	**Start Date**	**Compl. Date**	**Currently**	**Target Goal**	**Actual**	**Notes**
35	Build Personal Financial Spreadsheet (PFS)	mm-dd-yy	mm-dd-yy	$0	$0	$0	
36	Seek assitance of a financial advisor	mm-dd-yy	mm-dd-yy	$0	$0	$0	
37	Make payments to creditors on time	mm-dd-yy	mm-dd-yy	$0	$0	$0	
38	Create and monitor a monthly budget	mm-dd-yy	mm-dd-yy	$0	$0	$0	
39	Decrease discretionary spending	mm-dd-yy	mm-dd-yy	$0	$0	$0	
40	Review and reduce monthly fixed expenses	mm-dd-yy	mm-dd-yy	$0	$0	$0	
41	Reduce high-interest credit card debt	mm-dd-yy	mm-dd-yy	$0	$0	$0	
42	Add to an emergency fund savings account.	mm-dd-yy	mm-dd-yy	$0	$0	$0	
43	Add to an investment account (401K or IRA)	mm-dd-yy	mm-dd-yy	$0	$0	$0	
44	Check credit score and credit report	mm-dd-yy	mm-dd-yy	$0	$0	$0	
45	Review credit card and bank statements	mm-dd-yy	mm-dd-yy	$0	$0	$0	
46	Review insurance types and coverage	mm-dd-yy	mm-dd-yy	$0	$0	$0	
47	Shop insurance costs for savings	mm-dd-yy	mm-dd-yy	$0	$0	$0	
48	Other	mm-dd-yy	mm-dd-yy	$0	$0	$0	
49	Be Mindfully Aware and Be Here Now!	Every Day!					
50							

Appx. A, Figure A-19-4: PFS Tab - Fin-Plan - 4 of 4 (Sect. 2.1-3-Purch Plan Goals)

(Figure 19-4: Fin-Plan Sect 2.1-2.3 Major Purchases and Projects Goals)

	A	B	C	D	E	F
51	<<< Sect 2: Major Purchases and Projects >>>					
52						
53	< 2.1 Home Related Plans >					
54	Project Description	Start Date	Compl. Date		Amt. Budget	Amt. Spent
55	Gutter guards	mm-dd-yy	mm-dd-yy		$0	$0
56	Outdoor Electrical	mm-dd-yy	mm-dd-yy		$0	$0
57	New Toilets (2x)	mm-dd-yy	mm-dd-yy		$0	$0
58	Fence	mm-dd-yy	mm-dd-yy		$0	$0
59	Countertops	mm-dd-yy	mm-dd-yy		$0	$0
60	Replace stairs carpet	mm-dd-yy	mm-dd-yy		$0	$0
61						
62						
63	Total Home Projects Budget/Spent				$0	$0
64					=SUM(E55:E62)	=SUM(F55:F62)
65						
66	< 2.2 Vehicle Related Plans >					
67	New car	mm-dd-yy	mm-dd-yy		$0	$0
68	Car tires	mm-dd-yy	mm-dd-yy		$0	$0
69	Pontoon House boat	mm-dd-yy	mm-dd-yy		$0	$0
70						
71					$0	$0
72	Total Vehicle Projects Budget/Spent				=SUM(E67:E70)	=SUM(F67:F70)
73						
74						
75	< 2.3 Other / Big Ticket Plans >					
76	New bed	mm-dd-yy	mm-dd-yy		$0	$0
77	Refrigerator	mm-dd-yy	mm-dd-yy		$0	$0
78	Summer vacation	mm-dd-yy	mm-dd-yy		$0	$0
79						
80						
81	Total Other / Big Ticket Budget/Spent				$0	$0
82					=SUM(E76:E80)	=SUM(F76:F80)

Appendix B
Personal Financial Indicators (PFIs)

Table B-1 describes each of the 16 personal financial indicators with its name and abbreviation and whether it is measured in dollars ($) or as a ratio percentage (%). Note that these indicators may go by slightly different names depending on the financial professional. Most of the financial indicators are used in the Personal Financial Spreadsheet (PFS). Table B-1 indicates the Chapter and PFI number (e.g., 3-1) and the PFS sheet where the calculation is used and most of the data can be found. The table shows the formula used to calculate the indicator, a brief explanation, what data to include/exclude, and generally accepted values for the indicators.

Note: As a review, here are the Top 10 PFIs from Chapter 3, Part 5. All 16 of the PFIs used in the book are included in Appendix B Table B-1, referenced above. Make a copy of Table B-1 and use it to take notes.

The Top Ten PFIs
(Review from Chapter 3)
(Table 3-5: The Top Ten Personal Financial Indicators (PFIs))

Ratio Based (%) PFIs: Acronym/Name	Formula/Calculation	Chapt.
1. **DTI** - Debt-to-Income (%)	Monthly Reqd. Exp/ Gross Income	Ch. 3
2. **STI** - Savings-to-Income (%)	Monthly Savings/Gross Income	Ch. 7
3. **HTI** - Housing-to-Income (%)	Monthly Housing/Gross Income	Ch. 3
4. **TTI** - Transport-to-Income (%)	Monthly Transportation/Gross Income	Ch. 12
5. **DTC** - Debt-to-Credit (%)	Credit Used/Credit Limit	Ch. 9
6. **EFE** - Emerg. Fund-to-Expenses (%)	EF Balance/(Monthly Reqd. Exp. x 6)	Ch. 5
Dollar Amt. ($) PFIs: Acronym/Name	**Formula/Calculation**	**Chapt**
7. **PNI** - Personal Net Income ($)	Gross Income (minus) - Taxes = PNI ($)	Ch. 3
8. **EFG** - Emergency Fund Goal ($)	Monthly Reqd. Expense (times) * 6 = EFG($)	Ch. 4
9. **PCF** - Personal Cash Flow ($)	Monthly Net Income (minus) - Expenses	Ch. 3
10. **PNW** - Personal Net Worth ($)	Assets (minus) - Liabilities	Ch. 4

< Appendix B – Cont. >

Table B-1: Personal Financial Indicators (PFI) and Ratios

Use this form with Exercise 13-3 and Exercise 19-1

(Take notes in blank area of Calculation column)

Seq. Indicator / Ratio Name	Chapt-PFI, PFS Sheet	Calculation (Formula) and Notes
#1 Gross Income (GI) ($) (Monthly or annual)	3-1, Income-Exp	Total Income before taxes and deductions
#2 Net Income (NI) ($) (Monthly or annual)	3-2 Income-Exp	Total Income after taxes and deductions. (Take home pay from Paycheck and W2)
#3 Debt to Income (DTI) ratio (%) (Monthly comparison)	3-3 Income-Exp	Monthly Debt Payments divided by (/) Monthly Gross Income. (Should not exceed 40%)
#4 Personal Cash Flow (PCF) ($) (Monthly totals snapshot)	3-4 Income-Exp	Monthly Net Income minus (-) Monthly Total Expenses = (+ or -) PCF is also basis for Potential Saving Ratio (PSR).
#5 Potential Saving Ratio (PSR) (%) (Totals snapshot)	3-5, Income-Exp	Total Monthly Net Income minus (-) Monthly Total Expenses divided by (/) Monthly Net Income.
#6 Savings to Income (STI) ratio (%) (Monthly comparison)	4-1, Assets-Liab	Total Monthly Savings divided by (/) Gross Monthly Income. (Savings incl: Monthly Non-EF Savings accts, CDs, MMAs (Cash equivalents, 401Ks, IRAs etc.) (Should not exceed 30%)
#7 Emergency Fund Goal (EFG) ($) EF target (Total snapshot and EF goal)	4-2, Assets-Liab	Emergency Fund (EF) = Monthly Required Expenses x 6.
#8 Personal Net Worth (PNW) ($) (Totals snapshot)	5-1, Assets-Liab	Total Assets (equity) minus (-) Total Liabilities (Debt). (Result can be Pos/Neg.)
#9 Emergency Fund to Expenses (EFE) ratio (%) (Totals snapshot)	5-2, Assets-Liab	Emergency Fund current balance divided by (/) (Monthly Required Expenses x 6) (Normally > 0 and < 100%.)
#10 Liquid Assets to Expenses (LAE) projection (#M) (Totals snapshot) How many months w/out income based on assets.	5-3, Assets-Liab	Total Liquid Assets divided by (/) Total Monthly Required Expenses = No. Months of backup. (Liquid Assets include: All Savings accts. incl EF, CDs, MMAs, 401Ks, IRAs etc.)

#11 **Debt to Credit (DTC) ratio (%)** (Totals snapshot)	8-1, Cred-Cards	Total Revolving Credit Used divided by (/) Total of Revolving Credit Limits. (Should not exceed 30%)
#12 **Housing to Income (HTI) ratio (%)** (Monthly comparison)	11-1, Home-Info	Total Monthly Housing Expense divided by (/) Monthly Gross Income. (not exceed 30%) Mortgage or rental. Mortgage (PITI) + HOA dues + Utilities.
#13 **Income to Housing (ITH)** (Price Range Projection) ($-$) (Estimated price home you can afford)	11-2, Home-Info	Multiply your Gross Annual Income times 2 and then times 3. Range (x2 - x3) is appx price range home you can afford
#14 **Transportation to Income (TTI) ratio (%)**	12-1, Auto-Info	Total Monthly Transportation Expense divided by (/) Monthly Gross Income. Loan Payment + Insurance + gas + Monthly Maintenance + (Registration /12) (Should not exceed 10%)
#15 **Return-on-Investment (ROI) ratio (%)**	13-1	Investment Gain minus (-) Investment Cost) divided by (/) Investment Cost = ROI (%)
#16 **Investments to Income (ITI) ratio (%)** (Monthly comparison)	13-2, Assets-Liab	Total Monthly Investments divided by (/) Gross Monthly Income. (Investments incl: Stocks, Mutual funds, 401Ks, IRAs etc.) (Does not include Savings) (Should not exceed 30%).

Appendix C
Book Exercises Listed by Chapter

Chapter 1
Exercise 1-1: General Financial Knowledge Quiz
Chapter 2
Exercise 2-1: Compare Password Management Apps
Exercise 2-2: Download the Personal Financial Spreadsheet (PFS) Template
Chapter 3
Exercise 3-1: List PFS Income and Expenses
Chapter 4
Exercise 4-1: Create Personal Monthly Budget from Excel Template
Exercise 4-2: Compare Budgeting and Financial Apps
Chapter 5
Exercise 5-1: List PFS Assets and Liabilities
Chapter 6
Exercise 6-1: Compare Banking Features
Exercise 6-2: Automate Bank Accounts (Payments, Deposits, and Transfers)
Chapter 7
Exercise 7-1: Compare Automatic Savings Apps
Exercise 7-2: Compare Banking Products and Services
Exercise 7-3: Compare HELOC Lenders
Chapter 8
Exercise 8-1: Create Credit Bureau Account
Exercise 8-2: Obtain Your Credit Score and Report
Chapter 9
Exercise 9-1: Record PFS Credit and Credit Card Info
Exercise 9-2: Compare Credit Card Features
Chapter 10
Exercise 10-1: Compare Loan Amortization Calculators
Chapter 11

Exercise 11-1: Compare Home Mortgage Calculators
Exercise 11-2: Record PFS Home Info
Chapter 12
Exercise 12-1: Compare Auto Loan Calculators
Exercise 12-2: Record PFS Auto Info
Chapter 13
Exercise 13-1: Personal Investment Survey Questionnaire
Exercise 13-2: Compare ROI Calculators
Exercise 13-3: Evaluate Your PFI Status Using the Investing Checklist (optional)
Exercise 13-4: Record Investment Assets, Income, and Options
Chapter 14
Exercise 14-1: Compare Retirement Calculators
Chapter 15
Exercise 15-1: Calculate Income Tax and Effective Tax Rate
Chapter 16
Exercise 16-1: Compare Life Insurance Calculators and Policies
Exercise 16-2: Record PFS Insurance Policy Info
Chapter 17
Exercise 17-1: Research College Cost Calculators (optional)
Exercise 17-2: Research College Comparison Tools (optional)
Chapter 18
Exercise 18-1: Compare Computer and Smartphone Security Apps (optional)
Chapter 19
Exercise 19-1 (Fin-Plan Section 1): Gather Personal Financial Planning Data
Exercise 19-2 (Fin-Plan Section 2): Gather Major Purchases and Projects Data
Chapter 20
Exercise 20-1: None

References and Resources

American Institute of Certified Public Accountants. (2023, June 2). AICPA. *360 Degrees of Financial Literacy.* https://www.360financialliteracy.org

Arthur, M. (2022 June 5). Zillo. *10 Steps to Buying a House.* https://www.zillow.com/learn/10-steps-to-buying-a-home

Bankrate. (2023 October 12). Bankrate. *Retirement calculators on the Web.* https://www.bankrate.com/retirement/retirement-calculator

Bennet, K. (2023, May 17). Bankrate. *How a lack of financial literacy could be costing you thousands.* https://www.bankrate.com/banking/how-lack-of-financial-literacy-could-cost-thousands

Better Business Bureau. (2021, November 1). BBB. *Scam Alert: Home title fraud.* https://www.bbb.org/article/news-releases/22679-bbb-alert-home-title-fraud

Brown, J. (2021, July 27). Forbes Advisor. *How to Dispute Credit Report Errors Easily.* https://www.forbes.com/advisor/credit-score/how-to-dispute-credit-report-errors

Byrne, R. (2006). *The Secret.* New York City, NY: Atria Publishing Group.

Chopra, D. (1994). *The Seven Spiritual Laws of Success.* San Rafael, CA: Amber-Allen Publishing and New World Library.

Consumer Financial Protection Bureau. (2023, March 7). CFPB. *Mortgage help.* https://www.consumerfinance.gov/mortgagehelp

Consumer Financial Protection Bureau. (2023, May 11). CFPB. *Learn more: Navigating financial rules and regulations.* https://www.consumerfinance.gov/learnmore

Council for Economic Education and Jump$tart. (2022, May 11). CEE. *New National Standards for Personal Financial Education.* https://www.councilforeconed.org/new-national-standards-for-personal-financial-education

Covey, S. (1989). *The 7 Habits of Highly Effective People.* New York City, NY: Free Press.

Eisenberg, L. (2006). *The Number.* New York City, NY: Free Press.

Fair Isaac Corporation. (2023, June 24). FICO. *Credit Education.* https://www.myfico.com/credit-education

Fair Isaac Corporation. (2023, June 24). FICO. *Ninety percent of top lenders use FICO® Scores.* https://www.myfico.com

Federal Depositor Insurance Corporation. (2023, February 27). FDIC. *How Money Smart Are You?* https://www.fdic.gov/consumers/consumer/moneysmart/index.html

Federal Housing Administration. (2023, October 12). FHA. *Reverse mortgage information.*
https://www.fha.com/fha_reverse

Federal Trade Commission. (2022, May 1). FTC. *What To Know About Cryptocurrency and Scams.*
https://consumer.ftc.gov/articles/what-know-about-cryptocurrency-and-scams

Federal Trade Commission. (2022, August 1). FTC. *Reverse Mortgages.*
https://consumer.ftc.gov/articles/reverse-mortgages

Federal Trade Commission. (2022, December 2). FTC. *How To Secure Your Home Wi-Fi Network.*
https://consumer.ftc.gov/articles/how-secure-your-home-wi-fi-network

Federal Trade Commission. (2023, June 7). FTC. *Fraud alerts & credit freezes: What's the difference?*
https://consumer.ftc.gov/articles/what-know-about-credit-freezes-fraud-alerts

Federal Trade Commission. (2023, June 25). FTC Excerpts: *Credit Report Information - The Fair Credit Reporting Act (FCRA).*
https://www.annualcreditreport.com

Federal Trade Commission. (2023, September 12). FTC Credit report errors: *Disputing Errors on Your Credit Report.*
https://consumer.ftc.gov/articles/disputing-errors-your-credit-reports

Financial Literacy and Education Commission - U.S. Department of the Treasury. (2023-April 25). FLEC. *National financial education and a national strategy on financial education.* https://www.mymoney.gov

Free Application for Federal Student Aid. (2023, October 12). FAFSA. *2023–24 FAFSA Form.*
https://studentaid.gov/h/apply-for-aid/fafsa

Horymski, C. (2023, February 24). Experian. *Average Consumer Debt Levels Increase in 2022.*
https://www.experian.com/blogs/ask-experian/research/consumer-debt-study

Horymski, C. (2023, February 24). Experian. *What Is the Average Credit Score in the U.S.?*
https://www.experian.com/blogs/ask-experian/what-is-the-average-credit-score-in-the-u-s

Howard, C. (2005). *Clark Smart Parents, Clark Smart Kids: Teaching Kids of Every Age the Value of Money.* New York City, NY: Hachette Books.

Huston, S. and Texas Tech University (2014, Jan 21). AARP. *Test Your Money Smarts Financial Literacy Test.*
https://www.aarp.org/money/budgeting-saving/info-01-2014/test-your-money-smarts.html

Internal Revenue Service. (2022, October 1). IRS. *Health Savings Accounts and Other Tax-Favored Health Plans.*
https://www.irs.gov/publications/p969

Internal Revenue Service. (2022, October 1). IRS. *Retirement Plan and IRA Required Minimum Distributions FAQs.*
https://www.irs.gov/retirement-plans/retirement-plan-and-ira-required-minimum-distributions-faqs

Internal Revenue Service. (2023, October 6). IRS. *Online withholding estimator from the IRS.*
https://www.irs.gov/individuals/tax-withholding-estimator

Macrotrends. (2023, October 6). *Dow Jones - DJIA - 100 Year Historical Chart.*

https://www.macrotrends.net/1319/dow-jones-100-year-historical-chart

Macrotrends. (2023, October 6). *S&P 500 Index - Stock Market Performance over the Last 90 Years.*
https://www.macrotrends.net/2324/sp-500-historical-chart-data

National Financial Educators Council. (2023, June 2). NFEC. *Certified Financial Education Instructor (CFEI®) training, standards and course materials.* https://www.financialeducatorscouncil.org

Ohio Department of Education. (2023, May 12). ODE. *Learning Standards for Financial Literacy for grades K-12.*
https://education.ohio.gov/Topics/Learning-in-Ohio/Financial-Literacy/Financial-Literacy-in-High-School

Psychology Today. (2023, March 7). *Mindful Awareness.*
https://www.psychologytoday.com/us/basics/mindfulness

Ramsey Solutions. (2018, February 7). *Money Ruining Marriages in America.*
https://www.ramseysolutions.com/company/newsroom/releases/money-ruining-marriages-in-america

Schmidt, J. (2023, June 14). Forbes Advisor. *Return on Investment (ROI) Calculator.*
https://www.forbes.com/advisor/investing/roi-calculator/

Securities and Exchange Commission. (2023, Aug. 31). U.S. SEC. *Updated Investor Bulletin: An Introduction to 529 Plans.*
https://www.sec.gov/about/reports-publications/investor-publications/introduction-529-plans

Singer, M. (2007). *The Untethered Soul.* Oakland, CA: New Harbinger Publications/Noetic Books.

Tolle, E. (1999). *The Power of Now.* San Francisco, CA: New World Library.

Tolle, E. (2006). *A New Earth.* New York City, NY: Penguin Books.

TreasuryDirect. (2023, October 21). *TreasuryDirect.gov is the one and only place to electronically buy and redeem U.S. Savings Bonds.*
https://www.treasurydirect.gov

U.S. Government. (2023, June 27). *How to place or lift a freeze on your credit report.*
https://www.usa.gov/credit-freeze

Webster, Merriam. (2023, June 1). Book title dictionary definitions.
https://merriam-webster.com/dictionary

Wikipedia. (2023, June 1). *Financial Literacy Definition.*
https://en.wikipedia.org/wiki/Financial_literacy

About the Author

James Lorenz is an author and a Certified Financial Education Instructor^{SM} (CFEI®) living in Ohio. He holds a Bachelor of Science degree in Computer Information Systems and a teaching certificate in secondary education. He is a published author with Pearson Education and has over 30 years of teaching experience with community colleges and with private-sector companies such as Honda, Motorola, and Cisco Systems. He has worked with financial advisors over the last 20 years and has developed an understanding of personal finance based on first-hand experience. James is currently working with local community members to promote financial wellness and offer basic personal finance education with this book being an integral component. He is retired and has spent the past five years researching and writing this book with the goal of giving back to the community by helping to educate people on how to manage their finances. A portion of the profits from the sale of this book will be used to help promote financial literacy. James brings a fresh perspective and insight into the types of financial situations the average person might encounter during their lifetime while also providing many pertinent notes and money tips. Most of the scenarios presented in this book are his personal, real-life experiences including situations dealing with money management, investments, homes, vehicles, and college. He has had careers as an author/instructor in automotive technology, computer programming, and network engineering, as well as personal finance.

About the Editor

Todd Richardson is a Certified Public Accountant (CPA) living in Springfield, Ohio where he was born and raised. He has a Bachelor of Arts degree in Accounting and Business Administration from Wittenberg University, having also attended Bowling Green State University. He is a self-employed CPA with over 30 years of experience in the areas of personal taxation and small business tax and audit. He has worked closely with his own personal financial planner for over 25 years. They share over one hundred clients, with Todd providing the tax consulting and preparation services. He is happily married with three boys, all grown with families of their own, including four grandchildren. He has a passion for spreading financial knowledge to the broader population, in hopes of helping others avoid the financial pitfalls that so many people encounter.

Index